IMPORTANT:

HERE IS YOUR REGISTRATION CODE TO ACCESS
YOUR PREMIUM McGRAW-HILL ONLINE RESOURCES.

For key premium online resources you need THIS CODE to gain access. Once the code is entered, you will be able to use the Web resources for the length of your course.

If your course is using **WebCT** or **Blackboard**, you'll be able to use this code to access the McGraw-Hill content within your instructor's online course.

Access is provided if you have purchased a new book. If the registration code is missing from this book, the registration screen on our Website, and within your WebCT or Blackboard course, will tell you how to obtain your new code.

Registering for McGraw-Hill Online Resources

✓ **W9-BFA-747**

TO gain access to your McGraw-Hill web resources simply follow the steps below:

(1) USE YOUR WEB BROWSER TO GO TO: **www.mhhe.com/hybels7**

(2) CLICK ON **FIRST TIME USER**.

(3) ENTER THE REGISTRATION CODE* PRINTED ON THE TEAR-OFF BOOKMARK ON THE RIGHT.

(4) AFTER YOU HAVE ENTERED YOUR REGISTRATION CODE, CLICK **REGISTER**.

(5) FOLLOW THE INSTRUCTIONS TO SET-UP YOUR PERSONAL UserID AND PASSWORD.

(6) WRITE YOUR UserID AND PASSWORD DOWN FOR FUTURE REFERENCE. KEEP IT IN A SAFE PLACE.

TO GAIN ACCESS to the McGraw-Hill content in your instructor's **WebCT** or **Blackboard** course simply log in to the course with the UserID and Password provided by your instructor. Enter the registration code exactly as it appears in the box to the right when prompted by the system. You will only need to use the code the first time you click on McGraw-Hill content.

Thank you, and welcome to your McGraw-Hill online Resources!

* YOUR REGISTRATION CODE CAN BE USED ONLY ONCE TO ESTABLISH ACCESS. IT IS NOT TRANSFERABLE.

0-07-293564-2 T/A HYBELS: COMMUNICATING EFFECTIVELY, 7E

REGISTRATION CODE

signficant-59817504

Mc Graw Hill Higher Education

Communicating Effectively

Seventh Edition

Communicating
Effectively

Saundra Hybels

Richard L. Weaver II

Boston   Burr Ridge, IL   Dubuque, IA   Madison, WI   New York   San Francisco   St. Louis
Bangkok   Bogotá   Caracas   Kuala Lumpur   Lisbon   London   Madrid   Mexico City
Milan   Montreal   New Delhi   Santiago   Seoul   Singapore   Sydney   Taipei   Toronto

Publisher: *Phillip A. Butcher*
Senior Sponsoring editor: *Nanette Kauffman Giles*
Developmental editor II: *Jennie Katsaros*
Senior marketing manager: *Sally Constable*
Producer, Media technology: *Jessica Bodie*
Senior project manager: *Pamela Woolf*
Production supervisor: *Enboge Chong*
Design coordinator: *Mary E. Kazak*
Lead supplement producer: *Marc Mattson*
Photo research coordinator: *Nora Agbayani*
Art editor: *Jennifer DeVere*
Photo researcher: *Judy Mason*
Permissions editor: *Marty Granahan*
Cover and interior design: *Ellen Pettengell*
Cover images: *©Jeffrey Braverman/Getty Images; ©Diana Ong/Superstock; ©Ron Chapple/Picture Quest; ©Thinkstock*
Typeface: *10/12 New Aster*
Compositor: *Carlisle Communications, Ltd.*
Printer: *R.R. Donnelley and Sons*

Library of Congress Cataloging-in-Publication Data

Hybels, Saundra.
  Communicating effectively / Saundra Hybels, Richard L. Weaver II.--7th ed.
    p. cm.
  Includes bibliographical references and index.
  ISBN 0-07-256397-4 (softcover : alk. paper)
  1. Oral Communication. I. Weaver, Richard L. II. Title
P95.H9 2004
302.2'242--dc21   2003044549

www.mhhe.com

Brief Contents

Contents

Part One
Basic Principles of Communication

Chapter 1
The Communication Process   2

Chapter 2
Self, Perception, and Communication   32

Chapter 3
Intercultural Communication   62

Part Four
Communicating in Public

Preface

APPROACH

Communicating Effectively, Seventh Edition, has been written for the student who is taking a speech communication class for the first time. The book covers the theories of intercultural, interpersonal, group, public, and mass communication and shows how they apply to real-life situations at school, work, and home. The approach of the books is pragmatic, so that students can see and appreciate the practical application of the ideas, concepts, and theories in their own lives. The approach of the book also is problem-solution oriented, reflecting how I teach this material in the classroom. I not only post perplexing questions that ask for settlement, such as "How does this translate into the real-world?" but I offer realistic, applied, and worthwhile solutions. In this way, students can integrate what they are reading and learning directly into their lives.

There are numerous examples of this applied, problem-solution approach throughout the book. For instance, in the new intercultural communication chapter I ask, "How do you study culture?" In response, the six dimensions or frameworks for studying cultural differences are explained as solutions, and followed by corresponding, student-oriented examples of each dimension or framework. In this way students always will see the theory in use.

Another example of this applied, problem-solution approach occurs in Chapter 7, Interpersonal Relationships, the first of the two interpersonal relationships chapters. The perplexing problem is, "What is the glue that holds relationships together?" Old theories included similar interests, values, beliefs, and attitudes. But as it turns out, the key seems to be "bids and responses to bids," an approach championed by John Gottman and his team of relationship researchers. To apply Gottman's theory, I pose questions such as what determine your ability to bid, how common is it to bid, how important is it to bed, and what are some ways to encourage bidding. A similar approach can be framed for the new section on Baxter and Montgomery's relational dialectics: How can the "problem of" chaos that characterizes many relationships be explained and analyzed? The solution avails itself in their theory, and the examples I offer make their theory practical, realistic, and worthwhile.

This applied, problem-solving approach has four outcomes. It makes the book readable, interesting and challenging. Most important of all, it brings communication into the day-to-day lives of students. That is not just where it should be, but that is where these ideas can make the most difference.

ORGANIZATION AND COVERAGE.

Part One is devoted to the principles of communication. Chapters 1 through 6 present a model of communication, relate communication both to the self and culture, and show how communication works, both verbally and nonverbally, in our encounters with others. Chapter 3, Intercultural Communication, is new in this edition and explains different frameworks for studying cultural differences, barriers to intercultural communication, and ways to improve it.

The second part of the book focuses on interpersonal and small-group communication as well as communication at work. Chapters 7 and 8 cover interpersonal relationships, their dynamics, and how they can be evaluated and improved. Chapter 9, Communicating at Work, discusses informational interviews, informational interviews as precursors to job interviews, employment interviews, and presentations. Chapters 10 and 11 look at problem solving in small groups as well as leadership, participation, and conflict management in those groups.

The third part of the book examines public communication. Chapters 12 to 17, about public speaking, teach how to develop, organize, and deliver a speech. The Appendix, Mass Communication and Media Literacy, comprises a full chapter and focuses on mass communication, specifically on the Internet and the World Wide Web (WWW). It examines the relation of the media to the communication model, the reasons for studying media literacy, and how to assess information in general—information found on television and in newspapers and on the Internet. There is an additional section on the importance of ethics.

We continue to use many examples of key concepts in this book because this is the best way to bring theories to life. We draw these examples from familiar experiences of work, interactions with others, and campus life.

One of the goals for the text is to present the world beyond our local communities. Although this is true throughout the book, it is especially true in Chapter 3, Intercultural Communication.

A continuing goal of this edition is to connect readers to the Internet and WWW. Woven into the fabric of every chapter, we interlace specific *On the Web* boxes that ask readers to respond to Web information, access specific websites, evaluate Web material, or view related information carried on the Web. Web readings, too, are included in the Further Reading sections of each chapter. Chapter 13, Finding Speech Material, is oriented to using the Internet to discover and narrow speech topics as well as to learn about and research those topics. The Appendix is designed to underscore the need to study the effects of the Internet and WWW.

■ NEW TO THIS EDITION

Intercultural Communication

Chapter 3 examines culture and the reader's role as a cultural being. It discusses the importance of intercultural communication, relates intercultural communication to the model of communication, provides six dimensions or frameworks for studying cultural differences, discusses barriers to intercultural communication, offers ways to deal with barriers that include discussion of dominant and nondominant cultures, and provides practical suggestions for improving intercultural communication.

Assess Yourself

Within each chapter, a new chapter-relevant questionnaire, survey, or evaluation form challenges students to assess themselves. These boxes are designed to challenge knowledge foundations, examine assumptions, discover attitudes, look at feelings, question knowledge, assess ability, highlight awareness, analyze skills, check confidence, probe anxiety, review preparation, and survey understandings. Scaled responses with additional discussion, explanations, and motivation and suggestions for change are included on the *Communicating Effectively* student CD-ROM.

The FOXP2 Gene

Chapter 5, Verbal Communication, opens with an explanation of the multi-disciplinary approach taken to the discovery of the FOXP2 gene, its importance, and how it has contributed to the spread of speech and language throughout the human population. The FOXP2 gene is, perhaps, the most important new discovery with respect to the evolution of speech and language, and will open the way to new research. A related *On the Web* box provides students with Internet resources to supplement the opening example.

Student CD-ROM

The CD-ROM that accompanies the text provides students with multiple tools for learning. These tools are integrated with the text through the use of CD icons in the text margins that notify students which CD tool to use at the appropriate time. They include:

Video The video includes clips that illustrate basic communication concepts and excerpts of student speeches.

Self-Quizzes There are 15 multiple-choice and 5 true/false questions for each chapter.

Assess Yourself These provide scaled responses to the end-of-chapter questionnaires and surveys that challenge students to assess themselves.

Audio Flash Cards Students can use these digital flash cards to hear how key terms are pronounced and to study for exams.

PowerPoint Tutorial Students will learn the rules of design and helpful tips on implementation when working with presentation software.

Business Document Templates and Outline Tutor These tools enable students to prepare efficiently for class projects, assignments, and oral presentations.

Quick Guide to Public Speaking

The beginning of Part IV, *Communicating in Public,* features a Quick Guide to Public Speaking. This useful reference tool summarizes the goals students need to achieve to give a successful speech.

Impact of New Technologies

Ways of finding information have continued to change rapidly since our last edition as students have gained more access to computers. Almost every student with access to the Internet prefers doing computer research rather than using card catalogs, books of indexes, and library-housed reference material. Accordingly, we have added extensive computer and Internet information and advice in all chapters, and we have deleted most of the information formerly devoted to library-housed material.

On the Web boxes, found throughout every chapter in the book, and tied intimately and immediately to the information in each, not only ask readers to find information on the Internet, but ask them to respond, evaluate, and become involved with it. Many of these boxes provide specific websites where readers are asked to go and participate.

■ CONTINUING STRENGTHS—UPDATED

Communication Competencies

Chapter 1, The Communication Process, contains new, recent evidence about the need for communication competencies and skills that every college graduate should have.

Self, Perception, and Communication

Numerous new sections in Chapter 2 include information about how you can improve your self-concept, the relationship between perceptions and the self-concept, adjusting to perceptual influences, perceptual filters, and a new section on an individual's unique perceptual filter. Also, there is a new figure in the chapter that distinguishes between objective reality and subjective views of the world.

Intercultural Communication

The research of Mark P. Orbe discussing communication between non-dominant and dominant group members that was part of Chapter 2, is now in Chapter 3, Intercultural Communication. Orbe discusses assimilation, accommodation, and separation at each of three levels: nonassertive, assertive, and aggressive. His research raises interesting questions, suggests a different vision of what democracy may become, and relates directly to the intercultural domain discussed in Chapter 3.

Listening

In Chapter 4, there is an all-new opening section on the importance of listening in all of life's stages. Also, there is a list that compares the traits of good and poor listeners, and a new practical section on Note-Taking Skills. The chapter ends with a new section on Talking So Others Will Listen, which offers specific advice on how to focus others' attention on your ideas and feelings.

Nonverbal Communication

Chapter 6 is completely rewritten to incorporate the new research and writing in all the nonverbal areas. The Reference section of the chapter also reflects the new rewrite. The chapter includes new suggestions for evaluating the reader's own nonverbal effectiveness using videotapes.

Interpersonal Relationships

Chapter 7 includes three new practical sections. The first, Bids and the Bidding Process, builds on the work of John Gottman and presents specific ideas on what it takes to have successful relationships. The second section, "Owned Messages," outlines a specific method so that readers can take responsibility for the messages they send. The third, Relational Dialectics, builds on the theoretical work of Baxter and Montgomery, but makes their information accessible to readers and offers a specific method for examining interpersonal relationships.

The new section in Chapter 8, Evaluating and Improving Relationships, focuses on the elements that tend to draw people together and discusses verbal skills, emotional expressiveness, conversational focus, nonverbal analysis, conversational encouragement, care and appreciation, and commitment. Not only is there a discussion of these elements, there is special motivational encouragement for males to improve their ability in these areas.

There is an expanded section on Communication Problems in Relationships.

Communicating at Work

An expanded section on Electronic Resumes includes one sample. There is a new section on how to dress for an interview and one on the factors in interviews about which interviewees may be uninformed and over which they have no control.

Small Groups: Characteristics

There is a new section on the potential cultural element involved in groupthink.

Leadership, Participation, and Conflict Management

Situational leadership is compared with functional leadership as well as the traditional styles of autocratic, democratic, and laissez-faire leadership styles. The various skills of situational leadership including telling, selling, participating, and delegating are discussed with an emphasis on how to practice situational leadership.

Working in Groups

Because instructors continue to increase the time students spend in class working in groups, we include *Working Together* boxes that encourage group learning and discussion of the concepts in the text. The typical format of these boxes is either a series of questions, or a short passage to read, followed by questions. Many of these boxes have been updated in this seventh edition.

Getting Started
(the opening chapter on public communication)

There are new sections on Using the Internet to Discover a Topic, Internet Brainstorming, and a new running example on cyberrelationships. Much more emphasis in this chapter focuses on the use of the Internet as both a learning and research tool.

Finding Speech Material

The new focus on the Internet and WWW includes a table comparing subject directories with search engines, a new section on Taking Notes on Internet Information, a new section on the research burden that has fallen on speakers' shoulders with the advent and popular use of the Internet, and a new section, too, on effectively and efficiently printing information from the Internet. Information on library-housed material has been substantially reduced.

Organizing and Outlining the Speech

There is a new section on the Reference List and one on the ease of using the APA reference style.

Delivering the Speech

A new section presents the connection between emotionally charged incidents and memory—how to better remember your speech.

The Informative Speech

New examples are included for defining, etymology, example, comparisons, contrasts, describing, composition, fit, using numbers, arousing curiosity, presenting anecdotes, and rhetorical questions. Also, there is a new section with an example on using color.

The Persuasive Speech

This chapter includes numerous new examples as well as a new sample speech by Juanita E. Hill called "Unlock Your Full Potential" that will motivate readers to take advantage of all aspects of their college experience.

Mass Communication and Media Literacy

There is a new figure in the Appendix comparing face-to-face group communication and electronic group communication with respect to channels of communication and social cues to communication. A new section, too, compares synchronous and asynchronous communication. There is an expanded section on gatekeepers, new evidence presented in a rewritten section, "The Media Influences Behavior," as well as new evidence in an expanded section on "The Media Connect Us with the Global Community."

■ SUPPLEMENTS TO ACCOMPANY *COMMUNICATING EFFECTIVELY, SEVENTH EDITION*

As a full service publisher of quality educational products, McGraw-Hill creates and publishes an extensive array of print, video, and digital supplements for students and instructors. Communicating Effectively is accompanied by a comprehensive package of instructor resources that specifically address the challenges of teaching and managing the basic communications course. Orders of new textbooks support the substantial investment required to develop such important resources. Please consult your local McGraw-Hill representative for more information on any of the supplements.

Instructor's Manual/Test Bank

This manual is a source of both daily plans and activities for the classroom. Every chapter of the *Instructor's Manual* contains Learning Objectives, Tips for Teaching, Chapter Highlights, Activities, and Essay Questions. Additionally, the *Instructor's Manual* includes sample course outlines, annotated sample speeches, and a users guide to the videos. The Test Bank includes essay, multiple choice and true/false questions created by the author of this book.

Online Learning Center www.mhhe.com/hybels7

This free, web-based supplement for students and instructors features helpful tools for class and exam preparation, and links to revalent Internet websites. Designed specifically to complement each text chapter, the Online Learning Center offers:

- Chapter Objectives, Outline and Summaries which give students signposts for understanding and recognizing key chapter content while participating in class and while studying on their own or in groups.
- Self Quizzes which provide a place to practice at taking multiple choice and true/false tests for each chapter.
- Glossary Crossword Puzzles which allow students to test their mastery of key concepts when solving these puzzles.
- General Web links which provide revalent chapter-by-chapter links for further research.

Instructor's Resource CD-ROM

A source of both daily plans and activities for the classroom, the Instructor's Resource CD-ROM contains for each chapter: Learning Objectives, Tips for Teaching, Chapter Highlights, Activities and Essay Questions. Additionally, the Instructor's Resource CD-ROM includes sample course outlines, annotated sample speeches, and a user's guide to the videos. The Test Bank includes essay, multiple choice, and true/false questions—all developed by Richard Weaver. The Test Bank is available on the Instructor's Resource CD-ROM as a computerized testbank or as a basic Word document. The

Computerized Test Bank offers numerous multiple choice, true/false and short answer questions in an easy-to-use program that is compatible to both Windows and Macintosh computers. PowerPoint Slides include not only standard lecture support for the entire text, but incorporate illustrations and other special features from the text.

PageOut: The Course Website Development Center

All online content for this text is supported by WebCT, eCollege.com, Blackboard, and other course management systems. Additionally, McGraw-Hill's PageOut service is available to get you and your course up and running online in a matter of hours, at no cost. PageOut was designed for instructors just beginning to explore Web options. Even the novice computer user can create a course website with a template provided by McGraw-Hill (no programming knowledge necessary). To learn more about PageOut, ask your McGraw-Hill representative for details, or fill out the form at www.mhhe.com/pageout.

■ ACKNOWLEDGMENTS

We would first like to thank all the instructors and teachers who have chosen to use this textbook from among many. We appreciate your choice, and we consider it both a responsibility and a privilege to be working for you. Likewise, we wish to thank all the students. Although we know it wasn't your choice to read this textbook, we recognize your commitment—especially when you read the book—and we have worked hard on your behalf.

My coauthor, Saundra Hybels, died unexpectedly September 18, 1999. A dedication to her is printed in the sixth edition. Although I (Richard) did the work on the seventh edition, I continue to write as if Saundra is present (in my mind, she is), and we are writing as a team. Her presence is greatly missed.

I would like to thank my colleague and friend of more than 28 years, Howard W. Cotrell. When I met Howard he was a faculty facilitator at Bowling Green State University who worked with a variety of professionals to help them improve their teaching and research. We have coauthored more than 50 articles, and he has been a contributor to my thoughts, feelings, and ruminations on almost every project undertaken. Although his name does not appear on all my published works, he is there in both substance and spirit. Whenever I am stumped, I go to him first. Although Howard and I continue to meet on a monthly basis, our e-mail contacts take care of the time between. Thus, Howard's influence continues unabated.

A special thanks to my mother, Florence (Grow) Weaver, who died in 1998. My mother was always interested, encouraging, and supportive. I have dedicated my book on public speaking to her memory. After all, she was the one for whom I delivered my first public speech.

Thanks, too, to Marge Walker and Marilyn Hulett, my sisters, and to Jim Norris, who is Marge's friend. The Internet, and its online, real-time, private chat rooms, can be credited for pulling us even closer together as a family unit communicating with, concerned about, and supportive of each other.

Thanks to Edgar E. and Zella Willis, my in-laws. There is no way I can ever thank them enough for their love and kindness. Edgar's background in teaching and writing in the area of radio, television, and film has always proven instructive and valuable. Thank you, too, to Richard, Betsy, and Frank Willis, and to Frank's friend Kirstin Nielsen. You are all special and important people in my life.

I want to thank my friends for their continuing support and encouragement: Jim and Pat Angel, Gary and Linda (Lyn) Miller, Bob and Debbie Quigley, Larry and Sherry Bush, and David and Sharon Andersen.

Also, I want to thank my immediate family: Andrea, my wife, and Scott, Jacquie, Anthony, and Joanna have been inspirations to both my writing and life. Thanks to David Smeltzer and Jay Brooks and their families, Dale and Joyce Smeltzer, and Bud and Betty Brooks, our extended families. A special thanks to Karen Radford, Scott's wife. Thanks to my grandchildren: Madison, Morgan, Mckenzie, Amanda, Lindsay, Austin, and Grant. Many of the personal examples I have shared with readers over the years, even though often unattributed, have been drawn from a positive, supportive, close, loving, and productive family life.

A special thank you, of course, to Andrea for her support, contributions, and love. She is always there, willing to help, to share, to give, and make space in her life for my time at the computer. There is no way this book could have reached its seventh edition without the aid and assistance of my wonderful wife and family—both immediate and extended. I do not take them for granted. I am fortunate to have this incredibly valuable support system, and I know and appreciate it.

I would like to thank the following reviewers for their detailed and insightful comments:

Patreece R. Boone,
Saint Louis University

Tim Borchers,
Minnesota State University

Thomas D. Bovino,
Wallace Community College

Richard Cheatham,
Southwest Texas State University

Kristin Gatto Correia,
San Francisco State University

Carole Lewandowski,
Oral Roberts University

Michael McDevitt,
University of Colorado

Rajiv Ramil,
University of Texas at Austin

Heidi M. Rose,
Villanova University

Thomas E. Ruddick,
Edison Community College

Juliann Scholl,
University of Nebraska

Denise Solomon,
University of Wisconsin

Princess Williams,
Suffolk Community College

Paul Yerty,
Des Moines Area Community

Mark Zeigler,
Florida State University

Guided Tour

Contemporary Thought Encourages Critical Thinking

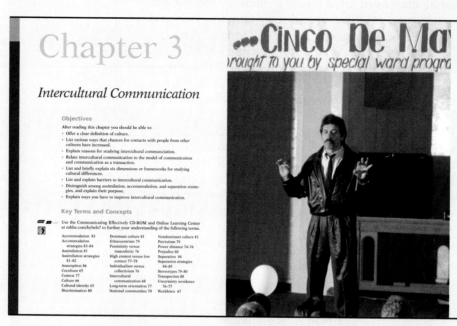

Chapter 3

Intercultural Communication

Objectives

After reading this chapter you should be able to:

- Offer a clear definition of culture.
- List various ways that chances for contacts with people from other cultures have increased.
- Explain reasons for studying intercultural communication.
- Relate intercultural communication to the model of communication and communication as a transaction.
- List and briefly explain six dimensions or frameworks for studying cultural differences.
- List and explain barriers to intercultural communication.
- Distinguish among assimilation, accommodation, and separation strategies, and explain their purpose.
- Explain ways you have to improve intercultural communication.

Key Terms and Concepts

Use the Communicating Effectively CD-ROM and Online Learning Center at mhhe.com/hybels7 to further your understanding of the following terms.

Accommodation 83	Dominant culture 81	Nondominant culture 81
Accommodation strategies 83–84	Ethnocentrism 79	Patriotism 79
Assimilation 81	Femininity versus masculinity 76	Power distance 74–76
Assimilation strategies 81–82	High context versus low context 77–78	Prejudice 80
Assumption 86	Individualism versus collectivism 76	Separation 84
Coculture 65	Intercultural communication 68	Separation strategies 84–85
Context 77	Long-term orientation 77	Stereotypes 79–80
Culture 66	National communities 70	Transpection 88
Cultural identity 65		Uncertainty avoidance 76–77
Discrimination 80		Worldview 67

The new Intercultural Communication chapter highlights contemporary thought (includes Mark P. Orbe's research) ways in which diversity enhances and enriches the quality of our civilization and helps students develop a sensitivity to various cultural heritages and backgrounds.

Communicating Effectively helps students recognize and appreciate how diversity in culture benefits our lives.

Because of the study of the genomes of people and chimpanzees ("Mutations eons ago . . .," 2002; "Lone gene linked . . .," 2002), progress leaped forward on why human beings developed language for communication. The work of Svante Paabo and his colleagues at the Max Planck Institute for Evolutionary Anthropology in Leipzig, Germany, is based on the discovery in 2001 of the first human gene—as one part of the human genome project—involved specifically in language. Known as **FOXP2,** the gene is directly linked to developing the fine motor skills needed to be a smooth talker. Dr. Anthony P. Monaco of the University of Oxford and his team of molecular biologists identified the FOXP2 as the gene responsible for switching on other genes during the development of the brain

Fox P2 Gene

Chapter 5, Verbal Communication, opens with an explanation of the multidisciplinary approach taken to the discovery for the Fox P2 gene and how it contributed to the spread of speech and language throughout the human population.

On the Web

The following articles on the Internet should give you some additional insights into the FOXP2 gene and its discovery and importance.

M. Balter. "Speech Gene' Tied to Modern Humans." August 16, 2002. *Science*: 297. Retrieved February 8, 2003, from http://www.sciencemag.org. In this article the caution scientists express against overstating the importance of FOXP2 in the evolution of language is presented.

A. Cubre. "FOXP2: To Speak or Not to Speak?" 2002. Department of Biology, Davidson College, Davidson, NC 28035. Retrieved February 8, 2003 from http://www.bio.davidson.edu/courses/ ics/2002/Cubre/project1.html. In this four-article, Cubre summarizes and compares the s announcing the discovery of the FOXP2 n both the popular press and scientific letters.

He concludes that the articles were "fairly accurate;" however, he points out that the conclusion that "the expansion of humans was associated with speech development" is pure speculation.

"First Language Associated Gene Identified." 2002. Applied Biosystems. *BioBeat* (Online Magazine). Retrieved February 8, 2003, from http://www.appliedbiosystems.com/biobeat/break throughs/bk65.cfm. This article offers a look at how the FOXP2 gene discovery was announced in a scientific publication.

"Gene Linked to the Dawn of Speech." 2002. Associated Press. MSNBC News; Health; Genetics. Retrieved February 8, 2003, from http://www. msnbc.com/news/794064.asp. This article provides a look at how the FOXP2 gene discovery was announced in the popular press.

On the Web box

On the Web boxes provide students with related Internet resources to supplement the chapter's opening example.

Consider This

Marsha Houston (2000), professor and chair of the Communication Studies Department at the University of Alabama, Tuscaloosa, discusses not just the fact that women's conversations with each other are different from their conversations with men, or that conversations between African-Americans and white women are different but too, and especially, that expectations are different. Notice in this brief excerpt how Houston first establishes the elements of communication then places conversations into the transactional framework:

A basic concept of contemporary communication theory is that a speaker does not merely respond to the manifest content of a message, but to his or her interpretation of the speaker's intention or meaning. In other words, I respond to what I think you meant by what you said. Such factors as the setting and occasion, the language variety or dialect, and the interpersonal relationship between speaker and listener influence message interpretation and response.

In addition, some understandings of talk are influenced by a speaker's gender or ethnicity. For

example, researchers have found that when the same message is delivered in much the same manner by a woman or by a man, listeners interpret it quite differently, in part because they expect women and men to use different styles of talk and to have knowledge of different subjects (p. 99).

Questions

1. Is it clear to you that Houston is working from a model of communication similar to the Hybels-Weaver model? What evidence do you have for this?

2. Can you see the three principles of trans al communication described (or alluded this excerpt?

3. To what extent will the interpretation of sage be determined by whether or nc delivered by a man or a woman? By whe not it is delivered by an African-America

Source: M. Houston. "When black women talk wit women: Why the dialogues are difficult." In A. Go M. Houston, & V. Chen. (eds.) *Our Voices: Es Culture, Ethnicity, and Communication* (Los Ange Roxbury Publishing Company, 2000), pp. 99–104.

Consider This box

Consider This boxes encourage students to think critically about real-life events.

Another Point of View

In his book, *West Side: Young Men & Hip-Hop in L.A.*, William Shaw discusses the importance of language:

How you talk is what you are. The increasing isolation of America's underclass is not just economic and spatial: It's linguistic, too. The African-American vernacular that thrives so richly in hip hop has its roots in West Indian creole, and in the eighteenth-century speech patterns of the Irish and Scottish immigrants. But linguists who have studied black English over the last few decades have noticed that instead of converging with what they call standard American English, it is fast drifting ever further away from it. The creative, fast-evolving language black Americans speak in the inner cities may be increasingly desirable on wax, as a cultural artifact, but it is becoming less and less like the language of the majority, the language of the schoolrooms, of mass media, of politics, and of the workplace."

Questions

1. Young boys from L.A. who were looking for work in the music industry often used "slangin" as their form of communication, but Mike Nixon, who had been in the music industry since the sixties, let them know that they weren't going to get anywhere in the music business if they couldn't communicate in a businesslike fashion. Do you find any analogous situations in today's world? That is, to succeed in business requires the adoption and use of communication that reflects a "busi-

nesslike fashion" as opposed to the everyday, common, ordinary speech that occurs between friends?

2. Have you any personal examples to support the insights that Shaw offers in this excerpt from his book? Have you detected, for example, the drift in black English farther and farther away from standard American English?

3. What do you think may be one reason why the fast-evolving language black Americans speak in the inner cities is becoming less and less like the language of the majority? Could it be, for example, that inner-city youth are creating a special language because they don't have as much power as the people around them? Are they doing it to exclude outsiders or members of the adult establishment?

4. Notice, in the example cited in question 1 above, that Mike Nixon understood why the young boys from the inner city of L.A. spoke the way they did, but he tried to encourage them to shift roles—to shift their speech—to adapt to a different language environment (business). How many different language environments do you adapt to in an average day? An average week? How about in an average month? With regard to effective communication, would you say that the more language environments to which one is exposed, the more effective communicator he or she is likely to be?

Source: W. Shaw, *Westside: Young Men and Hip-Hop in L.A.* (New York: Simon & Schuster, 2000), p. 480.

Another Point of View box

Another Point of View boxes offer interesting perspectives for student discussion. For example, Young Men and Hip Hop in L.A., the fast-evolving language of inner-city black Americans, the inner cities contrasted with the language of the media, politics, and the workplace.

Active, Everyday Applications Derived from Key Critical Concepts in Communication

Assess Yourself

Do You Have What it Takes to Be a Leader?*

Directions: Indicate the degree to which you agree or disagree with each statement by the following scale:

5 = Strongly agree
4 = Mildly agree
3 = Agree and disagree equally
2 = Mildly disagree
1 = Strongly disagree

Circle your response following each statement. When you have finished all seventeen statements, add up your responses, and put your total points in the "Total Points" blank.

1. I easily and comfortably question others' ideas and opinions.	5 4 3 2 1
2. I strive to find out and meet the needs of other group members.	5 4 3 2 1
3. I feel good when I measure the results of my hard work, rather than counting the time it took.	5 4 3 2 1
4. I feel comfortable thinking of others' needs.	5 4 3 2 1
5. I readily listen to the opinions of others.	5 4 3 2 1
6. I feel comfortable sharing power and control.	5 4 3 2 1
7. I seek out and move on to new opportunities.	5 4 3 2 1
8. I express my feelings easily to others.	5 4 3 2 1
9. I am able to easily share my accomplishments with others.	5 4 3 2 1
10. I am aware of my own strengths and weaknesses.	5 4 3 2 1
11. I feel comfortable with conflict.	5 4 3 2 1
12. I feel comfortable with change and making change.	5 4 3 2 1
13. I make goals.	5 4 3 2 1
14. I am able to motivate others.	5 4 3 2 1
15. I am constantly looking for ways to improve.	5 4 3 2 1
16. I feel comfortable knowing people look at me as a model for what is good.	5 4 3 2 1
17. In general I am a confident person.	5 4 3 2 1

TOTAL POINTS _____

 Find scaled responses on the Communicating Effectively CD-ROM or website.

Assess Yourself

Assess Yourself is a chapter-related questionnaire survey, or evaluation form that challenges students to examine their assumptions, attitudes, and feelings. Scaled responses are included on the Communicating Effectively student CD-ROM with additional discussion or explanation.

Source: Adapted from "Leadership Self-Assessment," ICANS (Integrated Curriculum for Achieving Necessary Skills), Washington State Board for Community and Technical Colleges, Washington State Employment Security, Washington Workforce Training and Education Coordinating Board, Adult Basic and Literacy Educators, P.O. Box 42496, 711 Capitol Blvd., Olympia, WA 98504. Retrieved February 19, 2003, from http://www.literacynet.org/icans/chapter05/leadership.html.

Consider This

Key Steps for Successful Interviewing

Step One: Be prepared. Adequate preparation and practice are essential to demonstrate that you are a knowledgeable and credible person.

1. Know the purpose and objectives of the interview.
2. Make certain the setting and time are satisfactory.
3. Remove any barriers that might interfere with a successful interview.
4. Make certain you have communicated effectively with the other interview participant or participants.
5. Dress appropriately.
6. Practice. Immediate impressions will be formed from your verbal and nonverbal communication; thus, make certain your self-confidence, personality, and speech habits convey a positive impression.

Step Two: Have an interview plan, but be adaptable and flexible. Even though the interview may not unfold exactly as your plan dictates, a plan shows that you are a thoughtful, knowledgeable, and organized. If there is dead space during the interview, having a plan will help provide material to move the interview forward. Having a plan, too, offers you any background information that might be helpful during the interview. If the interview moves far afield from where it should be, having a plan will help you refocus and redirect the interview[...] interview efficient[...] mary purpose and [...]

Step Three: Foll[...] interview requires [...] one who particip[...] minimum of a tha[...] you important in[...] from their regular[...] interview, a forma[...] short, timely lette[...] and further reinfo[...] credibility and tho[...]

Communication at Work

A thorough treatment of interviewing, business practices, and presentations prepare students for today's workplace.

The biggest difference between a presentation and a speech is the degree of visual support used and expected in presentations.

On the Web

A continuing goal of this edition is to connect readers to the Internet. In every chapter, On The Web boxes ask readers to respond to Web information and access and evaluate Web material.

On the Web

Compare and contrast each of the following models of communication with the Hybels-Weaver model of communication presented on page 9.

Model 1: (no author, no date). 6.2 *Shannon's and Moles' Communication Models*. Retrieved March 14, 2003 from http://www.uni-kassel.de/fb8/misc/lfb/html/text/6–2frame.html.

Model 2: (no author, no date). *The Elements of Communication: Communication Models (Transactional Model)*. Retrieved March 14, 2003, from http://historypages.org/elements/

Model 3: (no author, no date). *Introductory Models and Basic Concepts: Gerbner's General Model*. Retrieved March 14, 2003 from http://www.cultsock.ndirect.co.uk/MUHome/cshtml/introductory/gerber.html#means.

Questions

1. Do these models include elements not included in the Hybels-Weaver model? Should they be included?
2. Which model best represents the elements you think should be included in a communication model? Why?

On the Web

Internet Databases

- *Yahoo: www.yahoo.com/.* Yahoo is everybody's "favorite" subject guide; it is one of the first places that people register their sites so that it is fairly comprehensive, but its large size can make it unwieldy for precision searching. You can look for documents by moving through the menu categories or do a keyword search at any category level. You can search by Intelligent Default, exact phrase, AND, OR, limiting by date.
- *LookSmart: www.looksmart.com/.* LookSmart has reviewed and organized more than 2 million Web pages into a number of categories (200,000 organized hierarchically) covering everything from gardening and books to motor racing and space exploration in order. You can search by either keyword or drill down through the categories. The keyword search results give you both a list of relevant categories as well as the relevant sites.

hundreds of guides on as many topics, all put together by experts on each subject. You can search for information by keyword, or drill down through 36 categories to find what you want.
- *Librarians Index to the Internet: http://lii.org/.* This is an extensive index to great sites on the Internet compiled by librarians at the University of California and elsewhere. You can subscribe to a weekly list of new sites added to the index, which serves as a great way to keep up to date on good reference resources.
- *WWW Virtual Library: Data Sources by Subject:vlib.org/Overview.html.* This is another site where each subject is compiled and hosted by an expert in the field. The drawback to this distributed search guide is that the subject guides are erratically and infrequently updated.
- *Argus Clearinghouse for Subject-Oriented Internet Resource Guides (UMich):www.clear-*

Critically Acclaimed Public Speaking Chapters

■ A QUICK GUIDE TO PUBLIC SPEAKING

PREPARATION

Focus on your audience. The focus of all public speaking is the listeners—to gain a response from the audience. If you can get them to think, feel, or act in a certain way, you have achieved a measure of success. To accomplish this, you need to discover as much as you can about them and adapt your speech to their specific needs and interests.

Find a good topic. Select a topic that interests both you and your listeners and one on which you can complete some research.

Choose your purpose and central ideas. Choose your general purpose (to inform, to persuade, etc.), your specific purpose (what you want to achieve with your listeners), and your central ideas (a one-sentence statement of your message) with your specific audience in mind.

Carefully organize your speech. Devise two or three main points you want to explain and develop that will support your central idea.

Find strong support. Use personal experience, examples, facts, expert opinions, and statistics to develop each main point.

Use transitions. Smooth bridges are needed to help listeners know where you have been in the speech, where you are, and where you are going. Anytime you jump to a new point, it is helpful to have a signpost indicate the move: "My second reason is . . ."

Have an effective introduction. Begin your speech with information that will grasp listener attention and make them want to listen to the rest of your speech. Fascinating stories, intriguing questions, interesting facts and statistics, or engaging quotations are great attention-getters.

Develop a strong conclusion. Summarize the key points of your speech. Because it comes last in the speech, what you say in your conclusion is most likely to be remembered by your listeners.

Use an outline. Put all parts of the speech (introduction, main points, transitions, and conclusion) into an outline. Everything in the outline should explain, illustrate, or prove your central idea.

Prepare a speaking outline. From your complete outline, prepare a key-word outline that you will use when you deliver your speech.

Practice until you feel comfortable. Go over your speech using your key-word outline only. Speak your ideas differently each time you give your speech. Don't memorize it word-for-word.

Delivery

Reveal self-confidence. Strength comes from knowing your material, feeling you have something to share with your listeners, and having a positive attitude about yourself.

Channel your nervousness. Use it as a source of energy. Take a few deep breaths on the way to the lectern, pause before beginning your speech, and strive to be vital, enthusiastic, and involved.

Begin your speech. Walk confidently to the lectern. Arrange your notes, get your first sentence firmly in your mind, look directly at your listeners, and begin your speech. Throughout your speech, maintain eye contact, be expressive, and speak clearly.

Use your notes sparingly. Notes should never be a crutch. Avoid reading them or staring at them absentmindedly. Use them occasionally to pick up your next point.

End your speech with strength. After your conclusion, pause a few moments and, if appropriate, ask if there are any questions. The impressions you give as you move away from the lectern contribute to the overall effectiveness of you and your message.

Quick Guide

A Quick Guide to Public Speaking appears at the beginning of Part IV. This handy reference tool summarizes the goals students should strive to achieve in order to prepare and deliver a successful speech.

The Internet is the new focus of Chapter 13, Finding Speech Material. New material includes questions to ask to determine the reliability, validity, and objectivity of websites.

The Internet offers many opportunities related to speech topics. On the Internet you can brainstorm for them, find them, narrow them, as well as investigate and research them.

Using the Internet to Discover a Topic

There are numerous strategies you can use to discover topics via the Internet. One is no better than another; they are simply different approaches. Perhaps the easiest is to enter the words "Speech Topics" into the Google search engine. We received 5,500 hits (February 20, 2003), but we realized many of these were commercial sites advertising a list of topics that a particular speaker was announcing that he or she would be willing to speak on. However, we found three sites—and there are dozens more—where you can get a quick shot of mental adrenalin:

1. J. M. Books (2001). "Here Are over 850 of the Best Topics We've Seen." Retrieved February 20, 2003, from http://www.schoolelection.com/persuasive/speechtopics2.htm.

2. C. Gesell-Streeter, "Public Speaking: Help with Speech Topics." Gesell Webspinning, Cincinnati State Technical and Community College. Retrieved February 20, 2003, from http://faculty.cinstate.cc.oh.us/gesellsc/publicspeaking/topics.html.

3. (No author), "Speech Topics," District 70, Eastern Division, Area 35, Port Stephens, Toastmasters International. Retrieved February 20, 2003, from http://ww1.tpg.com.au/users/schleter/tie_sptc.htm.

A second approach is to begin with your **Web portal** (Smeraglia, 2000). Your Web portal is the home page your browser displays when you first connect to the Net. "Which portal you start with may be determined by your service provider (e.g., AOL.com, MSN.com, or ATT.net), or by your browser (Netscape.com). These home pages are called portals because they are designed to act as a gateway for your exploration of the Web. . ." (Smeraglia, 2000, p. 2). The advantage of beginning with your Web portal is that portals typically offer an alphabetical directory of topics designers of the portal thought might interest you. In addition, there are links to news, sports, and entertainment headlines, stock-market quotes, travel agencies, and local weather reports. Note, too, that the home page of any search engine is a second-level Web portal—second level simply because it requires your browser, the first level, to be activated before you can get to the search engine. Search engine home pages, too, include either a list of categories, or links to lists of categories. If you click on any of these categories, a more

Supplements That Make Sense

Interactive study tools match course concepts and motivate students to study and practice.

Communicating Effectively student CD-ROM includes: video clips, self-quizzes, Assess Yourself responses, audio flashcards, a PowerPoint tutorial, business document templates, and an Outline tutor. See the Preface for descriptions.

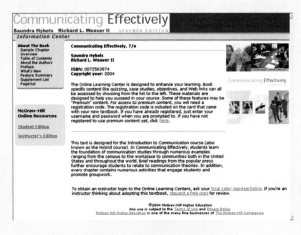

Online Learning Center website has distinct sections for instructors and students. The instructor site includes PowerPoint slides, the complete Instructor's Manual, additional box material (including Working Together and Consider This boxes from previous editions).

Create a custom course Website with PageOut, free with every McGraw-Hill textbook.

To learn more, contact your McGraw-Hill publisher's representative or visit www.mhhe.com/solutions.

www.pageout.net
Pageout helps instructors easily create professional-looking course websites. Compatible with Blackboard, WebCT, and eCollege.com.

Part One

Basic Principles of Communication

Chapter 1

The Communication Process

Objectives

After reading this chapter, you should be able to:

- Explain communication needs and relate them to your life.
- Define *communication* and explain it as a process.
- Identify the elements of communication.
- Explain how communication is a transaction.
- Explain how seeing communication as a transaction helps you understand it better.
- Describe the types of communication.
- Define and be able to explain *intercultural communication*.
- Discuss the ways you can improve your own communication skills.

Key Terms and Concepts

Use the Communicating Effectively CD-ROM and Online Learning Center at mhhe.com/hybels7 to further your understanding of the following terms.

Abstract symbol 10	Interpersonal communication 20	Sender-receiver 9
Channel 11		Setting 12
Communication 7	Intrapersonal communication 18	Small-group communication 21
Concrete symbol 10		
Culture 22	Mass communication 21	Subculture (coculture) 22
Ethical communication 23	Message 9	
	Noise 12	Symbol 9
External noise 12	Nonverbal symbol 10	Transactional communication 14–15
Feedback 11	Public communication 21	
Intercultural communication 23	Roles 15	Verbal Symbol 10
Internal noise 12	Semantic noise 12	

YOU ARE BEGINNING YOUR STUDY OF A SUBJECT THAT DATES BACK TO ANCIENT TIMES. As with any subject that has existed for a long time, it changes to meet the circumstances of the time in which it is used or studied. The earliest name for the subject, which we now call *communication* or *speech communication,* was *rhetoric,* and it was limited to the art of giving speeches.

In Western thought the philosopher who is best remembered is Aristotle, who wrote *The Art of Rhetoric* around 330 BC. One of his ideas, which is still discussed today, is that a speaker who is engaged in persuasion uses logical (*logos*), emotional (*pathos*), and ethical (*ethos*) appeals. When we get to the public-speaking part of this book, you will see that we still use some of these terms.

A few hundred years after Aristotle, Romans began to write about the art of giving speeches. The two most famous were Cicero (106–43 BC) and Quintilian (35–100 AD). Cicero's contribution described how to develop and find the material a speaker wanted to use in his speech.

The next scholar of note was St. Augustine, who lived in the fifth century. We still read his accounts of how he converted to Christianity, so it is not surprising that when he talked about speechmaking, he was concerned with how one should speak about Christianity. His was probably the first writing about the theory of preaching.

Scholars in the field look at others who made contributions throughout the centuries, but no one emerged who had the impact of those we have mentioned. In the twentieth century, however, many changes occurred in the field and shaped the subject that we study today.

During the twentieth century scholars realized that studying only speech was too limiting. It was becoming clear that the mass media, in particular movies, radio, and, later, television, were having an impact on their audiences, and several people began to study this. For example, hoping to have some influence in the World War II effort, researchers began to look at how messages from these media affected their audiences. One of the first studies, for example, looked at how a well-known singer used radio to sell war bonds. Since these studies went beyond public speaking, scholars labeled them *communication studies.*

In the late 1940s a Bell Telephone engineer developed a model of how communication worked. Although this model was mathematical and was intended to describe a technological process, some saw it as a way to describe the communication process, and so it became one of the first models to be used in the discipline. Some of the terms we use in this book, such as *sender-receiver, noise,* and *message,* came from this particular model.

Another major change entered the field in the sixties. Although interest in the analysis of speeches began to revive because the civil rights movement had spawned a new generation of speakers with new themes, the emerging hippie movement brought about a new interest in relationships. Scholars realized that relationships and communication go hand in hand, so scholars of communication began to look at how people communicate with each other in one-to-one relationships, small groups, and so on. Also, many communication scholars looked to the social sciences for existing work about relationships and found that some of the studies were relevant to the field. By this time, the subjects of communication had broadened so much that many departments became known as speech communication or communication departments. This is not to say, however, that the subject of rhetoric was no longer studied. In the decade between 1988 and 1998 more books about rhetoric were published than in the previous 75 years (Medhurst, 1998).

In the last decade or so, communication scholars have incorporated the field of cultural studies, which looks at who has power in society, what strategies they use to keep it, and how much society can be changed so that power can be shared. Studies of communication behavior and strategies are an important part of cultural studies. Also, we cannot overlook the impact of computers. Chat rooms and e-mail have opened new opportunities for people to talk to each other via computers. Many scholars regard this as a fascinating new area for study.

The study of speech and communication has had a long and honorable history because people in every age need communication skills. How about you? How do you fit into this picture? How much of your day have you spent in communication? Did people understand you the way you intended? Did you say what you wanted to say or get what you wanted to get? Could you have done it any better? These questions—and many others—will concern us in this chapter and throughout the book.

■ EVERYONE NEEDS COMMUNICATION SKILLS

As you prepare to enter the workplace and to engage in deeper relationships, your communication skills will be paramount to your success. "American workers surveyed about their educational preparation for the work force rate the ability to communicate and think critically as being more important than computer or other job-specific skills" (Morreale, 2000, p. 11). In this "national survey of 1,015 adult workers, 87 percent of the respondents rated communication skills as being 'very important' for performing their jobs. That compares with 50 percent who rated computer skills as being 'very important' " (Making the Grade?, 2000, p. 11). "It's ironic," writes Mary Boone in her book *Managing Inter@ctively*, "that most managers and executives spend a huge portion of their budget on communications bandwidth and hardware without stopping to think about their own communication skills or the quality of communication in their organizations. The *act* of communication," Boone writes, "is as important as the technologies we use to connect to each other" (2001, p. ix).

To even get a job, you must make a good impression in an interview. Over 90 percent of the 253 personnel interviewer respondents at 500 businesses in a midwestern city, responding to a questionnaire, indicated that communication skills are essential for success. Many job applicants, these interviewers said, lack effective communication skills in job interviews (Peterson, 1997). In an earlier study of 1,000 personnel managers, with a response rate of 428 usable sources, findings revealed that "the skills most valued in the contemporary job-entry market are communication skills (including oral communication, listening, and written communication)" (Curtis, 1988). Numerous other studies support the finding that "the most frequent factors deemed important in aiding graduating college students obtain employment are basic oral and written communication skills" (Winsor, Curtis, & Stephens, 1997, p. 179; U.S. Department of Labor, 1992; Rooff-Stefen, 1991; Report of the National Association of Colleges and Employers, 1998; Maes, Weldy, & Icenogle, 1997; & Lankard, 1990).

At work or in school you are likely to be asked to make presentations, to persuade your boss to take a particular course of action, or to work effectively in groups. As an adult, you hope that some of your relationships will become permanent. You need to communicate with the companion you choose to spend your life with; if you have children, you will have to communicate with them at various levels as they grow up; and you may have to make decisions with and about your aging parents. As well as communicating in couples and in families, you need to talk effectively to a number of people who affect your life in practical ways: computer technicians, plumbers, doctors, auto mechanics, salespersons, to name just a few. After completing a communication course at a large public university, students reported their most dramatic improvements were feeling more confident about themselves, feeling more comfortable with others' perceptions of them, experiencing greater ease in reasoning with people, and using language more appropriately (Ford & Wolvin, 1993). Also, communication courses contribute to improved critical-thinking skills (Allen, Berkowitz, Hunt, & Louden, 1999).

Even though you have been communicating since birth, you may not always be as effective as you want nor recognize the contribution of communication skills to your success. When communication doesn't work, you end up frustrated. You may get lost by not listening to directions, insult a friend through an e-mail statement you had intended as a joke, or bore an audience with a presentation. One study found that students commonly recognized communication skills as vital to their success, but they underestimated how essential some of these skills might be to their careers. For example, students underestimated how much time would be spent in meetings, the importance of interpersonal skills, how often they would be interacting with other employees, the importance of oral presentations, or the value placed on one's ability to use multimedia technology (McPherson, 1998).

Communication is vital in all areas of your life. You use it to persuade; to influence relationships; to inform; and to share, discover, and uncover information. You want a friend to go to a party; you want more friends; you want someone to join your club or to vote for a particular candidate—all these things require effective communication skills. Thus, it is not surprising that communication, and how to communicate, is so important to daily life that it has spawned an entire industry of books, articles, and seminars explaining how to do it better.

So, based on the evidence presented thus far, how would *you* answer the question, "What basic competencies or skills should every college graduate have?" When asked this same question, more than 1,000 faculty members from a cross section of academic disciplines said they should have skills in communicating (writing, speaking, reading, and listening), interpersonal skills, working in and leading groups, an appreciation of cultural diversity, and the ability to adapt to innovation and change (Diamond, 1997). One writer argues that communication is the ultimate people-making discipline because it teaches people how to think and speak well (Hart, 1993). Not only that, it frees us to be human: to apply our imagination, to solve practical problems, and to articulate our ideas.

In your own life you need communication to maintain and improve relationships. Through communication you discover others' needs and share your own. Any kind of relationship requires open and accurate lines of communication. Only when such lines exist will you feel free to voice important thoughts and feelings.

To live, then, is to communicate. To communicate effectively is to enjoy life more fully. On the premise that increased knowledge helps you do things better, let's begin with a discussion of how communication works.

■ COMMUNICATION IS A PROCESS

A Definition of Communication

Communication is any process in which people share information, ideas, and feelings. It involves not only the spoken and written word but also body language, personal mannerisms, and style—anything that adds meaning to a message.

To see how the communication process works, let's look at this exchange between Mark and Brian, who knew each other in high school but haven't seen each other since they graduated 10 years ago. They bump into each other in the park, where they are wheeling their children in strollers on a fine Saturday afternoon. First, they express their surprise at seeing each other. As they do this, they look each other over and begin to form some impressions. Mark notices that Brian looks thin and trim but that his hairline is receding. Brian looks at the stroller Mark is pushing and recognizes it as top of the line, one that he and his wife wanted but couldn't afford.

After they get over the surprise of bumping into each other, they begin to catch up on what they've done since high school. They start with their jobs; in American culture this is a way men have of assessing each other. Brian says that he works as the manager of a Uni-Mart (a convenience store), and Mark says that he is an account executive for a well-known advertising agency. Their conversation, though, is more than sharing information: As American men they are having a competitive conversation, and one way to win is to have a high-status job. In this case Mark wins because working at an advertising agency carries more status than being a Uni-Mart manager. Mark also has a high-priced stroller and that gains him points. Poor Brian: He loses a point or two for his receding hairline because Mark takes great pride in his own full head of hair.

Since they are both pushing strollers, they talk a little about their families. Brian says that he married his high school sweetheart, whom Mark remembers as very nice and pretty. But when asked about his wife, Mark loses some points. He says he is divorced and has custody of the baby in the stroller every other weekend. They talk a little more and then depart, both saying that they'll have to get together sometime but also realizing they will never do so.

Mark and Brian have communicated on all sorts of levels. Even without saying a word, they have sent out information about themselves by how they look, how they are dressed, and what objects they own. Their communication has a past. Because they knew each other long before they met in the park, they bring forth some of the old attitudes and feelings from high school.

Since one of them has a higher-status job and more money than the other, it is unlikely that they will make an effort at any kind of friendship. In American culture they are now separated by class.

The conversation between Brian and Mark illustrates communication as a process. When we say communication is a process, we mean that it is always changing (Berlo, 1960, p. 24). The conversation between the two begins with casual impressions of how they look. The conversation goes to a deeper level as they begin to catch up on their past, their families, and what they are doing now. On an even deeper level, after the conversation has continued for a while, both men realize that they probably won't be friends because the gap between them is too great.

The Elements of Communication

The communication process is made up of various elements: sender-receivers, messages, channels, noise, feedback, and setting. Figure 1-1

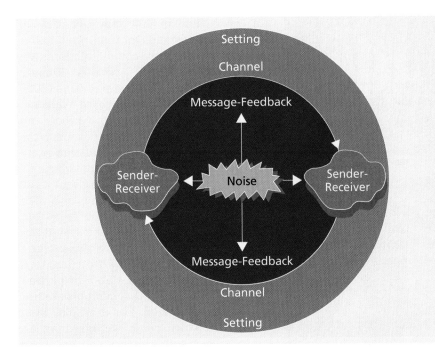

Figure 1-1

The Elements of Communication

shows how all these elements work together. The amoebalike shape of the sender-receiver indicates how this person changes—depending on what he or she is hearing or reacting to.

Sender-Receivers

People get involved in communication because they have information, ideas, and feelings they want to share. This sharing, however, is not a one-way process, where one person sends ideas and the other receives them, and then the process is reversed. In most communication situations, people are **sender-receivers**—both sending and receiving at the same time. For example, Janet and Al are discussing a problem their six-year-old daughter, Rebecca, is having at school. Janet has just come from a conference with Rebecca's teacher and is doing much of the talking. Al, by listening, is acting as the receiver. However, he is also sending messages that he is concerned: He pays careful attention, puts his hand on Janet's arm when she starts to get upset, and puts his arms around her when she starts crying. Through his actions, Al sends as many messages as he gets, even though he doesn't say a word.

Messages

The message is made up of the ideas and feelings that a sender-receiver wants to share. In the case of Al and Janet, Janet's message dealt with what had happened and what she was feeling about it, while Al's message was one of comfort and support.

Ideas and feelings can be communicated only if they are represented by symbols. A **symbol** is something that stands for something else. "Symbols

Feedback and nonverbal communication are important when we communicate with others.

are everywhere in our daily lives: We all know the eagle stands for the United States, the Statue of Liberty equals freedom, and roses express love," writes Deanna Washington in *The Language of Gifts* (2000, pp. 4–5). Then quoting Barbara Walker in *The Woman's Dictionary of Symbols and Sacred Objects*, she writes that "Any one symbol may have hundreds of interpretations according to the differing beliefs . . . Any basic symbol . . . can represent many disparate things in various times or places" (Walker, 1988, pp. 4–5).

All our communication messages are made up of two kinds of symbols: verbal and nonverbal. The words in a language are **verbal symbols** that stand for particular things or ideas. Verbal symbols are limited and complicated. For example, when we use the word *chair*, we agree we are talking about something we sit on. Thus, *chair* is a **concrete symbol,** a symbol that represents an object. However, when we hear the word *chair*, we all might have a different impression: A chair could be a recliner, an easy chair, a beanbag, a lawn chair—the variety is great.

Even more complicated are **abstract symbols,** which stand for ideas. Consider, for example, the vast differences in our understanding of words such as *home*, *hungry*, or *hurt*. How we understand these words will be determined by our experience. Since people's experiences differ to some degree, individuals will assign different meanings to these abstract words.

Nonverbal symbols are ways we communicate without using words; they include facial expressions, gestures, posture, vocal tones, appearance, and so on. As with verbal symbols, we all attach certain meanings to nonverbal symbols. A yawn means we are bored or tired; a furrowed brow indicates confusion; not looking someone in the eye may mean we have something to hide. Like verbal symbols, nonverbal symbols can be misleading. We cannot control most of our nonverbal behavior, and we often send out information of which we are not even aware.

Many nonverbal messages differ from one culture to another just as symbols differ from culture to culture. Black is the color for funerals in the Western cultures; in the Eastern cultures, that color is white. The crescent moon of male-oriented Islam used to be the symbol for female-oriented worship of the moon mother in ancient Arabia (Washington, 2000). In one culture, showing the sole of your foot when you cross your legs is an insult. In another culture, respectful behavior is shown with a bow; while in still another, deep respect is shown by touching the other person's feet. Whether or not you are aware of nonverbal messages, they are extremely important in all cultures. Albert Mehrabian, a scholar of nonverbal communication, believes that over 90 percent of the messages sent and received by Americans are nonverbal (1981, pp. 76–77).

Channels

The **channel** is the route traveled by a message; it is the means it uses to reach the sender-receivers. In face-to-face communication, the primary channels are sound and sight: We listen to and look at each other. We are familiar with the channels of radio, television, CDs, newspapers, and magazines in the mass media. Other channels communicate nonverbal messages. For example, when DeVon goes to apply for a job, she uses several nonverbal signals to send out a positive message: a firm handshake (touch), appropriate clothing (sight), and respectful voice (sound). The senses are the channels through which she is sending a message.

Feedback

Feedback is the response of the receiver-senders to each other. You tell me a joke and I smile. That's feedback. You make a comment about the weather and I make another one. More feedback.

Feedback is vital to communication because it lets the participants in the communication see whether ideas and feelings have been shared in the way they were intended. For example, when Deletha and Jordan decide to meet on the corner of 45th and Broadway in New York City, it would be good feedback for one of them to ask, "Which corner?" since the four corners at that particular intersection are among the busiest and most crowded in the city.

On the Web

Compare and contrast each of the following models of communication with the Hybels-Weaver model of communication presented on page 9.

Model 1: (no author, no date). 6.2 *Shannon's and Moles' Communication Models.* Retrieved March 14, 2003 from http://www.uni-kassel.de/fb8/misc/lfb/html/text/6–2frame.html.

Model 2: (no author, no date). *The Elements of Communication: Communication Models (Transactional Model).* Retrieved March 14, 2003, from http://historypages.org/hollywood/speech/commelements/models.html.

Model 3: (no author, no date). *Introductory Models and Basic Concepts: Gerbner's General Model.* Retrieved March 14, 2003 from http://www.cultsock.ndirect.co.uk/MUHome/cshtml/introductory/gerber.html#means.

Questions

1. Do these models include elements not included in the Hybels-Weaver model? Should they be included?

2. Which model best represents the elements you think should be included in a communication model? Why?

Sender-receivers who meet face-to-face have the greatest opportunity for feedback, especially if there are no distractions. In this kind of setting, they have a chance to see whether the other person understands and is following the message. A teacher working with a child, for example, can readily see by the child's face whether he is confused. She can also see when he is getting bored by the way he fidgets and begins to lose attention. A speaker in a large lecture hall, however, is not as aware of the feedback from his audience. The listeners he can see might look attentive, but the ones in the back rows may be having a quiet snooze. Little feedback occurs in messages sent out by the mass media. For example, if you want to respond to a newscaster, one way would be to write a letter. However, there is no assurance that he or she will receive it. In general, the fewer the people involved in the communication event, the greater the opportunity for feedback.

Noise

Noise is interference that keeps a message from being understood or accurately interpreted. Noise occurs between the sender-receivers, and it comes in three forms: external, internal, and semantic.

External noise comes from the environment and keeps the message from being heard or understood. Your heart-to-heart talk with your roommate can be interrupted by a group of people yelling in the hall, a helicopter passing overhead, or a weed wacker outside the window. External noise does not always come from sound. You could be standing and talking to someone in the hot sun and become so uncomfortable that you can't concentrate. Conversation might also falter at a picnic when you discover you are sitting on an anthill and ants are crawling all over your blanket.

Internal noise occurs in the minds of the sender-receivers when their thoughts or feelings are focused on something other than the communication at hand. A student doesn't hear the lecture because he is thinking about lunch; a wife can't pay attention to her husband because she is upset by a problem at the office. Internal noise may also stem from beliefs or prejudices. Doug, for example, doesn't believe that women should be managers, so when his female boss asks him to do something, he often misses part of her message.

Semantic noise is caused by people's emotional reactions to words. Many people tune out a speaker who uses profanity because the words are offensive to them. Others have negative reactions to people who make ethnic or sexist remarks. Semantic noise, like external noise and internal noise, can interfere with all or part of the message.

Setting

The *setting* is the environment in which the communication occurs. Settings can have a significant influence on communication. Formal settings lend themselves to formal presentations. An auditorium, for example, is good for giving speeches and presentations but not very good for conversation. If people want to converse on a more intimate basis, they will be better off in a smaller, more comfortable room where they can sit facing each other.

In many situations the communication will change when the setting changes. For example, in the town where one of your authors lives there

Settings can have a significant influence on communication.

was an ice cream stand just outside the city limits. People parked in front, got out of their cars, and walked up to a window to order their ice cream. On warm evenings, the place attracted many of the area's teenagers. After years of great success, the owner retired and sold the stand. The new owners decided to enclose it and make it more restaurantlike. You still had to order at the window, but because of the new addition at the front of the building, no one could see you anymore. Once you had your ice cream, you could take it to your car or eat it in the restaurant at one of the tables.

The new restaurant was certainly comfortable. You no longer had to stand in the rain, the place was open year-round, and you could sit down at a table and have dinner. However, comfort wasn't the issue: Every teenager deserted the place and headed for the Dairy Queen down the road. Why? So that they could be seen. For them, eating ice cream was secondary to

Working Together

Working with classmates as a group, create a model of communication. Drawing on everything that each person has read and all the information received in class, the group is to develop a complete model of communication by following each of these steps:

Step 1: Talk through the process of communication, making certain each group member contributes his or her thinking.

Step 2: Create a list of all the elements that need to be included in a model of communication.

Step 3: Have each member of the group create the same visual representation of the model in his or her own notebook. Each aspect of the model should be entered simultaneously, only when it is agreed upon by all members.

Step 4: One member of the group should explain the group's model to the entire class.

If there is time before this group exercise is complete, discuss (as a group) the question, "Why are visual representations effective tools for explaining a theory, idea, or process?"

Another Point of View

"It's no accident . . . that communication and community stem from a common root. Communities exist by sharing common meanings and common forms of communications. While this relationship seems obvious, it's often overlooked in discussions of communications, the implicit assumption being that communication is a phenomenon in and of itself, independent of the social context it interprets and reproduces. Anthropologists argue that communications cannot be divorced from community and culture. Neither can exist without the other. . . ."

Source: J. Rifkin. *The Age of Access: The New Culture of Hypercapitalism Where All of Life Is a Paid-for Experience.* (New York: Jeremy P. Tarcher/Putnam., 2000), p. 139.

participating in the social ritual of interacting with or being seen by their peers. In other words, the setting was an important part of their communication.

Setting often shows who has power in a relationship. The question "Your place or mine?" implies an equal relationship. However, when the dean asks a faculty member to come to her office, the dean has more power than the faculty member. When a couple meet to work out a divorce agreement, they meet in a lawyer's office, a place that provides a somewhat neutral setting.

The arrangement of furniture in a setting can also affect the communication that takes place. For example, at one college, the library was one of the noisiest places on campus. Changing the furniture solved the problem. Instead of having sofas and chairs arranged so that students could sit and talk, the library used study desks—thus creating a quiet place to concentrate.

All communication is made up of sender-receivers, messages, channels, feedback, noise, and setting. Every time people communicate, these elements are somewhat different. They are not the only factors that influence communication, however. Communication is also influenced by what you bring to it. That is the subject of our next section.

■ COMMUNICATION IS A TRANSACTION

A communication transaction involves not only the physical act of communicating but also a psychological act: Impressions are being formed in the minds of the people who are communicating (Wilder, 1979, pp. 171–86). What people think and know about one another directly affects their communication.

The Three Principles of Transactional Communication

Communication as a transaction—**transactional communication**—involves three important principles. First, people engaged in communication are sending messages continuously and simultaneously. Second, communication events have a past, present, and future. Third, participants in communication play certain roles. Let's consider each of these principles in turn.

Participation Is Continuous and Simultaneous

Whether or not you are actually talking in a communication situation, you are actively involved in sending and receiving messages. Let's say you are lost, walking in a big city that is not familiar to you. You show others you are confused when you hesitate, look around you, or pull out a map. When you realize you have to ask for directions, you look for someone who might help you. You dismiss two people because they look like they're in a hurry; you don't ask another one because she looks as though she might be lost too. Finally you see a person who looks helpful and you ask for information. As you listen, you give feedback, through both words and body language, as to whether you understand.

As this person talks, you think about how long it will take to walk to your destination, you make note of what landmarks to look for, and you may even create a visual image of what you will see when you get there. You are participating continuously and simultaneously in a communication that is quite complicated.

All Communications Have a Past, a Present, and a Future

You respond to every situation from your own experiences, your own moods, and your own expectations. Such factors complicate the communication situation. When you know someone well, you can make predictions about what to do in the future on the basis of what you know about the past. For example, without having to ask him, Lee knows that his friend Jason will not be willing to try the new Indian restaurant in town. Lee has been out to eat with Jason many times, and Jason always eats the same kind of food, burgers and fries. Lee also knows that Jason doesn't like changes of any kind, so he knows better than to suggest that they go out of town for a concert because he knows that Jason will respond that they should wait until the group comes to their town.

Even when you are meeting someone for the first time, you respond to that person on the basis of your experience. You might respond to physical traits (short, tall, bearded, bald), to occupation (accountant, gym teacher), or even to a name (remember how a boy named Eugene always tormented you and you've mistrusted all Eugenes ever since?). Any of these things you call up from your past might influence how you respond to someone—at least at the beginning.

The future also influences communication. If you want a relationship to continue, you will say and do things in the present to make sure it does. ("Thanks for dinner. I always enjoy your cooking.") If you think you will never see a person again, or if you want to limit the nature of your interactions, this also might affect your communication. You might be more businesslike and thus leave the personal aspects of your life out of the communication.

All Communicators Play Roles

Roles are parts you play or ways you behave with others. Defined by society and affected by individual relationships, roles control everything

Consider This

Marsha Houston (2000), professor and chair of the Communication Studies Department at the University of Alabama, Tuscaloosa, discusses not just the fact that women's conversations with each other are different from their conversations with men, or that conversations between African-Americans and white women are different but too, and especially, that expectations are different. Notice in this brief excerpt how Houston first establishes the elements of communication, then places conversations into the transactional framework:

A basic concept of contemporary communication theory is that a speaker does not merely respond to the manifest content of a message, but to his or her interpretation of the speaker's intention or meaning. In other words, I respond to what I think *you* meant *by what you said. Such factors as the setting and occasion, the language variety or dialect, and the interpersonal relationship between speaker and listener influence message interpretation and response.*

In addition, some understandings of talk are influenced by a speaker's gender or ethnicity. For example, researchers have found that when the same message is delivered in much the same manner by a woman or by a man, listeners interpret it quite differently, in part because they expect women and men to use different styles of talk and to have knowledge of different subjects (p. 99).

Questions

1. Is it clear to you that Houston is working from a model of communication similar to the Hybels-Weaver model? What evidence do you have for this?

2. Can you see the three principles of transactional communication described (or alluded to) in this excerpt?

3. To what extent will the interpretation of a message be determined by whether or not it is delivered by a man or a woman? By whether or not it is delivered by an African-American?

Source: M. Houston. "When black women talk with white women: Why the dialogues are difficult." In A. Gonzalez, M. Houston, & V. Chen. (eds.) *Our Voices: Essays in Culture, Ethnicity, and Communication* (Los Angeles, CA: Roxbury Publishing Company, 2000), pp. 99–104.

from word choice to body language. For example, one of the roles you play is that of student. Your teachers may consider you to be bright and serious; your peers, who see you in the same role, may think you are too serious. Outside the classroom you play other roles. Your parents might see you as a considerate daughter or son; your best friend might see the fun-loving side of you; and your boss might see you as hardworking and dependable.

Roles do not always stay the same in a relationship. They vary with others' moods or with one's own, with the setting and the noise factor. Communication changes to meet the needs of each of your relationships and situations. For example, even though Eduardo and Heidi have been married for 10 years and have three children, they still try to reserve Saturday night for a romantic date. While they are out, they try not to talk about children and family issues. Instead, they focus on each other and what the other is thinking and feeling. On Sunday morning, their roles change. Eduardo fixes breakfast while Heidi gets the children ready to go to church. Now their roles are children- and family-centered.

The roles you play—whether established by individual relationships or by society—may be perceived differently by different people. These perceptions affect the communication that results. For example, Tom, in his role of youth director, is well organized and maintains tight control over the activities he directs. The kids who play the games he coaches know they have to behave or they'll be in big trouble. Therefore they speak to him in a respectful voice and stay quiet when they're supposed to. To some kids, however, Tom's discipline seems rigid and inflexible. These kids avoid the youth center; they choose not to communicate with him at all.

The Principles in Action

Let's see how all three principles of transactional communication work as you listen to a conversation between a mother and her daughter, Lindsay:

Lindsay: Mom, can I borrow your stapler? I need it for my science assignment.

Mom: *(Steps back, slight frown)* You know Lindsay, I wouldn't mind lending it to you but you never bring it back.

Lindsay: *(Steps forward, slight whine in voice)* Mom, I really need it for this project. I promise I'll bring it back this time.

Mom: *(Steps back, puts her arms across her chest)* That's what you said the last time you took it.

Lindsay: *(Begs)* Pleeease. I promise to bring it back as soon as I'm done.

Mom: *(Stern voice)* OK, but this is the last time. If you don't bring it back, I won't lend it to you again.

Lindsay: Thanks, Mom. *(Runs off with stapler)*

You know right away in this scene that the mother does not want to cooperate, both from what she says and from her body language. As Lindsay speaks, her mother is simultaneously and continuously sending her signals: She frowns and steps back—both nonverbal symbols of resistance. Lindsay reinforces her verbal symbols by stepping forward and whining—a nonverbal way of showing assertiveness.

This scene between Lindsay and her mother would probably take no more than 30 seconds in real life, yet it is filled with symbols—some of which nonparticipants would be unable to detect. What are the past and future aspects of this communication? How many times has Lindsay borrowed something from her mother without returning it? How does the mother-daughter relationship influence the communication? How does the mother feel about Lindsay finishing her school project? Even if the mother knows the stapler might not be returned, she probably won't refuse to lend it because it's for a school project. Lindsay knows this, and that is why she asks for it, predicting that it will probably be given to her.

You must also look at the roles the mother and daughter play. In typical relationships, a parent provides what the child needs. Also, the mother wants to be an attentive parent—she doesn't want Lindsay to tell the teacher that her mother wouldn't let her use the stapler. In this dialogue, mother and daughter are pretty much equal: The mother knows that she controls the stapler, but Lindsay knows that she will be permitted to use it for schoolwork.

When you look at this conversation between Lindsay and her mother, you can see how complicated even a simple conversation can be. Still, you can never really understand what goes on in communication unless you look at it from a transactional perspective. Then you can begin to see the complexity and uniqueness of each communication event. As Heraclitus, the Greek philosopher, once observed, you cannot step into the same river twice: Not only are you different, but so is the river. The same is true of communication.

■ TYPES OF COMMUNICATION

As you can see in Figure 1-2, there are different kinds of communication. The figure shows four of the kinds most often used: intrapersonal, interpersonal, small-group, and public communication. Another commonly used type of communication is mass communication, which we will discuss along with the Internet, in the appendix.

Intrapersonal Communication

Intrapersonal communication is communication that occurs within you. It involves thoughts, feelings, and the way you look at yourself. Figure 1-3 shows some of the things that make up the self and, hence, intrapersonal communication.

Because intrapersonal communication is centered in the self, you are the only sender-receiver. The message is made up of your thoughts and feelings. The channel is your brain, which processes what you are thinking and feeling. There is feedback in the sense that as you talk to yourself, you discard certain ideas and replace them with others.

Even though you are not directly communicating with others in intrapersonal communication, the experiences you have had determine how you "talk" to yourself. For example, if you have had a good day, you are likely to look at yourself in a positive way. If a teacher was disappointed with your work, or if you had a fight with a fellow student, you are likely to focus on your feelings of failure or anger. You can never look at yourself without being influenced by the relationships you have had with others.

Figure 1-2

Types of Communication

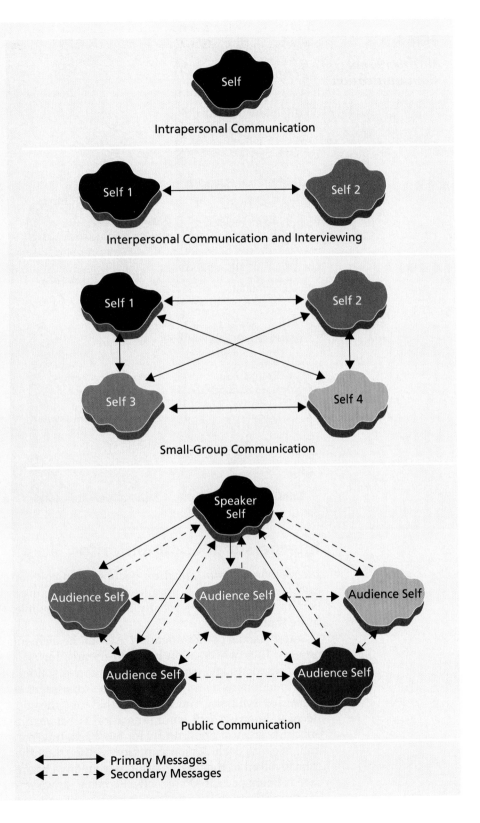

Intrapersonal Communication

Interpersonal Communication and Interviewing

Small-Group Communication

Public Communication

Primary Messages
Secondary Messages

Figure 1-3

Intrapersonal Communication

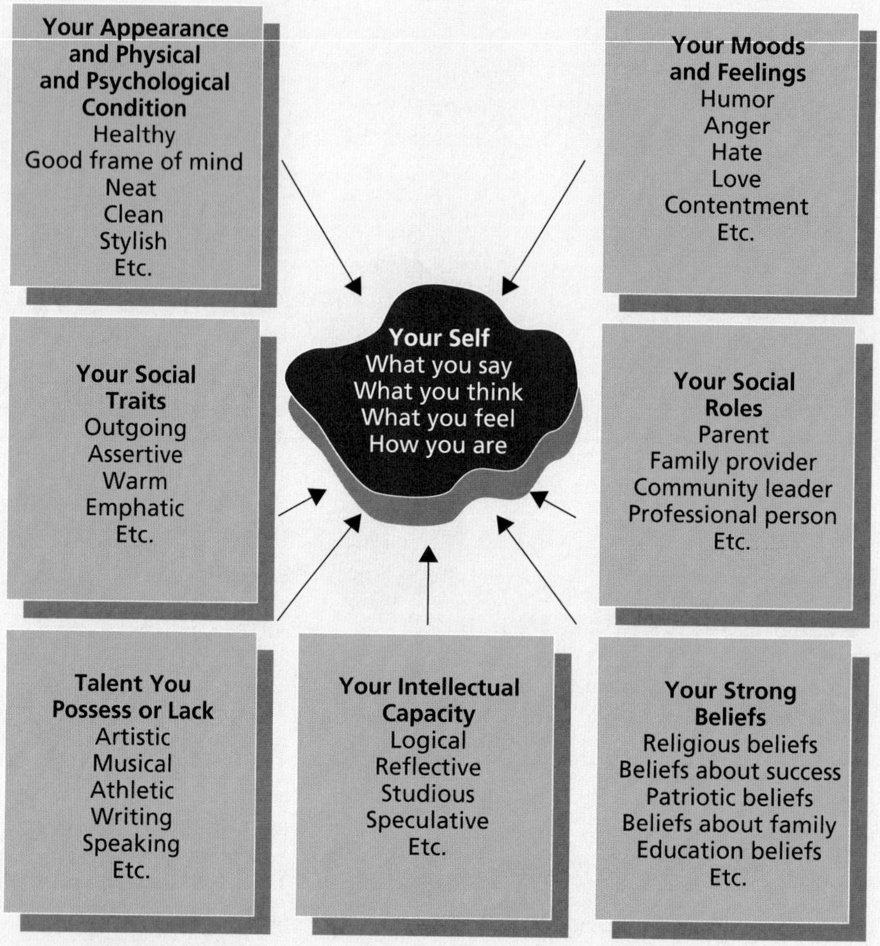

Your Appearance and Physical and Psychological Condition
Healthy
Good frame of mind
Neat
Clean
Stylish
Etc.

Your Moods and Feelings
Humor
Anger
Hate
Love
Contentment
Etc.

Your Self
What you say
What you think
What you feel
How you are

Your Social Traits
Outgoing
Assertive
Warm
Emphatic
Etc.

Your Social Roles
Parent
Family provider
Community leader
Professional person
Etc.

Talent You Possess or Lack
Artistic
Musical
Athletic
Writing
Speaking
Etc.

Your Intellectual Capacity
Logical
Reflective
Studious
Speculative
Etc.

Your Strong Beliefs
Religious beliefs
Beliefs about success
Patriotic beliefs
Beliefs about family
Education beliefs
Etc.

Interpersonal Communication

Interpersonal communication occurs when you communicate on a one-to-one basis—usually in an informal, unstructured setting. This kind of communication occurs mostly between two people, though it may include more than two.

Interpersonal communication uses all the elements of the communication process. In a conversation between friends, for example, each brings his or her background and experience to the conversation. During the conversation each functions as a sender-receiver. Their messages consist of both verbal and nonverbal symbols. The channels they use the most are sight and sound. Because interpersonal communication is between two (or a few) people, it offers the greatest opportunity for feedback. Internal noise is likely to be minimal because each person can see whether the other is distracted. The persons involved in the conversation have many chances to check that the message is being perceived correctly. People who want to engage in interpersonal communication usually look for informal and comfortable settings.

Small-Group Communication

Small-group communication occurs when a small number of people meet to solve a problem. The group must be small enough so that each member has a chance to interact with all the other members.

Because small groups are made up of several sender-receivers, the communication process is more complicated than in interpersonal communication. With so many more people sending messages, there are more chances for confusion. Messages are also more structured in small groups because the group is meeting for a specific purpose. Small groups use the same channels as are used in interpersonal communication, however, and there is also a good deal of opportunity for feedback. In keeping with their problem-solving nature, small groups usually meet in a more formal setting than people involved in interpersonal communication.

Public Communication

In **public communication** the sender-receiver (the speaker) sends a message (the speech) to an audience. The speaker usually delivers a highly structured message, using the same channels as in interpersonal and small-group communication. In public communication, however, the channels are more exaggerated than in interpersonal communication. The voice is louder and the gestures are more expansive because the audience is bigger. The speaker might use additional visual channels, such as slides or the computer program PowerPoint. Generally, the opportunity for verbal feedback in public communication is limited. The audience members may have a chance to ask questions at the end of the speech, but usually they are not free to address the speaker during the speech. However, they can send nonverbal feedback. If they like what the speaker is saying, they may interrupt the speech with applause. If they dislike it, they may fidget a lot or simply stop paying attention. In most public communication, the setting is formal.

Mass Communication

As with public communication, **mass communication** has highly structured messages and large audiences, often numbering in the millions. Many people create the messages of mass communication. In a television show, for example, there will be a producer, writers, a director, several people on the technical staff, and actors or any other people who are presenting the show. All of them will have some influence on the program.

The greatest difference between mass communication and other forms of communication lies in feedback. There is little exchange between the senders and the receivers, and what little there is is delayed, such as writing a letter to the producer. This lack of feedback affects the message: In order for a mass audience to understand it, it is kept simple. For example, most prime-time television programs can be understood by the average 12-year-old.

■ INTERCULTURAL COMMUNICATION

More than three decades ago Marshall McLuhan, a communication theorist, said that someday the whole world would be a mobile, global village. That day is here: We have a global economy, marketplace, and media. Few of us live in a place where our neighbors, fellow students, and co-workers are all like us. On campus, for example, in a single class you may find students of many nationalities and from a wide range of subcultures within the United States.

When we talk about **culture,** we mean "the ever-changing values, traditions, social and political relationships, and worldview created and shared by a group of people bound together by a combination of factors (which can include a common history, geographic location, language, social class, and/or religion)" (Nieto, 1995, p. 390). Cultures could include the Amish or Pennsylvania Dutch, groups with a common history. Cultures could include the Japanese or Taiwanese, groups with a common geographic location. Cultures could include those who speak the French or Islamic languages. Cultures could include just the socially elite, or just those in the top one-percent income bracket. And, cultures could include just the Baptists, Catholics, Unitarian-Universalists, or Jews. By **subculture,** we mean people who are part of a larger culture but also belong to a smaller group that has some different values, attitudes, or beliefs. Instead of subculture, we will use the term coculture—as explained in Chapter 3, Intercultural Communication—to mean the same thing. For example, in our society, African-Americans, Native Americans, Hispanic-Americans, and Asian-Americans make up large cocultures within the American culture. Within these cultures, and within the American culture as well, the disabled, elderly, and gays and lesbians, are cocultures.

Although people throughout the world have many characteristics in common, they also have many differences. Thus, if two or more cultural or cocul-

Every year the United States becomes more culturally diverse.

tural groups want to communicate, they must be aware that they may have different systems of knowledge, values, beliefs, customs, behaviors, and artifacts. If one group does not realize this, their communication will probably result in misunderstandings. For example, crossing your legs in the United States reveals a relaxed attitude, but in Korea it is a social faux pas. In West Africa, the comment "You've put on weight" means you look healthy and prosperous and is a great compliment; in America it is an insult. In Japan, they put business cards in safe places and handle them with great care, because they view them as an extension of the person; in America they are viewed as a business formality and convenience, and Americans are quick to put them away, a behavior insulting to the Japanese (Griswold, 1994, p. 1).

To help people understand each other better, scholars, teachers, and worldwide businesspersons have developed the field of **intercultural communication**—the communication that occurs whenever two or more people from different cultures interact. Different cultures could refer to racial, ethnic, or socioeconomic differences. This field studies how differences between people affect their perceptions of the world and, thus, their communication. Of course, there is no way to understand all cultures and cocultures. There are, however, certain characteristics that occur again and again, and the study of intercultural communication rests on these characteristics.

■ ETHICAL COMMUNICATION

Ethical communication is communication that is honest, fair, and considerate of others' rights. Communication is honest when communicators tell the truth; it is fair and considerate when they consider the listener's feelings. There are times, however, when honesty and fairness are in conflict. For example, when a friend shows you his new car and says, "Isn't it beautiful?", even if you don't agree, you should not tell him so. In our culture this is known as a "white lie"—one that preserves another's feelings—and since it is not about an important issue, it is ethically acceptable. On the other hand, when one of your friends goes out and drinks herself into oblivion every night and then asks whether you think she is an alcoholic, your answer should be "Yes." This is a situation where honesty is important because it concerns another person's well-being.

Being considerate of others' feelings is important in many types of communications. Might your words cause someone embarrassment? Teasing or telling stories about a person is often a way of embarrassing someone. Children and adolescents are often easily embarrassed, so special care should be shown with them.

Words that cause others pain are also ethically reprehensible. Anyone who is called "stupid," "faggot," or "clumsy" is hurt by these words. If criticism is important to your relationships, it should be carefully thought about before you use it. If you think back about times that were painful to you, you will often remember names that people called you or criticisms they made of you.

When you are making presentations in class, other ethical problems may arise. For example, it is unethical to conceal your motives—especially if you have something to gain. It is also unethical to conceal evidence that may not favor your cause. For example, if you are trying to persuade your

On the Web

Credo for Ethical Communication

Visit the website below. Read the "Credo"—the lead paragraph and the 10 bulleted items that follow it—and then answer the questions listed here. Website: (no author). *NCA Credo for Ethical Communication.* National Communication Association, January 6, 2000. Retrieved March 14, 2003, from http://people.csp.edu/winegarden/Common%20Links/nca_credo.htm.

Questions

1. Is this credo important or necessary? Why or why not?
2. Do you think such a credo is important for the kind of communication that occurs in a college speech-communication classroom? For all communication no matter where it occurs?
3. If you think this credo is important, and if you think it can make some difference in the communication that goes on in our world, how will you go about publicizing it?

audience to vote in the student government elections and you are a candidate, you should mention this or you could be seen as operating in your own self-interest. People who are making persuasive speeches must be particularly careful to disclose motives if they stand to benefit.

Much communication that is harmful to or disrespectful of others is done without thinking of the implications of the words. Think before you speak, and ask yourself if you are being honest and considerate of the other person's feelings. The Golden Rule still works: Ask yourself how you would feel if someone said the same thing to you.

■ COMMUNICATING EFFECTIVELY

Once you understand the process of communication, you can begin to understand why communication does or doesn't work. In an ideal communication situation the message is perceived in the way it was intended. But when messages don't work, it is useful to ask these questions: Was there a problem with the message? Was the best channel used? Did noise occur? Knowing the right questions to ask is essential to building skills in communication.

Most of us already have considerable communication skills. You have been sending and receiving verbal and nonverbal signals all your life. Nevertheless, you have probably had times when you have not communicated as effectively as you should. If you got a lower grade on a paper than you expected, you unintentionally hurt somebody's feelings, or if the instructor did not understand a question you asked in class, you are not communicating as effectively as you could.

Where to Begin

The information about communication is so vast that most of us could spend a lifetime studying the subject and not learn even a fraction of what

Consider This

Here, I (Richard) am writing to you—the reader—after over thirty years of teaching communication skills to undergraduate students. If your feelings match those of the majority of students just beginning a speech-communication course, then they probably fall along the lines "Why do I need to take this course, I already know how to communicate?" or "This course frightens me, I am really scared to stand up and speak in front of people." The number-one factor that will make a difference in what you learn from this course and how well you do in it will be your attitude:

Attitude is the key ingredient for living the life we desire. Our greatest tool for getting what we want is our ability to change our attitude, but attitude transformation is a skill that many of us have never learned. The truth is that our attitude will determine everything in our lives from whom we marry to what we do for a living. It will determine how we deal with our failures and how and if we achieve our successes; and it will determine our destinies. Our attitude is the defining factor that can make or break our careers, our personal relationships, our level of happiness and satisfaction. In fact, our attitudes will determine the evolution and the shape of our entire lives."

Source: L. Bassett *Life without Limits: Clarify What You Want, Redefine Your Dreams, Become the Person You Want to Be*. (New York: Cliff Street Books, an imprint of HarperCollins Publishers, 2001), p. 187.

Questions

1. Were you already aware that your attitude was that important? Does your attitude toward this course need to be changed? What information, or what circumstances, would be necessary to provoke a change in your attitude regarding this course?

2. Communication is another key ingredient (in addition to attitude), for living the life you desire. It is one of your greatest tools for getting what you want, and just like attitude, it is likely to determine everything in your life from whom you marry to what you do for a living. How are attitude and communication related? Can you cite any personal examples of how they are intimately and directly related?

3. Can it be said that if you change your attitude, your communication will improve? Can it just as easily be said that if you improve your communication, your attitude will likewise improve?

there is to know. However, as you begin your study of communication, the following five questions are a good starting point.

Which Communication Skills Am I Most Likely to Need?

Find out what communication skills are important to you. What do you intend to do in your life? What kind of work do you expect to do? What communication skills are required in this work? Which of these skills do you already have? Which ones need improvement? Which ones do you need to acquire?

For example, a career in business requires almost every communication skill. You need interpersonal skills to get along with the people you work with, intercultural communication skills if you are going to work with people from other countries, and public-speaking skills for making presentations. Although you may use some communication skills more than others, at one time or another you are going to need every one we have discussed in this chapter.

Assess Yourself

Have You Established the Foundations for Competent Communication?

Please give a qualitative evaluation of each of the twenty factors by circling the numerical score that in your judgment best represents your assessment of your performance, skill, or ability on that factor. This is not an opportunity to assess your desires, wishes, hopes, dreams, or even your potential.

7 = Outstanding (superb); 6 = Excellent; 5 = Very good; 4 = Average (good); 3 = Fair; 2 = Poor; 1 = *Very* minimal; 0 = No ability at all.

1. I have a sincere interest in improving my ability to communicate with others.
7 6 5 4 3 2 1 0

2. I have a sincere interest in increasing my own level of self-awareness—an interest in increasing my awareness of the often involuntary background activities (listening; verbal, nonverbal, and critical thinking) that control the display of foreground traits, skills, contexts, and emotions.
7 6 5 4 3 2 1 0

3. I want to increase my understanding of my own thinking patterns, assumptions, perceptions, prejudices, and biases.
7 6 5 4 3 2 1 0

4. I want to expand my mental capacity for new learning and for the challenges of life that will occur through my communication with others.
7 6 5 4 3 2 1 0

5. I want to engage in thoughtful communication with others.
7 6 5 4 3 2 1 0

6. I want to gain further experiences—in a variety of contexts— in communication.
7 6 5 4 3 2 1 0

7. I want to control my assumptions—the taking for granted of or suppositions that things are fact—before I have the evidence that confirms my generalizations as fact.
7 6 5 4 3 2 1 0

8. I sincerely want to show empathy and positive regard for the ideas and feelings of others.
7 6 5 4 3 2 1 0

9. I am prepared to display respect for others' ideas and feelings.
7 6 5 4 3 2 1 0

10. I am prepared to reveal a tolerance for ambiguity—a tolerance for facts, beliefs, and experiences that are capable of being understood in more than one sense.
7 6 5 4 3 2 1 0

11. I am prepared to show an interest in what others have to say.
7 6 5 4 3 2 1 0

12. I am prepared to remain nonjudgmental as I listen to the ideas and feelings of others.
7 6 5 4 3 2 1 0

13. I am prepared to be friendly, open, and polite to others as I converse with them.
7 6 5 4 3 2 1 0

14. I am prepared to reveal a sensitivity to the setting in which my communications with others take place—whether how it fits into history, how it fits into a relational setting, or how possible differences in expectations, styles, assumptions, values, body language, and privilege are likely to influence the communications.
7 6 5 4 3 2 1 0

Assess Yourself (continued)

15. I am prepared to take full responsibility for the ideas and feelings that I share with others. 7 6 5 4 3 2 1 0

16. I am prepared to be honest, fair, and considerate of others' rights when engaged in communication with them. 7 6 5 4 3 2 1 0

17. I am prepared to reveal my motives—especially when I have something to gain—when in communication with others. 7 6 5 4 3 2 1 0

18. I am willing to apologize and express regret for errors that I make when communicating with others. 7 6 5 4 3 2 1 0

19. I am prepared to watch for and detect, if possible, manipulation by others—to avoid being fooled, controlled, or too easily persuaded in the absence of compelling evidence. 7 6 5 4 3 2 1 0

20. I am prepared to experience the full range of possibilities that increased, effective, efficient communication with others will bring. 7 6 5 4 3 2 1 0

 Go to the *Communicating Effectively* CD-ROM to see your results and learn how to evaluate your attitudes and feelings.

Which Communication Skills Am I Most Lacking In?

Which kinds of communication are most difficult for you? Intrapersonal? Interpersonal? Intercultural? Small group? Public speaking? What are the symptoms of difficulties in these areas? What problems do you have to overcome before you can perform effectively?

Many people would prefer to avoid, rather than work in, the area that gives them the most trouble. For example, if you are anxious about public speaking, you might feel inclined to avoid any circumstance where you have to give a speech. A better approach, however, would be to get over this fear: You'll be able to offer a wedding toast, give a presentation at a meeting, consider many more job possibilities, and so forth. If you can conquer fear by plunging in and practicing the thing that gives you the most trouble, you will expand the possibilities in your life.

How Can I Get Communication Practice?

Are there situations, other than class, where you can practice communication skills that will be useful to you? Are there groups and organizations you can join that will help you develop these skills? It's always a good idea to take what you have learned in class and try it out on the world. Using new skills helps to develop and refine them.

Where Can I Get Help?

What people do you know who will help you develop communication skills and give you feedback on how you are doing? Are there people you can ask who will give you support when you are trying something new and threatening? Are you willing to ask them to support you? You can usually count on this kind of support from your friends. Don't you have a friend who would be willing to listen to one of your speeches and tell you whether it works and how you might improve it? Also, don't forget your instructors. Many of them sit in their offices during office hours hoping that students will drop by.

What Timetable Should I Set?

Have you set a realistic timetable for improvement? Knowing that it is difficult to learn new skills or break bad habits, are you willing to give yourself enough time? Your speech communication class is going to last for a semester or a quarter, and although you will be making steady progress in your interpersonal communication and public-speaking skills, change will not happen overnight. The act of communicating—whether with a single person or a classroom audience—takes time and effort. The most realistic timetable is one in which you say, "I'm going to keep working at this until I succeed."

Chapter Review

The study of speech goes back to the time of the Greeks and Romans. Important people during this time were Aristotle, Cicero, and Socrates. Later, in the Middle Ages, St. Augustine wrote about the art of giving sermons. Communication began to be studied toward the end of the twentieth century. In this discipline, interpersonal and group communication have been the focus of study, as well as verbal and nonverbal messages.

Everyone needs good communication skills. Effective communication helps bring us success and pleasure, helps us change the way others act and behave, and helps us in maintaining and improving relationships.

Communication is an ongoing process in which people share ideas and feelings. The elements of communication include sender-receivers, messages, channels, feedback, noise, and setting.

Every communication is a transaction. Viewing communication as a transaction focuses on the people who are communicating and the changes that take place in them as they are communicating. It also implies that all participants are involved continuously and simultaneously; that communication events have a past, present, and future; and that the roles the participants play will affect the communication.

Six kinds of communication are discussed in this book. Intrapersonal communication is communication with oneself. Interpersonal communication is informal communication with one or more other persons. Small-group communication occurs when a small group of people get together to solve a problem. Intercultural communication occurs whenever two or more people from different cultures interact. Public communication is giving a speech to an audience. Mass communication, which is discussed in the appendix, involves one message that goes out to many people via the mass media or the Internet.

Intercultural communication is communication that occurs when two or more people from different cultures interact. Culture means the ever-changing values, traditions, social and political relationships, and worldview created and shared by a group of people bound together by a combination of factors (which can include a common history, geographic location, language, social class, and/or religion).

Ethical communication is honest, fair, and considerate of others' rights.

Communication can be improved if you concentrate on several important areas. Find out what communication skills are important to you. Discover the kinds of communication that are most difficult for you and work to improve them. Seek out people who will help you develop these skills and give you support and feedback, and set a realistic timetable for improvement.

Questions to Review

1. Name the ways in which communication is important to our lives.

2. Why is communication called a process?

3. Why are people considered senders and receivers at the same time?

4. What kind of communication uses the greatest feedback? What function does feedback serve?

5. How can a setting influence the kind of communication that takes place? What is an example of a formal setting? An informal one?

6. Why is communication called a transaction? How are the past, present, and future important to a communication transaction?

7. Name some ways in which the roles you play will influence your communication.

8. How do intrapersonal and interpersonal communications differ from each other?

9. In mass communication how does feedback differ from the feedback in interpersonal communication?

10. Define *intercultural communication*. What do we mean by the term *culture*? What is a subculture or coculture? Name some of the subcultures found in the U.S. population.

11. When you consider the ethics of communication, what principles should you follow?

Go to the self-quizzes on the *Communicating Effectively* CD-ROM (side 2, track 10) and the Online Learning Center at mhhe.com/hybels7 to test your knowledge of the chapter concepts.

References

Allen, M., S. Berkowitz, S. Hunt, & A. Louden (1999). "A meta-analysis of the impact of forensics and communication education on critical thinking." *Communication Education,* 48, 18–30.

Berlo, D. K. (1960). *The process of communication: An introduction to theory and practice.* New York: Holt, Rinehart and Winston.

Boone, M. E. (2001). *Managing inter@ctively: Executing business strategy, improving communication, and creating a knowledge-sharing culture.* New York: McGraw-Hill.

Curtis, D. B. (1988, November). *A survey of business preferences for college grads.* Paper presented at the Annual Meeting of the Speech Communication Association, New Orleans, LA (ERIC Document Reproduction Service No. ED297407).

Diamond, R. (1997, August 1). "Curriculum reform needed if students are to master core skills." *The Chronicle of Higher Education,* B7.

Ford, W. S. Z., & A. D. Wolvin (1993). "The differential impact of a basic communication course on communication competencies in class, work, and social contexts." *Communication Education,* 42, 215–23.

Griswold, W. (1994). *Cultures and societies in a changing world.* Thousand Oaks, CA: Pine Forge Press.

Hart, R. P. (1993). "Why communication? Why education? Toward a politics of teaching." *Communication Education,* 42, 97–105.

Lankard, B. A. (1990). *Employability—The fifth basic skill.* ERIC Clearinghouse on Adult, Career, and Vocational Education, Columbus, OH (ERIC Document Reproduction Service No. ED 325659).

Maes, J. D., T. G. Weldy, & M. L. Icenogle (1997). "A managerial perspective: Oral communication competency is most important for business students in the workplace." *Journal of Business Communication,* 34, 67–80.

(No author). (2000, June 14). "Making the grade? What American workers think should be done to improve education." (The John J. Heldrich Center for Workforce Development, Rutgers University and the Center for Survey Research Analysis, University of Connecticut.) *The Chronicle for Higher Education.*

McPherson, B. (1998). "Student perceptions about business communication in their careers." *Business Communication Quarterly,* 61, 68–79.

Medhurst, M. J. (1998, Summer). "The rhetorical renaissance: A battlefield report." *Southern Communication Journal* 63:4, 309–14.

Mehrabian, A. (1981). *Silent messages: Implicit communication of emotions and attitudes,* 2nd ed. Belmont, CA: Wadsworth.

Morreale, S. (2000, September). "Survey of American workers reports communication as most important skill in workplace." *Spectra.* 36:9, 11.

Nieto, S. (1995). *Affirming diversity: The sociopolitical context of multicultural education* (2nd ed.). New York: Longman. In F. Yeo (1999, Fall). "The barriers of diversity: Multicultural education & rural schools." *Multicultural education*, 2–7. In Schultz, F., ed. (2001). *Multicultural education* (8th ed.). Guilford, CT: McGraw-Hill/Dushkin.

Peterson, M. D. (1997). "Personnel interviewers' perceptions of the importance and adequacy of applicants' communication skills." *Communication Education*, 46, 287–291.

(No author). (1998, Dec. 29). "Report of the national association of colleges and employers." *The Wall Street Journal, Work Week*, A1.

Rooff-Steffen, K. (1991). "The push is on for people skills." *Journal of Career Planning and Employment*, 52, 61–63.

Walker, B. G. (1988). *The woman's dictionary of symbols and sacred objects*. San Francisco: HarperSanFrancisco.

Washington, D. (2000). *The language of gifts: The essential guide to meaningful gift giving*. Berkeley, CA: Conari Press.

(No author). (1992). "What work requires or schools: A SCANS report for America." (U.S. Department of Labor). *Economic Development Review*, 10, 16–19.

Wilder, C. (1979, Winter). "The Palo Alto Group: Difficulties and directions of the transactional view for human communication research." *Human Communication Review* 5, 171–86.

Winsor, J. L., D. B. Curtis, & R. D. Stephens (1997). "National preferences in business and communication education." *Journal of the Association of Communication Administration*, 3, 170–79.

Further Reading

Beaulieu, L. J. (1999, May 28). "Communication process and leadership." Cooperative Extension Service, University of Florida. Retrieved March 14, 2003, from http://edis.ifas.ufl.edu/Body_CD013. Although Beaulieu discusses much of the same information as that in this chapter, he does so from a leadership point of view, acknowledging at the outset that "Communication is one of the essential elements of leadership." His "Suggestions for Leaders" toward the end of the article are useful. In evaluating this website, it is important to note that Beaulieu is a professor of extension and rural sociology in the Cooperative Extension Service, Institute of Food and Agricultural Sciences, at the University of Florida in Gainesville.

Condrill, J., & B. Bough, (1999). *101 ways to improve your communication skills instantly*. Palmdale, CA: Goalminds. This is a self-help book with many good tips. The book will not teach you communication theory, but it will give you useful pointers that will make your communication look more polished.

Gonzalex, A.; M. Houston; & V. Chen (2000). *Our voices: Essays in culture, ethnicity, and communication.*, 3rd ed. Los Angeles: Roxbury. The authors have included 34 essays grouped into categories such as "Naming Ourselves," "Negotiating Sexuality and Gender," "Representing Cultural Knowledge in Interpersonal and Mass Media Contexts," "Celebrating Cultures," "Valuing and Contesting Languages," "Living in Bicultural Relationships," and "Traversing Cultural Paths." This is an excellent collection of well-written essays.

Griffin, E. (2000). *A first look at communication theory*, (4th ed.). New York: McGraw-Hill. This introductory book describes over 30 theories that explain a wide range of communication phenomena, including sections on gender and intercultural theories. There is also an excellent reading list following each theory for students who want to do more investigation.

(No author). (1998). "How Americans communicate." Roper Starch—National Communication Association. Retrieved March 14, 2003, from http://wwwnatcom.org/research/Roper/how_americans_communicate.htm. In this survey you will discover how well Americans communicate, the methods they prefer for communicating, with whom Americans communicate well, and the factors affecting successful communication. The findings reinforce the positive impact most people's education has on their communication skills. Not only will you get the statistical results, but you will get an interpretation of those results as well. Useful and interesting.

Kitao, K., & S. K. Kitao, (1996; updated 2001). "Communication." Retrieved March 14, 2003, from http://ilc2.doshisha.ac.ip/users/kkitao/online/ www/communi.htm. This is a Web page link to organizations, conferences, journals and newsletters, useful information, areas in communication, mailing lists, programs, publishers, and people. It is a very comprehensive set of links.

Littlejohn, S. W. (1998). *Theories of human communication* (6th ed.) Belmont, CA: Wadsworth. Littlejohn offers a comprehensive examination of major communication theories. His discussion of the strengths and weaknesses of theories is useful; however, the book is designed for the more serious student of communication.

Ratey, J. J. (2001). *A user's guide to the brain: Perception, attention, and the four theaters of the brain.* New York: Pantheon Books (a division of Random House, Inc.). Ratey shows how the systems of the brain shape perceptions, emotions, actions, and reactions. With numerous examples from his psychiatric practice, research, and everyday life, he demonstrates how knowledge of the brain can improve our lives. Since much of his information has to do with language and the process of transforming information into function (communication), his material is directly relevant to most every section of this textbook. This is an enlightening and clear book written for those with no background or knowledge in brain composition or functioning.

(No author, no date). "Test your knowledge of human communication." Communication Institute for Online Scholarship (CIOS). Retrieved March 14, 2003, from http://www.cios.org/www/testme.htm. This quiz will test your knowledge of many aspects of communication, including electronic, mass, interpersonal, political, animal, nonverbal, computer mediated, persuasive, family, and its social history.

Wright, R., & M. Flores, (2001). "Comm 300— Communication theory." Retrieved March 14, 2003 from http://www.ic.arizona.edu/~comm300/mary/ alpha.html. At this website you can access communication theories either through their labels or through the names of the theorists. A complete explanation as well as an application of each theory is offered. This is a useful website for an overview of communication theories and theorists.

Chapter 2

Self, Perception, and Communication

Objectives

After reading this chapter, you should be able to:

- Explain self-concept and how it is formed.
- Define *reflected appraisal, social comparison,* and *self-perception.*
- Describe some of the ways you can improve your self-esteem.
- Describe how perception and self-concept are related.
- Explain the perceptual steps of selecting, organizing, and interpreting.
- Describe some of the things about the self-concept and perception that can be stated with certainty.
- Explain why perceptions are less than perfect because of deletions, distortions, and generalizations.
- Explain perceptual filters and the ways that they may influence your perceptions.
- Describe the process by which objective reality becomes a subjective view.
- Explain how you can adjust to perceptual influences.

Key Terms and Concepts

  Use the Communicating Effectively CD-ROM and Online Learning Center at mhhe.com/hybels7 to further your understanding of the following terms.

Deletions 50–51	Perceptual filters 51	Self-fulfilling prophecies 37
Distortions 51	Psychological risk 41	
Generalizations 51	Psychological safety 41	Self-perception 39
Map versus territory 54	Psychological sets 46	Social comparisons 37
Objective world/ reality 54	Reflected appraisals 36	Subjective view 54
Perception 46	Scripts 36	
	Self-concept 34	

"WHO AM I? AM I WHAT OTHER PEOPLE SAY I AM, OR AM I WHO I SAY I AM?" These are some of the most difficult and profound questions we can ask ourselves. How we answer them depends both on how we see ourselves and on how others see us. Rabbi Martin Siegel (Rubin, 1980) in his diary, describes the conflict between his own idea of himself and others' ideas of him:

> *People tend to make me a symbol. They say they know me, but they don't. They know only my roles. To some of them, I am a radical. To some of them, I am a signature on the marriage contract. To some of them I am the man who opposes the indulgence of the psychotic fear of anti-Semitism.*
> *People see me only as they care or need to see me.*
> *And poor Judith has to be a wife to all this.*
> *I can't recognize myself in their eyes, so how could she? We both have to live as exhibits in this community. While people are friendly, we have no friends. We have been made into what they want us to be. (pp. 187–88)*

In this passage, Rabbi Siegel is distressed that various people see only certain aspects of him. The people in his congregation never communicate to the whole man; instead, they communicate to the person he represents in their own eyes. For example, if they see him as a highly spiritual man, they may never talk with him about the ordinary problems of work or even the football game they saw on television. The passage, however, implies that he sees himself differently than the members of his congregation see him. Yet because all of them communicate to him on the basis of who they think he is, he (and his wife) have to struggle to maintain a fuller and more rounded self-concept.

■ SELF-CONCEPT

Your **self-concept** is how you think and feel about yourself. Our sense of self comes from our communication with others. Others tell us who we are ("You're really a good kid"), what we look like ("You have your grandfather's nose"), and how they feel about us ("I really feel that I can talk to you").

Your self-concept is based on the values of the culture and the community you come from. Your culture tells you what is competent and moral by defining attitudes and beliefs; the community you belong to tells you what is expected of you. The extent to which you reflect the attitudes and beliefs of your culture and live up to the expectations of your community will determine how you see yourself. If you were to spend your life in the town where you grew up, your self-concept would be formed by a fairly limited group of people. But if you moved from a small town to a big city, there would be many more influences. If you moved between two or more

On the Web

Visit the website below, take the personality self-rating scale, and then evaluate your score. This will give you some ideas for potential growth and alert you to the elements that one writer believes make up the composite "personality."

Website: D. Davies, Self Concept: Personality Self-Rating Scale. Department of Agricultural Education, University of Arizona, August 16, 2001. Retrieved March 14, 2003, from http://ag.arizona.edu/classes/aed301/scale.htm.

You will be asked to circle the appropriate number after 36 separate traits. A rating of 4 is outstanding, 3 is above-average, 2 is average, and 1 is poor. Following the scale, the author offers a system for evaluating your score.

cultures, the influences would be even greater. For example, Esmeralda Santiago explains how the American and Puerto Rican communities each wanted to define her in a different way. She says that her Puerto Rican mother expected her to be successful in American society but to stay 100 percent Puerto Rican. This was impossible.

> *To Puerto Ricans on the island during my summer there, I was a different creature altogether. Employers complained that I was too assertive, men said I was too feminist, my cousin suggested I had no manners, and everyone accused me of being too independent. Those, I was made to understand, were Americanisms.*
>
> *Back in the United States, I was constantly asked where I was from, and the comments about my not looking, behaving or talking like a Puerto Rican followed me (Santiago, 1994, pp. 34–36).*

Santiago realized that in order to move between the two communities she would have to resolve these conflicts:

> *I've learned to insist on my peculiar brand of Puerto Rican identity. One not bound by geographical, linguistic or behavioral boundaries, but rather, by a deep identification with a place, a people and a culture which, in spite of appearances, define my behavior and determine the rhythms of my days. (pp. 34–36)*

Although of Mexican rather than of Puerto Rican heritage, Santiago's experience is supported by Dolores Tanno (2000), a teacher of intercultural communication and rhetoric at the University of Nevada, Las Vegas. "We are indeed enriched by belonging to two cultures," she writes. "We are made richer still by having at our disposal several names by which to identify ourselves. Singly, the names Spanish, Mexican American, Latina, and Chicana communicate part of a life story. Together they weave a rhetorically powerful narrative of ethnic identity that combines biographical, historical, cultural, and political experiences" (p. 28).

Self-concept is made up of three distinct elements: reflected appraisals, social comparisons, and self-perception. Let's look at each of them.

Reflected Appraisals

Remember the story of Tarzan? Although Tarzan was a human, he believed he was an ape because he was brought up by apes and had no human experience. Tarzan's story reminds us that we are not born with an identity—others give it to us. Our parents, our friends, and our teachers all tell us who we are through **reflected appraisals**—messages we get about ourselves from others. Most reflected appraisals come from things people say about us. Your college speech instructor may say you are a good speaker, your peers may say you are a good friend, and your coach may tell you that you must work harder. All such messages from others help to create your self-concept.

Besides being given messages about ourselves, we are also given lines to speak (Murial & Joneward, 1971, pp. 68–100). These lines are often so specific that some people refer to them as **scripts.** Some scripts are given to us by our parents, and they contain directions that are just as explicit as any script intended for the stage. We are given our lines ("Say thank you to the nice lady"), our gestures ("Point to the horsie"), and our characterizations ("You're a good boy"). The scripts tell us how to play future scenes ("Everyone in our family has gone to college") and what is expected of us ("I will be so happy when you make us grandparents"). People outside our family also contribute to our scripts. Teachers, coaches, religious leaders, friends, and the media all tell us what they expect from us, how we should look, how we should behave, and how we should say our lines.

Writer and radio personality Garrison Keillor gives a list of scripts we get as we are growing up. Have you heard any of them or used them on your own children?

I. *I don't know what's wrong with you.*
   A. I never saw a person like you.
      1. I wasn't like that.
      2. Your cousins don't pull stuff like that.
   B. It doesn't make sense.
      1. You have no sense of responsibility at all.
      2. We've given you everything we possibly could.
         a. Food on the table and a roof over your head.
         b. Things we never had when we were your age.
      3. And you treat us like dirt under your feet.
   C. You act as if
      1. The world owes you a living.
      2. You've got a chip on your shoulder.
      3. The rules don't apply to you.

II. *Something has got to change and change fast.*
   A. You're driving your mother to a nervous breakdown.
   B. I'm not going to put up with this for another minute.
      1. You're crazy if you think I am.
      2. If you think I am, just try me.
   C. You're setting a terrible example for your younger brothers and sisters.

III. *I'm your father and as long as you live in this house, you'll—*
   A. Do as you're told, and when I say "now" I mean "now."
   B. Pull your own weight.
      1. Don't expect other people to pick up after you.
      2. Don't expect breakfast when you get up at noon.
      3. Don't come around asking your mother for spending money.
   C. Do something about your disposition.

IV. *If you don't change your tune pretty quick, then you're out of here.*
   A. I mean it.
   B. Is that understood?
      1. I can't hear you. Don't mumble.
      2. Look at me.
   C. I'm not going to tell you this again (Keilor, 1985, pp. 304–5).

If you were given positive reflected appraisals when you were young, you probably have a good self-concept; if the appraisals were largely negative, your self-concept may suffer. The messages we receive about ourselves can become **self-fulfilling prophecies**—events or actions that occur because we (and other people) have expected them. For example, at the beginning of the semester Professor Farley said to Kevin, "You're going to be a very good student." Because of this expectation, Kevin wanted to be a good student and worked hard to live up to Professor Farley's prophecy. Similarly, negative prophecies can have a negative impact. If someone tells a child that he or she will "never amount to much," there is a good chance the child will not.

Social Comparisons

When we compare ourselves with others to see how we measure up, we are making **social comparisons.** First of all, we compare ourselves with our peers. You might ask, "Do I look as good as she does?" or "What grade did you get on your midterm?" or "What kind of car do you drive?" If you are a parent, you might compare your child to your friend's child. "Can he talk yet?" "Did she get a position on the softball team?" In your job, you are likely to ask yourself if you are doing as well as your co-workers. Did you get as big a raise as the other guy got? Does the boss ever notice you and praise your work? The answers to these social comparison questions all contribute to your self-concept.

We get social comparisons from things or from people we don't even know. Take children's toys, for example. For years, people have complained that the Barbie doll gives little girls a false image of how a woman should look and dress. If a woman were to look like Barbie, she would have large breasts, a very small waist, and long, flowing hair. Her clothes would be very feminine, and her feet should fit into tiny little shoes. While Barbie has appealed to little girls, many little boys prefer G. I. Joe. First introduced in 1964, G. I. Joe has bulked up with each new version. Originally, he was the toy equivalent of 6 feet tall with normal biceps; 10 years later he was bulkier with a karate grip. By the mid-1990s he had a competitor who was even bigger, Gung-Ho, the ultimate marine. But G. I. Joe was not about to give

Working Together

Building a Self-Concept Map

Although you will be working in a group, you will be building your own self-concept map. The group should do each of the steps below, pausing after each step to allow each group member to record his or her own personal thoughts in a notebook. Each member should *write as many words or thoughts as time allows.* The purpose of the group responses is not confessional or self-revealing; the purpose is to generate words that can be used by group members when they record their own thoughts and ideas.

1: One at a time, each member of the group should orally complete the sentence "I want _____." To fill in the blank, members should use terminal values such as a comfortable life, intellectual growth, happiness, freedom, love, or friendship.

2: Again taking turns, each member of the group should orally complete the sentence "I am _____." To fill in the blank, members should use instrumental values such as honest, credible, ambitious, independent, optimistic, or caring.

3: Each member of the group, in turn, should orally complete the sentence, I like _____. To fill in the blank, members should use attitudes that explain why they like what they like. For example: I like sports for its competition; I like working out for its physical fitness; I like cats for their independence; I like hiking for its adventure; or I like friendships for their security.

4: In turn, each member of the group should orally complete the sentence I believe _____. To fill in the blank, members should use authority beliefs that we accept because of the source (society, religion, parents, or peer-group authority). Examples include "You should respect others' beliefs," "Going to church is good," "You should honor your parents," or "Studying is necessary to get through college."

5: You now have four lists in your notebook. Look at your lists and see how the items relate to each other. Devise a way to visually represent all these aspects of yourself. A visual representation could be a chart, graph, model, outline, picture, 3D structure, or whatever works best for you.

Source: Adapted from an exercise by A. M. Shubb, "The Communication Pages: Building a Self-Concept Map." GeoCities, 1999. Retrieved March 14, 2003, from http://www.geocities.com/Athens/Forum/7908/building.htm.

up; in the late 1990s he came out in a new incarnation called G. I. Joe Extreme—the biggest and bulkiest yet (G. I. Joe, 1999, p. 8A).

Some people argue that too much fuss is being made about such "ideal" forms in toys. Others argue that if this is how toy people are being represented to children, it is possible that as children grow up, they will think something is wrong with them if they don't look like the ideals. Toys, of course, are combined with many other images. The mass media are filled with the ideal "look." An evening of TV programs and commercials will convince you that everyone is tall, thin, well proportioned, and equipped with abundant hair. During prime time there are few representations of people who are even old, let alone of those with less-than-perfect bodies.

In a single day, you see many images of how people should look and behave. Magazines, movies, and videos all contribute to what the "ideal you" should be. Even if you can discount these images as being unrealistic,

The way we see ourselves is often a reflection of how we compare ourselves with others.

many of the people around you believe them and judge you and others by what they see and hear.

Self-Perception

In your earliest years, how you think about yourself comes largely from how people react to you—how parents and caregivers, for example, handle and care for you. "As they grow older," writes Valerie Wiener, in her book *Winning the War Against Youth Gangs* (1999), "teenagers broaden their people watching. At the same time teenagers are peering outward at others, they are also looking inward at themselves. Consciously or subconsciously, they weigh whether others' thoughts, attitudes, actions, and reactions will work for them" (p. 4). At some point, then, you begin to see yourself in your own way. The way in which you see yourself is called **self-perception.**

Self-perception comes from your experiences. If you have experiences that help you achieve the things you want, you will see yourself in a positive way. "One of the most important beliefs that influences [your] self-leadership capability is [your] view of [your] own ability to carry out a task," writes Manz and Sims, in their book *The New SuperLeadership* (2001, p. 110). They write that your "ability to perform successfully enhances the probability of actually *doing* it. Conversely, negative beliefs decrease the probability" (p. 110). Your state of mind about yourself clearly impacts your ultimate performance. Mary Boone, in *Managing Inter@ctively* (2001) claims that "At

Another Point of View

In his article, "Lacking in Self-Esteem? Good for You!," Andrew Sullivan writes that self-esteem isn't all that its cracked up to be. Drawing on the research performed by Brad Bushman of Iowa State University and Roy Baumeister of Case Western Reserve University, Sullivan writes:

Self-esteem can also be an educational boomerang. Friends of mine who teach today's college students are constantly complaining about the high self-esteem of their students. When the kids have been told from Day One that they can do no wrong, when every grade in high school is assessed so as to make the kid feel good rather than to give an accurate measure of his work, the student can develop self-worth dangerously unrelated to the objective truth. He can then get deeply offended when he's told he is getting a C grade in college and become *demoralized or extremely angry. Weak professors give in to the pressure—hence, grade inflation. Tough professors merely get exhausted trying to bring their students into vague touch with reality.*

Questions

1. Have you experienced people who think they are God's gift and who are offended if other people don't treat them that way?

2. Can you see how inflated egos can be substituted for a proper sense of self? That is, the distortion can become the reality?

3. What are some ways to enhance the realistic and natural development of self-esteem?

Source: A. Sullivan, "Lacking in Self-Esteem? Good for You!" *Time,* Oct. 14, 2002, p. 102.

the core of truly deep reflection is self-knowledge. In order to get over yourself," she writes, "you first have to know yourself well" (p. 126).

For most people, self-perception plays a greater role as they get older. Older people have learned and practiced being open to the ideas of others; they are okay with being wrong; they are not attached to particular outcomes; and they have learned how to be good listeners (Boone, 2001). Since they have gained confidence through life experiences, reflected appraisals and social comparison are no longer very important. Instead, they look at themselves from the point of view of the experiences they have had. Your parents, for example, might consider their lives to have been worthwhile because of you and your siblings.

Gender, Sex, and Self-Concept

Several research studies show that men and women gain their self-concept in different ways (Schwalbe & Staples, 1991). Two researchers found that when forming self-concept, men give the most importance to social comparisons, whereas women attach more importance to reflected appraisals. Men put more value on reflected appraisals from their parents, while women give more importance to reflected appraisals from their friends.

Other studies have shown that female self-confidence comes primarily from connections and attachments, while male self-confidence comes primarily from achievement (Joseph, Markus, & Tafarodi, 1992). This relates to research findings about gender and language. (In Chapter 5, Verbal

Communication, we discuss how women's language is tied to social networks, while men's language is tied to competition and achievement.)

Although your family and peers may influence how you act as a male or female, there is some evidence that your sexual identity is established when you are born. Researchers know this because of a terrible accident that occurred to an infant boy when he was eight months old. A surgeon was trying to repair a fused foreskin and accidentally cut off the boy's penis. Because the doctor thought he could never live as a boy, he recommended to the parents that they rear him as a girl. When the parents agreed, his testicles were removed and a vagina was constructed.

From this point on, the parents treated the child as a girl. They got her feminine clothes, gave her toys that girls liked, and even put her in the care of a female psychiatrist to help her adjust.

The child, however, never accepted her female identity. She tore off the dresses, refused the dolls, and looked for male friends. Instead of using makeup like her mother, she imitated her father by shaving and urinating standing up.

When she was 12, the doctors began estrogen treatments that enabled her to grow breasts. She did not like the feminizing effects of the drug and refused to take it. When she was 14, she refused any more treatment to feminize her. By this time she was so unhappy that her father told her what had happened to her, and her first feeling was that of relief.

At this point she went back to being a man. S/he took male hormone shots and had a mastectomy (an operation to remove breasts), and a surgeon began to reconstruct male genitals. Although the surgery was only partially successful, he married and he and his wife adopted children.

From this and other cases involving ambiguous genitals in newborns, many scientists have concluded that an infant with a Y chromosome will be a boy, regardless of his genitalia, and that nothing will ever change this.

Psychological Safety and Risk

Ask some second-semester seniors what they are afraid of. Chances are they will reply that they are very apprehensive about going out into the world. Will they find jobs? Can they survive outside the structure of university life? What is the world like? What is their place in it?

For most of us, **psychological safety**—the approval and support that we get from familiar people, ideas, and situations—is important. However, as the late psychologist Abraham Maslow, who worked in the area of self-fulfillment, pointed out, the needs for safety and growth pull us in opposite directions. Maslow believed that in order to grow, people have to abandon some of the safe areas of their lives and take some psychological risks (Maslow, 1970).

A **psychological risk** involves taking a chance on something new. It could be getting to know someone different from us, trying to understand a different point of view, or even moving to a new place. Taking a psychological risk helps improve one's self-concept. For example, when students go away to college, they must leave the safety of home, friends, and family. This is such a great risk that some first-year students spend a week or two away from home, decide they can't stand it, and drop out of school. The

Going away to school involves psychological risks—taking a chance on something new.

majority who remain, however, discover that they can cope on their own. This new knowledge helps to improve their self-concept.

New college students take risks not only in leaving home but also in being exposed to new ideas. For example, a student who has heard pro-choice ideas at home or in church will take a big risk if he or she tries to really understand a person who is pro-life, and vice versa. Similarly, it's risky for an athlete or a sports fan to try to understand the point of view that high schools might improve if they dropped competitive sports. The problem with taking the risk of really understanding a different point of view is that you might be changed. If you do change, you face the possibility that your family and friends probably will not change and you won't completely fit in anymore. Inevitably, whenever you take a risk, your circle of safety grows smaller.

Our first response to ideas that conflict with our own is to refuse to even listen to them. If we take this course, we choose psychological safety. When we take a psychological risk, we are ready to test our self-concept by considering ideas from another person's vantage point. Figure 2-1 shows some of the consequences of going abroad for a semester or quarter. As you can see, home is represented by religious values, family, and friends. As the two students get farther away from home, their connections to these things grow thinner and even threaten to break. For example, when you are in college, your religious beliefs might be threatened by a philosophy course or by late-night talks in the dorm with other students. If your beliefs are challenged, you might respond by no longer going to church or, in the extreme, by no longer believing in your church or even in religion. When this happens, you have taken a risk. When you go home, if you tell your parents what has happened, they probably are going to be upset; if you don't tell them, a gulf will grow between you and them as a consequence of your doing something so risky.

■ CAN YOU IMPROVE YOUR SELF-CONCEPT?

If you have any doubt that we, as a society, are obsessed with self-concept or self-esteem, look in the self-improvement section of any bookstore or library. You will find literally hundreds of books—each guaranteeing that if

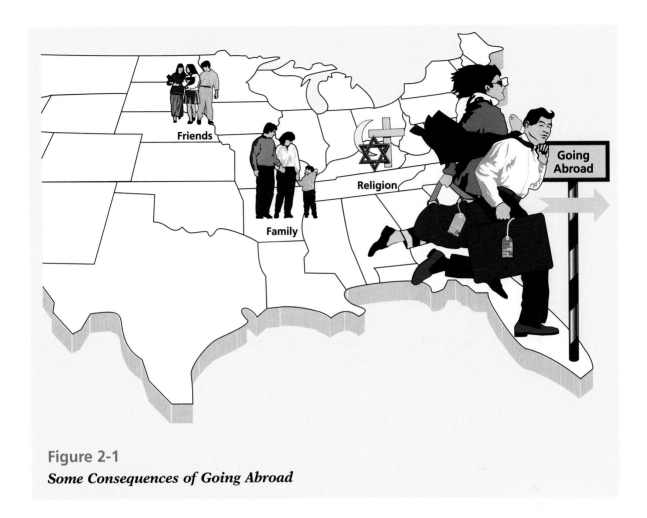

Figure 2-1
Some Consequences of Going Abroad

you read it, you will feel better about yourself and will change your self-esteem from negative to positive. One thing that many self-help books say is that the use of self-affirmations will assist you in raising your self-esteem. William Swann, Ph.D. (2001), of the University of Texas-Austin, suggests that self-affirmations, even when endlessly repeated, don't work and may even leave you more demoralized than before using them (Paul, 2001, p. 66).

According to Annie Paul, in her review article on "Self-Help" (2001), "The only way to change the final product—your self-esteem—is to change what goes into making it—feedback from other people." Then, she quotes Swann, who says "If you find yourself in bad relationships where your negative self-view is getting reinforced, then either change the way those people treat you by being more assertive, or change who you interact with" (p. 66). Then, in one of the most succinct, profound, and instructive summaries, she writes, "Stand up for yourself. Surround yourself with people who think you're great, and tell you so. Do your best to live up to their high opinions. And be patient. Self-esteem is the sum of your interactions with others over a lifetime, and it's not going to change overnight" (p. 66).

You should know that a positive self-concept may have nothing to do with success. Researchers have found that criminals and juvenile delinquents often have high self-esteem (Johnson, 1998). Even though self-esteem may not be connected to success, a positive sense of who you are is good because it will make you feel happier.

Unfortunately, as noted earlier, you can't change your self-concept by wishing it was more positive. It is going to change only when you have positive experiences and the accumulation of these experiences makes you feel better about yourself. The Internet has provided a useful medium for youthful posturing and experimentation regarding trying on a variety of selves (Kanter, 2001, p. 295; Nie & Erbring, 2000). Peter Doskoch, in an article "Personality Crisis? Not on the Net," has noted that those flocking to chatrooms and adopting new personae tend to have problems in real life. Other psychologists have found that most people are themselves online (Doskoch, 1998, p. 70).

What Do You Want to Change about Yourself?

Pick one area in which you would like to improve yourself. See if you can figure out why you have had problems in this area. Were you given a script saying you were inadequate in this area? Are you living out a self-fulfilling prophecy?

Are Your Circumstances Keeping You from Changing?

Are you living in circumstances that are holding you back? Do the people around you support you if you want to do something differently, especially if it involves taking a risk? Sometimes the people you live with try to hold you back—even though they might not be conscious of doing so. For example, one spouse says to the other, "Why do you want to go to Europe? We haven't seen all of the United States yet."

Sometimes you are locked into roles that are uncomfortable for you. Many women feel trapped when their children are small; some people hate their jobs; some students hate school. Are you in a role that you have chosen for yourself, or has someone else chosen it for you? Has someone else defined how you should play this role? Can you play this role in a way that will make it more comfortable for you? Can you change the role so that you can be more like the person you want to be?

Are You Willing to Take Some Chances?

Colleges and universities offer great chances to take some risks. Take a course from a professor who is rumored to be hard but fair. Study a subject you know nothing about. Join a club that sounds interesting—even if you don't know any of its members. Many colleges and universities also offer opportunities to study abroad or to take an internship. Going abroad is especially helpful in building self-confidence.

What Would Be a Realistic Goal?

Too often, people decide they are going to change their behavior overnight. Students who habitually get poor grades will often announce that this semester they are going to get all A's. This is an unrealistic goal. If you are going to try to change your behavior, see if you can break the problem down into steps you can handle. Let's say that you are shy but would like to speak up more in class because you often know the answers. Why not set a goal to speak up once a week in one class? That is probably a goal you can manage. Once you feel comfortable with that, you might increase your goal to speaking up two or even three times a week.

Can You Discipline Yourself?

The old saying "Nothing succeeds like success" applies to a positive self-concept: As soon as you experience success, you start feeling better about yourself. Sometimes people think they are not successful because they are not motivated enough. Typical thinking might be, "If only I could motivate myself, I would get better grades." People who think this way confuse motivation with discipline. There's no way to motivate yourself to take out the garbage, do the dishes, or study your class notes. These jobs can be done only through discipline: You say, "I am going to do this job for one hour—whether or not I want to do it is irrelevant." This sort of discipline is what leads to success, which, in turn, helps you feel better about yourself.

Are There People Who Will Support You?

Whenever we try to bring about a change in ourselves, we need to surround ourselves with people who will support us. These are people who understand how difficult it is to change and who understand our desire to do so. Take the example of speaking up in class. If you are very apprehensive about doing this, you might consider discussing the problem with an instructor you like and trust. Tell him or her that you are occasionally going to try to say something, and ask for his or her support. Also tell a couple of friends in your class what you plan to do. Just having other people know what you are trying to accomplish often provides good moral support. Not all people will support you, and some may even consciously try to defeat you. For them, the possibility that you might change is too threatening.

When you have found some people to support you, it's important that you tell them what you want to do and give them some direction as to how they can help you.

Can You Be More You-Centered?

People who lack self-esteem often spend a lot of time looking inward at their miseries, while people who seem happy and content with themselves seem to spend their time interacting with others. If you look inward all the time, you are probably making yourself more miserable. For a few days, experiment with relating more to the people around you. Just asking some one, "How was your day?" or "How is your semester (or quarter) going?" shows that you are interested.

If you have an opportunity to bestow some praise, do it. Look for situations around you in which you can praise people, and express your praise with genuine feeling. Tell your mother that her meatloaf tastes great, tell a professor that her class was really helpful on an internship, tell a friend that she looks wonderful in green. When you act positively toward others, they will act positively toward you, and this, in turn, will make you feel better about yourself.

■ PERCEPTION

Self-concept and perception are so closely related that they are often difficult to separate. While your self-concept is how you see yourself, **perception** is how you look at others and the world around you. Because your total awareness of the world comes through your senses, they all have a common basis and a common bias. How you look at the world depends on what you think of yourself, and what you think of yourself will influence how you look at the world.

Self-concept affects perception in another way as well. Acts of perception are more than simply capturing incoming stimuli. These acts require a form of expectation, of knowing what is about to confront you and preparing for it. These expectations or predispositions to respond are a type of perceptual filter called **psychological sets,** and they have a profound effect on your perceptions. "Without expectations, or constructs through which you perceive your world," writes John Ratey (2001), associate clinical professor of psychiatry at Harvard Medical School, "your surroundings would be what William James called a 'booming, buzzing confusion,' and each experience truly would be a new one, rapidly overwhelming you. You automatically and unconsciously fit your sensations into categories that you have learned, often distorting them in the process" (p. 56). Your self-concept not only helps create the psychological sets, assists in putting together the constructs, and aids in the formation of the categories, but is responsible for the distortions that occur in the process as well.

We can see how this works in the case of Chad and Karen, who are both emergency medical technicians (EMTs) at the local hospital. They work in the same crew and go out on ambulance runs together. They are used to working together, and each respects the other's ability. Chad admires how efficiently Karen can attach an IV to a patient, and Karen admires Chad's ability to comfort children who are in pain. On days when very little happens, they sit and chat and discover that they have many interests in common. They both like baseball, hiking, and camping. After a few months go by, they find that one of the pleasures of going to work is to see each other. Each would like to see the other outside of work, but neither has made a move in that direction. Then one day they bump into each other on a hiking trail, and they decide to walk the trail together. As they walk, Chad is thinking, "I really would like to ask her out. I wonder if she has a boyfriend." Karen is thinking along a similar line. "He really is a nice guy, I'd like to get to know him better. I think he likes me, but I'm really not sure."

You can see how their experiences together created the expectations in both about the possibilities of future contact. You can also see how constructs have been established—both Chad and Karen have constructed complete images of the other from what they have discovered. And you can see, too, how information has been stored in specific categories like common interests. You might even be able to project what might have occurred had either Chad or Karen had a weak self-concept and distorted some of the images of each other because of them. Chad might say, "She'd never go for me, she's too smart," or Karen might say, "I know he's too nice a guy for me. I could never keep such a nice guy, there is no point in even pursuing a relationship." You begin to see what Ratey was talking about when he said "We automatically and unconsciously fit our sensations into categories. . . ." (p. 56).

Although Chad and Karen's actual conversation and thoughts seem to be ordinary, each of them is going through a complicated perceptual process. Notice how expectations, constructs, categories, and distortions each play a role in the perceptual process. On one level, what Chad is saying and thinking reflects how he feels about himself ("I hate to ask someone out and then find out she has a boyfriend"). On another level, his thoughts reflect how he feels about Karen, or, his construct of Karen from what he knows of her thus far ("I like her, and I would like to know her better"). On yet a third level, they are influenced by how he thinks Karen sees him ("She seems to like me"). Although distortions could play a role at any level, this is a level where it often comes into play ("She'd never go for me, she's too smart").

Karen is going through a similar perceptual process. Her thoughts and what she says are influenced by how she sees herself, how she perceives Chad, and how she thinks Chad perceives her. Expectations, constructs, categories, and distortions will play just as important a role in her perceptual process as it did in Chad's.

The workings of self-confidence and perception make Chad and Karen's communication a complicated business. As is true in all transactional communication, many factors are occurring continuously and simultaneously. Chad's perception of Karen is influenced by how he sees himself and how he sees his past relationships just as Karen is influenced by her sense of self and her experiences with other men. Not only are there likely to be distortions here because of the strengths and weaknesses of one's self-concept, but think, too, about the psychological sets—expectations or predispositions to respond—based on past experiences. Has either just come out of a negative relationship? Has either come from a family full of separations and divorces—to name just two possible influences.

The complications, of course, don't stop there. Chad and Karen will be influenced by how they see their roles in a male-female relationship. Think of the influence here of the constructs created about male-female interactions. Karen might want to be more assertive in moving their friendship forward, but because of her idea of the role a woman should play in a relationship, she's worried about being too aggressive. Chad believes that it is his role to move the relationship forward, but he is too uncertain, and perhaps unsure of himself, to do so.

Just as Karen and Chad are slow in getting to know each other because of the way they see themselves, the way you view the world and communicate about it is greatly influenced by the way you view yourself.

Consider This

As you read this piece from Dr. McGraw (Dr. Phil), think about the effect that negative internal dialogue has on your perceptions of yourself, others, and the world around you:

Think of it this way: When you've lost your keys and then you find them, do you keep looking for your keys? If you've been searching for an answer and you believe you have it, do you continue investigating? No. You call off the search. Now suppose your conversation with yourself runs like this: "I am a knucklehead, I have always been a knucklehead, I will always be a knucklehead and no one will respect me." Once you begin believing yourself, why would you continue to process data? You might have ten experiences in the next week that run counter to your being a knucklehead, but your data processing window is shut, so you don't see the contrary information. You don't hear it. If your internal dialogue is that you are a knucklehead, and you believe that you are truthful with yourself then you absolutely will miss evidence to the contrary. You will miss it, even it it's served up to you on a silver platter. And you certainly won't go seeking out such evidence.

Questions

1. Are you comfortable with Dr. McGraw's explanation? Have you any personal examples to support his conclusion?

2. Are there times when you *have* continued to process data after one would expect the data-processing window to be closed? Under what circumstances?

3. What precautions could one take to make certain the data-processing window isn't closed too early—before all relevant data has been captured and considered?

Source: P. C. McGraw, *Self Matters: Creating Your Life from the Inside Out*. New York: Simon & Schuster, (2001), pp. 193–94.

The Perceptual Process

Your perceptions affect more than your direct interactions with people. They also influence your response to all the information around you. Whenever you encounter new information, whether it's from a television program, a newspaper, the Internet, or another person, you go through a three-step perceptual process: You select the information, you organize it, and you interpret it.

We do not all perceive information in the same way. Even when several people have access to the same information, they are likely to select, organize, and interpret it in different ways. Let's say, for example, that three different people read the same newspaper: Omar is a Syrian who is studying in the United States; Caroline is an American who has been an exchange student in Syria; and Jim is an American who has never traveled.

When Omar reads the paper, he looks for (selects) news about Syria. In his mind he organizes the information on the basis of what he already knows. He may interpret it by asking the meaning of certain government actions or by thinking that the reporter has the wrong slant on the story. Caroline goes through a similar process. She has a high interest in stories about Syria because she has been there. She, too, organizes what she reads

On the Web

And what is the connection between perception and communication?

Perception and communication are the twin skills needed by every good beer judge. Perception is the ability to see, taste, smell, and feel different elements in the beer, and to be able to recognize them for what they are and what *they tell a brewer or drinker about the beer in the glass. Communication is the ability to describe these perceptions to another brewer or knowledgeable beer drinker in a meaningful way.*

Source: M. Stevens, *Introduction to beer judging, tasting, and evaluation.* April 10, 1997. Retrieved March 14, 2003, from http://www.brewery.org/brewery/library/Tintro.html.

Whenever you encounter new information you go through a three-step perceptual process: You select the information, you organize it, and you interpret it.

according to what she knows about the country. However, she may interpret the news stories differently because she doesn't have as much information as Omar. Also, her interpretation will probably be from an American point of view. When Jim reads the newspaper, he skips all the stories about Omar's country. He has never been there and has no immediate plans to go there. In fact, he skips all the news about the world and goes directly to the sports section. These three people are all exposed to the same information, but they all perceive it differently.

Perceptions and the Self-Concept

There are a number of things that can be stated with certainty about the self-concept and perception (Purkey, 1988):

- Your self-concept is learned. It gradually emerges in the early months of life, but it is shaped and reshaped through repeated perceived experiences.

- Your self-concept is a social product that is developed through your perceptions of your experiences.

- Because of previous experiences and present perceptions, you may perceive yourself in ways different from the ways others see you.

- Your self-concept requires consistency and stability; it tends to resist change. If your self-concept were changed readily, you would lack a consistent and dependable personality; thus, your perceptions seek supportive information.

- Because your perceptions of yourself are quite stable, change takes time. Rome wasn't built in a day; neither is your self-concept.

- Your successes and failures impact on your self-concept. Just as failure in highly regarded areas lowers evaluations in other areas; success in prized areas raises evaluations in other areas as well.

- Your world, and all the things in it, are not just perceived, they are perceived only in relation to your self-concept.

- The development of your self-concept is a continuous process. Your perceptions are always alert to information. If you have a healthy personality, you will continually assimilate new ideas and discharge old ideas.

- You strive to behave in ways that are in keeping with your self-concept, no matter how helpful or hurtful to yourself or others.

- You continuously guard your self-concept against the loss of self-esteem, because such losses produce feelings of anxiety.

- Because your self-concept is constantly defending itself from assault, growth opportunities are limited (Purkey, 1988).

Of all the perceptions you experience in the course of living your life, none has more profound significance than those you hold regarding your own personal existence—your concept of who you are and how you fit into the world. But the perceptions you experience are subject to deletions, distortions, and generalizations, plus additional perceptual filters; thus, you do not come at the world in a pure, clean, untainted manner. The way you come at the world, instead, is—and has to be—totally unique. It is distinctive, exceptional, and unequaled—unmatched—in all the world. If you want something no one else has, you have it. It's the way you come at the world.

Deletions, Distortions, and Generalizations

Any perceptions you have are less than perfect because of deletions, distortions, and generalizations (External Reality, 1999). **Deletions**—blotting out, erasing, or canceling information—must occur, first, because your physical senses are limited. Your sight, hearing, touch, taste, and smell are the means you use to get information, but those senses focus only on those aspects of the environment that are most important for your survival. Your senses are not capable of perceiving everything in your external environment. Deletions occur, too, because of your beliefs. If you believe something to be true, you have an almost infinite capacity to delete information that contradicts that belief. In addition, if you believe something to be true, you will go through your life searching for information that supports that belief and ignore information that does not.

In addition to deleting information, you also distort much of the information from your environment. **Distortions** involve twisting or bending information out of shape. You distort information, first because you only observe a small part of your external environment. Since what you observe is such a small part of the whole, you must fill in the blanks—specifically add information—to make your information make sense. The other reason why you distort information is so that it will support your existing beliefs and values.

In addition to deleting and distorting information, you draw generalizations based on little substantial information. **Generalizations** involve drawing principles or conclusions from particular evidence or facts. Once you have observed something a few times, you conclude that what has proven true in the past will prove true in the future as well. Generalizations are important to your survival. Getting burned by putting a hand on a hot stove will give you a conclusion about the consequences of putting your hand on a hot stove in the future. If you had several bad experiences with members of the opposite sex, of a different race, of a different culture, or of a particular organization, you might generalize that *all* members of the opposite sex, a different race, a different culture, or a particular organization are bad (External Reality.). Then, all future experiences are filtered through that belief, information that contradicts the belief is deleted, and you distort other information so it will support the belief.

Keep these three activities in mind as you read the next section on perceptual filters. Realize that even before perceptual filters come into play and certainly while they are operating as well, deletion, distortion, and generalization are also influencing the information (External Reality, 1999).

Perceptual Filters

Deletions, distortions, and generalizations are important and affect your perceptions, but perceptual filters can be even more important. If self-concept and perception are as intimately intertwined as the section on "Perception and Self-Concept" above illustrates, then what factors influence your perceptions? There are a number of contributing factors. As you read through them, notice that for you, just as for others, some factors may be more influential than others (Yeager, 2001). As you read them, too, consider them **perceptual filters,** or limitations that result from the narrowed lens through which you view the world. For example, your biologic make-up has a significant influence. If your biologic makeup differs from that of the predominant society—if you are obese, short, or unattractive, for example—you may have difficulty securing and maintaining a positive self-concept because of the distortions your senses cause. You automatically see things differently than members of the predominant society.

Other significant influences on your perceptions include your culture, values, and beliefs. You, like most people, find it easier to communicate with members of your own culture. By *culture*, as noted in Chapter 1, The Communication Process, and as further discussed and explained in Chapter 3, Intercultural Communication, we mean "The ever-changing values, traditions, social and political relationships, and worldview created and shared by a group of people bound together by a combination of factors (which can include a common history, geographic location, language, social class, and/or religion)" (Nieto, 1995, p. 390). Many of your customs (e.g., Halloween), values (e.g., Everything should be clean: people, streets, buildings), and beliefs (All men are created equal)—as well as your manners, ceremonies, rituals, laws, language, religious beliefs, myths and legends, knowledge, ideals, accepted ways of behaving, and even your concept of self—are culturally determined. If you do not integrate American cultural practices, values, and beliefs, but those of another culture, you may have difficulty securing or maintaining a positive self-concept.

There are numerous other influences, too, such as the ways you have for coping with and tolerance for stress as well as your conflict resolution strategies (Yeager, 2001). If through your upbringing you have developed inadequate coping patterns to adapt to stress or resolve conflict you may have difficulty securing or maintaining a positive self-concept. One major influence would be the familial patterns you observed between your parents and between your parents and you or other siblings. For example, some of the patterns you may have observed could include the excessive use of denial, projection of blame and responsibility, hypersensitivity to criticism, and rationalizing of failures. Destructive behaviors may have included overeating, excessive smoking or drinking, the overuse of over-the-counter medications, or illicit drug use. Even high rates of illness as a result of high blood pressure, ulcers, irritable bowel syndrome, frequent headaches or neck aches, may, too, have been influential.

Other influences on your perceptions could include your previous experiences. Many failures rather than successes may create difficulty. If you attribute your successes to luck, chance, or the influence of powerful others rather than to your own personal behavior, this could be a factor. If you have suffered stressful life events such as financial difficulties, problems on a job, change or loss of a job, relationship concerns, sexuality concerns, divorce, or moving, particularly if they have been cumulative, your perceptions could be affected. Illnesses, traumas, and surgery, too, can create alterations in self-esteem, body image, and personal identity and can influence your perceptions. Even your current physiological state can influence your perceptions. Insufficient nutritional food, lack of sleep, or a serious night of drinking and the consequent hangover can be influential.

Our purpose here has not been to cast a negative light on the role of your perceptions in creating and maintaining your self-concept, rather, it is to show how many factors are likely to influence your perceptions, and, thus, how your perceptions of yourself, others, and the world are likely to be different from any other person's perceptions. Any changes from the norm—

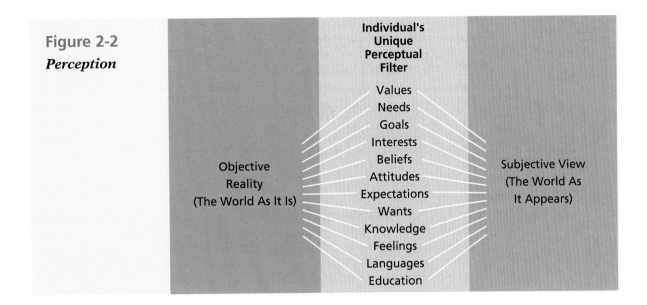

Figure 2-2
Perception

Individual's Unique Perceptual Filter

Values
Needs
Goals
Interests
Beliefs
Attitudes
Expectations
Wants
Knowledge
Feelings
Languages
Education

Objective Reality (The World As It Is)

Subjective View (The World As It Appears)

the perceptions of those who make up your predominant society—will influence your perceptions in some manner. Because there are so many influences, and because these influences are likely to combine in unknown ways and even have some cumulative effect, there is no way to predict or know how much effect the influences on your perceptions have nor how your self-concept is altered. What is interesting is that even self-assessments are likely to be distorted, since the self doing the assessing is also subject to the distortions!

Adjusting to Perceptual Influences

George A. Miller, the psychologist, said, "Most of our failures in understanding one another have less to do with what is heard than with what is intended and what is inferred." It would be great to believe that there were no such thing as perceptual filters. It would be great to believe that you come at the world straight on and that objective reality is, indeed, your reality. It would be great to believe, because of the truthfulness and honesty with which you conduct your life, that any observation you make is accurate, precise, and correct. That the conclusions you draw conform exactly to truth or to the standard set by the norm of others in your culture. Unfortunately, this is *never* the case. The fact is, your perceptions and the conclusions you draw from them represent, as noted in Figure 2-2, your reality, your subjective view, or the world as it appears to you.

If you think about it, if you were affected by any one of the perceptual influences listed above—lack of sleep, for example—you would experience some distortion from the norm. Whether or not you knew the distortion was occurring might depend on the severity of the influence—three nights without sleep—the circumstances in which you found yourself—taking a final exam—or whether you had other comparisons to make; that is, you had a way to compare your sensory data (observations) with that of others.

(Others thought the exam was fair; you thought it unfair.) You have drawn a conclusion that is true based on your perceptions.

Stay healthy, get rest, and exercise. Make every effort to come at the world as healthy, well-rested, and sufficiently exercised as possible. Because perception depends on your senses, the better condition that your senses are in, the more likely they will respond in proper ways. It is more likely that you will be able to be aware of and adjust to perceptual influences when you have a proper state of mind and body. For example, can you imagine getting physically and emotionally upset with an instructor because of an exam you felt was unfair after three days of no sleep, living on Mountain Dew, isolated in your room, and trying to study a semester's worth of notes in a day-and-a-half?

Avoid hasty conclusions. If you realize that you live in the same **objective world** as everyone else, the actual territory or external reality we all experience, and yet you have a different **subjective view** or personal mental map of that world—because of all your perceptual influences—then you realize at once that your experiences of the same external environment, whatever they are, have to differ. The **map is *not* the territory.** Your mental maps that you create, that is, your subjective experiences or subjective view, are different from the external, objective reality on which they are based. Thus, what are the chances that your conclusions about the objective world are going to be accurate? They will be based on *your* mental maps only, and therefore are likely to be just as inaccurate as anyone else's mental maps. That is why lawyers call on as wide a variety of witnesses as possible, hoping that through a combination of their views, they can get a closer, more accurate view of objective reality—realizing as they begin, no combination will get them the full picture they desire. Sometimes, of course, the selection of witnesses is specific and biased so the picture of reality will be the picture that will best help their client.

Getting back to avoiding hasty conclusions, if you feel it is necessary to publicly announce a conclusion, then state it tentatively rather than as a

On the Web

We think it makes sense to ask how self and perception relate to communication. At a website designed to provide an outline of a "Communication Workshop," the opening, introductory paragraph explains the importance of this chapter:

Communication is much more than a set of rules to follow. True communication involves not only the appreciation and expression of our different realities but also our ability to commune, to share and perceive the same reality. It involves skillful use of one's senses, one's heart, one's intellect to make authentic contact with another. It is the way we bridge our own internal state to get our needs met. After internal work, we can connect with the world, in ways that can be heard and accepted, if we listen as actively as we speak! (p. 1 of 7)

Source: (No author). *Communication Workshop.* Retrieved March 14, 2003, from http://www.growthandhealing.com/growthandhealing/comoutline.htm.

Assess Yourself

How Strong is Your Self-Esteem?

Please mark each statement in the following way:

If the statement describes how you usually feel, put a check in the column *Like Me.*
If the statement does not describe how you usually feel, put a check in the column *Unlike Me.*

For this inventory, there are no right or wrong answers.

	Like Me	Unlike Me
1. I'm pretty sure of myself.	___	___
2. I often wish I were someone else.	___	___
3. I'm easy to like.	___	___
4. I never worry about anything.	___	___
5. I find it very hard to talk in front of a class.	___	___
6. There are lots of things about myself I'd change if I could.	___	___
7. I can make up my mind without too much trouble.	___	___
8. I'm a lot of fun to be with.	___	___
9. I always do the right thing.	___	___
10. I'm proud of the college work that I do.	___	___
11. Someone always has to tell me what to do.	___	___
12. It takes me a long time to get used to anything new.	___	___
13. I'm often sorry for the things I do.	___	___
14. I'm never unhappy.	___	___
15. I'm doing the best work that I can.	___	___
16. I give in very easily.	___	___
17. I'm pretty happy.	___	___
18. I like everyone I know.	___	___
19. I like to be called on in class.	___	___
20. I understand myself.	___	___
21. Things are all mixed up in my life.	___	___
22. I'm not doing as well in college as I'd like to.	___	___
23. I can make up my mind and stick to it.	___	___
24. I have a low opinion of myself.	___	___
25. I don't like to be with other people.	___	___
26. I'm never shy.	___	___
27. I often feel upset in college.	___	___
28. If I have something to say, I usually say it.	___	___
29. I always tell the truth.	___	___

Assess Yourself (continued)

	Like Me	Unlike Me
30. Most people are better liked than I am.	_____	_____
31. I always know what to say to people.	_____	_____
32. I often get discouraged in college.	_____	_____
33. Things usually don't bother me.	_____	_____

 Go to the *Communicating Effectively* CD-ROM to see your results and learn how to evaluate your attitudes and feelings.

Source: Adapted from: S. Coopersmith, *The Antecedents of Self-Esteem*. (San Francisco: W. H. Freeman, 1967). In J. P. Robinson; P. R. Shaver; & L. S. Wrightsman, *Measures of Personality and Social Psychological Attitudes* (San Diego: Academic Press, 1991), p. 127–31.

conclusion. For example, rather than stating that you know that flying saucers exist because you saw strange lights in the sky last night, why not offer your observations in a tentative way that will allow exploration and discussion: "You know, I saw strange lights in the sky last night. Did anyone else see any strange lights?"

Take more time. The second method for adjusting to perceptual influences follows from the last one. Take more time. When it is said, patience is a virtue, nothing could be more succinct or accurate. Time has a number of benefits. It allows you to gather more facts. With more facts, it is likely your conclusions will change. Time also allows you to think about your observations and conclusions. For example, you might overhear another conversation about the strange lights in the sky, or read a newspaper article about a meteor shower last night, or the glow from locally launched weather balloons. How often have you discovered that your first impressions were wrong? That, for example, you could not tell what a book was about by its cover alone?

There is an important caution to be aware of as you search for information. As noted previously, when you believe something to be true, you will find information to support that belief. And that statement introduces the caution. Your external environment contains ample evidence to support all beliefs about a subject (External Reality . . ., 1999). If you believe, for example, that most people are bad and will lie, cheat, steal, and otherwise injure you, you can find plenty of evidence in the news and in your daily encounters with others to support that belief. If you believe that most people are good and will behave in honest, caring, and courageous ways, you can find plenty of evidence to support this belief as well. The point of gathering information is to seek evidence that might suggest your beliefs are in error or that other explanations exist for the conclusions you have reached.

Be available. Another method for adjusting to perceptual influences follows from the previous two methods. Be available to see the other person's viewpoint. Availability, here, means both physical and psychological openness. How often, for example, in the heat of an argument you could not stop long enough to really listen to another person's side? Rather, you were so upset you were framing your own ideas, choosing your own words, defending yourself from attack, and trying to outdo, outmaneuver, and outwit the other person? The advantage of counting to 10 to allow your emotions to calm, or stepping back and taking more time, or just trying to put yourself in the other person's shoes helps you become more available. The question, "Did anyone else see strange lights?" reveals availability and openness.

Be committed. Commit yourself to seeking more information. Commit yourself to having additional information before making any judgment. Commit yourself to being as fully informed as you would expect others to be with you before sharing their conclusions. Buy a local paper, for example, and examine it for possible explanations of strange lights in the sky. Listen to a local newscast for information. Go ask or make a call to a local expert who might have an answer. It is this kind of climate—the kind of climate in which educated and informed conversation and dialogue can take place—that is likely to produce additional perspectives, alternatives, and conclusions.

Be prepared to change. If everything has worked thus far, you are likely to get information, hear viewpoints, or gain perspectives, alternatives, or conclusions that you did not originally have. If this is true, you must be prepared to change accordingly. Whatever adjustments are necessary, you must be ready to make them. This is why it is important to avoid making hasty conclusions at the outset. In that way, changes at this point will be unnecessary. You simply adjust internally. If you expressed a hasty conclusion, now you must admit the error or openly reveal the adjustment necessary to accommodate the new information, viewpoint, perspective, alternative, or conclusion, and you can't save face, or protect yourself from embarrassment. Publicly admitting an error is difficult for anyone. As it turned out, the strange lights in the sky were a number of planes returning to the local airport at the same time, having all been at the same air show in another state. From the ground, at night, depending on your position or location, the planes lit up the night sky.

As you take steps to reduce the effect of perceptual influences on you, you will notice changes simply because the information you will get is likely to be more accurate and dependable. It will be better information for use in building a stronger self-concept.

Chapter Review

Self-concept is how you think about and value yourself. Self-concept comes from three sources: reflected appraisals, social comparisons, and self-perception. Scripts, roles, and self-fulfilling prophecies also influence your self-concept. If people are willing to give up some of their psychological safety and take some risks, their self-concepts will become more positive.

There are several ways to improve your self-concept. Decide what you want to change about yourself, consider your circumstances, take some chances, set reasonable goals, use a program of self-discipline, find people who will support you, and act positively toward others.

While self-concept is how you look at yourself, perception is how you see others and the world around you. Your perceptions come from interactions with others and from your cultural background. In the perceptual process you select information, organize it, and interpret it. Your education and experience will influence how you carry out this process.

There are a number of things that can be stated with certainty about the self-concept and perception including that they are intimately and intrinsically linked, each affecting the other in both subtle and profound ways. Your perceptions are essential to the building, maintenance, and sustained support of your self-concept.

Any perceptions you have are less than perfect because of deletions, distortions, and generalizations. Also, perceptual filters such as your biologic make-up, culture, values, and beliefs, coping with and tolerance for stress, conflict resolution strategies, previous experiences with failures and successes, illnesses, traumas, and sur-

gery will all have an effect on your perceptions. Because there are so many influences, and because these influences are likely to combine in unknown ways and even have some cumulative effect, there is no way to predict or know the effect of the influences on your perceptions nor on how your self-concept is altered.

There are a number of ways to adjust to perceptual influences. The first is to stay healthy and get rest and exercise. The second is to avoid hasty conclusions. The third is to take more time. Be available and be committed are four and five, and the sixth way to adjust to perceptual influences is to be prepared to change. But just because you have adjusted to perceptual influences, keep in mind that it is common to come to wrong conclusions; thus, it is extremely important to continually check out your interpretations of reality.

Questions to Review

1. How do reflected appraisals, social comparisons, and self-perception lead to a self-concept?

2. What is a self-fulfilling prophecy, and how does it contribute to one's self-concept?

3. What is psychological risk, and how does it contribute to one's growth and self-concept?

4. What are some of the ways by which self-concept might be improved.

5. What is perception, and how is it tied into self-concept?

6. What are the three steps of the perceptual process?

7. What are some things that can be stated with certainty about the self-concept and perception?

8. Why can it be said that the way you come at the world is distinctive, exceptional, and unequaled in all the world?

9. What role do deletions, distortions, and generalizations play in perceptions? Can you give an example of each one?

10. What are some of the perceptual filters that narrow the lens through which you view the world?

11. What are some of the ways you can adjust to perceptual influences?

Go to the self-quizzes on the Communicating Effectively CD-ROM (side 2, track 10) and the Online Learning Center at mhhe.com/hybels7 to test your knowledge of the chapter concepts.

References

Angier, N. (1997, March 14). "Sexual identity not pliable after all, report says." *New York Times*, A1, A18.

Boone, M. E. (2001). *Managing inter@ctively: Executing business strategy, improving communication, and creating a knowledge-sharing culture.* New York: McGraw-Hill.

Doskoch, P. (1998, March/April). "Personality crisis? Not on the net." *Psychology Today* 31:2, 70.

(No author). (1999, Dec. 28). "External reality and subjective experience." Western Michigan University. Retrieved March 14, 2003, from http://spider.hcob.wmich.edu/bis/faculty/bowman/erse.html.

(No author). (1999, July 7). "G. I. Joe: Is he really a self-esteem problem?" *Columbus Dispatch*, 8A.

Johnson, K. (1998, May 5). "Self-image is suffering from lack of esteem." *New York Times*, C7.

Joseph, R. A., H. R. Markus, & R. W. Tafarodi. (1992, Sept.). Gender and self-esteem. *Journal of Personality and Social Psychology* 63:3, 391–402.

Kanter, R. M. (2001). *E-volve: Succeeding in the digital culture of tomorrow*. Boston, MA: Harvard Business School Press.

Keillor, G. (1985). *Lake Wobegon days*. New York: Penguin/Viking Press.

Manz, C. C., & H. P. Sims, Jr., (2001). *The new superleadership: Leading others to lead themselves*. San Francisco, CA: Berrett-Koehler Publishers.

Maslow, A. H. (1970). *Motivation and personality*, 2nd ed. New York: Harper & Row.

Muriel, J., & D. Joneward (1971). *Born to win: Transactional analysis with gestalt experiments*. Reading, MA: Addison-Wesley.

Nie, N., & L. Erbring (2000, February 17). *Internet and society: A preliminary report*. Stanford University, CA: Stanford Institute for the Quantitative Study of Society; InterSurvey, Inc.; and McKinsey & Company.

Nieto, S. (1995). *Affirming diversity: The sociopolitical context of multicultural education* 2nd ed. New York: Longman. In F. Yeo, (1999, Fall). "The barriers of diversity: Multicultural education and rural schools." *Multicultural Education* 6th ed. 2–7. In F. Schultz (ed.). (2001). *Multicultural Education*, 8th ed. Guilford, CT: McGraw-Hill/Dushkin.

Paul, A. M. (2001, March/April). "Self-help: Shattering the myths." *Psychology Today*, 60–68.

(No author). *Perception and the self*. Retrieved March 14, 2003, from http://webhome.idirect. com/~kehamilt/ipsyperc.html.

Purkey, W. (1988). *An overview of self-concept theory for counselors*. ERIC Clearinghouse on Counseling and Personnel Services. Ann Arbor, MI (an ERIC/CAPS Digest: ED304630).

Ratey, J. R. (2001). *A user's guide to the brain: Perception, attention, and the four theaters of the brain*. New York: Pantheon Books.

Rubin, M., ed. (1980). *Men without masks*. Reading, MA: Addison-Wesley.

Santiago, E. (1994, Dec. 18). "A Puerto Rican stew." *New York Times Magazine*, 34–36.

Schwalbe, M. L., & C. Staples (1991). "Gender difference in self-esteem." *Social Psychology Quarterly* 54:2, 158–68.

Tanno, D. V. (2000). "Names, narratives, and the evolution of ethnic identity." In Gonzalez, A., M. Houston, & V. Chen, eds. *Our voices: Essays in culture, ethnicity, and communication* Los Angeles, CA: Roxbury Publishing Company, 25–28.

Wiener, V. (1999). *Winning the war against youth gangs: A guide for teens, families, and communities*. Westport, CT: Greenwood Press.

Yeager, S. (2001, Jan. 1). *Lecture notes: Self-concept*. DeSales University. Retrieved March 14, 2003, from http://www4.allencol.edu/~sey0/selfla.html.

Further Readings

Allen, R. L. (2001). *The concept of self: A study of black identity and self-esteem*. (African American Life Series). Detroit, MI: Wayne State University Press. Allen, a professor in the department of communication at the University of Michigan, examines past scholarship on African-American identity and explores a wide range of issues leading to the formation of an individual and collective sense of self. Using results of the National Study of Black Americans, he develops a model of African self. The three parts of his book illustrate his approach: 1) The Black Self, Trends, Influences, and Effects, 2) Theoretical and Empirical Examination of the Black Self, and 3) Theory Construction. A book designed for the serious student.

Branden, N. (1998). *A woman's self-esteem: Struggles and triumphs in the search for identity*. San Francisco, CA: Jossey Bass. In this 160-page book Branden has expanded on the articles on women's issues he wrote for *New Woman* magazine in the early 90s. His primary focus is on the challenges facing women: how to embrace their strengths, how to be assertive, and how to keep appropriate boundaries. Early in the book, Branden summarizes his overall theory in a succinct, meaningful way. This book will make readers think deeply and clearly about the role of self-esteem in their lives.

Dalrymple, T. (2001). *Life at the bottom: The worldview that makes the underclass*. Chicago, IL: Ivan R. Dee, Publisher. Dalrumple, a British psychiatrist, who treats the poor in a slum hospital and a prison in England, offers a searing account of life in the underclass and why it persists as it does. Of 22-chapters in this 263-page book, by far the most relevant for this chapter on self-concept, is "Choosing to Fail" in which Dalrymple offers realistic views of the nonverbal illustrations of failure, the self-fulfilling prophecies of doom, and the pernicious negative filters through which those who choose to fail, see the world. Dalrumple draws the conclusion for all members of our society: "for while we ascribe our conduct to pressures from without, we obey the whims that well up from within, thereby awarding ourselves carte blanche to behave as we choose. Thus we feel good about behaving badly" (p. 122). This is an excellent, readable, eye-opening book.

Eakin, P. J. (2001). *How our lives become stories: Making selves*. Ithaca, NY: Cornell University Press. Using life writings from works by Christa Wolf, Oliver Sacks, Henry Louis Gates, Melanie Thernstrom, and Philip Roth, Eakin draws on the latest research in neurology, cognitive science, memory studies, and developmental psychology to re-think the nature of self-representation. He shows how living in one's body shapes one's self-identity. He clearly demonstrates that the self and the story of self are constantly evolving in relation to others.

Friday, N. (1997). *My mother/my self: The daughter's search for identity*. Surrey, England: Delta Publishing. Friday uses self-disclosure and hundreds of interviews to underscore the feminine legacy of the mother/daughter bond, and she reveals the anger, hate, and love that daughters hold for their mothers. Although originally written twenty years ago, it has great meaning for both men and women because it uncovers the causes for pain in broken relationships and the embarrassing patterns that engender them. An excellent self-development book.

McGraw, P. C. (2001). *Self matters: Creating your life from the inside out*. New York: Simon & Schuster. Listen to some of McGraw's early chapter titles: Defining the Authentic Self, Your Self-Concept, Locus of Control, and Internal Dialogue. Although the information appears to be correct, although the book is well written with a large number of useful and interesting examples, and although McGraw (Dr. Phil) covers the topics thoroughly, he includes no references, footnotes, or bibliography, and even when he writes, "In an experiment some years ago." he gives readers no source and the experimenters no credit. That doesn't deny the value of the information, but readers have to rely on McGraw's credibility for the validity of what he writes. This is a great motivational book for those whose self-concept is in need of repair or for those who use excuses and fears to run their lives.

Nam, V. (2001). *YELL-Oh girls! Emerging voices explore culture, identity, and growing up Asian American.* Hillsboro, NH: Quill Publishers. Nam's main focus is on the tough work of establishing identity, and it is relevant for young women of all ethnic backgrounds. The 80 brief essays in this 336-page book cover such things as body image, interracial friendship, dating, adoption, "model minority" stereotypes, Asian-American feminist activism, sexuality, language and white boy's "Asian fetish." It is useful especially for young females who are trying to understand their cultural identity. A well written book that is totally relevant for today's society.

Shields, V. R. & D. Heinecken. (2002). *Measuring up: How advertising affects self-image*. State College, PA: University of Pennsylvania Press. Bringing together the literature of feminist media studies, feminist film theory, critical social theory, cultural studies, and critical ethnography, the authors examine the complex relationship between the idealized images of gender seen in advertising and one's own thoughts, feelings, and behavior in relation to these images. "They are technoenhanced labyrinths of unattainable appearances that leave women and men feeling horrified, estranged, and restricted by unrealistic, silent mandates," say the authors.

Tucker-Ladd, C. E. (1999). "Chapter 14—Methods for changing our thoughts, attitudes, self-concept, motivation, values, and expectations." *Psychological Self-Help* (An Online Book). Retrieved March 14, 2003, from http://mentalhelp.net/psyhelp/ chap14/. Although there are a number of sections in this work that are relevant to communication, this one is particularly useful because Tucker-Ladd, a licensed clinical psychologist, discusses changing self-concept, building self-esteem, and increasing self-awareness. He also offers help in improving one's self through motivation, straight thinking, common sense, and attitudes that will help you. A straightforward, encouraging book.

Whyte, D. (2001). *Crossing the unknown sea: Work as a pilgrimage of identity*. New York, NY: Riverhead Books (A division of Penguin Putnam, Inc.). Whyte views work not only as a means of support, but as a means for interacting with the world and developing self-expression and identity. He draws on the philosophical underpinnings of the self-help movement aimed at finding one's "inner compass," but there is no step-by-step format to follow here, rather an interesting and provocative look at the subject of work and its effect of individuals. This is a fascinating, insightful tour of the human psyche.

Chapter 3

Intercultural Communication

Objectives

After reading this chapter you should be able to:
- Offer a clear definition of culture.
- List various ways that chances for contacts with people from other cultures have increased.
- Explain reasons for studying intercultural communciation.
- Relate intercultural communication to the model of communication and communication as a transaction.
- List and briefly explain six dimensions or frameworks for studying cultural differences.
- List and explain barriers to intercultural communication.
- Distinguish among assimilation, accommodation, and separation strategies, and explain their purpose.
- Explain ways you have to improve intercultural communication.

Key Terms and Concepts

Use the Communicating Effectively CD-ROM and Online Learning Center at mhhe.com/hybels7 to further your understanding of the following terms.

Accommodation 83	Dominant culture 81	Nondominant culture 81
Accommodation strategies 83–84	Ethnocentrism 79	Patriotism 79
	Femininity versus masculinity 76	Power distance 74–76
Assimilation 81		Prejudice 80
Assimilation strategies 81–82	High context versus low context 77–78	Separation 84
Assumption 86	Individualism versus collectivism 76	Separation strategies 84–85
Coculture 65		Stereotypes 79–80
Context 77	Intercultural communication 68	Transpection 88
Culture 66		Uncertainty avoidance 76–77
Cultural identity 65	Long-term orientation 77	
Discrimination 80	National communities 70	Worldview 67

...Cinco De Mayo
...ought to you by special ward program

BEFORE COMING TO THE UNIVERSITY, I HAD NO thoughts about culture. It wasn't as if I was unaware of the differing cultures around me and the joy one should take within the classroom, demonstrating and celebrating the issue of diverseness, but rather the state where I resided all my life generally looked upon differences as accepted and not an issue that needed to be the basis of one's social existence. People are people, and they are accepted for who they are regardless of their ages, races, sexes, sexual orientation, or creeds.

In the public and Catholic elementary and secondary schools where I attended and taught, efforts—although they weren't all good—were made to provide students with the opportunity to express their identities, and teachers were willing to accept, assist, and allow students to foster a deeper sense of themselves at the spiritual, ethnic, and social levels.

While attending San Diego State University, many of my Hispanic companions born in the area stated that I was not Hispanic because of my ignorance of the Spanish language. One disturbing reality came to life while I discussed the issue with some friends. I noticed the racial separation on campus—Hispanics, African-Americans, Asians, and European-Americans congregated within their own groups without intermingling with people of other backgrounds. I was told, as my friends of color were, that we needed to "stick to our own kind" and not to associate with others. People used words like "coconut," "white-washed," and "sell out" toward us many times (Ramirez, Autry, & Morton, 2000, p. 65).

Fred Ramirez's experience, in the opening example above, is not unlike that of many other students. For most of his life, he had no thoughts about culture. It was only at college that it became an issue, and a negative one at that when, first, he noticed the racial separation, second, that various groups did not intermingle with people of other backgrounds and, third, that cultural slurs were used to keep people within their cultural groups. Although Fred cannot change the world, right the inequities he observed, or encourage others to live and work together in more harmonious ways, he can learn more about intercultural communication to establish a lifelong pattern of communication with the expressed purpose of bridging differences. Of course, that is exactly what Fred did as he became a teacher and writer about cultural issues and, indeed, does encourage others to live and work together in more harmonious ways.

In this chapter on intercultural communication we first look at the word *culture* and the importance of understanding your role as a cultural being. In the second section, we discuss the importance of intercultural communication. In the third section, we relate intercultural communication to the model of communication discussed in Chapter 1. In section four, we discuss six dimensions or frameworks for studying cultural differences. In section five, we discuss barriers to intercultural communication. In section six we look at how to deal with the barriers, which includes a discussion of dominant and nondominant cultures. Section seven is a practical section with suggestions for improving intercultural communication.

■ YOU ARE A CULTURAL BEING

One desired outcome from reading about *culture* is that you will recognize and accept *yourself* as a cultural being. **Cultural identity,** composed of ethnicity, culture, gender, age, life stage, beliefs, values, and assumptions, is the degree to which you identify with your culture, and it is determined by the values you support. If you were born and raised in the United States, your cultural identity involves the degree to which you identify with being American. But, it doesn't stop there. You have a number of cultural identities—being a member of the student body, a particular race, a specific age group, a religion, and so on. Although sometimes referred to as subcultures, the word *subculture* has the connotation of a culture beneath, lower, or under. We have chosen, instead, to use the word **coculture** to represent nonwhites, women, people with disabilities, homosexuals, and those in the lower social classes who have specific patterns of behavior that set them off from other groups within a culture (Gudykunst & Kim, 2003, p. 122). Which cultural identity is prominent depends on the situation, the people you are with, and the conversational topics.

There are three things that you need to understand about possessing a cultural identity. First, cultural identities are learned. You learn the ways of thinking, acting, and feeling from your family first, then from your friends and communities. You are not born knowing your culture; you come to know it through your interactions with others. Second, cultural identities vary in strength. Morgan, for example, had all the speech and language patterns, all the actions and reactions of a typical U.S. American student. All were so deeply embedded within her that she wasn't even aware of it until she visited Australia with her debate team. In a discussion with some Australian debaters, one challenged the American way of life as decadent, materialistic, and hedonistic. Morgan did not realize the strength of her cultural identity, and she was shocked at how fast, strong, and poised she was in articulating and defending her country and "the American way."

Third, cultural identities vary in their content. For example, not everyone would define what it means to be an American in the same way, just as students have different ways of defining what it means to be a student. The importance of this point becomes evident when you begin to generalize about cultures. To what extent do you value freedom, pleasure, social recognition, and being independent? These are values often ascribed to members of the U.S. American culture. What if you were a Japanese-American and you held cultural identities for both these cultures? The Japanese culture values self-sacrifice, harmony, and accepting traditions—values that, in part, directly contradict those of the U.S. American culture.

You can see from this example alone how cultural identities vary in their content, but when you realize all the cultural identities people possess, you also can see the perplexities associated with the *intersection* of issues of race and ethnicity, language, religion, gender and sexual orientation, generation and age, and so forth, as they operate within individuals. These factors interact and come out differently in different people. Understanding cultural identities offers insights into how individuals relate to the many groups to which they belong, but not only that, to understand others, and yourself, you need to realize the variety of groups that create their (and your) cultural identity. (Carnes, 1999, p. 50)

Cultural identity can be a complex issue. For example, a second-generation girl, living in a minority area, whose parents are Korean immigrants, whose friends are Spanish-speaking co-workers, identifies herself as Korean-American, Hispanic, a woman, or an American depending on the context. In another example, a student was born in Taiwan, moved to and grew up in Honduras, became thoroughly acculturated when he moved to the United States to attend college, but his primary language is Spanish, and he is an active member of the Chinese Student Association.

Cultural identity can be a simple issue, too. Some groups create their own cocultures to isolate themselves from others. The physically disabled (deaf and blind, for example) seem to do so, as does the homosexual community. In many cities the immigrants still seem to live and work in isolation and resolve to protect their heritage by maintaining all vestiges of their culture and not assimilating. Sometimes Blacks, Asians, or jocks on campus will always be seen together, isolating themselves from others, seldom assimilating, studying and working in isolation.

It is your culture that tells you what is appropriate to eat, how to dress, and what to say and do in varying contexts. At our local international festival, at a mosque within two miles of where my wife and I live, a minimum of a dozen different countries offered some of their local foods, which were served by individuals dressed in the characteristic clothing of their country. What intrigued us as we sampled the various foods, was not just how distinctive the various foods were, but in how different the clothing of each country was. Culture is important to you, and it influences all your thinking, acting, and doing on a daily basis.

■ WHAT IS CULTURE?

Culture, however, is not a box but, rather, a fluid concept that is an ever-changing, living part of you, reflecting your learned, socially acquired traditions and lifestyles. The following is a useful definition, however, as you read it, recognize that there are no hard edges, rather, there are phenomena that tend to overlap and mingle. **Culture** is:

> *The ever-changing values, traditions, social and political relationships, and worldview created and shared by a group of people bound together by a combination of factors (which can include a common history, geographic location, language, social class, and/or religion) (Nieto, 1995, p. 390).*

The word **worldview** means an all-encompassing set of moral, ethical, and philosophical principles and beliefs which governs the way people live their lives and interact with others. It governs the way people think, feel, and behave whether they realize it or not and affects in a major way how one views every aspect of life—physical, spiritual, emotional, moral, sociological, and mental. Although this chapter is about intercultural communication, it is important to understand the meaning of the word *worldview*, for it is used each time the definition of culture is repeated and illustrates the breadth of the definition of culture.

Culture is significant in your life because it is part of you. It includes your patterned, repetitive ways of thinking, feeling, and acting (Harris, 1983). Thus, it is not only maintained but often expressed through your communication. When Jonathan left a prominent position at a prestigious company, his best friend, Adam, explained his departure this way: "Voicing concern and choked with emotion, Jonathan was no longer able to step-up his efforts, as his American dream turned into a nightmare, his emotional roller coaster came to a full stop. Sending shock waves through family and friends, he said his final good-byes, and called it quits." Not only was Adam's communication full of cliches, but each one—eight in two sentences—was uniquely American. If you think about it, where do the words you choose come from? They reflect your culture because that is where you learned them, that is where they originated in the first place, and, if you are a typical, white, American, college student, they are likely to be all you know!

The words you choose reflect your culture because that is where you learned them, and that is where they originated in the first place.

Because it is part of you, culture not only influences your perception of your self and your perception of others (discussed in the last chapter) but your perception of everything in life with which you have contact. Think about what might be considered true American values and freedoms—things like democracy, individualism, property, equality, freedom, community, and justice. The degree to which you accept these as your own values is also the degree to which you measure your sense of self on those same values. For example, you would feel better about yourself if you were actively involved in your democracy (being informed of the positions of political candidates and voting), expressing your individualism (being assertive and sticking up for your rights), owning property (having a nice car), promoting equality (defending the rights of minorities), supporting freedom (revealing your appreciation for free speech), defending community (volunteering in local charitable organizations), and advocating justice (adhering to what is right, just, and true). And, regarding your perception of others, you might perceive them based on the same set of values—those that you hold dear.

"Culture is a mental set of windows through which all of life is viewed" (Beamer & Varney, 2001 p. 3). It is more than an environment or geographical location in which you live, and it is more than any single component of your personality or background, including your race, ethnicity, nationality, language, gender, religion, ability or disability, or socioeconomic status. These components—and certainly the way they combine and interact—impact one's social and educational status as well as one's family, community, and professional interactions. It is the way you make sense of your life (Rosaldo, 1989).

From this brief discussion of culture it is easier to understand intercultural communication. When a message is created by a member of one culture, and this message needs to be processed by a member of another culture, **intercultural communication** takes place (Samovar & Porter, 2001, pp. 2, 46).

■ THE IMPORTANCE OF STUDYING INTERCULTURAL COMMUNICATION

I have no culture. I am just White, I attended a mostly White school. We didn't have much diversity, I wish we had more multicultural students, and I have never known a multicultural person (Cruz-Janzen, 2000, p. 36).

Many white students in college today have been raised in predominantly white environments with little personal interaction with people of color, except, perhaps, the one or two who may have lived on their street or gone to their high school. Times are changing. The chances for contacts with people from other cultures have increased dramatically with changes in the workplace; U.S. businesses expanding into world markets in a process of globalization; people now connected—via answering machines, faxes, e-mail, electronic bulletin boards, and the Internet—to other people whom they have never met face-to-face; the ever increasing mobility of U.S. families; and the changing demographics within the United States and changing immigration patterns as well (Martin & Nakayama, 2001). It is precisely this increased contact that makes studying intercultural communication so important.

Understanding Your Own Identity. The first reason for studying intercultural communication is to develop a sensitivity to various cultural heritages and backgrounds in order to better understand your own identity. In a pluralistic national social environment, in which the demographics are continuing to change dramatically, decisions about the values you want to adopt or continue holding, the lifestyles or orientations you wish to pursue, and even the friends you want to have—much less, the major, occupation, or profession you desire—are affected by racial, cultural, gender,

Consider This

You have heard the term *melting pot*. You may have even used it yourself. From where did the concept of society as a melting pot come?

At the beginning of this century, as steamers poured into American ports, their steerages filled with European immigrants, a Jew from England named Israel Zangwill penned a play whose story line has long been forgotten, but whose central theme has not. His production was entitled "The Melting Pot" and its message still holds a tremendous power on the national imagination—the promise that all immigrants can be transformed into Americans, a new alloy forged in a crucible of democracy, freedom, and civic responsibility.

In 1908 when the play opened in Washington, the United States was in the middle of absorbing the largest influx of immigrants in its history—Irish and Germans, followed by Italians and East Europeans, Catholics and Jews—some 18 million new citizens between 1890 and 1920 (p. A1).

Source: W. Booth. "One Nation Indivisible: Is It History?" *Washington Post*, Feb. 22, 1998. Retrieved March 14, 2003, from http://www.washingtonpost.com/wp.srv/national/longterm/meltingpot/melt0222.htm.

and social-class factors that affect your personal identity, who you are and who you want to be (Schultz, 2001).

Enhancing Personal and Social Interactions. Perhaps it is too obvious that the broader your outlook and the more expanded your view of those different from you, the more tolerant and accommodating you become. The concept of society as a "melting pot" is a reality, and the chances of having close, personal, interactions with those different from you—whether it be in age, physical ability, gender, ethnicity, class, religion, race, or nationality—are increasing daily. Such relationships help you learn about the world, break stereotypes, and acquire new skills (Martin & Nakayama, 2001, p. 185). The concept of society as a "melting pot" is discussed in the Consider This box above.

Solving Misunderstandings, Miscommunications, and Mistrusts. This nation has a history of misunderstanding, miscommunications, and mistrusts regarding intercultural communication that is rooted in fear, neglect, and ignorance (Cruz-Janzen, 2000). It has been perpetuated by dominant groups, including white males, against disenfranchised ones who fan the flames of anger, fear, guilt, and shame. With such intense feelings associated with racism, sexism, and multiculturalism, conversations about equity and diversity have been largely forbidden, especially in mixed settings (Tatum, 1992, pp. 1–23). Our nation, especially white males, has not learned, nor has it needed to learn, to be multiculturally competent people (Cruz-Janzen, 2000; Howard, 1999).

The study of intercultural communication will not just unlock doors closed for generations; but it will open those doors, reduce the fear, neglect, and ignorance and, thus, resolve misunderstandings, miscommunications, and mistrusts through honest, open, positive, healthy communication. People not only fear, but they also distrust the unknown. Chapters like this one that help license and encourage conversation and discussion—which is just a first

On the Web

Sensitivity to cultural misunderstandings, miscommunications, and mistrusts may be a reason for studying intercultural communication, but it may be an understatement when it comes to the law. Certain people—and this may include you at some point in the future—really have no choice but to know more about intercultural communication:

Many small business owners are not ready to handle the problems associated with cultural diversity in the workplace. If not prepared, businesses may find themselves facing discrimination suits, litigation expenses, legal fees and settlements, high employee turnover, and negative community image.

Source: (No author) *Growing Your Business: Diversity Training in the Workplace.* WomanOwned.com, 2001. Retrieved March 14, 2003, from http://www.womanowned.com/growth/employees/diversity.htm.

step—assist in erecting a framework for tolerance, acceptance, change, and trust. Trust is gained through knowledge and understanding.

Enhancing and Enriching the Quality of Civilization. Recognizing and respecting ethnic and cultural diversity are important steps on the road to valuing the ways in which diversity enhances and enriches the quality of our civilization. Many people, according to Carlos Cortes, are galvanized by the issue of intermarriage. He says, "Many multiculturalists today seem unwilling to deal with the growing factor of intermarriage. Too much of multicultural education is frozen into a kind of group purity paradigm, when, in fact, intermarriage is one of the enormous changes that is taking place in America. For example, one-third of all Latinos born in the United States now marry someone who is not Latino. That says an awful lot about what the next generation's sense of ethnic identity is going to be; it's going to be much more unpredictable. What will these cultural blends be like?"(Carnes, 2001, p. 52). "The fastest growing student population is students of blended parentage" (Cruz-Janzen, 2000, p. 32). When you consider the potential for the new perspectives, cultural insights, and unique wisdom that intermarriages can produce, there is no doubt about the corresponding increase in the quality of our civilization.

Becoming Effective Citizens of Our National Communities. **National communities** are cocultural groupings within the country. National communities were established from the beginning as "our forefathers acquired the lands of Native Americans, 34 percent of the territory of Mexico in 1848, and the island of Puerto Rico in 1898" (Schultz, 2001, p. 113). Prior to the 1960s, most of the immigrants to the United States came from Europe (as noted in the previous Consider This), but of the million or so immigrants who now enter the United States every year, 90 percent are from Latin America and Asia. A study by the Population Reference Bureau suggests that by 2050 the United States will be a global society in which nearly half of all Americans will be from today's racial and ethnic minorities (Martin & Nakayama, 2001, p. 8).

Working Together

The word *multicultural* means different things to different people. To some people it is a red flag, perceived as strictly related to the betterment of people of a different color. Some scholars who write about the multicultural movement use the terms "African-Americans and other people of color." While this may not be intentional, it conveys a message of a "Black people versus White people movement." Allow each member of your group to express his or her ideas and feelings on the following questions:

1. If the word *multicultural* includes issues of race, class, gender, and disability (a more inclusive definition than color alone), does this more inclusive focus dilute attention toward ethnic studies and, thus incorporate groups not expressly cultural in nature?

2. Should the word *multicultural* reflect simply a fight against racism? Is that sufficient? Or, should it include struggles against sexism, heterosexism, classism, linguisism, and ableism as well? Why or why not?

Source: Adapted from information in A. Y. Ramirez; M. M. Autry; & M. L. Morton. "Sociopedagogy: A move beyond multiculturalism toward stronger community." *Multicultural Education*, Summer, 2000, pp. 2–9. In Fred Schultz, ed. *Multicultural Education*, 8th ed. (Guilford, CT: McGraw-Hill/Dushkin, 2001), pp. 63–69. This exercise was adapted from information on p. 66.

These statistics call attention to the importance of studying intercultural communication. First, regardless of where you come from (Mexico, Latin America, Asia) you must make an effort to become an effective citizen in our national communities. Second, you need to appreciate the benefit to our national communities of our diverse immigration patterns that bring us different ideas, arts, foods, styles, and so on. Third, you need to take responsibility for learning more about diversity and multiculturalism so that you can not only enjoy the benefits of what is occurring but become a more active participant in this diversity as well.

■ INTERCULTURAL COMMUNICATION AND THE COMMUNICATION MODEL

Using our broad definition of culture, and with the clear understanding that much of communication is intercultural, you can also see how much influence intercultural communication has had on the model of communication in Chapter 1.

It Influences Senders and Receivers. Values, traditions, social and political relationships, and worldview influence the brains of both senders and receivers and, any communication that occurs. If my values, traditions, social and political relationships, and worldview are different from yours, given the same subject to respond to and with everything else in the assignment the same, I will compose a significantly different response. Asked to observe and report on the interpersonal communication that occurs in one of the common spaces on campus, imagine the differences in the reports of males and females. Females are likely to be more sensitive to the relationships, connectiveness, and emotions of the people communicating, whereas males are likely to be more sensitive to the issues of assertiveness, competitiveness, or the easier to observe objective issues about the time, location, or positions of the communicators. As the differences among the observers become greater, the results in thoughts, feelings, and messages become more divergent as well.

It Influences Messages and Feedback. In Pakistan, for example, where this author's parents both had Fulbright scholarships to teach, they noted that students seldom, if ever, raised questions in the classroom. When my parents sought an answer to this "problem," they were told that raising a question in the classroom in Pakistan is considered an affront to a respected and esteemed authority—the teacher. It is seldom done. Instead of interpreting the lack of response as any of a number of things—indifference, dullness, lack of understanding, or apathy—my parents created unique classroom opportunities that nurtured and encouraged students to respond among themselves with the teacher as overseer, guide, and outside resource.

Both verbal and nonverbal messages are affected by intercultural communication. For most Americans, you pay attention and show respect in the classroom by maintaining eye contact with teachers. But Navajo students in the classroom show respect by avoiding eye contact. For many of those who leave the Navajo Nation to study, they must learn to look their professors in the eye.

In the United States, most Americans are quick to respond to any communication directed toward them. You might even call it standard procedure. And yet, the best verbal and nonverbal message in an intercultural situation—especially one in which there is confusion, doubt, or misunderstanding—might be a pause in verbal communication, reinforced with nonverbal eye contact with the other person and a smile. The least such a response is likely to signal is tolerance of the cultural components of the communication.

It Influences the Setting. Be aware that setting can refer to how this communication fits into history—past, present, and future events. One obvious example is the communication with Saudi Arabians in our country. According to some Saudis, communication seems to have—always present, whether overt or covert—the mistrust, suspicion, or hatred that resulted from the 9/11 experience. Before communication even occurs, the Saudi headdress, clothing, skin color, and accent are likely to establish a historical influence on the setting.

Setting can refer to how this communication fits into a relational setting, such as the influences of power and distance, individualism versus collectivism, or femininity versus masculinity, and will be discussed in a forthcoming section. The relationship might be dominance versus nondominance, also discussed later. It can refer to gender, or African, Asian, Native American, Hispanic, Anglo, or other related settings where differences in expectations, styles, assumptions, values, body language, and privilege would have influence.

Setting, too, can relate to your own position within a speech community. If you are the only African-American in an otherwise white community, the only physically disabled person in an otherwise abled environment, the only woman in a largely male environment, the only homosexual in an heterosexual environment, you may face specific expectations or have people project their motivations on your communication (Martin & Nakayama, 2001).

It Influences the Elements Involved in Any Transaction. The first of those elements, as you recall from the section Communication is a Transaction, in Chapter 1, is "Participation Is Continuous and Simultaneous." Your perception of others is conveyed when you communicate with them. It cannot be hidden. Whether accurate or not, the subtle or not-so-subtle verbal and nonverbal cues that you send will clearly signal your understanding and tolerance of the cultural components of the conversation. Thus, the more you learn and the broader your horizons, the more accepting of others you will become. When Mary Stewart was paired with Manolo Alejandro for a classroom exercise, Manolo immediately perceived Mary's nervousness even though she had tried to hide it. Manolo began the conversation with, "You have never spoken to an Hispanic person before, have you?" Mary said, "No." Manolo smiled, and very quietly said to her, "Don't worry, I won't bite," to which Mary smiled, and a delightful assignment and relationship ensued.

The second element of communication as a transaction is "All Communications Have a Past, a Present, and a Future." Because you respond to every situation from your own experiences, moods, and expectations, imagine how your responses are affected when you superimpose these ingredients: values, traditions, social and political relationships, worldview, common history, geographic location, language, social class, and religion. Imagine the complexity of a communication situation when you assess another person using these same variables. What happens to the communication if you know, for example, you want a continuing relationship with this person? What adjustments, adaptations, or modifications would you make to your communications? As the classroom assignment continued, in the example above, Mary became even more comfortable and relaxed with Manolo, finding his wit and humor delightful, his language patterns charming, and his thoughts and feelings intriguing. Her nervousness turned to coyness, flirtation, and charm when she realized Manolo had an interest in her.

The third element in communication as a transaction, is "All Communicators Play Roles." When Frank Marsh arrived on campus the first day he discovered he had an Hispanic roommate. At this very moment of discovery, Frank had to decide how he would present himself—what role would he play? He had grown up in a small midwestern town, found school challenging and enriching, graduated at the "top of the class," had the pick of virtually any college or university, and had received a full four-year scholarship. Frank had but a brief amount of time to think about this, but being white, coming from an upper-middle class family, and pursuing a course in premedicine helped make his decision critical. One thing he didn't want to do was put off his new roommate Domingo DeMilagros through arrogance or an overbearing nature.

In their first meeting, Frank decided to try out some of the Spanish he had learned in his advanced-placement high school Spanish classes and, as it turned out, it worked. Frank and Domingo not only became bosom buddies throughout their college career, but they became brothers-in-law as well, a situation beginning with a visit to campus by Domingo's sister, Maria Rosalia. Through constant contact with her via the Internet, visits to her home, and meetings with her friends, it was soon clear that Frank and Maria had fallen in love. Marriage followed much later, but if you ask Frank, he would tell you that it was his decision to speak Spanish—to play the role of an "equal" with a full admission of his inadequacies as a speaker of Spanish—which initiated the opportunities that followed.

■ STUDYING CULTURAL DIFFERENCES

There are a number of ways to contrast a group of cultures to another group of cultures (Triandis, 1990). Geert Hofstede (2001) examined cultural distinctions based on deeply rooted values and derived five dimensions. (*Dimensions* . . ., 2001). A sixth dimension, Edward T. Hall's (1976, 1994) high context versus low context, follows our discussion of Hofstede's five dimensions.

You may wonder how contrasting cultures might ever affect you as a student, citizen, or individual. Cultural differences are manifest in the cultural identities of the people, as the examples within each category will reveal. Cultural identity influences behavior including choices of symbols, heroes and heroines, rituals, and even the values one chooses.

The dimensions discussed here are general tendencies only. They are not always true of a culture, nor true of everyone in a culture. Jackie Low, from Perrysburg, Ohio (a suburb of Toledo), is a good example. Raised in Ohio, she has never been to China, never spoken a word of Chinese, and did not know much about China. She was a suburban American girl; however, anyone who assumed that Jackie was Chinese from her looks alone, would have been incorrect even though the assumption would have been easy to make based on her appearance.

Power distance—social inequality. You will notice power differences in family customs, the relationships between students and teachers, the young and the elderly, language systems, and organizational practices. When Lennie observed Tupac—who was from Africa, a high power-distance country—he noticed he always did as he was told by their boss, who Lennie thought was authoritarian, dictatorial, and unfair, and wasn't afraid to say so. When he talked to Tupac, he realized most people from Africa consider their boss a benevolent dictator and do as they are told. Because Lennie shared a class with Tupac, he asked him why he never asked questions in class. Tupac explained that in his country teachers possess wisdom, are automatically esteemed, and their authority is never questioned. These explanations not only helped Lennie understand Tupac, but cemented a valuable relationship as well.

Continents with high power distance include Africa, Latin America, and Near Eastern countries. Low power-distance countries include the United States, Germany, China, and Great Britain.

Our way to contrast a group of cultures to another group of cultures is to use the dimension of power distance—social inequality. The top picture reveals potential power distances between students and teacher as well as between the younger and the elderly. Examine the lower picture, and note the number of potential power distances represented.

View "Culture and Self," clip #9, on the CD to further understand the value of examining cultural differences.

If you were a student in an international student-exchange program, you would notice the power-distance factor quickly. In countries with low power distance, there is a strong emphasis on students, not leaders, and both genders are treated equally.

Individualism versus collectivism—the degree of integration and orientation of individuals within groups. When Elaine worked with the Peace Corps in Argentina for a Public Health Surveillance and Disease Control project, she learned about collectivist cultures. Working hand in hand with Eduardo Puerta, a native Argentinian, she noticed his concern for her training and skills. He had never worked side-by-side with a female. She noticed, too, his extreme concern for his family and especially his sons, and realized his need to be in control and to maintain face. In their discussions, she came to understand his preference for groups over individuals, and government control over the economy and press. Knowing about collectivist cultures helped Elaine not just understand Eduardo, but learn from and respect him as well.

You will notice that people in individualistic cultures such as Great Britain, the United States, Canada, France, and Germany, value self-expression, view speaking out as a way to solve problems, and use confrontational strategies to deal with interpersonal problems. In collectivist cultures such as many Arab, African, Asian, and Latin American countries, people have unquestioning loyalty to the group, and when in conflict they use avoidance, intermediaries, and other face-saving techniques.

Femininity versus masculinity—the division of roles between women and men. This dimension draws criticism because of its name. Anita Katz visited Israel (a high-feminine culture) when her family returned to their homeland to visit relatives. Tying her visit to a class paper in sociology motivated her to ask questions she would not have asked otherwise. When she was allowed to accompany her cousin Ravid to work, Anita discovered that many of the typical gender roles were relaxed. Ravid's immediate supervisor was a female, as was the head of the company. Where Ravid worked, for example, the entire work environment emphasized good relations with supervisors, peers, and subordinates. Not only were there excellent living and working conditions in the country, but complete employment security as well. Knowing that Israel was a high-feminine culture helped her put her discoveries in perspective.

High-feminine cultures believe women should be nurturant, concerned for the quality of life, and reveal sympathy for the unfortunate. In general, feminine cultures allow cross-gender behaviors. High masculine cultures believe men should be concerned about wealth, achievement, challenge, ambition, promotion, and that they should be assertive, competitive, tough, and recognize achievements. Masculine cultures are more likely to maintain strictly defined gender roles and, thus, have distinct expectations of male and female roles in society. High feminine cultures include Africa and the Nordic countries of Europe. High masculine cultures include Latin America, Great Britain, Japan, and the United States.

Uncertainty avoidance—tolerance for the unknown. When Amelia entered her math classroom on the first day, she was startled to realize her teaching assistant was from Japan. Although such situations raise concern with some students, Amelia accepted it as an opportunity to learn and grow.

Because Amelia knew Japan was a low uncertainty avoidance country, she was able to put into perspective much of what she learned from Juni Akimoto. Junji represented Japan well. Compared with her teaching assistants from the United States, Junji was less expressive, less openly anxious, and he behaved quietly without showing aggression or strong emotions. Easy-going and relaxed, he ran an open-ended class.

Cultures that feel threatened by ambiguous and uncertain situations and try to avoid them prefer formal rules to control social behaviors. The best example is China. Low uncertainty avoidance cultures need few rules and accept and encourage dissenting views and risk taking. Countries with low uncertainty avoidance include Latin America, Africa, and Japan. The United States is considered "medium" on this dimension—neither high nor low.

Long-term orientation—the trade-off between long-term and short-term gratification of needs. This dimension was added by Hofstede (1988) as a result of his work with Michael Bond. Bond labeled it Confucian dynamism. Elisha's roommate, Mei Li, explained to her what long-term orientation means in China. Mei Li told Elisha that China is a very stable society where the family is the prototype for all social organizations. In her family, she explained, her father carried the full authority of and responsibility for the family on his shoulders. Also noteworthy, Mei Li always spoke highly of her older brother, but seldom spoke of her sisters. Mei Li explained by example that virtuous behavior in China means acquiring skills and education, working hard, and being frugal, patient, and persevering. Mei clearly loved her country, her family, and her values. Knowing what a long-term orientation meant, helped Elisha bond with Mei Li and appreciate her incredible industriousness.

Those at one extreme on this dimension—having long-term orientation—admire persistence, ordering relationships by status, thriftiness, and having a sense of shame that emphasizes care for others and being loyal and trustworthy. China, Japan, and other Asian countries have an extraordinary long-term orientation toward life. At the other extreme—with short-term orientation—are countries like Finland, France, Germany, and the United States where people value personal steadiness and stability, but do not have as much respect for tradition because it prevents innovation, nor saving face, which can hinder the flow of business. These countries, too, favor reciprocation of greetings, favors, and gifts as related to social rituals.

High context versus low context—the degree to which most of the information is carried in the **context** (high) or most of the information is in the code or message (low). (Hall, 1976; Hall, 1994). In high-context communication most of the information is already in the person; very little information is in the coded, explicit, intentionally transmitted part of the message. For example, in the Japanese, African, Mexican, Asian, and Latin-American cultures most of the meaning of a message is either implied by the physical setting or is presumed to be part of the individual's beliefs, values, and norms. Often, in long-term relationships, communication is high context because the slightest gesture, quickest glance, or briefest comment is interpretable without explicit statements or extended explanations.

How does high context versus low context reveal itself in a work situation? When Hugh graduated from high school, he worked for awhile in an

American automobile manufacturing plant near his hometown. After college, he got a job at a high-profile Japanese automobile plant, and when Hugh began work, he was in for the shock of his life. Compared with competitive Americans who came from highly specific, individualistic, linear, and narrow low contexts, he had difficulty relating to high-context Japanese business people who worked in teams by consensus, shared rather than privatized, connected rather than fragmented, and worked together in lateral relationships rather than engaging in conflicted hierarchical relationships. When you experience all these differences, you begin to understand how having criteria to compare cultures can be helpful in the understanding of, expressing tolerance for, and adjusting to the communication differences.

Most Western cultures prefer low-context messages in which the majority of the information is in the communication itself—not in the context. Great examples of low-context messages are computer instructions. They are low context because they require that every space, period, letter, and number be precisely in the right location; there are no exceptions. All the information is in the instruction, or the instruction does not work.

The point of discussing these six dimensions is to offer you some specific vantage points, tools, for viewing cultural differences. They are basic frames of reference to help you appreciate differences. No culture is better than another; no culture is strange; no culture is unusual or foreign. Using these tools will help reduce misunderstandings by encouraging empathy, tolerance, respect, and, perhaps, a more accurate interpretation of messages from people of another culture group. It is a little like having a road map with some of the major roads indicated, even though many of the secondary roads are still missing.

■ BARRIERS TO INTERCULTURAL COMMUNICATION

As much as we may encourage empathy, tolerance, respect, and a quest for accurate interpretation, we also recognize inherent problems. Barriers occur because of socialization; they occur because of established habits; and they occur as part of the human condition. It should be pointed out that some people simply do not know about other cultures, and some people do not want to know. There is no doubt that both ignorance (lack of knowledge) and naivete (lack of sophistication) can be important barriers to intercultural communication.

In this section, we will briefly consider ethnocentrism, stereotyping, prejudice, and discrimination (Martin & Nakayama, 2001). These are barriers because each is constructed around a judgment made of individuals or groups formulated before any communication takes place that then biases the communication that follows. In communication as a transaction, where all communication has a past, present, and future, barriers are part of the past that influence the communication that takes place now, and affect all that follows in the future.

Ethnocentrism

When this author lectured in Perth, Australia, one of the things I was told by those who had arranged my visit, was that some Australians think that Americans believe that their (American) way is the best or the only way, and that in my lectures I must be careful never to show arrogance or, in any way to reveal condescension or become patronizing. It was wise advice and caused me to increase—but never falsely—my show of respect and admiration for the views, advice, and suggestions of those with whom I spoke. My hosts had warned me not to be ethnocentric—a common occurrence, they said, when Americans spoke to Australians.

Ethnocentrism is the belief that one's own cultural group's behaviors, norms, ways of thinking, and ways of being are superior to all other cultural groups. Ethnocentrism is not to be confused with **patriotism** which is devotion to one's country. Ethnocentrism carries devotion to the extreme point where you cannot believe that another culture's behaviors, norms, ways of thinking, and ways of being are equally as good or as worthy as your own. It becomes a barrier in intercultural communication when it prevents you from even trying to see another's point of view—that is, when it impedes all attempts at empathy.

Stereotyping

Stereotypes are oversimplified or distorted views of another race, another ethnic group, or even another culture. They are simply ways to categorize and generalize from the overwhelming amount of information we receive daily. If you were a white student from a small midwestern town and you had no contact with people of other races, but every night on the television news you saw angry people of other races creating civil disturbances, it would be easy for you to categorize this information—people of other races create civil disturbances—and generalize from it: I don't want to have contact with people of other races because they are violent and disruptive. You can easily see that this would be a stereotype because it is terribly oversimplified and certainly distorted, but also you can understand how such a stereotype, given the facts of the examples alone, could be formed.

Stereotypes also may be positive. If you were a white student from a small midwestern town and you had no contact with people of other races, but every night on the television news you saw people of other races in caring, comforting roles—assisting children in learning situations, helping the elderly attain necessary food and medicines, or serving in homeless shelters by serving food or doing counseling—you can easily see how you could form positive stereotypes regarding these situations. But, you can also see how these stereotypes could be distorted as well.

The problem with stereotypes is that once they are established, it is difficult to remove them. Sometimes they exist subconsciously; these are even more difficult to discard because they are just below our level of consciousness. Often, because of stereotypes, we tend to pick up information from our environment that supports the stereotypes rather than denies them. This simply embeds them more deeply. To remove them, we must first recognize them, then we must obtain individual information that will counteract them. This isn't easy.

Prejudice

"**Prejudice** is a negative attitude toward a cultural group based on little or no experience" (Martin & Nakayama, p. 43). The difference between stereotypes and prejudice should become clear in this example: When Chris was young, his parents told him never to go into the city because Mexican gangs ruled the city streets at night. The stereotype they conveyed was that Mexicans were ruthless, uncontrolled hooligans who raped, murdered, and robbed anyone who walked the city streets after dark. Chris, of course, then had the preconceived notion that all Mexicans were bad people. From the stereotype of Mexicans shared by Chris's parents, Chris formed a prejudice against Mexicans. The stereotype told him what a group (Mexicans) was like; the prejudice told him how to feel about the group. All this changed when Chris worked for the city to help pay his way through college, and almost all of his co-workers were Mexicans. Their attitude toward Chris as well as their behavior quickly changed the stereotype and altered his prejudice.

Discrimination

"**Discrimination** is the overt actions one takes to exclude, avoid, or distance oneself from other groups" (Martin & Nakayama, 2001, p. 44). Discrimination takes stereotypes and prejudice one step further—to action, whether it be overt or covert. You can discriminate against someone subtly by slightly turning your body away when in a conversation, or by avoiding eye contact with them. You can discriminate against people by hurling verbal insults at them. You can discriminate, too, by using physical violence, systematically eliminating the group from which the individual comes, or even in extreme cases by using genocide, as when autocratic tyrants exterminate racial or national groups. Yet another form of discrimination occurs when you exclude others from jobs or from other economic opportunities.

Obviously, discrimination can be interpersonal when you do it against another person, collective (when a number of individuals or a group perform the discrimination), or institutional (when a business or industry is involved). Institutional discrimination is represented when a restaurant chain chooses not to serve a particular group of people or when an auto-rental firm chooses not to rent cars to a specific group.

■ DEALING WITH BARRIERS TO INTERCULTURAL COMMUNICATION

For accurate communication to occur, sender-receivers must be operating from the same perceptual point of view. This is usually not a problem when we are interacting with people from our own race or culture, however, when we communicate with someone from a different race or background, we must realize that this person will be operating from an entirely different point of view.

The majority of the U.S. population is white. If you are a member of this majority, do you think that anyone stereotypes you as *white?* Chances are that many people do, especially if they are nonwhite themselves. What are the chances that you could be a victim of someone else's ethnocentrism, prejudice, or discrimination? Although you may not be aware of it today, within your lifetime—and sooner rather than later—there will be some major reversals in majority and minority populations, or the numbers of people in nondominant and dominant groups in the United States.

Communication between Nondominant- and Dominant-Group Members

Much of the literature about communication is written from the point of view of the dominant, or majority, culture. In the United States **dominant culture** includes white people from a European background, while **nondominant culture** includes people of color; women; gays, lesbians, and bisexuals; and those whose socioeconomic background is lower than middle class. When a person from a dominant culture encounters another from a nondominant culture, do they communicate differently when they are with each other? Consider these examples: When Mark and Janel, who are both middle-class African-Americans talk, they are communicating on the basis of shared experiences. However, Cedric, who went to a public school and grew up in the ghetto, and Janette, who went to a private school and is now attending Yale, have little in common. Because one of them is African-American, they have little shared experience, so they must learn how to communicate with each other.

The question, then, becomes, when people are not part of a dominant culture, how do they communicate with people who are? In a tantalizing piece of research, Orbe looked at how people from nondominant groups (people of color; women; gays, lesbians, and bisexuals; and those from lower socioeconomic backgrounds) communicated with people who were members of the dominant group (1998). He found that nondominant members adopted a series of strategies when they wanted to confront oppressive dominant structures and achieve success. Which strategy they used depended on the communication behavior that would get them what they wanted, and it fell into one of three categories: assimilation, accommodation, or separation.

Assimilation Strategies

When nondominants use **assimilation,** they drop cultural differences and distinctive characteristics that would identify them with the nondominant group. As you can see in Table 3-1, there are three types of assimilation.

Nonassertive Assimilation. In this type of assimilation, minority members want to belong to the majority group, but they do not want to use aggression to get there. In order to achieve acceptance, they emphasize what they have in common with the dominant group and sometimes censor themselves to fit in. For example, John, who is an African-American, is standing

Table 3-1 *Assimilation*

Nonassertive	Assertive	Aggressive
Emphasizing what the dominant and nondominant groups have in common	Carefully preparing for meeting dominant group members	Disassociating from one's own group
Acting positive	Manipulating stereotypes	Copying dominant-group behavior
Censoring remarks that might offend the dominant group	Bargaining	Avoiding interaction with other cocultural groups
Avoiding controversy		Ridiculing oneself

with several people from a dominant group. When someone tells a racist joke, John laughs at it and does not let on that it offends him.

People may assimilate because they want what the dominant group has, and assimilation is the only way to get it. However, it often comes at a terrible cost, as you can see in the following passage, written by a homosexual woman:

> *I spent the fifties essentially either going to graduate school or beginning my career as a teacher who was very much in the closet—and very much attempting to hide the fact that I was a lesbian. And that meant putting down and holding down a whole part of myself that was really vital to my being. I have these visions of faculty parties or church parties or picnics to which I would oftentimes go with a gay man friend of mine, and we would put on an incredibly good show (Adair & Adair, 1978).*

Assertive Assimilation. In assertive assimilation, people are likely to take a stronger approach to fitting in. They will often carefully prepare for an encounter with the dominant group. They may overcompensate by trying to be twice as smart, twice as witty, and so forth.

African-American writer Patricia Raybon (1996), in her book *My First White Friend*, describes her assertive assimilation stage, which occurred when she was a child living in a predominantly white culture:

> *I was reared to smile, to be polite, to say please and thank you and not to act ugly. I was reared to be the cleanest, nicest, smartest, kindest black child I could possibly be. That would make people like me. White people especially. (pp. 1–2)*

Aggressive Assimilation. In this type of assimilation, minority-group members want to fit into the dominant group at any cost. They will imply that there are no differences between the two groups and will be careful to not do or say anything that would indicate their difference, such as speaking in a dialect or making reference to their own group's behavior. They are so eager to be part of the dominant group that they might ridicule the group they belong to.

Accommodation Strategies

The next main category consists of accommodation strategies. **Accommodation** works toward getting the dominant group to reinvent, or at least change, the rules so that they incorporate the life experiences of the nondominant group. The three types of accommodation are summarized in Table 3-2.

Nonassertive Accommodation. In nonassertive accommodation, the person does not act in any way that would cause dominant-group members to be defensive or cautious but tries to make people more aware of the group she or he belongs to and tries to change stereotypes they might have. For example, Anna who is Mexican, often talks to her co-workers about her friends who are professionals, trying to break the stereotype of Mexicans as manual laborers. Also, in her office she has pictures of her family and artifacts from Mexico hanging on the wall.

Assertive Accommodation. Those who use this strategy try to achieve a balance between their own group and the dominant group. They try to get their own group's members to know them by sharing something about their lives; they also attempt to educate others about their group's members. Often they will choose a member of the dominant group as a mentor who can guide, support, and assist them.

They also try to educate the dominant group about their group's culture. Maria, for example, persuades some dominant-group members to go to a Mexican restaurant and then shows them how to order so they will get food that is tasty but not too spicy.

Aggressive Accommodation. The strategy in this approach is to get into a dominant group and try to change it with the goal of transforming it. Although nondominant-group members make efforts to work with the dominant group rather than against it, they may confront dominant-group members to gain an advantage. For example, a woman on a committee that brings international scholars to the university may point out that no women have been chosen. When, for the second year in a row, the committee chooses only men, she suggests that next year the committee find a topic that would be of interest to women. She also reminds the committee that it

Table 3-2 *Accommodation*

Nonassertive	Assertive	Aggressive
Increasing visibility	Letting DG members know who they really are	Confronting members of the DG when they violate the rights of others
Avoiding stereotypes	Identifying and working with DG members who have similar goals	Referring to DG oppression of NG
	Identifying members of the DG who can support, guide, and assist	
	Educating others	

Note: DG = dominant group; NG = nondominant group.

is well known on campus for not including women in its programs. Persons using aggressive accommodation may also warn dominant-group members of their history of oppression.

Separation Strategies

In the third category of strategies, separation, nondominant-group members have given up. In **separation,** nondominants do not want to form a common bond with the dominant culture, so they separate into a group that includes only members like themselves. During the 60s and 70s, many African-Americans and women, unhappy that power structures were not changing quickly enough, formed separate groups that excluded members of the dominant group' as well as nondominant-group members who did not share their views (e.g., Black Muslims exclude other blacks as well as whites). Some of these groups still exist today. Table 3–3 outlines the three types of separation.

Nonassertive Separation. In this type of separation, the nondominant person avoids the dominant group whenever possible. Although the nondominant may have a job involves working with dominant-group members, he or she won't go out to lunch with them or for a drink after work. Through verbal and nonverbal cues, the dominant group senses that this person wants to be left alone. For example, when Tom, who is gay, is asked whether he is going to the office Christmas party, he answers no, because he knows that the man he lives with would not be welcome.

Some nondominant groups make no attempt to become part of the dominant group. An example is the Hmong people who immigrated to the United States because they were no longer safe in Laos. Anne Fadiman (1997) describes them after they had lived for 17 years in the United States:

> *Seventeen years later, Foua and Nao Kao use American appliances but they still speak only Hmong, celebrate only Hmong holidays, practice only Hmong religion, cook only Hmong dishes, sing only Hmong songs, play only Hmong musical instruments, tell only Hmong stories, and know far more about the current political events in Laos and Thailand than about those in the United States . . . It would be hard to imagine anything further from the vaunted American ideal of assimilation, in which immigrants are expected to submerge their cultural differences in order to embrace a shared national identity (p. 182).*

Table 3-3 *Separation*

Nonassertive	Assertive	Aggressive
Maintaining barriers between themselves and the DG	Asserting their voice regardless of the consequences	Making direct attacks on DG members
Keeping away from places where DG members are found	Making references to DG oppression with the goal of gaining advantage	Undermining the DG by not letting its members take advantage of their privileged position

Note: DG = dominant group; NG = nondominant group.

Assertive Separation. Persons practicing assertive separation work to form organizations where they can be separate from the dominant group. While in these groups, they work against any dominant-group messages that imply the dominant group is superior and they are inferior. One communication strategy they use is reminding the dominant group of their oppression. Patricia Raybon (1996), whose passage we quoted in the assimilation discussion, describes some of the feelings that led to her assertive separation stage:

> *White people—that relentless, heavy presence. Never benign. Never innocent. "White people" as a category embodied in my view a clear and certain evil—an arrogant malevolence—that had done unspeakable things that I couldn't ignore because I knew the facts of these things. Names and dates and numbers. And the facts haunted me and the numbers justified my hate for all of the evil that I believed white people had done (pp. 1–2).*

Aggressive Separation. In aggressive separation, people separate from the dominant group and expect their fellow nondominant-group members to do so too. They are very critical of those who practice assimilation or accommodation. It is not uncommon for groups fighting against oppression to separate from the dominant group.

If members of these groups have to have interaction with the dominant group (e.g., at work), they will try to undermine the dominants by not letting them take advantage of their privileged positions. For example, an employee would bring legal action against his or her boss for discrimination.

The Consequences of Nondominant- and Dominant-Group Communication

The research that Orbe has done does not lead to a very optimistic picture of American society. If we depict his results on a continuum, as in Figure 3-1, on one end are people who want to belong so much that they are willing to give up or suppress their own cultures, while on the opposite end are

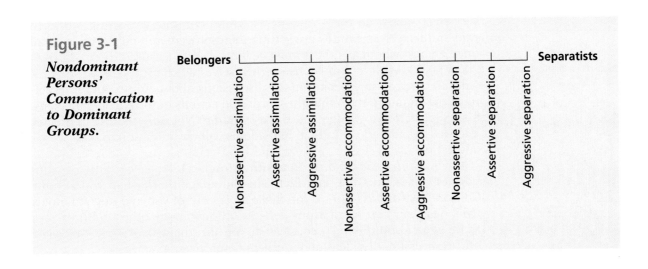

Figure 3-1

Nondominant Persons' Communication to Dominant Groups.

Belongers — Nonassertive assimilation — Assertive assimilation — Aggressive assimilation — Nonassertive accommodation — Assertive accommodation — Aggressive accommodation — Nonassertive separation — Assertive separation — Aggressive separation — Separatists people who have decided that they cannot live in the dominant culture of the United States and have gone off on their own. In a country that prides itself on being a place where people from all cultures can live in harmony, nothing on the continuum is acceptable to our vision of what democracy should be.

When you are communicating, even with someone you know, there is always the question of how authentic the communication really is. Many things happen in communication, some known and some unknown. However, given how power is handled by nondominant groups, the whole process becomes even more complex when people are deliberately miscommunicating. Few of us would like to live in a science-fiction world where everyone is just like us. Yet if we force people to assimilate to fit in or to separate when they won't, we might get that kind of world.

■ IMPROVING INTERCULTURAL COMMUNICATION

Sometimes when we are faced with an intercultural-communication situation with a person different from us, we may interpret the other person involved as *abnormal, weird,* or simply *different.* It is important to learn to control the human tendency to translate "different from me" into "less than me" (DuPraw & Axner, 1997). Rather, we need to raise questions. The important questions are, Are there *patterns* of difference on which I can draw to connect with them? Are there certain effective ways of dealing with different kinds of people? Can I develop a repertoire of five or six approaches that will help me reach others in real and meaningful ways?—as opposed to depending on one or two techniques that may or may not be helpful—my old standbys, you might say (Carnes, 2001, p. 53).

Pay attention to your words and actions. It is only through your thoughtful communication with others that you become aware of your own thinking patterns, assumptions, perceptions, prejudices, and biases (Pool, 2002). When students come to Cruz-Janzen's classes expecting to learn how to communicate with nonwhites, she tells them they are first going to study themselves, their gender, racial, ethnic, cultural, socioeconomic, and physical (ability, disability, and appearance) socialization. Cruz-Janzen has a very clear motive in this: "As long as whites continue expecting others to explain themselves, whites are setting themselves as the norm, the normal ones, against whom all others must be judged and measured" (Cruz-Janzen, 2000, p. 37). With a clear focus on themselves as cultural beings, she provides the appropriate backdrop for discussions about culture and intercultural communication so that the words and actions of the participants have a solid base in knowledge and understanding. Not only that, with greater knowledge and understanding, individuals will pay attention to their words and actions.

Control your assumptions. An **assumption** is a taking for granted or supposition that something is a fact. The old adage that "when you assume (look at the word ass-u-me), you make an ass out of you and me" still holds true. Yes, you can learn from generalizations about other cultures, but those generalizations turn sour when you use them to stereotype, "write off," or oversimplify ideas about others (Dupraw & Axner, 1997).

Another Point of View

One of the popular and quick ways to educate people who will be entering another culture is to provide them with lists of do's and taboos. The Internet, for example, is good at providing such lists. Here is what Linda Beamer and Iris Varner (2001) think of such lists:

The do's and taboos lists are usually accurate, but their helpfulness is limited. One-sentence advice on behavior is like seeing a snapshot from a movie. It is accurate, but without the content of the movie's story line, character development, or even the specific episode, the snapshot's significance may not be understandable. Lists of do's and taboos can't explain why you should or should not behave in a particular way in a particular place. Lists can't possibly be comprehensive. And even if a business traveler were armed with a very long list, who can consult a list for every nuance in every different country? It's no wonder that businesspeople may seem to discard tips on do's and taboos in favor of simply being themselves and acting the same way abroad that they would at home. And yet most businesspeople know that business as usual—doing what they do at home—can be counterproductive when doing business abroad (p. 11).

Source: L. Beamer, & I. Varner. *Intercultural Communication in the Global Workplace*. (New York: McGraw-Hill/Irwin, 2001).

Questions

1. Have you ever seen or used a list of do's or taboos? Have you found them helpful?

2. Do you think a list of do's and taboos would serve the purpose when the amount of time you have to prepare to enter another culture is brief, or when you just don't have time to study a thorough or comprehensive introduction to the new culture?

3. What do you rely on when you have no instructions of any kind and you are in a new culture? How do you behave? How do you know what to do?

- Don't assume that there is one right way (yours) to communicate. Question your assumptions about the "right way" to communicate.
- Don't assume that breakdowns in communication occur because others are on the wrong track. It isn't "who is to blame for the breakdown," it is "who can make the communication work?" (Dupraw & Axner, 1997). Remember, ineffective communication can occur for a variety of reasons:
  - You may not have transmitted your message in a way that can be understood.
  - Others may misinterpret what you say (Gudykunst & Kim, 2003).
- Don't assume that the preferred rules of interpersonal relationships you have learned in your culture apply universally across all cultures. They do not.
- Don't assume that your cultural definitions and successful criteria of conflict management apply universally across all cultures. They do not (Karim, 2001).
- Don't assume that because another's values and beliefs are not the same as your own you are being challenged. Tension often occurs in intercultural interactions when people feel their values and beliefs are being challenged.

- Don't assume that you can learn about intercultural communication by staying in your comfort zone. Even if awkward at first, you need to expose yourself to different cultures (Taylor, 2001).

- Don't assume you know what is best for someone else.

Engage in transpection. Instead of assuming—a process most people begin quickly, naturally, and often subconsciously, take a moment to relax and reflect. **Transpection** is the process of empathizing across cultures (Maruyama, 1970). "Achieving transpection, trying to see the world exactly as the other person sees it, is a difficult process. It often involves trying to learn foreign beliefs, foreign assumptions, foreign perspectives, and foreign feelings in a foreign context. Transpection, then, can only be achieved by practice and requires structured experience and self-reflection" (Martin & Nakayama, 2001, p. 320).

Striving *toward* transpection can be a self-imposed intervention strategy that will help you avoid assumptions and move you closer to tolerance, sensitivity, respect, empathic listening, and effective communication responses. By carefully listening to others, understanding others' feelings, being interested in what they have to say, being sensitive to others' needs, and trying to understand their points of view (Hwang, Chase & Kelly, 1980), you can utilize thinking, feeling, and communication components to not just forge a connection, but help you avoid making improper assumptions.

Gain knowledge. Education expands your mental capacity for new learning and for the challenges of life. In general, the greater your cultural and linguistic knowledge, and the more your beliefs overlap with those from other cultures, the less likelihood for misunderstandings (Gudykunst & Kim, 2003). You need to read, observe, ask questions, and visit places where there are people from different races and ethnic backgrounds.

Studies of immigrants to the United States have shown that the use of the mass media of the host society facilitates the adaptation process (Taylor, 2001). Using the mass media enables you to learn about a broad spectrum of elements. "In transmitting messages that reflect aspirations, historical forces, myths, work and play, and specific issues and events, the mass media explicitly and implicitly convey societal values, norms, and traditional perspectives for interpreting the larger environment" (Gudykunst & Kim, 2003, p. 366). Watching the media is fine, however, they may serve to distort or perpetuate stereotypes about certain cultural groups; thus, it is important to apply both your critical thinking and evaluation skills toward media messages.

If you know you will be engaging in an intercultural exchange, do research on the Internet to learn about the specific culture and cultural norms. For those of you who want instant access to background knowledge of specific cultures, cocultures, nationalities, races, minorities, or religions, the Internet provides a fast, efficient, and prodigious solution. Many websites offer tips and do's and don'ts; however, it is important to remember these are only guidelines or brief snapshots, as noted in the earlier Another Point of View box. It is important to avoid generalizations. The more you learn about other cultures, the more likely you will recognize and overcome ethnocentrism, unfavorable stereotypes, prejudices, and discrimination (Ramirez et al., 2000). A typical list of do's and don'ts is given in the following On the Web box.

On the Web

About Brazil

Cultural Do's and Don'ts

General Protocol
Brazilians resent being talked to in Spanish. They take pride in their Portuguese heritage. Avoid referring to yourself as American. Say you are from the United States. Brazilians do not like this appropriation of the adjective by the citizens of the United States.

Appointments/ Punctuality
Make appointments at least two weeks in advance.
Schedule meetings for 10 AM to noon, and 3 PM to 5 PM
A business lunch may likely last two hours.
Punctuality is important in Sao Paolo, but in Rio de Janeiro and other areas your business counterparts may arrive 10 or 15 minutes late. However, you are not supposed to be late.

Hospitality/ Gift Giving
If invited to dinner, send flowers and a thank you note to your hostess the following day. Do not send purple flowers (a symbol of death).

Cafezinho (very strong coffee often offered without asking) and caipirnha (very alcoholic citrus beverage) are standard drinks when showing hospitality.

Dress
Semicasual clothes are appropriate in Rio de Janeiro, but pack a suit if your destination is Sao Paolo. The corporate center is more formal.

Communication Style
Do not discuss Argentina and avoid ethnic jokes. Avoid also discussions of politics, religion, or other controversial subjects.
Soccer, local cuisine, and Brazilian music are welcomed topics. Also, Brazilians love to discuss their social activities and their children.

Hand Gestures and Body Language
The OK sign is considered vulgar and obscene. Thumbs up should make the point. Snapping fingers means something was done long ago or for a long time. The fig is a symbol of good luck.

Source: (No author). *About Brazil: Cultural Do's and Don'ts*. Retrieved March 14, 2003, from http://www.gwu.edu/~csol/culture/br-do.htm.

The On the Web box is but a single example, but it provides evidence regarding the communication considerations that are needed in bridging cultural barriers.

Gain Experience. You cannot learn how to be a good communicator just by reading, observing, asking questions, or doing research on the Internet. But gaining experience doesn't mean, although it could (and maybe should), actual visits to foreign countries or foreign cultures. There are a variety ways, of course, to gain experience. Find an individual of another culture, and ask if the two of you could have a conversation about intercultural communication. With that as your focus, ask some pointed, specific questions designed to help you better understand him or her and others of the same culture. The following 10 questions are designed to get your conversation started:

- How do you (the other individual in this discussion), or other members of your culture, cope with and adapt to unfamiliar cultural environments?

- What are some of the best ways that members of other cultures can begin to communicate with members of your culture?
- What factors can increase our effectiveness in communicating?
- If we had a conflict, what would be the most successful strategies for managing it?
- What are the most important factors that would contribute to the development of interpersonal relationships with you or with members of your culture?
- What are some of the changes you have noticed occurring in you as a consequence of your adaptive experiences in a (this?) new culture?
- How can we (whatever race, ethnicity, gender, or nationality you represent) become more *intercultural* as a result of our contact and communication with members of your culture?
- Can we develop community with members of your culture? (Gudykunst and Kim, 2003).
- What are some of the worst offenses people from outside your culture make in communicating with you or with members of your culture?
- What do you feel are some of the worst offenses you have made as you have become acclimated into this culture?

Another way to gain experience is to volunteer to serve on committees, teams, or in groups in which members of other cultures will be serving. Then, once in these situations, use them to not only observe and listen, but pursue questions that will assist you in better understanding these individuals. Some of the questions above might be useful. When working with members of other cultures on the job or in business make every effort to engage them in conversation as well. Much of what you learn about intercultural communication will depend on your willingness to find it out. To do this, of course, you have to be willing to move out of your current comfort zone, but once you do, you will find that the trade-off in the knowledge and understanding you gain is well worth any effort you put forth.

Assess Yourself

Cultural Awareness Self-Assessment Form?

Please give a qualitative evaluation of each of the 10 factors by circling the numerical score which in your judgment best represents your assessment of your performance on each factor. This is not an opportunity to assess your desires, wishes, hopes, dreams, or even your potential.

7 = Outstanding (superb); 6 = Excellent; 5 = Very good; 4 = Average (good); 3 = Fair; 2 = Poor; 1 = *Very* minimal; 0 = No ability at all.

1. I listen to people from other cultures when they tell me how my culture affects them.　　　　　　　　　　　　7 6 5 4 3 2 1 0

2. I realize that people from other cultures have fresh ideas and different points of view to bring to my life and to the workplace.　　7 6 5 4 3 2 1 0

3. I give people from other cultures advice on how to succeed in my culture.　　　　　　　　　　　　　　　7 6 5 4 3 2 1 0

4. I give people my support even when they are rejected by other members of my culture.　　　　　　　　　　　7 6 5 4 3 2 1 0

5. I realize that people outside of my culture could be offended by my behavior. I've asked people if I have offended them by things I have done or said and have apologized whenever necessary.　7 6 5 4 3 2 1 0

6. I realize that when I am stressed out that I am likely to make myself and my culture right and another culture wrong.　　7 6 5 4 3 2 1 0

7. I respect my superiors (boss, teacher, supervisor, group leader, or whatever) regardless of where he or she is from. I do not go over his or her head to talk to some one from my culture in order to try and get my way.　　　　　　　　　7 6 5 4 3 2 1 0

8. When I am in mixed company, I mix with everyone. I don't just stay with people from my culture, or only with people from the dominant culture.　　　　　　　　　　　　7 6 5 4 3 2 1 0

9. I go out of my way to work with, recruit, select, train, and/or promote people from outside the dominant culture.　　7 6 5 4 3 2 1 0

10. When people in my culture make jokes about or talk negatively about other cultural groups, I let them know that I don't like it.　7 6 5 4 3 2 1 0

TOTAL POINTS: _____

Go to the *Communicating Effectively* CD-ROM to see your results and learn how to evaluate your attitudes and feelings.

Source: Adapted from (No author). *Cultural Awareness Self-Assessment Form 3,* I CANS (Integrated Curriculum for Achieving Necessary Skills), Washington State Board for Community and Technical Colleges, Washington State Employment Security, Washington Workforce Training and Education Coordinating Board, Adult Basic and Literacy Educators, P.O. Box 42496, 711 Capitol Blvd., Olympia, WA 98504. Retrieved March 14, 2003, from http://www.literacynet.org/icans/chapter05/cultural3.html.

Chapter Review

In looking at the word *culture,* our emphasis was on recognizing and accepting yourself as a cultural being. We defined culture as the ever changing values, traditions, social and political relationships, and worldview created and shared by a group of people bound together by a combination of factors (which can include a common history, geographic location, language, social class, and/or religion). There are no hard edges to the word, rather, there are phenomena that tend to overlap and mingle.

In the second section, five reasons for studying intercultural communication included (1) Developing a sensitivity to various cultural heritages and backgrounds in order to better understand your own identity; (2) Enhancing personal and social interactions; (3) Understanding the basis for and at least on a personal level, helping to solve cultural misunderstandings, miscommunications, and mistrusts; (4) Recognizing and respecting ethnic and cultural diversity in order to value the ways in which it enhances and enriches the quality of our civilization; and (5) Assisting readers in becoming effective citizens of our national communities.

In the third section, the influence of intercultural communication on the model of communication discussed in Chapter 1 was discussed, then how intercultural communication dynamically impacts communication as a transaction. That dynamic impact occurs because the model of communication focuses more on the physical act of communication whereas communication as a transaction focuses more on the psychological act—where intercultural influence is most likely.

In section four, we looked at six dimensions of culture that allow you to study cultural differences. Power distance relates to social inequality. Individualism versus collectivism relates to the degree of integration and orientation of individuals within groups. Feminity versus masculinity relates to the division of roles between women and men. Uncertainty avoidance relates to the degree of tolerance for the unknown. Long-term orientation relates to the trade-offs between long-term and short-term gratification of needs. Finally, high context versus low context communication refers to either the amount of information already in the person or context [high context] or the amount of information in the coded, explicit, intentionally transmitted part of the message [low context].

In section five, we discussed four barriers to intercultural communication. These included (1) Ethnocentricism, the belief that one's own cultural group is superior to all other cultural groups, (2) Stereotyping, which is using oversimplified or distorted views of another race, ethnic group, or culture, (3) Prejudice, which is possessing a negative attitude toward a cultural group based on little or no experience, and (4) Discrimination., which includes the overt actions one takes to exclude, avoid, or distance oneself from other groups.

Section six discussed how barriers to intercultural communication are often dealt with. When members of a nondominant group work to get what they want from dominant group members, they use one or more of three main strategies: assimilation, working to fit into the dominant group; accommodation, trying to get the dominant group to change so that it includes experiences of the nondominant group; and separation, leaving the dominant group.

In the final section we provided five suggestions for improving intercultural communication: (1) Pay attention to your own words and actions. (2) Control your assumptions. (3) Engage in transpection—the process of empathizing across cultures. (4) Gain knowledge. (5) Gain experience.

Burns-Glover, A. (2002, June). "Culture, the classroom, and electronic contacts: Talk story and e-mail communications." *The Journal of Education, Community, and Values: Interface on the Internet.* Department of Psychology, Berglund Center for Internet Studies, Pacific University, Forest Grove, Oregon. Retrieved March 14, 2003, from http://bcis.pacificu.edu/journal/2001/10/ glover.php. In this lengthy online article, the author provides a look at oral culture in the U.S. classroom—with a particular focus on the college adjustment experiences of Asian and Pacific Island students. Burns-Glover examines students from collectivist cultures as they face the challenges of the academic expectations for particular forms of oral participation and the Western individualist culture preference for public demonstrations. This is an excellent, inciteful, interesting investigation.

González, A., M. Houston, & V. Chen (2004). *Our voices: Essays in culture, ethnicity, and communication,* 4th ed. Los Angeles, CA: Roxbury Publishing Company. In this 330-page, paperback anthology, the authors examine communication in a variety of cultural and personal settings. In over 40 essays, writers address the question, "What is a cultural explanation and interpretation for this communication phenomenon . . .?" Parts include "Naming Ourselves," "Negotiating Sexuality and Gender," "Representing Cultural Knowledge in Interpersonal and Mass Media Contexts," "Celebrating Cultures," "Valuing and Contesting Languages," "Living in Bicultural Relationships," "Economic Class and Cultural Identity," "Traversing Cultural Paths," and "Reflecting on 9/11."

Gudykunst, W. B., & Y. Y. Kim (2002). *Communicating with strangers: An approach to intercultural communication,* 4th ed. Boston: McGraw-Hill. In the first part of the book, the authors lay the conceptual foundations, and in the second, they examine cultural, sociocultural, psychocultural, and environmental influences on the process. Part three covers standard procedures involved in interpreting and transmitting messages. Part four, by far the most interesting, covers effective communication, managing conflict, developing relationships, adapting to new cultures, becoming intercultural, and community through diversity. The authors focus primarily on theoretical issues to provide readers with the conceptual tools to understand intercultural communication.

Hecht, M. L., R. L. Jackson II, & S. A. Ribeau (2003). *African American communication: Exploring identity and culture,* 2nd ed. Mahwah, NJ: Lawrence Erlbaum Associates, Inc. The authors offer a thorough examination of African American communication. They highlight the need for sensitivity to issues of power when discussing race, ethnicity, and culture. Taking a communicative, linguistic, and relational focus, they offer numerous recommendations designed to encourage understanding of African American communication.

James, K. (2001). *Dancing with the witch doctor: One woman's stories of mystery and adventure in Africa.* New York: William Morrow. Although James is a private investigator, the three stories here each reveal an unrelated mystery, and although she exposes us to warring political factions, communist borders, poachers, tribesmen, witch doctors, prostitutes, the poverty stricken, and the sick in her journeys, she recreates the remarkable people she encounters and therefore peels back the layers of culture to reveal the foundation of humanity that is Africa. This is a well-written, engaging look at the strength of women.

Kennedy, C. J. (2001). *Generally speaking.* New York: Warner Books, Inc. Kennedy, the first woman three-star general, and when she retired from the army in June, 2000, the highest ranking female officer of her time, gives specific and revealing insight into one of our country's largest cocultures—the military. As a woman, she shows us how the military continues to evolve in its treatment of women, how it corrects its mistakes, how an officer conducts her daily life, and how an effective leader makes decisions, handles crises, and manages subordinates. In this well-written, engaging book, Kennedy, from the inside, tells how one of our most revered and misunderstood institutions operates. This is a useful book, especially for those unfamiliar with military life or for those interested in what women can do given persistence, principles, and personal resolve.

Kim, E. Y. (2001). *The yin and yang of American culture: A paradox.* Yarmouth, ME: Intercultural Press. Kim takes an Eastern view of our culture and places it in the context of Asian value sets. Based on her decades of conversations and interactions with both Americans and Asians, she presents American virtues and vices from an Asian perspective using the Asian concepts of yin and yang. The book is full of personal experiences, anecdotes from numerous sources, quotes from both Asians and Americans, historical background, general wisdom, and proverbs. Clearly Kim is a woman straddling two cultures—those of her Asian birthplace and her adopted American home. Although this highly readable book may disconcert you because of her incisiveness about our vices, it will make you glow with pride about our virtues.

Martin, J. N., & T. K. Nakayama (2001). *Experiencing intercultural communication: An introduction.* Boston: McGraw-Hill Higher Education. This textbook is packed with information on the foundations of intercultural communication, intercultural processes, intercultural communication in everyday life, and intercultural communication in applied settings like tourism, business, education, and health care. With marginal boxes called "Info Bites," "Pop Culture Spotlight," "Surf's Up!" (Internet connections), and "What do you think?" and with pictures, suggestions for building intercultural skills, activities, key terms, and nonstop examples, this textbook makes a complete, readable, package.

_____ (2000). *Intercultural communication in contexts*, 2nd ed. Mountain View, CA: Mayfield Publishing Co. The authors discuss foundations, processes, and applications of intercultural communication. In addition to an explicit discussion of differing research approaches, their attention to history, popular culture, and identity, they include "Student Voices" boxes in which students relate their own experiences and share their thoughts, and "Point of View" boxes that offer diverse viewpoints from the news media, research studies, and other public forums. This is a complete textbook that incorporates the authors' personal experiences as well as examples from different religions.

Pipher, M. (2002). *The middle of everywhere: The world's refugees come to our town.* New York: Harcourt. Pipher, a psychologist, writes about the problems of newcomers in America, helping people understand the point of view of those who have very different lives from theirs. Her 1994 best seller, *Reviving Ophelia*, detailed the perils many girls face in adolescence. In 1999, her book *Another Country: Navigating the Emotional Terrain of Our Elders*, dealt with the generation gap between baby boomers and their aging parents. In this book, she discusses the resilient, those who adjust to change the best. For purposes of this chapter on intercultural communication, her "attributes of resiliency" are the most useful because they are designed to help everyone adjust to new and difficult environments, which could easily be new cultures.

Schultz, F. (Ed.). (2002). *Multicultural education* (8th ed.). Guilford, CT: McGraw-Hill/Dushkin. In this series of annual editions on multicultural education, coverage includes critical literature on gender, race, and culture in educational settings across the nation drawn from the academic literature in anthropology, sociology, social psychology, social history, sociolinguistics, and psychiatry. The purpose of the articles is to sensitize teachers to multicultural issues and move toward a greater understanding of diversity. There is a great deal of advice, numerous suggestions, and various opportunities for planning for the future. A very useful series for future teachers.

Storti, C., & L. R. Kohls (2001). *The art of crossing cultures*, 2nd ed. Yarmouth, MA: Nicholas Breaky International Press. Storti provides a brief 169-page introduction to cross-cultural communication. As founder and director of a Washington, D.C., intercultural-communication training and consulting firm, he details the challenges of anticipating cultural differences, managing the temptation to withdraw, and then gradually adjusting expectations of behavior to fit reality. Storti gives excellent advice on how to deal with country and culture shock.

(No author) (2002, February 28). *ViVa women's history*. International Institute of Social History. Retrieved March 14, 2003, from: www.iisg.nl/~womhist/vivahome.html. This is an up-to-date database of articles focusing on women's and gender history. All substantial articles and review essays about women and gender in history (1975 to 2001) are listed in the bibliography and is available at www2.iisg.nl/viva/. Related topics such as prostitution, witchcraft, housework, sexuality, birth control, infanticide, the family, gynecology, and masculinity are also included.

Winters, E. (2002, March). *Cross cultural communication*. Retrieved March 14, 2003, from http://www.bena.com/ewinters/xculture.html. This is a website of practical tips and ideas on context, environmental factors, nonverbal messages, official languages and dialects, social considerations, time, and who's in charge, that offers suggestions for the exploration of similarities and differences in cultures. The information here is written for leaders in business, industry, education, training, and the traveler. Winters also includes reading suggestions for those interested in cross-cultural communication.

Chapter 4

Listening

Objectives

After reading this chapter, you should be able to:

- Demonstrate the importance of listening from prebirth to predeath.
- Differentiate and give an example of each of the four kinds of listening styles.
- Explain the problems that lead to poor listening.
- Identify and explain the various parts of the listening process.
- List the benefits of active listening.
- Understand the meaning of listening for information and how to improve your skills in listening for information.
- Understand the meaning of critical listening and how to improve your skills in critical listening.
- Understand the meaning of empathic listening and how to improve your skills in empathic listening.
- Understand the meaning of listening for enjoyment and how to improve your skills in listening for enjoyment.
- Explain how you can talk so others will listen.

Key Terms and Concepts

Use the Communicating Effectively CD-ROM and Online Learning Center at mhhe.com/hybels7 to further your understanding of the following terms.

Action listening style 102	Critical listening 117	People listening style 102
Active listener 113	Empathic listening 121	Prediction 109
Assessment 112	Fact 119	Propriety 127
Central idea 114	Listening 102	Selective attention 110
Cognitive dissonance 104	Main heads 114	Supporting points 114
Content listening style 102	Opinion 119	Time-style listening 102
Credibility 118	Paraphrasing 123	
	Passive listener 113	

LET'S BRIEFLY LOOK AT THE VALUE OF LISTENING from before birth to just before death.

Before birth: Fetuses exposed to French speakers on a regular basis turned toward a French speaker and away from an English speaker (Wark, 1999). In another study, six weeks before they were born, fetuses were read *Cat in the Hat* twice a day. After a while, when the fetuses heard the familiar story, their heartbeats were lower (a sign of listening) than they were when the fetuses heard a new and unfamiliar story (Sones & Sones, 1999).

Young babies: Very young babies also show evidence of listening. When they are only two months old, they will respond to someone talking to them by trying to make sounds of their own. At three or four months they will show interest in nursery songs and games that involve body movement (Wark, 1999).

Within the family: Karin Klein, Administrator, Red Hill School, Red Hill, Pennsylvania, says "Once a decision is made to place a high priority on genuine listening within the family, parents can begin practicing the skills of listening. As children journey through childhood they will then reap the many benefits and pleasures of a home that knows how to listen" (Klein, 2002, p. 1).

In school: "Students who have good attention and concentration skills often finish homework quickly. They usually listen so well in class that they have learned much of what they need to know already. It is said that students who listen very carefully to what teachers are saying, can cut their study time by 45 percent. Other students, whose skills aren't so well-developed, may let their minds wander" (*Homework . . .*, 2001).

At college: "Learning is not a spectator sport. Students do not learn much just by sitting in classes listening to teachers, memorizing prepackaged assignments, and spitting out answers. They must talk about what they are learning, write about it, relate it to past experiences and apply it to their daily lives. They must make what they learn part of themselves" (Chickering & Gamson).

In relationships: "Listening well is at the heart of intimacy and connections. When we are able to listen to another person with attention and care, that person feels validated and enhanced. When we enhance the other person, we also enhance our own self" (Lerner, 2001). "Research has consistently demonstrated that ineffective listening habits present the most common barriers to success in relationships" (Barker & Watson, 2000).

In sales: Eugene Wilson (*How can . . .*, 2002, April–June), former DuPont Sales Trainer and Manager of Management Development, having analyzed 1,000 sales role-plays, discovered that the biggest reason for missed sales opportunities was poor listening. Wilson says, "The best way to sustain a career in selling is to become a good listener" (p. 2). Jerry Haasch, one of Sony's award-winning Western Zone account managers says, "Listening is the most important part of the sales technique" (*How can . . .*, 2002, April–June). "Being a good listener is more important in sales than being a good talker" (Mackay, 2001).

In business: "You probably understand the importance of listening and communication skills in your business. After all, people must listen to each other to work as a team, improve performance, and conduct business successfully" (*Listening skills . . .*, 2001).

In mentoring others: "One of the most important attributes of a mentor is good listening skills. Students need to feel that their questions and concerns are important to you to foster trust and good communication so that you both benefit from the mentoring experience" (Hackley & Gorman.).

On the death bed: "The patient is dying to everything he or she has ever known. As he or she begins to die, they become very reflective, and may want to share their reflections with their caregivers. Through these reflections, a patient gives meaning to their life. When we listen to a patient share their story, we are being invited into their soul" (*Gentle endings . . .*, 2002).

It is obvious that at whatever stage of life people find themselves, listening plays an important part. Effective listening can determine one's success within the family, in school, college, relationships, sales, business, mentoring, and for others on their death bed. If seeking proof for the importance of listening in other areas of life were pursued, we are certain it would be a major factor in how one succeeds in any aspect of life, profession, or pursuit. The problem is that people think they are already good listeners; ask them if they are and usually they'll say yes, and they are likely to add, "It's easy to be a good listener" (Mackay, 2001).

On the Web

Are You an Active Listener?

When you're conversing with another person—a colleague, a subordinate, a business acquaintance—do you listen with your whole body and mind? Do you actively listen? Take the simple self-scoring quiz at the website below to help find out. Website: R. G. Ensman, Jr. "Are You an Active Listener?" ISdesig.Net—*IS Magazine*—the Online Version of *Interiors & Sources Magazine.* Retrieved March 14, 2003, from http://www.isdesignet.com /isdesignet/Magazine/Apr'96/ Commentary. html.

Instructions

Score yourself on the 25 active-listening skills. If you usually practice the skill in question, score yourself with a 2. If you sometimes practice the

skill in question, score yourself with a 1. If you seldom practice the skill, give yourself a 0. Be honest with yourself; no one is looking over your shoulder.

Results

Total the numerical value of all your answers. If your total score is 40 or above, congratulations. You're a good conversation partner and practice active-listening skills quite effectively. If your total score is between 30 and 39, you're probably familiar with active-listening techniques—and you may well use them—but additional practice of these all-important communication skills won't hurt. If your total score is below 30, don't fret. You can increase your awareness of communication techniques, as well as your ability to be an effective listener.

The International Listening Association defines **listening** as the process of receiving, constructing meaning from, and responding to spoken and/or nonverbal messages (Wolvin, 1995). You might be surprised to read that part of listening is responding to nonverbal messages. However, when you think about it, it makes sense that some of the information being communicated to you is through the way the other person uses his or her body. A person who is resistant to what you have to say might show this by frowning and folding her arms across her chest. Do you remember a time when you were trying to communicate and you knew the other person wasn't listening? How did you know? Chances are that you could tell by the nonverbal behavior of the other person.

■ LISTENING STYLES

Most of us have discovered, after being in school for so many years, that there are different ways of learning and different ways of listening. Researchers have identified four different kinds of listening styles (Youaver & Kirtley, 1995). In a **people listening style,** the listener is concerned with the other person's feelings. Such listeners seek out common interests with others and respond to emotions. This listening is common among couples, families, and best friends.

In an **action listening style,** the listener wants precise, error-free presentations and is likely to be impatient with disorganization. A boss, for example, might ask for a report from one of the division heads on how the company is doing. She would expect this report to be focused and to the point.

In a **content listening style,** the listener prefers complex and challenging information. Since this information is generally abstract, people can listen without emotional involvement and then evaluate information before they make judgments. A doctor might, for example, ask for information from his colleagues on how a particular patient should be treated. Because of his training and experience he will not have difficulty understanding a complex medical explanation.

The final style is **time-style listening.** In this style, the listener prefers brief and hurried interaction with others and often lets the communicator know how much time he or she has to make the point. Newspeople, getting ready for a television newscast, need to get information quickly and efficiently because they are always working against the clock, so they are likely to be time-style listeners.

The most skillful listeners are able to adapt their listening styles to the circumstances. If listeners haven't learned to do this, they will have a problem in some of their interactions with others. For example, when a person is complaining about a co-worker, she would probably prefer a people-style listener. Yet her boss, who is short of time, wants her to state her problem, listen to his suggestions, and then leave his office—a reaction that will leave her feeling unsatisfied.

When you work with people, it's important you be aware of their listening styles. For example, if you want some critical reaction to a paper you have just written, a content-style listener will be more helpful than a people-style listener because the people listener wouldn't want to hurt your feelings by pointing out your mistakes.

Some research shows that a person's listening style might depend on the culture he or she comes from. One study that compared American, German, and Israeli speakers found that Americans were the most people-centered and were likely to pay careful attention to the feelings of the people they were talking to while Israelis concentrated more on the accuracy of the messages. Germans were the most active listeners and often interspersed questions as they listened (Kiewitz, Weaver, Brosius, & Weimann, 1970).

Gender and Listening

Anyone who has had some experience in the world might suspect that men and women listen differently. For example, how often have you heard the complaint, "My boyfriend/husband doesn't listen to me" or "You never listen to me"?

Scholars who have studied communication between men and women have discovered that men and women have different listening styles. In the study of cultural listening styles mentioned above, the researchers found that in all three cultures, women were more likely to be people listeners than were men (Kiewitz, et. al., 1997).

Deborah Tannen, a linguist whose work is discussed in detail in Chapter 5, Verbal Communication, maintains that men and women come from different communication cultures: Women are interested in relationships and networking, while men are more interested in competitive communication (O'Brien, 1993). This theory explains why a husband does not show much interest when his wife tells him about two people who were quarreling at her work. By the same token, the wife pays little attention when her husband talks about the batting averages of some of the players in the major leagues.

Tannen has also found that when men and women talk, women are more likely to be the listeners. Curious about how long this communication behavior has existed, Tannen went back to the literature of earlier times. She found that little has changed over the ages: In Shakespeare's fifteenth-century *Julius Caesar*, Portia begs Brutus to talk to her and not to keep his secrets from her. Tannen says that the culture of boys is based on status and that to maintain their status boys will hold the center of attention by boasting and telling jokes or fascinating stories; the same thing was true of the hero of *Beowulf*, an eighth-century saga (Tannen, 1999).

One problem women have to face when they enter the executive or professional world is getting men to listen to them. When Sandra Day O'Connor, the first female Supreme Court justice, was asked what problems she had in her career, she replied that the greatest problem was not being listened to. Finally she found a technique that made people pay attention to her: "I taught myself early on to speak very slowly—enunciating every word—when I wanted someone's undivided attention" (O'Brien, 1993). Her strategy makes sense: When we find that someone's attention seems to be fading, we are inclined to talk faster.

Another mistake women are likely to make in a business setting is to smile and wait their turn instead of using the male tactic of jumping into the discussion when they have something to say. Men don't follow the

Consider This

What are the challenges we face with respect to listening in the new technology-oriented world. Mary Boone, a leading authority on organizational communication and collaborative technologies, explains:

"Most of us have traditionally indicated that we're listening to each other by maintaining eye contact, orienting our bodies toward another person, and periodically through nods of our head indicating agreement or disagreement with what's being said. But these days people are "listening" in new ways. I've watched the teenagers of my friends do their homework, listen to the radio, have the TV on, be on a chat line and get instant messages—all at the same time! So they listen in a wholly different way than I listen."

Questions

1. Does Boone accurately capture the way you listen at times? Are there interfering ingredients that Boone has not mentioned?

2. Do you think additional technology is likely to introduce greater confusion in the communication between people? How and why?

Source: M. E. Boone, *Managing Inter@ctively: Executing Business Strategy, Improving Communication, and Creating a Knowledge-Sharing Culture.* (New York: McGraw-Hill, 2001.)

female system of taking turns. Patricia O'Brien (1993) advises that if women want to be listened to at work they should sit at the middle of the conference table where they can't be ignored, speak with conviction, avoid disclaimers such as "I might not be right but . . .," and go directly to the main point, omitting the details.

■ WHY DO PEOPLE HAVE PROBLEMS LISTENING?

Listening is hard work, and there are many reasons for our attention to go astray. Let's look at some of the problems that cause us to listen less effectively than we should.

Cognitive Dissonance

Cognitive dissonance, a psychological theory that applies to communication, states that a person feels conflict if he or she holds two or more attitudes that are in opposition to each other. For example, people might feel that their senator is doing a good job, but they might also believe that the charges of sexual harassment that are being made against him are probably true. People who hold these simultaneous beliefs (the senator is good but sexual harassment is bad) suffer from cognitive dissonance.

A common way that people reduce this dissonance is by ignoring the information that is causing the conflict. When the senator is accused of sexual harassment, for example, you think to yourself, "That can't be true. He's a good family man." As we pointed out in Chapter 2, Self, Perception, and Communication, listening to information that conflicts with your already-held beliefs is risky, especially if accepting the information might put you in conflict with people who are important to you. On the other hand, careful listening to such information is necessary if you are going to grow and respect others' ideas.

Anxiety

Some people don't listen well because their anxiety level creates psychological noise. Imagine you are driving to a new city and that you find yourself hopelessly lost. After driving for a long time and not seeing any highway numbers or signs indicating a nearby city, you probably feel like you're about to jump out of your skin. That's anxiety. When you finally stop to ask directions, you have completely lost confidence in yourself and your anxiety level is so high that you can't even listen. The result is that once you set out again, you probably still cannot find your way.

Anxiety certainly exists in the classroom setting. Research indicates that if teachers tell students they will be tested on difficult information, the students are likely to feel anxiety, which will interfere with how they listen (Ayres, Wilcox, & Ayres, 1995). For example, a student took a math course that he needed for graduation. Every time he came to a problem he didn't understand, his anxiety increased so much that he stopped listening. Finally he got to the point where he was so far behind that he stopped going to class. After enrolling in the class for the fourth time, he decided that he better try to get his anxiety under control so that he could listen well enough to pass the class.

Anxiety is not always a negative part of the listening process. One airline found that if passengers could use the airline's audio system to listen to conversations between the cockpit and the air-traffic controllers, it often reassured the more nervous fliers. A vice president of the airlines said that for some passengers, being involved in what was going on gave them a greater sense of reassurance (Kent, 1998).

The Controlling Listener

Many people don't want to listen at all. They take turns listening because they know it is expected of them, but they would prefer to be talking. When you talk to such a person, you and that person are each engaged in a monologue rather than a dialogue.

Controlling listeners always look for a way to talk about themselves and their experiences. If you talk about one of your own experiences, the controlling person comes up with a bigger and better one. If you own a 20-pound cat, he or she tells you about someone who owns a 25-pound cat. If you say you're going to Spain, he or she tells you that you really should go to Spain and Portugal to make the trip worthwhile.

Controlling people seldom notice the nonverbal cues they get from others. They ignore the fact that their listeners are glassy-eyed and often sneaking looks at their watches. They also ignore cues such as "I'd better get going" or "I just noticed how late it is."

The Passive Listener

People often believe that listening involves no work. Their attitude may range from "I don't have to do anything; I can just sit back and listen" to "If it's not going to be on the test, I don't have to listen." Listening without interest often occurs in the classroom, where not all professors are equally stimulating. Some may be better informed; they're just not as interesting and are therefore less popular. Also, some subjects are less interesting than others. A course in communication, for example, is probably more stimulating than one in economics. When the speaker or the subject is not very interesting, you have to make a real attempt to listen.

Depending on what you listen to, you need a variety of listening skills, for listening requires as much skill as speaking and writing. In the section that follows, you'll learn about the process of listening, the kinds of listening you do, and some ways to improve listening skills.

Cognitive dissonance, anxiety, controlling and passive listeners make up some of the problems of why people don't listen. In a study on barriers to effective listening, Steven Golen (1990) found that out of 23 potentially important barriers, six stood out. We have placed these barriers in Table 4–1 because you will recognize them, because they can be a serious handicap in the college classroom, and because awareness of the factors is the first step to overcoming them.

Consider This

From time to time everyone has lapses in listening. Yet you probably know people who are excellent listeners and know others who hardly listen at all. To find out what kind of listener you are, ask yourself the following questions and reply to each with either "Often" (O), "Sometimes" (S), or "Never" (N).

1. Have you ever done a class assignment incorrectly while the rest of the class did it right?

2. Have you asked an instructor to reexplain an assignment he or she gave the class?

3. Have you been lost because you didn't listen carefully to directions someone gave you?

4. Have your classmates ever laughed because you asked a question that had just been answered?

5. Have you asked a question that had nothing to do with what was being discussed?

6. Have you ever realized that you were not listening well because you were distracted by something?

7. Have you ever been accused of not listening?

8. Have you ever turned up in the wrong place when you were meeting someone because you forgot the directions you were given?

9. Have you had trouble finding something even when someone told you where to look?

How many times did you respond "Often" or "Sometimes" to these questions, and what do your answers tell you about the way you listen? Many people who reply to this questionnaire might be surprised to find that they don't listen very well.

Table 4-1 *Factors and Barriers to Effective Listening*

Factor	Barrier
Laziness	Avoid listening if the subject is complex or difficult.
	Avoid listening because it takes too much time.
Closed-mindedness	Refuse to maintain a relaxing and agreeable environment.
	Refuse to relate to and benefit from the speaker's ideas.
Opinionatedness	Disagree or argue outwardly or inwardly with the speaker.
	Become emotional or excited when the speaker's views differ from yours.
Insincerity	Avoid eye contact while listening.
	Pay attention only to the speaker's word rather than the speaker's feelings.
Boredom	Lack interest in the speaker's subject.
	Become impatient with the speaker.
	Daydream or become preoccupied with something else when listening.
Inattentiveness	Concentrate on the speaker's mannerisms or delivery rather than on the message.
	Become distracted by noise from office equipment, telephone, other conversation, etc.

Adapted from S. Golen, "A Factor Analysis of Barriers to Effective Listening," *The Journal of Business Communication* 27, Winter 1990, p. 32.

■ LEARNING TO LISTEN

Listening is a skill that can be improved by learning how it works. In a survey of *Fortune* 500 companies, 59 percent of the respondents said that they provided listening training for their employees. This interest in developing listening skills makes sense because research shows that employees of major corporations spend about 60 percent of their time listening while executives spend an average of 57 percent (Wolvin & Coakley, 1993). Researchers have found that there is a direct connection between good listening skills and productivity on the job. When employees were given training in listening before they received training in computer techniques, they were much more productive than employees who hadn't had the listening training (Papa & Glenn, 1988).

Figure 4-1 shows the average percentage of time people devote to the four communication skills: listening, speaking, reading, and writing. Although we spend the greatest amount of time listening, it is the skill that is taught the least (Sperry Corporation, 1980, p. 4).

Listening, like any skill, has to be learned and practiced. When researchers polled 450 graduates of business programs about what kind of communication skills they needed on the job, the graduates responded that listening was the most important skill for success. When they were asked what communication skill they wished they had been taught in college, listening ranked number one (DiSalvo, Larsen & Seiler, 1976).

Figure 4-1

Percentage of Time Devoted to Various Communication Skills

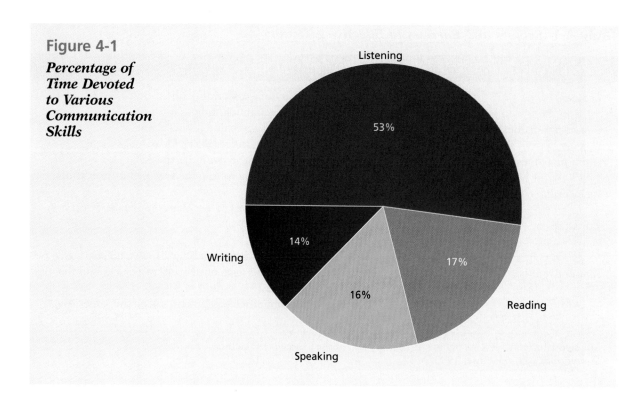

Michael Purdy (2002), writer and researcher on listening, conducted a study of 900 college and military students aged 17 to 70 which showed the traits of good and poor listeners:

A good listener:

1. Uses eye contact appropriately.
2. Is attentive and alert to a speaker's verbal and nonverbal behavior.
3. Is patient and doesn't interrupt (waits for the speaker to finish).
4. Is responsive, using verbal and nonverbal expressions.
5. Asks questions in a nonthreatening tone.
6. Paraphrases, restates, or summarizes what the speaker says.
7. Provides constructive (verbal or nonverbal) feedback.
8. Is empathic (works to understand the speaker).
9. Shows interest in the speaker as a person.
10. Demonstrates a caring attitude and is willing to listen.
11. Doesn't criticize, is nonjudgmental.
12. Is open-minded.

A poor listener:

1. Interrupts the speaker (is impatient).
2. Doesn't give eye contact (eyes wander).
3. Is distracted (fidgeting) and does not pay attention to the speaker.
4. Is not interested in the speaker (doesn't care; daydreaming).
5. Gives the speaker little or no (verbal or nonverbal) feedback.

Another Point of View

Do you think you listen well? Do you listen well to all others? Do you even listen well to the physically handicapped?

... *Studies of attitudes toward stutterers reveal widespread bias. In a 1997 survey, nurses filled out questionnaires about a hypothetical stuttering doctor and were asked to appraise the physician's personality traits. They deemed the stutterer more afraid and nervous and less mature, intelligent, and educated than a hypothetical physician who did not stutter. Even a poll of speech pathologists found that more than a third of the group expressed the view that people who stutter have psychological problems. Reviewing these findings, Gordon Blood, a professor of communication disorders at Pennsylvania State University, says that the persistence of such potent stereotypes can in itself worsen a stutterer's plight. "A listener's reaction plays a huge part in this disorder," he says.*

"What we're really asking is for people to be civil" (p. 50).

Questions

1. Do you think you would act differently toward a stutterer than is depicted in this excerpt?

2. How can those who are physically challenged increase the likelihood they will be listened to effectively by others? How can our society change the way they react to the physically challenged?

3. Is the problem one of poor listening? Or, is it more a problem of attitude? How do attitudes toward others and effective listening relate?

Source: R. K. Sobel, "Anatomy of a Stutter: New findings from brain studies and genetics are illuminating the causes of this ancient affliction." *U.S. News & World Report,* April 2, 2001, pp. 44-51.

6. Changes the subject.
7. Is judgmental.
8. Is closed-minded.
9. Talks too much.
10. Is self-preoccupied.
11. Gives unwanted advice.
12. Is too busy to listen (Purdy, 2002, pp. 2 of 3).

■ THE PROCESS OF LISTENING

Predicting

Listening plays a part in the transactional nature of communication. On the basis of your past experience with someone, you make a **prediction** about how he or she is likely to respond. For example, if you go to an instructor with a paper that is late, you know from past experience that she isn't going to be very happy with you and that you will probably have to listen to complaints about your shortcomings as a student. You also know that your best strategy is to listen—not to argue or give excuses.

Receiving Messages

In only a single day you probably receive more messages than you need or can process. Some of these messages we mentioned earlier: commercials, someone shouting in the hallway, an instructor's lecture, a conversation

Our first experiences of learning to listen usually come from our parents.

with a friend. You *hear* many of these messages, but you do not *listen* to all of them.

You hear sounds—such as words and the way they are spoken—but when you listen, you respond to much more. Hearing is a physiological process involving the various parts of the ear, whereas listening is a more complicated perceptual process involving your total response to others, including verbal as well as nonverbal communication.

Receiving messages, then, goes beyond mere hearing. Messages come in all forms and from a variety of sources. When you listen, you filter out the irrelevant messages. This brings us to the next step in the listening process—that of attending to what is important or interesting.

Attending

You are able to focus your attention on a particular stimulus. For example, if you're in the dorm in the early evening, you hear all kinds of noises: students shouting to each other, music playing, doors slamming. However, when your CD tracks to your favorite song, you are all attention: The song masks out all the other sounds around you.

The ability to focus perception—called **selective attention**—is quite extraordinary. For decades parents have told their children that it is impossible to study with the television set or stereo blaring away. If you like to study that way too and say that your parents are wrong, research will support you. In one study, listeners were seated in the middle of four loudspeakers, all with different messages, and each subject was told to pay attention to the message coming from only one particular speaker. In all cases, the listeners had an almost perfect performance in recalling the message from that speaker (Moray, 1969).

Although you may be able to focus your attention in specific ways, most people's attention spans are very short. Most individuals can hear about 600 words a minute; however, even fast talkers can speak only 100 to 150 words a minute. In the gap between hearing and speaking it's very easy to let your mind wander (Messmer, 1998). Few people can give full attention to a message for more than 20 seconds (Friedman, 1978, p. 274). Something in the message reminds you of something else, or you disagree with the message and let your mind wander in a completely different direction. Fortunately you are able to quickly refocus your attention on the message, but every listener and speaker should be aware of just how easily attention can go astray.

Attention span is closely tied to boredom. Researchers have found that the best listener is someone who is not easily bored and who has some basic skills in acquiring and organizing information (Bostrom, 1990). If you are easily bored, then, you must make a special attempt to focus your attention.

Assigning Meaning

When you decide to attend to a message, your next step is to assign it meaning. To assign meaning you must decide what in the message is relevant and how it relates to what you already know. Basically, then, the process of assigning meaning is one of selecting material and trying to relate it to your experience. In assigning meaning you might evaluate what the speaker has said against the personal beliefs you hold, question the speaker's motives, wonder what has been omitted, and challenge the validity of the ideas. As you understand *what* was said, you also consider *how* it was said. You assign meaning to the speaker's tone of voice, gestures, and facial expressions as much as you do to his or her words (Rubin & Roberts, 1987).

Remembering

The next step in the listening process is remembering. Again, remembering is a selective process of determining what is important and what is not. As students, few of you record the whole of an instructor's lecture. Instead, you take notes that help you remember the important points. Some students take too many notes and attempt to write down everything the instructor says rather than writing key words. Also, if you try to take too many notes, it might interfere with your listening; you're so busy writing that you are not paying attention to meaning. Another thing to keep in mind is not to write down anything you don't understand because you're not going to understand it when you look at it later. When you don't know what someone is saying, if possible, stop and ask for clarification.

Assessing

At the start of this discussion of the listening process, you were predicting what was going to happen when you asked your instructor to take a late paper. Although she took your paper, you know from her response that you better not try to hand in a late paper again: You predict from this experience that she would be really angry and not accept it. You have assessed the experience. **Assessment** is an evaluation of what occurred.

The actual listening process has six stages: predicting, receiving messages, attending to them, assigning meaning to them, remembering, and assessing. In an ideal listening situation, all these stages will be completed. If listening is ineffective, however, the process might break down at any stage. Figure 4-2 shows a student going through all the steps of a successful listening experience.

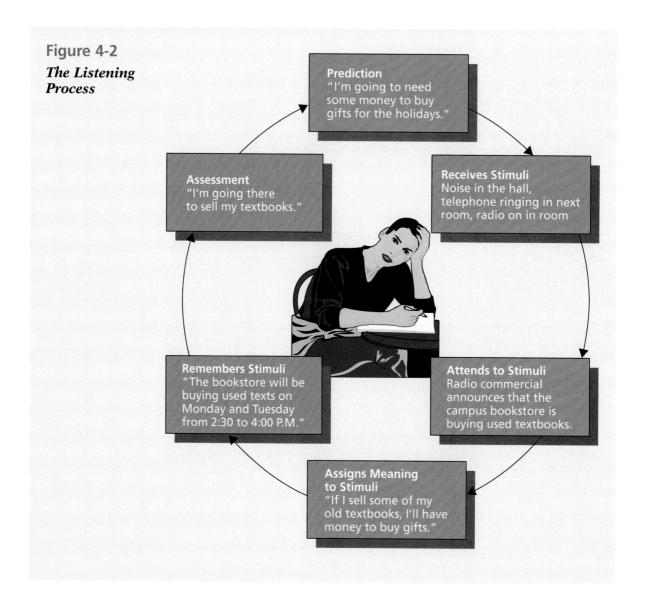

Figure 4-2

The Listening Process

Prediction
"I'm going to need some money to buy gifts for the holidays."

Receives Stimuli
Noise in the hall, telephone ringing in next room, radio on in room

Assessment
"I'm going there to sell my textbooks."

Attends to Stimuli
Radio commercial announces that the campus bookstore is buying used textbooks.

Remembers Stimuli
"The bookstore will be buying used texts on Monday and Tuesday from 2:30 to 4:00 P.M."

Assigns Meaning to Stimuli
"If I sell some of my old textbooks, I'll have money to buy gifts."

■ LISTENING FOR INFORMATION: ACTIVE LISTENING

Any college student will find that most class time is spent in listening, and this listening is primarily for information. Listening to various instructors talk about the reasons for the Civil War, the economic structure of the broadcast industry, or the definition of a paranoid individual is, in each case, an example of listening for information.

The business world also requires people to listen for information: The company receptionist finds out whom a visitor hopes to see and why; the service representative at an 800 number takes orders for computer parts; the mechanic receives information from the boss on how to install a new part. In business, listening can be seen in dollars-and-cents terms. The Sperry Corporation has pointed out that if 100 million U.S. workers each made a $10 listening error, the cost would total $1 billion (Sperry Corporation, 1980).

Even when careful listening is important for one's well-being, some people don't do it. A frequent traveler said that she always used to read magazines while the flight attendants explained safety features on the airplane. One day when her plane had made an emergency landing on the runway and she was crawling on the floor through the smoke toward what she hoped was the nearest exit, she wished she had paid attention to the flight attendants' messages.

The best way to focus on what is being said is to be a good **active listener.** You are an active listener when you make a mental outline of important points and think up questions or challenges to the points that have been made. Even though you might not say anything, you are mentally involved with the person who is talking.

Students have a special need to be active listeners because such listeners generally do better in school than **passive listeners,** who record but do not evaluate what they hear. Most teachers who lecture prefer that students take notes. Although there has not been a great deal of research about note taking, what is known is that passive listeners, who merely try to write down as much as they can of what an instructor says, will not do particularly well on examinations. (There is also little value in borrowing notes from a friend.) Active listeners, on the other hand, take notes that tie concepts together and distinguish between main and minor points. Students who take notes in this fashion and review them before the examination are likely to get better grades than students who passively record information (Kiewra & DuBois, 1991).

Active listening extends beyond the classroom. In interpersonal communication, for example, it involves looking for the literal and the emotional meaning in what someone is saying as well as showing interest with nonverbal cues, such as leaning forward, nodding, smiling, and frowning, and using audible cues, such as "Uh-huh," "Mmm," and "I see." In interpersonal communication there is also ample opportunity to give feedback by asking questions or commenting on what the person has just said.

Active listening helps you avoid boredom as well because you are less likely to be bored if you are participating rather than observing. Active listening is a way of involving yourself, and once you are involved, you are likely to get interested. If you use active-listening techniques when you listen to a lecture, you might be surprised to find how quickly the time passes.

The following are some ways in which you can be an active listener.

Consider This

Note-Taking Skills

Active listening is essential to effective note taking, and adequate notes are crucial to efficient study and learning in college. For more than 25 years, I (Richard) was a large-group lecturer for the basic speech-communication course in lecture halls that seated more than 300 students. One question that arose on a regular basis had to do with effective note taking for my lectures. Here is the essence of my advice to students on how to take effective lecture notes.

- Sit where you can easily see and hear the lecturer. Also, sit where you can see the chalkboard and any slides or overhead projections that might be shown.

- Do not try to write out everything that is said in a lecture. Think before you write, but don't get behind.

- Feel free to record the lectures using a small, inconspicuous recorder. (If you plan to do this in other classes, ask the lecturer for permission before making the recording.) If you record the lectures, make sure you have everything on the chalkboard and slides in your notes.

- Jot down notes of the main and minor points of the lecture.

- Listen carefully to verbal and nonverbal cues that indicate key or essential points.

- Write legibly, and use abbreviations wherever possible.

- If you recorded the lecture, compare your notes of the main and minor points with the information on the tape as you listen a second time.

- Fill in details missed the first time through; however, do not copy down everything.

- Annotate and highlight any key points or essential information.

- If you did not record the lecture compare and discuss your comprehension and notes with another student.

- Review your notes shortly after the lecture to help you better remember the contents.

- Once you have your notes reduced to the essence of the lecture, review them just before the examination.

A technique I found particularly valuable in classes I considered difficult or challenging was reducing my notes to their essence. I would then read them into a tape recorder so that I could listen to them in the car, at home in my room, or whenever a spare moment occurred. Listening to them over and over helped me learn the material thoroughly. (Some people complained that this was too much of a commitment; I would respond with, "It all depends on what you want out of college. A college education is what you make of it.")

Identify the Central Idea

If you are listening to a speech or lecture, you first should listen for and identify the **central idea**—the essential thought that runs through the passage. Then listen for **main heads**—the points that reinforce the central idea. Finally, you listen for **supporting points**—the materials that back up the main heads. It is important to identify the central idea, because all the main heads should relate to it. Also, identifying the central idea aids memory. If you remember the central idea, then the main heads will follow. If you remember only the latter, you may have unrelated points that make no sense, so you will quickly forget them. It is the central idea that ties them together and gives them meaning.

With interpersonal communication, the central idea is not always evident, and in some cases there might not be one. Central ideas are most likely to be present when you are having a heated discussion or an argument. A mother, for example, might have her teenager's safety in mind when she makes up the rules for using the car. Two people arguing about the best football team might each come up with a central idea to support a particular side.

When small groups are trying to solve a problem, they will work more effectively when they identify the central idea. If you have ever been in a group that did not accomplish very much, it's probably because the group strayed away from the central idea. For example, members of the food committee meet with the purpose of making suggestions on how the campus food service can improve. If they stick to this idea, they will be likely to come up with some useful advice. However, if the group members sit around and swap horror stories about the terrible meals they have had, they will not accomplish much.

Identify Supporting Material

In listening to a speech or a lecture, once you have identified the central idea, your next step is to look for the main heads that support it. The purpose of the main heads is to support the central idea in much the same way that the main branches of a tree support the smaller branches that lead off them. Supporting points build evidence for the main heads and often consist of illustrations and examples that make the main heads clearer to the listener. Let's suppose a speaker is trying to inform his audience about Americans' impressions of Arabs. His central idea is that the media are unfair in their representation of Arabs. Main heads might point out that Arabs are discriminated against in American economic, social, and political life. As a supporting point for the first main head (economic discrimination), he points out that when an Arab consortium bought out an American company, the purchase made negative headlines throughout the country. Yet when a British company made a similar purchase, there was almost no mention of it. As a supporting point for the second main head (social discrimination), he cites several examples of Arabs being portrayed as terrorists in American movies. To be more specific, he points out how Arabs are portrayed in a popular movie that is playing throughout the country. To support the third head (political discrimination), he points out that few people of Arab background are ever elected to political office or appointed to serve on the boards of government organizations.

Supporting material usually is not relevant to most interpersonal communication unless you are using it to support an argument. In small groups, however, it's often useful to break down the discussion topic into smaller, more manageable units. For example, the committee to improve campus food might want to offer supporting material in the form of new recipes that include more fruits and vegetables and more international dishes.

Form a Mental Outline

When you are listening to a speech or a lecture, try to form a *mental outline*. Identify the central idea and then listen for the main heads and their supporting points—this is the information to remember. The supporting points are illustrations and examples that help you remember the main heads better. In the overall organization of the speech, however, the examples might be trivial. If, after listening to a lecture about a "nutritional" food pyramid, you remember that you are supposed to eat a lot of fruit but forget the role that fruit plays in the whole nutritional plan, you have missed the main point.

Predict What Will Come Next

Earlier we discussed the role of prediction in the listening process. When you are listening for information, it helps to focus your attention by predicting what is coming next. Once you hear the speaker's main point—that the government has come up with a new nutritional pyramid—you can logically predict that she is going to tell you the foods that are part of this pyramid. Prediction might seem difficult, but you do it all the time. Take, for example, a TV sitcom. If you watch it often enough, you can predict what will happen next.

Relate Points to Your Experience

Another useful way to listen is to try to relate the points to your own experience. When a speaker makes the point that professional ice hockey is getting too violent, you might try to remember any particularly violent games you have seen. All good listeners attempt to relate material to their own experience—this is part of being an active listener. That's why adults usually do well in school; they have more experience.

Look for Similarities and Differences

Your understanding of a subject is often aided if you can discover similarities and differences in relation to what you already know. Sometimes the similarities and differences are obvious. When you hear that all Chinese people use chopsticks to eat their food, this is an obvious difference from the American and European practice of using forks. A more subtle difference begins to emerge when you examine the natural resources of each of these cultures to see how they might influence the creation of eating utensils. Bamboo, for example, is found throughout China, so it is not surprising to find that many chopsticks are made of bamboo.

Ask Questions

Questioning is an important aid to active listening. As you listen, you may ask questions of yourself. If you cannot answer them, it is important that you ask them of the speaker. Even if you have answers to your questions,

Working Together

Because we think at least four times faster than we speak, listening requires an expenditure of energy to compensate for the rate of presentation. Active listening involves intention—actively intending to listen. In your group, everyone should pretend that he or she is in charge of informing potential college students about how to use active listening, supported by active note taking, in college lectures. Develop a list of practical suggestions based on your own and others'

experiences in the following three categories: (1) before class, (2) during class, and (3) after class.

For someone else's suggestions (and to see where this Working Together idea originated), see the source note below.

Source: (No author). "A System for Effective Listening and Note Taking." Learning Skills Center, University of Texas–Austin, Feb. 5, 1999. Retrieved March 14, 2003, from http://www.utexas.edu/student/lsc/handouts/1415. html.

you might want to ask them of the speaker anyway so that you can check your perceptions with his or hers.

Although it would seem likely that college students would ask questions, most of them do not. When researchers studied classes in a variety of subjects, they discovered that over a 30-hour period students asked only 108 questions, or 3.6 per class. Of the 108 questions, 29 were about classroom procedures ("Will this be on the test?"); 27 were information-seeking ("What date did that happen?"); 23 were for clarification ("Will you repeat that definition again?"); 13 were confirmation ("Am I correct in thinking that . . . ?"); 13 were asking instructors' opinions; and 3 did not fit into any of these categories (Youst & Pearson, 1994).

These results are upsetting in two ways. One is that there are so few questions asked; the other is that questions of substance are so limited. You might find that your learning (and grades) will increase if you make a point of asking questions. To listen critically, the listener has to evaluate and challenge ideas. The next section, on critical listening, will suggest some ways you can do this.

■ CRITICAL LISTENING

Critical listening requires all the ingredients of listening for information. The listener still should identify the main idea and the supporting points. In **critical listening,** however, the listener also evaluates and challenges what has been heard. These challenges might take place in the listener's mind, or they might be expressed directly to the speaker.

Ideally, all communication should be listened to critically. When you are receiving new information, however, it is sometimes difficult to evaluate it critically because you do not know very much about the subject—or possibly about the speaker either.

When people are persuading us to do something or believe something, critical listening is vitally important. Just imagine what might have happened if people had asked more questions during the rise of the Nazi party.

In our own country, democracy can work only if citizens ask questions of their leaders.

Another area where questions are important is advertising. Products are advertised every day with the promise that they will bring romance, adventure, or success into our lives. It takes no genius to be critical of those sorts of messages! Other persuasive messages occur in politics. A candidate wants your vote; you are asked to sign a petition to impeach the mayor; you are asked to show up and vote. All these messages require evaluation and questioning.

Determine the Speaker's Motives

In critical listening, your first job is to question the communicator's motives. With commercials, this is easy. Someone wants to sell a product. With political candidates, determining the motive is more complex. Obviously they want to be elected to office, so the most important question is, Why? Are they after money or power? Do they want to bring about social change? Do they want to keep things the way they are?

A petition to impeach the mayor is an even more complex issue and requires more in-depth questions. You need to know what the mayor has done to deserve such drastic treatment. You also might ask whether a petition is the right way to remove the mayor, how a new mayor will be appointed (or elected), and the broader question of whether impeachment will best serve the interests of the community.

When you are involved in persuasive situations, questioning the persuader's motives is a normal, proper response. For example, when someone presents a speaker, there is often a lengthy introduction. This is to convince the audience that the speaker is worth listening to. In public-speaking situations the speaker's motives can be examined by looking at his or her background. Some lengthy introductions are designed to establish speakers' **credibility,** or believability. Not every speaker has to be an expert; it is enough to have done a sufficient amount of homework to give a credible speech.

Challenge and Question Ideas

Critical listening also involves challenging and questioning ideas. Where did the speaker get his or her information? Did it come from a source that is generally regarded as credible? Is the speaker quoting the information accurately or taking it out of context? Does the speaker identify his or her sources of information so that the audience can check them later?

In persuasive situations, speakers sometimes omit information that does not support their cause. If you have information contrary to what a speaker presents, keep it in mind so that you can ask questions later. You can assess whether information has been omitted by asking questions about the speaker's sources. In a political speech, for example, is all the supporting material from one particular party or viewpoint—say, liberal or conservative? Does this mean that important information may have been omitted?

Distinguish Fact from Opinion

Part of challenging ideas and questioning their validity is the ability to distinguish fact from opinion. A **fact** is something that can be verified in a number of ways, which might include experiments, direct observation, or books by authorities. Everyone who applies the same test or uses the same sources should be able to get the same information. That cinnamon comes from the bark of a tree is a fact that can be found in any number of books and encyclopedias. That cinnamon is very tasty in foods, especially cookies, is an **opinion**—a personal belief—because some people will disagree. During the course of a day, you hear many more opinions than facts, so it is important that you, the listener, make the distinction.

Although all facts are equally true, some opinions are more reliable than others. You are more likely to trust the opinions of speakers who have similar beliefs to your own, who have been right before, who have a high degree of authority or credibility, or whose opinions have been (or are) supported by people you respect.

Recognizing Your Own Biases

Sometimes there are messages you don't want to hear because they contradict your attitudes and beliefs. If you're a Democrat, you don't go to Republican rallies; if you're a religious liberal, you don't go to revival meetings. If, for some reason, you are forced to go to either of these, you would probably disregard most of what you heard there.

In some cases, you might not even be aware that you are blocking out messages. For example, one study found that although jurors had heard instructions about the rules of circumstantial evidence, only 40 percent correctly followed those instructions. The authors of the study concluded that this misunderstanding of the law was not merely a matter of poor listening. They believed that jurors were likely to misinterpret the law when they didn't believe in it (Pryor, Taylor, Buchanan & Strawn, 1980). This tendency to interpret information in the light of our beliefs can lead us to distort the information we hear. As a listener, you have to be aware of your own values and attitudes—especially when you hear information you might resist or disagree with.

Assess the Message

Earlier in this chapter, we discussed listening as an ongoing process that includes assessment of the communication. This assessment can take place while the event is happening and can continue long after the event is over. Assessment is basically a critical process; it is chewing over what you have heard before you swallow it. An idea that may seem acceptable when you first hear it may not be so palatable when you have had time to think about it. This is especially true for important ideas: It is essential to reflect on them before they become part of us and of our thinking. You must learn to delay taking a position until you receive all the facts and other evidence, until you have had a chance to test the facts in the marketplace of ideas, and until you have chewed everything over sufficiently for digestion. Figure 4-3 shows a checklist for assessing a speech or lecture.

Figure 4-3

Critical Listening Evaluation Checklist for a Speech or Lecture

1. Were you able to make any accurate predictions about what the speaker was going to say? What helped you to do so?

2. What was the speaker's central idea? Was it clearly stated?

3. Do you have any ideas of the speaker's motive for giving this speech? If you know the motive, does it make the speech more or less believable?

4. What kinds of supporting points were used to back up the speaker's ideas? Were these points based on evidence you respect?

5. What questions would you like to ask the speaker? Are they questions that clarify what the speaker has said or questions that ask for more information?

6. Think of one or two ways you would like to challenge the speaker.

7. How would you evaluate this speech? What did the speaker do well? Was there anything the speaker could have done to make the speech better?

■ EMPATHIC LISTENING

We engage in both informational and critical listening when we talk to friends and family, but we often use another kind of listening as well: *empathic*—listening, recognizing, and identifying the speaker's feelings.

Listening for Feelings

You are often asked or expected to listen for feelings, and you often want to share your feelings with others. Most people are upset or happy at one time or another; sharing these feelings with someone else permits you to reveal yourself and helps you cope with them. Often when you talk your feelings over with other people, you can gain control of them or deal with them better. Listening to other people's feelings is a way of giving emotional support, and the ability to do this creates intimacy with others.

If the feelings you hear are directed toward another person, not you, you are likely to find them much easier to listen to. However, if you are the target of someone's feelings, especially negative ones, it is much more difficult to listen with empathy. Michael P. Nichols, who has written about listening, points out that when you listen with empathy, you have to suspend your ego and immerse yourself in the other person. Only by doing this will you be able to enter into his or her feelings (Nichols, 1995, p. 62).

Many of us have habitual responses to messages from others, responses learned from our families or friends. We use them whenever we get into particular situations. Some of these responses, which may work if you are listening critically, do not work when you are listening to someone's feelings. In this context, their effect is actually negative.

Negative Listening Responses

Let's assume that your friend has been feeling depressed for the last few days. You ask her what is wrong, and she responds that she is having a terrible time at her job because her boss is picking on her. Below are some possible ways you could respond—responses that would not be very helpful.

Deny Feelings

If you respond, "You shouldn't feel that way—everyone knows how hard it is to get along with him," you are focusing on the personality of the boss rather than on what your friend is feeling. When your feelings are intense, you want them recognized. You don't want them pushed aside while other, less important items are dealt with.

Compete

If you have had a terrible boss at some point in your life, you might be tempted to bring up the story of this boss and how you dealt with the problem. This response, however, is not helpful to your friend. Her boss is making her feel bad; how she feels about him should be the focus of your conversation.

Give Advice

"Go out and get a new job. Your boss will never get any better." This is concrete and specific advice. When people have problems, however, it is better to let them find their own solutions. Your job is not to give advice but to listen in such a way that your friend can solve the problem on her own. Deborah Tannen (1990), who writes about language, points out that men, in particular, are more interested in "fixing" problems than in listening to them (pp. 49–53). Also, telling someone to "calm down" is usually not helpful.

Respond Defensively

Let's say you respond with, "You shouldn't feel that way" and your friend angrily replies, "You are always telling me I shouldn't feel a certain way." You, in turn, say, "Well, I was just trying to help you. If you don't want my help, just say so!" That reply is a defensive response, the kind of response we often make when we feel we are being criticized. Such a response, however, changes the whole nature of the conversation. You're not talking about the boss any more—now you are talking about you.

All the above responses are weak because they do not deal with the problem on the level of feelings. They all, in one way or another, lead the person with the problem away from her feelings. How, then, can you respond so that you focus on feelings?

The Empathic-Listening Response

The best way to listen for feelings is through **empathic listening**—in which you try to understand what the person is feeling from his or her point of view and reflect these feelings back. As the listener, your job is to put aside your own feelings and enter into the feelings of the person who is speaking.

This African-American woman shows through her nonverbal communication that she is an empathic listener.

To do this, you need to recognize what feelings are involved, let the speaker tell you what has happened, and then encourage him or her to find the solution to the problem.

Identify the Emotion(s)

First, and this is often the most difficult part, you need to listen to what the person is *really* saying. If, for example, a friend comes over and says, "I am going to kill my boss!" he is obviously not saying that he literally plans to kill him. What is he really saying? In this case, it would be reasonable to assume that the speaker is feeling anger. If you respond with "Boy, you really sound mad," you create the opportunity for your friend to tell you what has happened.

Listen to the Story

Another part of an empathic response is to listen attentively. As the whole story comes out, there is no need to respond with anything very specific. At this point the person just wants to be listened to. You can show your interest and concern if you listen and look sympathetic.

Let's go back to your friend and her problem with her boss. What happened to make her so angry? She explains that she was promised a raise with this week's paycheck. Not only did she not get a raise, but someone who has been there a much shorter time got one.

Working Together

Perhaps one of the most difficult barriers to empathic listening is judgments and becoming aware of judgments as they arise. In your group, begin a conversation about a topic that is highly value-oriented (e.g., interracial dating, underage drinking, sexual promiscuity, cheating). All group participants should be active contributors to the discussion and should feel free to express their opinions about the topic of discussion.

When one of the group's participants makes a judgment, any other group member should stop that member and point out the judgment that has been made. Whether that member who points out the judgment is correct or not must not be debated. The group member who has made the judgment must imagine that she is grabbing that judgment in her hand—literally. Then, holding it out in front of her, she must create a space between herself and the judgment. She must now continue to listen through that space—allowing any other member of the group allowing the words and reasoning of any other member of the group to enter.

As the group discussion proceeds, other judgments must be identified and singled out in the same manner. Those finding and labeling judgments are allowed to explain why the comment is a judgment. Once the discussion proceeds again, those making the judgments can bring their hands down.

The point is for group members to make themselves see the space between themselves and the judgments so that they can learn to listen with curiosity and to withhold judgments.

Questions

1. How does judging affect group members' ability to listen?

2. When group members are judging, are they empathizing?

3. What is the real purpose of grabbing judgments in your hand, holding them out in front of you, and creating a space between yourself and the judgment? Could you see yourself doing this in a real conversation with another person?

Source: S. Keeva, *Transforming Practices: Finding Joy and Satisfaction in the Legal Life*. (Chicago, IL: Contemporary Books, 1999.) Keeva credits: L. Ellinor, & G. Gerard, *Dialogue: Rediscover the Transforming Power of Conversation*. (New York: John Wiley & Sons, Inc., 1998), for this idea.

After your friend has told you the whole story, she is not quite so mad, but she is still pretty upset. As you listen, you discover other feelings in addition to anger. She feels betrayed because the boss had told her she would get a raise. She also feels humiliated because her co-workers know that an employee who was hired after her got a raise while she did not. Usually people do not feel just one emotion—they have a whole assortment of them.

If you can let your friend talk through the entire problem, without making judgments but by offering support, it is likely that the full range of the problem will be revealed. One way to reach this point is through **paraphrasing**—restating the other person's thoughts or feelings in your own words. If she says, "I'm going to go in and tell him I quit," an appropriate paraphrased response might be, "You sound too upset to go on working there." This response not only helps identify the feelings; it also helps find out whether you have been hearing accurately and shows that you are paying attention. A paraphrased response provides a mirror for the other person's remarks.

Let the Person Work Out the Problem

Sometimes just listening for people's feelings and letting them explain what is upsetting them largely solves the problem. You often hear someone say, "I feel better just because I've talked to you." People frequently want to vent their feelings, and once they have done so, they feel better.

But sometimes merely listening is not enough; your friend has a problem, and he or she wants some help in solving it. In such a situation, the best approach is usually to trust the other person and his or her ability to work out the problem. This does not mean, however, that you ignore the problem. Empathic listening includes helping the other person find a way to solve the problem.

The last step in empathic listening, then, is to give the person a chance to work out the problem. In the case of your friend, you don't want to say, "You should quit!" Let her decide what she wants to do. If the emotion in the situation has died down, it might be appropriate to ask some very broad and general questions, such as "What are you going to do now?" It might also be possible to ask some questions that might lead to a solution the other person has not thought of: "Do you think if you talked to your boss, he might change his mind?" or "Do you think he may have made a mistake?"

The important thing to remember at this stage is that you do not have to solve the problem. If you try to solve every problem that people bring you, you will put a heavy burden on yourself. Think of the person with the problem as "owning" that problem. This attitude also will help the other person to grow in his or her ability to deal with problems. If parents, for example, tried to solve all their children's problems, the children would never learn how to do so for themselves.

If you are the kind of person who feels burdened because everyone comes to you with problems, you are probably taking on more responsibility than is required. Rather than focusing on solutions, try focusing on feelings and listening empathically. You will be surprised at how well this system works.

The important thing to remember is that when strong emotions are involved, people often just need a sounding board. To be there and to utter an occasional "Oh," "Mmm," or "I see" is often enough. Much comfort is derived from just being listened to.

■ LISTENING FOR ENJOYMENT

Few people have difficulty listening to things they choose. You turn on the television, for example, or the radio, lean back, and relax. If you like what you hear, you have no problem remembering it. You can probably recite, with perfect fidelity, song lyrics from a recording or a dialogue from a movie.

You probably find it more challenging, however, when your instructors ask you to enjoy information that is complex and difficult to listen to. When your English teacher puts on a recording of a famous actor reading from *Hamlet,* he hopes that you will both understand and enjoy it. Your theater instructor does not stick to uncomplicated Broadway plays and musical comedies; she also wants you to enjoy George Bernard Shaw and Wendy Wasserstein. As a student, you too are probably interested in increasing your ability to listen with enjoyment to more complex information.

When you want to listen to something for enjoyment but it is too complex for you to understand, you can try listening in the same way you listened for information, listen critically, and listen for feelings. A course in music appreciation is a good example of a place to employ all these skills. Since most of us enjoy music, it is not unreasonable to assume that you will enjoy some of the music you hear in such a class. In addition to enjoying the music, however, you will be asked to use other listening skills. Your informational skills might be tested: Can you identify the theme? What is the rhythm of the piece? What does *allegretto* mean? Your critical skills might be tested if you are asked to listen for the way two different composers treat the same theme or to indicate whether you agree with the way the musician interprets the piece. Since music involves feelings, you will probably be asked to listen for the mood of the piece: Is it solemn or light? How does it make the listener feel? By requiring listening skills other than those needed for enjoyment, the music instructor is hoping to increase the pleasure you find in music—because the more one knows about music, the more one is able to appreciate and savor more complex forms of it.

Listening for enjoyment, then, can be a more sophisticated process than merely sitting back and letting the sounds wash over you. Complex material, even when you enjoy it, involves greater listening skills. In music, for example, if you had not worked on these skills, you would still be listening to "Twinkle, Twinkle, Little Star."

The same skills can be applied when you listen to a play. Listen for information: What is the play about? What is the plot? Listen critically: Do the scenes flow into one another? Are the characters believable? Listen with empathy: What is the character feeling? How does she relate to the other characters?

Listening is often more enjoyable if you can relate what you are hearing to your own experience. Someone who plays the violin can enjoy a violin concerto because he or she knows what to look for and is aware of the discipline and practice that it takes to play such a piece. Watching a play, you may think, "I have felt that way too."

You will find it worthwhile working to enjoy more complex information. Remember, however, that listening for enjoyment can require skills just as complex as those needed in any other listening situation. The only difference is the rewards. What could be better than listening to enjoy yourself?

■ TALKING SO OTHERS WILL LISTEN

There is a downside to the technology-oriented, information-driven society that you are experiencing, and that is a corresponding reluctance to listen. Whether it is distractions, preoccupations, time limitations, or the difference in the slow rate of others' speaking to you versus the rapid pace of gaining information from the media and from the Internet—how accustomed you've become to having your attention span satisfied by video games, chat room banter, and fast-paced television programs—the fact is,

Consider This

The doctor-patient relationship represents one significant example where listening is often a problem:

Next time you visit your doctor keep in mind one crucial if little-known rule: catch 23.

The catch works this way: Doctors typically will listen to a patient's "opening statement" little more than 23 seconds before changing the subject or "redirecting" the talk.

That means you, the patient, must talk not only fast, but compellingly, even knowledgeably, to get his or her attention. That's important for your doctor to fully grasp what's bothering you.

Too often doctors don't. In fact, researchers increasingly are finding that one big reason treatments don't work—or aren't prescribed at all—is because of problems in the way doctors and patients communicate.

Or, more precisely, fail to communicate. And when communication fails, the results can be disastrous.

Late last year the National Academy of Sciences (NAS) reported that some 7,000 patients die every year because of medication errors.

Even more alarming, the NAS found medical errors in hospitals cause between 44,000 and 98,000 deaths every year.

Some mistakes can be avoided, experts believe, if doctors and patients do a better job talking to each other.

Questions

1. Have you ever had this happen to you? How have you handled it?

2. Are there other situations—other than doctor-patient relationships—in which you have discovered that effective listening was a problem? Lawyer–client? Salesperson–buyer? Parent–child? Teacher–student?

3. What are the barriers, hurdles, or restrictions that cause you to be reluctant to deal with the other person in such relationships in an effective manner?

Source: L. Greider, "Talking Back to Your Doctor Works." *AARP Bulletin,* February 2000.

you do not listen well nor does anyone else. Whether or not this represents a societal change or simply a continuation of a well-documented, ongoing problem is not the point. The point is, what can be done when you realize others are not and will not be listening to you? Is it a hopeless situation?

Although there are numerous techniques for reaching out and grasping the attention of others, the following are some that may work. Often, a combination of techniques works best. We'll briefly discuss assertiveness, getting to the point, being prepared, writing ideas down, being flexible, and changing your vocal style.

First, and perhaps most obvious, you need to be more assertive. In the article, "Talking Back to Your Doctor Works" (Greider, 2000), the writer says, "Studies show that doctors remember best the cases of assertive patients. Medical outcomes are also likely to be better" (p. 25). See the Consider This box above. These results are likely to apply across communication contexts. It has long been an established research result that assertive behavior tends to be associated with positive outcomes.

Second, knowing that the other person is likely to be a weak or indifferent listener, avoid idle chit-chat and friendly conversation, and get to the point fast. In advance of the conversation, think about what you want to say, how you plan to say it, and what you want from the other person. Then, try to follow your plan. The point isn't to memorize a speech; rather, it is to move rapidly toward your point rather than beat around the bush.

Third, do your homework. That is, know what you are talking about. If some research is necessary to gather facts and relevant information, go to the library or use the Internet to ferret out the facts that will make your case or back up your position. Well-informed people tend to get the ear of others, as opposed to those who either do not know what they are talking about or are simply willing to hear the ideas of others and make no significant contribution of their own.

Fourth, write down your most important points or questions, and prioritize them. A list of ideas has always been associated with a rational, judicious, well-thought-out approach. Even if you do not use your notes, writing them out will assist you in organizing your ideas and phrasing them in the most effective way. When you put your most important ideas first, it is more likely they will be heard or noticed. Otherwise, they may be hidden in the middle or end of your conversation, or they may come too late for the attention span of your listener.

Fifth, have some options in mind, and be willing to listen. You are more likely to get the attention of others when you appear flexible and willing to listen yourself. The old adage, "It takes one to know one," suggests that if you want someone to listen to you, you must also be willing to listen to them. But preparation and forethought does not necessarily mean all the alternatives have been considered. Thus, remember that this is a conversation; it is two-way. You must be willing to prepare your ideas and, in turn, listen to the ideas of others.

Sixth, try to change your vocal style. For some people—as indicated earlier in this chapter—this may mean slowing down your rate of delivery. If your pace tends to be slow already, or plodding, speeding up may be a useful approach. Often, it may simply be a need for variety. A change in volume—either louder or softer depending on the circumstances—may also help.

There are many ways to talk so others will listen. These suggestions will get you started, but overriding any of them are, of course, the courtesy and respect you need to demonstrate. Being assertive, for example, is not an excuse for being aggressive and thoughtless. "Avoiding idle chit-chat and friendly conversation" is not an excuse for overlooking necessary or important human concerns and connectiveness. You should make all decisions in the context of good judgment, common sense, thoughtfulness, and **propriety**—the character or quality of being proper, especially in accordance with recognized usage, custom, or principles.

Throughout all of this—your use of techniques to get others to listen to you—you need to recognize that there are some people who will not listen to you no matter what you do. Fortunately, these people are likely to be few and far between. This doesn't mean that you should not try to talk so they will listen, but more important, perhaps, is that you should not be disappointed if the techniques you use do not work. A significant learning in all

Assess Yourself

Are you a Good Listener?

How effective are you as a listener? Give a qualitative evaluation for each of the following factors by circling the numerical score next to each of the factors that best represents your listening ability: 7 = Outstanding; 6 = Excellent; 5 = Very good; 4 = Average/good; 3 = Fair; 2 = Poor; 1 = Minimal ability; 0 = No ability demonstrated.

1. I listen for the other person's feelings, not just to the words he or she says.	7 6 5 4 3 2 1 0
2. I paraphrase what other people say to me.	7 6 5 4 3 2 1 0
3. I don't interrupt.	7 6 5 4 3 2 1 0
4. I am open-minded to ideas, some of which I don't think I agree with.	7 6 5 4 3 2 1 0
5. I remember what people say.	7 6 5 4 3 2 1 0
6. I am willing to express my feelings.	7 6 5 4 3 2 1 0
7. I don't complete other people's sentences even when I think I know what they are going to say next.	7 6 5 4 3 2 1 0
8. I make eye contact.	7 6 5 4 3 2 1 0
9. I don't think of what I'm going to say next while the other person is talking.	7 6 5 4 3 2 1 0
10. I ask the person questions in order to get more information and show that I am interested in what he or she is saying.	7 6 5 4 3 2 1 0
11. I am comfortable with silence.	7 6 5 4 3 2 1 0
12. I am aware of a person's body language and my own body language.	7 6 5 4 3 2 1 0

TOTAL POINTS: _____

 Go to the *Communicating Effectively* CD-ROM to see your results and learn how to evaluate your attitudes and feelings.

of this is: Communication involves a large number of factors or variables. No situation is the same as any other. No one has or ever will have control of all the factors or variables. No one has that kind or level of control. The more experience you have, the more practice that you engage in, and the more you believe in yourself and your abilities, the more likely you will be successful. Success is never guaranteed; it could never be.

Chapter Review

Of all the communication faults people are accused of, not listening probably ranks as number one. Listening is a skill, and like any other skill it must be learned and practiced. Obstacles to effective listening include cognitive dissonance, anxiety, a need to control communication, and passivity. Listening is also a process and a transaction. You make predictions about messages before you hear them. How you listen is determined by the attention you give to a message. You are able to tune out unwanted messages through the process of selective attention. Once you hear a message, you must assign meaning to it by organizing the material you have heard and selecting what you need to remember. The last step is assessing what you have heard.

To be a good listener, you must become actively involved in the process of listening. As an active listener, you should evaluate and criticize material while you listen to it. When you listen actively, you are less likely to become distracted or bored. In many situations you have a responsibility to listen carefully.

There are four kinds of listening: listening for information, critical listening, empathic listening, and listening for enjoyment. Listening for information involves listening for facts. In this kind of listening it is important to identify the central idea and distinguish it from the main points. Critical listening involves evaluating the material you hear. To listen critically, you listen for the motives of the speaker and mentally challenge the speaker's ideas and information. Critical listening is especially important when you are listening to persuasive messages.

Empathic listening is listening for feelings. This kind of listening is most often done in interpersonal communication, and it often helps the speaker cope with his or her feelings and problems. Listening for enjoyment is the listening that you choose to do for your own pleasure. You can learn to enjoy complex material by using all the other listening skills.

When you discover that those you want to listen to you are not listening, or will not, it does not have to be a hopeless situation. We discussed the techniques of assertiveness, getting to the point, being prepared, writing ideas down, being flexible, and changing your verbal style as possible ways—or combinations of ways—for reaching out and grasping the attention of others. Whatever techniques you choose, you need to avoid being aggressive and thoughtless and show courtesy and respect. All decisions should be made using good judgment, common sense, thoughtfulness, and propriety.

Questions to Review

1. How is listening defined, and why is it regarded as a process?

2. What are the four kinds of listening styles? Why is it helpful to know someone's listening style if you are communicating something important?

3. How might cognitive dissonance, anxiety, passivity, and the need for control impair your ability to listen?

4. What are the six steps that take place in the process of listening?

5. How does active listening contribute to better listening?

6. How does identifying the central idea and the supporting points and forming a mental outline contribute to better listening?

7. In addition to listening for information, what must be added when you are listening critically?

8. When listening critically, how does the listener distinguish fact from opinion?

9. What is empathic listening, and when does one use it?

10. What are some of the negative responses to empathic listening? What are the positive responses?

11. What are some of the techniques you can use to reach out and grasp the attention of others when you must talk so others will listen?

mhhe.com/hybels Go to the self-quizzes on the Communicating Effectively CD-ROM (side 2, track 10) and the Online Learning Center at mhhe.com/ hybels7 to test your knowledge of the chapter concepts.

References

Ayres, J. A., K. Wilcox, & D. M. Ayres (1995). "Receiver apprehension: An explanatory model and accompanying research." *Communication Education* 44, 223–35.

Barker, L. L., & K. W. Watson (2000). *Listen up: How to improve relationships, reduce stress, and be more productive by using the power of listening.* New York: St. Martin's Press.

Bostrom, R. N. (1990). *Listening behavior.* New York: Guilford Press.

Chickering, A. W., & Z. F. Gamson (No date) "Seven principles for good practice in undergraduate education." Guidebook, Faculty Development Committee, Hawaii Community College. Retrieved March 14, 2003, from http://www.hcc.hawaii.edu/intranet/committees/FacDevCom/guidebk/teachtim/7princip.htm.

DiSalvo, V., D. C. Larsen, & W. J. Seiler, (1976). "Communication skills needed by people in business." *Communication Monographs* 25, 274.

Friedman, P. G. (1978). *Listening processes: Attention, understanding, evaluation.* Washington, D.C.: National Education Association.

(No author) (2002). "Gentle endings, preparing for a peaceful departure: Lessons from a hospice spiritual counselor." HealthandAge.com, Novartis Foundation for Gerontology. Retrieved March 14, 2003, from http://www.healthandage.com/htm/min/gentle_endings/web/counselor.htm.

Golen, S. (1990, Winter). A factor analysis of barriers to effective listening. *The Journal of Business Communication* 27, 25–36.

Greider, L. (2000, February). "Talking back to your doctor works." *AARP Bulletin.*

Hackley, D. & R. Gorman. "Call for mentors." ASME. Retrieved March 14, 2003, from http://www.asme.org/ementoring/.

(No author) (2001). "Homework & studying at home: How long should my child spend on homework?" Learning Resources, Apple Learning Interchange, Apple Computer, Inc. Retrieved March 14, 2003, from http://henson.austin. apple.com/edres/parents/pfet/howlong.shtml.

(No author) (2002, April–June). "How can salespeople improve listening skills?" *HighGain Inc.,* 2150 Blucher Valley Road, Sebastopol, CA 95472. Retrieved March 14, 2003, from http://www.highgain.com/newsletter/hg-enews-current.html.

Kent, T. (1998, August 30). "Listening in on pilots eases fears." *San Diego Union-Tribune.* Online: Lexis-Nexis, Academic Universe.

Kiewitz, C.; J. B. Weaver H-B. Brosius; & G. Weimann (1997, Autumn). "Cultural differences in listening style preferences: A comparison of young adults in Germany, Israel, and the United States." *International Journal of Public Opinion Research* 9:3, 233–47. Online abstract retrieved March 14, 2003, from http://www3.oup.co.uk/intpor/hdb/Volume_09/Issue_03/090233.sgm.abs.html.

Kiewra, K. A., & N. F. Du Bois (1991, June). "Notetaking functions and techniques." *Journal of Educational Psychology* 83:2, 243.

Klein, K. (2002). "Parent connection: Learning to listen." Pre-K Smarties. Retrieved March 14, 2003, from http://www.preksmarties.com/connection/.

Lerner, H. (2001). *The dance of connection: How to talk to someone when you're mad, hurt, scared, frustrated, insulted, betrayed, or desperate.* New York: HarperCollins.

(No author) (2001). "Listening skills: How to recognize and repeat them." The PAR Group. Retrieved March 14, 2003, from http://www.thepargroup.com/articles/listeningskills.html.

Mackay, H. (2001, May 24). *Minneapolis Star Tribune.* Reprinted: H. Mackay (2001, December 29). "Listening is the hardest of the 'easy' tasks." International Listening Association. Retrieved March 14, 2003, from http://www.listen.org/pages/mackay.htm.

Messmer, M. (1998, March). "Improving your listening skills." *Management Accounting* 79. Online Infotrac, Expanded Academic ASAP.

Moray, N. (1969). *Listening and attention.* Baltimore: Penguin.

Nichols, M. P. (1995). *The lost art of listening*. New York: Guilford Press.

O'Brien, P. (1993, February). "Why men don't listen . . . and what it costs women at work." *Working Women* 18:2, 56–60.

Papa, M. J., & E. C. Glenn (1988, Fall). "Listening ability and performance with new technology: Case studies." *Journal of Business Communication* 25, 13.

Pryor, B. K., P. Taylor, R. W. Buchanan, & D. U. Strawn. (1980). "An affective-cognitive consistency explanation for comprehension of standard jury instructions." *Communication Monographs* 47, 69.

Purdy, M. (2002). "Listen up, move up: The listener wins." (Monster Career Center). Retrieved March 14, 2003, from http://content.monster. com/listen/ overview/.

Rubin, R. B., & C. V. Roberts. (1987, April). "A comparative examination and analysis of three listening tests." *Communication Education* 36, 142–53.

Sones, B., & R. Sones (1999, Mar. 28). "Sunday news: Strange but true." *Chicago Sun-Times*. Online at Lexis-Nexis Academic Universe.

(No author) (1980). Sperry Corporation. *Your personal listening profile*. Falls Church, VA: Sperry.

Tannen, D. (1999, May 6). "Listening to men, then and now." *New York Times Magazine*, 56ff.

_____ . (1990). *You just don't understand*. New York: Morrow.

Wark, K. (1999, Feb. 13). "Life story: How babies learn." *Daily Telegraph* (London). Online at Lexis-Nexis Academic Universe.

Wolvin, A. D. (1995, July). "On competent listening." *Listening Post*, 54.

Wolvin, A. D., & C. G. Coakley (1993). "A survey of the status of listening training in some *Fortune* 500 corporations." *Communication Education* 40: 152–53.

Youaver, J. B., III, & M. D. Kirtley (1995). "Listening styles and empathy." *Southern Communication Journal* 60:2, 131–40.

Youst, R., & J. C. Pearson (1994). "Antecedent and consequent conditions of student questioning: An analysis of classroom discourse across the university." *Communication Education* 43:4. CommSearch 95, CD-ROM, National Communication Association, first release, no date.

Further Reading

Barker, L. L., & K. W. Watson (2000). *Listen up: How to improve relationships, reduce stress, and be more productive by using the power of listening*. New York: St. Martin's Press. This is an easy-to-read guide on listening by two listening experts. The authors begin by outlining the payoffs for improving listening skills, offer instruction on identifying listening styles and bad listening habits, and then teach skills that will help readers gain more control when communicating. There is a chapter on listening differences between men and women. This is a conversational, anecdotal book full of research-based, sound advice.

Clemmer, J. (1998, March 30). *Why smart managers master the art of listening well*. Retrieved March 14, 2003, from http://www.clemmer.ca/ globe/listen.htm. Clemmer discusses the one crucial ingredient that many companies that talk passionately about being market-driven and customer-focused overlook—the ability to listen well. He points out that good customer listening helps organizations avoid expensive service or quality overkills. There is great use of examples in this brief article.

Gerlach, P. K. (2002, April 26). "Stepfamily in formation—project 2: Coparents learn and use five mental/verbal skills to problem solve—skill #3: Empathic listening." Stepfamily Association of Illinois, Inc. Retrieved March 14, 2003, from http://www.stepfamilyinfo.org/listen.htm. Gerlach introduces five communication skills that coparents can learn and use together to effectively resolve stepfamily conflicts. The skill that most concerns us here is empathic listening—the benefits, the steps, and what it sounds like. This is a practical, useful, important website.

Lovitt, J. W. (2002). *Who's listening anyway? A guide to effective listening*. Austin, TX: Landmarc Publishing. In this 125-page book, Lovitt, teacher of courses in organizational development, corporate and personal coach, consultant, trainer, and writer living in San Antonio, Texas, writes that listening is essential for personal and professional success. The book covers the nature of the listening process, roadblocks and traps to avoid, and conditions necessary for listening. There are scales and inventories to measure listening skill, workplace examples relevant to leaders, managers, and team members, and imaginative and humorous drawings. This is an enjoyable book.

Milne, H. (1998). *The heart of listening: A visionary approach to craniosacral work,* 2nd ed. Berkeley, CA: North Atlantic Books. In this 500-page work, Milne describes, in detail, the anatomy, physiology, and energetics of the craniosacral system. Here, readers will find the most complete list of craniosacral techniques in print with clearly written descriptions of each technique, along with technically accurate photographs. This a complete text for practitioners who want to expand and deepen the healing process with their clients. There is great wisdom here and Milne's depth of experience and valuable insight are not only genuine and worthwhile, but can be read and digested again and again.

Nichols, M. (1996). *The lost art of listening.* New York: Guilford Press. In this 251-page book, Nichols distills years of clinical wisdom and forthrightly explains why listening is the fundamental psychotherapeutic skill. The book serves as a wake-up call to remind professionals that listening is difficult, and it should not be an assumed skill. His practical advice is specifically designed to improve our most important relationships and, ultimately, who we are. Although written in an academic style, the information is presented in a clear, interesting manner and is intended for anyone who wants to relate to and connect with people.

Palmer, P. J. (1999). *Let your life speak: Listening for the voice of vocation.* San Francisco, CA: Jossey-Bass. In this 128-page book, Palmer avoids how-to formulas and five-step plans and uses, instead, intricate metaphors, poetry, self-revelation, and fireside wisdom to share his mistakes and stories as he has sought to listen to the voice within. He reflects upon vocation, spirit, and the life journey with depth, insight, inspiration, and challenge.

The book is personal without being preachy. It is also conversational and useful for those struggling to make early decisions about vocation.

Shafir, R. Z. (2000). *The zen of listening: Mindful communication in the age of distraction.* Wheaton, IL: Quest Books. Shafir, chief of speech pathology at Massachusetts's Lahey Clinic, with over 25 years of clinical experience helping patients learn to speak, goes beyond the mechanics of good listening behavior to an approach requiring relaxation, focus, and a desire to learn from the speakers' perspective. She defines listening as "The willingness to see a situation through the eyes of the speaker." The book includes specific exercises, activities, and strategies for improving awareness, and her practical advice is especially valuable for counselors and those in the helping professions.

Shapiro, S. (2000). *Listening for success: How to master the most important skill of network marketing.* Winnipeg, Canada: Chica (Community and Hospital Infection Control Association) Publications. Shapiro's 50-page, how-to book, is written in a clear, simple, entertaining style. He includes a how-to model for listening. This easy-to-read book is full of personal stories that illustrate the power and pitfalls of listening. For greater personal power, increased attractiveness, improved human relations skills, and more personal and professional success, this quick-read is especially good for those involved in sales and network marketing.

Wolvin, A. D. & Coakley, C. G. (1995). *Listening,* 5th ed. New York: McGraw-Hill. This comprehensive textbook on listening examines the need for, process of, and types of listening. The authors look at appreciative, discriminative, comprehensive, therapeutic, and critical listening. This is a useful, well-documented resource.

Chapter 5

Verbal Communication

Objectives

After reading this chapter, you should be able to:

- Explain the importance of the FOXP2 gene and its contribution to the development of language in humans.
- Briefly describe how you acquired your ability to use words.
- Describe the importance of language.
- Explain how language is symbolic.
- Explain what is expected of a speaker in a particular language environment.
- Give examples of the ritual use of language.
- Explain the function of role in a language environment.
- Define *style*.
- Describe differences between women's language and men's language.
- Define report-talk and rapport-talk.
- Explain differences between standard English and dialect.
- Describe the ways in which speaking is more transactional than writing.
- Describe some of the ways to make your verbal style clearer, more powerful, and more vivid.
- Define and give examples of *metamessages*.

Key Terms and Concepts

  Use the Communicating Effectively CD-ROM and Online Learning Center at mhhe.com/hybels7 to further your understanding of the following terms.

Clarity 156	FOXP2 gene 136	Rapport-talk 151
Connotative meaning 141	Language environment 145	Report-talk 151
Denotative meaning 141	Metamessage 161	Ritual language 145
Dialect 153	Paralanguage 154	Style 149
Doublespeak 147	Powerful talk 157	Vividness 159
Euphemism 146		

ONE OF THE GREAT HUMAN MYSTERIES OF ALL TIME HAS perhaps been solved. The mystery of why human beings developed a language for communication has continued for centuries. Because there are no "linguistic fossils" dating prior to the development of writing systems, theories about the origin and evolution of language have been speculative. For this reason, the topic was banned from discussion by Societe de Linguistique de Paris in 1866. It was more than 100 years later—in the 1990s—that we saw the first major resurgence of interest in the evolution of language.

What were the factors that caused this renewed interest? New insights in a variety of disciplines created the need for an interdisciplinary focus. Examining the syllabi of courses in "Origins and Evolution of Language" (Carstairs-McCarthy) will give you an idea of the interdisciplinary approach. In Professor Carstairs-McCarthy's course, students studied linguistic, primatological (the study of primates), anthropological, archaeological, neurobiological, and philosophical approaches. In another course, students looked at evidence from psychology, the cognitive neurosciences, comparative psychology, and computational modeling of evolutionary processes. It is only from a combination of approaches that researchers feel any adequate explanation will arise (*"Library of Excerpts"*).

However, the mystery may be solved with an interdisciplinary approach. It was Rosalind Franklin, James Watson, and Francis Crick who offered an accurate model of the DNA molecule in 1952—for which Watson and Crick received the 1962 Nobel Prize in physiology/medicine. Without that model, molecule work on the human genome (the entire package of genes) would not and could not have proceeded. Genetic scientists provided the complete sequence of the DNA in the human genome using new technologies for mapping and sequencing that were developed only in the previous 10 years.

Because of the study of the genomes of people and chimpanzees ("Mutations eons ago . . .," 2002; "Lone gene linked . . . ," 2002), progress leaped forward on why human beings developed language for communication. The work of Svante Paabo and his colleagues at the Max Planck Institute for Evolutionary Anthropology in Leipzig, Germany, is based on the discovery in 2001 of the first human gene—as one part of the human genome project—involved specifically in language. Known as **FOXP2,** the gene is directly linked to developing the fine motor skills needed to be a smooth talker. Dr. Anthony P. Monaco of the University of Oxford and his team of molecular biologists identified the FOXP2 as the gene responsible for switching on other genes during the development of the brain

("Mutations eons ago . . . ," 2002). Paabo's group at the Max Planck Institute worked with Monaco's team to begin tracing the gene's evolutionary history.

Paabo claims the gene remained largely unaltered during the evolution of mammals, but it suddenly changed in humans after the hominid line split off from the chimpanzee line of descent. This evolutionary, mutational change (in two amino acids) suggests that it conferred some overwhelming benefit to human beings—the ability for rapid articulation. As a new, must-have gene, it swept through the human population—providing the finishing touch to the acquisition of language—at about the same time as the explosive invasion of modern humans out of Africa and across the planet between 50,000 and 120,000 years ago. It has been estimated that all humans likely had made the change (in amino acids) less than 120,000 years ago and with virtual certainty, earlier than 200,000 years ago. All this, of course, is speculation; however, it appears to be speculation that rests on more solid footing now that the FOXP2 gene has been discovered.

What is interesting about the discovery of the FOXP2 gene—the study of how it swept through the population because it was so advantageous and the approximate dates when all of this occurred—is that it corresponds precisely with a novel theory advanced by Dr. Richard Klein, an archaeologist at Stanford University ("Mutations eons ago . . . ," 2002). Klein argues that the emergence of behaviorally modern humans 50,000 years ago was set off by a major genetic change, most probably the acquisition of language. Paabo's findings can now reinforce Klein's account of the sudden appearance of novel behaviors such as art, ornamentation, and long-distance trade.

There are a couple of important cautionary notes. As with any new theory, it is easy to overstate the importance of the FOXP2 gene in the evolution of language ability. After all, it is the first gene to be correlated with speech. It may not be the only gene—and probably isn't—that evolved to permit the emergence of speech and language; there may be other genes that influence speech, and FOXP2 is just a first step of many in figuring out when it was that human language separated us as the dominant species. Even if it is not solely responsible for the ability to talk, it is extremely important and serves as a benchmark for further research.

The point of this discussion about how and why human beings developed a language is simply that if Paabo's and Monaco's teams are correct, one of the great human mysteries of all time has been solved, and many of the questions that have perplexed researchers for centuries can now be answered. This discovery no doubt will stimulate more research as well as additional theories and questions.

Now that we have a reasonably sound theory of why human beings developed a language, we can look at how *you* acquired your ability to use words. It depended on three factors: (1) native architecture, (2) cognitive development, and (3) environmental influences. As a human being, you have inborn language-acquisition devices—native architecture—that transform the surface structure of language into an internal deep structure that you readily understand. Your cognitive ability and your language development progressed together. You were analyzing language content before you were discovering and understanding grammatical structures. Finally, your environment provided you with the requisite learning experiences necessary to acquire language, and your parents facilitated your language acquisition by providing you a language-acquisition support system.

No matter what the theory is of why human beings developed a language for communication, and no matter what the quality of your own personal native architecture, cognitive development, and environmental influences, you cannot deny the importance of language. Language is central to your intellectual, social,

On the Web

The following articles on the Internet should give you some additional insights into the FOXP2 gene and its discovery and importance.

M. Balter. "Speech Gene' Tied to Modern Humans." August 16, 2002. *Science:* 297. Retrieved March 14, 2003, from http://www.sciencemag.org. In this article the caution scientists express against overstating the importance of FOXP2 in the evolution of language is presented.

A. Cubre. "FOXP2: To Speak or Not to Speak?" 2002. Department of Biology, Davidson College, Davidson, NC 28035. Retrieved March 14, 2003, from http://www.bio.davidson.edu/courses/genomics/2002/Cubre/project1.html. In this four-page article, Cubre summarizes and compares the reports announcing the discovery of the FOXP2 gene in both the popular press and scientific letters.

He concludes that the articles were "fairly accurate;" however, he points out that the conclusion that "the expansion of humans was associated with speech development" is pure speculation.

"First Language Associated Gene Identified." 2002. Applied Biosystems. *BioBeat* (Online Magazine). Retrieved March 14, 2003, from http://www.appliedbiosystems.com/biobeat/break throughs/bk65.cfm. This article offers a look at how the FOXP2 gene discovery was announced in a scientific publication.

"Gene Linked to the Dawn of Speech." 2002. Associated Press. MSNBC News; Health; Genetics. Retrieved March 14, 2003, from http://www.msnbc.com/news/794064.asp. This article provides a look at how the FOXP2 gene discovery was announced in the popular press.

Consider This

How important is verbal communication? In his book, *Coloring Outside the Lines: Raising a Smarter Kid by Breaking All the Rules,* Roger Schank begins his chapter on "How to Raise a More Verbal Kid," with this paragraph:

Let's begin with a simple premise: The more verbal a child is, the more intelligent she seems. No matter what your child decides to do with her life, verbal ability will have an enormous impact on her degree of success. People who communicate clearly, respond quickly and cleverly, tell interesting stories, and make compelling arguments have a distinct advantage. Those who don't are put at a disadvantage; we assume that their halting speech and poorly phrased utterances are signs of stupidity."

Questions

1. Have you ever stereotyped someone just from hearing the person talk? What are some of the stereotypes you attribute to those with excellent verbal ability?

2. Do you have any personal examples of how your own verbal ability (or inability) has contributed to a success (or failure) you have had?

Source: R. Schank, *Coloring Outside the Lines: Raising a Smarter Kid by Breaking All the Rules.* (New York: HarperCollins, 2000), p. 87.

and emotional growth and is a crucial tool for learning in all areas. Whether you are studying literature or history, or learning science, you need fundamental language skills to understand information and express your ideas. Through language learning, you acquire skills that are essential in the workplace; for example, you learn to analyze ideas and information and to communicate them clearly, both orally and in writing. Through a study of literature, you can understand other people and yourself and can appreciate the power of words and the many different uses of language. By examining media productions, you can develop the ability to understand and interpret a range of media messages.

The flip side to acquiring and using proper languaging skills can be devastating. In his book *A User's Guide to the Brain,* John Ratey, the clinical professor of psychiatry at Harvard Medical School cited previously, states it succinctly, "When people . . . fail to make proper language connections, or do not stop and consider what they are saying, they wind up not only with speaking, reading, or writing problems—which are bad enough—but with difficulty sustaining social relationships, making moral decisions, controlling anger, and even feeling emotions" (Ratey, 2001, p. 253). The potential repercussions of poor language acquisition and use are enormous, to say the least. There is even evidence that a poor command of language may inhibit your ability to imagine and think up new ideas ("Let's talk").

So, when you learned to use language in the elementary grades, you did more than master the basic skills. You learned to express feelings and opinions, and, as you matured, to support your opinions with sound arguments and research. You became aware of the many purposes for which language is used and the diversity of forms it can take to appropriately serve these purposes and a variety of audiences. You learned to use the language and forms appropriate for different formal and informal situations—for example, the formal language of debate, the figurative language of poetry, the technical language and formal structures used in report writing. In sum, through your mastery of language, you have experienced expressive and communicative powers, and you appreciate language as both a source of pleasure and an important medium for recording and communicating ideas and information.

Language is just as important in your personal life. How you use language will affect your relationships with friends and loved ones. Failures in relationships with friends and family are often attributed to a failure of language. In fact, in a Roper Starch poll of 1,001 Americans, 44 percent said that a lack of effective communication was the leading cause of their marital breakup (Roper Starch, 1998), and you can be sure that language was part of the problem.

This chapter is largely concerned with the language behavior of speakers and listeners and the context within which they operate. To divorce words from how they are spoken and heard is to look at them in isolation—and words are never isolated in communication. For this reason, it is impossible to discuss language behavior without discussing the people who are using the language. This applies equally to both speakers and listeners.

Protests and demonstrations will probably have a lot of connotative language.

Successful communication depends on the completion of the transaction, and much of the emphasis in this chapter is on how the sender-receiver conveys thoughts and emotions through language.

An understanding of language will help you express what you really want to say in a clear and straightforward way. When a message is misunderstood or has no effect on the listener, it may be that the speaker's language is at fault. And no matter how skillful you may think your language is, if it is not understood, the communication is a failure. Barbara Wallraff (2000), in her book *Word Court*, offers one additional incentive to studying language: She says "Our ability to communicate will break down if we don't work together at maintaining our language" (pp. 9–10).

■ HOW WORDS WORK

When you say a word, you are vocally representing something—whether that thing is a physical object, such as your biology textbook, or an abstract concept, such as peace. The word is, as noted in Chapter 1, The Communication Process, a symbol: It stands for the object or concept that it names. This is what distinguishes a word from a random sound. The sounds that are represented in our language by the letters *c a t* constitute a word because we have agreed that these sounds will stand for a particular domestic animal. The sounds represented by the letters *z a t* do not make up a word because these sounds do not stand for anything. A word that stands for a concrete and emotionally neutral thing—such as the word *mailbox*—can usually be interpreted with good fidelity because most people respond primarily to its **denotative meaning**—that is, its dictionary definition.

Other words stand for abstract concepts that evoke strong feelings. Words such as *freedom* and *love* are easily misunderstood because they carry a lot of **connotative meaning**—the feelings or associations each individual has about a word. For example, when you hear the word *love*, you don't just think about the word; you probably associate it with a person or an experience you have had. The connotative aspect of words may cause problems in communication because a single word may evoke strong and varied feelings in listeners. Think, for example, of the many different reactions people have to the phrases *affirmative action* and *axis of evil*.

Although we need abstract connotative words to express ideas, precise denotative words work best when we want to convey information or get things done. Figure 5-1 shows the usefulness of precise, concrete words.

There are situations when abstract language works best. For example, when you want others to know some general information (like about a dying parent, or a crash that killed a close friend), but details would not be necessary. Here is a story that circulated via the Internet with just the sender's name attached, that reveals the power of abstract over concrete language:

The Smiths were proud of their family tradition. Their ancestors had come to America on the Mayflower. They had included senators and Wall Street wizards. They decided to compile a family history, a legacy for their children and grandchildren. They hired a fine author. Only one problem arose—how to handle that great-uncle George, who was executed in the electric chair. The author said he could handle the story tactfully. The

Figure 5-1

*Using Precise,
Concrete Words*

I'd also like a Coke with that, please.

Would you like small, medium, or large? Original, Cherry, or Vanilla Coke? Regular or Diet? With or without caffeine? Do you want ice with that too?

Never mind—I'll have a milk instead.

We have white, chocolate, whole, 2%, and skim...

book appeared. It said, "Great-uncle George occupied a chair of applied electronics at an important government institution, was attached to his position by the strongest of ties, and his death came as a great shock" (Cotrell, 2001).

When you study a language, whether it is your native tongue or a foreign one, you must learn what the words stand for; that is, you have to know both their denotative and their connotative meanings. You must also know how to put the words together to make the phrases and sentences that express relationships between the words. This is the *grammar* of a language.

Notice, however, that your idea of an object or a concept is never exactly the same as another person's, because each individual has had different

Consider This

Words work differently in different cultures. In an article about "Identity and Struggle in Jamaican Talk," Dexter B. Gordon (2000), who teaches at the University of Alabama, Tuscaloosa, says that "Jamaicans can be readily distinguishable by their talk" (p. 141). Gordon directly addresses how words work in Jamaica:

Jamaican language provides its speakers a sense of identity, comfort, and shared solidarity. It bestows a feeling of uniqueness, especially in the face of the alienating function of the dominant, mainstream European American culture. Jamaicans living in the United States conduct their private conversations, with family or with Jamaican friends, in their local language and sometimes in a mixture of Jamaican and standard English.

In their language Jamaicans find contact with a shared world and ready access to important aspects of that world. The word irie for example, is understood by Jamaicans as a greeting of good-will, a commentary on the state of one's being, and a cultural celebration of the inventiveness of the marginalized. Irie emerged out of the Jamaican Rastafarian subculture. To describe

everything as kosher comes closest to the idea of everything irie" (p. 147).

Questions

1. Could the same be said for the language you speak as for the Jamaican language? That it provides you "a sense of identity, comfort, and shared solidarity"? Why or why not?

2. Edward Sapir and Benjamin Whorf suggest that the language of one's culture determines how you see and think about the world. Does Sapir and Whorf's theory apply to the Jamaican language? If you knew that Jamaicans use their language "to survive external domination" (p. 147), to conserve "aspects of their (Jamaican) culture" (p. 147), and "to exclude those who do not share (their) cultural marker" (p. 147), does this make Sapir and Whorf's theory clearer and more applicable?

Source: D. B. Gordon. Identity and Struggle in Jamaican Talk. In A., Gonzalez; M., Houston; & V. Chen, eds. *Our Voices: Essays in Culture, Ethnicity, and Communication.* (Los Angeles: Roxbury Publishing Company, 2000), pp. 141–49.

experiences. Your notion of what *cat* means comes from all the cats you have ever known, read about, seen on television, heard others talk about, and so on. This composite cat is unique to you, but you can use the sound of the word to refer to cats in general because cats have certain qualities on which we all agree.

A theory of language developed by Edward Sapir and Benjamin L. Whorf suggests that the language of one's culture determines how you see and think about the world. Cheryl Pawlowski, in her book, *Glued to the Tube*, quotes Ludwig Wittgenstein, who says "Language is not only a vehicle of thought, it is also the driver of the vehicle." "He contends," writes Pawlowski, "that individual languages create foundations for the cultures that use them. These languages define the cultures' perceptions of the world around them, specifying what constitutes an event, action, or thing. Language even designates the importance of each object or action" (Pawlowski, 2000, pp. 9–10; Postman, 1992, p. 124). Em Griffin (2000), who writes about communication theory, shows how the word *you* is used in three different cultures: In English-speaking cultures you use *you* to refer to anyone—regardless of your relationship with him or her. In German, however, you use *si* if you have a formal relationship and *du* if the relationship is informal. The use of *you* in Japanese is very complicated to a nonspeaker of the language: There are 10 different words, and the one you use will depend on the gender, age, and status of the person you are talking to (p. 43).

Because the United States has been a one-language nation, many Americans do not understand how language and perception of the world are connected. Americans sometimes complain that immigrants to the United States do not learn and use English. However, if you accept the theory that language defines your world and your perception of it, you see that learning a language is not just a matter of learning a sign system: It is also learning a different way of looking at the world. For example, one of your authors taught a student who had immigrated to the United States when she was a child. Although she was fluent in English, she said she always prayed in Polish; if she used English, the prayer didn't seem real to her.

■ PEOPLE DETERMINE MEANINGS

For the listener to understand what a speaker intends, the speaker should have something definite in mind. If an idea or impression is vague in the speaker's mind, the resulting message will be confused and ambiguous. Understanding is the core of meaning, and understanding is a two-way process; that is, the speaker is responsible for presenting the idea clearly, and the listener is responsible for trying to understand it accurately. Meanings are ultimately determined by people, not by words.

When speaking of some subjects, you have to use a very specialized vocabulary. As Mary Boone, in her book *Managing Inter@ctively* says, "The accountants have their language, the marketing people have their language, the businesspeople have their language, the IT people have their language. . . . That's what they've gotten their degrees in" (2001, pp. 109–10). Here is how Keith Moffatt and Ytaka Shimomura, mathematicians, explain the forces at work on a spinning egg: "We may note that a raw egg does not rise when spun, simply because the angular velocity imparted to the shell must diffuse into the fluid interior; this process dissipates most of the initial kinetic energy imparted to the egg, the remaining energy being insufficient for . . . the state of gyroscopic balance to be established" ("Egg mystery," 2002).

Understanding debates over educational policy can be difficult without a background in the jargon used by educators and reformers. To discuss educational policy, for example, you would need to know terms like ability grouping, block scheduling, charter schools, norm-referenced tests, outcomes-based education, performance-based assessment, and vouchers. In fact, you probably need to know abbreviations such as ESL, ESEA, Title I, Title VII, and Title IX. The language of education is an excellent example of a very specialized vocabulary.

Language differences might even occur within a family. The world of adults is different from the worlds of children or adolescents. Parents might wish, for example, that their child were popular. But "popular" to a teenager may mean "being able to stay out late and own a car"—possibly unacceptable conditions to the parents. Because the experiences of the teenager and parent are so different, their values and vocabulary also differ.

New meanings are continually created by all of us as we change our ideas, our feelings, and our activities. As we think, read, travel, make friends, and experience life, the associations and connections that words have for us are changed.

■ THE LANGUAGE ENVIRONMENT

All language takes place within a particular environment. A minister speaks in the environment of a church; two friends have a conversation in the student center; an instructor gives a lecture in a classroom. Language that is appropriate to one environment might appear meaningless or foolish in another. The language you use in a dormitory, for example, might be completely inappropriate in a classroom.

People, Purposes, and Rules

According to Neil Postman, who writes about language and education, the **language environment** is made up of four elements: people, their purpose, the rules of communication by which they achieve their purpose, and the actual talk used in the situation (Postman, 1977, p. 9). To illustrate these elements, let's take the simple example of John and Mary, who greet each other:

Mary: Hi. How are you?

John: Fine. How are you?

Mary: Good.

The rules for this sort of conversation are known to you, since you often participate in it yourself. If John had failed to follow the rules, however, and had stopped to talk for five minutes about how miserable he felt, Mary might have been annoyed. John would have gone beyond the limits of that sort of conversation.

The kind of conversation Mary and John had illustrates language as a ritual. **Ritual language** takes place in environments where a conventionalized response is expected of you (Goffman, 1971, p. 62). Greetings are a ritual; you briefly respond to someone—usually only half listening to what the other person has said—and then go about your business.

The rituals you use are determined by the language environment. If you are at a baptism or *bris,* you are expected to say how good-looking the child is or how well he or she behaved during the service. At a wedding you wish the couple happiness and tell the bride she looks beautiful.

Every society's language rituals are determined by the cultural values of that society. In rural East Africa, it would be rude to pass a man you know well with a brief "Hello." You are expected to stop and inquire about the person, his home, his livestock, and his health. In some cultures it is appropriate to tell a couple at their wedding that you hope they will have many sons; in American society, such a comment would be considered inappropriate.

You learn ritualized language when you are very young, from your parents or other adults around you. Researchers have found that young children do not automatically make the conventional responses of "Hi," "Good-bye," or "Thanks"—even though they hear adults doing so. If children are going to use these conventional terms, they must be taught (Greif & Gleason, 1980, pp. 159–66).

As children grow older, they begin to learn and use ritual language. Anyone who has handed out candy on Halloween can tell you that although the younger children may have to be prompted, this is no longer necessary with the older children; they offer their thanks spontaneously.

Appropriate Language

For any society to function it must have some sort of understanding about which words are inappropriate. As children grow up, they try out the new words they hear and, from the reactions of the adults around them, learn the words they shouldn't use. Generally, Americans (and probably most cultures) would agree that the following are inappropriate: First are racial or ethnic epithets against members of groups to which you do not belong. For example, a white person should never use the word *nigger* to describe an African-American. African-Americans, however, can use this word within their own culture because in that context it has a different emotional meaning. Second are words that insult others' appearance or behavior. These words may range from *stupid* or *ugly* to *clumsy* or *incompetent.* Third are words that are blasphemous (religious words) or obscene (body-function words). Fourth are aggressive words intended to control others, such as *shut up* or *drop dead.* Words in any of these categories are highly loaded, emotional words that can do serious damage to human relationships.

Sometimes you have to refer to something for which it would be impolite to use the direct word. To do this you use a **euphemism**—an inoffensive word or phrase that is substituted for other words that might be perceived as unpleasant. For example, you ask "Where's your bathroom?" even when you don't intend to take a bath. If somebody has died, you might use the phrase "passed away." In one instance, when a restaurant in Taiwan

Working Together

Here, now, is an opportunity for your group to make a significant contribution to the whole world. Based on the combined backgrounds and experiences of the members of your group, you are to combine all of your knowledge and expertise to establish a set of rules for members of YOUR generation. We will call these rules "Handy Reminders for Comfortable Communication." These are rules that could be distributed to every member of your generation that would absolutely ensure the use of appropriate language.

Come up with as many rules as you can given the amount of time you have. Then, as you have established the fundamental rules, arrange them in the order of most importance, with the most important rules at the top of your list. Brainstorm, first, for rules on which every member of the group can agree. Arrange them only after a set of 5 to 10 rules has been agreed upon.

wanted to serve dog meat, the owners knew that it would offend some people, and so rather than admit what it was, they called it "fragrant meat." Closer to home, you call your own meat "beef," "veal," and "pork" to veil that it is really dead cow, calf, and pig.

Sometimes government agencies, businesses, or other institutions create euphemisms to either cover up the truth or make the truth more palatable. When euphemisms are created by government or institutions, they are often referred to as **doublespeak.** Often doublespeak is used to further evil ends. Adolf Hitler used the phrase "final solution" when he meant the killing of all Jews, gypsies, and homosexuals in Nazi Germany. In the late 1990s, Slobodan Milosevic created an equally offensive phrase when he used the term "ethnic cleansing" for the killing of Albanians and other non-Serbian peoples. The United States is not without its doublespeak. William Lutz, an expert on doublespeak, found 96 ways that companies said they were laying off workers ("Tangled Web," 1998, p. 22A).

You learn appropriate language as you become more sophisticated and mature. By the time you reach late adolescence, you probably know what language to use for a particular language environment. Whether you want to use the prescribed words is largely irrelevant. The language environment dictates the language that is expected of you. If you violate these expectations, you run the risk of having people respond to you negatively.

Specialization

Most language environments have words that are specialized and are used only in those environments. If your plumber tells you that your toilet needs a new sleeve gasket, you probably won't know what that means. You would understand if the plumber told you that the toilet needs a new seal at the bottom to keep the water from leaking out onto the floor. Most professions and occupations have a language that only its practitioners understand. Professional cooks make a *roux,* teachers write up their *behavioral objectives,* and contractors install *I-beams.* Members of an occupational group must learn their specialized language in order to master their field.

Some language environments can be specialized even if the communicators are trying to reach a mass audience. For example, if you watch a jewelry show on a home shopping network on television, you soon discover that there are many words for describing jewelry. For example, the clasp used to keep the jewelry on your body may be a *lobster claw clasp,* a *box closure,* or a *snap bar* closure. Do you want a *faceted stone,* an *emerald cut,* or a *diamond cut?* You can't make choices until you learn this language. The language of the Internet, as noted previously, is an excellent example of specialization.

Other groups develop a language that is never intended to be understood by outsiders. Car-lot salespersons, for example, have many words for describing customers who are out of earshot. A *tire-kicker* is a person who pretends expertise but has none. A *roach, flake,* or *stoker* is a person with a bad credit rating, while a *be-back* is a customer who promises to return but probably won't (Bennett, 1995, D1 & D5). Sometimes people create a special language when they feel they don't have as much power as the people around them. Quite often it is a language that those in power do not understand, and it is deliberately used to keep information from them. Students,

Another Point of View

In his book, *West Side: Young Men & Hip-Hop in L.A.*, William Shaw discusses the importance of language:

How you talk is what you are. The increasing isolation of America's underclass is not just economic and spatial: It's linguistic, too. The African-American vernacular that thrives so richly in hip hop has its roots in West Indian creole, and in the eighteenth-century speech patterns of the Irish and Scottish immigrants. But linguists who have studied black English over the last few decades have noticed that instead of converging with what they call standard American English, it is fast drifting ever further away from it. The creative, fast-evolving language black Americans speak in the inner cities may be increasingly desirable on wax, as a cultural artifact, but it is becoming less and less like the language of the majority, the language of the schoolrooms, of mass media, of politics, and of the workplace."

Questions

1. Young boys from L.A. who were looking for work in the music industry often used "slangin" as their form of communication, but Mike Nixon, who had been in the music industry since the sixties, let them know that they weren't going to get anywhere in the music business if they couldn't communicate in a businesslike fashion. Do you find any analogous situations in today's world? That is, to succeed in business requires the adoption and use of communication that reflects a "businesslike fashion" as opposed to the everyday, common, ordinary speech that occurs between friends?

2. Have you any personal examples to support the insights that Shaw offers in this excerpt from his book? Have you detected, for example, the drift in black English further and further away from standard American English?

3. What do you think may be one reason why the fast-evolving language black Americans speak in the inner cities is becoming less and less like the language of the majority? Could it be, for example, that inner-city youth are creating a special language because they don't have as much power as the people around them? Are they doing it to exclude outsiders or members of the adult establishment?

4. Notice, in the example cited in question 1 above, that Mike Nixon understood why the young boys from the inner city of L.A. spoke the way they did, but he tried to encourage them to shift roles—to shift their speech—to adapt to a different language environment (business). How many different language environments do you adapt to in an average day? An average week? How about in an average month? With regard to effective communication, would you say that the more language environments to which one is exposed, the more effective communicator he or she is likely to be?

Source: W. Shaw, *Westside: Young Men and Hip-Hop in L.A.* (New York: Simon & Schuster, 2000), p. 480.

especially those in high school and college, are one example of special-language groups. They use slang or a special meaning to exclude outsiders or members of the adult establishment. When away from adults, they may also use some of the language the culture considers inappropriate.

When a group has created a special language, you usually cannot step into that group and use its language unless you have some legitimate claim to membership. Students, for example, might secretly make fun of a teacher who tries to talk as they do. How you are expected to speak in a language environment depends on the role you are playing.

Whenever you shift roles, you shift your language environment and your speech as well. Let's say that in a single day you talk to your roommate, you go to class, and you speak to your mother on the telephone. Your role has shifted three times: from peer relating to peer, to student relating to instructor, to child relating to parent. Each circumstance has entailed a different language environment, and you have probably changed your speech accordingly—perhaps without even realizing it.

The important thing to remember about a language environment is that you must choose language that is appropriate to it. The language used in one environment usually does not work in another. When you think about the environment, you need to ask yourself who it is you are going to be talking with and in what context your language is going to be used. If you don't adapt to the environment, your language will not work, and you will lose the chance for effective communication.

■ STYLE, ROLES, AND GROUP MEMBERSHIPS

The words you use are determined by all your past experiences, by everything in your individual history. Stephen King (2000), in his book *On Writing*, says it this way, "You undoubtedly have your own thoughts, interests, and concerns, and they have arisen, as mine have, from your experiences and adventures as a human being" (p. 208). You learn words in order to express thoughts, and thought and language develop together. The way you think and the way you talk are unique; they form a distinctive pattern. In a sense, you are what you say because language is the chief means of conveying your thoughts. Neither language nor thought can be viewed in isolation because they are so interrelated. Together, they determine your verbal style.

Sheryl Perlmutter Bowen, a teacher of communication and women's studies at Villanova University, describes her own language and verbal style in this way: "My own speech. . .is often marked by a preference for personal topics, abrupt topic shifts, storytelling (in which the preferred point is the teller's emotional experience), a fast rate of speech, avoidance of inter-turn pauses, quick turn-taking, expressive phonology, pitch and amplitude shifts, marked voice quality, and strategic within-turn pauses. Given these characteristics," she adds, "my complaining and teasing should both be seen as normal interaction strategies" (Tanno, 2000, p. 33).

Style is the result of the way you select and arrange words and sentences. People choose different words to express their thoughts, and every individual has a unique verbal style. Not only do styles vary among people, but each person uses different styles to suit different situations. In the pulpit, a minister usually has a scholarly and formal style. At a church dinner, however, his or her style is likely to be informal and casual. When a football player signs autographs for fans, he speaks to them in the role of athlete— even though he might drop this role when he is with friends and family.

Sometimes style can negate a communicator's other good qualities. You probably know someone who is extremely shy and speaks in a faltering manner. You might also know some people who can never seem to get to the point. If you are critical of these people, it is probably because of their style.

Style, because of its power and influence, is just as important to the acceptance of ideas as all the other aspects of communication. Even if you have the

On the Web

Crafting a Positive Online Persona

An "old" saying goes, "on the Internet, no one knows if you're a dog." Since you are not physically present with the other person when you communicate via e-mail, you can be whomever you choose. Or at least, you can be whomever you can write like. Your identity when you use e-mail is based to a large extent on what you write. In essence, you are what you write.

So what sort of person do you want to be online? If you want people to think positively of you, you should try to construct an "expert persona" for yourself. You want people who receive your e-mail to respect what you have to say. Gaining this respect is a process of continually posting in a manner that lets people know that you are knowledgeable, and that your messages are worth reading. So how do you construct an expert persona? Here are some guidelines:

- *Stick to facts.* Don't spread rumor or inferences. If you don't know something for sure, be sure to preface your remarks with a disclaimer. Better yet, don't send the message at all.

- *Stick to what you know.* If you have a certain degree of expertise, share your knowledge with others. If you don't know much about the topic, don't say anything. Someone else who is an expert on that topic will be sure to chime in when necessary.

- *Don't just ask questions, answer them.* Offer thoughtful responses. Take the time to craft your answers—one of the major benefits of e-mail is that you have a chance to make your message as artistic and polished as possible.

- *Be a resource for others.* Stretch ideas that others have posed. Make connections to others' concepts. Offer summaries when lots of ideas have been thrown out and the discussion starts to lose coherence. Push others to think harder.

If you consistently stick to facts that you know, answer questions well, act as a resource for others, and follow the rules of netiquette . . . you'll soon be considered an expert by the people who read your mail. Who knows—someday you may even become a cyber-celebrity!

Source: N. Clark, "E-mail: Online Personae & Netiquette." Department of Communication, Appalachian State University, October 22, 1997. Retrieved March 14, 2003, from http://www.asucom.appstate.edu/emailnet.htm.

proper information, the right occasion, and a listener interested in your message, what you have to say may be lost if your style is inappropriate.

Impressions of personality are often related to verbal style. When you characterize a person as formal and aloof, your impression is due in part to the way that person talks. Since your style partially determines whether others accept or reject you, it also influences how others receive your messages. Style is so important that it can influence people's opinion of you, win their friendship, lose their respect, or sway them to your ideas.

Like language environment, verbal style is often connected with the roles you play. Professionals, for example, are expected to speak grammatically correct English—both in private and in professional life. A college student is also expected to use correct grammar. Yet if he takes a factory job during summer vacation using correct grammar might get him into trouble with his fellow workers, for his verbal style could identify him as a "college kid."

Gender and Language

In recent years there have been numerous studies of the different language styles used by men and women. Sociolinguist Deborah Tannen (1990) has found that men and women have almost completely different styles of speaking (pp. 42–43). In fact, she maintains that their languages are so different that they might as well come from different worlds. According to Tannen, when women have conversations, they use the language of **rapport-talk.** This language is designed to lead to intimacy with others, to match experiences, and to establish relationships. Men, however, speak **report-talk.** In this type of speech the speaker's goal is to maintain status, to demonstrate knowledge and skills, and to keep the center-stage position (Tannen, 1990, p. 76). Because of their different ways of speaking, men and women often have problems when they try to talk to each other, Tannen says. For example, a stock cartoon shows a man and woman at the breakfast table, with the man reading the newspaper and the woman trying to get his attention. The man is using the newspaper as a source of information he needs for future report-talks. The woman, however, is looking for interaction, or rapport-talk.

Tannen also says that men are more likely than women to look at problems in terms of "fixing them." A woman, for example, might tell her husband that someone insulted her. Her husband's reaction is to take revenge as a way of fixing the problem. For the woman, this probably is not a satisfactory solution; she would prefer a statement of understanding or an expression of empathy from him (1990, pp. 51–52).

Other researchers have also looked at differences between the way men and women interact. They have found that when men and women talk together, men are more likely to interrupt ("Let's go on to the next topic") and give directives ("Why don't you write this down?"). Women use more personal pronouns and more intensive adverbs ("I really like her"). The researchers also found that women use more questions and more justifiers ("The reason I say this . . . .") (Mulac, Wiemenn, Widenmann, & Gibson, 1988).

Tannen believes that gender differences in language are important considerations in the college classroom. In a typical classroom, she says, male students are likely to say what they know before the whole class and to welcome arguments and challenges from their classmates. They are also likely to reject anecdotal information as unimportant. Female students, on the other hand, do not find much pleasure in verbal conflict and are much more comfortable when they work in small groups and offer personal anecdotes. Since most classrooms are organized on the male model, Tannen believes that many women find the classroom to be a hostile space (Tannen, 1992).

An interesting example of gender differences in language occurred when a teacher asked her students to make up words that described experiences unique to their sex but that did not already exist in English. She found that women's and men's words were in entirely different categories. Women created words that tended to put women into passive roles, such as *perchaphonic* ("waiting for someone to phone you") and *herdastudaphobia* ("fear when passing a group of strange men"). Men, however, created words that focused on competency and the power to change things, such

Another Point of View

Some Criticisms of Tannen's Work

Seems to be based on anecdotes.

Seems to overgeneralize.

Seems to consider only white middle class women and men.

Seems to focus on heterosexual women and men.

Sees problems in relationships between men and women as based in difference and not dominance.

Seems to ignore political and economic differences between men and women.

Relies on individuals' intentions ("He didn't intend to dominate") rather than on facts and also others' interpretations.

Tries to separate dominance and gendered culture.

Doesn't explain why men and women have these different styles.

Questions

1. To what extent does criticism of an author automatically convey truth? How difficult would it be to verify the criticisms above?

2. Does criticism of a work nullify the value of or findings in that work? To what extent do sales of a work or the effect of a work mitigate (cause to become less harsh or harmful) criticism of that work?

3. If you were the author of a work and received criticism of that work, how would you go about addressing that criticism?

Source: "Language and Gender." University of Colorado, 1998. Retrieved July 27, 2002, from http://www.colorado.edu/linguistics/sp98/2400/tannen.hyp.

as *gearheaditis* ("making your car the best on the road") and *beer muscles* ("believing you are tough after you have had something to drink") (Turner, 1992).

Where does gender-specific language come from? Tannen believes that it begins in childhood and that children learn it from their peers. She reports that one researcher who observed preschool children found that when the children wanted to do something, the girls would start with, "Let's . . . ." while the boys would give direct commands, "Sit down" (Tannen, 1990, p. 153). In looking at videotapes of second-graders, Tannen says that in language and behavior, second-grade girls were more similar to adult women than they were to second-grade boys (Tannen, 1990, p. 245). When the same second-graders were put in pairs and were asked to talk about "something serious," the girls did so. The boys, however, resisted or mocked authority (pp. 255–56). Since language behavior starts so young, it's not surprising that it soon becomes automatic.

While some scholars have criticized the emphasis put on differences between male and female language because they feel that those who do the studies often interpret the results in a way that reinforces stereotypes society already holds about men and women (Weatherall, 1998), others attempt to explain the female advantage in language aptitude. In her book, *The War Against Boys*, Christina Hoff Sommers, the W. H. Brady Fellow at the American Enterprise Institute in Washington, D.C., who has a Ph.D. in philosophy from Brandeis University and was formerly professor of philosophy at Clark University, offers research to support her contention that physiological sex differences correlate with differences in preferences and aptitudes. She cites the research of Bennett and Sally Shaywitz, neuroscientists at Yale University (Shaywitz, 1995). Using brain-imaging technologies—specifically functional magnetic resonance imaging (MRI)—to look for sex differences in the brain, they gave 19 men and 19 women volunteer subjects a simple language task. "In both men and women," writes Sommers, "the front of the cortex in the left hemisphere lit up brightly, indicating that to be the area where this task is carried out. But in 11 of the 19 women—and none of the men—an area in the right hemisphere also lit up. If two parts of the female brain focus on language, this might explain the female advantage in this area" (pp. 89–90).

Other scholars have pointed out that language use is not tied to gender; rather, it is connected to role. Faye Crosby and Linda Nyquist (1977) discovered, for example, that when women are in positions of authority, they use basically the same speech as their male counterparts (p. 314). Likewise, men may cross over into what has been considered women's language. For example, as presidents, Clinton and Reagan often used an anecdotal style that is generally associated with women. George W. Bush, on the other hand, tends to use men's language littered with metaphors and aphorisms associated with the wild west.

Dialect

Toward the end of the summer in central Pennsylvania, many cooks begin to fry or preserve "mangoes." Outsiders are always surprised that Pennsylvania cooks are so interested in this tropical fruit. What they don't know is that in that part of the country a mango isn't a fruit at all; it's what everyone else calls a green pepper or a bell pepper. The central Pennsylvanians' use of the word *mango* is an example of dialect.

A **dialect** is the habitual language of a community. It is distinguished by unique grammatical structures, words, and figures of speech. The community members who use the dialect may be identified by region or by such diverse factors as education, social class, or cultural background. Many people will hold on to their dialects because they are a tie to their own community.

When radio and television became widespread, linguists predicted that their popularity might herald the end of dialect because people would imitate the standard American speech they heard on these media. However, it didn't work that way. Linguists have found that dialect is growing stronger, especially in many urban areas (Hummel, 1999).

Linguists refer to dialects as "nonstandard" forms of language. They generally try to avoid such questions as whether a dialect is a correct form of speech or whether one dialect is superior or preferable to another.

African-Americans, the second largest dialectal group in the United States, have kept their dialect. Hispanics have edged past blacks as the nation's largest minority group. One study shows that the African-American dialect is moving further and further away from standard English. The linguists who conducted the study believe that this has happened because African-Americans are becoming increasingly segregated from whites—particularly in urban areas. They point out that African-American children often do not meet a white person until they enter school. This segregation, which led to dialect originally, still contributes to new, unique sentence structures and idioms that are not found in standard English (Stanbeck & Pearce, 1981). In Sapphire's novel *Push* (1996), her main character, an urban teenage girl, uses dialect when she tells her story. In the example below, she is describing her first day in the classroom of her new alternative school. Her dialect is especially apparent in her verb use:

> *The first thing I see when I step through the door is the windows, where we is high up, no other buildings in the way. Sky blue blue. I looks around the room now. Walls painted an ugly green. Miz Rain at her desk, her back to me, her face to the class and the windows. "Class" only about five, six other people. Miz Teacher turn around say, Have a seat. I stays standing at the door. I swallow hard, start to, I think I'm gonna cry. I look Miz Teacher's long dreadlocky hair, look kinda nice but look kinda nasty too. My knees is shaking, I'm scared (pp. 41–42).*

Although there are no clear-cut rules for where and when it is appropriate to use a dialect, it is possible to make some generalizations. A dialect is appropriate in a group with a strong ethnic identity, but it may be inappropriate in situations where standard English is used. Linguistic scholars agree that some dialects have more prestige than others and that prestige is determined by both the people who speak the dialect and those who hear it. Thus, if you want to be accepted by and identified with people who use a dialect or who use a standard English different from your own, you might have to adapt to their way of speaking. Many people in America have discovered that it is not difficult to speak two "languages," a dialect and standard English. By so doing, they find it possible to keep their ethnic identity as well as function in a world where expectations are different.

Speaking and Writing

We use language in both speaking and writing, but the transactional nature of speaking makes it very different from writing.

When two people are engaged in conversation, they interact continuously and simultaneously. Both get and give information, form impressions, and respond to each other. On the basis of each other's responses, both can change their comments to explain, backtrack, hurry up, slow down, or do whatever is necessary to be understood.

Sometimes conversation reflects the participants' past knowledge of each other. They can use a kind of shorthand because of the experiences they've had together. If you are in a close relationship or desire one, you know that the words you speak may affect your present and future relationship. If the relationship is more impersonal, the choice of words might not be so important.

You also are able to change your language to reflect the circumstances. When you get negative feedback, you can change language to appease your listeners. You can use simpler words or concepts if listeners don't seem to understand. Spoken language is also accompanied by **paralanguage**—vocal cues, or the way you say your words. For example, your meaning can be influenced by your pitch and rate (high and fast if you are excited), your

Consider This

". . . Speech is characterized by all the things writing teachers tell students to eliminate from their prose in the interest of clarity: repetition, contradiction, exaggeration, run-ons, fragments, and clichés, plus an array of tonal and physical inflections—drawls, grunts, shrugs, winks, hand gestures—unreproducible in written form. People talk for hours without uttering a single topic sentence. Yet we generally understand speech perfectly and instantaneously. We don't have to keep going over the same sentence three times to figure out what the person is trying to say. People communicate with their bodies much more effectively than they do on paper. You cannot make a semicolon mistake when you're talking. You can stick that emphasis any place you want, baby."

Source: L. Menand, "Comp Time: Is College Too Late to Learn How to Write?" *The New Yorker*, September 11, 2000, pp. 92–94.

volume, and how often you pause. This kind of adaptation occurs in every conversation. Whether you are talking to your father, a professor, or a friend, your language will reflect your impression of this person, the kinds of experiences you have had together, and the role you are playing.

In contrast, it's not so easy to change your written language. In fact, writers have an entirely different set of problems than speakers do. When you are speaking, people are reacting to you as the message occurs. For writers, reaction from their audience is unusual, and they have no way of knowing if they have pleased or offended someone, or if they have even communicated their ideas. This means that their words must be chosen very carefully. Also, they have time to go over their words, polish their phrases, and check their grammar. Their readers have more time too. They can always reread the words if they're not clear the first time. Writers are more likely to use a larger vocabulary than speakers do, and readers can look up the words if they don't understand them. Writers do not have the paralanguage of speakers to add to their meaning. If the words they choose don't work, their attempt at communication fails.

Writers have no way of taking the future effects of their words into account. When an Indian author, Salman Rushdie, wrote *The Satanic Verses*, he could not predict that his words would be seen as blasphemous and would be condemned by an Iranian religious leader, who "gave permission" for any Moslem to kill the author.

■ WORKING ON YOUR COMMUNICATION

When you set out to communicate verbally, you are more likely to be successful if you use words and ideas that have the same meaning to the person with whom you are communicating as they do to you. Sometimes, although you think you are being clear, the other person might not perceive what you think you have communicated.

Communication can go awry at various stages. Let's look at some of the places where this might happen.

What Do You Want to Say?

In 1938, Orson Welles broadcast *The War of the Worlds,* a radio play about martians invading the United States. You can assume that in writing this play, Welles intended to entertain his audience. Although Welles's intent was clear to him, at least one million people misunderstood it and believed that the play was real: They believed that martians really had landed and that their lives were in peril. By the time the network announced that the broadcast was only a play, many people had already reacted to it by fleeing their homes to find a place of safety.

Although this is an extreme example of intent going astray, most of us have had times when people's responses were different from those we intended. You intend to tell your roommate to meet you at 7:00, but she thinks you said 7:30. You intend to make a joke, but you end up insulting someone. When you are involved in one-to-one communication, you often have a chance to clear up misunderstandings. If you see that the other person looks confused or annoyed or if the response you get indicates that you have not communicated something as precisely as you had intended, you can attempt to clarify what you said.

When you are talking to an audience, however, it is not so easy to clear up misunderstandings. In a public-speaking or mass-communication setting, you may not have a chance to respond to feedback or you may not be able to respond until the communication is over. Therefore, when you are going to communicate to a large audience, you must prepare your words much more carefully than you do in an interpersonal setting.

The first thing you must consider is, What exactly do you want to say? Students who are new to public speaking often do not think through this step clearly enough. Speakers who do not know precisely what they want to say frequently end up confusing their audience. The same may happen if they have not clearly thought out their words.

How Do You Want to Say It?

Although you are often told that you should make careful language choices, you might not know how to go about doing so. Command of language requires years of practice and study. Since it is impossible to lay down strict rules that govern the choice of language for all occasions and for all circumstances, the discussion here is limited to four important aspects of language choice: clarity, power, vividness, and ethics.

Clarity

A pilot died in the crash of a private jet because the instructions on how to open the emergency door were so unclear that she could not get it open. Although a lack of clarity is usually not a matter of life or death, it can lead to frustration and misunderstanding. In most situations, you have to speak as clearly as possible if you want to be understood. **Clarity** is that property of style by means of which a thought is so presented that it is immediately understood, depending on the precision and simplicity of the language. Clarity is especially important when there is little opportunity for feedback. For example, if you are saying something of special importance, making a formal speech, or being interviewed by the media, clarity is essential since you will probably not get another chance.

Jargon is a language that can be so specialized that it is inappropriate to use it outside the field where it originated. Emanuel Rosen, in his book *The Anatomy of Buzz* (2000), writes this about the use of jargon: "From ancient fortified cities to current gated communities, people have always put walls and other barriers around themselves to keep intruders away to differentiate themselves from others. Networks have their own walls and fences, but instead of wire or bricks, people use dialect, jargon, and acronyms to keep strangers out" (p. 215). Physicians often use a highly specialized language to describe illnesses and injuries. Although doctors can communicate with each other, sometimes they have problems communicating with patients because of the walls and fences. Many newspapers carry a column in which a physician answers questions from readers who do not understand what their own doctors told them—a way to break down the walls and add gates to the fences.

Other language that might not be clear to everyone is slang. Slang has its place when you are talking informally with your friends. However, many slang words have such broad and vague meanings that they could apply to almost anything. If you use the word *cool* to compliment someone's shirt and use it again to describe beautiful scenery, you reduce everything to a common element.

Sometimes people feel that if they have taken the trouble to learn long and complicated words, they should use them whenever they can. On a bottle of fluoride solution, the consumer is advised to "hold the solution in the mouth for one minute and then expectorate." In case the consumer doesn't understand the word *expectorate,* the phrase *spit it out* follows in parentheses. Since the purpose of this message is to communicate with the consumer, the simpler words, *spit it out,* should have been used in the first place.

Use more complicated words only when they help make your meaning clearer. For example, if you want your car painted red, you'll be happier with the final results if you use a more precise description than *red.* What shade do you prefer? Burgundy? Crimson? Vermilion? Garnet?

When you increase your vocabulary, you increase your chances of getting your intended meaning across to your listener. The more words you have at your command, the more precise you will be. This does not mean that you should search for big words; on the contrary, familiar words are often the best.

One of the delights of language is that it offers many subtleties and shades of meaning. Choosing the same words to express all our ideas is like eating a Big Mac for dinner every night. Language is a marvelous banquet providing us with a vast array of choices for anything and everything we want to say.

Powerful Talk

Many communication researchers have been looking into the issue of what makes speech powerful. **Powerful talk,** they agree, is talk that comes directly to the point—talk that does not use hesitation or qualifications. People who engage in powerful talk are found to be more credible, more attractive, and more persuasive than those who do not (Johnson, 1987). In the college classroom, teachers who used powerful language were considered by their students to be more believable and to have more status (Haleta, 1996).

Working Together

According to Eric Golanty, in his online article, "Effective Communication," clarity in communication boils down to *I-statements* and *you-statements*. Here is a condensation of his comments. Read the explanation, followed by the brief dialogue. Then, working with others as a group, answer the questions that follow.

Explanation

- *A clear message is one in which the symbols represent as closely as possible the sender's intent.*
- *Clear messages are best delivered with* I-statements—*sentences that begin with (or have as the subject) the pronoun "I."*
- *I-statements identify clearly the sender as the source of a thought, emotion, desire, or act, as in "I think . . . ," "I feel . . . ," "I want (need). . . ," or "I did (will do) . . ."*
- You-statements, *which begin with (or have as the subject) the pronoun "you," as in "You always . . . ," "You never . . . ," "You are . . . ," or the interrogatives, "Why don't you . . . ?" or "How could you . . . ?" often are put-downs or character assassinations.*

Dialogue

Ron: Beth! Why didn't you answer the phone?

Beth: I'm not your secretary.

Ron: You don't care what happens around here, do you?

Beth: Oh yeah, who pays for the damn phone, anyway?

Ron: Money, money, money. That's all you ever think about. You're as materialistic as your father.

Beth: At least he cared about getting ahead. All you care about is playing golf with your pals.

Ron: I'd play less golf if you were more fun to be around. All you do is work around the house.

Beth: If I don't do it, who will? You're just an irresponsible kid.

Ron: And you're just an old nag.

Questions

1. What was the intent of Ron's original message? Was it ever discussed?

2. Could Ron have begun this discussion in such a way that Beth would have known what was bothering him? Give some examples of possible opening lines.

3. How might Beth have begun her part of this discussion so that she would find out why Ron's upset? That is, when Beth heard Ron's attack, what choices did she have? Would any of her choices have been more likely to get them on the road to greater understanding? What did she need to say to accomplish this?

4. When you are drawn into the game of *attack-counterattack* or *blame-accuse-blame-accuse*, whose responsibility is it to stop the game? Could the above discussion have been stopped early so that the potentially hurtful exchange would not have occurred?

Source: E. Golanty, "Effective Communication." College Health—Las Positas, 1999. Retrieved March 14, 2003, from http://www.webcom.com/ergo/health/comm.html.

To achieve powerful talk, you should avoid certain communication behaviors. First, avoid hedges and qualifiers—expressions such as "I guess" and "kind of"—because they weaken the power of your speech. Next, eliminate hesitation forms such as "uh" and "you know." These words make speakers sound too uncertain. Third, be careful not to use too many tag questions—comments that start out as statements but end as questions ("It would be nice to go on a picnic, wouldn't it?"). Tag questions make the speaker seem less assertive. Finally, do not use disclaimers. These are words and expressions that excuse or ask the listener to bear with the speaker. Examples are "I know you probably don't agree with me, but . . ." or "I'm really not prepared to speak today" (Johnson, 1987, p. 167).

Many of us dilute our conversations and speeches with powerless words and expressions. However, the use of these expressions is mainly a matter of habit. Once you recognize your bad habits, you can start to break them.

Besides using powerful language, you can use several other techniques to make your language more lively. A sense of urgency is communicated mainly by verbs—the action words of language. "Judy slapped him" and "The children jumped up and down" are both sentences that sound energetic. Language is also livelier when you put sentences in the active rather than the passive voice. "The boy hit the ball" is more energetic than "The ball was hit by the boy."

Vividness

Remember those ghost stories you heard when you were a child? The best ones were those that filled you with terror—the ones laced with blood-curdling shrieks, mournful moans, mysterious howling. They were usually set in dark places, with only an occasional eerie light or a streak of lightning. If any smells were mentioned, they were sure to be dank and musty.

The teller of a ghost story usually speaks in the first person. Any narrative told from the point of view of "I was there" or "It happened to me" is particularly vivid. By re-creating an experience for your listeners, you can often make them feel what you felt. **Vividness** is the property of style by which a thought is so presented that it evokes lifelike imagery or suggestion.

Vividness also comes from unique forms of speech. Some people would say that a person who talks too much "chatters like a magpie," a phrase that has become a cliché. To one southern speaker, however, this person "makes a lot of chin music." When we say that language is vivid, we often mean that someone has found a new way of saying old things. Children often charm us with the uniqueness of their language because they are too young to know all the clichés and overused expressions. Another place to look for vivid language is in poetry and song. Although more words have been written about love than any other subject, many songwriters have given us new expressions and therefore new ways of looking at the experience. Their unique perspectives make an old idea sound original and exciting.

To Whom Are You Talking?

As you talk to people, become conscious of them as particular individuals for whom you need to adapt your message. Note the language environment in which your conversation is taking place, and make the adjustments that are necessary. Also, when you are talking about a particular subject, see if you can find words that are unique to the subject—even if you have to define them. Often, learning about a subject is also learning the vocabulary of the subject. Be conscious of what you are saying. This added consciousness will increase your sensitivity to other people as well as your awareness of language choice and use.

Consider This

Dalton Conley (2001), a sociologist, grew up as one of a few white boys in a neighborhood of mostly black and Puerto Ricans on Manhattan's Lower East Side. Early in his book he looks back on his childhood and reflects on the languages spoken:

I even felt culturally more similar to my darker-hued peers than to the previous generations of my own family. For one, I didn't talk like my parents, who had migrated to New York from Pennsylvania and Connecticut. I spoke like the other kids in the neighborhood. On the playground everyone pretty much spoke the same language with the same unique accent, no matter where our parents came from. While adults might speak only Spanish, or talk with a heavy drawl if they came from down South, our way of talking was like a layered cake; it had many distinctly rich flavors, but in our mouths they all got mixed up together. When we 'snapped' on each other (playing one-upmanship with quick witty retorts), little did we know we were using the same ironic lilt and intonation once employed in the Jewish shtetls of Central Europe. This Yiddish-like English had mixed with influences from southern Italians, Irish, and other immigrant groups to form the basic New Yorkese of the mid-twentieth century. We spoke with open vowels and dropped our r's: quarter was quartah, and water was watah. To this European stew we

added the Southern tendency to cut off the endings of some words—runnin', skippin', jumpin'—a habit that came northward with many blacks during the Great Migration. We also turned our t's into d's, as in "Lemme get fiddy cents." The latest and most powerful influence was Puerto Rican. Within the Spanish-speaking world, Puerto Ricans were notorious for their lazy r's, just as New Yorkers were, so the fit was perfect. Whenever someone said mira, the Spanish term for look, it came out media" (pp. 8–9).

Questions

1. Put yourself in Conley's peculiar situation: How would you talk? Would you tend to assimilate and use the language of your parents, or would you take up the language of your peers on the playground? Why?

2. Do you think Conley was unusual in his ability to note the language environment in which his conversations took place? Did he make the adjustments necessary, as the textbook recommends? In similar circumstances, do you think you would be as observant of the language use occurring around you? Why or why not?

Source: D. Conley, *Honky* (New York: Vintage Books (A Division of Random House, Inc.), 2000).

Sometimes people confuse personal authenticity with inflexible language usage, and they equate undisciplined speech with spontaneity. "Telling it like it is" becomes an excuse for allowing the first words that come into your head to spill out in a torrent. Such language choices reflect a kind of self-centered indulgence that says to your listener, "Never mind who you are—listen to me." Adapting your language to the individual with whom you are talking can result in a more satisfying exchange.

What Metamessages Are You Sending?

You probably choose your words carefully when you are making a public presentation. It might not occur to you, however, to be so careful when you are talking to a friend or conversing with a small group of people. Yet you might occasionally have had a conversation that made you feel uneasy—the words all sounded right, but there was something else going on.

In such cases, you need to think about the **metamessage** (sometimes called *subtext*)—the meaning apart from what actual words express. For example, when one spouse tells the other, "We need to talk," he or she really might be saying, "I want to complain."

Metamessages take many forms. At a graduation ceremony, the president of the university introduced everyone on the stage except one of the deans. The dean realized that this was more than a simple oversight, that he might be in serious trouble. He was right—he was fired the next semester.

Many metamessages don't involve words at all. Deborah Tannen believes that American men refuse to ask directions because it puts them in an inferior position and the person they ask in a superior position (Tannen, 1990, p. 62).

Sometimes metamessages are recognizable to people within a specific culture but not to outsiders. A Polish professor complained that when she was in the United States, one of her American colleagues kept saying, "Let's have lunch sometime." When she tried to pin him down, he looked annoyed. What she didn't realize until much later was that this is an expression that some Americans use to terminate a conversation.

Language is filled with metamessages, and you have to listen for this kind of talk and understand its meaning if you are going to have accurate communication. You also should be aware of the metamessages you yourself send. For example, it is not unusual for a student speaker to begin a speech by implying that the speech will not be very good: "I just finished this speech this morning," "I couldn't find any research on this topic," or "You'll have to excuse me because I am feeling sick." If you say anything of this sort, you may be engaging in a metamessage; what you may really be saying is, "I am feeling extremely nervous and anxious about giving this speech."

Ethics

Ray Penn (1990), a communications professor, points out that "a choice of words is a choice of worlds" (p. 117). He reminds us that we can cause considerable damage to others by choosing the wrong words. For example, if you are asked to remember your most painful moment, the response will most likely be something someone said.

Penn asks us to consider whether "our analogies create a self-fulfilling prophecy that will ultimately keep us from relating to others unless we get our way." For example, how often in life do you talk of "winners" and "losers," condemning the losers to permanent failure? On the international scene, does calling Saddam Hussein "another Hitler" create a self-fulfilling prophecy? When political figures in the Middle East refer to the United States as "Satan" or "the devil," does such labeling influence the way we, as a country, react to them?

Penn also reminds us that language choices can influence people's perceptions of themselves. Insulting words, he points out, can reduce an individual to a mere trait ("dyke," "queer"); they can reduce someone to less-than-human status ("pig," "chicken"); or they can tell the person "I know all about you and you have no mystery" by means of labels ("hillbilly," "redneck," "geek") (p. 117).

Assess Yourself

Verbal Communication Self-Evaluation Form

How effective is your verbal communication? Give a qualitative evaluation for each of the following six factors by circling the numerical score next to each of the factors that best represents your verbal communication. Select an event, a situation, a context, and a time when you recently gave a speech or presentation, and provide yourself a self-analysis by using the following verbal communication criteria: 7 = Outstanding; 6 = Excellent; 5 = Very good; 4 = Average/good; 3 = Fair; 2 = Poor; 1 = Minimal ability; 0 = No ability demonstrated.

1. *Did you use extended conversation?* That is, did you use language that was not highly formal, that was easy for you to use (not a stretch), that seemed like normal conversation, and that revealed a natural, comfortable, relaxed vocabulary and approach?   7 6 5 4 3 2 1 0

2. *Did you reveal clarity in your word choices?* That is, were your words immediately meaningful? Did they arouse specific and definite meanings? Was there no ambiguity or confusion revealed?   7 6 5 4 3 2 1 0

3. *Did you reveal simplicity in your word choices?* That is, did you use simple words? Was your vocabulary instantly understandable? Did you avoid using vague and confusing words? Were you sensitive to audience knowledge and background?   7 6 5 4 3 2 1 0

4. *Did you reveal accuracy in your word choices?* That is, did your words seem to convey exactly what you meant? Did you give your listeners enough, but not too much, information? In your examples, did you give complete details such as names, places, dates, and other facts? When you used an uncommon or technical word, did you accurately define it for your listeners?   7 6 5 4 3 2 1 0

5. *Did your verbal communication reveal appropriateness?* That is, did the words you chose have a direct relationship to your listeners? Did all your facts, examples, illustrations, opinions, statistics, and personal experiences relate directly to your audience? Did you use personal pronouns such as you, us, we, and our? Did you ask your listeners questions or use rhetorical questions that did not require an answer but which created the impression of direct audience contact?   7 6 5 4 3 2 1 0

6. *Did you reveal dynamism in your choice of words?* That is, was your language vivid? Was it impressive? Did your language appear planned and prepared—like you had given it some specific thought? Did your language reveal your own personal imprint?   7 6 5 4 3 2 1 0

TOTAL POINTS: _____

 Go to the *Communicating Effectively* CD-ROM to see your results and learn how to evaluate your attitudes and feelings.

Penn reminds us that we make moral choices when we choose the language we are going to use. Many of the choices you make not only determine how you present yourself to others but also decide the nature of your relationships in the years to come. For this reason, it is important that you choose your words wisely and well.

Chapter Review

The mystery of why human beings developed a language for communication has, perhaps, been solved. With the combined efforts of physiologists, medical doctors, genetic scientists, anthropologists, molecular biologists, and others, the FOXP2 gene, the gene directly linked to developing the fine motor skills needed for communication, has been identified. Your own ability to use words, however, depends on your native architecture, cognitive development, and environmental influences. Language is one of our species' most important abilities (Kepp, 2000).

A word is a symbol; it stands for the object or concept it names. For us to understand one another, we must agree on what the particular word symbol stands for—in both its denotative and its connotative meanings.

Language is directly linked to your perception of reality and to your thought processes. Your perceptions and your thought processes begin in earliest childhood. Each person creates meanings for words as ideas, feelings, and activities change. Because meanings are determined by each person, it is important for the speaker to present ideas as clearly as possible while the listener tries to understand.

For language to be successful, it must be appropriate to the language environment. The language you should use in a particular environment is often determined by the role you are playing in that environment. Certain language rituals, conventionalized responses, are predetermined for you by the values of your society. You learn these and other forms of appropriate language during your childhood. When you become an adult and enter the work world, you often must learn a specialized language used by your occupational or professional group.

Style, the way you express yourself, is an important aspect of language. The style that is expected of you is often determined by the roles you play. If you do not modify your language to fit your role, you may speak in ways that are inappropriate for the occasion.

Your gender might determine the language style you use. Men are more likely to use report-talk, a language that maintains their status, demonstrates their knowledge and skills, and keeps them at the center of attention. In contrast, women are more likely to use rapport-talk, a language that leads to intimacy with others, establishes relationships, and compares experiences. Some scholars think, however, that looking for language differences between men and women may reinforce gender stereotypes.

If you belong to an ethnic group, you may use a dialect—the habitual language of your community. The advantage of dialect is that it helps a person fit into an ethnic community; the disadvantage is that it might not have prestige in a community where standard English is spoken.

Speaking and writing differ in that oral communication is more transactional. In oral communication, people interact continuously and simultaneously, and their conversation reflects their past knowledge of each other.

When you work on your communication, you have to decide what you want to say and how you want to say it. In choosing how you wish to communicate, you should aim for clarity, vividness, powerful talk, and ethical choices. Then you should ask to whom you are speaking and what metamessages—the meaning apart from the actual words—you are sending.

Questions to Review

1. What is the importance of the FOXP2 gene, and how did it contribute to the development of language in humans?

2. What do you mean when you say that a word is a symbol?

3. What is the difference between denotative meaning and connotative meaning?

4. Using a personal example, how does language define your world and your perception of it?

5. What are the four elements that make up a language environment?

6. Using an example of each, what is the definition of *euphemism* and *doublespeak?*

7. What do you mean when you talk about verbal style?

8. What is the difference between report-talk and rapport-talk, and who uses each?

9. How does gender affect learning in the classroom?

10. What is dialect, and what does it have to do with one's cultural background?

11. How do speaking and writing differ?

12. What is paralanguage, and how does it influence meaning?

13. What is powerful talk? When people use it, what kind of impression do they make?

14. What are some of the moral choices you should make in choosing the words you use?

15. What are metamessages, and how do they change meaning?

mhhe.com/hybels Go to the self-quizzes on the Communicating Effectively CD-ROM (side 2, track 10) and the Online Learning Center at mhhe.com/ hybels7 to test your knowledge of the chapter concepts.

References

Bennet, J. (1995, March 29). "A charm school for car salesmen." *New York Times,* pp. D1, D8.

(No author) (2001). "Birth of a language." Evolution Library, WGBH Educational Foundation and Clear Blue Sky Productions, Inc., PBS (Public Broadcasting Service). Retrieved March 14, 2003, from http://www.pbs.org/wgbh/evolution/library/07/2/1 072 04.html.

Boone, M. E. (2001). *Managing inter@ctively: Executing business strategy, improving communication, and creating a knowledge-sharing culture.* New York: McGraw-Hill.

Carstairs-McCarthy, A. "LING 408: Origins and evolution of language." Retrieved March 14, 2003, from http://www.ling.cantergury.ac.nz/408.html.

Cotrell, H. W. (2001). "Spice up that family history." Retrieved December 2, 2001, from e-mail.

Crosby, F., & L. Nyquist (1977). "The female register: An empirical study of Lakoff's hypothesis." *Language in Society* 6: 314.

(No author) (2002, April 2). "Egg mystery boils down to physics: Mathematicians unravel gyroscope effect." *The Blade* (Toledo, OH), 3A.

Friend, T. (2002, August 15). "Lone gene linked to language skills" (Science & Education). *USA Today,* p. 7D. Goffman, E. (1971). *Relations in public.* New York: Basic Books.

Greif, E. B., & J. B. Gleason (1980). "Hi, thanks, and goodbye: More routine information." *Language in Society* 9:159–66.

Griffin, E. (2000). *A first look at communication theory,* 4th ed. New York: McGraw-Hill.

Haleta, L. L. (1996, January). "Student perceptions of teachers' use of language on impression formation and uncertainty." *Communication Education* 45: 20–27.

Hummel, S. (1999, January 25). "Do you speak Bostonian?" *U.S. News and World Report,* 56–57.

Johnson, C. E. (1987, April). "An introduction to powerful talk and powerless talk in the classroom." *Communication Education* 36: 167–72.

King, S. (2000). *On writing: A memoir of the craft.* New York: Scribner.

Kopp, B. (2000, June 1). "Chimpanzee communications and the evolution of human language." University of Chicago. Retrieved March 14, 2003, from http://geosci.uchicago.edu/~rekopp/writings/chimps.html.

(No author). "Language." Retrieved March 14, 2003, from http://www.criticalthinking.org/K12/k12class/4–6/language.html.

(No author). "Let's talk about it: Fostering the development of language skills and emergent literacy." The Whole Child, For Early Care Providers, (PBS) Public Broadcasting Service. Retrieved March 14, 2003, from http://www.pbs.org/wholechild/providers/talk.html.

(No author). "Library of excerpts: Language, neoteny, heterochrony, and human evolution." Retrieved March 14, 2003, from http://www.humanevolution.net/a/language.html.

Mulac, A., J. M. Wiemenn, S. J. Widenmann, & T. W. Gibson, (1988). "Male/female language differences and effects in same-sex and mixed-sex dyads: The gender-linked language effect." *Communication Monographs* 55: 316–32.

(No author). (2002, August 15). "Mutations eons ago may be key to human speech." *The Blade* (Toledo, Ohio), AIO. (Original source: *New York Times*.)

Pawlowski, C. (2000). *Glued to the tube: The threat of television addiction to today's family*. Naperville, IL: Sourcebooks, Inc.

Penn, C. R. (1990, December 1). "A choice of words is a choice of words." *Vital Speeches of the Day*, 116.

Postman, N. (1977). *Crazy talk: Stupid talk*. New York: Delta Books.

Postman, N. (1992). *Technopoly: The surrender of culture to technology*. New York: Vintage Books.

Ratey, J. J. (2001). *A user's guide to the brain: Perception, attention, and the four theaters of the brain*. New York: Pantheon Books (A Division of Random House, Inc.).

(No author) (1998). "Roper Starch: How Americans communicate." Retrieved March 14, 2003, from www.natcom.org/research/Roper.

Rosen, E. (2000). *The anatomy of buzz: How to create word of mouth marketing*. New York: Doubleday.

Sapphire, R. L. (1996) *Push*. New York: Knopf.

Shaywitz, B. A. (1995, February 16). "Sex differences in the functional organization of the brain for language." *Nature* 373: 607–8.

Sommers, C. H. (2000). *The war against boys: How misguided feminism is harming our young men*. New York: Simon & Schuster.

Stanbeck, M. H., & W. B. Pearce, (1981). "Talking to the man: Some communication strategies used by members of 'subordinate' social groups." *Quarterly Journal of Speech* 67: 24–25.

(No author) (1998). "A tangled web of words." *Atlanta Constitution*. Retrieved April 27, 1998, from www.lexis~nexis.com.

Tannen, D. (1992, February). "How men and women use language differently in their lives and in the classroom." *Education Digest* 57: 3–6.

Tannen, D. (1990). *You just don't understand*. New York: Morrow.

Tanno, D. V. (2000). Jewish and/or woman: Identity and communicative style. In Gonzalez, A., M. Houston, & V. Chen, eds. *Our voices: Essays in culture, ethnicity, and communication*. Los Angeles, CA: Roxbury Publishing Co., 31–36.

Turner, L. H. (1992). "An analysis of words coined by women and men: Reflections on the muted group theory and Gilligan's model." *Women and Language* 15: 21–27.

Wallraff, B. (2000). *Word court: Wherein verbal virtue is rewarded, crimes against the language are punished, and poetic justice is done*. New York: Harcourt, Inc.

Weatherall, A. (1998). "Re-visioning gender and language research." *Women and Language* 21:1, 1.

Further Reading

Baron, N. S. (2000). *Alphabet to e-mail: How written English evolved and where it's heading*. London, UK: Routledge. Baron examines the effect of technological change on language to see if historical patterns repeat themselves in the virtual world. This is not a book for academics. In her glib style, she explains linguistic concepts and gives a dynamic picture of the changes that have occurred as formal written English has evolved toward spoken language patterns. This is a well-reasoned, highly credible, enjoyably informative book for those interested in language, communication, or the social effects of the Internet. She includes a lengthy bibliography as well.

Corballis, M. C. (2002). *From hand to mouth: The origins of language.* Princeton, NJ: Princeton University Press. Corballis's theory is that language evolved from manual and facial gestures. Using evidence from anthropology, animal behavior, neurology, molecular biology, anatomy, linguistics, and evolutionary psychology, he makes the case that language developed to supplant gestures. This is a lively, well-constructed read for those interested in how humans became the extraordinary creatures they are.

Gonzalez, A., M. Houston, & V. Chen, (2000). *Our voices: Essays in culture, ethnicity, and communication,* 3rd ed. Los Angeles, CA: Roxbury Publishing Company. The theoretical view that guides this edition, as previous editions, is "that race, culture, gender, class, and ethnicity are not 'external' variables but rather inherent features in an ongoing process of constructing how collectively we understand and participate in the larger social, cultural, and political discourse" (p. xiv). Collectively, the essays here "explore the rich variety of communication practices within a broad cultural spectrum" (p. xvi).

Levy, D. M. (2001). *Scrolling forward: Making sense of documents in the digital age.* New York: Arcade Publishing. This is a fascinating examination of written forms from grocery-store receipts and greeting cards to identity papers and e-mail messages. Levy examines the continuing transition from print to digital and what this means at both practical and symbolic levels. This is a book that you can read thoroughly and about which you can think deeply.

Mindell, P. (2001). *How to say it for women: Communicating with confidence and power using the language of success.* Englewood Cliffs, NJ: Prentice-Hall Press. Mindell, an expert on professional communication, shows women how to transform themselves by transforming their language. Empowerment, according to Mindell, comes through shedding weak words, phrases, and gestures and choosing the right word or sentence as well as speaking, reading, writing, leading, dressing, and interviewing effectively. She has packed this book with practical tips, techniques, and examples. This is a commonsense approach to successful business communication.

(No author, no date). "Owl handouts indexed by topic." Writing Laboratory, Purdue University. Retrieved March 14, 2003, from http://www.owl.english.purdue.edu/writers/by-topic.html. At this website there are hundreds of links to writing resources of all kinds grouped under such topics as writing, punctuation, professional writing, spelling, sentence construction, parts of speech, writing in the job search, English as a second language (ESL), and research papers. This is an excellent resource for anyone interested in improving his or her use of language.

Roman, K., & J. Raphaelson, (2000). *Writing that works,* 3rd ed. New York: Harper Resource. Roman and Raphaelson offer numerous practical tips for helping your written and oral communication. This is a guide to effective business writing and to written business etiquette. The guidance with reference to computers and e-mail communications is especially useful. This book is the antidote to interminable memos, pointless presentations, and endless e-mail messages.

Tannen, D. (2001). *Talking from 9 to 5: Women and men in the workplace: Language, sex, and power,* Reprint edition. London, UK: Quill. This is the third, after *That's Not What I Meant: How Conversational Style Makes or Breaks Your Relations with Others* (1986) and *You Just Don't Understand: Women and Men in Conversation* (1990), in this series of investigations into what we say and how we say it. In this book, Tannen focuses on informal and formal conversations in the workplace, especially gender differences in conversational style, although age, class, ethnic, and geographical distinctions are also discussed. The book is designed to assist women in the workplace in becoming confident and competent.

Wallraff, B. (2001). *Word court: Wherein verbal virtue is rewarded, crimes against the language are punished, and poetic justice is done.* New York: Harcourt, Inc. Although this is a collection of some of the pieces from Wallraff's column in *The Atlantic Monthly,* where the senior editor at the magazine settles disputes about words and the ways in which we use them, if you are a speaker or writer today, this is an important book. Here, she deals with newly coined vocabulary, grammar, slang, jargon, misused words, clarity of phrasing, tone, punctuation, pronunciation, and much, much more. Her concern is as much for the written as it is for the spoken word, and that is precisely what makes this warm, witty, and wise book invaluable for speakers. This is a 368-page book that can as easily be read for pleasure as for advice.

(No Author). "Writing resources." Allan K. Smith Center for Writing & Rhetoric, Trinity College. Retrieved March 14, 2003, from www.trincoll.edu/depts/writcent/writ.html. This is a website of links to writers' desk references, documentation and citation guides, and other aids and references. On the home page are links to research tools, teaching resources, and more, such as 10 writing online centers; rhetoric, writing, and language websites; and miscellaneous sites. A useful resource.

Chapter 6

Nonverbal Communication

Objectives

After reading this chapter, you should be able to:

- Frame a clear definition of nonverbal communication and provide examples to reveal its use.
- Explain why it's important to study nonverbal communication.
- Clarify the relationship of nonverbal communication to the model of communication and to communication as a transaction.
- Point out differences between verbal and nonverbal communication.
- List various functions of nonverbal communication.
- Explain the characteristics of or the basic principles that govern nonverbal communication.
- Describe and provide an example of each of the various types of nonverbal communication.
- Explain some of the ways you have for becoming more aware of and improving your own use of nonverbal communication.

Key Terms and Concepts

Use the Communicating Effectively CD-ROM and Online Learning Center at mhhe.com/hybels7 to further your understanding of the following terms.

Adaptors 182	Feng shui 173	Proxemics 189
Attractiveness 184	Illustrators 181	Public distance 192
Body adornment 188	Intimate distance 190	Quality (of voice) 180
Body movement (kinesics) 181	Leisure clothing 188	Rate (of speech) 180
	Mixed message 177	Regulators 181
Chronemics 195	Nonelective characteristics 185	Social distance 191
Control 171		Space and distance 192
Convergence 180	Nonverbal communication 170	Territory 189
Costumes 188		Touch 193
Displays of feelings 182	Occupational dress 188	Uniforms 187
Elective characteristics 185	Paralanguage 179	Vocal fillers 181
	Personal distance 191	Volume (of vocal sound) 180
Emblems 181	Pitch 180	
Eye messages 183		

SHANNON MCVICKER COULD NOT CONTAIN HER EXCITEMENT; it showed in her pace, in her warm, self-contained smile, in the sparkle in her eyes, and in the way she held herself. The newly acquired ring on her finger from her now-fiancé, friend for two years, Austin, might explain part of her enthusiasm. The firm handshake she received the day before from Amy Goodbody, the top campus recruiter for The Star Group, a popular, sought-after, and successful advertising firm, that had given her every assurance that the job she had so aggressively researched and sought was hers, could have been part of the motivation as well. Probably the best explanation, however, was moving the tassel on her mortarboard cap from one side to the other, announcing to the world that she had changed her status from student to graduate.

Interesting isn't it? McVicker did not have to say a word, and yet anyone who knew her well would have detected her feelings. Anyone who knew her might have spotted the newly acquired ring on her finger. And anyone who knows what it means to move the tassel would have understood the change from student to graduate and what that might mean to students and to their identity. These are all fairly common nonverbal actions, and, too, they are all actions that convey specific feelings and ideas—at least to most people in our society and culture.

Something else has occurred, however, because of a single nonverbal cue given in the example. From one nonverbal cue, you can—using your imagination, of course—answer a number of related questions: What was the context, setting, or occasion for this example? Who are likely to be the people with McVicker? How many people are likely to be involved in this event? Are any members of McVicker's family with her today? Is this a happy or a sad time? Will there be any speeches given at this occasion? What was McVicker doing this morning? What is she likely to be doing tonight? Will her evening activities involve the use of alcohol? Why or why not? What will likely be the setting where McVicker will be tonight? Think of all the additional questions you could probably answer about McVicker, because you know she moved the tassel on her mortarboard cap from one side to the other, signifying her college graduation.

Nonverbal communication is information that is communicated without using words. Much of it—like the pace, self-contained smile, sparkle in the eyes, and posture in the McVicker example—is unintentional. People may not even be aware they are sending some nonverbal messages. On the other hand, the ring, firm handshake, and tassel move are, indeed, intentional and specifically designed to convey meanings.

■ WHY STUDY NONVERBAL COMMUNICATION?

As much as 93 percent of communication is nonverbal (Mehrabian, 1981, pp. 76–77), with 55 percent sent through facial expressions, posture, and gestures and 38 percent through tone of voice (Brody, 1992, C12). With so much of communication being nonverbal, it is essential that you understand how it works and how you can learn to communicate better when you use it. This chapter examines how nonverbal communication is an essential part of every message you send.

Nonverbal Communication and Our Model of Communication

In relating nonverbal communication to the model of communication we presented in Chapter 1, The Communication Process, and to communication as a transaction, we will also show how verbal and nonverbal communications differ. We'll look at the model elements of sender-receiver, message-feedback, noise, channel, and setting. Then we'll examine the relationship of nonverbal communication to communication as a transaction.

Sender-Receiver

Many of the differences between verbal and nonverbal communication result from sender-receiver characteristics. For example, the formal rules for verbal communication, such as grammar, are taught in a structured, formal environment, such as a school. You are also taught what style is appropriate for particular situations—that formal English is required for essays, whereas informal English is more suitable for speech. The better you are at acquiring these formal rules, especially when they are reinforced at home or reinforced through increased education, the more likely your verbal communication will be better.

In contrast, much nonverbal communication is not formally taught; you pick it up by imitating others. Young children commonly imitate the nonverbal communication of their parents, siblings, and peers.

Another clear difference between verbal and nonverbal communication within the element of senders and receivers is control. **Control** means having a governing influence. You do not always have control over your nonverbal communication. The area where you have the least control is your emotional responses. When you are happy, surprised, hurt, or angry, most of your nonverbal signals are spontaneous, arising out of the occasion or setting. This differs from verbal communication, where you can choose your words—you have control over them.

Message-Feedback

Unlike verbal communication, which begins and ends with words, nonverbal messages are continuous. For example, you are talking to a person you have recently met but with whom you think you would like to have further contact. While you are speaking the words, you notice the other person giving you her undivided attention when speaking by looking you in the eye and not diverting her attention. You notice the other person's manner of dress, the way she carries her book bag, and her overall comfortable, relaxed style. You notice, too, how she responds to what you are saying by nodding her head, smiling, and turning slightly more toward you—all signs of positive reinforcement and agreement. As you watch all this nonverbal communication, you think, "Nice person."

As well as reacting verbally to others, you give a lot of nonverbal feedback as shown in the example above. The other person showed she was interested in what you were saying by smiling, nodding her head, and turning slightly toward you. It isn't just positive reinforcement, it is feedback. She could have revealed a lack of interest by fidgeting, looking at her watch, giving you no eye contact, or using facial signs of apathy. Much of a person's emotional response is expressed by facial expression and body positioning.

Noise

Since noise is simply any interference that keeps messages from being understood, and since they can be external, internal, and/or semantic, you can see how much noise is likely to be nonverbal. You're standing talking to this person, above, with whom you would like to have further contact, and another person walks by and accidentally sideswipes you, or waves, or makes an intrusive sound. All of these are nonverbal, external stimuli. Examples of internal noise, in the same on-campus situation, could be such things as your being emotionally distraught from coming out of an exam you thought was unfair and on which you know you did horribly, the feelings you are now experiencing for the person with whom you are talking, or the feelings you have because tomorrow begins your weekend, and you have big plans. Semantic noise can also be nonverbal. For example, what if the other person, in the same example, aroused emotional reactions in you because of poor grammar, racist remarks, or the use of profanity?

Channel

Verbal communication, in general, uses one route—sound—to reach the sender-receivers. Nonverbal communication can use this route, sound, but often uses many more than one channel. In the example of standing on campus talking with a person with whom you would like to have further contact, look first at the nonverbal channels you have noticed to make this judgment (that you would like further contact): You might have noticed that when you met, the other person reached out and gently touched your shoulder or, you could have shaken hands or hugged (touch), or, you might have noticed her good taste in clothing (sight), her fragrance (smell), and her relaxed, comforting voice (sound). Each of these—touch, sight, smell, and sound—are channels used to communicate nonverbal messages.

In verbal communication, much of your information is conveyed through words. Nonverbal communication, however, uses the senses. Because so much nonverbal communication occurs unconsciously, it follows no planned sequence. Unlike verbal communication, which has a grammar that determines how you build your sentences, nonverbal communication lacks formal structure and uses numerous channels at the same time. Standing talking to someone, you don't plan to look away toward a passing student, reach down to pick up a dropped set of keys, or look at the other person. These nonverbal actions occur in response to what happens during the conversation. The only rules that govern nonverbal communication are those that determine whether a behavior is appropriate or permissible. When you learned manners, you were being taught appropriate behavior for public places.

Setting

In contrast to much verbal communication, nonverbal communication can take place when you aren't around for people to get an impression of you directly. For example, the rooms you live in tell a good deal about you. The pictures of family members show the important people in your life; the stack of CDs and DVDs give away both your musical and film tastes; and the posters on your wall show whether you prefer art, music, or sports. In **Feng Shui** (pronounced *fung shway*), "The ancient Chinese art of improving every aspect of your life by enhancing your environment according to the principles of harmony and energy flow" (Kennedy, 2001, p. 41), the relationship between you and your living environment is of primary significance; thus the Feng Shui saying, "Your house is you" (p. 41). The saying is a symbolic way of conveying that your house (its structure, shape, condition, and so on) represents and reflects you, your body, your mind, and your spirit—the very state of your psyche and your life (Kennedy, 2001, p. 41).

Another Point of View

There is no question about the importance of nonverbal communication in our interactions with others, but here, from an excerpt in the book, *What Your Face Reveals,* Henry B. Lin indicates its importance in the Chinese culture:

Face reading provides us [the Chinese] with a very convenient and powerful tool to reveal the secrets of the fortune and personality of ourselves and others whom we may not even know. As the world becomes more and more integrated, and contact with others becomes increasingly frequent and important, the art of face divination (or, decoding the secrets of fortune. "Chinese divination uses tools to induce supernatural forces to reveal the secrets in the course of human affairs and that of nature.") can be of tremendous help in your decision making and interpersonal skills regarding hiring and promotion, making friends, establishing relationships, finding a spouse, or selecting business partners.

Questions

1. When you learn that the Chinese also use other methods of divination, including astrology, palmistry, and numerology, does this help you better understand or provide a more inclusive context for face reading?

2. Knowing what is revealed in the excerpt above, and knowing that face reading is a profound art in the truest sense of the word, taking years of experience to master, does it strike you as something you would want to pursue?

3. If you understand the importance of nonverbal communication—specifically face reading—in the Chinese culture, why do you suppose it has never become as important in American culture? What do you think would be the constraints or restrictions for it remaining, primarily, a Chinese phenomena?

Source: H. B. Lin, *What Your Face Reveals: Chinese Secrets of Face Reading.* (St. Paul, MN: Llewellyn Publications [a division of Llewellyn Worldwide, Ltd.], 1998), p. xvii.

The settings you choose can also tell something about you. You are talking to this other person on campus, as in the example on pages 171–172, and you decide to take a chance and invite her to dinner. You give one message if you take her to a restaurant with plush seating, indirect lighting, and a French menu. You give quite another message if you take her to a place with plastic chairs, fluorescent lighting, and a menu posted on the wall. In addition to telling something about yourself, your choice of restaurants will tell something about how you feel about your relationship with this new-found friend.

Nonverbal Communication as a Transaction

The transactional nature of communication is very evident in nonverbal communication. Participation is continuous and simultaneous. Without saying a word, you could be communicating by your choice of clothing, your facial expressions, your posture, or any number of nonverbal signals. In just the simple act of walking across campus, you are giving signals to and getting signals from people passing you whom you might not even know. You think, "Nice coat—wonder where he got it?" "She's in my dorm—I'd like to know her better," "Wow! He's hot!" As these people see you, they may be making similar assessments of you.

When you attend a class for the first time, some of the judgments you make of the instructor are based on her nonverbal behavior. Remember, though, all communications have a past, present, and future. She hands out the syllabus and then discusses some of the assignments for the class. As you listen to her, you think, "She sounds tough. I'd better get my work in on time." In making these assessments, you are comparing her with past instructors who may have looked and acted the way she does. You are also predicting what you will have to do to get a good grade. At the same time, she may be assessing you—judging you by your posture and clothes, thinking about past students you may resemble, looking to see where you sit, and predicting whether you'll be a good student.

Information about roles is communicated nonverbally as much as it is verbally. When you visit your instructors in their offices, you will probably wait to be asked to sit down. If you're smart, you won't plop your book bag on anyone's desk since that would be a violation of someone else's territory.

■ FUNCTIONS OF NONVERBAL COMMUNICATION

Nonverbal communication has four functions. Nonverbal cues *complement* a verbal message by adding to its meaning. When you are talking to someone with a problem, for example, you might say, "I'm really sorry," and complement the message with a pat on the shoulder or a hug.

Nonverbal cues also *regulate* verbal communication. How would your boss or one of your teachers tell you that it's time for a conversation to end? He or she might do something obvious, like getting out of the chair, or something more subtle, like arranging papers on the desk, in order to communicate to you that the conversation is over.

Consider This

Examine the importance of being able to read nonverbal messages in this excerpt from LaDonna Harris's book, *LaDonna Harris: A Comanche Life*. Harris, a Native-American from the cultural group known as the Comanche Indians, is the wife of Oklahoma Senator Fred Harris:

He was verbal and I was still the stoic Indian, calling on all the things that helped me get through school and protect myself. (This refers to her protection against prejudice and verbal abuse within the public-school system.) Because I had always avoided anything that might be hurtful, I used all my senses in knowing how to read people's body language. Fred depended on my interpretation of behavior and especially liked me to go to any of his committee hearings and react to them. He was in one position to hear something *and I, as part of the audience, was in another position . . . .*

This was the relationship we built up through the years. He relied on my evaluation of people and always wanted to know what I thought and what my observation was . . . .

. . .We were such kids ourselves and were just thrown into this political situation, but our partnership was one of the best things in our relationship. I depended on him to be our voice. He was so articulate. Because I didn't speak, my senses were much more attuned to what was going on. When you have the ability to speak, you lose some of those senses.

Source: From L. Harris, *LaDonna Harris: A Commanche Life* (Lincoln, NE: University of Nebraska Press, 2000).

Nonverbal messages can also *substitute* for verbal messages. Your instructor looks up, looks specifically at a couple of class members who are talking, then waits a couple of seconds until everyone is quiet before she begins to speak. Her look says, "All right, everyone be quiet now, it's time to begin." Your roommates wave at you as you look back down the hallway and head out for an important engagement. Your best friend has balloons delivered to your room on your birthday. All these nonverbal messages substitute for verbal ones.

Often, nonverbal messages *accent* what you are saying. The instructor's voice is strong and firm when she tells the class she will accept no late papers; the teenager leans forward while she is trying to persuade her parents that she needs a new dress; a man communicates to his family, by his posture, that he is feeling energetic and ready for the family outing. Whenever people are communicating something they consider important, they often accent it with a nonverbal message.

■ CHARACTERISTICS OF NONVERBAL COMMUNICATION

All forms of nonverbal communication have four characteristics in common. First, much nonverbal communication is unique to the culture or subculture to which you belong. Second, verbal and nonverbal messages may be in conflict with one another. Third, much nonverbal communication operates at a subconscious level—you are often not aware of it. Fourth, your nonverbal communication shows your feelings and attitudes. These characteristics are considered basic principles that govern nonverbal communication.

Nonverbal Communication Is Culturally Determined

Much of your nonverbal behavior is learned in childhood, passed on to you by your parents and others with whom you associate. Through the process of growing up in a particular society, you adopt the traits and mannerisms of your cultural group. When meeting people for the first time, Americans put a high value on eye contact and usually limit their touch to firm handshakes. Arabs do not mind noise and interference during conversations. People from the Micronesian islands in the Pacific neither speak nor touch when they pass each other; instead, they greet each other by raising their eyebrows or giving a nod.

What happens when people from different cultural groups share a common space? Dr. Elizabeth Lozano, a teacher in the Department of Communication at Loyola University, offers one explanation for when its Latin- and Anglo-Americans share a common space. She says that in addition to language acquisition, survival in this new cultural setting requires "an ability to perform according to the local rules of public interaction and to recognize patterns and rituals in daily encounters with others" (Lozano, 2000, p. 233). But, she says, the adaptation required never involves the substitution of one cultural style for another. Rather, it involves the interpretation and integration of styles and, as a result, each acquires new features. "Another style, a cultural, bilingual language, emerges from those who cannot consider themselves as Latin-Americans any longer but are now Hispanic-Americans: Hispanic citizens of the United States" (p. 233).

In most cultures, the nonverbal behavior of males differs from that of females. In American culture, for example, there is a good deal of difference in the way men and women position their bodies. As Deborah Tannen observed after watching videotapes of communication between males and females of different ages, girls and women sit closer together than do boys and men and look directly into each other's faces. Boys and men, on the other hand, sit at angles to each other and hardly ever look at one another directly (Tannen, 1990, p. 246). She finds that men usually sit in a relaxed, sprawled-out way whether they are with groups of men or in mixed groups. In contrast, women sit in ladylike poses when they are in mixed groups but sprawl out and relax when they are in all-female groups (pp. 235–36).

Nonverbal Messages May Conflict with Verbal Messages

View "Nonverbal Messages," clip #4, on the CD.

Nonverbal communication is so deeply rooted, so unconscious, that you can express a verbal message and then directly contradict it with a nonverbal message. Sometimes, of course, the contradiction can occur simultaneously. For example, this is one way experts have of detecting lies. Lie detection has become incredibly sophisticated. Terrence Sejinowski, of the Salk Institute for Biological Studies in La Jolla, California, has developed a computer program that can detect lies by analyzing fleeting facial expressions (Boyce, 2001, p. 42). The computer is trained to analyze in real time the almost imperceptible expressions like eyelid flutters and strained smiles—the same expressions it used to take Paul Ekman, a psychologist at the University of California-San Francisco, and his team of researchers hours to catalog. It took experts like Ekman an hour to catalog all the microexpressions on one minute of videotape. With the new computer program, people can be screened for lying without them even knowing it (Boyce, 2001, p. 42).

Another example is meeting a fellow who is all smiles, handshakes, and concern about your business and health. Although his words say one thing, in numerous other ways the fellow communicates a profound lack of sincerity. His body language and attitude tell you that he's on the prowl for personal benefits (Ross & Ross, 2000, p. 134).

Getting messages like this can be confusing. You have received a **mixed message**—a message in which the verbal and the nonverbal contradict each other. In the above incident, the fellow tells you one thing ("I'm personally interested in you and your health"), but his nonverbal behavior communicates something else ("I'm personally interested in how much money I can make from you").

In mixed messages, the nonverbal communication is often more reliable than the verbal content. You can learn to manipulate words, but you might find it difficult to manipulate your nonverbal communication. The fellow probably was not aware of the negative nonverbal message he was giving. The message, however, was coming through loud and clear.

Nonverbal Messages Are Largely Unconscious

You wake up feeling that you might be getting a cold. It's not yet bad enough to stay home, so you go to classes. The minute one of your classmates sees you, she says, "You look like you aren't feeling very well." She is reading this information nonverbally. She can tell from your posture that you're not feeling well, or maybe she can hear it in your voice or see it on your face. She is making a nonverbal assessment: You don't have to say a word for her to know how you're feeling.

Often you don't recognize your own nonverbal behavior. For example, you probably stand farther away from people you don't like than from people you like. Your body position, such as crossed arms, might show that you are resisting what is being said. You use your head and eye movements to begin and end conversations with others. When you consider the amount and ordinariness of your nonverbal behavior, it is hardly surprising that you are unaware of much of it.

If you doubt the unconscious nature of nonverbal messages, look at Table 6-1. How much of this nonverbal behavior are you aware of?

Nonverbal Communication Shows Your Feelings and Attitudes

Facial expressions, gestures, body movements, the way you use your eyes—all communicate your feelings and emotions to others. The feelings and emotions others can detect in your face include happiness, sadness, surprise, fear, anger, interest, contempt, shame, shyness, and guilt (Ekman & Friesen, 1975; Izard, 1977). In one of her columns, Ellen Goodman (2002) discussed Botox, the microbe created by the U.S. Army to inflict botulism

Table 6-1

Nonverbal Cues That Indicate a Woman's Interest in Dating

Cue	High Interest	Moderate Interest	Low Interest
Eye contact	Looks at him constantly	Looks at him half the time	Looks at him very little
Smiling	Smiles almost constantly	Smiles half the time	Does not smile
Lean	Leans toward	Sits straight up	Leans backward
Shoulder orientation	Faces directly (shoulders parallel)	Partially faces (shoulders at 45-degree angle)	Faces away (shoulders at 90-degree angle)
Distance	18 inches	4 feet	7 feet
Touching	Brief touch above the knee	Brief touch on forearm	No touch
Catches his eye (while hearing joke)	Laughs and catches eye	Laughs, does not catch eye	Does not laugh or catch eye
Attentiveness	Stops what she is doing and looks at him	Looks away while listening, toward while talking	Glances at beginning, but then looks away
Attentiveness (looking at other people)	Does not look at other people	Looks at other women	Looks at other men
Avoids public grooming	Does not groom	Mild grooming	Excessive grooming
Animated speech	Speaks quickly, accentuates, varied facial expressions	Average tone and movement	Slow monotone with little movement

Source: Charlene L. Muehlenhard et al., "Cues That Convey Interest in Dating," in Joseph A. DeVito and Michael L. Hecht, eds., *The Nonverbal Communication Reader* (Prospect Heights, IL: Waveland Press, 1990), p. 364.

poisoning on our enemies that is now being used for domestic and aesthetic purposes—specifically as a cosmetic for forehead injections to erase aging lines. Goodman writes: "This is the real symbolism of Botox. It eliminates lines temporarily by paralyzing muscles. It offers an actual trade-off. You trade the ability, literally, to express your emotions—furrow that brow, crinkle that eye—for a flawless appearance. In the search for approval from others, you hide what you are feeling. Especially anger" (p. 11A).

In addition to detecting feelings and emotions in your face—if Botox has not reduced some of that possibility—research shows that other people are as accurate, if not better, at detecting them through your vocal cues (Kappas, Hess, & Scherer, 1991; Planalp, 1998). As a matter of fact, researchers Planalp and her associates have shown that vocal cues are the most recognizable signs of emotions (Planalp, 1998; Planalp, DeFrancisco, & Rutherford, 1996).

Your body is also quite capable of expressing emotions. In her report on communicating emotion in everyday life, Planalp (1998) reports that people easily interpret a person's emotional state from cues such as "being physically energetic, bouncy, jumping up and down, clenching hands or fists, making threatening movements, holding the body rigidly, shuffling, or having a slumped, droopy posture, dancing around, and using hand emblems" (p. 34). If you wanted to demonstrate greater warmth and immediacy to another person, you might reveal a happy facial expression, enthusiastic gestures, closer interpersonal distances, and friendly touches (Andersen & Guerrero, 1998). You could easily conclude from the comments in this paragraph that it is often the face, gestures, body movements, and eyes in some combination of cues that communicate emotions. Certainly it doesn't require all these parts working together; any single part could do the job.

■ TYPES OF NONVERBAL COMMUNICATION

In this section, we will consider paralanguage, body movement, eye messages, attractiveness, clothing, body adornment, space and distance, touch, and time. The goal is to provide a brief introduction only to each of these elements.

Paralanguage

Verbal communication consists of the words you use to communicate; nonverbal communication has a **paralanguage**—the way in which you say the words. Paralanguage, or paralinguistic cues, exist beside language and interact with it. For example, a parent tells a child in a mild voice to clean up his room. When the room is still in the same condition two hours later, the parent says, "I thought I told you to clean up your room." This time the parent's voice communicates "If you don't do it soon, you're in big trouble," and the child, reading the sound of the voice, gets busy. "Don't talk to me in that tone of voice" is an example of paralanguage in parent-child interaction.

One of the fathers of nonverbal communication, Ray Birdwhistell (1970), shows how important paralanguage can be in its ability to modify everything that is said and by placing it into context:

> These cross-referencing signals [paralanguage] amplify, emphasize, or modify the formal constructions, and/or make statements about the context of the message situation. In the latter instance, they help to define the context of the interaction by identifying the actor or his audience, and furthermore, they usually convey information about the larger context in which the interaction takes place (p. 117).

An important aspect of paralanguage—and one noted in the quotation above when Birdwhistell says "by identifying the actor"—paralinguistic cues can create distinct impressions of you, the communicator. For example, what characterizes an attractive, influential voice? Researchers suggest that it is resonant and calm, less monotonous, lower-pitched (especially for males), less regionally accented, less nasal, less shrill, and more relaxed (Addington, 1968; Pearce, 1971; Zuckerman & Driver, 1989; Zuckerman, Hodgins, & Miyake, 1990).

Paralanguage includes such vocal characteristics as rate (speed of speaking), pitch (highness or lowness of tone), volume (loudness), and quality (pleasing or unpleasant sound). When any or all of these factors are added to words, they can modify meaning. Albert Mehrabian (1968; Mehrabian, 1981, pp. 42–47), a nonverbal guru, writer, and researcher in nonverbal communication, estimates that 39 percent of the meaning in communication is affected by vocal cues—not the words themselves but the way they are said. In languages other than English, this percentage may be even higher.

Rate

The **rate** (speed) at which one speaks can have an effect on the way a message is received (MacLachlan, 1979). Researchers have discovered that speaking rate has a major effect on first impressions. Faster speakers are seen as more competent, credible, and intelligent (Ray, 1986; Buller & Aune, 1988; Street & Brady, 1982). But, they are also seen as less honest and trustworthy than slower speakers (Burgoon, 1978).

Another aspect of rate is how one person will accommodate or adapt to another's rate. It's called **convergence.** Fast talkers slow down when interacting with slow talkers; slow talkers speed up when talking with fast talkers (Street & Giles, 1982). So what? People who converge to another's rate are seen as more attractive and persuasive (Buller & Aune, 1988).

Pitch

Pitch is the highness or lowness of the voice. Pitch can determine whether a voice sounds pleasant or unpleasant. Some people believe that high-pitched voices are not as pleasant as low-pitched voices. However, the same researchers who studied rate of speaking also found that speakers were judged more competent if they used a higher and varied pitch (Ray, 1986, p. 273). Lower pitches are more difficult to hear, and people who have low-pitched voices may be perceived as insecure or shy because they don't seem to speak up. Pitch can be changed, but it requires working with someone who has had professional training in voice modification.

Volume

The meaning of a message can also be affected by its **volume**—how loudly a person speaks. A loud voice is fine if it's appropriate to the speaker's purpose and is not used all the time. The same is true of a soft voice. Expert teachers know at what points to increase or decrease their volume when they want a class to be quiet.

Quality

The overall **quality** of a voice is made up of all the other vocal characteristics—tempo, resonance, rhythm, and articulation. Voice quality is important because researchers have found that people with attractive voices are seen as more youthful, more competent, and more honest. However, people with immature voices were seen as less competent and powerful but more honest and warm (Berry, 1992, pp. 41–54).

Vocal Fillers

A related aspect of paralanguage but not part of it is **vocal fillers**—the sounds you use to fill out your sentences or to cover up or fill pauses. Paralanguage involves the way you say the words; vocal fillers are what you use when you are searching for words. In real life you use many vocal fillers to let others know you are still speaking even though you may not know specifically what to say. They may be nonwords such as "uh," "um,"and "er," or they may be words and phrases such as "you know," "like," or "whatever," when used to fill a pause. Although the latter may be words, they are used in these instances as if they have no meaning.

Body Movement

Body movement, also called *kinesics,* comes "from the Greek word for 'movement' and refers to all forms of body movement, excluding physical contact with another's body" (Burgoon, Buller, & Woodall, 1996, p. 33). Ekman and Friesen (1969), researchers on nonverbal communication, divide body movement into five categories: emblems, illustrators, regulators, displays of feelings, and adaptors.

Emblems are body movements that directly translate into words. The extended thumb of a hitchhiker is an emblem that means "I want a ride." A circle made with the thumb and index finger can be translated into "OK." These emblems are known by most of the people in our society, and they are used to send a specific message. Emblems often cannot be carried from one culture to another. Shaking your head back and forth in southern India, for example, means "yes."

Emblems are often used when words are inappropriate. It would be impractical for a hitchhiker to stand on the side of the road and shout, "Please give me a ride!" Sometimes emblems can replace talk. You might cover your face with your hands if you are embarrassed, and you hold up your fingers to show how many of something you want. Subgroups in a society often use emblems that members of the group understand but whose meanings are intentionally kept from outsiders—the secret handshake of a fraternity is an example.

Illustrators accent, emphasize, or reinforce words. If someone asks how big your suitcase is, you will probably describe it with words and illustrate the dimensions with your hands. If someone is giving you directions, she will probably point down the road and gesture left or right at the appropriate times. Illustrators can help make communication more exact. If someone tells you he caught a huge fish, you will have an idea of how big the fish was by how far apart he holds his hands. He could tell you the size in inches, but you have an even better idea if he uses his hands as illustrators. Illustrators can go beyond gestures. When an instructor underlines something she has written on the blackboard, she is telling you that this point is particularly important. When a car salesperson slams the car door, you can hear how solid it sounds and assume the car is well built.

Regulators control the back-and-forth flow of speaking and listening. "They are the 'traffic cops' of conversation" (Burgoon, Buller, Woodall, 1996, p. 42). They are made up of hand gestures, shifts in posture, and other body movements that signal the beginning and end of interactions. At a very simple level, a teacher uses a regulator when she points to the person she wants to speak next. On a more subtle level, someone might turn away slightly when you are talking, perhaps indicating "I don't like what I'm hearing" or "I don't want to continue this conversation."

Displays of feelings show, through facial expressions and body movements, how intensely a person is feeling. If you walk into a professor's office and the professor says, "I can see you are really feeling upset," he or she is responding to nonverbal cues you are giving about your feelings. You could also come in with a body posture indicating "I'm really going to argue about this grade"—with your clenched hands or stiff body position showing that you are ready for a confrontation.

Adaptors are nonverbal ways of adjusting to a communication situation. They are behaviors that satisfy your physical or psychological needs. What do you do, for example, when you have to go to the bathroom, or when you need to manage your emotions? What do you do when you feel anxious, relaxed, crowded, or defensive? What do you do when you want to maintain interpersonal contact with another person? In general, adaptors are habits and are usually not intended to communicate (Burgoon, Buller, Woodall, 1996, p. 42). However, despite the intention not to communicate, often they convey a great deal of information.

Because people use such a wide variety of adaptors, and because they are so specific to each person's own needs and the individual communication situation, they are difficult to classify or even to describe generally. Let's look at how they work in some specific communication situations: You

Consider This

Tears could be classified as displays of feelings when they show how intensely people are feeling. They could be classified as adaptors when used to adjust to a communication situation, for example, the sudden, unexpected news that a close friend has died. There is no question that tears are a form of communication:

As a communication medium, tears are like very early radio: they grab everyone's attention, and sometimes the signals can be picked up quite clearly, but they are at best diffuse in their broadcast and spotty in their reception.

And like any language, they can be used to persuade or evade, to clarify or obscure, to reveal or disguise the self and its motives. They can be used, like any language, in the full gamut of human projects, from the sublime to the ridiculous.

Questions

1. Could tears also be considered emblems, illustrators, or regulators? Why or why not?

2. Could you cite examples from your personal experience where tears have been used to evade? Examples where tears have been used to clarify? To obscure? To reveal the self and its motives? To disguise the self and its motives?

3. Would tears be classified as eye messages? Why or why not?

4. What rules (or restrictions) govern the use of tears in your society?

Source: P. T. Reardon, "The Crying Game: What Goes On behind Those Tears? *The Blade*, February 16, 2000, pp. 36–37. Reardon is quoting T. Lutz, *Crying: The Natural and Cultural History of Tears* (New York: W. W. Norton, 2001). Tom Lutz is an English professor at the University of Iowa.

have rented your first apartment, and your mother has come to visit. While she is there, she spends a great deal of time moving objects and furniture around. By moving things around, she is using adaptors. What does her nonverbal behavior mean? On a simple level, she might be telling you that you are not very tidy. On a more complicated level, she might be telling you that you are still her child and that she, your mother, is still in charge.

People often use adaptors when they are nervous or uncomfortable in a situation. You might play with jewelry, drum on the table, or move around a lot in your seat. Each of these behaviors is an adaptor—a way of helping you cope with the situation. We all use adaptors, but we are generally not aware of them unless someone points them out.

Eye Messages

Eye messages include all information conveyed by the eyes alone. The most important aspect of eye messages is eye contact, and in American culture, meeting another's eyes is a sign of honesty and credibility as well as warmth and involvement. In many cultures, conversing without eye contact can be considered rude, indicate disinterest, show inattention, or reveal shyness or deception (Andersen, 1998, p. 40).

Based on eye messages alone, think about all the personal qualities you attribute to other people: "Evil eyes," "bedroom eyes," "shifty eyes," "sad eyes," and "all eyes." When living in Hawaii, our family members learned that prolonged eye contact with an Hawaiian, known as "stink eye," was an invitation to fight. In our culture it is called "giving someone the eye." But, just as "giving someone the eye" may have negative connotations, it can be perceived positively when it is used to signify, "I'm interested," or, "I like what I see." When you agree with others, you "see eye-to-eye," when you think another should be condemned to death for the murder of another, you "take an eye for an eye," and when you take a drink of liquor early in the morning, it's known as an "eye-opener."

When you think about the functions that eye messages can perform, you quickly realize their importance. Eye messages provide turn-taking signals in conversations that regulate interactions. By receiving numerous messages from the other person, eye messages are used to monitor interactions. They signal attentiveness, express involvement, show immediacy, and offer connection to others. By using prolonged stares, especially along with negative facial expressions, they can be intimidating. But one of their most delightful and wondrous aspects is their role in flirtation (Kendon, 1967; Exline, Ellyson, & Long, 1975; Fehr & Exline, 1987; Andersen, 1985; and Silver & Spitzberg, 1992). The first rule of a successful flirt is to make eye contact ("Successful flirts . . . ," 2002, p. 4E).

Although eye messages have received but marginal attention by intercultural scholars (Gudykunst & Kim, 1997; Jensen, 1985; Samovar, Porter, & Jain, 1981), an African proverb says, "The eye is an instrument of aggression" (Richmond & Gestrin, 1998, p. 95). Many Asians and Pacific Islanders would agree, as noted in the "stink eye" reference in a previous paragraph. In these countries young people never make eye contact with their elders. In most African countries and many other parts of the world, if a person has more status than you, you should not look him or her in the eye.

Working Together

In a group—preferably with a mix of males and females—discuss male and female attractiveness. First, what are the general parameters of male and female attractiveness? Second, do the parameters change according to which sex you are discussing? Third, when looking for an attractive person to date, what are the features of attractiveness that appeal to you? Fourth, put male features of attractiveness on one list with the most important features—agreed upon by group members—at the top, second most important features next, etc. Fifth, put female features of attractiveness on a second list organized in the same way as the male list.

When all groups have completed their tasks, have a class leader place a combined set of male features on the chalkboard. Then, do the same for a combined set of female features. As a class discussion: Are there any problems that you can see from creating lists of attractive features? Finally, for full class discussion, if you had to choose between an incredibly beautiful or handsome person of less than average intelligence and no sense of humor and a very smart person of less than average good looks who had a great sense of humor, what would your choice be?

Attractiveness

Let's say you are interested in finding a date. What is attractive to you? **Attractiveness** is having the power or quality of drawing, pleasing, or winning. Did you know that your answer to the question, "What is attractive to you?" will depend on whether you are male or female? Sure, whether you are male or female, you want a physically attractive date, no doubt about that, but physical beauty is much more important to males (Feingold, 1990). And the importance of physical beauty to males is universal; men in all cultures around the world prefer young, nubile (of suitable age to marry) women. Young, nubile women are a sign of health and fertility. More than health and fertility, however, men prefer having a physically attractive mate because it is a sign of status (Andersen, 1999, p. 113).

Females, on the other hand, have a significantly different impression of what is attractive. Seeking to select men with sufficient resources to care for them, women have stronger preferences for intelligent, considerate, and outgoing dates and, just as men of all cultures want young, nubile females, women of all cultures are attracted to wealth, power, and status (Andersen, 1998, p. 113; Berscheid, Dion, Walster, & Walster, 1971; Berscheid & Walster, 1969, 1972, 1974; Brislin & Lewis, 1968; Coombs & Kenkel, 1966; Walster, Aronson, Abrahams, & Rottman, 1966).

Several research studies have found that people who are perceived as attractive get a more positive response from others and have an easier time in life. Researchers have discovered that attractive women have more dates, receive higher grades in college, persuade males to do things with greater ease, and receive lighter court sentences than do other women (Knapp, 1978, pp. 153–61). Men or women rated as attractive are also perceived as being more sensitive, kind, strong, sociable, and interesting than unattractive people (Berscheid & Walster, 1978). In business, attractiveness pays off in several ways, including finding jobs and obtaining higher starting salaries (Rosenfeld, 1979, pp. 22–26).

There is another factor in determining another's attractiveness with which most of you are familiar. In a series of research studies over the past two decades, researchers have shown that judgments of attractiveness (ourselves and others) depend on the situation in which you find yourself (Levine & Marano, 2001). Psychologists Sara Gutierres and Douglas Kenrick of Arizona State University have demonstrated that if you first saw a highly attractive person, then you saw a person of average attractiveness of the same sex, the average person would seem a lot less attractive than he or she actually is. If you were in a bar talking to a beautiful person, and then you were joined by a less attractive person of the same sex, the second person will seem relatively unattractive. The reverse of this is also true: People of average attractiveness will seem more attractive than they are if they enter a room full of unattractive people of the same sex. The point is: "Context counts" (Levine & Marano, 2001, p. 41).

Physical characteristics you can control are called **elective characteristics** and include clothing, makeup, tattoos, and body piercing. **Nonelective characteristics,** things you cannot change, are height, body proportion, coloring, bone structure, and physical handicaps. Many of the nonelective traits influence how you see the world. A six-foot woman, for example, would see life quite differently from her five-foot sister (Dimitrius & Mazzarella, 1998, p. 31). Of course, plastic surgery has the potential of changing some physical characteristics once considered nonelective.

Clothing

Because clothing gives such a strong and immediate impression of its wearer, it is enormously important to nonverbal communication. Besides communicating, however, clothing may serve as protection, sexual attraction,

Clothing projects a message; by choosing particular clothing, wearers commit themselves to the statements clothing makes.

On the Web

When we entered the words "Dress for Success" (in quotation marks) into the Google search engine on March 14, 2003, the search engine came up with 47,100 hits. You should have no trouble getting advice on how to dress for a job interview and what is appropriate on-the-job attire. Here are three websites that provide just a sampling of what's available online:

"Dress and Grooming for Job Success." (Creative Job Search, Minnesota WorkForce Center, December, 2001). Retrieved March 14, 2003, from http://www.mnwfc.org/cjs/cjs_site/dress.htm. Here is a one-page guide that offers excellent suggestions. The site says: "Your appearance is a statement of who you are. Your clothing and grooming should create the image that will help you get the job offer."

"Dress for Success." (Kiwi Brands, 1999). Retrieved March 14, 2003, from http://www.kiwicare.com/dress.htm. This one-page site offers the latest in dress for success tips from shoe care to casual wear and everything in between. This site is full of *Dos* and *Don'ts* for both men and women.

L. Plotkin, "Dress for Success." (Worktree.com, 1999). Retrieved March 14, 2003, from http://www.worktree.com/tb/IN_dress.cfm. Plotkin tells why dress is important, how to dress, covers some of the fine points of the subject, and then gives specific tips and advice to men and then to women.

self-assertion, self-denial, concealment, group identification, and provide indications of status and role (Schwartz, 1963). In addition, think of how much information you can gain from a person's clothing: sex, age, nationality, relation to opposite sex, socioeconomic status, group and occupational identification, mood, personality, attitudes, interests, and values (Kelly, 1969). In his book, *You Are What You Wear*, William Thourlby suggests that there are 10 decisions people make about others based on clothing: (1) Economic level, (2) Educational level, (3) Trustworthiness, (4) Social position, (5) Level of sophistication, (6) Economic background, (7) Social background, (8) Educational background, (9) Level of success, and (10) Moral character (1978, pp. 143–51).

Clothing "has the most variability and the largest number of cues of any adornment feature"(Burgoon, Buller, & Woodall, 1996, p. 52). When you go out and select clothing to adorn your own body, you make choices based on color, style, comfort, fabric texture, pattern and design, neatness, interest, conformity, conventionality, economy, mood, and fashionableness. And, it goes without saying, those are precisely the dimensions on which you interpret the clothing of others (Aiken, 1963; Bickman, 1974; Birren, 1952; Compton, 1962; Gibbons & Gwynn, 1975; Pinaire-Reed, 1979).

Even though people may appear to dress in similar ways, they don't always see themselves as similar: An Amish woman points out that although Amish women wear dark clothes that cover the body, they are still aware of style. She writes: "Every culture has its own fashion expectations and requirements, and my people are no exception. They are concerned about how they look. They do not all wear black. They have individual color and style preferences. They enjoy shopping. And they talk about styles and fashions among themselves. . . .To these women, high and proper fashion means busy sewing machines, solid-colored, store-bought fabrics, and patterns passed down from generation to generation" (Stolzfus, 1998, pp. 134–35).

As you can see in Figure 6-1, clothing falls into four categories: uniforms, occupational dress, leisure clothing, and costumes. Each of these categories conveys a different meaning and results in different interaction patterns.

Uniforms identify wearers with particular organizations. They are the most specialized form of clothing. There is little freedom of choice in a uniform. Its wearers are told when to wear it (daytime, summer) and what they can and cannot wear with it (jewelry, medals, hairstyles).

Figure 6-1

Each of the four categories of clothing conveys a different meaning and results in different interaction patterns.

Category	Meaning	Interaction Patterns
UNIFORMS	Asserts the presence of social controls in the workplace. Interaction occurs for the sake of the group or organization rather than the person wearing the uniform—the representative of the group or organization.	The uniform precludes the intrusion of personal considerations; thus, interaction tends to be formal, structured, and controlled.
OCCUPATIONAL CLOTHING	Conveys organizational affiliation without the power revealed by uniforms. Permits the intrusion of norms from outside the group or organization. —Both uniforms and occupational clothing indicate structure, group or organizational affiliations, and functions.	Facilitates interaction with customers or clients and places interaction on the desired level of intimacy.
LEISURE CLOTHING	Announces a respite from work, social mobility, the expression of moods and identity, loose structure, and great autonomy. Because it is the antithesis of uniforms and occupational dress, it declares an absence of the social controls of the workplace.	Interaction here is open and lacks most formality, structure, and control.
COSTUMES	Symbolize doing away with ordinary social relationships and engagement in extraordinary and spontaneous behaviors. Conventional social structure, formality, and control vanishes!	Because they represent a removal of the customary forms of responsibility and accountability—a suspension of the usual norms—costumes facilitate interaction spontaneity and easy sociability.

Source: Nathan Joseph, *Uniforms and Nonuniforms* (New York: Greenwood Press, 1986).

The most common uniforms are worn in the military. By showing rank, military uniforms tell what positions the users hold in the hierarchy and what their relationships are to others in the organization. The uniform also implies that its wearer will follow certain norms (Joseph, pp. 2–3, 15). For example, you expect that someone in military uniform will always respect the flag.

Occupational dress is clothing that employees are expected to wear, but it is not as precise as a uniform. Occupational clothing indicates the performance of a certain kind of job, and it is designed to present a specific image of the employer (Joseph, p. 143). Unlike wearers of uniforms, employees who wear occupational dress have some choices. Flight attendants are required to wear specific pieces of clothing, but they can mix blouses, scarves, trousers, or skirts according to their own preferences. Nurses might be required to wear white, but they can select the style they like. People who wear business clothing have even more choices. A company might expect its employees to wear suits, but the employees can choose both color and style.

What teachers wear affects student perceptions. In a study of teaching assistants, researchers found that those who dressed the most informally were viewed the most positively by students. In this case, informal dress was faded jeans, T-shirts, and flannel shirts (Morris, Gorham, Cohen, & Hoffman, 1996).

Leisure clothing is worn when work is over. Because wearing this kind of clothing is up to the individual, some people assert their personal identities through it (Joseph, pp. 168–69). However, not everyone sees styles of leisure wear as a choice. Many teenagers will wear only a particular brand of jeans because when their group agrees on a brand, everyone wears it. Skiers might use a certain brand of skis, parkas, and goggles—even though other brands would work equally well. The mass media have had such a great influence on leisure clothing that it's hard to separate media influence from individual preference.

Costumes are a form of highly individualized dress. One example of a costume is imitation cowboy dress: boots, bandanna, and hat. By putting on a costume, the wearer announces, "This is who I want to be." Such a costume might have symbolic importance; the cowboy costume, for example, announces a macho kind of individuality (Joseph, pp. 124–25). Few people are interested in wearing costumes in daily life. Costumes not only require thought regarding the image they convey but also go against many norms. As one student shrewdly observed as he changed his shoes for a job interview at a supermarket in the Northeast, "I better not wear my cowboy boots. They look too aggressive."

Body Adornment

Body adornment includes any addition to the physical body designed to beautify or decorate. Throughout the world people have found ways of changing the body they were born with. Americans are no exception. Hairstyles, facial hair, and makeup are conservative changes that are widely accepted. In fact, it's hard to believe that early in the century people were shocked when women used makeup and cut their hair short. As late as the

Another Point of View

Unfortunately, the communicative ability of material objects has a limited range of expression. Facing a wide age difference between popular piercers and the influential members of society, there is a low degree of mutual understanding. While youth wear piercings as a way to not fit in, older, established members of society look upon popular piercings as unclean and unsightly. The message the piercing conveys is lost in the translation between age groups and socioeconomic classes. Instead of presenting an image calling for social change, the interpretation states alternate views; that of disgust and contempt for cultural ideals. This miscommunication creates tension between age and social groups, and has lead to a common perception of youths as being unclean and unfit to inherit our society.

Source: C. Terrien, "Body Adornment," November 26,1997. Retrieved March 14, 2003, from http://www.bmezine. com/ritual/971207/temien.html.

1960s, many people objected to men having long hair and complained that they couldn't tell males from females; next, they were just as upset when men began to wear earrings.

The greatest creators of body adornment are usually students in the 12 to 22 age range. The most innovative in this group are those who try to set themselves apart from the adult world. The most adventurous choose a combination of flamboyant hairstyles and colors, tattoos, and body piercing. Usually this style is not only about looks; it also has to do with getting a reaction from the adult world. Body piercing would probably disappear overnight if all parents admired it and urged their children to do it.

Space and Distance

The study of space and distance, called **proxemics,** concerns the way people use the space around them as well as the distance they stand or sit from others. The minute you enter a classroom, you are faced with a decision that relates to how you use space. You have to decide where to sit. As you can see in Figure 6-2, your choice of where to sit depends on how much interaction you want to have with the instructor: If you are in the "action zone," you may be indicating that you want to participate in the class. However, if you sit in the back or corner seats, you may be communicating to the instructor that you don't want to be involved.

People also map out certain spaces as their territory. **Territory** is the space that a person considers as belonging to him or her—either temporarily or permanently. For example, you would probably be upset if you came into the classroom and found someone sitting in "your"chair. When my wife and I go to the movies, we like to sit in the center about two-thirds of the way back from the screen. When someone else is already occupying "our" seats, we always feel a bit put out. Most of us have territories that we consider our own, and other people can enter them only with our permission. If they don't follow the rules, we get upset.

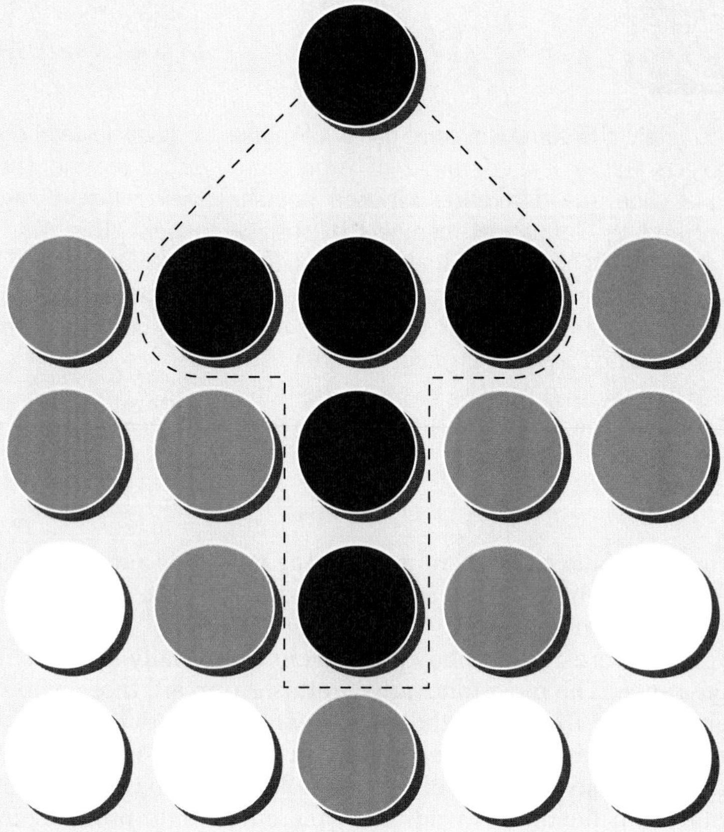

Figure 6-2

A Traditional Classroom Arrangement

In such an arrangement, those students occupying the purple seats will account for a large proportion of the total interaction that occurs between teachers and students. Those in the green seats will interact some; those in the white seats will interact very infrequently. The area enclosed in dotted lines has been called the "action zone."

Sometimes people unwittingly send out a mixed message about their space. Four students who rented a church that had been converted to student housing with four sleeping lofts found that they had little control over their space. Other students dropped in night and day—probably because the building looked more like a public than a private space. The minute their lease ended, they moved into more traditional housing. Look at the next Another Point of View (page 192) to see how even when the use of space is culturally determined, it can still be a problem.

Every culture has rules—usually informal—about the use of space and distance. Edward T. Hall, author of *The Silent Language* and *The Hidden Dimension*, two classic books on nonverbal communication, coined the term *proxemics* for the study of space and distance (Hall, 1959, 1969). From his observations and interviews, Hall discovered that North Americans use four distance zones when they are communicating with others: intimate distance, personal distance, social distance, and public distance (Hall, 1969, pp. 116–25).

Intimate distance, a range of less than 18 inches apart, places people in direct contact with each other. Look at a mother with her baby. She picks him up, caresses him, kisses him on the cheek, holds him on her lap.

The distance people keep from other people is determined both by culture and occasion. The people in the left picture are Americans waiting in line at an airport. Those in the right picture are Chinese.

All her senses are alert when she is this close to the baby. She can touch him, smell him, and hear every little gurgle he makes. People also maintain an intimate distance in love relationships and with close friends. Intimate distance exists whenever you feel free to touch the other person with your whole body.

When your intimate distance is violated by people who have no right to be so close, you feel apprehensive. If you are on a crowded bus, subway, or elevator and people are pressed against you, they are in your intimate distance. You ignore these people by not making eye contact. In this way you can protect your intimate distance psychologically, if not physically.

Personal distance, from 18 inches to 4 feet, is the distance you maintain from another person when you are engaged in casual and personal conversations. It is close enough to see the other person's reactions but far enough away not to encroach on intimate distance. If you move closer than 18 inches, the person will probably back away. If you move farther away than 4 feet, it will be difficult to carry on a conversation without having the feeling that it can be overheard by others.

Social distance, from 4 to 12 feet, is the distance you are most likely to maintain when you do not know people very well. Impersonal business, social gatherings, and interviews are examples of situations where you use social distance.

Whenever you use social distance, interaction becomes more formal. Have you ever noticed the size of the desks in the offices of important people? They are large enough to keep visitors at the proper social distance. In her book *Managing Inter@ctively,* Mary Boone writes, "A colleague of mine has this amazing desk. It looks like it should belong to Henry VIII. It's huge and imposing and he used to have it placed perpendicular to the far wall as you walked into his office. Two chairs (that look like they belonged to Anne

Another Point of View

Elaine Sciolino, a correspondent for *Newsweek* and *The New York Times* who reported on the key events of Iran for two decades, describes the use of space and distance in Iranian society:

Negotiating the space between men and women is . . . hard work. The existence of the hejab (hejab literally means "curtain" which is defined as any dress that follows Islamic principles) is apparently not enough to separate men and women, and male-female relationships work themselves out in public spaces in irrational ways. There is no clear-cut definition of a sexually inte-grated public space. Women may be segregated from men in government offices, but are squeezed close to them in the buildings' overburdened ele-vators. Men and women are required to use sepa-rate entrances at airports, but they sit next to each other on domestic flights. Buses are segregated (women ride in the back), but communal taxis are not. In fact, men and women can sit so tightly packed in taxis that there is a popular expression for going on a date: going for a taxi ride.

Source: E. Sciolino, *Persian Mirrors: The Elusive Face of Iran* (New York: The Free Press, 2000), p. 147.

Boleyn) were placed across the desk from him. The impression it conveyed was that he was in charge and granting you an audience" (2001, p. 51).

Public distance, a distance of more than 12 feet, is typically used for public speaking. At this distance, people speak more loudly and use more exaggerated gestures. Communication at this distance is more formal and permits few opportunities for people to be involved with each other. Figure 6-3 shows the dimensions of the four distance zones.

Space/Distance in Relationships

Space and distance are those distances people maintain between them-selves and others that convey degrees of intimacy and status. Degrees of intimacy are communicated through the use of space. When you observe the distances that people maintain between themselves and others, you can tell which people have close relationships and which have more formal rela-tionships. If you enter the college president's office and she remains behind her desk, you can assume that your conversation is going to be formal. If she invites you to the corner where there are easy chairs and you sit side by side, she has set up a much more intimate situation, and the conversation is going to be more informal.

As you get to know people better, you are permitted into their more per-sonal space. Remember when you were in middle school and went to the movies with a boy or a girl for the first time? When your hands met in the popcorn box, you were exploring the possibilities of moving from a per-sonal to an intimate distance. The opposite can also happen. A married couple experiences a lot of intimate distance. If there are problems in the marriage, however, the couple's communication is conducted mostly at a personal distance. If they start to negotiate a divorce, they will probably carry out most of their negotiations at a social distance.

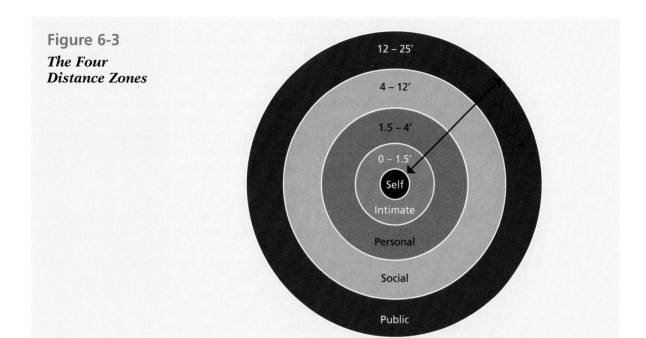

Figure 6-3

The Four Distance Zones

12 – 25'
4 – 12'
1.5 – 4'
0 – 1.5'
Self
Intimate
Personal
Social
Public

Degrees of status in relationships are also communicated through the use of space. Executives, presidents of colleges, and government officials all have large offices with expansive windows and elaborate furnishings. These privileges are so carefully guarded that one company sent out a memo regarding who could have what kind of plants: Anyone who was a vice president or above could have one floor plant and one table plant. However, the executive assistant to the vice president could have only a table plant. The memo further warned that plants were attached to the position: If you lost your position, you had to surrender your plant to the person who took your place! ("Office-plant politics," 1999, p. 24)

Children have the least amount of space. Even if they have their own rooms, that space is controlled by adults. It is usually planned and decorated by an adult, and the adult sets the rules for how the space will be used. Sometimes adults also punish chilren by depriving them of space. Commands such as "Get to your room" or "Stay out of my room" limit children's access to space within the household.

Touch

The closer you stand to someone, the more you increase the likelihood of touching. **Touch** is to be in contact or come into contact with another person. You are familiar with the use of touch in intimate situations: You kiss babies, hold hands with loved ones, and hug family members. Touch "is a key component in growing, learning, communicating, and living" (Ratey, 2001, p. 76). The importance of touch for babies was shown in a study of premature babies. In order for them to thrive, they had to be touched.

When babies are touched, brain chemicals are released that promote growth. Premature infants who were massaged three times a day for 15 minutes gained weight 47 percent faster than those who were left alone in their incubators. They were also able to leave the hospital an average of six days earlier. Eight months later, they still held their advantage in weight and did much better on tests of mental ability and motor ability than premature infants who were not touched as much (Goleman, 1988). If you doubt the importance of touch to newborns, just ask an experienced nurse in any neonatal care center. "Touch is the first of the five senses to develop, and is far more developed than hearing or seeing in newborns" (Ratey, 2001, p. 76).

Dr. John Ratey, a Harvard Medical School professor of psychiatry, explains the importance of touch: "Human beings possess an instinctive urge to touch and be touched. It is part of the human drive to explore and interact with the world. Touch," Ratey continues, "is unique because it is the only sense that allows us to experience the world through direct physical contact. Touch is also our most powerful and intimate form of communication. A touch can move us, and hurt us, in a way that no spoken word can, sending messages from comfort to hate across language and cultural barriers" (2001, p. 76). Researchers found that when people who did not even know each other began interacting, if one person touched the other, he or she was seen as affectionate, relaxed, and informal (Burgoon, Walther & Baesler, 1992).

When and where people touch one another is governed by a strict set of societal rules. Richard Heslin has described five different categories of touch behavior (1974; Winter, 1976; Thayer, 1988). The first is *functional-professional touch,* in which you are touched for a specific reason, as in a physical examination by a doctor or nurse. This kind of touch is impersonal and businesslike. *Social-polite touch* is used to acknowledge someone else. The handshake is the most common form. Although two people move into an intimate distance to shake hands, they move away from each other when the handshake is over. In close relationships people use the *friendship-warmth touch.* This kind of touch involves hugs and casual kisses between friends. Touching is one way to communicate liking (Anastasi, 1958; Mehrabian, 1970; Mehrabian, 1971). In more intense relationships the *love-intimacy touch* is common. Parents stroke their children; lovers and spouses kiss and fondle each other. The final touch Heslin describes is *sexual arousal touch*—touch used as an expression of physical attraction (Heslin, 1974; Winter, 1976).

The factors influencing touch include the type of touch it is, degree of liking or disliking in the relationship, and the situation at hand (Hickson & Stacks, 1993). Another significant factor in touching behavior, too, is whether or not you like to be touched. Peter Andersen and Kenneth Leibowitz, researchers in nonverbal communication, have suggested that the variables that affect perceptions of touch include your age, race, and religion (1978). When is touching acceptable? You are likely to accept touch in most professional situations. You are likely to accept it, too, if it is consistent with the relationship and the message or messages of the moment. But, touch can quickly become a violation, too, when it is unexpected or out of the message context. The most serious violation of touch, of course, is in assault and battery (Hickson & Stacks, 1993).

Time

The study of time is called **chronemics.** To say that time is very important in American culture is a huge understatement; we are obsessed with time. Even that is an understatement. Our daily life is infused with a sense of urgency that involves beating the clock. Burgoon, Buller, and Woodall (1996) write, "Time is seen as a precious resource, a valuable and tangible commodity. We spend time, save it, make it, fill it, and waste it. It is seen almost as a container with defined boundaries. This tangible view of time is also reflected in how we mark its passage. It is highly divisible: we break it into years, months, weeks, days, hours, minutes, seconds, tenths of seconds, even nanoseconds. The average American thinks of time in five-minute blocks, which are very small chunks of time. The way we schedule events also reflects the urgent and precise way we deal with time. We expect classes to start on time (within a minute or so), and when they don't we wait only so long (20 minutes at the most) before leaving" (pp. 127–28).

On a personal level, time seems to fall into two categories—persons who are always on time and those who are always late. Have you ever noticed that certain students always come late, whereas others are always in their seats when the class begins? From the viewpoint of an instructor, the person who is always late may be communicating considerable negative information. He is really not interested in this class, he doesn't respect the instructor, and so on. By the same token, students might resent an instructor who is always late. They might think he doesn't plan well enough or doesn't respect the class.

You can use time for psychological effect. If you have a date with someone you don't know very well, you will probably not arrive too early because this might make you appear too eager. If you dent the family car, you might wait for the right time to tell your parents about it. Your control of time, then, is an important form of nonverbal communication.

Time is often connected with status. The higher your status, the more control you have over your time. Children have little control over time. A parent can interrupt children's play to have them eat dinner or to make them go to bed far earlier than they want. Professionals in our society often make others wait for them. How long do you wait in the doctor's office before your examination? Students have little say in how their time is spent. If they want a particular class and it is offered only at 8 A.M. they have little choice but to take it then. They also have no choice about when papers are due or when exams are given. If you want to discover who has the most status in society, watch who waits for whom.

Chronemics is the most discussed and best-researched nonverbal code in the intercultural literature (Bruneau, 1979; Burgoon, Buller & Woodall, 1996; Gudykunst & Kim, 1997; Hall, 1959, 1976, 1984). Time differs greatly from one culture to another. Figure 6-4 shows what people in the United States regard as fashionably late, but South Americans would answer the figure's question differently. For example, suppose you were invited to a

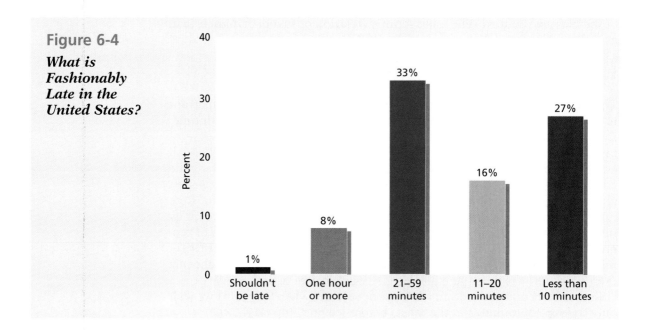

Figure 6-4

What is Fashionably Late in the United States?

party in Venezuela, and the host said it would begin about 8 P.M. If you arrived at that time, you would be the only one there—the Venezuelans wouldn't arrive until 9 or 10 P.M. The lesson is that when interacting with people from different cultures, simply assume that their sense of time is different from yours. And, when visiting a third world culture, it is "safe to assume that all your assumptions about time are false" (Andersen, 1999, p. 77).

■ IMPROVING YOUR NONVERBAL COMMUNICATION

View "Nonverbal Messages," clip #4, on the CD.

Because your nonverbal behavior is so tied in with your social and cultural conditioning, it is not easy to change. Fortunately, you probably don't need to make any drastic changes. You should be concerned with nonverbal communication that distracts from what you want to say or that contradicts your verbal messages. If you find that people regularly misunderstand you, you would do well to ask whether this is because of nonverbal cues people are picking up. Below are some questions it would be useful to ask about your nonverbal communication.

How Do People React to You?

Do people ever react to you in a way that surprises you? It may be because you are sending nonverbal messages that are being interpreted differently from the way you intended. For example, you may intend to tease someone but instead hurt his or her feelings. If you see that the person looks upset, you then have a chance to explain what you really meant.

Sometimes people don't know how they are perceived. For example, at school a student with a disability was ignored by most of the other students—probably because they didn't know how to react to someone who is disabled. When he had an opportunity in his speech communication class to talk about his disability, and what he could and couldn't do, students began to speak to him much more. Several audience members also revealed their anxiety about dealing with persons who have disabilities.

What Can Videotapes Show You about Your Nonverbal Communication?

Videotape can tell you a great deal about yourself that you might not know. Since home video cameras are so common, it is not difficult to get someone to tape you or, for that matter, for you to tape yourself. A speech you are going to give in class will be better if you can see it on video first. Undoubtedly you will discover some behaviors you were not aware of and ones that you want to get rid of. Here are just a few items that you might look for when you see your tape (Ritts & Stein):

Eye contact. Since it signals interest in others, increases credibility, and opens the flow of communication by conveying interest, concern, and warmth, make certain your eye contact is comfortable and natural, but direct.

Facial expressions. Your face transmits happiness, friendliness, warmth, liking, and affiliation; thus, it pays to smile frequently. By smiling you will be perceived as more likable, friendly, warm, and approachable.

Gestures. By not gesturing you are likely to be perceived as boring, stiff, and unanimated. By being lively and animated, you capture others' attention, make your information more interesting, and provide conversational positive reinforcement.

Posture and body orientation. Posture and body orientation includes the way you walk, talk, stand, and sit. By standing erect, but not rigid, and by leaning slightly forward, you will communicate that you are approachable, receptive, and friendly.

Proximity. Cultural norms dictate the distances you need to stand for interacting with others. By increasing your proximity to others when in conversation, but not excessively, you not only make better eye contact, but you become more sensitive to the feedback of others.

Paralinguistics. You need to modulate your voice by changing such features as tone, pitch, rhythm, timbre, loudness, and inflection. Check closely for a monotone, because it is likely to reveal a dull or boring voice. Variances in the features above are likely to reveal enthusiasm and interest in your ideas.

Humor. When you reveal a willingness to laugh, you foster an inviting, warm, and friendly conversational environment. Laughter also releases stress and tension.

Is Your Nonverbal Communication Appropriate to the Role You Are Playing?

Like your language, your nonverbal communication should change as you play different roles. To learn about this, observe people in their roles. How does a good boss act? How much of this communication is nonverbal? What kind of nonverbal communication does a teacher show in her role? Is it something you would want to imitate if you became a teacher? What people don't you want to be like? Is it their nonverbal behavior that turns you off? Do you do any of the same things? Can you stop doing them?

How Do You Use Your Space?

Are you aware that the space you live in communicates something about yourself? What messages are you sending out through the posters on your walls? Through the cuddly animals on your dresser? What do they say about you?

How tidy is your space? What does your tidiness or lack of it communicate about you? One of our neighbors was having some remodeling done on her home. As I was jogging one morning, I passed one of the worker's cars parked at the curb outside our neighbor's home. To me, it looked as if the inside of the car had been trashed with old beer and pop cans, candy wrappers, the wrappings off different kinds of hamburgers, and a variety of other kinds of trash. I wondered what all of this communicated about the worker doing the remodeling?

How much space do you occupy? Are you a sprawler, or do you keep your arms close to your body and your legs together? Are you conscious of certain space as "belonging" to you? Is it important that you have some spaces that you can call your own? What does the way you regard space tell others about you?

How Do You Use Time?

Are you on time or always late? What does your sense of time say about you to others? Are you a procrastinator, leaving everything until the last minute? If you are, does your procrastinating have anything to do with your inability to make decisions—for example, you don't prepare a speech because you are changing your topic every day?

Are you aware of the relationship between time and status—that there are some times when you can make people wait but other occasions when you should be on time? When is it important for you to be on time? When can you be late? On what occasions do you expect others to be on time? If your use of time creates a bad impression, is it possible for you to change your ways?

When you look at all the things you communicate about yourself nonverbally, you will see that you should give nonverbal communication attention and care. Although nonverbal behavior is difficult to change, it can be done, especially if you are aware of how you use it.

Assess Yourself

Are You Aware of Nonverbal Communication?

How nonverbally aware are you? Give a qualitative evaluation for each of the following factors by circling the numerical score next to each of the factors that best represents your nonverbal awareness: 7 = Outstanding; 6 = Excellent; 5 = Very good; 4 = Average/good; 3 = Fair; 2 = Poor; 1 = Minimal ability; 0 = No ability demonstrated.

1. I look others directly in the eye when communicating with them.	7 6 5 4 3 2 1 0
2. I gesture with my hands and arms when communicating.	7 6 5 4 3 2 1 0
3. I turn my body fully toward the person with whom I am speaking.	7 6 5 4 3 2 1 0
4. I use a pleasant, appropriate tone of voice when speaking to others.	7 6 5 4 3 2 1 0
5. I use a vocal volume that is appropriate when speaking to others.	7 6 5 4 3 2 1 0
6. When listening to another person, I notice and respond to their nonverbal responses to me—their vocal tone, eye contact, facial expressions, posture, gestures, and body movement.	7 6 5 4 3 2 1 0
7. When listening to another, I am quiet when they are talking and allow them to express their ideas without interruption.	7 6 5 4 3 2 1 0
8. When listening to another person, I smile when the person uses humor, and I nod at appropriate times.	7 6 5 4 3 2 1 0
9. When listening to another person, I reveal my full support and attention through my nonverbal cues.	7 6 5 4 3 2 1 0
10. I feel the nonverbal cues I use when speaking, and those I use in responding to others when they are speaking, reveal my comfort, poise, and confidence as an effective communicator.	7 6 5 4 3 2 1 0

TOTAL POINTS: _____

 Go to the *Communicating Effectively* CD-ROM to see your results and learn how to evaluate your attitudes and feelings.

Chapter Review

You send more messages through nonverbal communication than you do through verbal communication. Verbal communication and nonverbal communication often reinforce each other, but there are clear differences between them. The differences become clear as you relate nonverbal communication to the model of communication and to communication as a transaction. Verbal communication begins when a word is uttered, and it requires a single channel. It is under your control; it is structured; and it is formally taught. Nonverbal communication, on the other hand, is continuous; it is multichanneled; it is mostly habitual and unconscious; it is largely unstructured; and it is learned through imitation.

Nonverbal communication serves important functions. It can complement, regulate, substitute for, or accent a verbal message. Most non-verbal communication takes culturally determined forms. It may conflict with verbal messages. It is sent subtly, perhaps even unconsciously, and it communicates feelings and attitudes.

There are several types of nonverbal communication. They include paralanguage, eye messages, attractiveness, clothing, space/distance, touch, and time. Space and distance relate to relationships in the way they can communicate both intimacy and status.

One way of evaluating your nonverbal communication is to ask some questions about how you use it: How do people react to you? Can you use videotapes to improve your nonverbal communication? How do you use your space? How do you use time? The answers to these questions will indicate areas in which you can improve.

Questions to Review

1. What is an example of nonverbal communication? How does this example demonstrate communication as a transaction?

2. How do verbal communication and nonverbal communication differ? How do they differ in the areas of senders and receivers? Message and feedback? Channel and setting?

3. By using an example, can you show how nonverbal communication is culturally determined?

4. What is it called when verbal and nonverbal messages conflict? Have you any examples of this occurring?

5. What is paralanguage? What are the vocal qualities that contribute to paralanguage?

6. Can you give an example of nonverbal communication in each of the following body movements: Emblems? Illustrators? Regulators? Displays of feeling? Adaptors?

7. What does clothing communicate about you? How do the following kinds of clothing differ? Uniforms? Occupational dress? Leisure clothing? Costumes?

8. What is the study of space and distance called? What are the four distance zones, and how do they differ?

9. How do space and distance communicate important relationship information? What kinds of information are related?

10. Can you give an example of how one's use of time communicates status? How does the use of time differ from culture to culture?

mhhe.com/hybels Go to the self-quizzes on the Communicating Effectively CD-ROM (side 2, track 10) and the Online Learning Center at mhhe.com/hybels7 to test your knowledge of the chapter concepts.

References

Addington, D. W. (1968). "The relationship of selected vocal characteristics to personality." *Speech Monographs,* 35, 492–505.

Aiken, L. R. (1963). "The relationship of dress to selected measures of personality in undergraduate women." *Journal of Social Psychology,* 59, 119–28.

Anastasi, A. (1958). *Differential psychology.* New York, Macmillan.

Andersen, P. A. (1985). "Nonverbal immediacy in interpersonal communication." In A. W. Siegman & S. Feldstein, eds. *Multichannel integrations of nonverbal behavior.* Hillsdale, NJ: Erlbaum, pp. 1–36.

Andersen, P. A., & L. K. Guerrero (1998). "The bright side of relational communication: Interpersonal warmth as a social emotion." In P. A. Andersen & L. K. Guerrero, eds. *Handbook of communication and emotion: Research, theory, applications, and contexts.* San Diego, CA: Academic Press, pp. 303–24.

Andersen, P. A., & K. Leibowitz (1978). "The development and nature of the construct touch avoidance." *Environmental Psychology and Nonverbal Behavior* 3, 89–106.

Berscheid, E., K. K. Dion, E. H. Walster, & G. W. Walster (1971). "Physical attractiveness and dating choice: Tests of the matching hypothesis." *Journal of Experimental Social Psychology,* 7, 173–89.

Berscheid, E., & E. H. Walster (1969, 1978). *Interpersonal attraction,* 2nd ed. Reading, MA: Addison-Wesley. (1972, September). "Beauty and the best." *Psychology Today,* 5, 42–46, 74.

————— (1974). "Physical attractiveness." In L. Berkowitz, ed. *Advances in experimental social psychology,* Vol. 7. New York: Academic, 158–215.

Berry, D. S. (1992, Spring). "Vocal types and stereotypes of vocal attractiveness and vocal maturity on person perception." *Journal of Nonverbal Behavior* 16(1), 41–54.

Bickman, L. (1974). "The social power of a uniform." *Journal of Applied Social Psychology,* 4, 47–61.

Birdwhistell, R. L. (1970). *Kinesics and context.* Philadelphia: University of Pennsylvania Press.

Birren, F. (1952). "Emotional significance of color preference." *American Journal of Occupational Therapy,* 6, 61–65, 72, 88.

Boone, M. E. (2001). *Managing Inter@ctively: Executing business strategy, improving communication, and creating a knowledge-sharing culture.* New York: McGraw-Hill.

Boyce, N. (2001, January 15). "Truth and consequences: Scientists are scanning the brain for traces of guilty knowledge." *U.S. News & World Report,* p. 42.

Brislin, R. W., & S. A. Lewis (1968). "Dating and physical attractiveness: Replication." *Psychological Reports,* 22, 976.

Brody, J. (1992, Aug. 19). "Personal health: Helping children overcome rejection." *New York Times,* p. C12.

Bruneau, T. (1979). "The time dimension in intercultural communication." In D. Nimmo, ed. *Communication yearbook* 3. New Brunswick, NJ: Transaction Books, pp. 423–33.

Buller, D. B., & R. K. Aune (1988). "The effects of vocalics and nonverbal sensitivity on compliance: A speech accommodation theory explanation." *Human Communication Research,* 14, 301–32.

Burgoon, J. K. (1978). "Attributes of a newscaster's voice as predictors of his credibility." *Journalism Quarterly,* 55, 276–81.

Burgoon, J. K., D. B. Buller, & W. Gill Woodall (1996). *Nonverbal communication: The unspoken dialogue,* 2nd ed. New York: McGraw-Hill.

Burgoon, J. K., J. B. Walther, & E. J. Baesler (1992, December). "Interpretations, evaluations, and consequences of interpersonal touch." *Human Communication Research* 19(2), 237–63.

Compton, N. H. (1962). "Personal attributes of color and design preferences in clothing fabrics." *Journal of Psychology,* 54, 191–95.

Coombs, R. H., & W. F. Kenkel (1966). "Sex differences in dating aspirations and satisfaction with computer-selected partners." *Journal of Marriage and the Family,* 28, 62–66.

Dimitrius, J. E., & M. Mazzarella (1998). *Reading people: How to understand people and predict their behavior—Anytime, anyplace.* New York: Random House.

Ekman, P., & W. V. Friesen (1969). "The repertoire of nonverbal behavior: Categories, origins, usages, and coding." *Semiotica,* 1, 49–98.

————— (1975). *Unmasking the face: A field guide to recognizing emotions from facial clues.* Englewood Cliffs, NJ: Prentice-Hall.

Exline, R. V., S. L. Ellyson, & B. Long (1975). "Visual behavior as an aspect of power role relationships." In P. Pliner, L. Drames, & T. Alloway, eds. *Nonverbal communication of aggression,* New York: Plenum, Vol. 2, 21–52.

Fehr, B. J., & R. V. Exline (1987). "Social visual inter-action: A conceptual and literature review." In A. W. Siegman, & S. Feldstein, eds. *Nonverbal behavior and communication*, 2nd ed. Hillsdale, NJ: Erlbaum, 225–36.

Feingold, A. (1990). "Gender differences in effects of physical attraction on romantic attraction: A comparison across five research paradigms." *Journal of Personality and Social Psychology*, 59, 981–93.

Gibbons, K., & T. K. Gwynn (1975). "A new theory of fashion change: A test of some predictions." *British Journal of Social and Clinical Psychology*, 14, 1–9.

Goleman, D. (1988, February 2). "The experience of touch: Research points to a critical role." *New York Times*, C1.

Goodman, E. (2002, May 1). "Some prefer to smile, furrow brows to Botox." *The Blade* (Toledo, OH), 11A.

Gudykunst, W. B., & Y. Y. Kim (1997). *Communicating with strangers: An approach to intercultural communication*, 3rd ed. New York: McGraw-Hill.

Hall, E. T. (1959). *The silent language*. Greenwich, CT: Fawcett.

_____ "A system for the notation of proxemic behavior." *American Anthropologist*, 65, 1003–26.

_____ *The hidden dimension*. Garden City, NY: Anchor Books.

_____ *Beyond culture*. Garden City, NY: Anchor Books.

_____ *The dance of life: The other dimension of time*. Garden City, NY: Anchor Press.

Harrison, R. P. (1974). *Beyond words: An introduction to nonverbal communication*. New Jersey: Prentice-Hall.

Heslin, R. (1974). "Steps toward a taxonomy of touching." Paper presented at the Western Psychological Association Convention, Chicago, 1974.

Hickson, M. L. III, & D. W. Stacks (1993). *NVC—Nonverbal communication: Studies and applications*, 3rd ed. Boston: McGraw-Hill.

Izard, C. E. (1977). *Human emotions*. New York: Plenum.

Jensen, J. V. (1985). "Perspective on nonverbal inter-cultural communication." In L. A. Samovar, & R. E. Porter, eds. *Intercultural communication: A reader*. Belmont, CA: Wadsworth, 256–72.

Kappas, A., U. Hess, & K. R. Scherer, (1991). "Voice and emotion." In R. S. Feldman, & B. Rime, eds. *Fundamentals of nonverbal communication*.

Cambridge, England: Cambridge University Press, 200–37.

Kelly, J. (1969). "Dress as nonverbal communication." Paper presented at the Annual Conference of the American Association for Public Opinion Research.

Kendon, A. (1967). "Some functions of gaze direction in social interaction." *Acta Psychologica*, 26, 22–63.

Kennedy, D. D. (2001). *Feng shui for dummies*. Foster City, CA: IDG Books Worldwide.

Knapp, M. L. (1972, 1978). *Nonverbal communication in human interaction*, 2nd ed. New York: Holt, Rinehart and Winston.

Leathers, D. G. (1976). *Nonverbal communication systems*. Boston: Allyn & Bacon.

Levine, M., & H. E. Marano (2001, July–August) "Why I hate beauty." *Psychology Today*, 41.

Little, K. B. (1965). "Personal space." *Journal of Experimental Social Psychology*, 1, 237–47.

Lozano, E. (2000). "The cultural experiences of space and body: A reading of Latin American and Anglo American comportment in public." In A. Gonzalez, M. Houston, & V. Chen, eds. *Our voices: Essays in culture, ethnicity, and communication*. Los Angeles, CA: Roxbury Publishing Company, 228–34.

MacLachlan, J. (1979, November). "What people really think of fast talkers." *Psychology Today* 113–17.

McCroskey, J. C., T. J. Young, & V. P. Richmond (1977). "A simulation methodology for proxemic research." *Sign Language Studies*, 17, 357–68.

Mehrabian, A. (1968, September). "Communication without words." *Psychology Today*, 53.

_____ "Some determinants of affiliation and conformity." *Psychological Reports* 27, 19–29.

_____ "Verbal and nonverbal interaction of strangers in a waiting situation." *Journal of Experimental Research in Psychology* 5, 127–38.

_____ *Silent messages: Implicit communication of emotions and attitudes*, 2nd ed. Belmont, CA: Wadsworth.

Morris, T. L., J. Gorham, S. H. Cohen, & D. Hoffman, (1996, April). "Fashion in the classroom: Effects of attire on student perceptions of instructors in college classes." *Communication Education* 45, 142–48.

(No author) (1999, August). "Office-plant politics." *Harper's Magazine*, 24.

Pearce, W. B. (1971). "The effect of vocal cues on credibility and attitude change." *Western Speech*. 35, 176–84.

Pinaire-Reed, J. A. (1979). "Interpersonal attraction: Fashionability and perceived similarity." *Perceptual and Motor Skills*, 48, 571–76.

Planalp, S. (1998). "Communicating emotion in everyday life: Cues, channels, and processes." In P. A. Andersen, & L. K. Guerrero, eds. *Handbook of communication and emotion: Research, theory, applications, and contexts*. San Diego, CA: Academic Press, 29–48.

Planalp, S., V. L. DeFrancisco, & D. Rutherford (1996). "Varieties of cues to emotion occurring in naturally occurring situations." *Cognition and Emotion*, 10, 137–53.

Ray, G. B. (1986). "Vocally cued personality prototypes: An implicit personality theory approach." *Communication Monographs* 53, 272.

Richmond, Y., & P. Gestrin, (1998). *Into Africa: Intercultural insights*. Yarmouth, ME: Intercultural Press.

Ritts, V., & J. R. Stein. "Six ways to improve your nonverbal communications." (Faculty Development Committee, Hawaii Community College). Retrieved March 14, 2003, from http://www.hcc.hawaii.edu/intranet/committees/FacDevCom/guidebk/teachtip/commun-1.htm.

Rosenfeld, L. B. (1979, April). "Beauty and business: Looking good pays off." *New Mexico Business Journal*, 22–26.

Ross, D., & D. Ross, (2000). "Nonverbal networking." *Masters of networking: Building relationships for your pocketbook and soul*. Marietta, GA: Bard Press (an imprint of Longstreet Press).

Samovar, L. A., R. E. Porter, & N. C. Jain (1981). *Understanding intercultural communication*. Belmont, CA: Wadsworth.

Schwartz, J. (1963). "Men's clothing and the Negro." *Phylon*, 24, 224–31.

Silver, C. A., & B. H. Spitzberg (1992, July). "Flirtation as social intercourse: Developing a measure of flirtatious behavior." Paper presented at the Sixth International Conference on Personal Relationships, Orono, ME.

Stolzfus, L. (1998). *Traces of wisdom: Amish women and the pursuit of life's simple pleasures*. New York: Hyperion.

Street, R. L., & R. M. Brady (1982). "Speech rate acceptance ranges as a function of evaluative domain, listener speech rate and communication context." *Communication Monographs*, 49, 290–308.

Street, R. L., & H. Giles (1982). "Speech accommodation theory: A social cognitive approach to language and speech behavior." In M. Roloff & C. Berger, eds. *Social cognition and communication*. Beverly Hills, CA: Sage, pp. 193–226.

[No author] (2002, December 29) "Successful flirts know how to follow a few simple rules." *Toledo Blade* (Toledo, OH), P 4E.

Tannen, D. (1990). *You just don't understand: Women and men in conversation*. New York: Morrow.

Thayer, S. (1988). "Touch encounters." *Psychology Today* 22, 31–36.

Thourlby, W. (1978). *You are what you wear*. New York: New American Library.

Walster, E., V. Aronson, D. Abrahams, & L. Rottman (1966). "Importance of physical attractiveness in dating behavior." *Journal of Personality and Social Psychology*, 4, 508–16.

Winter, R. (1976, March). "How people react to your touch." *Science Digest* 84, 46–56.

Zuckerman, M., & R. E. Driver (1989). "What sounds beautiful is good: The vocal attractiveness stereotype." *Journal of Nonverbal Behavior*, 13, 67–82.

Zuckerman, M., H. Hodgins, & K. Miyake (1990). "The vocal attractiveness stereotype: Replication and elaboration." *Journal of Nonverbal Behavior*, 14, 97–112.

Further Reading

Andersen, P. A. (1999). *Nonverbal communication: Forms and functions*. Mountain View, CA: Mayfield Publishing Company. There are three parts to this excellent textbook by one of the premier researchers in the field: fundamental forces, affective exchanges, and implicit influence (which includes persuasion, deception, and power). With up-to-date research, interesting stories and examples, practical strategies to help readers improve their nonverbal communication, and an engaging writing style, this is one of the best books on nonverbal communication yet available.

Burgoon, J. K., D. B. Buller, & W. G. Woodall (1996). *Nonverbal communication: The unspoken dialogue*. New York: McGraw-Hill. The authors divide this textbook into two major parts: codes and functions. Codes covers the standard elements of kinesics, vocalics, haptics, proxemics, environment, artifacts, and chronemics. Functions covers structuring interactions, creating and managing identities, forming impressions, communicating emotions, managing relationships, conversations, and impressions, and influencing and deceiving others. Although sophisticated and research oriented, this is a readable text with application boxes inserted for additional illustration and interest.

Cole, J. (1999). *About face.* Boston: MA: MIT Press. This is a philosophical book about the face written by a neurophysiologist. His many insights are based on patients who have come to him who are unable to read facial expressions or do not have the ability to make facial expressions. Cole also discusses the link between the face and the inner self.

(No author) (2000, June 14). "Contract pricing reference guides Vol 5—Federal contract negotiation techniques: Chapter 5—Nonverbal communication." Department of Defense, United States Government. Retrieved March 14, 2003, from http://www.acq.osd.mil/dp/cpf/pgv10/pgv5/pgv5c5.html. This is a good introduction to nonverbal communication that covers forms (conscious, subliminal, involuntary, voluntary), and how body language, physical environment, and personal attributes affect negotiations. Although this guide is basic and includes no sources, it is well-written and interesting.

Dunn, L. J. (1999, January 14). "Nonverbal communication: Information conveyed through the use of body language." Department of Psychology, Missouri Western State College. Retrieved, March 14 2003, from http://clearinghouse.mwsc.edu/manuscripts/70.asp. A useful starting point for developing an interest in nonverbal communication. With less than fifteen sources, this undergraduate research paper ends with the admonition, "In a new age where increasing population is decreasing personal space, it is imperative to understand cultural and personal communication differences and similarities" (p. 5 of 7).

Given, D. B. (2002). "The nonverbal dictionary." Center for Nonverbal Studies. Retrieved March 14, 2003, from http://members.aol.com/nonverbal2/ entries.htm#Entries. A fascinating set of over 250 words associated with nonverbal communication. Click on any one of them, then sit back and enjoy a thorough explanation from an etymology, to its use in other disciplines, consumer products related to the term, other related nonverbal behavior, cultural explanations, and research reports. A truly unique and enjoyable experience.

Guerrero, L. K., J. A. Devito, & M. L. Hecht, eds. (1999). *The nonverbal communication reader: Classic and contemporary readings.* Prospect Heights, IL: Waveland Press. In 51 articles by some of the outstanding and best known writers and researchers in the field and in four major parts that cover perspectives, codes, functions, and theories, the editors introduce basic terms and concepts; provide an overview of research methods used to investigate nonverbal behaviors; explain individual nonverbal codes and how different codes work together; and discuss theories about how people respond to the messages of others. This is an excellent and comprehensive look at the field of nonverbal communication.

Hewitt, K. (1997). *Mutilating the body: Identity in blood and ink.* Bowling Green, Ohio: Bowling Green Popular Press, Bowling Green State University. This is a scholarly book about the various ways people change their bodies by piercing, tattooing or not eating. The book, based on psychological theory and ritual theory, includes interviews with people who have changed their bodies. The author also talks about body modification as a cultural phenomenon.

Madonik, B. G. (2001). *"I hear what you say, but what are you telling me?" The strategic use of nonverbal communication in mediation.* San Francisco: CA: Jossey-Bass Publishers. Madonik offers practical information and real-world strategies for mediators. As an international consultant, she helps readers understand, analyze, and utilize nonverbal communication in mediation. She offers a seven-step process that can be widely applied in employment, labor, commercial, consumer, family, community, and governmental disputes. Her book is easy-to-read and full of examples.

Roecker, F. (2002, April 1). "Nonverbal communication." Library User Education, Ohio State University. Retrieved March 14, 2003, from www.lib.ohio-state.edu/gateway/bib/nonverbal.html. This site provides a vast resource of links in either different categories: background information, books and journals, quick facts, people and organizations, opinions, and further research. Although useful, many sources are not specific to the subject of nonverbal communication.

Shedletsky, L. J. ed. "Nonverbal communication." ComResources Online, National Communication Association. Retrieved March 14, 2003, from http://www.natcom.org/ctronline/nonverb.htm. This two-page resource is simply a link first to aspects of nonverbal communication such as body language, eye gaze, facial analysis, graphic symbols, other nonverbal communication links, a nonverbal communication research page, senses, and more. Second, it is a link to the websites of some nonverbal researchers such as Andreas Altorfer, Diane Berry, Judee K. Burgoon, Ross Buck, Kari Edwards, Paul Ekman, Robert Feldman, Howard Friedman, Judith A. Hall, Marvin A. Hecht, Albert Mehrabian, Robert Rosenthal, Joan Tucker, Leslie Zebrowitz, and many others.

Wainwright, G. (2000). *Teach yourself body language,* 2nd ed. New York: McGraw-Hill. In this 208-page paperback, Wainwright, a specialist in communication studies, provides elementary information on learning to use and interpret body language. The first part of his book covers skills, the second, contexts. He offers numerous practical exercises to enhance understanding and uses personal and professional situations to make reading enjoyable and worthwhile.

Part Two

Interpersonal Communication

Chapter 7

Interpersonal Relationships

Objectives

After reading this chapter, you should be able to:

- Define *interpersonal communication*.
- Explain emotional intelligence.
- Tell why people are attracted to each other.
- Define and explain *interpersonal needs*.
- Discuss how roles influence interpersonal communication.
- Give some ways of beginning a conversation.
- Provide an example of a bid and a response to a bid and give their purpose.
- Explain the parts of an owned message, and give an example.
- Define *self-disclosure*, and tell why it is important.
- Describe the four panes of the Johari Window.
- Explain the systems theory of family.
- Discuss the factors likely to affect intimacy in couples and families.

Key Terms and Concepts

Use the Communicating Effectively CD-ROM and Online Learning Center at mhhe.com/hybels7 to further your understanding of the following terms.

Affection 219	Empathy 214	Reaffirmation 245
Attitudes 217	Family 239	Recalibration 245
Balance 245	Inclusion 219	Relational dialectics 244–245
Beliefs 217	Integration 245	
Bid 223	Interpersonal communication 211	Response to a bid 223
Compatibility 217		Segmentation 245
Control 220	Intimacy 241	Self-disclosure 230
Control messages 247	Johari Window 232	Small talk 222
Denial 245	Owned message 228	Spiraling alteration 245
Disorientation 245	Proactive 247	Support messages 247
Emotional intelligence 212	Proximity 218	Systems theory of family 239
	Reactive 247	

THERE IS LIKELY TO BE NO MORE IMPORTANT OR AVAILABLE source for information on relationships than the Internet. Almost every search engine has a "relationships" icon on its home page. If you enter "relationships" into the Google search engine, you will come up with 11,600,000 hits (March 24, 2003). We put each of the following categories in quotation marks and entered them in the Google search engine to find out how many Web pages were associated with each. Here, we have listed them according to how many hits Google reported were available with the sites with the most Web pages listed first:

personal relationships	301,000	homosexual relationships	14,700
family relationships	269,000	marriage relationships	11,400
sexual relationships	89,300	heterosexual relationships	10,700
dating relationships	68,800	Internet relationships	6,160
love relationships	60,700	teen relationships	4,130
abusive relationships	31,300	intercultural relationships	3,270
interracial relationships	22,000		

If you add together the related relationships—personal, sexual, love, and dating—you come up with a total of 519,800 websites, and you get a picture, albeit a dim one, of Internet usage. "In 1995, online dating sites barely existed. Today there are thousands, including the popular Match.com and Yahoo Personals" (Peterson, 2003, p. 9D; Kurlantzick, 2001, p. 43). In addition to these kinds of sites, there are numerous others for advice, books, and divorce, R- and X-Rated, singles, and weddings, too. And if new relationship-related issues arise, you can bet a series of Internet sites will soon be created to correspond to them. There are many places to post personal advertisements. Also, there are date guides, gift guides, communities, and chat rooms. There are sites for rating friendships and romances. Many sites are advice columns with FAQs (frequently asked questions) and responses, opportunities to post your own questions, and numerous specific benefits outlined on each home page. College and university sites, too, offer advice and counsel specifically for students. Our point here really isn't the number of websites available, although that is interesting; our point is that the subject "relationships" is a hot topic, and if you are looking for information it is readily available.

You need to go no farther than your local newsstand to find advice about relationships. Pick up *Glamour* and read, "Blind Date Do's and Don'ts." If you want information about young teens, take a look at *Teen* and read

"Guy Likes . . . Guy Gripes." If *Good Housekeeping* is your favorite, you can find out what to do about that pesky friend in "The Frustrating Friend." Even your daily newspaper has a toe in the relationship business; chances are that it carries an advice column or two.

Magazines and newspapers don't have a monopoly on advice on relationships. When you turn on the TV, relationship themes prevail again. Soap operas are all about relationships; watch an episode of *Days of Our Lives* if you have any doubts. You can ponder relationships during prime time with numerous, popular shows based on relationships. There are host- or hostess-controlled audience-response shows that convey "true-life" relationship experiences and even game shows based on togetherness. Reality-TV offers a number of shows as does MTV that feature real-life relationship situations and experiences.

If you want more depth than a magazine or TV show can give, try a book. Barnes and Noble, at their online website, will give you seven categories under the heading "In Relationships": dating, divorce, love & romance, marriage, relationships, sexuality, and weddings. For just these categories, 14,349 "bestsellers" are listed. Then each of these categories has subtopics. For example, under relationships, interpersonal relationships has 55 subcategories, friendship has 16, and social interactions in relationships has 11 (March 24, 2003). Similarly, Amazon.com, an online mail-order company, will give you a list of 32,000 book titles for the keyword *relationships,* 32,000 book titles for *romance,* and 21,524 for *marriage.*

When you see how much time and space are devoted to relationships in the media, you might wonder why we are adding even more with this chapter. We want to approach the subject from a more scholarly view than that presented in the mass media or on the Internet. We are interested specifically in the best way to communicate in relationships—whether you are beginning a new relationship or trying to keep your present relationships in good condition.

Interaction with others is called **interpersonal communication,** and it occurs whenever one person interacts with another—usually in an informal setting. You cannot survive in society without interpersonal communication skills. They enable you to function socially and to maintain relationships that are important to your life.

According to Clyde Lindley, Director of the Center for Psychological Services, Silver Springs, Maryland, and former psychology and abnormal psychology lecturer at George Washington University, "Much research shows the importance of interpersonal relationships to well-being, happiness, and satisfaction with life"

(Lindley, 1996). One study showed that lack of contact with others doubles the chance of getting sick or dying (Goleman, 1995, p. 179). In a study of college roommates, the researchers discovered that the more roommates disliked each other, the more likely they were to go to the doctor and to come down with colds and the flu. Isolation has more impact on men than on women. Men without close social ties are two to three times more likely to die earlier than men who have them (Goleman, 1995, p. 178).

■ EMOTIONAL INTELLIGENCE

"In 1995," writes Stephen Ceci (2001), in his article called "Intelligence,"

> Yale psychologist Robert Sternberg and colleagues developed new evidence that practical and analytical intelligence are two different things. They demonstrate that the skills of practical intelligence, such as common sense, are important in predicting life outcomes, but are not associated with IQ-type analytic intelligence. There may be at least seven or eight different kinds of intelligence, says researcher Howard Gardner of Harvard, including interpersonal, intrapersonal, linguistic, motoric and musical intelligence (2001, p. 50).

Anyone who has taught long enough to see students mature can tell you stories of some who were smart in the classroom but never went anywhere and of others who did not do particularly well in school but went on to have successful careers and relationships. This success is due to what Daniel Goleman calls "emotional intelligence" (Goleman, 1995). At its simplest level **emotional intelligence** is the ability to understand and get along with others. Goleman and other researchers see this kind of intelligence as made up of five characteristics: being self-aware, managing emotions, motivating yourself, recognizing emotions in others, and handling relationships. Let's look at each of these in turn (Goleman, 1995, pp. 43–44).

Being Self-Aware

Before you can deal with the emotions of others, it is important to recognize your own by paying attention to how you feel. Self-awareness requires the ability to get a little distance from the emotion so that you can look at it without being overwhelmed by it or reacting to it too quickly. For example, if you are having an argument with someone and act on your anger, you might tell the other person that you never want to see him or her again. On the other hand, if you can recognize how angry you are feeling, you might be able to say, "Let me think about this some more and talk to you about it later."

Distancing yourself from an emotion should not be a denial of it ("I shouldn't feel this way"). Rather, it's a way to articulate to yourself what you are feeling so that you can act on it appropriately.

Managing Emotions

Managing your emotions means expressing them in a manner that is appropriate to the circumstances (Goleman, 1995, pp. 81–82). You may not be able to do this easily because emotions often come from below the surface of your consciousness. For example, there may have been a time that unexpected tears came to your eyes, or other times when you felt a terrible rage well up inside you. An example of this kind of rage occurred with a student who stayed after class to discuss a paper he had just gotten back from his instructor. When he asked why he had failed the paper, the instructor said he had not followed the assignment and the paper had several spelling and grammatical errors. The student abruptly left the classroom and, in leaving the building, set off the fire alarm. You would probably agree that this was an inappropriate response. Unless this student could find a way to get his emotions under control, he was going to have difficulty learning anything in the future—especially if it involved criticism of him.

Another emotion that gets out of control is anxiety (Goleman, 1995, p. 193). When anxiety is out of control, you feel so worried or so upset that it interferes with how you function. In a university setting, for instance, most teachers have had students who have been so worried about the right way to do an assignment that they didn't do it at all or did it poorly because they were afraid to take any chances.

Managing your emotions does not mean that you should never feel angry, worried, or anxious. These emotions are all part of being human, and if you don't find a way to express them, they can result in depression or antisocial acts. For emotional intelligence, it's important that you control these emotions rather than letting them control you.

One interesting finding about emotions is that women are better than men at detecting them. In a study where men and women were shown video clips in which someone was having an emotional reaction, 80 percent of the time women were better than men at discerning the emotion (Goleman, 1998, pp. 322–23; Covey, 1998, pp. 22–23, 238).

Motivating Yourself

Motivating yourself is setting a goal and then disciplining yourself to do what you have to do to reach it. Whether you are an athlete or a writer, talent is not enough to make you win the race or get your story published. Both writers and athletes will tell you that they worked hard on many boring activities before they mastered their discipline.

Much of self-motivation involves resisting impulses. If you are studying for a test, for example, it might be tempting to turn on the computer and chat with a friend. If you give in to this impulse, you might become so engrossed in the computer that you completely forget the test.

Some of the most fascinating research on impulse control was done on a group of four-year-old preschoolers (Goleman, 1995, pp. 86–90). When a child was put into a room with a researcher, he or she was offered a marshmallow. However, the children were told that the researcher had an errand to run and that if they didn't eat the marshmallow, they would get two when the researcher returned. The researcher was gone 15 to 20 minutes—an eternity for a child. The minute he was gone, one-third of the children ate their marshmallows; the remainder found ways to distract themselves from eating them: They tried to go to sleep, they talked to themselves, or they engaged in play.

Later these same children were studied when they were teenagers. Those who waited when they were children were much better in social skills, more assertive, and better able to handle themselves in a crisis. Academically, they were far superior as students, and they had an average of 210 points higher on SAT scores (Goleman, 1995, p. 193).

Other influences on motivation, according to Goleman, were positive thinking and optimism. Those who had a strong sense of self could bounce back after they had a negative experience. Rather than dwelling on the failure, they looked at ways in which they could improve (Goleman, 1995, pp. 86–90).

Recognizing Emotions in Others

Empathy, the ability to recognize and share someone else's feelings, is essential to human relationships. It comes from hearing what people are really saying—both by listening to their words and by reading body language such as gestures and facial expressions, and recognizing what is meant by a particular tone of voice. When someone has the same feelings or experiences you have had, it's not difficult to feel empathy. You are really put to the test when you haven't had the other person's feelings or experiences. For example, how can you feel empathy with an African student who hasn't been home for three years and stays in the dorm over Christmas? You can feel sorry for him, and you could tell him that you would feel terrible if you couldn't go home for the holidays. However, these emotions are pity (feeling sorry for him) and sympathy (saying that you'd feel bad too), but they are not empathy because you have not shared his experience. You may go in the direction of empathy if you talk to him for a while, look at the pictures of his brothers and sisters, hear about all the delicious things his mother cooks for Christmas, and so on. Empathy is the extent to which you can sit in his place, see what he sees, and taste what he tastes.

Empathy has a strong moral dimension. Being able to recognize and share someone's distress means that you will not want to hurt him or her. Child molesters and sociopaths, for example, are people lacking in empathy (Goleman, 1995, pp. 106–110). Sharing empathy with others also means that you are able to reach out and help them because when you can feel as they feel, they are no longer alone.

Handling Relationships

What are some of the characteristics of popular people you know? Chances are that they are people who are largely positive and energetic and that being with them makes you feel positive too. Most likely, they are also the people who organize others (such as the child who suggests a game), negotiate solutions when there is a problem to be solved, and generally connect with others emotionally (Goleman, 1995, pp. 111–26).

Another Point of View

John Ratey, Harvard professor of psychiatry, offers this opinion about emotional intelligence:

Emotional intelligence is an attractive concept because it can provide a convenient scapegoat for today's epidemics of violent crime, marital strife, and teenage drug abuse. Conversely, we'd like to believe that if we improve levels of emotional intelligence in the young they will be better equipped for life's trials. Much of the how-to advice that is supposedly a reflection of emotional intelligence, however, is just plain common sense. Obviously, being able to control rage or develop empathy, say, will enable a person to have better future success in life than someone who doesn't have these abilities.

There are two central questions in the debate over emotional intelligence: Can it really be measured in a meaningful way? And can it be "taught" as a skill to children and adults? We don't know the answers yet, but you can be sure there will be plenty of research in coming years to find out.

Questions

1. After having read about emotional intelligence, do you think improvement in it is likely to have positive results with respect to social relationships? Communication with others?

2. Is the concept of emotional intelligence completely obvious? Common sense?

3. Do you agree with Ratey that the essential questions regarding emotional intelligence are "Can it be measured in any meaningful way?" and "Can it be taught?" Do you think the elements of emotional intelligence are important enough, in and of themselves, that they *should* be taught?

J. J. Ratey, *A User's Guide to the Brain: Perception, Attention, and the Four Theaters of the Brain.* (New York: Pantheon Books (a division of Random House, Inc.), 2001), p. 251.

Being popular, however, is not their only goal. People also need a sense of balance; they need to recognize their own needs and know how to fulfill them. For example, you might be popular if you are always willing to stop studying to go to a party. This, however, would not meet your own need to pass your courses.

■ ATTRACTION TO OTHERS

In the course of a week, most of us have hundreds of casual encounters with other people. With most of the people you meet, you conduct your business and go on your way. You probably don't remember the waitress who served you the last time you ate out or the guy who delivered your pizza last week. These people recede into a kind of human landscape. Occasionally, however, you have an encounter where you think, "I would like to get to know that person better." Out of all the people you meet, how do you pick some you want to know better? What ingredients make up your attraction to others? What do you have to gain?

There are many factors that make up attraction to others. Physical attraction, perceived gain, similarities, differences, and proximity are some of them. What are the likely factors at play here?

Physical Attraction

We are often attracted to others because of the way they look; we like their style and want to get to know them better. In some cases physical attraction may be sexual attraction. In most cases, however, it goes beyond that. Sometimes we are attracted to people because of the way they dress. For instance, someone chooses a style of clothing that is your own style or is a style you would like to imitate.

Physical attraction is particularly important to teenagers. For them, what matters is "Is he [or she] cute?" If a high school student is able to date someone whom other teenagers consider desirable, this fact raises that student's status.

For adults who have had experience in the world, physical attraction is more superficial; it usually recedes into the background as they get to know a person. Physical attraction, then, can be a reason for getting to know someone, but it is usually not the basis for a long-term relationship.

Perceived Gain

Often we are attracted to people because we think we have something to gain from associating with them. For example, you join the Spanish club because you know it's planning a members-only trip to Spain. Or you join the ski club to get discounted lift tickets. Someone else joins a business management club because she believes that meeting certain people will help her network with them when she enters the working world. Other people like to make friends with those who have status or power, hoping that this association will confer status and power on them too.

One subject that needs more study in this country is social class. Although Americans believe they are a classless society, if you look around, you will discover that this is not true. In high school, for instance, the highest-status kids are usually those with professional mothers and fathers, followed by students with parents who work in business, while the next class is made up of children of working-class parents. Students who are able to transcend their class either are very attractive or have unusual athletic ability. Colleges and universities also have a social hierarchy: Private schools (especially those in the Ivy League) have the most status, while junior and community colleges have the least. Public state colleges and universities rank somewhere in the middle. Colleges that stress religion and are supported by a church are in a category of their own, although there is status ranking within that category.

What does this have to do with attraction? People will usually seek out others in their own class. Sometimes, however, they are motivated to move up and they try to blend into a higher class because the perceived awards will be greater. Most people will not try this because they feel more comfortable with their own social class.

Similarities

Many times we are attracted to people because we like what they say and they belong to our own social class. Thus you may be attracted to someone when you discover that he or she shares your attitudes and beliefs or seems knowledgeable about topics you find interesting and significant. Your **beliefs** are your convictions; your **attitudes** are the deeply felt beliefs that govern how you behave. Although it's often said that opposites attract, when it comes to a strongly felt belief, you probably look for people who believe as you do. For example, in today's world it would be difficult for an Albanian and a Serb to be close friends—their politics have put them in opposing camps. Although a fundamentalist Christian and an Orthodox Jew might share similar ideas about home and family, they would be so far apart in religious beliefs that they probably would not seek each other out.

As adults grow older and meet more and more people, they become aware of the kinds of people they like and dislike, and they recognize the importance of compatibility. **Compatability** is made up of attitudes, personality, and a liking for the same activities (Hatfield & Rapson, 1992). For example, one couple decides to live in the city and focus on their careers rather than have a family. Their personalities are the same in that they like drama and excitement in their life—something the city provides. They also like the same activities: They often attend hockey and basketball games, and they spend their money on trendy clothes and eating out. Because they like the same things, their relationship is likely to last.

Differences

Although two people who have very different beliefs are unlikely to form a strong and lasting relationship, people with different personality characteristics might be attracted to each other. For example, a person who doesn't like making decisions might be attracted to a strong decision maker. Because these characteristics complement each other, they might help to strengthen the relationship.

Sometimes you have a chance to meet people from a different race or culture. In this situation you might expect your attitudes and beliefs to be different from theirs. Specific interests, however, may be so similar that they outweigh anything else. An American who runs in the Boston Marathon might have more in common with a runner from Kenya than with someone who spends every Sunday morning reading the newspaper and eating doughnuts. A white American and an African-American may share similar beliefs about child rearing. Association with a group might bring people together. Although a Rotary member from Indiana would have a different cultural background than a Rotary member from India, the fact that they both belong to Rotary will create a common ground for some of their interactions.

Proximity

A quick look through the engagement and wedding notices in the newspaper will show the importance of proximity. **Proximity** is the close contact that occurs when people share an experience such as work, play, or school. Through this contact, people meet their friends and often find their mates. Even when people might not otherwise have been attracted to each other, they may begin to know and like each other because they are together so much. For example, being in the same study group for a semester, sharing an office, or standing side by side on an assembly line are activities that place people in close proximity. Once they begin to share their lives on a day-to-day basis, they may find themselves becoming friends or even forming a romantic relationship.

After people finish school, they are most likely to make new friends in the place where they work. These friendships go through three stages: *co-worker to friend,* where people get to know each other and do some socializing outside work; *friend to close friend,* where personal and work experiences and difficulties are shared, and *friend to almost best friend,* where they share life and work experiences and communication becomes more intimate (Sias & Cahill, 1998).

Sometimes people who are attracted to each other form a strong friendship but lose touch when they no longer have proximity. Typically, friends who move to different cities vow to stay in touch. However, if they can't afford telephone calls or if they don't have access to e-mail, it's not unusual for contact to drop to a yearly holiday card. Proximity, then, is important not just for starting relationships but also for keeping them going.

■ MOTIVES FOR INTERPERSONAL COMMUNICATION

Interpersonal communication is valuable to people because it serves so many important purposes. Your sense of self comes from your communication with others; the communication you use to meet needs is most likely to be spoken rather than written.

Everyone has needs that will vary with personality and moods. When you seek out others, you are trying to meet one or more of the following interpersonal needs: pleasure, affection, inclusion, escape, relaxation, and control (Rubin, Perse, & Barbato, 1998).

Pleasure

We engage in a lot of interpersonal communication because it's fun. This kind of communication is a form of entertainment. You gossip on the telephone with your best friend; you sit around and argue about sports teams with your buddies; you stop at the student center to have coffee, but also in the hope of meeting someone you know. In the evening you go out with your friends to enjoy yourself and to meet others.

Affection

Affection is the feeling of warm attachment you have for people you appreciate and care for. Whether it is expressed nonverbally (hugging, touching) or verbally ("I'm really glad you called me today"), affection is important to human happiness.

Affection is a one-to-one emotion. Unlike inclusion, which can involve many people, affection is a matter of singling out a particular person.

Inclusion

Inclusion—involvement with others—is one of the most powerful human needs. At one time or another, you've probably had the experience of being excluded, especially if you have an older brother or sister who tried to get rid of you when you were a kid. You can be excluded by not knowing the language everyone is speaking, by not getting into a fraternity you want to join, or by not being 21 and able to go out with your friends.

Although nearly everyone has had the experience of being excluded, most people have had more experiences of being included. They may eat with a certain group at the cafeteria, go to parties at friends' houses, or join a club at the university. Belonging in this way is important to everyone's sense of well-being.

Escape

At one time or another, we all engage in interpersonal communication to try to avoid the jobs we are supposed to do. For example, before you begin writing your term paper, you decide to wander down the hall of your dorm to talk to a friend.

A new form of escape that has emerged in recent years is escape by computer. Chat rooms, e-mail, and surfing the Internet are particularly popular and enable you to escape without even going anywhere. More than one student has gone to the computer to do an assignment and ended up spending hours computer socializing.

Relaxation

You often talk to your friends or families to relax and unwind from the activities of the day. You might sit with co-workers during a break, spend a few minutes with your spouse after work, or go out with a group of friends on the weekend.

Control

In a broad sense **control** is defined as being able to make choices. Control in relationships sometimes means getting other people to do what you want them to do. It could involve something minor, such as going to a movie instead of watching television, or something major, such as persuading your spouse to buy the car that you like the best. Because controlling others implies a certain amount of manipulation, it is sometimes seen as the least satisfying of communication behaviors (Rubin, Perse, & Barbato, 1998, p. 618). For example, a parent who tells a child that she can have a sleepover party if she cleans up her room would probably prefer that the child clean up without having to be offered a reward.

In the best relationships, the persons try to share control, depending on the situation. Also, control may change due to circumstances. For example, a couple we know moved to a new place where the wife had to commute two hours a day. This meant that she was not home to cook the evening meal, so her husband had to do it. He took control by reorganizing the kitchen to his liking—a legitimate action since he was now the main cook. The wife, however, had difficulty giving up control of the kitchen that she had always considered hers. Then one night when she came home, she discovered that her husband had cleaned the stove so thoroughly that he had "washed" all the numbers off the oven dial. Whether this was deliberate will never be known. However, the wife decided that it was time to give control of the kitchen to him.

Researchers have found that people who have control over their own lives are healthier both mentally and physically (Goleman, 1988, pp. C1, C11). Students learn better when teachers give them some independence, and workers feel better about their jobs when they can make some decisions about how their work should be done. Elderly people in nursing homes live longer if they have some say about what they eat and how to arrange the furniture in their rooms (Goleman, 1988). In these and similar interactions, people have the sense that they are in control of their lives and are thus meeting one of their deepest needs.

■ TALKING TO EACH OTHER

Roles, Relationships, and Communication

All relationships are governed by the roles that the participants expect each other to play. Sometimes these roles are tightly defined; other times the participants have the flexibility to define them. A traditional elementary school teacher, for example, would expect his students to sit quietly at their desks and raise their hands if they want his help. When they are working at their desks, they are not supposed to talk to the other students without his permission. The teacher next door, however, doesn't play such a traditional role. At story times she lets the children call out questions without raising their hands, and if they are working at their desks, they can ask classmates for help as long as they don't make too much noise.

Often the roles you know best are those that are the most traditionally defined. You have certain expectations of teachers, coaches, and employers. In families, parents decide what time young children should go to bed and whether they should be permitted to eat junk food. In public schools, the state, the school board, the principals, and the teachers decide what children should learn. Health care workers recommend what is best for a patient. Even though the people who work in these roles might want more flexibility than is allowed by traditional definitions, they often feel social pressure to conform to traditional roles and thus to traditional behavior.

As roles get further away from the nuclear family or the institutions of society, they are not so tightly defined. Usually at the beginning of a relationship with someone your own age, you can choose the roles you want to play. Friends, for example, often decide on the role they will play within a friendship. Once the relationship is established and functioning, the role expectations become fixed and friends expect each other to react in certain ways.

Roles in intimate relationships are probably the hardest. The closest relationship is probably the marital one, so a critical question you have to answer is whether, in marriage, you want to play the role your father or mother played. If you don't want to, how will you set out to define your own role? Sherod Miller, a psychologist, says that this creates a lot of problems for a couple because once the partners give up old roles—the ones that were based on gender—the couple has to work out new ones—a process that leads to negotiating every aspect of their lives, especially when the first baby arrives (Marano, 1997, p. C8).

Other psychologists who have studied marriage found that the most successful marriages are ones where the male partners listen to their female partners rather than reacting defensively to complaints and criticism. A husband's willingness to listen shows that he understands and respects his wife's needs, and when this occurs, there is a much better chance of marital stability (Marano, 1997).

As well as roles for your intimate relationships, there are roles for all aspects of your life and communication that works best in each of them. Your job is to find out which communication works best for all the roles you play. You will see, then, that much of your success in playing a role will depend on how well you communicate in that role.

Beginning Conversations: The Art of Small Talk

Have you ever felt nervous about entering a classroom where you didn't know any of the students? If someone invites you to a party and you don't know anyone but the host, will you go? Are there some social occasions that make you feel uneasy? What are they?

In many new social situations you might feel uneasy. You may wonder whether you will be able to begin a conversation and whether you will find people you like and, just as important, people who like you. The uncertainty you are feeling will probably be shared by other people in the room. How do you go about reducing it?

When most people begin conversations, they engage in **small talk**—social conversation about unimportant topics that will allow a person to maintain contact without making a deep commitment. You may often be in situations where it would be uncomfortable to stand around without talking. Therefore, there are all sorts of conventions in small talk. Scholars who have studied conversation have found that it follows a routine which varies only slightly. Figure 7-1 shows this conversation pattern.

As you can see in this figure, many of the conversational responses are based on questions. Some questions are asked to find out information; others are used to find a way of establishing common ground. In certain situations questions are asked just to fill time or to be sociable. Since most people like answering questions about themselves, they are flattered when someone shows interest in them.

Dianna Booher (1996), a business communications consultant, offers the following tips for beginning conversations (p. 5).

- *Introduce yourself in a way that gives the other person a way to respond to you.* This approach will give the other person a chance to find out what the two of you have in common, and it will probably lead to subjects for conversation. Here, for example, is how a person who was much younger than most of the guests at the university president's party introduced himself: "Hi, I'm Jim Dolan, and I'm the student member of the Board of Trustees at the university."

Figure 7-1

How People Begin Conversations

If you follow this figure from top to bottom, you will see how conversations begin, progress, and end. In the sections that are numbered, there is some variation: people may speak about one or more of these topics.

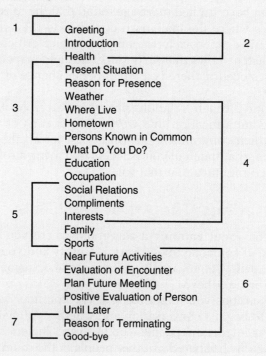

- *Give people a way to remember your name.* The author of this text whose last name is Hybels told people that it rhymes with *Bibles.* Not only did people learn how to pronounce her name, but often they remembered it when they met her again.
- *Personalize your greeting.* If you know something about the person, try to work it into your greeting. For example, "I liked the presentation you made in class last week."

Booher also suggests that when you end the conversation, you do it as gracefully as possible. "Excuse me, I've enjoyed talking to you" is a short and graceful ending.

Because small-talk topics and questions are socially sanctioned, they create a safe meeting ground. They provide you with a chance to establish who you are with others. They also permit you to find out more about yourself through the eyes of others. Although you don't give away a lot of personal information in small talk, the image you give to others and the image you receive of them will let you know if you want to see them again.

Bids and the Bidding Process

If you knew specifically what it was that holds relationships together, and you knew that it was within your control, would knowing those specifics change the way you conducted yourself in your interpersonal relationships? If you knew exactly the characteristics that drove married couples together rather than toward divorce, would you make every attempt you could to achieve and nurture those characteristics? What holds relationships together and the characteristics that drive married couples together are the same. It has to do with bids and with the bidding process. A **bid,** according to John Gottman (2001) and his team of relationship researchers, "can be a question, a gesture, a look, a touch—any single expression that says, 'I want to feel connected to you.' A **response to a bid** is just that—a positive or negative answer to somebody's request for emotional connection" (Gottman & DeClaire, p. 4).

What Determines Your Ability to Bid and to Respond to Bids?

Before discussing bids and the bidding process further, we want to recognize some of the many factors that may affect people's ability at bidding and responding to bids. Some people are likely to be better at it than others. There are three major influences at work. First, it may be a function of the way people's brains process feelings. Second, it may be a function of the way emotions were handled in the homes where people grew up. And third, it may be a function of people's emotional communication skills. These three influences can be complex, interacting variables. Despite their influence, however, sometimes just knowing what ingredients can influence a relationship, or just knowing specifically what you can do to make a relationship you cherish a success, is enough. Knowing about placing and responding to bids may be sufficient.

Nobody knows exactly what factor it is that pulls the trigger and causes us to respond in a certain way. It could be a comment from a friend or teacher, a television program or Internet article, or it could be something

Consider This

How important is the bidding process to relationships?

. . .Husbands headed for divorce disregard their wives' bids for connection 82 percent of the time, while husbands in stable relationships disregard their wives' bids just 19 percent of the time. Wives headed for divorce act preoccupied with other activities when their husbands bid for their atten-

tion 50 percent of the time, while happily married wives act preoccupied in response to their husbands' bids just 14 percent of the time."

J. M. Gottman & J. DeClaire, *The Relationship cure: A Five-Step Guide for Building Better Connections with Family, Friends and Lovers.* (New York: Crown Publishers, 2001), p. 4.

you read in a required textbook. Everyone knows the importance of knowledge in loading the gun. Having this knowledge available is important, and it can be valuable and worthwhile to creating successful relationships. Placing bids and responding to bids is a skill that can be learned, practiced, and mastered (Gottman & DeClaire, p. 25).

How Common Is the Bidding Process?

Let's say you have a joke you want to share with a relationship partner, or you are interested in gaining some affection, or you want to contradict an opinion he or she just shared with you, or you want to complain about your job. How do you do it? To begin a conversation with another person, an emotional connection is necessary, but that connection—and the degree to which it will be accessible—is part of a larger context. That larger context includes the hundreds of ordinary, day-to-day exchanges of emotional information and interest that preceded the current bid. These ordinary, day-to-day exchanges of emotional information and interest are called bids. They occur when you are seeking empathy, respect, friendly conversation, sexual intimacy, forgiveness, or to fit in. They occur as well when you want to be recognized, feel accepted, seek affection, or feel appreciated. To be successful in any of these situations you must gain the attention of another person—so you make a bid for their attention.

In successful relationships, bids for emotional connection are responded to positively. Bids from either relationship partner are neither ignored nor dismissed, whether they are simple or mundane. It is the simple and mundane bids that weave the fabric that forms the backdrop for all future bids. Many come nonverbally and include vocalizing, affiliating gestures (like opening a door or offering a place to sit), playful touching, facial expressions, or affectionate touching (Gottman & DeClaire, p. 31). Sure, some bids may be unseen, unheard, or overlooked just as some may be sent in a subtle, camouflaged, confused, or nonspecific manner. That is precisely why the statistics are important. It is the overall pattern of behavior that is important, not necessarily any single, solitary bid. Remember, in most positive relationships there are thousands of bids that take place daily.

Does Bidding Have Anything to Do with Relationship Conflict?

The answer is clearly yes. Many conflicts arise because of misunderstandings and feelings of separation. Many of these can be avoided if a person's emotional needs are acknowledged on an ongoing basis. Because couples don't have the conversations they need to have, they will argue instead. Bidding and responding to bids in positive ways will result in keeping the channels of communication open by clearing up misunderstandings when they occur and maintaining and nurturing the contact that keeps people feeling wanted, needed, and valued—but most important of all, included.

How Do Relationships Develop?

Complex, fulfilling relationships don't just appear out of nowhere, fully formed, well-developed, and successful. Rather, they are developed one encounter at a time, bid after bid after bid. Each encounter in a relationship is made up of many smaller exchanges—bids and responses to those bids. These exchanges of emotional information will either strengthen or weaken the connections between people, and these connections form the fabric we referred to earlier. Here, in the first two examples of bids and responses to bids, the response to the bid is negative. In the next two, the responses to the bids are positive:

> *Hey Chris. Did you get that class report finished?*
> *Would you stop nagging at me? You sound just like my mother!*

> *Are we going to be able to go out Friday night as we talked about last week?*
> *You gotta be kidding. Weren't you listening to me? I have so much work to do.*

> *Would you get me a beer while you are up?*
> *No problem. Do you want anything else? Some chips, maybe?*

> *Could we talk? We really need to talk.*
> *Okay. But, let's not sit here, let's go somewhere where we can talk in private. All right?*

The point is not the content, and the point has nothing to do with timing or circumstances. The point is that a positive response to a bid typically leads to continued interaction. Often, this means that both parties will be extending more bids, and with more bids and positive responses, the chances for a successful relationship become better and better. And the reverse is just as clear. Negative responses to bids will shut down communication. Bids cease, and the relationship terminates.

With negative responses to bids, you might wonder what hope remains for the relationship? Is there such a thing as rebids? Gottman and his associates found that the likelihood that a bid will be rebid once a bid has been rejected is close to zero. Let's take the second example above: *"Are we going to be able to go out Friday night as we talked about last week?" "You gotta be kidding. Weren't you listening to me? I have so much work to do."* Will there be a rebid? Probably not, but had the response *"You gotta be kidding. . . ."* been rephrased, the chances for a rebid would have become more likely:

Consider This

Here, John Gottman writes about his findings:

My insights into the process of bidding for emotional connection are a result of many years of observing human interaction in a variety of real-life settings. My research colleagues and I have studied the dynamics of friendships, parent-child relationships, adult siblings, and couples in all stages of marriage and child rearing.

J. M. Gottman & J. DeClaire, *The Relationship Cure: A Five-Step Guide for Building Better Connections with Family, Friends, and Lovers.* (New York: Crown Publishers, 2001), p. 15.

"I'm so sorry. I'm not going to be able to follow through since I'm so busy. Could we put it off until next Friday?" Now, a rebid has not only been encouraged, it has been invited, and in that positive response the person has also accepted a bid for emotional connection.

How Important Is the Bidding Process?

Although all this bidding and responding to bids may sound trite and trivial to you—especially when you think of the weight of having couples possess similar values, interests, beliefs, and needs—the point that Gottman and his associates discovered is that it is precisely all those interactions that we often take for granted on a daily basis that form the base—the emotional connectiveness, or glue—that holds relationships together. How can two people with seemingly diverse values, interests, beliefs, and needs not only remain happy, but remain together as well? If you check out their bidding process, there is no doubt you will discover an emotional connectiveness that both cements the partners and satisfies them with each other. No doubt these two people show an interest in each other's world, but undoubtedly, too, they understand how each other is feeling. That is an emotional connection that can rise above a similarity of values, interests, beliefs, and needs. We're not saying that similarity of values, interests, beliefs, and needs isn't important, we're simply saying emotional connectiveness is more important.

Gottman and his associates discovered, too, that the bidding process is more important than three other things commonly thought to hold relationships together. After examining couples and their dialogue in realistic settings, they found it wasn't the depth of intimacy in conversations, whether couples agree or disagree, or even the content of their conversations. Paying attention to each other was the key: bids and the responses to bids.

What Are Some Ways You Have to Encourage Bids?

How can you make certain you respond positively to the bids of others if you choose to do so? Gottman and his researchers discuss six ways to encourage and reinforce the bids of others. Although they appear to be common sense, just keeping them in mind is likely to nurture strong interpersonal relationships because if kept in mind, they will be available to implement and employ whenever appropriate.

First, focus on the people around you by noticing their bids and how you respond to them. Shift your attention from your own concerns to the concerns of others. If your goal is to build intimacy and understanding with others, this is a positive first step with or without bids and the bidding process.

Second, set a positive tone as you begin conversations. The best way to encourage bids is to weave the appropriate fabric. When bids begin negatively—*"Why didn't you just fill out the form when you got it?"*—with blame or criticism, the outcomes are predictable. Gottman and his associates found they could predict the outcome of 15-minute conversations based on what happened in the first 3 minutes of those conversations (Gottman & DeClaire, p. 70). The best advice is to watch how you begin conversations. A soft, gentle beginning is likely to establish the proper framework. *"Do you remember getting the form?"* And, with the next response, you could help guide the other person: With a *"Yes,"* you could say, *"Can I help you look for it?"* With a *"No,"* you could say, *"You know, I'm sure we'll be able to get another copy of that form."*

The third way to encourage bids is to couch any concerns you have as helpful complaints, not as harmful criticism. Complaints focus on specific problems; Criticism is judgment and global, often accompanied by attacks on a person's character, negative labels, and name calling. When carefully lodged, complaints help others understand one another and solve problems.

The fourth way to encourage bids is to avoid becoming physically or emotionally overwhelmed. Gottman labels being swamped physically or emotionally as flooding. The best thing to do when signs of flooding occur—pounding heart, sweaty hands, and irregular or shallow breathing—is to take a break of at least 20 minutes. Watch television, play a video game, read a book or magazine, or go for a run. Think of anything else but the immediate conflict. After 20 minutes try to get back to discussing the problem.

The fifth way to encourage bids is more difficult to approach or overcome if it happens to be one of your traits. Gottman calls it "practicing a crabby habit of mind" (p. 78). It's a habit of looking for the worst in others and in the world—finding the faults, mistakes, human weaknesses, foibles, and frailties. If this "crabby habit of mind" is truly a response to a chemical imbalance, therapy and treatment (sometimes with Prozac) may be merited. Although it is not easy to reverse any habit, Gottman and his associates suggest making a choice to look at the world differently. Create a new climate of praise and gratitude. Gottman says, "Instead of getting bogged down in people's faults and mistakes, you should get swept up in a fruitful search for reasons to say "Thank you" (p. 78).

Sixth, and finally, hold the conversations you need to have. Gottman says, "Self-disclose and connect" (Gottman & DeClaire, p. 83). The best place to begin these conversations is to focus on your feelings of the moment. Here are some examples:

"I'm so upset. I want to leave."

"I feel so defensive. I can't even talk straight right now."

"I am so angry, I want to shout."

"I feel so threatened, I think I'm going to lose you forever."

Working Together

In a group, discuss bids and responses to bids by answering the following questions one at a time around the group:

1. Have you noticed the way you made bids for connection with important people in your life today?

2. How did you feel about the way people responded to your bids?

3. Did you notice anyone responding positively to your bids? In what ways?

4. Did you notice anyone turning away from your bids? In what ways?

5. Did you notice anyone turning against your bids? What did your behavior look like?

6. How have you responded today to other people's bids for connection?

7. Did you respond positively? How?

8. Did you turn away? How?

9. Did you turn against any bids for connection? How and why?

10. Do you think bids and responding to bids is an accurate way to assess the quality of interpersonal relationships?

J. M. Gottman & J. DeClaire, *The Relationship Cure: A Five-Step Guide for Building Better Connections with Family, Friends, and Lovers,* (New York: Crown Publishers, 2001), p. 15.

Expressing your feelings—which we will discuss in the following section on Owned Messages—creates opportunities to connect (Weaver, 1996, pp. 149–54). Although difficult—it is always hard to discuss feelings—taking the risk of self-disclosure in a trusting relationship where both partners are willing to talk about an issue, express their feelings of fear, reluctance, or anxiety, will bring couples closer together and move relationships in a positive direction.

Owned Messages

An **owned message** (also known as an I-message, as coined by Thomas Gordon (1975)) is *"an acknowledgment of subjectivity by a message-sender through the use of first-person-singular terms* (I, me, my, mine). 'Responsible' communicators are those who 'own' their thoughts and feelings by employing these pronouns" (Proctor, 1991, p. 11).

Owned messages tend to provoke less interpersonal defensiveness than you-messages, and they are useful for conveying negative information. Some simple examples of owned and unowned messages will demonstrate the problem. To say "You make me mad" is an example of an unowned message (a you-message) and, as is obvious, has the potential for creating defensiveness in another person. To say "I'm feeling angry" is an example of owning a message and is less likely to create defensiveness. Clearly, you have a problem (potential defensiveness) when you use unowned messages; the solution is to use owned messages (owning your feelings) (Weaver, 1996).

Gordon said owned messages can be called "responsibility messages" because those who send them are taking responsibility for their own inner condition (listening to *themselves*) and assuming responsibility for being open enough to share their assessment of themselves with others. In addition, they leave the responsibility for the other person's behavior with them (Gordon, 1974, p. 139).

What does an I-message look like? Gordon suggests a behavior/feelings/effects formula for constructing I-messages. An example will illustrate its ease of construction:

1. A description by the one concerned of the other's unacceptable (disruptive) behavior.
2. The feelings of the one concerned in reaction to the other's unacceptable behavior.
3. An explanation of how the other's behavior interferes with the one concerned's ability to answer his or her own needs.

Example: "Jennifer, when you leave things everywhere (1) I get frustrated (2) because I cannot do what I have to do (3)."

Example: "Paul, when you take such long shower (1) I get annoyed (2) because there is no hot water left for me to take a shower, to do dishes, or to do the laundry (3)."

Example: "Susan, when you come home early in the morning (1) I get angry (2) because you wake me up from a deep sleep (3)."

Remember as you use owned messages, any given behavior can be an asset or a liability, depending on the goal or situation. Interpersonal skills are competent when communicators employ them sensitively and sensibly according to the requirements of a particular social setting. Using owned messages is a skill that is generally perceived to be competent across contexts. It can increase your sense of control and responsibility, and control and responsibility are issues that are basic and paramount to interpersonal competence (Parks, 1985, pp. 171–201).

■ SELF-DISCLOSURE: IMPORTANT TALK

Much interpersonal communication is made up of small talk. You talk to your classmates about a party, you discuss the weather with a stranger, or you talk with a friend about a ball game you saw on TV. Although this kind of talk is important in keeping society functioning, if you used only small talk, you would probably end up feeling frustrated. The problem with small talk is that it's not important enough. It doesn't touch on the central issue of who you are and what you need and want from life.

The Importance of Self-Disclosure

"Speaking our mind and heart is the most precious of human rights," writes Harriet Lerner in her book, *The Dance of Connection* (2001). "The ability to speak our own truths forms the core of both intimacy and self-regard." The poet Adrienne Rich puts it beautifully, Lerner writes, "It is not, she writes, that we have to tell everything, or to tell it all at once, or even to know beforehand all that we need to tell. But an honorable relationship, she

Telling a secret might be one form of self-disclosure.

reminds us, is one in which 'we are trying, all the time, to extend the possibilities of truth between us . . . of life between us' " (Rich, 1995). Lerner concludes, "When we are not able to speak authentically, our relationships spiral downward, as does our sense of integrity and self-regard" (pp. 4–5).

In order to communicate who you are to other people, you have to engage in **self-disclosure**—a process in which one person tells another person something he or she would not reveal to just anyone. To see how self-disclosure works, let's look at the case of Natalia and Misha.

One day Natalia comes home from work, and without saying anything to her husband or children, she begins to prepare dinner. When her husband asks her how her day went, she replies "OK" and continues with her work. She pulls pots and pans out of the cupboard with a big bang. When one of her daughters comes in to ask if she can help, Natalia answers, "I've got it under control." After dinner is finished and the dishes are done, Misha says to Natalia, "I know something is wrong. Do you want to talk about it?"

Natalia responds by telling him about a problem she is having with her new clerk. For the third time this week, the clerk misfiled important documents. Although Natalia says she has discussed the problem with her, she has the sense that the clerk is not paying very much attention—behavior that is making Natalia very irritated.

Natalia is able to tell Misha what is bothering her because they are in a close relationship. She trusts him: Not only is he her husband; he is her best friend. Her willingness to tell him what is bothering her is part of self-disclosure. She is able to tell him what has happened and, more important, to tell him how she is feeling about it.

Self-disclosure clearly shows the transactional nature of communication. Natalia can tell Misha what is bothering her because she knows from past experience that she can trust him to show concern for her problems. Misha

Consider This

In her article, "Overcoming Sex: Can Men and Women Be Friends?" Camille Chatterjee (2001) talks about the importance of self-disclosure in male–female friendships where sex is part of the dynamic:

Whatever the challenges of male–female friendship, researchers agree that to succeed as friends, both genders have to openly and honestly negotiate exactly what their relationship will mean—whether sexual attraction is a factor and how they'll deal with it—and establish boundaries. In Afifi's and Reeder's studies, (2000) the friendships that survived—and even thrived—after sex or attraction came into play were those in which the friends extensively discussed the meaning of the sexual activity and felt confident and positive about each other's feelings. Once they got past that, they were home free.

If sex is part of the dynamic, addressing it explicitly is the best strategy for making sure the friendship survives, says Werking (1997), "The issue will fester if friends try to ignore it." So in the end, male–female friendship does have something in common with romantic relationships: To work, communication is key (p. 67).

Questions

1. From your own personal experience, or the experience of friends you know, to what extent is sex part of male-female friendships?

2. How does one partner's willingness to self-disclose with the other—sharing his or her personal feelings about the relationship and about the role of sex in the relationship—bear on whether or not the friendship will survive?

3. Do you agree with the assessment that for friendship to work, "communication is key"?

4. From your experience, is it easier for same-sex pairs to be friends than it is for opposite-sex pairs? Why or why not?

5. In most opposite-sex pairings of college students, do you think those involved prefer friendship over sex? (". . .Of more than 300 college students surveyed, 67 percent reported having had sex with a friend. Interestingly, 56 percent of those subjects did not transition the friendship into a romantic relationship, suggesting that they preferred friendship over sex") (Chatterjee, 2001, p. 67).

Sources: W. Afifi, *Journal of Social and Personal Relationships*, 2000; C. Chatterjee, "Overcoming Sex: Can Men and Women Be Friends? *Psychology Today*, September/October; 2001, p. 67; and Kathy Werking, *We're Just Good Friends*. New York: Guilford, 1997.

is secure enough in the relationship to realize that Natalia is not mad at him—something else must be the cause of her behavior. Both of them know that when one talks, the other will show concern and understanding. In their conversation, they are communicating continuously and simultaneously. While Misha is wondering what Natalia is thinking, Natalia is sending out verbal and nonverbal signals.

You also rely on your past experience when deciding whether to engage in self-disclosure. Like Natalia and Misha, you are likely to disclose things about yourself to people you trust. Generally, you trust the people who you predict will react to you in the way you want them to. They are not likely to tell you that you are bad or that you have done a wrong thing. For example, you could confess to a friend that you once flunked out of school because you would expect him to react sympathetically. You can predict his reaction because you know him well and have experienced his reactions to you and to other situations. Self-disclosure, then, occurs when you discover people who believe the way you do and who react to situations and events the way you would; you trust these people enough to tell them about yourself (Wheeless & Grotz, 1970). The forthcoming Assess Yourself box on trusting others (pages 236–237) directly addresses the concept of trust.

The Process of Self-Disclosure

You should consider what to disclose and what to keep to yourself. One way to look at how this process operates was developed by Joseph Luft and Harry Ingham. Combining their first names, they labeled their model the **Johari Window** (see Figure 7-2) (Luft, 1970).

The "Free to self and others" area—the *open pane*—involves information about yourself that you are willing to communicate, as well as information you are unable to hide (such as a blush when you are embarrassed). When students meet for the first time in a class, they follow the instructor's suggestion and introduce themselves. Most of them stick to bare essentials: their names, where they come from, and their majors. When people do not

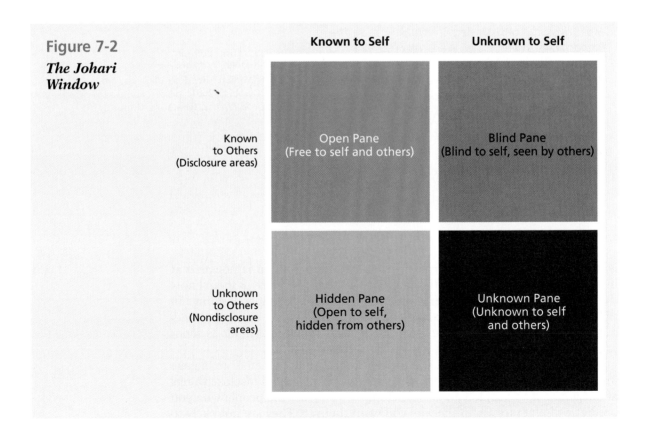

Figure 7-2

The Johari Window

	Known to Self	Unknown to Self
Known to Others (Disclosure areas)	Open Pane (Free to self and others)	Blind Pane (Blind to self, seen by others)
Unknown to Others (Nondisclosure areas)	Hidden Pane (Open to self, hidden from others)	Unknown Pane (Unknown to self and others)

know one another very well, the open pane is smaller than when they become better acquainted.

The area labeled "Blind to self, seen by others"—the *blind pane*—is a kind of accidental disclosure area: There are certain things you do not know about yourself that others know about you. For example, a husband complains that every time his wife comes home from work, she looks mad—something she didn't realize until he pointed it out.

The *hidden pane*—self-knowledge hidden from others—is a deliberate nondisclosure area; there are certain things you know about yourself that you do not want known, so you deliberately conceal them from others. Most people hide things that might evoke disapproval from those they love and admire: "I was a teenage shoplifter"; "I don't know how to read very well." Others keep certain areas hidden from one person but open to another: A young woman tells her best friend, but not her mother, that her grades are low because she seldom studies.

The *unknown pane* is a nondisclosure area; it provides no possibility of disclosure because it is not known to the self or to others. This pane represents all the parts of you that are not yet revealed. You might think, for example, that you are very brave, but you really don't know how you will react when you are faced with personal danger. The unknown area is sometimes revealed when a person undergoes psychological counseling. It is sometimes revealed, too, when people are willing to take risks—moving out of their comfort zones.

The disclosure and nondisclosure areas vary from one relationship to another; and they change all the time in the same relationship. Figure 7-3 shows how the Johari Window might look in a close relationship. In such a relationship, the open pane becomes much larger because a person is likely to disclose more. When disclosure increases, people not only reveal more

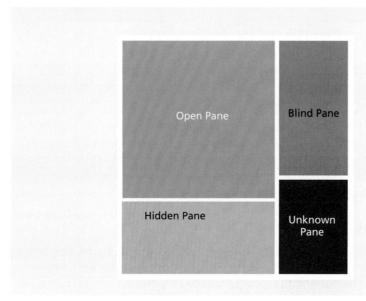

Figure 7-3

The Johari Window after a relationship has developed

information about themselves but also are likely to discover things about themselves that they had not known before. If you apply the Johari Window to each of your relationships, you will find that the sizes of the panes are different in each one. In other words, you are likely to be more self-disclosing in some relationships than you are in others.

Self-Disclosure and Intimacy: Rewards and Fears

Self-disclosure is the most rewarding when it leads to greater intimacy. Only intimate relationships give you a chance to really be yourself, to share who you are with another person. This kind of intimacy can be found in romantic relationships and among family members and close friends. A recent study has found that both men and women are willing to self-disclose to about the same degree (Dindia, Fitzpatrick, & Kenny, 1997).

Although in this chapter we take the position that self-disclosure is very important if you are going to have deep and satisfying relationships, we also acknowledge that many people fear the consequences of revealing themselves to another.

Fear of Having Your Faults Exposed

Self-disclosure in a relationship may lead to communicating that you are not perfect and exposing things from your past that you would rather keep hidden. Once your fears, anxieties, or weaknesses are known to another person, that person could tell them to others or use them against you. With students from a wide variety of age groups, one of the worst things that can occur is having their secrets told.

Fear That Your Partner Will Become Your Critic

By telling someone you are vulnerable, you open yourself to attack. A wife, for example, tells her husband how bad she felt when she wasn't invited to the senior prom. One day when they are having a fight, he says, "Don't tell me how much people like you. You didn't even get invited to the prom!"

Fear of Losing Your Individuality

Some people feel that if they reveal too much, they lose their sense of self, that there are private things that only they should know. This might be especially true during the years when teenagers are trying to gain autonomy from their families. Part of being autonomous is making decisions on your own and not telling everything to your parents.

Fear of Being Abandoned

Sometimes one partner is afraid that if the other knows something about him or her, he or she will be abandoned. For example, someone might not want to tell another about his struggle with alcoholism for fear that the other person will no longer love, accept, or want him.

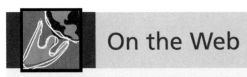

On the Web

Self-Disclosure on Computer Forms

Do people disclose more on a computer form than they do in an interview or on a paper form? With increased use of computers, the number of computer forms has likewise increased. These forms include mental health questionnaires, personality scales, job attitude scales, cognitive selection tests, and training inventories. Also, electronic surveys are used to gather personnel, medical, and consumer information. Researchers conducted a statistical meta-analysis of 39 studies from 1969 to 1994 using 100 measures, and they found that computer administration increased self-disclosure:

Among the reasons offered as to why people disclose when using a computer are that comput-er interfaces as compared with traditional formats create in respondents an inattention to audience, immersion in the immediate task along with a sense of invulnerability to criticism, an illusion of privacy, the impression that responses "disappear" into the computer, or other misattributions that cause respondents to be careless about their responses. For example, people can be induced to behave as if computers are human, suggesting that human-computer interaction is fundamentally social.

Source: S. Weisband and S. Kiesler, "Self-Disclosure on Computer Forms: Meta-Analysis and Implications." CHI96—Electronic Proceedings, August 11, 1999. Retrieved March 24, 2003, from http://www.acm.org/sigs/sigchi/chi96/proceedings/papers/Weisband/sw_txt.htm.

When Should Self-Disclosure Occur?

Disclosure should occur only in relationships that are important to you. People who do not know you very well are likely to feel uncomfortable if you tell them too much about yourself too soon. Wait until you have some signs that a relationship has the possibility of developing further. For example, if someone seeks you out to invite you to go out with him or her, after three or four times this is a sign that the person wants the relationship to develop.

For disclosure to work, both parties must be involved in it. If one person does all the disclosing and the other party just sits back and listens, disclosure is not likely to continue. Remember that disclosure means taking a risk. You will never know how another person will respond to your openness until you give it a try. To avoid getting hurt, try testing the water before you plunge in. One way of doing this is to talk about a subject in general terms and see how the other person reacts before you talk about your own experience with it.

Finally, examine your own motives for self-disclosure. Why do you want the other person to know this information? Will it really enhance the relationship, or can it do harm? All of us have some secrets that we should probably keep to ourselves. Sharing them may cause injury or make the other person lose trust in us. Although some secrets are a burden to keep, it may serve the interest of the relationship to do so. Those in relationships who believe in full and complete disclosure with partners risk the possibility of damage and even loss.

Assess Yourself

Trusting Others Scale*

Directions: Indicate the degree to which you agree or disagree with each statement by the following scale:

1 = strongly agree
2 = mildly agree
3 = agree and disagree equally
4 = mildly disagree
5 = strongly disagree

Circle your response following each question, but do not add the total until you have first consulted the Communicating Effectively CD-ROM and followed the directions for the "Assess Yourself," Chapter 7, Interpersonal Relationships, "Trusting Others Scale."

1. Most people in my life are reliable and dependable.   5 4 3 2 1

2. In general, when there is a task to be done, I prefer doing it myself rather than asking someone else to do it.   5 4 3 2 1

3. Other people, in general, possess what I consider to be core (essential) skills and abilities.   5 4 3 2 1   5 4 3 2 1

4. In general, people share relevant information with me.   5 4 3 2 1

5. I get overly anxious when an important job that directly affects me and that I could do is carried out by someone else.   5 4 3 2 1

6. In general, the actions others take live up to the values they claim to live by.   5 4 3 2 1

7. Sometimes I feel I am being taken advantage of when someone else is taking actions that directly affect me, and yet I have no control over those actions.   5 4 3 2 1

8. In general, other people have a benevolent attitude toward me.   5 4 3 2 1

9. When in a group, I prefer working independently rather than as part of the group.   5 4 3 2 1

10. People tell white lies.   5 4 3 2 1

11. I have confidence in the integrity, ability, character, and truth of most other people.   5 4 3 2 1

12. In general, when others promise they will do something, I believe it will be done.   5 4 3 2 1

13. When others perform actions that directly affect me, I expect positive outcomes to occur.   5 4 3 2 1

14. In general, other people are open and honest with me, sharing all of their information, not just selected facts or opinions.   5 4 3 2 1

15. Other people voluntarily share their information with me.   5 4 3 2 1

16. I prefer to let those around me work independently, even if their work directly affects me.   5 4 3 2 1

17. Other people listen to me and to my ideas.   5 4 3 2 1

Assess Yourself (continued)

18. In general, others do not do what they say they will do.	5 4 3 2 1
19. I prefer situations where people with whom I am working have full opportunities for mutual influence—me influencing them and they influencing me.	5 4 3 2 1
20. In general, people are considerate of the ideas and feelings of others.	5 4 3 2 1
21. I prefer to monitor the behavior of others when I know their actions will affect me in some way.	5 4 3 2 1
22. I am willing to allow others to take actions that are important to and directly affect me, even though I have no control over how those actions will be done.	5 4 3 2 1
23. In general, other people are not as important as I am.	5 4 3 2 1
24. In general, I prefer to work with others to obtain a mutually acceptable outcome rather than to work alone.	5 4 3 2 1
25. In general, most people meet my expectations.	5 4 3 2 1

Be certain to consult the Communicating Effectively CD-ROM before computing your total score. Once you have read the directions on the CD-ROM, compute your total score and put it here: _____

 Go to the *Communicating Effectively* CD-ROM to see your results and learn how to evaluate your attitudes and feelings.

See: Messina, J. J. and Messina, C. M. (2002). "Tools for personal growth: Building trust. Coping.org Tools for Coping with Life's Stressors." (Provided as a Public Service) Retrieved August 13, 2002, from http://www.coping.org/growth/trust.htm. I have quoted from their Web page, and I have refrained from using quotation marks simply because quotation marks form a minor barrier to the ease of reading the information.

■ FAMILY COMMUNICATION

"There are many kinds of success in life worth having. It is exceedingly interesting and attractive to be a successful businessman, or railroad man, or farmer, or a successful lawyer or doctor, or a writer, or a President, or a ranchman, or the colonel of a fighting regiment, or to kill grizzly bears and lions," William J. Bennett (2001) quotes Theodore Roosevelt as having said this six years before his death in 1919, and looking back on a lifetime of great goals, deeds, and honors, he also said, "But for unflagging interest and enjoyment, a household of children, if things go reasonably well, certainly makes all other forms of success and achievement lose their importance by comparison" (p. 173).

Robert Reich (2001), professor at Brandeis University and former secretary of labor under President Bill Clinton, listed the four criteria most families conform to: (1) Members of a family are expected to remain committed to each other. (2) They spend a lot of time together under the same roof. (3) Families reproduce themselves biologically and help their offspring grow

Families have a shared history and future. Strong families find support at spiritual, intellectual, emotional, and physical levels. What indicators do we have that this family finds support at these levels?

into adulthood. (4) They support one another—financially and with caring attention. But, Reich claims that "every trend line is moving in the opposite direction" (p. 174). "Connections are becoming more temporary, people spend less time together, couples are having fewer children, financial support between spouses is eroding, and care and attention are being subcontracted. Extend these trends into the future," writes Reich, "and 'family' may mean something entirely different from what it used to" (p. 174).

Julianne Malveaux, (2001) in her column titled "What Constitutes a Family Nowadays?" supports Reich's observations. She writes, "According to the 2000 Census just 23.5 percent of households now are 'traditional' families—a married couple and minor children" (p. 13A). She notes that other percentages are up, "families headed by single mothers or fathers, people living alone, and unmarried couples, heterosexual or homosexual" (p. 13A).

The point here is not the trends nor the statistics, it is that the notion of "family" means something different today than it did just 10 years ago for many people. And, extending current trends into the future, "family" will mean something entirely different ten years from today than it does now. Attitudes about the ideal family have changed, and certainly there have been strains, tensions, hurt, and disappointment along the way. There will certainly be different kinds and patterns of communication resulting from all the changes that are continuing to occur. Especially when there is emotional harm or violations from people you thought you could trust to love and respect you, and when deep resentment, anger, or rage has resulted, it is important to take the self-responsibility to heal the wounds so the relationship pain does not continue to deteriorate at spiritual, intellectual, emotional, and physical levels. Relationships have the potential to provide joy and even ecstasy, but the strains, tensions, hurt, and disappointments must be dealt with (Afua, 2000, p. 300).

What is the single place where you have had the greatest amount of interpersonal communication? Most people would probably say that it is at home, with family members. Families engage in interpersonal communication all the time: Their members discuss problems with each other; they sit around the dinner table and chat about their day; and they use communication to feel closer to each other.

To understand how interpersonal communication is used within a family, we must start with some definitions. A **family** is made up of two or more individuals who are joined together at a particular point in time through the biological or sociological means of genetics, marriage, or adoption (Noller & Fitzpatrick, 1993, pp. 2–3). This definition encompasses many different kinds of families. For example, one of your authors has a wife and four biological children; the other lived with her husband and his 12- and 14-year-old nieces (who also have biological parents). Both of these groups are families. Families are also made up of a single parent and a child, same-sex parents, and couples with no children.

All family communication is transactional. Families engage in continual and simultaneous communication; their members have a shared history and future. For children, this shared history may have begun with their birth. The transactional model may be very complex because each family member has a separate relationship with every other family member, and each relationship affects the family as a whole (Noller & Fitzpatrick, 1993, pp. 6–12).

The Systems Theory of Family

Because relationships and communication within a family are interconnected, researchers often look at a family as a system. The **systems theory of family** holds that a family is "a dynamic whole composed of constantly shifting interrelationships but still bounded and rule-governed" (Noller & Fitzpatrick, 1993, pp. 39–40).

The Whole Family Is Greater Than the Sum of Its Parts

Although you can look at family members as individuals, they can usually be best understood as members of the whole. When a child needs discipline, this often affects the whole family; if a teenage son has a lot of conflict with his father, this conflict has an impact on the entire family.

A Change in One Member Affects the Whole Family

Let's say a new baby is born in the family. Both the parents and the child's siblings will be affected. Attention is drawn from the other members of the family, and the next youngest child may feel slighted. Also, the baby's cries can interrupt anything else that is going on in the home.

We cannot predict whether families that face similar experiences will react in the same way or differently. For example, two families suffer from an earthquake and lose all their possessions. Members of one family work together by sifting through the rubble and supporting each other emotionally; members of the other family are so frightened and depressed that they are unable to do anything.

Family members tend to work to restore household equilibrium when there is tension in the household. For example, Cindy and Tom are always angry at their children for not doing their chores. They decide that rather than yelling, they will pay for each chore. The children like this system, usually do their chores, and peace is restored.

Communication about important change is very important in families. One study found that if parents were not open about an impending divorce, it would have a long-term impact on their children: The children would be dissatisfied with their parents' communication, and their own self-esteem would be affected (Thomas, Booth-Butterfield, & Booth-Butterfield, 1995).

Behavior Is More Revealing Than Words

The most important information about a family can be observed more through how the family members behave than by what they say. A wife, for example, may tell her husband that she loves him, but the real information about her feelings comes from the way she treats him. If she humiliates him in front of their friends or ignores him when he talks, she might be showing that she has little respect for him.

Family Members Conform to Rules

Families have rules about how individual members should behave and interact. Anyone who has lived in a family is familiar with such rules. Some rules are known even though nobody talks about them. Children know, for example, that there are appropriate ways to speak to their parents; all family members know that they are expected to be present for certain meals at certain times; a father knows that he is expected to spend some time with his children and to drop his daughter off at her job. Many of these rules change as circumstances change. For example, the rules about dropping a teenager off at her job and at social events change when she gets her driver's license. At this point the family develops new rules about cars and driving behavior.

Intimacy in Couples and Families

Although there are many kinds of families in the United States, the most common one begins with a man and a woman who decide to marry. Once the couple marries, they become a family. If children are born, the family expands.

To understand how a family functions, it is useful to begin by examining intimacy in couples, since the couple is usually the foundation of the family. Although many people may regard intimacy only as sexual, even the dictionary recognizes it as close or confidential friendship, the first definition there (*New Illustrated*, 1992, p. 513). Anyone, of course, can assemble a series of factors that make up or characterize intimacy. According to Patricia Noller and Mary Ann Fitzpatrick (1993), writers and researchers in the area of *Communication in Family Relationships*, the name of their book, **intimacy** is defined by some or all of the following characteristics: spontaneity, self-disclosure, motivation, interdependence, and tension and balance—what your authors have relabeled relational dialectics (pp. 243–245). If you have ever been in an intimate relationship, we think you will find that the following five characteristics truly meet the "eye-ball" test—they look, sound, and feel correct.

Spontaneity

In a close personal relationship, a key factor is *spontaneity*—the ability to be yourself, showing both your good side and your bad. In this relationship, you shouldn't have to play a role that is uncomfortable; when you are with your partner, you should be able to relax.

Whether you can reach this kind of intimacy during marriage might depend on what went on during your courtship. If you and your mate were on best behavior while you were dating, marriage might be a rude awakening (Noller & Fitzpatrick, 1993, p. 201). If a marriage is going to be successful, it is a good idea for you and the person you are dating to risk being who you really are.

But what happens if a couple is *not* spontaneous? First, Noller and Fitzpatrick defined intimacy by including *some* or all of these characteristics; thus, spontaneity—or any of the following—are not essential and necessary elements. The fact is, there are people who are *not* spontaneous—who cannot act from their own impulse, prompting, or desire. Spontaneity is a desirable element and important when present, but we are certain there are personal, individual, couple-related elements that may be just as important and may well substitute for the nonexistence of spontaneity—like the presence of laughter, surprise, or unusual caring. It may be a little like a sight-impaired person whose hearing is enhanced or a hearing-impaired person whose sight is enhanced because of the impairment.

Self-Disclosure

Being yourselves requires that you and your mate have the ability to open up and expect that your disclosures will be received warmly and sympathetically. When we talk about self-disclosing, we're talking about sharing your thoughts and feelings about life experiences, personal circumstances, emotions, dreams, opinions—everything. Do not disregard our discussion of self-disclosure in a previous section of this chapter. In the following table, we have listed some of the benefits of self-disclosure along with some of the risks:

Benefits	Risks
Helps gain information about others	Others may not respond favorably
Helps predict thoughts and actions of others	Others may gain power with new information
Gains access to other's thoughts and feelings	Has potential of damaging a relationship
Encourages others to self-disclose	Can lead to rejection
Deepens trust in relationships	Can lead to criticism
Makes you feel better about yourself and the relationship when accepted	
Offers truths, not just your good side or your social mask	
Leads to closer, more enjoyable relationships	
Enables deeper looks into yourself	
Helps resolve problems and interpersonal conflicts	

One additional note about the importance of self-disclosure. Researchers have shown that self-disclosers are more self-content, more adaptive and competent, more perceptive, more extroverted, more trusting and positive towards others than nondisclosing persons (Johnson, 1986). What should you do if you tend to be a nondisclosing person? Gradually work up to being more open. Start with telling a friend some facts about your work or classes. Save opinions and feelings for later. Once you feel okay about doing this, then select a trusted friend, and tell him or her what you think and how you feel about a movie, a political candidate, your boss, your parents, or your occupation. Try this with several people. Lastly, practice "here and now" talk with friends. Disclose what you are feeling towards and needing right now from the friend. This last stage is the most difficult. (*Psychological Self-Help.*) Self-disclosure is too important to the development of true, deep intimacy with another person, to allow a relationship to develop without it.

Motivation

Motivation is anything that incites you to action. Intimacy cannot exist unless both members of the couple want it and want to work toward it. If a relationship is what both members want, then there must be some action taken to establish and maintain that relationship; it cannot exist with apathy, complacency, and lethargy on the part of either partner. What action? The action can involve taking steps to be with the other person or taking steps to actively communicate with the other person. The action can involve your willingness to listen to your partner's point of view, share in his or her success and failures, communicate about your feelings, and unite with him or her against a world that might sometimes feel hostile. The action, too, should involve taking steps to make a "go" of the relationship under any circumstances—including, of course, the worst circumstances.

Interdependence

Interdependence has to do with the idea that each partner's well-being is dependent on the other's input. Both individuals have to function as one unit. Interdependence does not mean living under the same roof but leading parallel, nonintersecting lives. It might involve discussing the possibility of a new job with a partner, but, as a major and important aspect of that discussion, it should involve discussing the impact of a job change not only on the other person but the impact of any change on them as a couple as well. For example, when Melanie had the opportunity for a promotion to a new job with new responsibilities, she discussed it first with her significant other, Aaron. Melanie wanted to accept the new opportunity, but it would not simply require that the couple move, Aaron would have to find another job at the new location, and the couple would probably not see as much of each other because the new job would involve major traveling requirements as well. Because of the increased responsibilities, Melanie would be also doing more work at home, and her stress level would be increased.

After a week of discussion between Melanie and Aaron, lists of benefits and weaknesses of the new job and new location, and dozens of Internet searches for jobs for Aaron at the new location, Aaron not only told Melanie to take the job, but that he would do everything he could to support her in her new position—knowing, of course, that Melanie's happiness and increased income and status, would result in greater benefits for both of them. Melanie and Aaron functioned as a single unit—interdependence—knowing, in this instance, that what was good for Melanie would be good for Aaron and good for the couple as well. Aaron felt good that his input was a significant part of Melanie's decision making, and Melanie felt good that Aaron had provided significant input into her decision making.

Relational Dialectics (Tension and Balance)

Leslie Baxter and Barbara Montgomery (1996), offer, perhaps, the best explanation for the tensions couples in relationships experience. The premise that guides their research is that "relationships are organized around the dynamic interplay of opposing tendencies as they are enacted in interaction" (Baxter & Montgomery, 1996, p. 6). "Contradiction is the central concept of relational dialectics" (Griffin, 2000, p. 164). Their approach is dependent on the fact that relationships are always in flux, and the only certainty in relationships is certain change (Baxter, 1992). It is not just change, however, to which couples must adapt. Relationships are complex, messy, and always somewhat on edge (Griffin, 2000, p. 166). That is why communication is so important to couples and families: They are always having to deal with issues, ideas, and, yes, change. That is also why men oftentimes have more difficulty in relationships; they want the relationship, and they want to know it's there for them—a settled state. Because it is settled, they prefer not talking about it. An outline of Baxter and Montgomery's approach is available online (Shedletsky, 1999).

Baxter and Montgomery call their approach **relational dialectics,** the dynamic interplay between unified oppositions (1996, p. 8). They claim that

To hear Barbara Montgomery discuss her theory on "Relational Dialectics," view clip #10 on the CD.

contradictions occur "whenever two tendencies or forces are interdependent (the dialectical principle of unity) yet mutually negate one another (the dialectical principle of negation)" (Baxter, 1988, p. 258). It involves dealing with the natural forces couples must endure. Some of these are internal; some are external to the couple. For example, if you have ever been in a serious relationship, you know the struggle you have had as a couple with setting the degree you want to be connected to each other or separated from each other—the struggle you face between wanting intimacy and yet wanting independence. Connectedness versus separateness are unified oppositions. At times partners like to be very connected, but at the same time a degree of separateness is appreciated. We know a couple, for example, where the female wanted to continually smother the male with attention and affection—connectedness—but the male, although he loved his relationship partner, needed his freedom, independence, and distance—separateness—and it was the differences they experienced in this connectedness-separateness opposition that drove them apart.

According to Baxter and Montgomery, all relationships face this same tension, and rather than deal with it negatively or bemoan the difficulties it causes, they suggest that couples take advantage of the tension as an opportunity for better communication, for working out ways to deal with their conflicting desires, and for pulling themselves closer to each other because, "Bonding occurs in both interdependence with the other and independence from the other" (Baxter & Montgomery, 1996, p. 43), and "One without the other diminishes the relationship" (Griffin, 2000, p. 164).

Baxter and Montgomery list two other internal continua: certainty versus uncertainty and openness versus closedness. Regarding certainty versus uncertainty, think first about how much you want predictability in your relationship and how much you search for interpersonal certainty—both guarantees about the strength and stability of the relationship. And, yet, there is an equal desire for novelty. You want some mystery, some spontaneity, some surprise that will keep you interested in the relationship and having fun. Otherwise your relationship will become bland, boring, and, in the end, dead (Griffin, 2000, p. 168).

Regarding openness versus closedness in a relationship, think about how much each of you want to reveal about your past, how much you think about someone else, or how much you want to reveal about your feelings about your future with this partner—openness versus closedness—and how much you want to keep private. The pressures for openness and closedness wax and wane in relationships.

There is an external dialectic as well that includes three other continua that reveal the tensions created between relationship partners and the outside community: inclusion versus seclusion, conventionality versus uniqueness, and revelation versus concealment. And these offer a dynamic interplay between unified oppositions as well. Think first about how much partners want to include others into their intimate circle, or how they want to seclude themselves from others and the world. Think second how much partners want to conform with society's conventions, or how much they want to deviate from them by being unique. And, think third how much partners want others to know about them as opposed to how much they want to conceal.

Baxter and Montgomery offer eight ways couples have for dealing with or responding to dialectical tension (Griffin, 2000, pp. 171–72). Remember that the problem is that couples face opposing elements and have to, in some way, face the resulting dilemmas. **Denial** involves responding to one element of a dialectic while ignoring the other. **Disorientation,** a nonfunctional response, involves couples becoming overwhelmed by the contradictions dialectics present. **Spiraling alteration** involves separating the dialectical forces and responding to one pull now, the other pull later. **Segmentation** is a strategy of compartmentalizing different aspects of a relationship. Couples decide, for instance, to reveal some topics but suppress others. Although **balance** appears to be a useful approach because it is a compromise that promotes dialogue about both opposing dialectical extremes, and while both extremes are seen as equally legitimate, the balance strategy falters when couples try to meet the conflicting demands of the dialectic. **Integration** is a way that partners simultaneously respond to opposing forces without dilution or delusion. For example, a couple who successfully dealt with their opposing relational needs for certainty and uncertainty said, "We have one steadfast rule that every Friday night we do something new that we have never done before" (Montgomery, p. 211). Using **recalibration,** couples reframe situations so the tugs and pulls on partners do not seem to be in opposite directions; however, recalibration is simply a mental exercise and does not offer a permanent solution. Finally, **reaffirmation** involves an active recognition by both partners that dialectical tensions will never go away. Dialectical tensions, they would agree, are a relational fact of life, so why not acknowledge and celebrate the rich complexity of the relationship? Relational closeness generates problems. It is the rare, mature, and alert couple who can acknowledge, "If we weren't so close, we wouldn't be having all these problems" (Shedlesky, 1999). Also, using reaffirmation, couples are likely to face opposing forces as they arise in a positive, genuine, mutually supportive, and open manner. They become a test of competency: "A couple is interactionally competent to the extent that they can sustain an honest dialogue about the tension" (Griffin, 2000, p. 171).

Happily Married Couples

The traditional Protestant marriage ceremony puts it, "To have and to hold from this day forward, for better, for worse, for richer, for poorer, in sickness and in health, to love and to cherish, till death do us part." In their book, *The Case for Marriage,* Linda Waite and Maggie Gallagher (2000) say this about that vow: "As frightening, exhilarating, and improbable as this wild vow of constancy may seem, there is no substitute. When love seeks permanence, a safe home for children who long for both parents, when men and women look for someone they can count on, there are no substitutes. The word for what we want is *marriage*" (p. 203).

What makes a happily married couple? David Myers (1993, 1999) has compiled a list of factors that predict a lasting, happy marriage. Couples are more likely to stay together if they get married after the age of 20, date for a long time before marriage, are well educated, have a stable income from a good job, live in a small town or on a farm, grew up in stable two-parent

Another Point of View

William J. Bennett, in his book *The Broken Hearth*—a book first about the siege that has befallen the American family and, second, about the matchless benefits marriage bestows on individuals and society as a whole—provides a summary of his comments about cohabitation:

To sum up: Widespread cohabitation delivers, in practice, nothing of what it promises in theory. To the contrary, it undermines lasting attachments, mutual obligations, successful child-rearing, and sexual fidelity. It undermines those precious things themselves, and it undermines our belief in them. What it offers instead is a kind of institutionalized adolescence: a dream of free love freely bestowed, a love relying solely on the springs of mutual emotion and independent of the legal and other constraints imposed by state and society and their surrogates in the form of traditional family arrangements.

"It is a pretty enough dream—even if, like many an adolescent dream, fundamentally irresponsible. The only hitch is that in actual experience it has led directly to injury upon injury upon injury."

Questions

1. Do you have any friends or family members who would offer evidence (personal experience) of the injuries that cohabitation can provide?

2. To what extent is the freedom to leave a partner at any time—the freedom cohabitation provides—a freedom you would trade for the deep intimacy, commitment, and mutual support that marriage provides?

3. Do you believe that cohabitation is simply "institutionalized adolescence," or do you believe this is simply a label attached to it by those who disagree with it?

4. Do you believe that the state has any business interfering in people's private lives, curtailing their freedom of personal action, and regulating their domestic arrangements? Should these decisions be left to individuals alone with no interference from the state?

Source: W. J. Bennett, *The Broken Hearth: Reversing the Moral Collapse of the American Family* (New York: Doubleday [a division of Random House, Inc.]), 2001, p. 81.

homes, are of similar age, faith, and education, did not live together or become pregnant before marriage, are religiously committed, enjoy frequent laughter (not at one another's expense), have a minimum tendency to criticize and disapprove, and experience high instances of agreement. Though a couple will likely stay married the more of these factors that are true, none of them alone is enough to maintain or derail a stable relationship.

In a survey of 576 couples who had been married for at least 50 years, most of the partners agreed about what made them a couple. Ninety-eight percent said they did not try to change their partners; 91 percent said they confided in their spouses; 83 percent said they showed affection every day; and 89 percent said they felt their spouses were understanding. However, the men were more likely to define their marriages in a positive light than the women were (Peterson, 1994, p. 5D).

And if you want to become a happily married couple, what is being asked of you? "Great relationships aren't 50/50. They're 100/100," writes Gregory Godek (2000) in his book on romance. Although fifty-fifty sounds terrific, like I'm willing to meet you halfway, love means giving 100 percent. You might say, "But I can't give 100 percent of myself all the time, it's impossible," and you will be right. But, you can try for it, and when you fall short it'll be all right. "The problem is," writes Godek, "when you're both trying to limit your giving to 'your fair share'—usually defined as 50 percent—you'll *definitely* fall short of 100 percent" (p. 94).

Communication between Parents and Children

Hundreds of studies show that how parents communicate with their children will have long-lasting consequences on their children's emotional lives. Whether parents treat their children with harsh punishment or empathy, with indifference or warmth, is particularly important. Also, couples who have good emotional intelligence pass these qualities along to their children (Goleman, 1995, p. 92).

In regard to how parents communicate with their children, there has been much more research on mothers than on fathers. Generally, mothers send support or control messages to their children. **Support messages** make a child feel comfortable and secure in the family relationship. They include praise for the child's competence and reassurance when the child is feeling anxious. Children who get support messages from their mothers have higher self-esteem, engage in less aggressive behavior, and conform more to what their mothers want (Noller & Fitzpatrick, 1993, p. 201).

Control messages are designed to get children to behave in ways that are acceptable to the mother. These messages may take different forms. Some messages force children to obey. They may be threats, such as "If you don't . . . I will. . . ." These messages may involve physical punishment or taking away children's privileges ("You are grounded for a week"; "You can't use the car anymore.") Strong control messages have a negative effect on children. These messages increase aggression and decrease self-esteem, creativity, and academic achievement (Noller & Fitzpatrick, 1993, p. 202).

Mothers have two styles of responding to undesirable behavior. One style is **reactive,** in which the mother punishes the child when the behavior appears. The other style is **proactive.** In this style the mother anticipates that the undesirable behavior is coming and tries to divert the child. For example, children are usually bored in restaurants. The reactive mother scolds the child who misbehaves; the proactive mother brings along some books or toys. Proactive intervention takes more effort from the mother, but the long-term result is better behavior (Noller & Fitzpatrick, 1993, pp. 17–18).

Communication between fathers and children is not well documented because until recently mothers were regarded as the primary caregivers. Fathers have reported distress because work keeps them from spending as much time with their children as they would like. Some cross-cultural studies have shown that men are as good at caretaking as are women. However, it seems that only a few men take total responsibility for the care of a child. Their role is much more likely to be to help out when help is needed (Noller & Fitzpatrick, 1993, pp. 204–5).

Adolescent girls and boys have more communication with their mothers than with their fathers. Adolescents see their mothers as more interested in their problems, more open and understanding, and more able to negotiate agreements. Fathers, however, are perceived as more authoritarian, more judgmental, and less willing to listen. Because some adolescents see their fathers as stern and rigid, they are more likely to react defensively to fathers than to mothers (Noller & Fitzpatrick, 1993, p. 209).

Stepfamilies

Because of high divorce rates in the United States, many of the children born in the 1980s and 1990s are likely to spend some part of their childhood or adolescence in stepfamilies. The most common stepparent pair is the biological mother and a stepfather (Noller & Fitzpatrick, 1993, p. 238).

Problems in stepfamilies are likely to follow a pattern. Discipline is difficult in a "step" relationship, especially if the children are older when the stepfamily forms. Stepparents, for example, have to negotiate the difficult balance of forming a relationship with the stepchild while still being able to discipline him or her.

One of the greatest problems in a step relationship is that children do not want to accept the new stepparent. Many children fantasize that their biological parents will get back together, but a remarriage means that they must give up this fantasy. As a result, children often resent the new partner in a marriage, thinking, "If you hadn't come along, everything would have worked out."

In the new marriage it is inevitable that the natural parent will have less time to spend with the children. Because the children have often spent more time with the parent between the marriages, they resent the new parent for taking this time away from them.

Perhaps the main problem with stepfamilies is that there is no institutionalized set of rules and roles. The stepparent doesn't know how to act,

The beginning of a stepfamily is often perilous because there is no institutionalized set of rules and roles.

and the children don't understand the role they should play. Although these problems may work out in time, the beginning of a stepfamily is often perilous (Noller & Fitzpatrick, 1993, pp. 238–40).

Quality Communication in a Family

Researchers have found that four factors lead to good communication among family members: openness, confirmation, rules for interaction, and adaptability (Noller & Fitzpatrick, 1993, pp. 17–18).

Openness

Openness is the ability to disclose feelings in the family. Not only should children be able to tell their parents what they are feeling, but parents should be able to do the same with their children as long as they do not burden them with adult problems.

Confirmation

Family members should be able to be themselves within the family structure. This does not mean that they must always agree; it means that when they disagree, they will still be loved. If children cannot be themselves at home, they will have problems developing relationships with others, both friends and future partners. Like all members of the family, children play roles, but it is important that these roles not be too confining.

Rules for Interaction

All families have rules for how members interact with each other. A child usually learns these rules while growing up ("Don't talk to me in that tone of voice"; "Don't interrupt your sister"). These rules change as the children get older, since what works for younger children will not work for adolescents.

Adaptability

Children and parents need to adapt their communication to the situation. When parents must decide an issue that affects them as a couple, they are not likely to discuss it with their children. However, children should be consulted when an issue affects them. This may range from "Do you want to take your lunch or buy it in the cafeteria?" to "Do you want to rent a cottage on the lake or go away to summer camp?"

These four principles of communication are equally important if all family members are to be happy.

Subjects Better Left Unsaid in Families

Both of the following events actually occurred: A 16-year-old went home one night and told his churchgoing parents that he was an atheist; he thought his parents would be pleased that he was thinking on his own. A 13-year-old girl told her mother that she was having sex but that she had acted responsibly and first gone to a clinic to get contraceptives; she thought that since she had been responsible about the contraceptives, her mother would not be alarmed. As you can probably imagine, all the parents were greatly upset by these disclosures, which became points of conflict in their relationships with their children for many years.

Most kids know, and it has been confirmed by research, that there are certain subjects that are avoided in families (Guerrero & Afifi, 1995). Sex is one of them: Researchers discovered that if teenagers talked about sex with anyone in the family, it was most likely to be to a same-sex brother or sister. Children are also more likely to talk to their mothers than to their fathers about relationships, activities with friends, and romantic feelings for others.

Many teens do not want to talk about these subjects to anyone in their family because they don't want to lose their individuality or privacy, and they fear a negative reaction. As they mature into adults, however, there are fewer topics that are avoided because they develop a mature mutual relationship with their parents. In most people's lives there is a transitional time when parents stop being parents and become friends.

Chapter Review

Interpersonal communication, or one-to-one communication, is necessary for you to function in society. It helps you connect with others and develop empathy, and it contributes to your mental and physical health.

Emotional intelligence is an important part of interpersonal communication. It is made up of being aware of your feelings, managing your emotions, motivating yourself, recognizing emotions in others, and handling relationships.

All relationships begin with attraction. Although the basis of attraction might vary greatly from one relationship to another, you probably are most attracted to people with whom you have similarities and frequent contact. Sometimes you might form a relationship because you see something you can gain from it. To form a relationship, you need proximity—frequent contact with the other person.

The motives for seeking out interpersonal relationships are pleasure, affection (warm emotional attachments with others), inclusion (involvement with others), escape, relaxation, and control (getting others to do as you want them to or being able to make choices in your life).

Relationships with others are governed by the roles you are expected to play. Roles that reflect the structure of society are more rigidly defined than roles you establish with friends. Much of the communication you have in relationships depends on the role you are playing.

First contacts with others begin with small talk. An important part of small talk is asking questions because doing so helps you discover common ground with others.

Bids and the bidding process are the glue that holds relationships together. Bids can be questions, gestures, looks, or touches; and responses to bids are positive or negative answers to somebody's request for emotional connection. We discuss your ability to bid and respond to bids, how common the bidding process is, whether or not bidding has anything to do with relationship conflict, how relationships develop, the importance of the bidding process, and how to encourage bids.

Owned messages are acknowledgments of subjectivity by message senders through the use of first-person singular terms. Their value is that they provoke less interpersonal defensiveness than you-messages; thus, they not only assist the bidding process but encourage it as well because of the likely decrease in conflict and the protection of an environment in which bids and responses to bids can take place.

If you want a relationship to grow beyond superficiality, you must engage in self-disclosure. Self-disclosure is the process of communicating oneself to another person, telling another who you are and what you are feeling. Self-disclosure can be understood through the Johari Window, which has four panes: open, blind, hidden, and unknown. As a relationship develops and disclosure increases, the open pane gets larger.

Much of your interpersonal communication occurs within your family. A family is two or more individuals who are joined together at a particular point in time through the biological or sociological means of genetics, marriage, or adoption. In systems theory, a family is a dynamic group of people who shift interrelationships often but are still bound by rules. The foundation of a family is usually a couple. Intimacy within couples requires spontaneity, self-disclosure, motivation, interdependence, and tension and balance (or relational dialectics).

Relational dialectics is the dynamic interplay between unified oppositions—the conflicts that occur naturally in relationships that must be faced by couples. There are numerous potential internal and external factors that reveal the tensions couples must deal with, and there are eight ways for facing the dilemmas: denial, disorientation, spiraling alteration, segmentation, balance, integration, recalibration, and reaffirmation. Reaffirmation involves active recognition by both partners that the tensions exist and must be faced in a positive, genuine, mutually supportive, and open manner.

Communication between parents and children takes two forms: support messages and control messages. In their relationships with children, mothers are more effective if they are proactive rather than reactive (reacting to). Most adolescents communicate more with their mothers and see them as more sympathetic than their fathers.

Because divorce is common in America, many children are part of stepfamilies. Typical problems in stepfamilies include forming a relationship with a stepparent, finding time to spend with the biological parent, and dealing with a lack of institutionalized rules and roles.

Quality communication in a family seems to have four components: openness, confirmation, rules for interaction, and adaptability. There are some things that are better avoided in family communication. Generally, sex, if it is discussed at all, will be talked about more often with same-sex siblings rather than with parents.

Questions to Review

1. How is *interpersonal communication* defined, and when do you use it?

2. What is emotional intelligence, and how are the following characteristics part of it: being self-aware, managing emotions, motivating yourself, recognizing emotions in others, and handling others?

3. Explain how and why you are attracted to other people.

4. How do your roles and relationships influence your communication?

5. What is a bid, what is the bidding process, and how do they contribute to relationships?

6. What are the parts of an owned message, and how do they assist in conflict reduction?

7. What are the various positive influences on relationship maintenance? Negative influences?

8. What is self-disclosure, and how is it important to maintaining relationships?

9. Explain the Johari Window and its four panes.

10. What is family communication, and how do you explain it through a systems theory?

11. How do couples and families show and communicate intimacy?

12. What contribution does relational dialectics make toward explaining and dealing with the tensions couples must face?

13. In parent-child communication what is the difference between support messages and control messages? Give an example of each.

14. What makes up quality communication in a family?

Go to the self-quizzes on the Communicating Effectively CD-ROM (side 2, track 10) and the Online Learning Center at mhhe.com/hybels7 to test your knowledge of the chapter concepts.

References

Afua, Q. (2000). *Sacred woman: A guide to healing the feminine body, mind, and spirit.* New York: One World (Ballantine Books).

Baxter, L. A. (1988). "A dialectical perspective on communication strategies in relationship development." In S. Duck, ed. *A handbook of personal relationships.* New York: John Wiley & Sons.

———— (1992). "Interpersonal communication as dialogue: A response to the 'social approaches' forum." *Communication Theory* 2, 330.

Baxter, L., & B. Montgomery (1996). *Relating: Dialogues and dialectics.* New York: Guilford.

Bennett, W. J. (2001). *The broken hearth: Reversing the moral collapse of the American family.* New York: Doubleday (a division of Random House, Inc.).

Boone, M. E. (2001). *Managing inter@ctively: Executing business strategy, improving communication, and creating a knowledge-sharing culture.* New York: McGraw-Hill.

Booher, D. (1996, May). "How to master the art of conversation." *Vitality.*

Ceci, S. (2001, July-August). "Intelligence: The surprising truth." *Psychology Today,* 50.

Covey, S. (1998). *7 habits of highly effective families.* New York: Golden Books.

Dindia, K., M. A. Fitzpatrick, & D. A. Kenny (1997, March). "Self-disclosure in spouse and stranger interaction: A social relationships analysis." *Human Communication* 23:3, 388.

Fein, E., & S. Schneider (2001). *The rules for marriage: Time-tested secrets for making your marriage work.* New York: Warner Books.

Godek, G. (2000). *The author's annotated edition: 1001 ways to be romantic.* Naperville, IL: Casablanca Press.

Goleman, D. (1995). *Emotional intelligence.* New York: Bantam.

———— (1988, October 7). "Feeling of control viewed as central in mental health." *New York Times,* C1, C11.

Gordon, T. (1975). *P.E.T.—Parent effectiveness training: The tested new way to raise responsible children.* New York: New American Library.

———— (1974). *T.E.T.—Teacher effectiveness training.* New York: Wyden.

Gottman, J. M., & J. DeClaire (2001). *The relationship cure: A five-step guide for building better connections with family, friends, and lovers.* New York: Crown Publishers.

Griffin, E. (2000). *A first look at communication theory,* 4th ed. New York: McGraw-Hill.

Guerrero, L. K., & W. A. Afifi (1995, Summer). "Some things are better left unsaid: Topic avoidance in family relationships." *Communication Quarterly* 43:3, 276–96.

Hatfield, E., & R. L. Rapson (1992). "Similarity and attraction in close relationships." *Communication Monographs* 59: 209–212.

Infante, D. A. (1995, January). "Teaching students to understand and control verbal aggression." *Communication Education* 44:1, 51.

Johnson, D. W. (1986). *Reaching out: Interpersonal effectiveness and self-actualization,* 4th ed. Englewood Cliffs, NJ: Prentice Hall.

Knapp, M. L., L. Stafford, & J. A. Daly, (1986). "Regrettable messages: Things people wish they hadn't said." *Journal of Communications* 36: 40–57.

Kurlantzick, J. (2001, June 4). "Hello, goodbye, hey maybe I love you? Fast dating spawns a fast-growing industry." *U.S.News & World Report.*

Lerner, H. (2001). *The dance of connection: How to talk to someone when you're mad, hurt, scared, frustrated, insulted, betrayed, or desperate.* New York: HarperCollins.

Lindley, C. (1996). "Clyde's corner." International Personnel Management Association Assessment Council. Retrieved March 24, 2003, from http://www.ipmaac.org/acn/dec96/clyde.html.

Luft, J. (1970). *Group process: An introduction to group dynamics,* 2nd ed. Palo Alto, CA: Science and Behavior Books.

Malveaux, J. (2001, May 18). "What constitutes a family nowadays?" *Toledo Blade,* 13A.

Marano, H. E. (1997, May 28). "Rescuing marriages before they begin." *New York Times,* C8.

McCluskey, A. (2000, April 28). "Emotional intelligence." *Connected,* an online magazine. Retrieved March 24, 2003, from http://www.connected.org/learn/emotion.html.

Messina, J. J., & C. M. Messina (2002). "Tools for Personal Growth: Building trust." coping.org. Tools for Coping with Life's Stressors (Provided as a Public Service). Retrieved March 24, 2003, from http://www.coping.org/growth/trust.htm.

Montgomery, B. M. (1993). "Relationship maintenance versus relationship change: A dialectical dilemma." *Journal of Social and Personal Relationships* 10.

Montgomery, B. M., & L. A. Baxter (1998). Dialogism and relational dialectics. In B. M. Montgomery & L. A. Baxter eds. *Dialectical Approaches to Studying Personal Relationships* (155–183). Mahwah, NJ: Laurence Earlbaum Associates.

Myers, D. G. (1993, July/August). "Pursuing happiness." *Psychology Today*, 32–35, 66–67.

_____ G. (1999, January/February). "The pursuit of happiness." *Horizons*, 9–11.

(No author). (1992). *New illustrated Webster's dictionary of the English language*. New York: PMC Publishing Company, Inc.

Noller, P., & M. A. Fitzpatrick (1993). *Communication in family relationships*. Englewood Cliffs, NJ: Prentice-Hall.

Parks, M. R. (1985). "Interpersonal communication and the quest for personal competence." In M. L. Knapp & G. R. Miller, eds. (1985). *Handbook of interpersonal communication* (171–201). Thousand Oaks, CA: Sage Publication.

Peterson, K. S. (2003, February 11). "Dating game has changed." *USA Today*, 9D.

_____ (1994, November 15). "Sharing is the key ingredient to a long-lasting marriage." *USA Today*, 5D.

Proctor, R. F. II (1991). "An exploratory analysis of responses to owned messages in interpersonal communication." Unpublished doctoral dissertation, Bowling Green State University, Bowling Green, OH.

(No author). "Psychological self-help." Mental Help.net. Retrieved March 24, 2003, from http://mentalhelp.net/psyhelp/chap13/chap13i.htm.

Reich, R. B. (2001). *The future of success*. New York: Alfred A. Knopf.

Rich, A. (1995). "Women and honor: Some notes on lying." In *On lies, secrets, and silence: Selected prose, 1966–1978*. New York: W. W. Norton & Company.

Rubin, R. B., E. M. Perse, & C. A. Barbato (1998). "Conceptualization and measurement of interpersonal communication motives." *Human Communication Research* 14: 602–28.

Shedletsky, L. (1999, February 15). "Relational dialectics of Leslie Baxter & Barbara Montgomery." University of Southern Maine. Retrieved March 24, 2003, from http://www.usm.maine.edu/com/dialectic.

Sias, P. M., & D. J. Cahill (1998). "From co-workers to friends: The development of peer friendships in the workplace." *Western Journal of Communication* 62:3, 173–299.

Thomas, C. E., M. Booth-Butterfield, & S. Booth-Butterfield (1995, Summer). "Perceptions of deception, divorce disclosures, and communication satisfaction with parents." *Western Journal of Communication* 59:3, 228–45.

Vaches, A. (1994, August 28). "You carry the cure in your own heart." *Parade*, 4.

Waite, L. J., & M. Gallagher (2000). *The case for marriage: Why married people are happier, healthier, and better off financially*. New York: Doubleday.

Weaver, R. L. II (1996). *Understanding interpersonal communication*, 7th ed. New York: Harper/ Collins.

Wheeless, L. R., & J. Grotz (1970, Spring). "The measurement of trust and its relationship to self-disclosure." *Human Communication Review* 3: 250–57.

Further Reading

(No author). (2002, April 5). "Ask mr. relationship." Retrieved March 24, 2003, from http://members.ad.com/jfree81350/index.htm. Although we are reluctant to put a "Dear Abby" type of reading in our "Further Reading" list, and although we are unable to check out all of "Mr. Relationship's" answers, we found much of the advice here valuable. Go to the "Problem Solver Mailbox" in the left margin, click on "Relationship Letters and Answers" and you will get topics such as "fooling around," "relationship change," "threesomes," "breaking up," "feelings for ex," and "what makes a good relationship." There were over 70 topics as of March 24, 2003.

Boone, M. E. (2001). *Managing inter@ctively: Executing business strategy, improving communication, and creating a knowledge-sharing culture*. New York: McGraw-Hill. Boone has written a book for managers in an Internet-transformed world, but more important and relevant, it is a communication book for all people managers. She discusses power, conflict, and conversation, but her chapter "Get Over Yourself" on interpersonal communication as well as the ongoing and interwoven information on online discussion is informative and insightful. Her stories from CEOs, executives, and managers are impressive and valuable. Here is proof that the Internet has increased the need for superb communication and collaboration.

Dane, J. (2001). *Romantic stability*. Los Angeles, CA: Seven Arrows Publishing, Inc. In this 186-page book, the author itemizes romantic stability into six rungs: (1) Choose Your Favorite Style, (2) Discover Your Romantic Energy, (3) Consider What You Bring to the Table, (4) Clean Up Your Language and Determine Your Wants, (5) Evaluate Your Game, and, (6) Reflect on Your Purpose. This book is easy to read, understand, and use. Dane, using charm and compassion, and with information and support, urges us to continue to work on connecting with our partners in healthy, innovative ways.

Fischer, A. H. ed. (2001). *Gender and emotion: Social psychological perspectives*. Cambridge, UK: Cambridge University Press. This is a sophisticated, research-oriented book, in which scholars, using the most recent social-psychological research, address such issues as "When do people call someone emotional?" "Why is it generally accepted that women are emotional and men are not?" "What are the actual differences between men and women with regard to specific emotions?" "Under what circumstances are these differences most pronounced?" and "How can we explain these alleged differences?" The book is full of empirical evidence and theoretical explanations.

Foster, D. G. & M. Marshall, (2001). *How can I get through to you?* New York: MJF Books. The authors offer the "3R" system of read, respond, and reciprocate, to diagnose both you and your partner's styles (either feeler, analyzer, driver, or elitist), and then work to pinpoint the areas of stress between the two styles and solve the communication problems that arise. This book teaches you how to understand, celebrate, and use the differences between yourself and your partner to sustain and deepen mutually nurturing relationships.

Gottman, J. M., & J. DeClaire (2001). *The relationship cure: A five-step guide for building better connections with family, friends, and lovers*. New York: Crown Publishers. There is no question in our mind that Gottman's concept of the "emotional bid" can be a revolutionary idea for building (or assessing) successful relationships. Since a bid can be any look, comment, question, or gesture, this becomes a basic communication book. With questionnaires and exercises, it is a hands-on guide for improving connections with others through interpersonal communication. This is a well-written, enjoyable book full of interesting and useful advice.

Greenhalgh, L. (2001). *Managing strategic relationships: The key to business success*. New York: The Free Press (a division of Simon & Schuster, Inc.). From the front inside jacket description, ". . . Today's successful managers are primarily negotiators who are judged on their ability to foster, coach, protect, and support collaborative relationships—and manage conflict—with peers, workers, bosses, suppliers, customers, regulators, competitors, and stakeholders." With chapters on "Relationships between People in Organizations," "Relationships Involving Groups in Organizations," "Relationships Involving Organizations," and "Personalities and Relationships," Greenhalgh offers a well-written, thoughtful, and insightful book on interpersonal relationships. It is valuable for those involved or not involved in business.

Guilmartin, N. (2002). *Healing conversations: What to say when you don't know what to say*. New York: Jossey-Bass (a Wiley Company). What Guilmartin does is simply give you appropriate and caring things to say when you are at a loss for words. What do you say when a friend tells you she's lost her job? When a colleague's test results confirm cancer? When neighbors who are like family are moving away? When your best friend's mother is diagnosed with Alzheimer's? When your spouse's father suddenly dies? The table of contents lists close to 75 different situations, and Guilmartin's words teach you how to be gentle, human, and kind.

Lerner, H. (2001). *The dance of connection: How to talk to someone when you're mad, hurt, scared, frustrated, insulted, betrayed, or desperate*. New York: HarperCollins. Lerner teaches readers how to talk to the most difficult people in the most difficult situations, as when you are betrayed, rejected, insulted, or cut off. Lerner offers help when you can't figure out whether to stay or leave a relationship, when you can't make yourself heard, or when a partner or family member can't or won't apologize. The response to Lerner's other books, *The Dance of Anger*, *The Dance of Intimacy*, *The Dance of Deception*, and *The Mother Dance*, were positive, but many think this is her best book. Focusing on the authentic expressions of self, maximizing the chance of being heard, and keeping connections open, she provides concrete guidance on how to speak out in a wide variety of problem situations.

Lieberman, D. J. (2002). *Make peace with anyone: Breakthrough strategies to quickly end any conflict, feud, or estrangement*. New York: St. Martin's Press. Lieberman claims that the ingredients of all conflicts are fear and perceived loss of respect, and when people and events don't respond as we planned, we fear a loss of control. We compensate and translate this fear and lowered self-esteem into anger. Conflict resolution is accomplished, he further claims, by offering the injured party the ingredients for restoring self-regard and a sense of control. In this book, are step-by-step scenarios or scripts for resolving all types of conflicts. In the end, the book will help you keep your cool and choose your language better so that peace can be assured.

Olson, D. H., & A. K. Olson (2000). *Empowering couples: Building on your strengths.* Minneapolis, MN: Life Innovations, Inc. Based on over 20 years of clinical experience and research with couples, in this self-help book for couples, partners are led to identify their strengths, build and increase their couple strengths, identify some stumbling blocks, and develop a plan for building a stronger, more satisfying couple relationship. The authors cover couple communication, conflict resolution, roles, finances, spiritual beliefs, sexuality, couple closeness and flexibility, parenting, and couple goals. There are couple quizzes, stepping stones for building strengths, and couple discussion exercises.

Preece, J. (2000). *Online communities: Designing usability and supporting sociability.* New York: John Wiley & Sons. Preece, once again (in addition to her book on *Human-Computer Interaction*) beautifully synthesizes the sociological needs that communities require and the design elements of online activities, virtual spaces, and cybervillages. What makes this book interesting is her approach. Through the use of examples and case studies from actual websites and other electronic communications, she sheds light on tools that work to make them sustainable—that is, places where humans will want to live, work, and communicate. This is a well-researched, well-thought-out exposition of the human interface and social issues underlying virtual community design.

Rosenberg, M. B. (1999). *Nonviolent communication: A language of compassion.* Encinitas, CA: PuddleDancer Press. Rosenberg claims that the language of modern life is a language of judgment and criticism, a language that easily creates guilt and fear, and that easily plants seeds of violence. He shows that language can be a bridge to deep connection, and he challenges readers to be more mindful and conscious about the way they choose to use language. He offers a step-by-step approach, numerous exercises, as well as simple, inspiring stories that are profound, deep, and have lasting impact—all designed to grow and nourish your relationships with others.

Sommers, C. H. (2000). *The war against boys: How misguided feminism is harming our young men.* New York: Simon & Schuster. In this provocative, fascinating, well-written book, the author analyzes the work of leading academic experts who have suggested that girls are suffering from a decline in self-esteem, need extra help in school and elsewhere, and exist in a society that favors boys. With more than 500 footnotes, Sommers shows there is no girl crisis. Indeed, it is boys who need help catching up with girls academically. It is boys who need love, discipline, respect, moral guidance, and understanding. This is a book about gender differences between males and females.

Sone, D., B. Patton, S. Heen, & R. Fisher (2000). *Difficult conversations: How to discuss what matters most.* Bergenfield, NJ: Penguin USA. This is a how-to book from the Harvard Negotiation Project. It is designed for those honestly interested in elevating their communication skills who have endured hostile, annoying, and utterly unproductive talks with family members, bosses, co-workers, neighbors, and acquaintances. The authors walk readers through both mistakes and remedies in a way designed to boost confidence when unavoidable clashes arise. They offer real-world strategies and an ongoing road map to difficult conversations.

Tannen, D. (2001). *I only say this because I love you: How the way we talk can make or break family relationships throughout our lives.* New York: Random House. In a book aimed mostly at adult family interactions, Tannen, one of the world's most famous linguists, notes that it is metamessages–the unstated meanings based on tone, relationship, and past associations–that are the real messages. Using anecdotes filled with dialogues, she illustrates why we hear criticism when caring is conveyed and how family members create alignments with secrets and broken confidences. She examines the dynamics of arguments, the power of apologies, and gender patterns in family talk, and communication with teens. There are no quick-and-easy answers, ten-step programs, or proven solutions to family-relationship problems, just useful insights and helpful advice.

Williams, M. A., M. W. Williams, & D. O. Clifton (2001). *The 10 lenses: Your guide to living & working in a multicultural world.* Dulles, VA: Capital Books Inc. This is a sophisticated, intellectually grounded, and constructive framework for thinking about diversity issues. It helps readers understand different perspectives, even those dramatically different from their own. The new framework and new language allow greater freedom to talk about diversity and move towards greater understanding. This book is especially helpful in promoting communication among members of a highly diverse workforce.

Chapter 8

Evaluating and Improving Relationships

Objectives

After reading this chapter, you should be able to:

- Summarize the stages of a relationship in coming together and coming apart.
- List and explain the essential elements of good relationships.
- Tell how the following can become communication problems: aggressive talk, regrettable talk, criticism, complaints, avoidance, and defensive behavior.
- List the strategies for changing defensive communication.
- Explain how roles and expectations, renegotiating roles, and costs and rewards contribute to evaluating your relationships.
- Explain how empathic listening, I/you messages, and assertiveness can help communication.
- List and explain the steps in conflict resolution.
- Summarize the characteristics of relationships that work

Key Terms and Concepts

Use the Communicating Effectively CD-ROM and Online Learning Center at mhhe.com/hybels7 to further your understanding of the following terms.

Aggression 273	Conflict resolution 287	Empathy 280
Aggressive talk 272	Control 279	Evaluative
Assertiveness 286	Costs and rewards 283	statements 279
Avoidance 278	Criticism 276	Indirect aggression 273
Commitment 271	Defensive	Regrettable talk 274
Complaint 277	communication 278	

ON THE FIRST DAY OF CLASS, LENORE JARMANN WATCHED him walk into her business communication class at the university. Although she clearly thought he was attractive, she immediately put him out of her mind as the class began. But because the class was small and the instructor conducted numerous exercises and activities, over the next few weeks Lenore found herself in many dyads and groups with this fellow. She discovered his name was Marc Adams, and as she engaged in conversations and discussions, she found Marc saying many of the things she was thinking. By his nonverbal observation of her, obviously choosing seats next to her in class and in the group discussions, and revealing his sense of humor when they talked, Lenore knew that he noticed her, too. Marc also realized Lenore contributed interesting ideas to class discussions and seemed to smile and respond positively to his sense of humor.

One day toward the middle of the term, Marc saw Lenore sitting alone in the student union and asked to join her. She agreed, and they started talking about their class, the instructor, and their exercises and activities. Talk between them came naturally and easily. It was as if they had known each other for years. As they became more and more comfortable, they talked about what they liked to do in their free time and they discovered they both loved movies. Marc asked Lenore if she would like to see a new film opening at the end of the week, and she readily agreed.

Lenore and Marc have had an experience that occurs in various forms on campuses all over the country. People who don't know each other get together for a variety of reasons. They might, like Lenore and Marc, be attracted to each other. They could be co-workers who want to get to know each other outside work. They could be people who want to make new friends. On the basis of what they discover when they meet, they decide whether they should explore the possibility of a relationship.

■ THE STAGES OF A RELATIONSHIP

Most relationships begin with superficial communication; then, if the people like each other, they take steps to see each other again. Mark L. Knapp, a writer and researcher who focuses on relationships, has found that relationships develop along rather predictable lines. He describes five stages of how relationships come together and another five of how they fall apart. Each stage is characterized by certain kinds of communication (Knapp &

Vangelisti, 1995). In an analysis of Knapp's relational stages completed 20 years after their introduction, researchers report, "Taken together Knapp's (1978) stages represent the most complete possible progression of a relationship" (Avtgis, West & Anderson, p. 281). To support their conclusion that his model represents a full treatment of the relational life cycle, these researchers, using focus groups, identified specific thoughts, feelings, and behaviors at each of the stages. Whereas other approaches have been limited in scope because they addressed only particular behaviors or part of the process, Knapp's stages are complete. Let's begin with a relationship that is coming together, using the example of Lenore and Marc.

Coming Together

Stage 1: Initiating

Michael Levine and Hara Estroff Marano (2001), in an article entitled "Why I Hate Beauty," explain the importance of beauty in the initiating stage. They claim that "In the world of abstract logic, marriage is looked on as a basic matching problem with statistical underpinnings in game theory." They claim, "Logic says that everybody wants to do as well as they possibly can in selecting a life partner. And when people apply varied criteria for choosing a mate, everybody ends up with a partner with whom they are more or less satisfied. Not everybody gets his or her No. 1 choice, but everybody winds up reasonably content" (p. 42).

When Marc and Lenore started talking together, they began the *initiating* stage. As they talked, they probably assessed each other on various factors—such as clothes, physical attractiveness, and beliefs and attitudes. From all these observations each began to make judgments about the other: "He seems like a nice guy"; "She sounds like she is very smart."

Marc and Lenore were interested enough in each other to begin a conversation, but not all people will begin the initiating stage. On the basis of first impressions, we often decide the other person isn't interesting enough or doesn't seem to want to pursue a relationship with us. Often, too, although those experiencing the initiating stage may be curious, this stage is characterized by nervousness, caution, and a degree of hesitancy (Avtgis, West & Anderson, p. 283).

Stage 2: Experimenting

In the *experimenting stage,* people make a conscious effort to seek out common interests and experiences. They experiment by expressing their ideas, attitudes, and values and by seeing how the other person reacts. For example, someone with strong feelings about the equality of all races might express an opinion to see if the other person agrees or disagrees.

Marc and Lenore find they have common interests and values, and they both decide that they want to talk even more. They experience some connectedness and comfort with each other. They start going for coffee after class. They tell each other about their families and their friends. They meet outside class to eat a meal or watch a movie. At this stage of a relationship, everything is generally pleasant, relaxed, and uncritical, although still uncertain (Avtgis, West, & Anderson, p. 283). Many relationships stay at this

Consider This

"For many," according to Kamika Dunlap (2002) writing an article on "Online Love Connections" for the *San Jose Mercury News,* "online dating sites have become the new singles scene compared to more traditional places like clubs and bars. These sites attract a variety of people looking for romantic relationships, from receptionists to executives and long-time singles to widowers. Online matchmaking services can even accommodate specialized dating requirements for singles over 50, African-American singles, Jewish singles, gay and lesbian singles, and singles in the same profession. . . .

" 'Dating online is more about control and less about chance,' said Lawrence Cohen, a professor of anthropology at the University of California-Berkeley. 'This is a scary time and people are looking for security.' Many of the lifestyle questions added to online dating questionnaires are to help users define their ideal mate. They incorporate a number of variables including age, location, smoking and drinking tendencies, and education. In addition, users can type freeform in a text box detailing more insights about themselves and their interests" (pp. 1–2).

Source: K. Dunlap, "Online Love Connections: Computerized Dating Services Are Getting More Personal," *The Blade,* (Toledo, Ohio), Peach Section, March 15, 2002, pp. 1–2.

particular stage—the participants enjoy the level of the relationship but show no desire to pursue it further.

Stage 3: Intensifying

Lenore and Marc have discovered that they like each other quite a lot. They spend more time with each other because they are happy, loving, and warm (Avtgis, West, & Anderson, p. 284). This is the *intensifying stage* of their relationship. They swap DVDs and CDs and spend free time together. Not only do they enjoy each other's company, but closeness is both wanted and needed, so they hold hands, kiss, and hug. They start to open up to each other—telling each other private things about their families and friends. They talk about their moral values. They also begin to share their frustrations, imperfections, and prejudices.

Other things happen in the relationship. They call each other by nicknames; they develop a "shorthand" way of speaking; they have jokes that no one else understands. Their conversations begin to reveal shared assumptions and expectations. Trust becomes important. They believe that if either one tells the other a secret, it will stay between them. They start to make expressions of commitment such as making plans together: "Let's go to Ocean City to work next summer." Expressions of commitment involve buying gifts for each other or doing favors without being asked (Avtgis, West & Anderson, p. 284). They also start engaging in some gentle challenges of each other: "Do you really believe that, or are you just saying it?" Openness has its risks in the intensifying stage. Self-disclosure makes the relationship strong, but it also makes the participants more vulnerable to each other.

Stage 4: Integrating

Lenore and Marc have now reached the *integrating stage*—the point at which their individual personalities are beginning to merge. People expect to see

On the Web

Here is a selection of some online dating or personals sites:

- Date.com: Browse function displays photos and brief information about prospective dates within age groups but not by location.

- Jdate.com: Jewish singles network claims 300,000 members.

- Kids.com: Features breakdowns by gender and age of members online at any given time.

- Match.com: Quick search shows photos' age, location, and whether they are signed on at the time.

- Matchmaker.com: Established pre-online in 1984. Allows searching by ZIP code, age, religion, gay, or lesbian.

- Udate.com: Claims to be No. 1 site for singles 25 and older.

Source: K. Dunlap, "Online Love Connections: Computerized Dating Services are getting more Personal, *The Blade*, Toledo, Ohio, Peach Section, March 15, 2002, pp. 1–2.

them together, and they are unhappy when apart (Avtgis, West, & Anderson, p. 284). If people see just one of them, they ask about the other. The friendship has taken on a specialness. They do most things together and reflect about their common experiences—the things they do together. They go to the same parties and have a lot of the same friends; their friends assume that if they invite one, they should invite the other. Each of them is able to predict and explain the behavior of the other. They feel like one person.

The integrating stage is reached only when people develop deep and important relationships. Those who reach this stage are usually best

At the bonding stage participants make a formal commitment that announces their relationship to those around them.

friends, couples, or parents and children. It is at this stage—if it hasn't happened before—that partners meet one another's family and friends.

Stage 5: Bonding

The last coming-together stage of a relationship is the *bonding stage.* At this point, the participants make some sort of formal commitment that announces their relationship to those around them. For Lenore and Marc, an announcement of their engagement or marriage would be an example of bonding. In other cases, such as those between friends, the bonding agreement might be less formal—for example, signing a lease together. Whatever form it takes, bonding makes it more difficult for either party to break away from the relationship. Therefore, it is a step that is taken when the participants have some sort of long-term commitment to their relationship.

At this stage, the partners experience true unity as they make plans for the future, pledge their love to each other, make agreements and promises about the future, and talk about birth control and children as well as financial and career issues. They are relaxed and often overcome with joy and happiness as they move in together, think about each other constantly, and have joint possessions (Avtgis, West & Anderson, 1998, p. 284).

What may not be clear from our discussion of bonding is that the term *bonding* can apply in many nonromantic relationships as well. For example, good friends become best friends often because of some especially meaningful (good or bad) "bonding" experience. Dorm roommates are often randomly assigned, but nonromantic apartment mates, who must depend on each other for bill paying, housekeeping, amenities, and the like, are more likely to be successful if they've reached a bonded relationship before moving in together. Partners in business, in the police, or in the military—where their success, reputations, and even survival depend on close bonding with and trusting of each other—learn to "think alike" or at least to think in such a way that each knows exactly what to expect from the other in critical situations. This same kind of bonding can occur between dancers and ice skaters as well.

Although there are times when you may want to believe it isn't so, sex on its own, or a "one-night stand" with a virtual stranger, is not bonding. For some partners, such events can lead to pregnancy and then years of often-hostile dealings with each other. The relationship never experienced true bonding. It may even reach a point at which the partners refer to each other as "my baby's father" or "my son's mother."

Advancing from Stage 1 to Stage 5

The five coming-together stages build on one another. Whether a relationship will move from one stage to the next depends on both participants. If one wants to move to the next stage, doing so will not be possible unless the other agrees. Because most of us have only limited time and energy for intense relationships, we are willing to let most of our relationships remain at the second or third stage. The first three stages permit us to become involved in friendships and to carry out normal social activities. The fourth and fifth stages, integrating and bonding, demand much more energy and commitment—they are reserved for very special relationships.

Consider This

A Man, a Woman, and a Cat: Stages in a Relationship

At the beginning of a relationship. . .

Woman: *Darling, I'd like you to meet my cat.*

Man: *(under his breath: Ugh. I hate cats.) Uh, hi. Nice kitty.*

As the relationship progresses. . .

Woman: *Dear, I get the impression that you don't like my cat.*

Man: *That's ridiculous. I love Poopsie. (Under his breath: This cat is ruining our relationship.)*

As the relationship reaches a more stable level. . .

Woman: *Oh, Poopsie looks just so cute sitting there on your lap.*

Man: *(Darn thing's shedding all over my new suit.) Well, I guess she's not so bad.*

Later. . .

Woman: *I swear, you like that cat more than you like me.*

Man: *You know that's not true. I can't help it if she follows me around all the time.*

The final stages. . .

Man: *Honey, have you seen my cat anywhere?*

Woman: *What do you mean,* your *cat?*

Source: From "A Man, a Woman, and a Cat: Stages in a Relationship" by Colin McEnroe, columnist for the Hartford Courant. Retrieved from Tina Mancuso, "A Man, a Woman, and a Cat: Stages in a Relationship," Monster-Island, Aug. 14, 1999. Retrieved March 24, 2003, from www.monster-lisland.org/tinashumor/humor/relcats.html.

Another point should be made about these stages: People in a new relationship should not try to progress too quickly beyond stage 1 or 2. In all relationships it is important that each participant be sensitive to feedback from the other. It is this feedback that will determine whether it is time to advance to another stage. Since stage 3 is the first in which there is self-disclosure, moving from stage 2 to stage 3 is particularly sensitive. If one person opens up too quickly, the other might feel so uncomfortable that he or she will be unwilling to go on to a new stage in the relationship.

Coming Apart

For a relationship to continue, both participants must grow and change together. If they cannot do this in ways that are satisfying to both of them, the relationship will come apart. Although it is more satisfying to look at relationships coming together, we all know that relationships also fail. Relationships that are failing can also be described in five stages—stages that reverse the process of coming together.

Stage 1: Differentiating

Time has passed, and Lenore and Marc have been married for over a year. The first months were a little rocky, but now serious problems are beginning to emerge. Lenore likes to go out several nights each week; Marc wants to stay home. Marc likes to cook new and exotic food; Lenore wants to eat meat and potatoes. Even their love for movies is causing conflict: Lenore wants to see them as soon as they open; Marc wants to wait until they are released as videos so that they can watch them at home.

Lenore and Marc have entered the *differentiating stage.* The interdependence of their courting stage is no longer so attractive. Now they are beginning to focus on how different they are, and much of their conversation is about their differences rather than their similarities. There is noticeable arguing, with talk about being incompatible (Avtgis, West, & Anderson, 1998, p. 284).

To some extent, the differentiating stage is a healthy phase that most couples experience. Many couples work out their differences by being autonomous some times and interdependent other times. For example, Lenore and Marc go together to family gatherings and to parties. However, when Marc goes hunting, Lenore goes shopping.

The differentiating stage can be worked out if the differences are not too great. Marc, for example, wants to begin a family right away, but Lenore isn't sure that she wants to have children. Since this issue doesn't lend itself to compromise, their conversations begin to take on a quarrelsome tone. Marc says, "I think we should have our children while we are still young." Lenore replies, "If I don't work on my career now, I'll be left behind."

The differences the two recognized and tolerated during the stages of coming together become focal points for discussion and argument. Lenore says, "It's a lot better to watch movies on the big screen than on video. Can't you tell the difference?" On another occasion Marc says, "Didn't your family ever eat anything different? I'm sick of roast beef and potatoes."

The most visible sign of differentiating is conflict. But differentiating can take place without conflict. Even if nothing specific is bothering the couple, they may discover, as they mature and find new interests, that they have less and less to talk about. Lenore, for example, reads the newspaper every day and follows world events. Marc, on the other hand, gets his news from television and finds it too depressing to talk about. Each experiences slight loneliness because the two of them are no longer as close as a couple, and regarding the relationship itself, there is some confusion and inadequacy creeping in (Avtgis, West, & Anderson, 1998, p. 284). What is happening? Where is the relationship going? How long can it go on like this? Am I at fault? Should I admit that I am to blame so that we can mend the relationship and go on? These are a few of the questions that one or the other partner may be considering; usually they are internalized and never expressed at this stage.

Stage 2: Circumscribing

When a relationship begins to fall apart, less and less information is exchanged. It seems better to stay away from mentioning points of conflict in the relationship in order to avoid a full-scale fight. Thus this is called the *circumscribing stage.*

Now conversation is superficial; everyday matters are discussed: "Your mail is on the desk." "Did I get any telephone calls?" "Do you want some popcorn?" The number of interactions is decreased, the depth of discussions is reduced, and the duration of each conversation is shortened. Because communication is constricted, the relationship is constricted.

Most people who find themselves in this stage try to resolve their problems by discussing the relationship itself. In response, the negative turn in the relationship might change. For example, Marc could go out to a movie with Lenore, and Lenore could agree to try some different food. In other cases, discussion about the relationship might reveal greater differences between the participants. In such cases, discussion about the relationship leads to even more conflict, so the participants limit discussion to "safe" topics. Lenore and Marc, for instance, stay away from the topic of children because they know they will fight about it.

Often, people at this stage pursue different activities. Sometimes, too, they act aloof from each other. These experiences reveal coldness and distance. With respect to each other, partners are uncaring, and one or the other may become depressed or frustrated, feeling unloved and misunderstood (Avtgis, West & Anderson, 1998, p. 285).

Persons who are in this stage often cover up their relationship problems. Although they might reveal problems to very close friends, in social situations they give the appearance of being committed to each other. They create a social or public face—in essence, a mask.

Stage 3: Stagnating

The *stagnating stage* is a time of inactivity. The relationship has no chance to grow, and when the partners communicate, they talk like strangers. The subject of the relationship itself is now off limits. In some cases they may want to talk about the relationship but then may decide not to. Rather than try to resolve the conflict, they are more likely to take the attitude of "Why bother to talk? We'll just fight, and things will get even worse"; thus, for self-protection, they give short answers to questions.

How long this stage lasts depends on many things. If Lenore and Marc lead busy lives and just come home to sleep, they might go on in this stage for months or even years. However, if Marc stays home and broods about the relationship, he may look for some kind of resolution to their conflict. Most couples whose relationship reaches this stage feel a lot of pain. The partners may find it hard to separate and may hold on to the hope that they can still work things out. Either partner at this stage may feel unwanted, scared, bored, and sentimental (Avtgis, West & Anderson, 1998, p. 285).

Stage 4: Avoiding

The *avoiding stage* involves physical separation. The parties avoid face-to-face interaction. They are not interested in spending time together, in building any kind of relationship, or in establishing any communication channels.

This stage is usually characterized by unfriendliness, hostility, and antagonism. Sometimes the cues are subtle: "I only have a minute. I have an appointment." They can also be direct and forceful: "Don't call me anymore" or "I'm sorry, I just don't want to see you." Often, responses are "I don't care" and "I don't know." If communication occurs, it covers general matters only; there is no talk about the relationship.

In relationships where physical separation is impossible, the participants may act as if the other person does not exist. Partners eat in silence, stay busy, and, if possible, spend a lot of time away (Avtgis, West & Anderson, 1998, p. 285). Each one carries on his or her activities in a separate room and avoids any kind of interaction. In the case of Lenore and Marc, Lenore might sleep in the bedroom and Marc on the living room couch. Often, partners feel some sense of nervousness, as well as helpless and annoyed (Avtgis, West & Anderson, 1998, p. 285).

Stage 5: Terminating

In the *terminating stage,* the participants find a way to bring the relationship to an end. Each party is preparing for life without the other. Differences are emphasized, and communication is difficult and awkward. They may talk about staying in touch and discuss what went wrong. A goal at this stage may be to divide up their belongings. There are feelings of unhappiness, but these are accompanied by a sense of relief. Other feelings likely to occur during this stage are sadness and depression—and sometimes happiness, too. Often one partner or the other is lonely or scared because of having to face life alone again. Sometimes the reality of termination causes one or the other partner to cry (Avtgis, West & Anderson, 1998, p. 285).

In an article entitled "The Rhetoric of Goodbye," Knapp (1973) and his colleagues describe three distinct types of statements that commonly occur in terminating relationships. First, there are summary statements: "Well, we certainly have tried to make a go of it," or "This isn't the end for either of us; we'll have to go on living." Second are statements that signal the likelihood of decreased access: "It might be better if we didn't see each other quite so often." Finally, there are messages that predict what the future relationship (if any) will be like: "I don't ever want to see you again," or "Just because we aren't going to live together doesn't mean we can't be friends" (Knapp, Hart, Friedrich & Shulman, 1973).

Some relationships cannot be entirely terminated. There are cases in which the parties have to have some contact. Partners who have children cannot entirely end their relationship if the children are going to see both parents. In this kind of situation, the parents might terminate their relationship with each other as marriage partners but decide to continue in some kind of relationship as parents to the children. The more amicably this can be done, the better it is for the children involved. To do so peacefully, partners might set down a list of rules that will govern the new relationship (Banks, Altendorf, Greene, Cody, 1987). When the termination is a divorce, the court is the one that establishes the rules.

Sociologist Diane Vaughan (1990) has studied the patterns that occur when a relationship is about to end. She says that one member of the couple, realizing he or she is unhappy, begins the process of ending the relationship. This person typically begins by finding alternatives—often in the form of a transitional person. Although the transitional person might be a romantic interest, the person could also be a minister, a therapist, or a good friend. When one partner begins to find satisfaction elsewhere, the couple's relationship becomes less endurable. At this point the dissatisfied person lets the other know of his or her discontent through body language and words.

Finally the time comes when the dissatisfied person lets the partner know that he or she wants to end the relationship. The partner typically feels betrayed, hurt, and shocked—and is often unprepared. Vaughan says

Another Point of View

How does the institution of marriage measure up in our high-tech society? Dr. Robert Epstein, the editor in chief of *Psychology Today,* University Research Professor at California School of Professional Psychology at Alliant International University, and Director Emeritus of the Cambridge Center for Behavioral Studies in Massachusetts, and Harvard Ph.D. has an answer:

The problem is that the marriage contract isn't worth the paper it's written on. Prenuptial agreements are now harder to break than marriage contracts. Marriage is no longer a vehicle for permanent commitment, because it's too easy to change one's mind. As singer Paul Simon might have said, there are 50 ways to leave your spouse.

So what can couples do who want to stay together forever? I say, let's create a new institution—call it moorage, maybe, after the way we secure a ship to a dock. And let's create a moorage contract, one that's really binding. All it will take to get things going are a few committed couples, acting on their own, jotting down some special words on a piece of paper, loving each other and standing by what they write.

Knowing that you've just entered into a permanent arrangement keeps you working hard to make that arrangement work. Stresses and strains are inevitable in a relationship. With a high level of commitment, people get through rough times—often with marvelous times ahead, born in part of the stresses a couple has shared and conquered.

Moorage isn't for everyone, of course. We also need to recognize the short-term commitment—yes, mereage—rather than trying to fold it into the institution of marriage. And for those who are willing to commit to raising children through the age of majority but who aren't interested in that lifetime thing, we probably need yet another type of contract—moreage, perhaps?"

Questions

1. What do you think of the premise for this whole article, "The marriage contract isn't worth the paper it's written on"? True or false?

2. Are there any problems with Epstein's idea? What are they?

Source: R. Epstein, "M Words: Marriage, Mereage, Moorage, and More," *Psychology Today,* January/February 2002, p. 5.

that during the breakup, both partners suffer emotional pain and go through the same stages of disengagement—the process just happens at different times for each of them (p. 124).

■ ESSENTIAL ELEMENTS OF GOOD RELATIONSHIPS

Most authors who look at relationships between couples and among family members and friends believe that they have certain elements in common. Once you have begun using bids and owned messages, as discussed in the previous chapter, and a relationship has truly begun, you need to grow the relationship. Here is our list of the elements that tend to draw people together. Following our list of positive elements, we offer several negative ones. You may be good at implementing some of these elements and weak in others, but knowing the factors may be helpful to maintaining interpersonal relationships.

Verbal Skills

Verbal skills, as noted in Chapter 5, Verbal Communication, include not just your vocabulary and understanding of language, and not just your ability to use language, although all of these are part of verbal skills. More than anything else, it depends on your willingness—motivation—to talk. Bids and the bidding process require verbal skills. Partners in good relationships must have ongoing conversations, or dialogues, about the relationship itself. They must be able to search together for ways of reducing conflict, to discuss expectations they have of each other, and to explore anything else that might affect the relationship. In her article, "Finding Real Love," Cary Barbor (2001) ends by saying, "Learning how best to communicate with each other and treat one another will help us enjoy loving, lasting relationships" (p. 49).

Not only do females begin talking earlier than males, on most national assessment tests they score well ahead of males in reading and writing, and many more major in English, comparative literature, and foreign languages (Kimura, 1999, p. 26; Hedges & Nowell, pp. 41–45; Halpern, 1992; Blum, 1997). Michele David claims that "Men sometimes get overloaded with words and they stop listening. When that happens, it doesn't matter *how* their wives say things, they're not going to be able to get through to their husbands with words. It's in one ear and out the other" (David, 2001, p. 118). This should not serve as an excuse for men to stay quiet. To level the playing field, males may need to apply themselves more when it comes to verbal skills because for partners to continue in a relationship, they must find mutually beneficial ways of communicating. Also, males need to alter their perception of relationships as stable, static commodities that once achieved never need discussion or reexamination.

Emotional Expressiveness

Gottman (2001) noted that your ability to bid and to respond to bids depends on the way your brain processes feelings, the way emotions were handled in your home, and your emotional communication skills (pp. 65–87). Christina Hoff Sommers, to whom we have referred earlier in this book, claims that the increased ability of females over males in verbal skills, "may be responsible for their superior emotional expressiveness" (Sommers, 2000, p. 87). Her claim is supported by Daniel Goleman in *Emotional Intelligence* (1995), who says "Because girls develop language more quickly than do boys, this leads them to be more experienced at articulating their feelings and more skilled than boys at using words to explore and substitute for emotional reactions such as physical fights" (p. 131). Not only are females more expressive and responsive to others, they "invite others into conversations" (Wood, 1998, p. 69). Once again, to level the playing field, males need to improve their ability at emotional expressiveness.

Emotional expressiveness may involve discussing points of conflict. This is particularly important if relationships are to be successful. Some people are conditioned to stay away from conflict. Childhood messages such as "Hold your tongue," and "I don't ever want to hear you talk that way again," lead us to believe that it's wrong to say words that other people do not want to hear.

Working Together

One area of difficulty often expressed by couples is getting men to open up and express their feelings to women. In this mixed-sex group discussion, the purpose is to explore some of the reasons why this area of difficulty continues. In the first part of the group discussion, group members are simply to express their point of view and any relevant supporting experiences, on the following topic:

Men in relationships often have difficulty expressing their feelings or openly discussing their relationships with their relationship partner.

This is not just an opportunity to gang up on men; it is a chance to confront one of the major gender issues in male-female interpersonal relationships. Women as well as men should feel free to express their feelings on this topic, and where possible to provide some examples that would support their point of view.

After everyone in the group has had an opportunity to talk about the topic above, the group can proceed to the second part of the discussion. Once again, everyone in the group should have an opportunity to contribute to the constructive/instructive portion of the discussion:

What can be done in a relationship to facilitate better communication between relationship partners?

Write the suggestions down. At the end of this discussion about what can be done, arrange the suggestions in hierarchical order with the most important suggestion listed first and the least important listed last. Now, have a full-class discussion using the chalkboard to list the suggestions from the various groups.

As adults, however, we have to recondition ourselves to discuss areas of conflict: withdrawing from or avoiding conflict is too harmful to relationships.

Conversational Focus

A third factor likely to affect your ability to handle relationships is what you choose to talk about. Sommers claims that "Males, whether young or old, are less interested than females in talking about feelings and personal relationships" (2000, p. 151). Researchers at Northwestern University analyzed the conversational focus of college students gathered around a cafeteria table (Levin & Arluke, 1985). They discovered that 56 percent of the women's targets were intimates, close friends, boyfriends, and family members, but only 25 percent of the conversational focus of men was friends and relatives (pp. 281–285). When researchers simultaneously presented male and female college students with two images on a stereoscope, one of an object, the other of a person, male subjects more often saw the object while female subjects more often saw the person (McGuinness & Symonds, 1977). Males need to increase their focus on feelings and relationships—to not only make their feelings known, but to make other people, especially their relationship partner, know how they feel about them and about their relationship.

Nonverbal Analysis

A fourth factor that will affect your ability to handle relationships is your ability to read between the lines, to analyze the nonverbal cues of the other person. There are dozens of experiments that confirm "that women are much better than men at judging emotions based on the expression on a stranger's face" (Sommers, 2000, p. 151; Brody & Hall, 1993, p. 452). Not only are women better at observing the nonverbal cues of others, they also "tend to give obvious visual and vocal clues to signal they are following what others say and are interested in it" (Wood, 1998, p. 69). Clues might include nodding their heads, smiling, establishing eye contact, and offering responsive gestures (p. 69). Males need to increase their sensitivity to nonverbal cues. Because they are not conditioned to be as observant in this area, they need to be especially vigilant and aware.

Conversational Encouragement

Often, men listen to others without showing their feelings; they keep their responses and feelings to themselves, as noted in the section on emotional expressiveness above. This can be interpreted as an unwillingness to listen or lack of interest (Wood, pp. 69–70). Women, on the other hand, encourage others to continue talking. Using listening noises such as "um, hmmm," "yes," "that's interesting," "so," "and," and so forth. They are encouragers, and these vocalizations not only reveal they are listening and interested, they prompt others to continue talking and to elaborate on their ideas (Wood, p. 69).

Roger Axtell, in his book *Do's and Taboos Around the World for Women in Business*, quotes Kathi Seifert, group president of North American personal care products for the Kimberly-Clark Corporation, who says "Women are naturally more caring, nurturing, and better listeners. They like to help and to respond to people's needs" (Axtell, 1997, pp. 161–62). Shmuley Boteach, dean of the L'Chaim Society, which hosts world figures and statesmen and concentrates on values-based leadership, says women "when speaking to their husbands, . . . stop talking in midsentence because they know they are not being listened to. They feel like a piece of furniture, and this experience of being ignored is a denial of their value. Their spirit is crushed" (2000, p. 165). Fein and Schneider, in *The Rules for Marriage*, write "Learn how to listen without interrupting or offering advice, so that you can understand your spouse's perspective on things" (2001, pp. 187–88). Men need to open up more, show their feelings, listen better, and reveal their responses. It may help, too, if men view conversations as Mary Boone describes them: "The purpose of a conversation is not to *agree* with each other, it's to learn from each other on both an intellectual and emotional level" (2001, p. 223).

Care and Appreciation

Scholars have found that people consistently use ways to communicate whether they want to have a relationship with a person or whether they want to avoid him or her (Mottet & Richmond, 1998). The approach people use most often to foster a relationship is expressing *caring and appreciation* for the other person. Typical remarks might be, "We had such a good time last night, I would like to see you again," or "I am so glad that we are friends"—bids expressing "I want to feel connected to you." The second most used technique is giving *compliments:* "That was such a funny joke

When people have a commitment to a relationship they not only enjoy doing things together, but doing things together improves both their connectiveness and communication.

you told last night," or "You look great today"—more bids seeking connection. The third technique they use is engaging in *self-disclosure*—(also a bid) telling someone something about themselves that they wouldn't tell most people: "I felt so bad when I failed the test," or "I really like her: I wish she would pay some attention to me."

Commitment

All relationships need **commitment**—a strong desire by both parties for the relationship to continue and a willingness on both parties to take responsibility for the problems that occur in the relationship. Trying to force a partner to make a commitment, however, is a waste of time, claims Adreinne Burgess (2002), in an article "I Vow to Thee" in the *Guardian*. She says, "Not only does it (commitment) provide no guarantees, but it also causes resentment and hostility, which undermines any loving feelings. In relationships with a real future, therefore, commitment usually develops at much the same rate on both sides. But promises of commitment are meaningless in the long-term, too—commitment isn't an act of will (while we can promise to stay with someone physically, we can't promise the same emotionally), and isn't something we do in any active sense. Commitment is a spin-off from other things: how satisfied we are with our relationship; whether we see a viable alternative to it; and whether moving on would cause us to lose important investments (time, money, shared property, and children)" (Burgess, 2002).

All relationships have some kind of commitment as their foundation, but sometimes the partners to the commitment have different expectations. *Unconditional* commitments are those in which you commit yourself to another regardless of what may happen. Marriage vows are often cited as examples of unconditional commitments; however, with divorce rates hovering around 50 percent, it is clear that nearly one out of every two couples who accept the unconditional commitment do not fulfill it. *Conditional* commitments set forth the conditions of the commitment and carry with them the implication of "only if." "I will commit to you only if I do not find something better in the meantime," or "I will commit to you only if something extraordinary doesn't happen."

Although commitments are important and reassuring, it is, perhaps, better to accept them for what they are worth, based on the trust and faith in the person making the commitment and with hope for a positive future. With all of that, however, it is best to prepare for the fact that most commitments are conditional, and it is unlikely that all conditions will be, or even could be, revealed or even known. Of course marriage should be an unconditional commitment, but we live in a transient society where planned obsolescence, endless technological advances, and instant millionaires guarantee a rapid and regular turnover of products, information, and fortunes; why should we expect relationships, including marriages, to be anything other than of short duration? Dreams, faith, optimism, visualizations, and confidence are all fine, but they really don't prepare you for a realistic conditional future. Only you can do that.

■ COMMUNICATION PROBLEMS IN RELATIONSHIPS

Just as there are essential elements of good relationships, there are numerous negative influences that will affect bids, the bidding process, and the maintenance of relationships. All the motivation and willingness to communicate, assertiveness training, owned messages, and listening and communication skills in the world cannot prevent relationships from becoming fertile ground for silence and stonewalling, for anger and frustration, or for just plain hard times. No speech, article, book, or expert can protect you from the range of painful emotions that make you human (Lerner, 2001). The communication problems we will discuss here include aggressive talk and aggression, regrettable talk, criticism and complaints, avoidance, and defensive communication.

For an example of aggressive dialogue, view clip #2, "Aggressive Communication."

Aggressive Talk and Aggression

Aggressive talk is talk that attacks a person's self-concept with the intent of inflicting psychological pain (Infante,1995, p. 51). This kind of talk includes disparaging words such as *nigger, faggot,* or *dummy* and phrases such as *You'll never amount to anything, You're so stupid. I'm ashamed you are my son.* Such aggressive talk has the effect of making the recipient feel inadequate, embarrassed, or angry. If a parent uses it on a child, the effect may last a lifetime (Vaches, 1994, p. 4). Although not as powerful or serious, an obvious manifestation of this same kind of talk occurs when kids say to one another, *You are such a loser.*

Because of its impact on the receiver, aggressive talk is seldom justified, be it in a sports competition, in response to an insult, or in an Army sergeant's training session. Further, there is considerable evidence that aggression breeds aggression. Children who suffer from this kind of emotional abuse grow up to be parents who use it on their own children. When the Army recruits get promoted to sergeants, it is likely that they, in turn, will abuse their own recruits. Also, verbal aggression can easily lead to physical aggression.

People who can control verbal aggression are people who can recognize their anger and control it when it occurs—usually by giving themselves a cooling-off period. Goleman maintains that children of verbally or physically aggressive parents have to be taught to handle their anger and recommends that this training start in the schools in the early elementary grades (Goleman, 1995, pp. 237–38).

Although people believe that verbal aggression is bad, this does not mean that people should never criticize others or complain. It is not the act of criticizing nor complaining, it is the way it is communicated that makes the difference.

Aggressive talk often leads to **aggression,** a physical or verbal show of force. Some people resort to physical aggression when they are unhappy in a relationship. Unless the partners can get professional help, these relationships are usually doomed. People who are tempted to use verbal aggression should be aware that such actions can destroy a relationship.

A more subtle act, and one we are often not aware of committing, is **indirect aggression** (also called *passive aggression*). People who use this form of communication often feel powerless and respond by doing something to thwart the person in power. For example, a teenager whose mother forces him to clean the kitchen might do such a poor job that she never asks him again. A student who is forced to go to college might show indirect aggression by flunking all her courses. One of the authors had a friend whose mother played hymns loudly on the piano whenever her daughter brought home someone she didn't like. All these are acts of indirect aggression.

Sometimes indirect aggression is not a conscious act. The student, for example, might not realize she is failing her classes to thwart her parents. At other times the behavior is planned and deliberate—as in the case of the hymn-playing mother.

When one partner in a relationship commits an act of indirect aggression, it is often useful for the other partner to bring it to his or her attention. This should be done carefully, or it is likely to result in more aggression or a defensive response. For example, a parent can ask the child who failed, "Did you really find your classes that difficult, or did you fail because you don't want to go to school anymore?"

Regrettable Talk

At one time or another, you have probably said something that you regretted. This **regrettable talk** may have been something that embarrassed you or another person. It may have hurt someone, or it may have been a secret you were not supposed to tell. Mark L. Knapp, Laura Stafford, and John A. Daly (1986) have studied "regrettable words" with the aim of finding out (1) whether they fell into certain categories, (2) what people did once they realized the impact their words had on the other person, (3) why they said the words in the first place, (4) how the other person responded, and (5) the short- and long-term effects the words had on the relationship.

The researchers discovered that 75 percent of regrettable words fell into five categories. The most common was the blunder—forgetting someone's name or getting it wrong, or asking "How's your mother?" and hearing the reply "She died." The next category was direct attack—a generalized criticism of the other person or of his or her family or friends. The third was negative group references, which often contained racial or ethnic slurs. The fourth involved direct and specific criticism, such as "You never clean house," or "Don't go out with that guy; he's a sleezeball!" The fifth category—revealing or explaining too much—included telling secrets or reporting hurtful things said by others.

When they used words they regretted, 77 percent of the people in the study said they realized it immediately and felt bad, guilty, or embarrassed. Some of them responded nonverbally: They winced or covered their mouths. Commonly the speaker apologized, corrected, or rephrased what he or she had said. Others discounted what they said by covering up their words or denying them.

When people were asked why they had made the remark in the first place, the most common response was, "I was stupid. I just wasn't thinking." Some said their remarks were selfish—intended to meet their own needs rather than the other person's. Others admitted to having bad intentions. They deliberately set out to harm the other person. On a less negative level, people said that they were trying to be nice but the words just slipped out. Some people said that they were trying to be funny or to tease the other person, and the words were taken in the wrong way.

How did the people who were the objects of the regrettable words respond? Most often they felt hurt. Many got angry or made a sarcastic reply. Some hung up the phone, walked away, or changed the subject. Others were able to dismiss the statement or to laugh about it. When the speaker acknowledged the error, the listener often helped to "cover" the incident by offering an explanation or justification.

One of the most interesting aspects of this study addressed whether regrettable words had a negative impact on the relationship. Of the respondents, 30 percent said there was a long-term negative change, 39 percent said there was no change in the relationship at all, and 16 percent said that the change was positive—for example, "In the long run, I think our relationship is stronger since it happened."

In looking at the entire range of regrettable messages, the researchers concluded that regrettable messages seem to be part of our interactions with others and that although they might be hurtful to the other person when they occur, their effects can be overcome and the relationship has a good chance of recovering from them.

Criticism and Complaints

Most people experience anger from time to time in close relationships. Many of the signs are nonverbal: They clench their fists, scowl, and talk louder and faster. Anger does not have to destroy a relationship: University of Michigan researchers found that the average couple has one serious fight a month and several small ones (Guerrero, 1994). John Gottman, psychologist at the University of Washington, found that anger is not the most destructive emotion in a marriage, since both happy and miserable couples fight. He calls the real demons "the Four Horsemen of the Apocalypse"—criticism, contempt, defensiveness, and stonewalling (Kantrowitz & Wingert, 1999, p. 54).

Experts agree that it's *how* partners fight that makes the difference. The most effective kind of anger is that which expresses one's own feelings while conveying concern for one's partner ("The Rat"..., 1993). Since most anger begins with a complaint or criticism, let's look at the most effective way to express it.

Gottman suggests that he can predict, within three minutes of the onset of a quarrel between partners, whether the couple will divorce. The way couples begin a discussion about a problem—how one partner presents an

Another Point of View

In her book, *The Dance of Connection,* Harriet Lerner writes about some of the advantages of anger:

"My point is not that you should deny your anger or ignore its sources. On the contrary, anger is an important signal that something is wrong. It always deserves our attention and respect. Anger can sharpen our passion and clarity and inspire us to speak honestly and truly. It can motivate us to say no to the demands and expectations of others, and yes to the dictates of our inner self. Our anger can help us clarify where we stand, what we believe, and what we will and won't do. Our anger tells us when the other person has crossed a line that shouldn't be crossed. In all these ways, our anger preserves the very dignity and integrity of our voice. If we didn't have our anger to motivate us, our fear might lock us into passivity, silence, and accommodation."

Questions

1. Do you have any personal examples of the positive expression of your own anger?

2. Do you think anger when expressed tends to be more positive than negative? Do you think when anger is expressed, it is more frequently negative than positive?

3. Taking the oppositive point of view, what are some negative things that occur because of anger?

4. How can the negative outcomes of anger be changed to positive by our own efforts? In a relationship, what can you do specifically to help encourage anger to become positive and not negative?

Source: From H. Lerner, *The Dance of Connection: How to Talk to Someone When You're Mad, Hurt, Scared, Frustrated, Insulted, Betrayed, or Desperate.* (New York: HarperCollins, 2001.)

Most people experience anger from time to time in close relationships. Anger doesn't have to destroy relationships. It is *how* people fight that makes the difference.

issue and how the other partner responds—is absolutely critical. Newlyweds heading for divorce start an argument by sending out hostile vibes through their tone of voice, facial gestures, and what they say, Gottman's six-year study finds. The biggest problems occur when the woman brings up an issue "harshly" and critically and the man responds with great negativity, says Gottman and study coauthor Sybil Carrere. (Gottman's earlier research showed that women initiate discussions about problems approximately 80 percent of the time) (Peterson, 1999, p. 1).

We have all probably said at one time or another that we don't mind hearing criticism as long as it is constructive. The questions, then, are, what is criticism, and what do we consider constructive criticism?

Criticism is a negative evaluation of a person for something he or she has done or the way he or she is. In more distant relationships, criticism usually originates from a higher-status person and is directed toward one with lower status (Tracy, Van Duesen & Robinson, 1987). A teacher, for example, criticizes a student; a parent criticizes a child. If the participants are equals, such as friends or a couple, criticism could come from either partner.

Researchers have discovered that criticism has five targets: appearance (body, clothing, smell, posture, and accessories); performance (carrying out a motor, intellectual, or creative skill); personhood (personality, goodness, or general ability); relationship style (dealing with others); and decisions and attitudes (opinions, plans, or lifestyle). They found that the target of most criticism is performance, followed by relationship style, appearance, and general personhood (Tracy, Duesen, & Robinson, 1987, p. 48).

The researchers also looked at what the recipients perceived as "good" and "bad" criticism. Some criticism was perceived as bad because of the relationship between the criticizer and the person being criticized (Tracy, Duesen, & Robinson, 1987, p. 50). Most of the study's respondents believed that those who did not know them very well didn't have the right to criticize them. They also felt that in the case of an argument, a good friend should side with them—not with the criticizer. Another feature of bad criticism was an inappropriate setting. People were much more likely to identify criticism as bad if it was given in front of others rather than privately. Students, for example, felt particularly humiliated if a teacher criticized them in front of their classmates.

The study also found that good criticism was distinguished from bad by five stylistic points. First, criticism was labeled "bad" if it contained negative language (profanity or judgmental labels such as "stupid jerk") or if it was stated harshly by screaming or yelling. Second, criticism was better received if it was specific and gave details on how to improve ("If you are going to be home after midnight, please call and let me know where you are"). Third, criticism was considered good if the person who made it also offered to assist in making the change ("If it's hard for you to find a telephone when you are out of town, maybe we should get a cellular phone"). Fourth, criticism was better accepted if its receiver could see how it would be in his or her best interest to change ("If you called me when you are going to be late, I wouldn't be so upset once you got home"). Fifth, good criticism places negative remarks into a broad and most positive context ("If you called, it would reduce a lot of tension and anxiety in our relationship").

Good criticism, the researchers found, leads to positive consequences. When the recipients of criticism did not feel threatened, they were able to take the comments seriously and make changes. In contrast, poorly given criticism was likely to evoke negative emotions and be seen by the recipient as inaccurate. Gottman discovered that when partners have a deep understanding of each other's psyche, they can navigate the relationship roadblocks without creating emotional gridlock (Kantrowitz & Wingert, 1999, p. 54).

Research conducted about criticism on the job has found that harsh or inept criticism in the work setting undermines work relationships, increases the likelihood of future conflicts, and prevents people from doing good work. Like criticism in relationships, the best criticism on the job is specific. It is also important that criticism be timely. The researchers found that people reacted angrily to criticism when the boss stored up grievances and then communicated them all at once. Finally, good criticism at work focuses on what the person has done incorrectly rather than suggesting that poor work is a form of character deficiency, such as laziness or incompetence (Goleman, 1988, p. C1).

A **complaint** is an expression of dissatisfaction with some behavior, attitude, belief, or characteristic of a partner or of someone else. A complaint differs from criticism in that it is not necessarily directed at any specific person.

In studies of complaints between partners, researchers found that, as with criticism, some responses to complaints were more useful than others (Alberts & Driscoll, 1992). First, when complaints are trivial, they can probably be ignored. "This spaghetti is overcooked," or "Why do I have to be the only one to shovel the snow?" are trivial complaints. Second, a complaint should not be directed at anyone specifically. When you say, "Why doesn't anyone ever close doors?" you are not pointing to any one person, so the guilty party can change his or her behavior without losing face. Third, a complaint should be softened or toned down so that the complainer can express his or her frustration or dissatisfaction without provoking a big argument. Fourth, if the complaint is serious, the partners should discuss it and try to arrive at a solution or a compromise before the complaint turns into a serious conflict.

The researchers also found that complaints were least manageable when the partners were unresponsive or the conflict escalated. Among the couples studied, if a partner ignored important complaints, the result was increased anger and dissatisfaction. Also, if the complaint escalated during the exchange, the partners were likely to end up angry with each other. Couples who had the weakest relationships were those who were likely to withdraw from any complaints or to escalate them (Alberts & Driscoll, 1992).

Avoidance

Many people who are in unsatisfying relationships try to dodge any discussion of their problems. Some people use silence; others change the subject if their partners try to begin a discussion. Often people who refrain from discussing relationships are trying to avoid any kind of conflict. The dilemma of **avoidance**—refusing to deal with conflict or painful issues—is that unless the problem is discussed, it probably will not go away.

Sometimes people refuse to engage in discussion because they believe that nothing is ever resolved or that their partners will not give them a fair hearing. In such cases, discussion can often be facilitated by calling in a third party to listen to both sides. Ideally, this should be a person who is able to listen objectively and not take sides. In the case of roommate conflict, a dorm counselor might be helpful. Partners in marriage often seek out marriage counselors.

Defensive Communication

For an example of defensive communication, view clip #1, "Defensive Communication."

Defensive communication occurs when one partner tries to defend himself or herself against the remarks or behavior of the other. If a teacher tells a student, "This is the worst paper I have ever read," the student is likely to think (if not say), "And you are the worst teacher I have ever had." Obviously, this communication is not off to a good start.

The problem with defensive communication is that we are so busy defending ourselves that we cannot listen to what the other person is saying. Also, defending ourselves is dealing with past behavior; it gives us no chance to think about resolving the problem.

How can we avoid defensive communication? A researcher, in a classic article, came up with six categories of defensive communication and supportive strategies to counter each of them (Gibb, 1961).

Evaluation versus Description

Evaluative statements involve a judgment. If the judgment is negative, the person you are speaking to is likely to react defensively. If you tell your roommate, "It is inconsiderate of you to slam the door when I am trying to sleep," he might respond, "It's inconsiderate of you to snore every night when I am trying to sleep." Obviously such statements do not lead to solving the problem. On the other hand, a descriptive statement is much more likely to receive a favorable response. If you tell your roommate, "I had trouble sleeping last night because I woke up when I heard the door slam," he is much more likely to do something about the problem. Since you have merely described the problem, the message is not as threatening.

Control versus Problem Solving

People who consistently attempt to exert **control** believe that they are always right and that no other opinion (or even fact) is worth listening to. Those who feel they must control communication argue for their point of view, insist that their position be accepted, and sometimes even raise their voices to get people to accept what they believe (Witteman, 1992).

Most of us will not choose to be with someone who must always have control. However, when the controlling person has status and power, we may have no choice. Parents have a good deal to say about controlling their children, but once the children reach adolescence, there are often struggles for control. We learn lessons about control from our parents. A boy who has a stern, controlling father is likely to grow up to be a controlling father, too.

People tend to respond negatively if they think someone is trying to control them. For example, if you are working on a class project with a classmate and you begin by taking charge and telling him or her what to do, you will probably be resented. A better approach is for you and your classmate to engage in problem solving together. The same applies to close relationships. If conflict arises and you decide what should be done ("I'll take the car and you take the bicycle"), your partner is not likely to respond positively. It is better to discuss the transportation options together.

Strategy versus Spontaneity

Often strategy is little more than manipulation. Rather than openly asking people to do something, you can try to manipulate them into doing what you want by using strategies such as making them feel guilty or ashamed. A statement that begins "If you love me, you will. . . ." is always manipulative. A better approach is to express your honest feelings spontaneously: "I am feeling overwhelmed with all the planning I have to do for the party. Will you help me out today?"

Neutrality versus Empathy

Have you ever asked someone "Where shall we go to eat?" or "What movie should we see?" or "What do you want to do tonight?" and heard the person respond, "I don't care"? This kind of neutral response indicates a lack of interest, and it is likely to make you feel defensive enough to respond,

"Why do I always have to come up with the ideas?" or "If you don't care enough to make a suggestion, then we'll stay home."

On other occasions, we want and expect family members and friends to take our side. If you receive a low grade on a paper and are feeling bad about it, you don't want your friend to say, "Maybe the teacher was right. Let's look at both sides." When feelings are high, no one wants a neutral, objective response. That can be saved for later. What is needed in such a situation is for the other person to show **empathy**—the ability to recognize and identify with another's feelings. An empathic response to a poor grade in a course might be, "You must feel bad. You studied hard for that class."

Superiority versus Equality

None of us likes people who act as though they think they are superior to us. Feelings of superiority are communicated in a variety of ways. People who always take charge of situations seem to imply that they are the only ones who are qualified to do so. Others feel superior because of their roles: "I am the boss and you are the employee, and don't you forget it." It's not uncommon for parents to issue statements of superiority: "I am your father, and I will set the rules." Even if we have a position that is superior to someone else's, people will react less defensively if we do not communicate this superiority. An attitude of equality—"Let's tackle this problem together"—produces much less defensive behavior.

Certainty versus Provisionalism

There are people who believe that they are always right. One label for these people is "dogmatic." It is important that we don't confuse people who are confident and secure with people who think they are always right. Confident and secure people may hold strong opinions; they are likely, however, to make many provisional statements—statements that permit another point of view to be expressed. For example, someone might say, "I feel strongly on this subject, but I would be interested in hearing what you have to say." People who are willing to take a more provisional approach are also able to change their own positions if a more reasonable position is presented.

Table 8-1 lists the categories of defensive and supportive behavior.

Table 8-1
Categories of Defensive and Supportive Behavior

Defensive Climate	Supportive Climate
1. Evaluation	1. Description
2. Control	2. Problem solving
3. Strategy	3. Spontaneity
4. Neutrality	4. Empathy
5. Superiority	5. Equality
6. Certainty	6. Provisionalism

Avoiding Defensive Communication: A Practical Example

Although we have discussed each of the six defensive categories separately, in most communication situations several of them appear simultaneously. You can see how this works in the following situations:

A Defensive Dialogue

Boss: You're an hour late. If you're going to work here, you have to be on time. (superiority, control)

Employee: My car wouldn't start.

Boss: That's no reason to be late. (certainty, evaluation) You should have called. (evaluation)

Employee: I tried, but. . . .

Boss: When work starts at 8 AM, you must be here at 8 AM (superiority, control) If you can't make it, you should look for another job. (superiority, control, certainty) If you're late again, don't bother coming to work. (superiority, control, strategy)

This dialogue leaves the employee feeling defensive, angry, and unable to say anything. Let's take a look at how it might have gone if the boss had been more willing to listen:

A Supportive Dialogue

Boss: You're an hour late. What happened? (description, equality)

Employee: My car wouldn't start.

Boss: Weren't you near a phone? (still no evaluation)

Employee: Every time I tried to call, the line was busy. I finally decided that it would be faster to walk here than to keep trying to call.

Boss: When people don't get here on time, I always worry that we're going to fall behind schedule. (spontaneity) Wasn't there any way of letting me know what happened? (problem solving)

Employee: Yeah. I guess I panicked. I should have asked my sister to keep trying to call to let you know what happened. If it ever happens again, that's what I'll do.

Boss: Good. Now let's get to work. There's a lot of catching up to do.

Working Together

Imagine that you have caught your relationship partner in a boldface lie, and it is clear that he or she cannot deny it, explain it away, or otherwise retreat from the situation. Go around your group, and have each member supply first a defensive statement and then a supportive statement of the same level—or a supportive statement designed to offset, dispel, or otherwise ameliorate the defensive one. For example, the first person in the group supplies an evaluative statement: "You really annoy me when you lie to me like that. We both agreed that is unacceptable behavior." The next person will supply a descriptive statement. The next student will offer a controlling statement, and the next a problem-solving one. The next student will offer a manipulative statement, the next a spontaneous one. The next student will offer a neutral statement followed by the next student with an empathic one. A superior statement is offered and then an equal one. And, finally, the next-to-the-last student offers a statement of certainty, and the final one a provisional comment.

In this conversation, neither boss nor employee is left feeling defensive or resentful. Although the role of boss is superior to that of employee, this boss tries hard not to use his position of power. The result is a more equal conversation, which leads in turn to better communication between the two.

■ EVALUATING YOUR RELATIONSHIPS

Roles and Expectations

In successful relationships, the participants have usually worked out their roles and expectations. These roles, however, change through the course of a relationship. A young couple, for example, might share housekeeping chores. However, if they decide to have a baby, it is important that they discuss how their roles will change once the baby is born. "Who's going to take care of the baby during the day?" and "Who's going to get up at night when the baby cries?" are some of the questions the couple will have to answer.

Friends who are in conflict might benefit from looking at their role expectations. Let's say that whenever a man asks her out, Jenn cancels her plans with her friend Beth. Beth feels hurt and angry because, in her opinion, this behavior implies that Jenn thinks a date is more important than their friendship. Jenn indeed does believe that male-female relationships are more important than female-female ones. Unless the two women can decide the roles they will play in regard to each other, their friendship is in jeopardy. Similarly, if a husband expects his wife to cook dinner every night and she does not have the same expectation, it is time for them to redefine their roles and expectations. Besides defining their roles, both people in a relationship have to reach agreement on them. Finally, the roles and expectations that people have in a relationship must be satisfying to both parties.

Renegotiating Roles

Sometimes relationships have to be renegotiated when the participants' roles change. Let's say, for example, that a 19-year-old college student marries someone who is 35. In this marriage it is likely that the younger person will depend on the older person to make decisions, to provide reassurance, and so forth. Once the 19-year-old finishes school and takes a job, it is likely that his or her self-confidence will increase and that he or she will no longer depend on the spouse as much. Such change may be threatening to the spouse. To help this relationship, the partners must discuss the roles they have been playing with a view to changing them. How can this be done?

When we have been in a role for a long time, we develop habitual ways of behaving as well as assumptions about how our partner will behave. The young spouse, for example, may have let the older partner pay the bills, advise on clothes, and make decisions about what social occasions they should attend. If, feeling newly independent, the younger spouse announces a desire to change things, this will come as a shock to the older spouse.

The best chance for this relationship would be a renegotiation of roles. The younger spouse might say, "I'm feeling more secure now, and I would like to make my own choices about what to wear." Since this is not an unreasonable request, agreement is likely. The older spouse may see this as an opportunity to renegotiate his or her role as well, and may say something like "Now that you're feeling more comfortable by yourself, I'd like to rejoin my Thursday evening tennis league."

It is much easier to make role changes when they are seen as being in the best interest of both partners. For example, some parents are willing to give up the role of being on an ambitious career path in order to spend more time with their children. However, if a person sees this change as a loss, it will be very difficult for him or her to agree to it. The ease with which role changes are made within a relationship also depends on the flexibility of the individuals. When relationships and roles are rigidly defined, change is very difficult.

Costs and Rewards

In a relationship, the **costs and rewards** need to be weighed against each other. The *costs* are the problems in the relationship; the *rewards* are the pleasures. In a work situation, for example, you don't have much choice about your boss or the people you work with. Usually, the only way of terminating a relationship at work is to quit your job. This is a great cost, and it must be balanced against the rewards. You might worry that you won't find another job, so keeping the job outweighs its costs and you decide not to quit. People sometimes remain in relationships that are not entirely satisfying when the rewards of staying are greater than the costs of getting out.

People may stay in an unsatisfying marriage because the emotional and economic costs of divorce are too great. A middle-aged woman who has never worked, for example, might stay in a marriage because she has no way of supporting herself and can't imagine living alone. Other partners stay together for the sake of the children, or because it is too much of a problem to divide property, or for any number of other reasons.

Consider This

Know Your Relationship Partner

Test the strength of your relationship by taking this quiz prepared especially for *Newsweek* by John Gottman. Happy couples have a deep understanding of their partner's psyche.

	True	False
1. I can name my partner's best friends.	___	___
2. I can tell you what stresses my partner is currently facing.	___	___
3. I know the names of some of the people who have been irritating my partner lately.	___	___
4. I can tell you some of my partner's life dreams.	___	___
5. I can tell you about my partner's basic philosophy of life.	___	___
6. I can list the relatives my partner likes the least.	___	___
7. I feel that my partner knows me pretty well.	___	___
8. When we are apart, I often think fondly of my partner.	___	___
9. I often touch or kiss my partner affectionately.	___	___
10. My partner really respects me.	___	___
11. There is fire and passion in this relationship.	___	___
12. Romance is definitely still a part of our relationship.	___	___
13. My partner appreciates the things I do in this relationship.	___	___
14. My partner generally likes my personality.	___	___
15. Our sex life is mostly satisfying.	___	___
16. At the end of the day my partner is glad to see me.	___	___
17. My partner is one of my best friends.	___	___
18. We just love talking to each other.	___	___
19. There is lots of give and take (both people have influence) in our discussions.	___	___
20. My partner listens respectfully, even when we disagree.	___	___
21. My partner is usually a great help as a problem solver.	___	___
22. We generally mesh well on basic values and goals in life.	___	___

Score your results: Give yourself one point for each "True" answer. Above 12: You have a lot of strength in your relationship. Congratulations. Below 12: Your relationship can stand some improvement and will probably benefit from some work on the basics, such as improving communication.

Source: B. Kantrowitz, and P. Wingert. "The science of a good marriage," *Newsweek*, April 19, 1999, pp. 52–57. Although the survey was intended for married partners since that is the focus of the entire article, it seems to work as well for most established relationships.

If you are in a relationship that is not very satisfying, you will have to ask yourself some probing questions and determine from your answers whether the relationship is worthwhile.

Mira Kirshenbaum (1996), a therapist who works with families and couples, suggests that the answers to some of the questions she poses might help people make up their minds about relationships. For example, she says that if a person answers "Yes" to the question of whether there has been more than one incident of physical violence, he or she should get out of the relationship. Some of the other areas she deals with include communication, power, sex and physical attraction, love, respect, and differences between partners.

Kirshenbaum does not believe that making a list of pros and cons about a relationship will help a person decide whether he or she should break it off. Rather, she holds that since the dynamics of a relationship are constantly shifting, it is better to ask questions about the relationship that go right to the heart of it. For example, she maintains that the answer to a question like the following will tell a lot about a relationship: "Does it seem to you that your partner generally and consistently blocks your attempts to bring up topics or raise questions, particularly about things you care about?" (p. 94)

■ COMMUNICATION SOLUTIONS IN RELATIONSHIPS

Once people have a commitment to a relationship, they can usually improve their communication within it. We will make this section brief since most of these solutions have been discussed earlier. For example, review the previous chapter on interpersonal relationships as well as the section earlier in this chapter on the essential elements of good relationships. Better communication, including empathic listening, "I/you" messages, and assertiveness, can lead to better relationships.

Empathic Listening

Chapter 4, Listening, discusses the subject of empathic listening in detail. Because this kind of listening is so important to relationships, it is worthwhile to review the main points here.

Empathic listening is listening for feelings from the other person's point of view. In this kind of listening, you put aside your own feelings and try to hear what the other person is really saying. If your partner says, for example, "Everyone is picking on me today," as an empathic listener you would be sympathetic to your partner and indicate, both verbally and nonverbally, that you are ready to listen to what is bothering him or her.

The most important thing about empathic listening is that you don't try to evaluate the other person's feelings. If you respond to "Everyone is picking on me," with "You're really paranoid today," communication is likely to end. A more appropriate response might be, "You sound upset. What happened?" This response sets the stage for the other person to talk about the problem. In empathic listening, the most important thing to remember is that people often just need a sounding board. Everyone feels happier when the other person in a relationship is a sympathetic listener.

I/You Messages

Chapter 7, Interpersonal Relationships, discusses the subject of owned messages in some detail. The point was that it is possible to make changes in relationships by changing our ways of communicating. Also, "I" messages create the positive, supportive environment in which bids and responses to bids can take place. Rebecca Cline and Bonnie Johnson (1976) have done some valuable research that shows the importance of making careful language choices when dealing with criticism. They found that people react negatively and defensively when conversation is filled with "you" messages ("You didn't empty the garbage"; "You always foul up the checkbook"; "You never change the oil in the car").

Cline and Johnson found that this kind of "you" talk makes the other party feel defensive. "I" messages, however ("I am afraid we will need a new car if we don't change the oil more often"), are likely to receive a much less defensive response. The reason for this is that an "I" message takes the pressure off the other person—and this makes him or her more likely to focus on the feelings of the person who believes there is a problem. Here are some typical "I" messages: "When I am left alone at a party, I feel shy and embarrassed"; "I can't concentrate when the room is such a mess"; "I feel uncomfortable when we have the only yard in the neighborhood where the grass isn't cut."

Assertiveness

For an example of assertive communication, view clip #2, "Assertive Communication."

Sometimes communication goes astray because we don't express ourselves clearly or we are not certain what we want. **Assertiveness** is taking the responsibility of expressing needs, thoughts, and feelings in a direct, clear manner. Let's say, for example, that you always put things away, but your roommate seldom does, so your apartment is always a mess. You have several options in this situation. You could clean up after yourself and your roommate with a lot of sighs and significant looks showing you are unhappy, or you could make an indirect verbal comment ("I wish our apartment were a little tidier") and hope your roommate will get the hint. These approaches, however, are not assertive. If you want to make an assertive statement that might change your roommate's behavior, you should say something on the order of "I'd like it if you would wash the dishes and put them away after you use them." You could also make a statement about how you feel: "I feel like the whole kitchen is dirty when there are dirty dishes in the sink." Neither of these comments should make your roommate feel defensive since you are not evaluating his or her behavior.

Often it's hard to tell what another person is feeling, so it is useful to make clear statements about your emotional state:

I feel anxious if you don't call me when you are going to be late.

I'm not mad at you. I'm mad at my boss, and I need some time to cool down before I can talk to you.

I feel that if we go to your mother's house over the holidays, I will be too rushed and I won't be able to meet my deadlines.

Our definition of assertiveness includes the responsibility to be as clear as possible. You can fulfill this responsibility by planning what you want to say before you say it. This is particularly useful when a situation is charged with emotions. Thinking your words through in advance helps make the situation clear in your own mind.

■ RESOLVING CONFLICT

From time to time, all of us face conflict in our interpersonal communication. Sometimes conflict destroys a relationship; other times, if the participants can work it out, the relationship becomes stronger.

When two people are in conflict and have decided that nothing will be served by avoidance or aggression, the option left open to them is **conflict resolution**—negotiation to find a solution to the conflict. Conflict arises because two individuals do not have compatible goals. Through the negotiation process, the two try to find out how they can both reach their goals. For the negotiation to be considered successful, both sides must be satisfied and feel that they have come out ahead. This is often referred to as *win-win negotiating*.

Deborah Wieder-Hatfield (1981), a researcher in this area, has suggested a useful model for resolving conflict. In this model, each individual looks at the conflict intrapersonally. Then the partners get together interpersonally to work out the problem.

In the first stage, *intrapersonal evaluation,* each person analyzes the problem alone. This analysis is accomplished through a series of questions: How do I feel about this problem? How can I describe the other person's behavior? What are the facts?

It is important not to confuse facts with inferences. If you have an untidy roommate, for example, a fact might be that he doesn't pick up his clothes. An inference would be that he is trying to irritate you by not cleaning up. Throughout the intrapersonal process it is important to describe—not judge—the other person's behavior.

In the second stage, the parties in the conflict get together to work out an *interpersonal definition* of the problem. It is important that both parties believe there is a problem and can define what it is. Partners in conflict often do not see the problem in the same light; in fact, one person might not even believe there is a problem. Therefore, in this stage, it is important that each person listen carefully. To aid in listening, it is useful for each person to check the accuracy of what he or she has heard by paraphrasing what was said. The same is true for feelings. Because feelings are intense in a conflict, it is important for each partner both to express his or her own feelings and to make sure he or she is listening accurately by trying to paraphrase the feelings of the other. Then it is useful for each person to describe the other person's behavior. At the end of this stage, both partners should agree on the facts of the problem.

In the third stage, the partners should discuss *shared goals.* Still focusing on the problem, the individuals should ask, "What are my needs and desires?" and "What are your needs and desires?" Then they should work to see whether their needs and goals overlap. Let's look at the tidy and untidy roommates. The tidy roommate wants to have things picked up and the dishes washed. The untidy roommate hates doing housework and doesn't care if the apartment is in disorder. Thus their goals in housework are incompatible. Nonetheless, they like each other and like sharing an apartment. Each is also concerned that the other partner be happy. In this case, then, they have found some goals in common.

Consider This

There are a number of different strategies or approaches for resolving conflicts. If you don't believe this, type "Resolving Conflicts" into a search-engine window (Google, 75,300 hits; March 24, 2003) or "Strategies for Resolving Conflicts" (Google, 609 hits, March 24, 2003). We offer an approach to "Managing Group Conflict" in Chapter 11, Group Leadership. So many interpersonal conflicts occur spontaneously and get resolved without structure; here are 15 strategies for resolving conflict constructively that will help you maintain the proper, supportive conflict-reducing atmosphere. These are written for groups, but apply to two-person conflicts just as well.

1. Do everything possible to create a supportive environment for resolving the conflict. Hold a special meeting so people will know they will have a chance to be heard. Allocate plenty of time to avoid having to rush. Stipulate that no one can be interrupted while speaking.

2. Choose an appropriate time to deal with the conflict, preferably after people have had a chance to calm down and look at facts more objectively.

3. Focus on issues rather than personalities. Be as specific as possible in describing the problem to be solved.

4. Differentiate between reality and perception. People have a tendency to see what they want to see.

5. Periodically remind one another of what you have in common and of the interests you share. Focus on these potential bridges more than on your differences.

6. Break the conflict into smaller "bite-size" pieces, which can be dealt with one by one.

7. Don't seek a premature solution—better to move more slowly and cautiously toward a solution that will stand the test of time.

8. Invite a neutral party to listen, counsel, and play a peacekeeping role.

9. Use personal statements (I, my, our) rather than blaming or attacking (you, your).

10. Describe feelings rather than acting them out or attempting to disguise them.

11. Rather than stating your inferences or assumptions about others' motives as if they were true, state your concern as a guess and ask for confirmation or denial.

12. As much as possible, stay with descriptions of behavior rather than guesses at what the behavior means.

13. Acknowledge your share in creating the conflict or tension.

14. Before stating your position, respond to others in ways that show understanding (silence or arguments do not let others know you see any merit in their case).

15. Make no threats.

Questions

1. Are these strategies you already practice? Which of them are you more familiar with? Are there certain strategies that appeal to you that you do *not* currently use? Which ones?

2. Do you think that a set of strategies like these makes more sense than laying out a very specific, structured set of steps to follow? Why or why not?

Source: (No author), "16 Strategies for Resolving Conflict Constructively." The Vine, 1999. Retrieved March 24, 2003, from http://www.tabcom.org/TheVine/1999/10–99/05.htm. One strategy was deleted because it had to do with prayer.

At the fourth stage, the partners must come up with *possible solutions* to the problem. Here it is useful to create as long a list as possible. Then each individual can eliminate solutions he or she considers unacceptable. One partner's list might look like this:

- Clean the apartment every week.
- Pay someone to clean the apartment.
- Move out.

The other partner's list might be:

- Clean the apartment once a month.
- Use paper plates and plastic cups.
- Eat only fast food.

When the roommates look at each other's lists of solutions, they both decide there are some items they can't live with. Neither can afford to hire someone to clean, and they decide that disposable dishes are not good for the environment. One also says she really doesn't want to move out, and the other admits that a steady diet of fast foods is not very appealing.

In the fifth stage, the partners move on to *weighing goals against solutions*. Since the roommates want to live together and they want each other to be happy, their task is to choose a solution or solutions that will help them reach these goals. Looking at their lists, they discover that only two items remain ("Clean the apartment once a week" and "Clean the apartment once a month.") Some compromises are inevitable at this stage. In this particular situation, the roommates decide to do a thorough cleaning of the apartment every two weeks. Also, the tidy roommate agrees to stop nagging, and the untidy roommate agrees to pick up after herself in the common living areas. These solutions may not be entirely satisfactory to either party, but they are a compromise that both hope they can live with. Negotiators would label this a win-win solution.

Since all resolutions are easier to make than to keep, the last stage of the process is to *evaluate the solution* after some time has passed. Did the solution work? Does it need to be changed? Should it be discussed again at a later date? As we mentioned earlier, it is not easy to change human behavior. When partners work to resolve conflict, even when they come up with good solutions there is likely to be some backsliding. It therefore makes good sense to give partners a chance to live up to their resolutions. Letting time pass before both negotiators are held accountable helps achieve this goal.

Although these guidelines can be useful in many situations, it must be pointed out that not all conflicts can be resolved. If partners cannot find any goals that they share or if they cannot agree on solutions that will enable them to meet their goals, the conflict will probably not be resolved. Also, although this model looks good on paper, it is much like the chair you see advertised in the local discount store. The sign says, "A child can put it together in 10 minutes," but when you get it home, you find there are 30 nuts and bolts and a dozen separate pieces, and after two hours' work you have something that only vaguely resembles a chair. In the same way, this model sounds simple in theory, but it is not always easy to put into practice.

Assess Yourself

Faith in People Scale
Please place an "X" in the blank which most closely matches your response to the question.

1. Some people say that most people can be trusted. Others say you can't be too careful in your dealings with people. How do you feel about it?

   Most people can be trusted. _____   You can't be too careful. _____

2. Would you say that most people are more inclined to help others, or more inclined to look out for themselves?

   Tohelp others. _____   To look out for themselves. _____

3. If you don't watch yourself, people will take advantage of you.

   Agree. _____   Disagree. _____

4. No one is going to care much what happens to you, when you get right down to it.

   Agree. _____   Disagree. _____

5. Human nature is fundamentally cooperative.

   Agree. _____   Disagree. _____

Go to the *Communicating Effectively* CD-ROM to see your results and learn how to evaluate your attitudes and feelings.

Source: M. Rosenberg, *Organizations and Values* (Glencoe, IL: Free Press, 1957), pp. 25–35. This scale was published in: J. P. Robinson, P. R. Shaver, & L. S. Wrightsman, *Measures of Personality and Social Psychological Attitudes* (San Diego: Academic Press, 1991), pp. 404–6.

Human communication is so complex, and there are so many ambiguities and subtleties in meaning, that each person in a negotiation must bring careful thought and analysis to each stage of the process. When both partners are committed to a relationship, however, there is a good chance that conflict can be worked out using this or a similar process.

■ RELATIONSHIPS THAT WORK

If you were to focus on just one thing that causes most of the problems in relationships it is that we take them for granted. We don't invest the same attention, thought, time, and energy in them that we do in building our careers or pursuing other interests. Often, we think love or familiarity is sufficient, says Stedman Graham (2001) in his book, *Build Your Own Life Brand.* "Love is a powerful force," he says, "but love doesn't live or grow in a vacuum. To keep love alive, you have to feed it with a rich supply of consideration, loyalty, trustworthiness, sensitivity, thoughtfulness, cooperation, compromise, tolerance, and responsibility" (pp. 186–187).

Most relationships can be improved when the partners understand how to communicate with each other. Conflict occurs in all relationships; it's how conflict is worked out that allows the partners to find satisfaction and happiness together.

Partners must learn new styles of conversing with each other. One way to do this is to avoid linguistic booby traps that leave no room for a partner to respond. For example, using names and epithets ("You sexist pig"), diagnoses ("You're only saying that because you're so tired"), direct commands ("Take off that awful tie"), prophecies ("You're going to hate yourself in the morning"), sermons ("Decent people stick to a budget and don't spend the way you do"), unsolicited advice ("Here's what I'd do if I were you"), and hijackings ("You think you had a bad day? Listen to what happened to me today"). Although you may not be able to eliminate all of these structures at once, if you become aware of them, and realize they can block your efforts to foster intimacy, you will be able to ask yourself before using one of them, "What can my partner possibly respond to what I'm about to say?" If you can't think of an answer, let this be a clue. Say something for which you yourself can think of a range of responses. That is exactly what constitutes good communication—not just thinking before speaking, but thinking of the other person before speaking (Lewis, 1997, p. 50).

Gottman, from all of his research on couples, says that happy couples have a different way of relating to each other during disputes. Partners make frequent "repair attempts," reaching out to each other in an effort to prevent negativity from getting out of control in the midst of conflict. Humor, too, is often part of a successful repair attempt. If partners can work together and appreciate the best in each other, they learn to cope with the problems that are part of every relationship (Kantrowitz & Wingert, 1999, p. 56). Partners must learn to love each other not just for what they have in common but for things that make them complementary as well (Kantrowitz & Wingert, 1999, p. 56).

What is a relationship that works? It is one in which there is intimacy and self-disclosure. When you save up the good things that have happened to you to tell to your partner, that is a good relationship. As a matter of fact, Gottman says that one quick way to test whether a couple still has a chance to mend a broken relationship is to ask what initially attracted them to each other. If they can recall those magic first moments and smile when they talk about them, all is not lost (Kantrowitz & Wingert, 1999, p. 57). Thus, a relationship that works is one in which you can share the good and the bad things you feel. It is a partnership in which you can solve problems and feel happy that you have solved them. Most importantly, a relationship is the psychological space where you and another person are closest to being your truest selves. It can happen with a marriage partner, with a best friend, or with a parent or child. For an individual to be happy, it is important that it happen with someone.

But there is one more test of a relationship that works. Is your partner one whom you can lean on for strength and support in difficult times? This is a key because this is one of the important functions of relationships. If you've ever gone to a loved one or friend for support in a time of crisis or challenge and received an indifferent or negative response, then it may be, according to Stedman Graham (2001), that "You did not put enough into that relationship to expect anything out of it" (p. 187). Graham adds that "If you haven't invested in the welfare of the people around you, it's not very realistic to expect them to take an interest in you and your problems, is it?" (p. 187).

Chapter Review

The most important relationships in our lives go through five stages: initiating, experimenting, intensifying, integrating, and bonding. Relationships that remain superficial go through only the first or second stage.

Relationships that come apart also go through five stages: differentiating, circumscribing, stagnating, avoiding, and terminating. When a relationship is ending, the participants often make statements that summarize the relationship and comments that indicate whether the relationship will continue in any form. Many relationships end when a third person intervenes in some way.

There are a number of elements that could be considered essential for good relationships. Among those, we discuss verbal skills, emotional expressiveness, conversational focus, nonverbal analysis, conversational encouragement, care and appreciation, and commitment. On many of these elements, women already have a significant edge with respect to effectiveness, and to level the playing field, men may need to work harder and concentrate more to have an effect on making their relationships successful.

There are communication problems, too, that partners in a relationship must overcome. We discuss aggressive talk and aggression, regrettable talk, criticism and complaints, and defensive communication. Strategies for avoiding defensive communication include describing rather than evaluating, problem solving with a partner rather than trying to control him or her, being spontaneous rather than manipulative, using empathy rather than remaining neutral, aiming for equality rather than superiority, and being provisional rather than certain.

When people evaluate their relationships, they should look at their roles and expecta-tions they have of their partners. As circumstances change, it is important to renegotiate roles. When a relationship is in trouble, it's a good idea to look at costs and rewards. Costs are the problems in the relationship, and rewards are the pleasures.

Several communication strategies can help improve a relationship. Assertiveness helps both partners because needs, thoughts, and feelings must be expressed in a direct, clear manner before they can be acted upon. Empathic listening involves concentrating on the other person's feelings without evaluating what he or she says. It is useful for persons involved in disagreement to use "I" rather than "you" messages—owned messages.

Using a model of conflict resolution can help reduce conflict in a relationship. The steps involve evaluating the conflict intrapersonally, defining the nature of the conflict with your partner, discussing the goals you and your partner share, deciding on possible solutions to the problem, weighing goals against solutions and deciding on a solution that will reach the goal, and evaluating the solution after some time has passed.

Most of us take relationships for granted, and that is, perhaps, one of the biggest problems in relationship care and maintenance. A relationship that works is one in which there is intimacy and self-disclosure. It is a partnership in which you can solve problems and feel happy you have solved them. But most important of all, a relationship is a psychological space where you and the other person can be your truest selves. One test of a relationship that works is its availability to the other partner in difficult times or times of crisis or challenge. Can you count on your partner for strength and support in such times?

Questions to Review

1. When a relationship comes together, it goes through five stages: initiating, experimenting, intensifying, integrating, and bonding. What happens in each stage?

2. When a relationship breaks down, it goes through the following stages: differentiating, circumscribing, stagnating, avoiding, and terminating. What happens in each of these stages?

3. What are considered some of the essential elements of good relationships? Which of these elements do you consider most important?

4. What are considered some of the communication problems in relationships?

5. When it comes to aggressive talk and regrettable talk, can it be avoided in relationships?

6. How can one make criticisms and complaints about a relationship without causing damage to it? What are some examples of good criticism?

7. What is defensive communication?

8. What are the six types of defensive communication, and how can each one be changed to supportive communication?

9. How are roles and expectations important in relationships? How can roles be negotiated as relationships change?

10. What are some of the costs and some of the rewards of relationships?

11. Why are "I" messages and assertiveness important communication behaviors in relationships?

12. What are the six stages of conflict resolution?

13. What are some of the characteristics of good relationships?

Go to the self-quizzes on the Communicating Effectively CD-ROM (side 2, track 10) and the Online Learning Center at mhhe.com/hybels7 to test your knowledge of the chapter concepts.

References

Alberts, J. K., & G. Driscoll, (1992). "Containment versus escalation: The trajectory of couples' conversational complaints." *Western Journal of Speech Communication* 56, 394–412.

Avtgis, T. A., D. V. West, & R. L. Anderson (1998, Summer). "Relationship stages: An inductive analysis identifying cognitive, affective, and behavioral dimensions of Knapp's relational stages model." *Communication Research Reports* 15:3, 280–87.

Axtell, R. E. (1997). *Do's and taboos around the world for women in business.* New York: John Wiley & Sons, Inc.

Banks, S. P., D. M. Altendorf, J. O. Greene, & M. J. Cody, (1987). "An examination of relationship disengagement perceptions: Breakout strategies and outcomes." *Western Journal of Speech Communication* 51, 19–41.

Barbor, C. (2001, January/February). "Finding real love." *Psychology Today*, 42–49.

Blum, D. (1997). *Sex on the brain: The biological differences between men and women.* New York: Viking.

Boteach, S. (2000). *Dating secrets of the ten commandments.* New York: Doubleday.

Brody, L., & J. Hall, (1993). "Gender and emotion." In M. Lewis, & J. Haviland, (1993). *Handbook of Emotions* New York: Guilford, 452.

Burgess, A. (2002, January 26). "I vow to thee." *Guardian.* Retrieved March 24, 2003, from http://www.guardian.co.uk/Archive/Article/0,4273,4342138,00.html.

Cline, R. J., & B. M. Johnson (1976). "The verbal stare: Focus on attention in conversation." *Communication Monographs* 43, 1–10.

David, M. W. (2001). *The divorce remedy: The proven 7-step program for saving your marriage.* New York: Simon & Schuster.

Farley, M. A. (1986). *Personal commitments.* San Francisco: Harper & Row.

Fein, E., & S. Schneider, (2001). *The rules for marriage: Time-tested secrets for making your marriage work.* New York: Warner Books.

Gibb, J. (1961). "Defensive communication." *Journal of Communication* 11, 141–48.

Goleman, D. (1995). *Emotional intelligence.* New York: Bantam.

Goleman, D. (1988, July 26). "Why job criticism fails: Psychology's new findings." *New York Times,* C1.

Gottman, J. M., & J. Declaire. (2001). *The relationship cure: A five-step guide for building better connections with family, friends, and lovers.* New York: Crown Publishers.

Graham, S. (2001). *Build your own life brand! A powerful strategy to maximize your potential and enhance your value for ultimate achievement.* New York: The Free Press (a division of Simon & Schuster, Inc.).

Guerrero, L. K. (1994, Winter). "I'm so mad I could scream: The effects of anger expression on relational satisfaction and communication competence." *Southern Communication Journal* 59:2, 125–41.

Halpern, D. (1992). *Sex differences in cognitive ability.* Hillsdale, NJ: Erlbaum.

Hedges, L., & A. Nowell, (1995, July 7). "Sex differences in mental test scores, variability, and numbers of high-scoring individuals." *Science* 269, 41–45.

Infante, D. A. (1995, January). "Teaching students to understand and control verbal aggression." *Communication Education* 44:1, 51.

Kantrowitz, B., & P. Wingert (1999, April 19). "The science of a good marriage." *Newsweek,* 52–57.

Kimura, D. (1999, Summer). "Sex differences in the brain." *Scientific American Presents* (Special Issue) 10:2, 26.

Kirshenbaum, M. (1996). *Too good to leave, too bad to stay.* New York: Dutton.

Knapp, M. L., R. P. Hart, G. W. Friedrich, & G. M. Shulman (1973). "The rhetoric of goodbye: Verbal and nonverbal correlates of human leave-taking." *Speech Monographs* 40, 182–98.

Knapp, M. L., L. Stafford, & J. A. Daly (1986). "Regrettable messages: Things people wish they hadn't said." *Journal of Communication.* 36, 40–57.

Knapp, M. L., & A. Vangelisti (1995). *Interpersonal communication and human relationships,* 3rd ed. Boston: Allyn and Bacon.

Lerner, H. (2001). *The dance of connection: How to talk to someone when you're mad, hurt, scared, frustrated, insulted, betrayed, or desperate.* New York: HarperCollins.

Levin, J., & A. Arluke (1985). An exploratory analysis of sex differences in gossip. *Sex Roles* 12: 281–85.

Levine, M., & H. E. Marano (2001, July–August). "Why I hate beauty." *Psychology Today.*

Lewis, M. (1997). "Making your intimate conversations better." In D. H. DeFord, ed. *Are you old enough to read this book? Reflections on midlife.* Pleasantville, NY: Reader's Digest.

McGuinness, D., & J. Symonds (1977). "Sex differences in choice behavior: The object-person dimension." *Perception* 6:6, 691–94.

Mottet, T. P., & V. P. Richmond (1998). "An inductive analysis of verbal immediacy: Alternative conceptualization of relational verbal approach/ avoidance strategies." *Communication Quarterly* 46:1, 35–40.

Peterson, K. S. (1999, September 29). "A hostile start makes the argument for divorce." *USA Today,* 1 (Life Section).

(No author). (1993, September–October). "The rat in the spat." *Psychology Today,* 12.

Sommers, C. H. (2000). *The war against boys: How misguided feminism is harming our young men.* New York: Simon & Schuster.

Tannen, D. (1986). *That's not what I meant!* New York: Morrow.

Tracy, K., D. Van Duesen; & S. Robinson (1987). "'Good' and 'bad' criticism: A descriptive analysis." *Journal of Communication.* 37, 46–59.

Vaches, A. (1994, August 28). "You carry the cure in your own heart." *Parade.*

Vaughan, D. (1990). *Uncoupling: How relationships come apart.* New York: Random House.

Wieder-Hatfield, D. (1981). "A unit in conflict management education skills." *Communication Education* 30, 265–73.

Wilmot, W. W., D. A. Carbaugh, & L. A. Baxter (1985). "Communication strategies used to terminate romantic relationships." *Western Journal of Speech Communication* 49, 204–16.

Witteman, H. (1992). "Analyzing interpersonal conflict: Nature of awareness, type of initiating event, situational perceptions, and management styles." *Western Journal of Speech Communication* 56, 248–80.

Wood, J. T. (1998). "But I thought you meant . . . Misunderstandings in human communication." Mountain View, CA: Mayfield Publishing Company. In D. Vaughan, (1990). *Uncoupling: How relationships come apart.* New York: Random House.

Further Reading

(No author). (2000, September 5). "Common questions about relationships, and some answers." Counseling Center, University at Buffalo, State University of New York (SUNY). Retrieved March 24, 2003, from http://ub-counseling.buffalo.edu/questions.shtml. The staff of the Counseling Center, Division of Student Affairs at the University at Buffalo, offers an excellent set of important, relevant, and specific relationship questions especially designed for college students, along with very specific answers to each question. A great place to begin if you are new to relationships or dating.

Davis, L. (2002). *I thought we'd never speak again: The road from estrangement to reconciliation.* New York: HarperCollins. In this 368-page book, Davis covers every sort of connection, from seemingly minor differences that can escalate over time to larger issues of abuse, neglect, and dysfunction. Based on her own personal odyssey as well as numerous interviews, she illustrates ways to reconcile without necessarily forgiving. This loving, thoughtful book is useful for adults dealing with personal issues or families undergoing emotional trauma.

Davis, M. W. (2001). *The divorce remedy: The proven 7-step program for saving your marriage.* New York: Simon & Schuster. More than just a remedy for divorce, Davis, an author, marriage therapist, and relationship expert, provides a skills book for successful marriages. This is a well-written guide full of inspirational anecdotes, in-depth case studies, and down-to-earth strategies for getting relationships back on track. The most effective part of the book for our purposes is her identification of ineffective, hurtful ways of interacting. Getting partners to ask for what they want—step three—is a useful tactic for serious couples. This is a guidebook for creating strong, loving relationships.

Ellison, S. (1998). *Don't be so defensive! Taking the war out of our words with powerful nondefensive communication.* Kansas City, MO: Andrews McMeel. Ellison has developed a communication process that gives each person the ability to communicate effectively without engaging in power struggles. It is innovative, practical, and has unlimited potential to strengthen interpersonal relationships, increase organization effectiveness, and build a more productive and harmonious society. Ellison uses numerous examples which cover interactions among strangers, couples, families, friends, and professional relationships.

Isenhart, M. W., & M. L. Spangle. (2000). *Collaborative approaches to resolving conflict.* New York: Sage Publications (A division of John Wiley & Sons). The authors offer a variety of different tools to cover a variety of relationship problems. They explain the major approaches to managing disputes at home, in the workplace or school, within communities, or in the international arena. Each approach is illustrated with recent examples of what can go wrong and how to respond appropriately. The approaches covered include negotiation, mediation, facilitation, arbitration, and judicial processes.

Kheel, T. W., & W. L. Lurie. (2001). *The keys to conflict resolution: Proven methods of resolving disputes voluntarily,* 2nd ed. New York: Four Walls Eight Windows. Kheel tells how he helped resolve some of the great showdowns between labor and management over the past 50 years in America. He is a veteran of more than 30,000 labor disputes, and in this book he teaches readers how to stress the art of persuasion and the techniques of compromise. His main focus is on the three types of alternative dispute resolutions: mediation, arbitration, and negotiation—the voluntary techniques of conflict resolution. This is a straightforward approach, couched in easy-to-follow language, illustrated with numerous personal examples. An accessible, thought-provoking, inspiring book.

Lerner, H. (2001). *The dance of connection: How to talk to someone when you're mad, hurt, scared, frustrated, insulted, betrayed, or desperate.* New York: HarperCollins. This book could as easily be listed as a further reading for the chapter on the self and communication, listening, or for the chapter on interpersonal relationships. It is about protecting yourself, listening with care and concern, taking conversations to the next level, as well as evaluating and improving relationships. The author provides specific advice for healing betrayals, inequalities, and broken connections and shows how to speak with honor and personal integrity in marriages, families, and friendships. This is a wise, sensible, knowledgeable, and intelligent approach to dealing with difficult relationships.

Sheth, J., & A. Sobel (2000). *Clients for life: How great professionals develop breakthrough relationships.* New York: Simon & Schuster. This is not a book full of a laundry-list how-tos, but a book full of interesting real-life examples designed to show readers how to secure clients. It is a book on relationships, true, but designed specifically for advisers and the attributes required that include selfless independence, empathy, deep conviction, integrity, judgment, and synthesis. One of the authors' points is that you have to be a consummate teacher, student, and observer of life to deliver on the promise of being a great adviser, because most of their traits come through the school of hard knocks and years of experience. The deeper insights they offer make this book good for professional advisers, lawyers, accountants, and marketing professionals.

Stern, E. S. (1999). *He just doesn't get it: Simple solutions to the most common relationship problems.* New York: Pocket Books. Stern, a nationally known relationship counselor, offers simple solutions to the problems women have with the infuriating, confusing, difficult—and absolutely wonderful—guys they love including such topics as why are men so selfish, how can they be so oblivious, are they intimacy-impaired, will they ever grow up, and will they ever understand us and love us the way we long to be loved? She focuses on the 15 most common relationship problems, and she supplies the answers along with specific advice on what to do. Straightforward and inspirational.

Tillett, G. (2000). *Resolving conflict: A practical approach,* 2nd ed. New York: Oxford University Press. Tillett is an Australian conflict resolution academic and practitioner and, in this book, provides an easy-to-read, comprehensive approach to interpersonal, neighborhood, workplace, and environmental conflicts. He does not cover international conflict resolution. Combining practical skills and processes, and clear explanations of underlying theory, arguments, and criticisms, he discusses conflict analysis, collaborative problem solving, mediation, negotiation, and arbitration. The book is conversational, user-friendly, and easy to absorb.

Turndorf, J. (2000) *Till death do us part (Unless I kill you first): A step-by-step guide for resolving marital conflict.* New York: Henry Holt & Company. Based on 15 years of clinical and laboratory research,

Turndorf has developed a proven 12-step program that breaks the conflict cycle of marital warfare and resolves it before it turns ugly and abusive. She makes a good case that fighting is not only not healthy, but it can cause massive destruction in a relationship. She claims that fighting creates a chemical imbalance in males that leads to more aggressive and negative behavior. Her suggestions can help cool down a combative climate so relationship partners can reapproach each other. Full of humorous anecdotes, case examples, and concrete suggestions.

Waite, L. J. & M. Gallagher (2000). *The case for marriage: Why married people are happier, healthier, and better off financially.* New York: Doubleday. This is a fascinating, well-written book in which the authors argue that being married is better physically, materially, and spiritually than being single or divorced. Not only is the institution of marriage thoroughly analyzed, the authors offer cultural criticism as well as practical advice for strengthening marriages. Also, they provide guidelines for reestablishing marriage as the foundation for a healthy, happy society. Although this is a well-researched study that provides 15 pages of bibliography and 25 pages of footnotes, it offers refreshing support for the 93 percent of Americans who say they hope to form a lasting and happy union with one person.

Zeldin, T. (2000). *Conversation: How talk can change our lives.* London, UK: HiddenSpring. This 103-page book by Zeldin, the Oxford University historian, was originally broadcast in Britain as a BBC radio series. It covers many aspects of conversations among friends, family, lovers, and especially among people at work. Zeldin claims we talk at cross purposes, don't listen to what the other person has to say, or talk at someone rather than to them. One of his bold ideas is to be able to spend time learning the essence of a profession by shadowing or working with someone in the field as a step toward a more humane type of education and as a way to improve our lives.

Chapter 9

Communicating at Work

Objectives

After reading this chapter, you should be able to:

- Define *informational interviews*.
- List some of the ways information interviews are used.
- Tell how information interviews can enhance information gathering.
- Construct the following kinds of questions: primary, follow-up, open-ended, closed, neutral, and leading.
- Explain the purpose of, preparation for, and execution of information interviews as precursors to job interviews.
- Describe your preparation for employment interviews.
- Explain electronic résumés, the types of delivery systems, and the file formats.
- Prepare an effective résumé that follows the suggestions and is a scannable plain-text document.
- Explain the employment interview—preparation, questions, and the process of being interviewed.
- Describe your preparation for a presentation.

Key Terms and Concepts

 Use the Communicating Effectively CD-ROM and Online Learning Center at mhhe.com/hybels7 to further your understanding of the following terms.

Appraisal interview 303	Follow-up questions 308	Open format 307
Closed format 307	Information interview 303	PETAL 335
Closed questions 308	Internet-ready résumé 322	Policy information 306
Cover letter 325	Interview 301	Precursor 314
Disciplinary interview 303	Leading questions 309	Presentation 332
Electronic résumé 322	Letter of application 326	Primary questions 308
Employment interview 316	Letter of inquiry 325	RDAT 336
Exit interview 303	Natural delivery 333	Résumé 318
Factual information 306	Neutral questions 309	Scannable résumés 322
File 325	Online résumé 322	Semiopen format 307
File format 325	Open-ended questions 308	Stress interview 303

CHARLES VANBELLE, AN EMPLOYEE OF A CITY COMMUNITY Development division, and a resident of Shawnee Trace, a subdivision located on the periphery of the same city, was concerned about the prospect of a 350-unit apartment complex being built on land abutting his development and, thus, decreasing the property values of his and surrounding homes and increasing the already heavy burden on the city's overtaxed school system. The first thing Charles did was to research the process by which the land was annexed and to fully inform himself about the pending development. This involved searching city records, examining newspaper accounts, and conducting a number of interviews with city officials. Next, he prepared a flyer that, on one page, outlined the information he had discovered. Then, he circulated around his neighborhood and informally interviewed his neighbors and solicited their support. When he gave each family a copy of his flyer, he had them sign a petition that simply expressed their negative position on the zoning that allowed multifamily units on the abutting land. Before the city council's Zoning Committee had its formal meeting on the zoning of the abutting property, Charles asked to make a presentation at the meeting.

Using his computer's presentation software, Charles prepared a short presentation that outlined each of the major concerns of his neighbors, showed the potential negative effect of the 350-unit complex on surrounding property, and revealed the potential burden that would fall upon the local school system. His presentation, utilizing the city's available tools, took the full 10 minutes he was allowed, and he followed it by submitting the signed petitions to the committee. Knowing that the council's Zoning Committee was simply a recommending agency of the full Planning and Zoning Committee, and knowing, too, that he would be asked to put his allegations in writing, Charles prepared an 11-page document, which he distributed to each of the members of the council's Zoning Committee. A copy of the document went to the city law director as well. When the full Planning and Zoning Committee met, the president, having heard of the effectiveness of his first presentation, invited Charles to give a second presentation.

Because of the extensiveness of his research, the strength of his presentations, and the signed petitions he submitted, the Planning and Zoning Committee decided to assign permanent zoning to the land in question that reduced zoning from multifamily housing to single-family and two-family dwellings only. Charles's combined usage of interviews and presentations resulted in a solid, positive effort that had concrete results for his city in general and for his housing development, Shawnee Trace, in particular.

When Loreta Velazquez looked for a permanent job with a local company, she began an investigation to learn more about the company, its products, and the industry in general. She had heard that coming to interviews without this knowledge is a leading weakness of job applicants. She acquired much objective background information on the Internet; by conducting information interviews of company customers, competitors, and employees, she learned additional, subjective information, such as the attitudes of those who run the company, the status of the company in the community, and the various problems the company was trying to solve. Loreta was taking a business communication course at a local technical college, and she assembled her information about this company for a presentation in her class.

Both of these examples, Charles VanBelle and Loreta Velazquez, involved interviews and presentations. Not only were VanBelle and Velazquez well prepared, but their communication skills reflected positively on them as well. In our own lives, we spend time conducting interviews and being interviewed, giving presentations and listening to the presentations of others. The first part of this chapter is about interviewing (informational and employment); the second part is about presentations.

An **interview** is a series of questions and answers, usually exchanged between two people, that has the purpose of getting and understanding information about a particular subject or topic. Thus, when you ask a professor about a low grade you received on a paper, you are engaged in interviewing. You go in with a purpose—to find out why you received a low grade—and your conversation with the professor involves a series of questions and answers. If you go to pick up your car that has been in the garage being repaired, you are likely to have an interview with the mechanic who fixed it. You might ask what was wrong with the car, what parts had to be replaced, how long the repair is likely to last, and whether you should even keep the car.

What makes an interview different from interpersonal communication is that it is task-oriented—it has the goal of finding out specific information. You interview someone for information you need to put together a speech, or you go into a job interview with the goal of presenting yourself so well that the interviewer will want to hire you.

The interview is another form of transactional communication. Because of the interview's back-and-forth nature, communication is continuous and simultaneous. Not only are interviewer and subject (interviewee) responding verbally to each other; they are also making assessments. The interviewee is assessing the knowledge, poise, and preparation of the interviewer. The interviewer is thinking about what is the best way to ask a question, how to rephrase a question to get a more specific answer, or how to probe certain points that have come up in the interviewee's comments. Roles are quite specific in interview situations: One person plays the role of information seeker and the other of information giver. During the course of the interview, questions, answers, and perceptions are determined by each person's background, education, and experience. Because

Consider This

Key Steps for Successful Interviewing

Step One: Be prepared. Adequate preparation and practice are essential to demonstrate that you are a knowledgeable and credible person.

1. Know the purpose and objectives of the interview.
2. Make certain the setting and time are satisfactory.
3. Remove any barriers that might interfere with a successful interview.
4. Make certain you have communicated effectively with the other interview participant or participants.
5. Dress appropriately.
6. Practice. Immediate impressions will be formed from your verbal and nonverbal communication; thus, make certain your self-confidence, personality, and speech habits convey a positive impression.

Step Two: Have an interview plan, but be adaptable and flexible. Even though the interview may not unfold exactly as your plan dictates, a plan shows that you are thoughtful, knowledgeable, and organized. If there is dead space during the interview, having a plan will help provide material to move the interview forward. Having a plan, too, offers you any background information that might be helpful during the interview. If the interview moves far afield from where it should be, having a plan will help you refocus and redirect the interview. Help make certain that the interview efficiently and effectively fulfills its primary purpose and objectives.

Step Three: Follow-up. Any commitment to an interview requires both time and effort, and anyone who participates on your behalf requires a minimum of a thank you. If they have provided you important information, taken time away from their regular job, or if it is an employment interview, a formal thank you in the form of a short, timely letter of appreciation is important and further reinforces and underscores both your credibility and thoughtfulness.

an interview is a structured form of interpersonal communication, most take place in a setting appropriate for serious, goal-oriented communication.

The interviews we are most likely to be involved in are information interviews and job interviews. Of course, interviewers may discard the regular one-on-one interview and opt for either doing it over the phone or meeting you for lunch. On a Career Journal website from Jobpilot entitled "Types of Interviews and How to Handle Them" (2002), the unknown author discusses six types of interviews: phone, lunch, screening, group, panel, and job interviews.

One thing all interviewers will look for, despite the type or format of the interview, is communication skills. All interviewers know the value of communication. "Improved communication is a key to retaining employees" (Morreale, 2001). Sherry Morreale, associate director of the National Communication Association, cites a study, "Three Out of Four Say Better Communication Equals Greater Employee Retention" (2000), which reports the results of a survey of 4,000 human resource professionals conducted by KnowledgePoint. Seventy-one percent of the respondents cited solid communication skills as the major way to retain employees. To foster a culture of communication, interviewers will seek people who reveal effective communication skills. These are people, too, who will "gravitate to workplaces where they feel valued, have good working relationships with their managers, and understand how their work contributes to the organization's objectives."

■ THE INFORMATION INTERVIEW

An **information interview** is an interview in which the goal is to gather facts and opinions from someone with expertise and experience in a specific field. Types of information interviews include the **appraisal interview** where a supervisor makes a valuation by estimating and judging the quality or worth of an employee's performance and then interviews the employee in connection with the appraisal. A **disciplinary interview** concerns a sensitive area, where the employee is notified, and the interview involves hearing the employee's side of the story and, depending on the outcome, instituting disciplinary action. An **exit interview** occurs at the termination of an employee's employment and is designed to resolve any outstanding concerns of employers and employees. Some exit interviews occur by questionnaire only. Many employees are often willing to point at deficiencies in the company at exit interviews. A final kind of informative interview is a **stress interview,** which is sometimes part of the job search. A stress interview is designed to see how you act under pressure—to give interviewers a

The goal of the information interview is to gather facts and opinions from someone with expertise and experience in a specific field.

realistic sense of your response to difficult situations. Stress interviews went out of fashion in the 1990s but were designed for positions such as air traffic controllers, stockbrokers, military special forces, surgeons, some sales jobs, test pilots, and submariners.

Interviews are a flexible means of information gathering. No longer does the term *interview* suggest an interviewer sitting face-to-face, or speaking over the telephone, with a single interviewee. We can credit technology for expanding the media through which interviews are conducted; thus, often they are carried on in electronic chat rooms, in teleconferences, or via e-mail. The information interview is a useful tool when you are collecting information for a speech, a group discussion, or a paper. Also, it can serve as a way to get answers to questions you may have about a certain occupation, a career field, education, training, or work conditions. It can serve as a precursor to job interviews because the answers to questions you pose about a career, work opportunities, or the education and training needed for certain occupations can guide you to the appropriate job interviews. There is more on information interviews as precursors to job interviews in the next section.

The information interview can be used to supplement more traditional research sources—such as books, periodicals, and Internet searches. It may also produce information that is not available from these sources—like the subjective information Loreta Velazquez gathered on attitudes, status, and problems regarding the company she was investigating in one of the opening examples of this chapter.

Information interviews help us to get the most up-to-date information. Reporters, for example, make extensive use of information interviews. They interview the mayor of the town about her plans for increasing taxes. They talk to the governor of the state about his plans for reelection. On campus, an interview is the most effective way of getting information from members of the college community. A student interviews the vice president for administration about whether tuition will increase next year; another interviews a department head about the new requirements for a major.

Interviews are also very effective in getting personal reactions to events. You might read about the damage a hurricane has caused in a small town, but an interview can give you a chance to discuss someone's experience in the hurricane. Personal experience adds another dimension to your information; it tells you what it feels like to be in that situation.

One of the greatest advantages of the information interview is that it allows an opportunity for feedback and follow-up. If you don't understand something, you will have a chance to ask questions. An interview also permits you to explore interesting points of information as they arise—points you may not have been aware of beforehand. For example, if you are interviewing a member of the college administration about a tuition increase, she might mention that electricity costs have gone up this year. You can explore this area: Have they gone up because the utility company has raised its rates or because of greater electricity use on campus?

The information interview is the most personal way of getting information. You can interact with the person being interviewed; you can observe nonverbal behavior; you can ask for clarification. The interview gives you a way of learning and of sharing information in a human setting.

Preparing for the Interview

Preparation is one of the essential keys to success in most interviewing situations. Preparation has three important benefits. First, it means you are less likely to waste the time of the interviewee, because you will be able to focus on just the information you need. You will avoid using the interviewee's time to randomly explore the subject area. Second, you will be able to gain greater depth into the subject. With adequate preparation, you will have already surveyed the subject area; thus, with focused questions and pertinent follow-up questions, you are likely to gain a depth of understanding not available otherwise. These benefits depend, of course, on whether you have chosen the right person to interview.

There is a third benefit of preparing for the interview. You will increase your credibility. Preparing for an interview gives you an unexpected and unmeasurable advantage. If the people you are interviewing see that you have taken time to prepare, they are much more likely to be willing to spend their time with you. If you start out with such questions as "How do you spell your name?" or "I don't know much about this topic; do you have any ideas for questions?" you will not inspire confidence in your skills as an interviewer. On the other hand, if you show that you know something about the interviewee and about the topic, you will likely find much more willingness to discuss the topic seriously, and you will get better and more specific information.

Choosing the Person to Interview

Once you have chosen the topic you want to research, how do you decide whom you should interview? Basically, the answer depends on the kind of information you are looking for. For a class project, most interviews will focus on either **policy information** (data on how an organization should be run) or **factual information** (data dealing with who, what, where, when, and the like). Some colleges have background information about their faculty online. Also available online are numerous biographical sources. Using your college's online reference materials may provide you with access to the whole series of *Who's Who* resources plus many others.

Policy Information. Every organization has people who make policy and others who carry it out. In the public schools, for example, the school board makes the policy and the principals carry it out within their own individual schools. Therefore, if the budget for music has been cut and you want to know why, you should interview a member of the school board. If, however, you want to know the impact this cut has had on individual schools, you should interview a principal. By the same token, if you want to know the impact of food stamps being cut, it would be useful to interview someone from the local welfare office.

In colleges and universities, policy making is usually divided into two areas: administrative and academic. The administrative area sets policies on the due date for tuitions, allocation of parking spaces, food services, law enforcement, and so on. The academic area sets policies on such matters as curriculum, faculty, class schedules—anything that might influence teaching and learning. If you want to find out why the parking spaces for students are so limited, you should interview someone in the administrative area. If you wonder why so few courses are scheduled for summer school, you should talk to someone in the academic area.

Factual Information. When you are gathering material for a speech or term paper, quite often the information you need is of a factual nature. For example, you might want to know how China controls its population or how well women do at getting jobs in advertising. In such cases, you should seek out the best-informed person on the subject. One of the best places to look is among the faculty on your campus. Everyone on the faculty is an expert on some subject. If you want to do research on population control in China, for example, you might start with the sociology or political science faculty. If you do not know which instructors specialize in which areas of expertise, ask the department head.

People who work in the community are also valuable sources of information. City council members and county commissioners can tell you about the workings of local government. And don't forget city employees. The tax assessor can tell you how taxes are calculated and collected. His or her office will also have information on who owns what property. Police officials and lawyers can offer valuable information on how the legal system works. The welfare office and the children's services office can often provide insight into social problems in the community. Researching a medical subject? Why not talk to some local doctors? You will be surprised how many experts are available once you look around.

Gathering Background Information

Anyone who is planning to conduct an interview should know something about the person being interviewed. Typical information you should have beforehand includes the proper spelling of the person's name and his or her title. If the person is well known, you might be able to discover some biographical information before the interview. *Books in Print*, for example, lists all the titles and names of authors of books recently published in the United States. *Who's Who in America* contains biographical information about prominent Americans. Don't forget to check out the specialized editions, such as *Who's Who in the South, Who's Who in American Women*, and so on. If you are going to talk to someone who works for the college or university, the public relations office is likely to have some biographical information about the person.

You should also have background information on the topic of your interview. The purpose of an interview is not to give you a crash course on a particular topic; it is to give you information that is not commonly known or new insight into an old topic. For example, if you want to interview someone about using computers for research, you need to know something about what is available. If you're going to interview someone about using the Internet, you should have some experience in actually using it so that you can speak with some authority.

As you prepare your background information, decide on the angle you want to take in your interview. The *angle* is the information on which you want to concentrate. If, for example, you decide to interview someone on the status of women in the Middle East, your topic would be so broad that it might be impossible to get any useful information. Women are treated very differently in Saudi Arabia than they are in Jordan. Would it be better to concentrate on just one country? Also, should you narrow the topic even more by concentrating on one aspect of women's lives, such as education, politics, or homemaking? Once you have an angle for the interview, it will be much easier to get information you can use.

Along with deciding the angle, you should decide on the format as well.

Deciding on the Format

Interviews vary in their degree of structure or format. **Open-format** interviews are relatively unstructured. As interviewer, you take note of or record the participant's statements but do not exert a great deal of control. In open-format interviews, you may ask interviewees to respond to a general topic or concern, and they determine the direction of the interview as they react to the points raised.

Closed-format interviews are highly structured. They are as formal, buttoned-down, and structured as the open format is freewheeling. As interviewer, you know exactly what you want to ask, and you work to keep your interviewee on track by asking one of your standardized questions and recording the respondent's answers to each one before moving on to the next question. Although this is an efficient technique for getting information because it is highly scripted, it doesn't allow much spontaneous information to emerge.

Semiopen format interviews occur when you have a core set of standardized questions that you ask in a standard manner and carefully record. However, this format allows you to deviate from the script with spontaneous follow-up questions if they are germane to the interview.

The best way to prepare an interview is to ask a variety of different kinds of questions, many of which emerge as the interview progresses. Thus, for most information interviews, our position is that the semiopen format works best because it most successfully accommodates this approach—requiring effective listening on the part of the interviewer and flexibility in adapting to what transpires. There may be a script or plan for the interview, but it serves as a general template rather than as a precise menu. Once an angle and format have been planned, the next stage is preparing questions.

Preparing Questions

In a closed-format interview, you know exactly what you want to ask and you work to keep your interviewee on track. Although this is an efficient technique for getting information, it doesn't allow much spontaneous information to emerge. On the other hand, in an open-format interview you might wander off the topic. For example, students interviewing college professors often get a five-minute answer to their questions. When this happens, you lose control of the interview and it's hard to get it back.

The best way to conduct an interview is to ask a variety of different kinds of questions. In this section we will look at primary, follow-up, open-ended, closed, neutral, and leading questions.

Primary Questions. These are the questions that often come first in the interview or that come first with each new topic the interviewer introduces. **Primary questions** are designed to cover the subject comprehensively, and should be based on your background research. Let's say you are interviewing a member of your counseling staff about depression. Some of the primary questions you might ask are:

- What is the clinical definition of depression?
- How does depression differ from being in a bad mood?
- What are the signs of a serious depression?
- Where can a student go to get help?
- How is depression treated?

Follow-Up Questions. Although you should always go into an interview with some preplanned primary questions, these will not be the only questions you will ask. As the interview proceeds, you will think of other questions based on the answers given by your interviewee. These **follow-up questions** are useful when you want to go into a subject in greater depth. They also enable you to pursue an area that might be new to you or to clarify something you don't understand.

Follow-up questions require that the interviewer listen carefully and think about the answers. Often the answers to follow-up questions lead into such interesting areas that interviewers get information they hadn't planned on.

Open-Ended Questions. **Open-ended questions** permit the person being interviewed to expand on his or her answers. They lead to explanations, elaboration, and reflection. Most in-depth questions are open-ended.

Closed Questions. Questions worded in ways that restrict their answers are **closed questions.** A question that can be answered with a yes or a no is a closed question: "Do you plan to stay in this job?" "Are you going to

Working Together

Working with others as a group, come up with follow-up questions to these answers from an interview:

1. The people I hate most are drunken drivers. Ever since our family suffered such a tragic loss, I have been determined to devote my efforts to getting them off the roads.

2. The United States government is taking care of Native Americans through the reservation system.

3. People who live in earthquake-prone areas should take some basic safety precautions.

4. Once the United States has invaded a country, they have an obligation to stay and help the country become stable and functioning again.

5. The harmful chemicals and wastes that are discharged into the air and water of our nation not only make us sick but cause death as well.

6. Burnout, which is stress caused by the inability to cope and adjust to the demands of certain situations, causes irritability, fatigue, and low motivation.

Now the group should create several more statements that will lead to follow-up questions. Pass them along to another group so that they can come up with follow-up questions.

graduate from school?" Other closed questions require only a short answer; for example: "Do you work better at home or in your office?" "What city would you most like to live in?" Closed questions have some advantages. They are designed to get a lot of information quickly, and they are good for eliciting facts.

Closed questions can be very useful when the subject of your interview is too talkative. If his or her answers are so long that you don't have a chance to ask the rest of your questions, you have lost control of the interview. By interjecting a series of short, closed questions, you can regain control. If, for example, you are interviewing the director of athletics about the mix of athletics and academics and she begins to talk at great length about the many stereotypes people have about athletics, you might ask: "What are some of the stereotypes?" "Can you cite specific examples to disprove the stereotypes?" "Do you have the statistics of graduation rates for student athletes compared with those for all students?" "Are there academic benefits to being involved in athletics?" When you prepare your interview's primary questions, they should be a mixture of closed and open-ended questions.

Neutral Questions versus Leading Questions. Questions that do not show how the interviewer feels about the subject are **neutral questions.** For example, a reporter interviewing the mayor about a tax increase might ask this neutral question: "Many people think this tax increase will create a hardship for people who live in the city. What do you think?"

Leading questions point the interviewee in a particular direction. If you were to ask the dean, "When is the college going to stop exploiting women?" you would be implying that the college is currently exploiting women. A more neutral way of phrasing this question would be, "Do you think men and women have equal opportunities at this college?" or, if you want to get more specific, "Men's intramural sports are allotted twice as much money as women's. Why is that?"

Leading questions often show the bias of the interviewer, and if there is a negative bias, it might arouse hostility in the person being interviewed. Sometimes, however, leading questions can be used effectively. If you are interviewing a member of Alcoholics Anonymous, it might be appropriate to ask, "How did AA improve your relationships in your family?" Sometimes interviewers use a leading question to get a strong emotional reaction from the person being interviewed. Reporters and talk-show hosts often ask persons they are interviewing provocative questions like "How do you deal with the kind of negative comments being made about you?" or "What is it like to be known for your bad temper and rudeness?"

It's important to know when to ask leading questions. Since some questions can lead to hostility, especially when feelings run high, the inexperienced interviewer should leave them for the end of the interview and concentrate on neutral questions at the beginning. You should also remember that some leading questions can result in explosive replies, and so you should not ask them if you are not prepared for the answers they might evoke.

Here are some examples of leading questions (LQ) rephrased as neutral questions (NQ):

LQ: Why are you so afraid of being interviewed?

NQ: Some people have noticed that you seem to be apprehensive about being interviewed. Why do you think they have this idea?

LQ: Why do you run student government like a tyrant?

NQ: Some people have called you a tyrant for the way you run the student government. Do you think you have done something to make them feel that way?

LQ: Why don't you ever get anything done on time?

NQ: Do you ever have problems meeting deadlines?

Questions can be worded in many different ways. A good interview will have a variety of questions. Not only will these questions get at different kinds of information, but they will also be interesting to the person being interviewed.

Using Tape or Notes?

Before you conduct an interview, you should decide whether you want to record it on audiotape or videotape. The main advantage of either form of taping is that it allows you to record the interview without taking notes. If you are not tied to note taking, you can concentrate on listening and pay more attention to the nonverbal cues you receive from the person you are interviewing. Taping also permits you to get precise quotations. This is particularly useful if the topic is controversial. If you are looking only for background information, however, exact quotations might not be your goal.

The main advantage of videotaping is that you can concentrate on listening and pay more attention to the nonverbal cues you receive from the person you are interviewing.

Note taking has advantages of its own. You don't have to worry about equipment, and it is easier to review notes to find what you want than it is to go through a tape cassette.

One advantage of conducting an online interview is that you can print out an exact copy of what transpired. In doing research for a speech, this would allow you to use just the portion or portions you want, cite the wording precisely, and preserve the interview for posterity.

The popularity and inexpensive nature of video cameras allows them to be used instead of audio tape recorders. An advantage of a video recording, too, is that a portion of the actual interview can be used as visual support for a speech or presentation if appropriate. Be certain to check the lighting and sound conditions before using a video camera. Familiarity with the equipment is essential. If you are doing your own taping, remember that your credibility is as affected by your professional handling of the equipment as it is by your conduct of, and in, the interview itself. Make certain you have a long-enough videotape to cover the entire interview—even if it goes longer than the planned time, as often happens.

Taping interviews also has disadvantages. Some people just do not like to be taped. Sometimes tape recorders or video cameras make people feel self-conscious, and some of the spontaneous nature of an interview can thus be lost. In other cases, a very controversial interviewee might not want to be pinned down to his or her exact words. A city council member who calls the mayor a fool would probably prefer not to have those words on tape. Another disadvantage of taping is that if you have a very long interview, you will find it time consuming to watch or listen to the tape and pick out the main points.

If you decide to tape an interview, you should follow these basic procedures:

1. When setting up the appointment for the interview, ask if you may tape the person's comments.

2. Before you go into the interview, make sure you know how to use the recorder.

3. Most recorders have built-in microphones. Some of these work quite well, but others will pick up a lot of background noise. If you are going to be in a noisy place, take along a microphone that plugs into the recorder or camera and can be placed close to the participants.

4. Each recorder shows its length in time. Make sure you have adequate cassettes for your interview.

5. Let the person you are interviewing know how you are going to use the recording. He or she might react differently if you are going to use it for background information as opposed to airing the interview on the campus radio or television station.

If you decide to take notes instead of making an audio or video recording, it is useful to devise your own form of shorthand. After the interview is over, you should immediately write out your notes in greater detail. More than one interviewer has discovered, two or three days after the interview, that he or she has no idea what some of the notes mean. Looking at your notes immediately after the interview will help you fill in the gaps while the comments are still fresh in your mind.

Conducting the Interview

Whenever you conduct an interview, the most important thing you can do is know what you are talking about. Most people will be pleased if you let them know you have been researching the topic of the interview and have taken the time to find out something about it.

People who are not accustomed to being interviewed might feel nervous, so it is important to help them feel at ease. You can best do this by thanking them for agreeing to the interview and expressing your interest in the topic you will be talking about. If you are taping the interview, try to put the recorder in an unobtrusive place so that it will not make the interviewee feel self-conscious.

Once you begin asking questions and listening to answers, don't be afraid to ask for clarification. Sometimes interviewers do not do this because they are afraid of appearing ignorant. If the person you are interviewing, for example, mentions a Supreme Court case you have never heard of, you should immediately ask for background information on the case.

It is important that you, as interviewer, keep control of the situation. As you ask your questions, you should set the tone for the interview and establish your authority, the course the interview will take, and your relationship to the interviewee (Misler, 1975). When you are talking to people in their own area of expertise, quite often they will digress or tell you more than you want to know. If you have scheduled a half-hour interview and after the first 10 minutes you are still on your first question, you are losing control of the interview and won't have time to pose all the questions you want to ask. If this happens, the only thing you can do is interrupt. This can be done with such statements as "This is really very interesting and I would like to talk more about it, but I want to ask you a few more questions."

Although we have stressed the importance of preparing interview questions in advance, an interview will occasionally take a completely different and more interesting direction. Let's say that you are interviewing the director of campus security about the use of alcohol on campus. During the course of the interview, she reveals that two fraternities are on probation for alcohol abuse. You should immediately follow up on this information: "What are the violations?" "What is meant by 'probation'?" "Who makes the decision to put them on probation?" "How long does probation last?" One of the advantages of getting information by interview is that the discussion can always take a more interesting and provocative direction. If you stick rigidly to your prepared questions, you can miss some good opportunities.

When you are interviewing, watch for nonverbal cues. If the issue is sensitive, is the interviewee giving you cues that he or she is dodging the questions? Is he or she avoiding eye contact? Tapping a pen nervously on the desk? Nonverbal cues can often tell you whether to follow up on a point or to steer away from it.

If you are interviewing someone who is on a tight schedule, don't run beyond the time you have scheduled. If you need more time, ask for it at the interviewee's convenience or call back to tie up the loose ends over the telephone. Occasionally, when you listen to your tape or read your notes, you will discover something you missed or something that needs clarifying. The telephone is a good way to get this information after the interview is over.

Once the interview is completed, thank the interviewee. If it was a good interview, don't be afraid to say so. Even people who are interviewed frequently are pleased to hear they have been helpful. Also, let the person know how you plan to use the interview.

Analyzing the Interview

When the interview is over, spend some time thinking about how well you did. Your success can be measured by how the interviewee responded to you and whether you got the information you needed.

You can tell if your questions were well worded by the way the person answered them. If he or she never quite dealt with the points you raised, the problem may have been with the questions. If he or she asked for clarification, that is another indication your questions weren't well structured.

Looking at your notes will tell you whether you were listening carefully. Are your notes confusing? Are there gaps in them? Your notes will also tell you whether you covered the subject thoroughly enough. Sometimes, after an interview is over, an interviewer thinks of all sorts of questions that should have been asked. Finally, did you conduct the interview in a professional manner? Did you arrange the questions in a logical order beforehand? Had you researched the topic of your interview? Did you know how to run the equipment? The main measure of your professionalism is whether your interviewee took you and your questions seriously.

Consider This

As part of the process of acquiring information—perhaps hand-in-hand with information interviews as precursors to job interviews—should be your use of the Internet. Here, Sheila Wellington (2001) in her book, *Be Your Own Mentor,* gives suggestions for searching the Web.

By now, we all know about the job listings on the Internet—most big-newspaper classified sections, for example, are there, or you can go to a portmanteau site (they bring together lots of different subjects under one virtual roof) such as Headhunter.net, where you'll find 140,000 listings worldwide. More interesting are the newest additions to e-search, sites such as WetFeet.com, where you can get the lowdown on companies and industries, learning about their history and their culture as well as their pay scales, who they're hiring and in what field, and their approach to diversity. Look up Avon, for example, and you'll learn that it won Working Mother's Leadership Award seven years in a row as a "Best Company for Women to Work For," as well as being on Fortune's list of "America's 50 Best Companies for Minorities" (pp. 338–48).

Questions

1. Have you found quality Internet sites for job listings? What are they?

2. If you were a woman looking for a job, what are the key factors you would want to know about before accepting a new job? What are the key questions you would ask at an interview?

3. If you were a member of any minority, what are the key questions you would ask to determine whether or not a job would be acceptable to you?

Source: S. Wellington *Be Your Own Mentor: Strategies from Top Women on the Secrets of Success.* (New York: Random House, 2001).

■ INFORMATION INTERVIEWS AS PRECURSORS TO JOB INTERVIEWS

A **precursor** is simply something that precedes or comes before something else. One use of information interviews is to become more knowledgeable about your field of interest. Information interviews can help clarify and define career goals, introduce potential employers, and establish a network of contacts that could lead to future employment. Unlike job interviews, information interviews do not require that you sell yourself to employers. Employers may not grant you a job interview because vacancies do not exist, but information interviews often can be arranged regardless of existing vacancies. They are arranged with individuals who are most likely to provide information directly or with those who can refer you to persons with information. The best feature of information interviews as precursors to job interviews is that they are a way of exploring your possibilities—choosing academic majors, making career choices, changing careers, or beginning a job hunt.

There are several steps involved to using informational interviews as precursors to job interviews. First, you need to analyze your skills, scrutinize your interests, and clarify your career goals. Second, you need to research the "world of work." Select occupational fields that fit your career interests and needs, and research these fields. Third, you need to write a résumé. The process of writing résumés is discussed later in this chapter.

Now, locate appropriate people to interview. The first and most immediate source of information consists of friends, family, neighbors, colleagues, former employers, and anyone else you know who might either supply an information interview or offer you a referral. Think, too, about contacting faculty, career center personnel, staff at other university offices, alumni, and any employer contacts the career center can provide. Other sources are community service agencies and trade and professional organizations such as the chamber of commerce, women's organizations, or the Information Management Association. You might, too, scan the *Yellow Pages* and articles in newspapers, magazines, and journals. Consider, as well, attending local, state, regional, or national meetings for professional associations in your career-interest field.

Once you locate someone to interview, prepare a variety of questions in different categories. Tailor your list of questions specifically to the individual and his or her organization. Background questions might include "Tell me about how you got started in this field," "What was your education?" and "What educational background or related experience might be helpful in entering this field?" Work-environment questions might include "What do you do during a typical workday or workweek?" "What skills are most essential for effectiveness in this job?" and "What are the most difficult or challenging elements to the job?" Questions on career preparation might include "What credentials, educational degrees, licenses, and so on, are required for entry into this career field?" "What kinds of prior experiences are absolutely essential?" and "What kind of lifestyle does your job permit?" Other areas of concern might include hiring decisions, supply and demand concerns involving current and future job availability and potential job advancement, any personal advice, and referrals to others to whom you could talk.

Setting up appointments requires that you be resourceful and sincere and, above all, show interest in what your target person does. Most people enjoy the opportunity to discuss their work. If they are too busy to meet you during their office hours, explore the possibility of meeting over lunch or after work. In addition to reviewing the date and time of the appointment, be sure to ask for directions and parking information. If a person cannot meet with you, ask whether you can ask her or him a few quick questions over the telephone. Find out exactly how many minutes you can have.

Here are some final reminders for conducting information interviews as precursors to job interviews:

1. Remember that this is not a job interview. Your purpose is to acquire information. Nevertheless, dress as if it were an actual job interview. First impressions are always important.

2. Get to your appointment a few minutes early, and be courteous to everyone you meet.

3. Take the initiative in conducting the interview. The interview is in your ball park; thus, you ask the questions, and you interview the person.

4. Indicate your strengths and interests. It is all right to do this at appropriate times.

On the Web

The Internet is full of information about interviews, interviewing, and the entire job-search process. Entering "The Job Interview" into the Google search engine (March 24, 2003) produced 40,700 hits. Here are three sites we found especially useful.

1. D. Curtis, "The Job Interview," Office of Career Services, Harvard University, 1995. Retrieved March 24, 2003, from www.ocs.fas.harvard.edu/html/interview.html. Curtis offers concrete steps you can take to increase the probability that a job interview will be successful. She discusses the interview, informational interviews, the recruiting interview, second interviews, consulting interviews, and preparing for consulting interviews. She offers a great deal of practical, specific advice.

2. (No author). *"Making a Good Impression on Job Interviews,"* Careerbuilder, 2002. Retrieved March 24, 2003, from http://www.careerbuilder.com/gh_int_htg_impression.html. This site offers specific suggestions regarding inter-

view preparation, interview types, good impressions, common questions, asking questions, and common mistakes. There is information on how to make a good impression before, during, and after the interview.

3. D. Taylor, & J. J. Guidry, "Going to Work: Make a Good Impression." Texas Agricultural Extension Service, The Texas A & M University System, December 1999. Retrieved March 24, 2003, from http://agpublications.tamu.edu/pubs/fdrm/12364.pdf. The article begins, "Your goals, self-image, personality, attitude, cleanliness, and concern for your family can make a major impression on an employer"(pg. 1). There follows, then, a section on each of these six elements with specific suggestions under each one.

There is no way one chapter, Communicating at Work, can compete with the Internet with respect to coverage or number of suggestions regarding the topic of interviews. Use the Internet to obtain much valuable, up-to-date, and available information.

5. Do not exceed your requested time, but be prepared to stay longer in case the contact indicates a willingness to talk longer.

6. Before you leave, ask your contact if he or she could refer you to others in the same career. By doing this, you can establish a referral list and build a job-search network.

7. Write a thank-you note. Your contact has given you valuable work time. Thank the person for his or her time and interest and cite any conclusions or decisions resulting from the interview.

8. Keep a record of each organization you visit. Record the information you obtained, too: names, comments, and new referrals for future reference.

■ THE EMPLOYMENT INTERVIEW

The **employment interview** is an interview used by an employer to determine whether someone is suitable for a job. In an employment interview you have two goals: to distinguish yourself in some way from the other applicants, and to make a good impression in a very short time. The key to reaching both these goals is careful preparation.

The employment interview is a structured form of communication.

Evaluating the Job Description

Usually the first notice of a job comes from some kind of written description—a newspaper advertisement, an online listing on the computer, or a request filed with an organization such as a college placement service. If you think the job suits your abilities and you want to get an interview, begin by making a list of the major job responsibilities and the skills you need to do the job. For example, let's say you see the following job advertisement and think you want to apply:

Administrative assistant to design director/department coordinator. Wanted for art department of weekly magazine. Varied responsibilities, basic computer skills, processing of all department bills. Good phone manner, organizational skills, quick thinking, some pressure. College graduate.

In defining this position, first list the skills needed. Your list might include major job skills such as basic computer skills, processing of department bills, handling phone calls, organizing, and quick thinking under pressure. Second, in assessing the skills needed for this job, consider the following: Basic computer skills means that you will not be using it all the time, but you should know basic word-processing skills, the keyboard, and be able to type about 40 words per minute. Although the ad is vague about the processing of department bills, if you are good with numbers and have some knowledge of bookkeeping, you could probably qualify in this category. Handling phone calls requires that you answer the telephone and make calls in a businesslike manner. Organizing requires that you be able to find information when it is needed and that you set priorities for the work that should be done first. The need for quick thinking and the presence of some pressure implies that this job is in a busy office. In this situation you may be overworked at times and may have to make decisions on your own.

Listing the job responsibilities and the skills needed is a good way to discover whether you qualify for a job and whether it's worth your time to apply. If you have a skill for each point in the job description and can back it up with an example (for instance, "When I was a reporter for the campus newspaper, I always had to work under pressure"), you are probably a good candidate for this position. Not only will this assessment of responsibilities and skills help you decide whether you qualify, but it will also help you clearly identify what you need to know in order to write a strong letter of application and perform effectively if you get an interview.

Preparing a Résumé

For help in creating a résumé, use the "Business Documents Templates" on the CD.

A **résumé** is a summary of your professional life written for potential employers. It should give an idea of your career direction, present your achievements, and cite examples of your skills. An employer going through a stack of résumés may spend little more than 20 or 30 seconds on each one, so it is important that you present yourself in as efficient a way as possible.

In any campus community there are many businesses, even online Internet sources, that offer résumé-writing services. Many of the résumés they produce tend to be more style than substance—bland, cookie-cutter types that look like they came off a conveyor belt in a résumé-production facility. Writing your own résumé will add the substance, warmth, and personality it needs to be effective. Also, with your own writing skills, it is more likely that your résumé will be unique and distinctive.

The Career Center at the University of Maine offers the following suggestions for developing a résumé:

1. *Sell yourself.* Create a good first impression by highlighting your skills and abilities appropriate to the position.

2. *Use active language.* Articulate marketable skills acquired through your positions. For example: *Salesperson,* Smith Shoe Store, Portland, Maine. Assisted clients with selection of shoes, developed and promoted special marketing events, trained new employees, monitored cash. Store increased in sales by 7 percent in a six-month period.

3. *Be consistent.* Choose a pattern of spacing, an order of information presentation, or a format of highlighting and be consistent throughout.

4. *Present information in reverse chronological order within categories.* List education and work experiences starting with the most recent first.

5. *Check for grammar.* Misspellings and poorly constructed sentences communicate negative impressions about a candidate.

6. *Ensure that it is neat and visually appealing.* Choose high-quality paper in white, off-white, or another conservative color. Have the final version professionally reproduced. ("Guide to Résumé Writing")

On the Web

Action Verbs

Many Internet sites contain lists of action verbs for use in creating résumés—in line with our suggestion to use active language. Google produced 8,360 hits for "Action verbs for résumés" on March 24, 2003. Here are four sites to consult:

1. (No author), "Action Verbs," Student Employment Services, Student Affairs, University of Manitoba, Canada. Retrieved March 24, 2003, from http://www.umanitoba.ca/student/ employment/ book1/berbs.html.

2. (No author), "Action Verbs for Resumes," Career Services, University of Alabama at Birmingham.

Retrieved March 24, 2003, from http://www.careercenter.uab.edu/gethired/resumes/actionverbs.htm.

3. (No author), "Action Verbs for Resumes." Employment, Human Resources, The University of Kansas Medical Center, 2002. Retrieved March 24, 2003, from http://www2.kumc.edu/hr/employ/actverb.html.

4. (No author), "Action Verbs for Use in Resumes," Careers Handbook, Massachusetts Institute of Technology, December 17, 1998. Retrieved March 24, 2003, from http://web.mit.edu/career/www/handbook/ resumeverb.html.

Résumé Components

Identification. The top portion of the résumé should have your name, address, and phone number. If you have temporary and permanent addresses and phone numbers, give all. If you have an e-mail and/or a FAX address, put those in, too.

Career Objective. Your job objective is extremely important in your résumé. If your objective is too vague, it will be meaningless ("I am seeking a position that will use academic achievements"). On the other hand, if you are too specific, you might limit yourself too much. Often, when people are considering several different positions, they will write résumés with different job objectives. Then they can match the job objective with the position for which they are applying.

Education. Your highest degree should be listed first. Begin with the name of the college, followed by the degree, major, and date of graduation. If you are looking for a position where your major might not be relevant, list the job-related courses you have taken. List your grade point average if it's 3.0 or above.

You don't have to limit yourself to formal degrees in this section. Depending on their relationship to the job you are seeking, you can also list certificates, minors, workshops, honors programs, or study abroad.

Experience. In this section, you should list only the positions that directly relate to your career goals. Usually the most recent job information is listed first. However, if you have had experience that ties in directly with the job you are seeking, you might consider putting that at the top. Another way to handle experiences you have had that tie in directly with the job you

Another Point of View

In his book, *The Future of Success* (2001), Robert Reich, professor at Brandeis University and former Secretary of Labor under President Bill Clinton, following a paragraph about the value of a college education having more to do with who one has met there than what one has learned, writes this about the relationship of résumés and businesses:

Businesses looking to hire are placing greater reliance on referrals from people they trust, for the same reason that trustworthy brand-portals are becoming more important to buyers who are drowning in information and need guidance as to what's good. Even in a tight labor market, the sheer volume of résumés in circulation at any moment is beyond the power of employers to process. Entire galaxies in cyberspace will soon be taken up with Internet job boards deploying millions of electronic resumes, from young people entering the job market as well as others who want better jobs. Several of my students already have mastered the art of filling resumes with "scannable" keywords guaranteed to be picked up by every digital resume-management system in the civilized world. They're also "blast-faxing" their credentials to thousands of additional employers, and combing Internet databases for more addresses. One student told me proudly that she'd sent more than 5,000 "personalized" *resumes, each highlighting aspects of her education and experiences most likely to be attractive to a particular target.*

Questions

1. Are you aware of the necessity that Reich points out, the value of the connections you acquire during your college education? Reich claims, "The more prestigious the university, the more valuable such connections are likely to be" (p. 134).

2. If you do not have the connections necessary to impress companies, what kinds of things can you do that would compensate for this lack?

3. Reich writes in the paragraph following the one excerpted above, "Personal job referrals are like letters, e-mails, and phone calls from familiar names in this era of communication overload. They're convenient filters" (p. 134). Knowing that a communication overload exists, what tactics can you use in writing your resumes, or applying for jobs, that would help you stand out from the crowd? That would help you break through this communication overload?

Source: R. B. Reich, *The Future of Success*. (New York: Alfred A. Knopf, 2001.), p. 134.

are seeking is to highlight them in the cover letter. In addition to jobs you have held, experience may include student teaching, internships, management trainee positions, or significant volunteer experiences. For each position list your job title, the organization, its location, and the dates you worked there. After listing these, write a job description that includes the skills you used, your responsibilities, and any outstanding results ("increased sales by 5 percent").

If you haven't had very much professional experience, you should also include summer and part-time jobs.

References. Many students have their references on file with the placement service on their campus. If this is true in your case, give the name, address, e-mail address, and telephone number of the service. If you don't have a file with a placement service, put "References Furnished upon Request" at the bottom of your résumé.

When you have accomplishments that don't fit into the basic sections of your résumé, you can add additional categories. Here are some possibilities:

Special Skills and Interests. High-level skills such as fluency in another language, knowledge of computers, artistic ability, or a pilot's license should be listed in this category. Cite anything that could make you more desirable for the position.

Activities. Include extracurricular activities, community involvement, and membership in professional organizations if they are relevant to the job you seek. If you have held a leadership position in any of these activities, mention that too.

Honors and Awards. Include this category if you have received several awards. Typical awards and achievements might include being included on the dean's list or being awarded a scholarship, special recognition on campus, or membership in an honorary society. If you do not have enough awards to justify a separate heading, include them in your education or experience section.

While you are putting your résumé together, experiment with your headings and text to see what works and looks best. Proofread and check for

On the Web

When we entered "Sample Résumés" into Google, it produced 243,000 hits. Many of the websites produced are commercial ones and although you can find sample résumés and cover letters at many of these sites, their purpose is to sell you their services. One good commercial site was:

(No author). "Monster.com's Résumé Builder," Monster Career Center, March 24, 2003. Re-trieved February 17, 2003, from http://content. monster.com/resume/samples/resumes/. There is a link, here, to "Tips for creating a scannable resume."

All of the rest of the sites we refer you to here are educational sites that provide this information as a free service through college career service centers—and try to sell you nothing. Also, you might want to check out your own college career center for information.

1. (No author). "Sample Résumés." Career Services, Earlham College Richmond, IN 2000. Retrieved March 24, 2003, from http://www. earlham.edu/~career/resume/sample.html.

2. (No author). "Sample Resumes." Office of Career Development, Stevens Institute of Technology, February 6, 2003. Retrieved March 24, 2003, from http://attila.Stevens-tech.edu/ocs/sampler. htm.

3. (No author). "Sample Résumés." OMI College of Applied Science, Professional Practice & Career Placement Department, University of Cincinnati. Retrieved March 24, 2003, from http://www.ocasppcp.uc.edu/help/help8.htm.

4. (No author). "Sample Résumés guide." Business Career Center, University of Wisconsin-Madison School of Business, January 22, 2003. Retrieved March 24, 2003, from http://www.bus.wisc. edu/career/pubs/SampleResumes/.

spelling and grammar. If your intent is to produce a computer-scannable document, make certain your headings follow those prescribed for such documents. See the bulleted list of tips in the section that follows.

When you have completed the first draft of your résumé, take a critical look at it, and consider these points:

- Have you overused the word *I*?
- Are you absolutely sure of your grammar and spelling?
- Have you been consistent in your use of capital letters and underlining?
- Does your résumé have enough white space to avoid looking crowded?

Once you are satisfied with your résumé's basic format, ask someone with professional experience to read and critique it. Remember that this résumé is going to be advertising you. If it's effective, it should open some doors for interviews. (Review Figure 9-1.)

Electronic Résumés

Electronic résumés (Internet-ready résumés or online résumés) are designed to apply for jobs online that produce interviews. They contain the information discussed in the previous section, Résumé Components, but they differ from a traditional, non-electronic version, with respect to format. Each résumé must be properly formatted for the specific delivery system used. For example, the print verion, with its bulleted lists, italicized text, and other highlights, is formatted for printing and mailing to potential contacts or handing to interviewers. In preparing résumés it is wise to have a print version in addition to electronic versions.

Scannable résumés are those that can be scanned into a computer using document imaging technology ("Scannable . . . ," 2002). They are designed to be sent by e-mail, and employers use scanning technology to sort, store, and search them ("Make sure . . . ," 2002). Tips for maximizing scannability are the same for preparing plain-text résumés—a discussion of which follows.

- "Use white or light-colored 8½" × 11" paper, printed on one side only.
- Laser printed original is best.
- Use standard typefaces (Helvetica, Futura, Times, Palatino, or Courier).
- Use a font size of 10–14 points (avoid Times 10 point).
- Don't condense spacing between letters.
- Use boldface and/or all caps for section headings.
- Avoid italics, underlining, or shadows.
- Avoid vertical and horizontal lines, graphics, and boxes.
- Avoid two-column or newspaper/newsletter format.
- Place your name at top of each page.
- Use standard address format below your name.
- List each phone number on its own line" ("Scannable . . .").

Figure 9-1 is a sample scannable/electronic, plain-text résumé adapted from a sample provided by the Career Development Center at Indiana University.

```
Consuelo Kanaga
3333 College Avenue
Sherman, ME 04777
(207) 555-1742
ckanaga@eagle.umaine.edu

OBJECTIVE
A challenging office administrator position leading to increased
responsibility, advancement, and growth.

EDUCATION
 • University of Maine at Machias, May 2004
   Major: Bachelor of Arts in Speech Communication
   Minor: Computer Science
   GPA 3.8, Honors Division

RELEVANT COURSEWORK
 • Administration Office Management; Business Communication; Business,
   Professional, and Technical Writing; Public Speaking; Human Behavior
   in Organizations; and Personnel Management
 • Installed and configured web server software; wrote practical Java
   and CGI applications.

TECHNICAL CERTIFICATIONS
 • COMPTIA A+ Certified Computer Service Technician
 • Microsoft Certified Professional (MCP)

WORK EXPERIENCE
 • Supervisor, Information Management Center (IMC), University of
   Maine/Machias, September 2001-May 2003.
 • Trained and supervised word processing operators using Corel's
   WordPerfect Office 2000.
 • Delegated daily assignments via e-mail and online postings. This
   position was a promotion from word processor the previous year.
 • Webmaster; maintained Center's website.
 • Redesigned website and implemented new Information Management
   Center web-tracking based on an all-Center, needs-analysis profile.
 • Edited text for brevity and target audience; managed information.
 • Created presentation to inform campus personnel about IMC using
   Adobe PageMaker and Adobe Persuasion.
Chairperson, Business Opportunities Conference, January 2003.
 • Organized and administered a student-run job fair consisting of
   41 firms and attended by 750 students.
 • Managed a 12-member preparation committee and 30 volunteers.
 • Communicated with company recruiters and human-resource departments.
 • Created Information Hot Line to keep all parties informed.
 • Served as liaison between Department of Business Administration,
   Career Center, and sponsoring organizations on recruiting.
 • Created a website for the Division using HTML editors at Microsoft
   FrontPage. Website was selected by Point Survey as one of top 5
   percent of all web pages.
```

Figure 9-1

Computer Scannable, Plain-Text, Sample Résumé

Figure 9-1

Computer Scannable, Plain-Text, Sample Résumé

```
• Developed an online slide presentation explaining the purpose and
    services of the Division using PowerPoint 4.0.
• Assistant to the Director, Job Start, Resource Development Department,
    WHCA, Millbridge, ME, January 2001-May 2001.
• Implemented the Job Start program.
• Offered technical assistance to clients and responded to inquiries.
• Compiled online handbook for business support groups using Word 2000.
• Organized filing system and entered confidential information using
    PFS-File for data entry.
• Computer Technical Consultant, self-employed, June 2000-present.
• On-site installation and configuration of software and hardware,
    troubleshooting, and computer skills tutoring for more than 50 clients.
• Installed ethernet cards and remedied network connection problems.
• Demonstrated problem solving and verbal communication skills.

COMPUTER PROFICIENCY
 • Languages: Visual Basic, SQL, Perl, JavaScript, HTML
 • Databases: Oracle, Microsoft Access
 • OS: UNIX, Windows 3.x/95/98/01, Windows NT
 • Graphics: Adobe Photoshop, Adobe Illustrator, Adobe PageMaker,
    Microsoft FrontPage, Microsoft PowerPoint
 • General: Microsoft Office, Corel WordPerfect, Lotus Notes

KEYWORDS
business communication, chairperson, computer science, consultant,
consulting, honors division, human behavior, information management,
leadership, management aid, personnel management, project management,
supervisor, technical writing, technical support, UNIX, web designer,
web developer, webmaster, Windows NT

ACTIVITIES
 • Chair, Dormitory Council
 • President, Honors Program
 • Secretary, Kappa Eta Academic Society
 • Student Ambassador, University of Maine
 • Supervisor, Special Olympics
 • Sales representative, Yearbook Staff
 • Member, Executive Committee, Association for Industrial Management
    and Economics (AIME)

ACADEMIC HONORS
 • Honors Division Scholarship
 • UM Faculty Scholarship
 • Alpha Lambda Delta Scholarship

REFERENCES
 • Available upon request.
```

There are three delivery systems and three file formats. Submitting or posting your résumé, or file, for computer audiences requires e-mail, an electronic form, or a Web page. A **file** is a complete, named collection of information. A **file format** exists so that the information can be stored and retrieved electronically. The file formats are coded in ASCII (pronounced ask-ee), which stands for the American Standard Code for Information Interchange. The formats are plain text, rich text, and hypertext.

At the end of the URL (uniform resource locator—or, computer address) that identifies the file of information, and set off by a period, is an extension that identifies the format: (1) plain text is .txt; (2) rich text is .rtf; and (3) hypertext is .htm or .html. These endings identify the kinds of computers that can handle and transfer these files as well as what computer programs may be used to create and post the resume.

Plain text is the most popular ASCII file format. As e-mail has become more popular as a way of sending and receiving information so, too, have plain text résumés. They are easy to use and alter. Their major disadvantage is that they are plain with no formatting.

Rich-text-file format résumés provide for the fancy formatting options plain text do not, and they are compatible across word processors. Problems are that destination computers may not recognize them, and there may be problems when trying to send them via e-mail. Saving résumés in rich-text-format requires consulting word processor user manuals.

HTML provides the means for publishing résumé on the World Wide Web (WWW). It allows for the integration of printed résumé development with Web-page design strategies. They can include links to other websites, and they are most effective when used as part of a comprehensive self-marketing program. Two problems are that they may be difficult to print out, and working with HTML documents requires a Web browser, Internet access, and an HTML converter application. For the non–Internet-savvy, it may be better to stay with printed, scannable, and plain-text documents.

Cover Letters

There are two general types of cover letters—the letter of inquiry and the letter of application. They are called **cover letters** because in both cases they provide a "cover" to your résumé. A **letter of inquiry** accompanies your résumé and is designed to determine if an employer has an opening for which you may qualify. It should be short and to the point—no longer than one page. In the first paragraph, tell why you are writing by inquiring about positions in your field. Use the first sentence to get the employer's or reader's attention so that he or she will read the entire letter. In the second paragraph, tell why you want to work for the organization, but in doing so, try to stimulate interest in yourself as a possible employee by giving an example of your accomplishments and qualifications. In the third paragraph, tell why the company should hire you and why you would be effective. You should indicate the significant experience and training you have in your field which makes you a desirable employee and the contributions you would make to the organization. In the fourth and final paragraph, refer to your enclosed résumé and state your availability for interviews,

For help in writing cover letters, use the "Business Documents Templates" on the CD.

giving specific dates if possible. Ask for an appointment, state that you look forward to hearing from the employer, and ask for some type of action.

A **letter of application** should accompany your résumé and other requested materials, such as transcripts and letters or recommendation, when you know an employer has an opening in which you are interested. The application letter introduces you to the employer, tells why you are writing, emphasizes the contributions you can make to the job, and asks for a job interview. Its purpose is to "sell" you to the interviewer and interest him or her in interviewing you.

There are strong similarities between letters of inquiry and letters of application. Like the letter of inquiry, the letter of application should be short and to the point, limited to one page and not more than four brief paragraphs. The first tells the reader why you are writing by identifying the position for which you are applying and briefly mentioning your source of information about the opening. It tries to get the reader's attention so that he or she will read the entire letter. The second paragraph tells why you are interested in working for this particular organization and briefly points out your achievements, training, and related experience in the field that would make you effective on this job. Here, you stimulate the interest of the reader in you as a possible employee. The third paragraph tells why he or she should hire you and tries to create a desire to know more about you. An example of your accomplishments and qualifications helps create this desire. Finally, the fourth paragraph refers to your enclosed résumé, asserts the availability of your references, or indicates that your credentials including references are enclosed or are being sent by your college's career services center by a separate mailing. Also, in the fourth paragraph you restate your interest and availability, request an interview, and ask for some type of action.

Cover letters, whether letters of inquiry or letters of application, should accompany each résumé. They should be neat and free from error, easy to read, and personalized. Avoid long sentences and paragraphs that will cause readers to lose interest. These letters should sum up what you have to offer and serve as an introduction to your résumé. The following are guidelines that will help when you are writing these letters:

Address your letter to a specific person when possible. If this is not possible, write, "To whom it may concern," "Dear Search Committee," or something similar that is general but appropriate to the situation.

- Show interest in the firm by making a reference to something you know about it.
- Describe your skills and refer to your résumé for further details.
- Suggest that you will telephone the firm for an interview.
- Let your letter reflect your individuality, but avoid appearing aggressive, familiar, cute, or humorous. ("Composing a letter . . . ")

View "The Employment Interview," clip #3 for two examples of employment interviews

The Interview

The big day comes when an employer calls to schedule an interview with you. Of all the application letters and résumés the company has received, yours has stood out enough for the employer to want to see you. However, it's likely that he or she will interview several other people too. During your interview you are going to have to sell yourself as the best candidate for the position.

Again, you have some work to do.

Preparing for the Interview

In preparing for an employment interview, find out about the company and what it does. Research shows that applicants who do their homework about potential employers ask better questions and feel more confident during interviews (Babbitt & Jablin, 1985, p. 529).

How do you go about this research? Lisa Vallino looked for a job with an advertising agency. She began her search on the Internet. She entered "Advertising Agencies" into the Google search engine and received a list of 289,000 Web pages. She began examining some of these to gain an overview, obtain first impressions, and learn general information. Some of the sites offered specific information such as the work the agency had done (samples were provided), what the agency specialized in, some of its major accounts, and the size of the agency. Sometimes the size of an agency could be determined by the items listed in the agency's index, sometimes by the number of contacts or representatives within the agency and the specialties each of the contacts or representatives had. Some sites were directories to a variety of different agencies. At one, the directory included the following items: advertising, direct marketing, editorial services, graphic design, integrated marketing communications, marketing consulting, marketing research, photography, printing, professional organizations, promotional products, publications, public relations, web development, and writing. Clicking any of these topics led Lisa to a specific company, a contact person, an e-mail address, a postal address, and a Web address (URL). This is why it is necessary to narrow your focus when preparing for the interview. Although Lisa was interested in working for an advertising agency, her specific areas of expertise included public relations, web development, and writing.

When she clicked on a relevant agency, the name of a contact person was mentioned. By clicking her mouse on the e-mail address, she could have direct contact with that person. Lisa then asked for further information such as brochures and sample work. Also, Lisa established a file for all her contacts. Into the file she put a printout of her first e-mail contact; thus, she could keep a record of all her contacts with an agency, their responses, and their literature.

Many companies are *public*—meaning that their stock can be bought by the public. Every public company is required to issue an annual shareholders' report, which can provide valuable information, particularly about profits and losses. If the company is a local one, it has probably been the subject of articles in the local newspaper. The Chamber of Commerce or the Better Business Bureau can also give you information about local businesses. If the company is national, it may have been written about in magazines such as *Business Week* or *Fortune* and in the *Wall Street Journal*. Most businesses are also covered by trade publications—magazines that concentrate on a particular line of business. In advertising, for example, one trade publication is called *Advertising Age,* and is likely to be available in your college library. Such magazines concentrate on trends, and they are an excellent way of finding out what important things are happening in a particular line of business. Professional groups—doctors, lawyers, and teachers—also have specialized magazines that discuss important occupational issues. Most companies have Web pages on the Internet. To find your company, use one of the search engines, such as WebCrawler, and type in the company's name, or put the company name in the search window at http://business.lycos.com/companyresearch/crtop.asp.

Interview Questions

Most employment interviews follow a predictable line of questioning. Discussed below are some of the kinds of questions you are likely to be asked in a job interview. Before you go to the interview, you should think about how you would answer them.

Job Expectations. The interviewer will want to find out if what you are looking for in a job is compatible with the job the company has to offer. You will be asked what you want in a job, what kind of job you are looking for, and whether you would be content in this particular job. The best way to prepare for such questions is to study the job description carefully and see whether your qualifications and expectations match the job description. Sometimes people go into a job interview thinking they can redefine the job to meet their own needs. This is seldom a successful strategy. Employment ads are written with a specific job in mind, and if your education and experience don't qualify you, you won't even be considered.

Academic Background. The interviewer will want to know whether you have had enough education to do the job. To find this out, he or she will ask you questions about the schools you attended, the degrees you have, and your grades. This is a good time to mention extracurricular activities that might be pertinent to the job. If you are a social work major, for example, and you spent time teaching jail inmates to read and write, this is part of your education too.

Knowledge of the Organization. All interviewers expect you to know something about the organization they represent. They assume that if you are interested enough in the job, you will have taken the trouble to find out something about the employer. Sometimes you will be asked a direct question: "Why do you want to work for this company?" An answer might be, "I know several people who work here, and they like the company very much," or "I am impressed by your management training program."

Even if you are asked no direct questions, you should be prepared to ask some questions yourself about the company or organization. For example, "Why is this position open?" "Is it a new position?" "How important is this position to the organization?" "To what extent does the company promote from within versus hiring from the outside?" "What plans for expansion (or cutbacks) are in the immediate future?" "On average, how long do most employees stay with this company?" "If you had to briefly describe this organization, what would you say?"

Work Experience. The interviewer will want to know about other jobs you have had and whether anything in your work experience might relate to the job you are applying for. Even though your work experience might not be directly related to the job at hand, don't assume it is necessarily irrelevant. Let's say you are applying for a job as manager of a local store and your only job experience has been taking junior high students on canoe trips every summer. Although this summer job might not be directly relevant, it would certainly show that you are a responsible person—a characteristic an employer will be looking for in a manager. You should also consider whether any volunteer experience might be relevant to the job. Someone who has served as chairperson for the annual heart fund drive, for example, has a good deal of administrative and management experience that might be useful in many jobs.

Career Goals. Most interviewers will be interested in knowing your short- and long-term goals in relation to the job. *Short-term goals* concern what you want to do in the next year or so. *Long-term goals* are directed to a life-time plan. Typical questions about long-term goals might be "Where do you see yourself 10 years from now?" and "What kind of career do you want with our company?" Interviewers ask these kinds of questions to discover whether you are thinking about your future, to gauge your ambition, and to see whether you will fit into the company's long-term goals. If you are interviewing for a management trainee position in a bank, for example, the interviewer will try to find out whether you can foresee a long-term career with the bank and whether the bank is justified in putting you in its training program.

Strengths and Weaknesses. Most interviewers will want to find out whether hiring you will enhance their organizations. To this end you might be asked directly "What do you see as your greatest strength?" or "What is your greatest weakness?" Think about both these points in relation to the job being offered before you go to an interview. Even if you are not asked directly about your strengths, you should be prepared to sell yourself on your good points during the interview. If on your last job you reorganized a department and improved its efficiency by 50 percent, now is the time to mention it. Be honest if you are asked about your weaknesses. If you are doing something about them, mention what it is. For example, "I am not always as well organized as I could be, but I am working on setting priorities and that seems to help" lets the interviewer know you are working on the problem.

Since the above kinds of questions will probably make up the bulk of the interview, you should think about how you will answer them. The most important thing to remember is that every interview is different: Even if the questions are the same, the answers will vary. Your success will depend on how well you can answer in relation to the job being offered.

Being Interviewed

Once you have researched the company, prepared your résumé, and thought about the questions you are likely to be asked, you are ready for your interview.

On the Web

Behavioral Interviewing

Behavioral interviewing is a structured interviewing strategy built on the premise that past behavior is the best predictor of future performance in similar circumstances (Fox, 2000). Although behavioral interviewing is a relatively new mode of job interviewing, although it is generally accepted as the most effective interviewing technique available ("Course Description," 2000)—it "is said to be 55 percent predictive of future on-the-job behavior, while traditional interviewing is only 10 percent predictive" (Hansen)—and although employers such as AT&T and Accenture (the former Andersen Consulting) have been using behavioral interviewing for about 15 years now (Hansen), only "30 percent of all organizations are using behavioral interviewing to some degree" ("Behavioral Interviewing"). Just the same, "understanding how to excel in this interview environment is becoming a crucial job-hunting skill" (Hansen).

But all the information you need on behavioral interviewing is available on the Internet—Google came up with 8,230 hits for "Behavioral Interviewing" (March 24, 2003)—and the following are some of the best websites for obtaining it:

1. (No author). "Behavioral Interviewing." Career Services, The University of Montana-Missoula. Retrieved March 24, 2003, from http://www.umt.edu/career/behavior.htm This is a complete explanation of behavioral interviewing with a full example of a PAR (problem, action, result) story, and excellent preparation suggestions.

2. (No author). "Behavioral Interviewing." Job Search Preparation, MU Career Center, University of Missouri, 2000. Retrieved March 24, 2003, from http://www.missouri.edu/~cppcwww/behavioralinterviewing.shtml. This site explains what it is, discusses important points about it, and provides all-in-all, an excellent one-page overview.

3. (No author). "Behavioral Interviewing," September 26, 1998. Retrieved March 24, 2003, from http://www.uwstout.edu/place/ behavior.html. This site offers specific behavioral-type questions on your focus and dedication, technical and professional knowledge, teamwork, analysis, adaptability, work standards, job motivation, initiative, ability to learn, planning and organizing, communication, customer service orientation, and sensitivity. There is an excellent "Table of Performance Skills" included and a discussion of the "Evaluation System" often used.

4. K. Hansen, "Behavioral Interviewing Strategies." Quintessential Careers. Retrieved March 24, 2003, from http://www.quintcareers.com/behavioral_interviewing.html. Katharine Hansen is a former speechwriter and college instructor and has written three books for job seekers. Here, she provides an excellent introduction, how job candidates need to respond, the three-step S-A-R or P-A-R response process, and specific suggestions for preparing for behavioral-based interviews. This is the most succinct, complete explanation uncovered.

Dress for it. How you dress reveals your professionalism, how seriously you consider the interview, how aware you are of the need to look good, and what you want your first impression to be. The way you dress will certainly have an effect on the first impression you make. Women: Wear a solid color, conservative suit with a coordinated blouse and moderate shoes. Limit the amount of jewelry you wear; have a neat, professional hairstyle; wear tan or light hosiery; put on sparse makeup and perfume; make sure your nails are manicured; and carry a portfolio or briefcase. Men: Wear a solid color, conservative suit with a white, long-sleeved shirt; a conservative tie; dark socks; and professional shoes. Wear very limited jewelry, have a neat, professional hairstyle, go easy on the aftershave, have neatly trimmed nails, and carry a portfolio or briefcase.

Research suggests that the first few minutes of an interview are the most important, for it is then that many interviewers establish their biases and make their decisions. So it's important that you make a good impression right from the start. Much of the good impression you convey is nonverbal: being on time, being dressed appropriately, and giving a firm handshake. It will also help if you can appear confident—even though you might not be feeling that way. When William N. Yeomans asked managers from several companies what they looked for in a candidate for a job, they mentioned personal characteristics such as appearance, enthusiasm, tact, and honesty. Although they mentioned job-related characteristics such as work experience, leadership, and communication skills, no one listed "a demonstrated ability to do the job." This would indicate that a personality that fits the job is even more important than specific job skills.

You should be aware when you interview that there are some factors in the mix of what employers are looking for over which you have no control and of which you may not be informed. One is likely to be diversity, which describes employers' desire to maintain a workforce that more accurately represents the complexity of today's society. It may describe a firm's efforts to recruit more women and minorities; it could describe efforts to address differences in management style between men and women; also, it could describe how different work environments affect worker productivity. Many companies consider workplace diversity to be a smart business practice, especially as industries grow more dependent on a global marketplace (Liu, 2002).

The Follow-Up Letter

After every interview, you should write a follow-up letter. This shows your interest in the organization and helps keep your name in the employer's mind.

Follow-up letters are generally short and to the point. In the standard five-step format, you (1) Thank the employer for the interview, (2) State your interest in one or two specific aspects of the position or the company discussed in the interview, (3) Supply any additional information that was requested during the interview, (4) Express your continuing interest in the position, and (5) Thank the interviewer for the interview.

■ PRESENTATIONS

At one time, presentations were the exclusive domain of engineers, product specialists, and business professionals. Now, they are the exclusive domain of nobody. Urvashi Vaid gave a presentation to the student governance board trying to obtain more student support for international groups on

View clip #5, "Presentation Skills," for examples of business presentations.

campus. Her slides showed statistical tables regarding the growth of the international-student population, fund dispersement for other campus groups, and the uses international students intended for the funding.

In another example of a student presentation, Hayden Katen gave one to his fraternity that supported a new volunteer program that would involve all fraternity members. His slide presentation included the name of the program and its various services, the needs for increased participation, and a breakdown of services the fraternity members could provide. In a third example, Yvonne Vera was asked by the local Rotary Club to give a presentation on the role that college students can play in civic-service enterprises. Yvonne, through extensive research and interviewing, found the names of other civic organizations in which students participated, offered the hours of current participation, demonstrated how increased participation could be gained, and named specific areas of current Rotary work where students could have an impact.

A wide variety of people are called upon to make presentations, explain concepts, communicate complex data, make recommendations, or persuade and motivate others. A **presentation** is created to communicate ideas in a compelling and graphic manner. One writer on presentations said, "I find it difficult to provide a clear, detailed description of all the facets of an excellent . . . presentation—like most of us, I know it when I see it" (Price, 1998). Presentations may be informative or persuasive. In an explanation of the difference between presentations and speeches, another writer noted that presentations are often easier, devoid of memorization and note cards, and convey more information (Wang, 1998). One of the major differences between speeches and presentations is the assumed and expected emphasis on visual support. It should be noted, too, that there are many similarities between speeches and presentations.

Why do presentations deserve special attention? There are several reasons. First, they require a different emphasis and a different approach. Second, with the ready availability of and access to high-quality computer-generated graphics, presentations are within the reach of everyone, not just people who have access to professionals who can prepare the visual support. Third, they have become popular. Entering "Technical presentations" into any single search engine, such as Google, yielded more than 40,400 Web pages (March 24, 2003); entering "Presentations" yielded 6,580,000 pages (March 24, 2003). Some of the Web pages, too, offer online slide presentations on preparing presentations, and in almost any bookstore, there is usually a current book on the subject. Fourth, we wanted to put all relevant information about presentations—even though some will duplicate what is discussed later in this book—in the same location.

The following comments are *not* designed to be different from other information to be presented later in this textbook; they simply emphasize the important elements of every presentation. The most important guiding principle that governs all aspects of presentations is the requirement for careful planning—not unlike the advice offered throughout the public-speaking chapters. There are three phases of successful presentations: (1) Thorough preparation, (2) Natural delivery, and (3) Effective visuals. The specific tasks required to create a presentation should be chosen with the goal of communicating ideas in a compelling and graphic manner.

The biggest difference between a presentation and a speech is the degree of visual support used and expected in presentations.

Thorough Preparation

Effective presentations result from thorough preparation. Before they do anything else, presenters must know the constraints under which they are operating. Audience size and arrangement, room size, and the equipment provided are important considerations. One of the most important constraints, however, is the time allowance. Because presenters often have so much material they could present, they must spend time deciding what they want to achieve and can achieve in the time frame given. It is this kind of thinking that helps them determine what they should present.

Presenters must carefully appraise their audiences. Audience analysis is challenging when delivering presentations, especially when communicating to diverse audiences with varying knowledge levels and technical expertise. It is impossible for us—the writers of this textbook—to know the relationship between the presenters' information and the listeners' background, knowledge, and technical expertise, but it is important that this relationship be determined and the appropriate adjustments be made. If audience knowledge or technical expertise is slim, it might require more definitions, a gradual development of the ideas, simplified charts and graphs, and, perhaps, the elimination of some of the more technical or sophisticated information.

Presenters must establish a clear central idea, sometimes referred to as the *thesis, goal, objective,* or *purpose.* Every element of the presentation should support the central idea, and any element that detracts in any way must be eliminated or minimized. To accomplish this, presenters need to determine (1) what is to be done, (2) how it will be done, and (3) what will be the significance. When these steps are completed, presenters should know how they want their listeners to respond.

Natural Delivery

Effective presentations result from natural delivery. **Natural delivery** is the collection of speech and actions that best represents your true self—that is free from artificiality, affectation, and constraint. Natural delivery requires an extemporaneous style: carefully preparing the thoughts, but not deciding on the words in advance. It requires that presenters refrain from reading their presentations. If presenters' thoughts are so cloudy, foggy, or murky that they need to be written and read, the presenters are not ready to make a presentation. How do you prepare for an extemporaneous presentation? (Price, pp. 1–3).

- Develop a key-idea outline (key ideas only)—but not a complete-sentence outline. (Do not write out the speech or commit any substantial portion of it to memory.)

- Use the key-idea outline as the basis for practice. Use it as the basis for preparing your visual support. Fit your words to the ideas. Also, fit your visual support to the ideas.

- Present your talk, working from your outline, in front of friends, family, or anyone else you can get to listen. You are ready to give your presentation when you can go through all your material without faltering. (This does not require memorization; it requires extreme familiarity with your key ideas.)

Presentations require a high degree of professionalism. It is expected. Presenters must refrain from being sarcastic, cute, flippant, or entertaining. If they concentrate on the general purpose, they are more likely to attain it. Often, this advice isn't heeded. Because presentation software can add so much to a presentation, such as sounds, images, animation, dissolves, multimedia, and more, creating presentations becomes fun. Humorous asides sometimes cannot be resisted, nor can slides that lend "a light touch" to the presentation. Our advice: Resist the temptation. Keep focused on the central idea. As one writer advises, "Sell steak, not sizzle" (Price, p. 6).

One author lists the top 10 negative nonverbal cues (before, during, and after a presentation): A weak handshake is number one; sloppy clothes are number two. These are followed by too much jewelry, inappropriate hairstyle, slouching, staring at your notes, bad breath, dirty fingernails, repeated hand mannerisms, and general bad manners. The final category includes having poor eye contact, arriving late, using crude language, rubbing an ear, or taking more time for the presentation than allotted (Templeton & Fitzgerald, 1999, pp. 146–48).

A variety of outline patterns are recommended by authors writing about presentations. One suggestion is to tell a story in the form of a presentation by creating a clear beginning, middle, and end (Ringle, 1998, pp. 120–21). Another suggestion involves using an introduction, giving the results of the investigation, discussing the results and suggesting future work, and offering conclusions (Price, p. 4). Still another suggestion is to use the inverted pyramid approach: Present your conclusions first, then the general supporting background information, and finally the detailed support ("Technical". . . , 1999). If you have a great deal of theory or a substantial amount of data to present, this is the approach we support. If your presentation is a report on scientific research, we suggest you follow the normal organizational pattern of published research (Tham, 1997). Whatever pattern presenters select, an essential requirement is that they don't switch patterns midway through the presentation. Consistency throughout the presentation is crucial.

Effective Visuals

Effective presentations result from effective visuals. Perhaps *the* biggest difference between a presentation and a speech, as noted earlier, is the degree of visual support used and expected in presentations. The overall advice regarding visual support is that it must reinforce and expand the message, focus listener attention on key ideas, and clarify meaning. Emphasizing again what we said moments ago, presenters must not allow the availability and ease of use of visual support to seduce them into using too much, using it to entertain, or using it in any way that detracts from the central idea of the presentation.

For guidance in creating Powerpoint presentations, see "Powerpoint Tutorial" on the CD.

One author writing about presentation graphics suggests using the acronym **PETAL** to conceptualize every presentation (Birdsell, 1998, pp. 8–11). Develop *pertinent* materials, choose an *engaging format,* present your materials in a *timely* manner, satisfy yourself that they are *appropriate* to the audience, and ensure that everything is *legible.* Everything in the presentation should be pertinent to the topic; no element should be added just for effect. An engaging format results from the judicious use of color, a consistent, uncluttered design format, and relatively limited text. The word *timely* refers to the placement of slides. They should be placed where they are needed in the presentation, not before and not after their oral complement has been delivered. They must be appropriate to the audience, topic, and situation. And they must be legible: large enough and clear enough to be seen by everyone.

Presenters' first slides, just like first impressions of themselves, will generate quick judgments:

- Is he or she professional?
- Does he or she care about this presentation?
- Does he or she care about me (the listener)?

Good visuals must be visible, clear, and simple (Price, p. 6). Make certain the visuals are large enough. Our best suggestion is to prepare visuals and try them out. Presenters need to sit in the back of a room and see if they can be seen. Also, regarding visuals, strive for variety. A series of step-by-step slide buildups—sometimes called *progressive disclosure,* or the *reveal technique*—can put listeners to sleep just as easily as a series of similar slides with just one or two words on them.

Regarding presenting with the visuals, there are a number of suggestions as well (Nordgren, 1996). Practice with the equipment—whether it is a computer, projection system, screen, lighting, installed software, or microphone. Have backups if you are unsure of the situation. Dominate the presentation. (To dominate the presentation means presenters need to be introduced, or they need to introduce themselves, without a visual.) The room should not be totally darkened; this allows you to share the platform with the visuals and still maintain eye contact with listeners. If presenters stand within two feet of the visuals, they maintain control and do not need to walk too far if necessary to point. If, with reference to the visuals, they stand "opposite handedness," they will not have to turn away from the audience to point to their visuals. (This means right-handed people will stand to the left of the display screen when looking at the audience.) They need to step forward to get the attention turned on themselves, and turn off the projector when not using a slide or transparency.

Presenters, too, need to use transition statements between visuals. One writer suggests following the words represented by the acronym **RDAT:** *Read* the visual, *describe* its meaning or significance, *amplify* it with an explanation or illustration, and, finally, make a *transition* to the next slide (Dershem, 1998, p. 20). Presenters should disclose visuals only after the transition statement. Although the visuals control the message, with the suggestions in the previous paragraph about dominance, lighting, and standing position, speakers still maintain overall control. Presenters should not digress; they should read the entire visual immediately when it is disclosed, use gradual disclosure of information sparingly, and only spend one to three minutes per visual—which also will govern how much information is on a single slide or overhead transparency.

Remember that just because presenters *can* prepare a very elaborate slide presentation doesn't mean they *should*. Simplicity is a virtue, and often simplicity goes hand in hand with professionalism and elegance as well. Fancy fades, wipes, and dissolves can detract from the essential message. A variety of fancy colors can do the same. Think about it: Formal attire is often just black and white and that "little black dress" is considered classy. Simplicity can refer to the use of technical equipment as well. Equipment should never be overtly revealed; that is, it should be so smooth and natural that the audience hardly notices its use. Strive to avoid having to adjust slides, focus them, or move them up and down. If you have to use a slide twice, don't go back; create a second slide.

Assess Yourself

Job Involvement Scale*

Please place an "X" in the blank which most closely matches your response to the question.

1. How often do you do some extra work for your job which isn't required of you? Would you say you do this:

   Often: _____ ; Sometimes: _____ ; Rarely: _____ ; Never: _____ .

2. On most days of your job, how often does time seem to drag for you?

   Often: _____ ; Sometimes: _____ ; Rarely: _____ ; Never: _____ .

3. Some people are completely involved in their job—they are absorbed by it night and day. For other people, their job is simply one of several interests. How involved do you feel in your job?

   Very little: _____ ; Slightly: _____ ; Moderately: _____ ; Strongly involved: _____ .

4. How much effort do you put into your job beyond what is required?

   A lot: _____ ; Some: _____ ; Only a little: _____ ; None: _____ .

5. How often do you think about your job when you're doing something else?

   Often: _____ ; Sometimes: _____ ; Rarely: _____ ; Never: _____ .

6. My main satisfaction in life comes from my work.

   Strongly disagree: _____ ; Disagree: _____ ; Agree: _____ ; Strongly agree: _____ .

7. How much do you agree or disagree that the most important things that happen to you involve your job?

   Strongly disagree: _____ ; Disagree: _____ ; Neither agree nor disagree: _____ ; Agree: _____ ; Strongly agree: _____ .

Go to the *Communicating Effectively* CD-ROM to see your results and learn how to evaluate your attitudes and feelings.

Source: Lorence, J., & J. Mortimer, "Job involvement through the life course." *American Sociological Review,* **50,** 1985, pp. 618–738. This scale was published in: J. P. Robinson, P. R. Shaver, & L. S. Wrightsman, *Measures of Personality and Social Psychological Attitudes* (San Diego: Academic Press, 1991), pp. 346–47.

Chapter Review

An interview is a series of questions and answers, usually between two people, which has the purpose of getting and understanding information about a particular subject.

Interviews can be used for a wide variety of purposes, including speeches, group projects, and research papers. Careful preparation is essential. The person conducting the interview should gather background information—both about the person being interviewed and about the topic. Questions should be prepared beforehand, and the interviewer should strike a balance between informational and thought-provoking questions.

Before the interview, the interviewer should decide whether to use tape or take notes. Tape offers the advantage of greater accuracy, and it frees the interviewer from note taking. The disadvantages of tape are that it is time-consuming to listen to after the interview has been completed and that some interviewees will react differently if they are being taped.

Information interviews also can serve as precursors to job interviews. They are designed to get job information, make contacts, and offer practice. They require special preparation. Interviewers must determine whom to contact, how to find these people, what questions to ask, how to arrange for the interview, how to conduct it, and how to follow it up.

Gaining employment usually involves a several-step process. You begin by evaluating the job description; then you write an application letter and a résumé that are tailored to the position. Before you go to an employment interview, it's important that you research the organization that is offering the job.

During the employment interview be prepared to talk about all of the following: your job expectations, your academic and work backgrounds, your knowledge of the organization, your career goals, and your strengths and weaknesses as a potential employee. After the interview, write a follow-up letter or call the interviewer, indicating that you are still interested in working for the organization. You should also thank the interviewer again for the interview.

Presentations involve a variety of skills. They are popular because they serve an important purpose—providing information and/or motivating others—and because the means for providing the visual support they require are readily available. Presenters must thoroughly prepare their presentations. This means checking out the facilities, doing a complete audience analysis, and establishing a clear central idea, sometimes referred to as a thesis, goal, objective, or purpose. Presenters must demonstrate natural delivery. Develop a key-idea outline (key ideas only)—but not a complete-sentence outline. Use the key-idea outline as the basis for practicing and for preparing visual support. Present your speech, working from your outline, to anyone you can get to listen. Finally, use effective visuals. Find visual support that reinforces and expands the message, focuses listener attention on key ideas, and clarifies meaning. Good visuals must be visible, clear, and simple. Also, be both technically efficient and knowledgeable so that professionalism is revealed throughout the presentation.

Questions to Review

1. What is an information interview, and when do you use it?

2. What is the difference between policy information and factual information?

3. What kind of information should you know before you go to an interview?

4. What are the differences among open-format, closed-format, and semiopen format interviews?

5. What are the differences among primary, follow-up, open-ended, closed, neutral, and leading interview questions?

6. What are the factors that will help you decide whether to tape or take notes during the interview?

7. How do interviewers keep control in interviews?

8. What preliminary planning must take place before you conduct information interviews that are precursors to job interviews?

9. Why use information interviews as precursors to job interviews?

10. Where do you find people who are appropriate interviewees for information interviews that are precursors to job interviews?

11. What are suggestions for developing résumés?

12. What is the difference between letters of inquiry and letters of application?

13. What are the guidelines for preparing letters of inquiry and letters of application?

14. How are presentations different from speeches?

15. What are the phases of successful presentations?

16. What is the meaning of thorough preparation, and what does it involve with respect to presentations?

17. What are the guidelines for acquiring a natural-style delivery for presentations?

18. What overall advice should guide the choice of visual support for presentations?

Go to the self-quizzes on the Communicating Effectively CD-ROM (side 2, track 10) and the Online Learning Center at mhhe.com/hybels7 to test your knowledge of the chapter concepts.

References

Babbitt, L. V., & F. M. Jablin, (1985, Summer). "Characteristics of applicants' questions and employment screening interview outcomes." *Human Communication Research* 11, 507–35.

(No author) "Behavioral interviewing." Student Life & Services, SUNY Brockport. Retrieved March 24, 2003, from http://www.brockport.edu/career/behave.htm.

Birdsell, D. S. (1998). *The McGraw-Hill guide to presentation graphics*. Boston: McGraw-Hill.

(No author). "Composing a letter of application." School-to-Career Partnership, Colorado. Retrieved March 24, 2003, from http://www.205.168.238.42/letterapp.

(No author). (2000, January 26). "Course description: Behavioral interviewing." Performex. Retrieved March 24, 2003, from www.employeetrainer.com/management/behavior.htm.

Dershern, H. L. (1998, June 24). "How to give technical presentations." Retrieved March 24, 2003, from http://www.cs.hope.edu/~dershern/reu/howtopresent/.

Fox, P. G. (2000). "Behavioral interviewing." Fox Performance Training, Connecticut. Retrieved March 24, 2003, from www.foxperformance.com/employment2.html.

(No author). "Guide to resume writing." Career Center, University of Maine. Retrieved March 24, 2003, from http://cardinal.umeais.maine.edu/~career/res.html.

Hansen, K. "Behavioral interviewing strategies." Quintessential Careers. Retrieved March 24,

2003, from http://www.quintcareers.com/behavioral_ interviewing.html.

(No author). "Job search tools & basics: Scannable resumes." Center for Career Services, Columbia University. Retrieved March 24, 2003, from http://www.columbia.edu/cu/ccs/99website/99student/bassics/scanresume. html.

Liu, W. (2002). "Start thinking about diversity." WetFeet.com. Retrieved March 24, 2003, from http://www.wetfeet.com/asp/article2.asp?aid=247&atype=Diversity.

(No author). (2002, April 17). "Make sure your resume is e-ready." *The Blade*, Toledo, Ohio, EC-6.

Misler, E. G. (1975). "Studies in dialogue and discourse: II. Types of discourse initiated by and sustained through questioning." *Journal of Psycholinguistic Research*. 4: 99–121.

Morreale, S. (2001, May). "Communication important to employers." *Spectra*, 8.

Nordgren, L. (1996, September 23). "Designing presentation visuals." Media Services, Robert A. L. Mortvedt Library, Pacific Lutheran University. Retrieved March 24, 2003, from http://www.plu.edu/~libr/media/designing_visuals.html.

Price, R. M. (1998, April 29). "Technical presentations: Hints & Suggestions." University of Mississippi. Retrieved March 24, 2003, from http://home.olemiss. edu/~emprice/lectures/badpres.html

Ringle, W. J. (1998). *TechEdge: Using computers to present and persuade*. (Essence of Public Speaking Series) Boston: Allyn and Bacon.

(No author). (2000, December 8). "Three out of four say better communication equals greater em-ployee retention." Knowledgepoint, Press Release via Business Wire. Retrieved March 24, 2003, from http://www.knowledgepoint.com/coinfo/press/2000–7dec.html.

(No author). "Scannable resumes." Career Development Center & Arts & Sciences Placement Office. Retrieved March 24, 2003, from http://www. indiana.edu/~career/fulltime/scannableresumes. html.

(No author). (2002). "Scannable resumes." Online Writing Lab (OWL), Purdue University. Retrieved March 24, 2003, from http://owl.english.purdue.edu/handouts/pw/p scanres.html.

(No author). (1999, February 4). "Technical presentations." (Toastmasters International). Retrieved March 24, 2003, from www.toastmasters. bc.ca/ed-program/man-technical.html.

Templeton, M. & S. S. Fitzgerald, (1999). *Schaum's quick guide to great presentations*. New York: McGraw-Hill.

Tham, M. (1997). "Poster presentation of research work." Chemical and Process Engineering, University of Newcastle upon Tyne. Retrieved March 24, 2003, from http://lorien.ncl.ac.uk/ming/ dept/tips/present/posters.htm.

(No author). (2002). "Types of interviews and how to handle them." Career Journal, Jobpilot. Retrieved March 24, 2003, from http://www.jobpilot.co.th/content/channel/journal/type-interview.html.

Wang, E. (1998, Oct. 2). "Technical presentations." Retrieved March 24, 2003, from http://www.scs. unr.edu/mecheng/me/50/presentations/sld001.htm.

Further Reading

Adamy, D. L. (2000). *Preparing and delivering effective technical presentations* (Artech House Technology Management and Professional Development Library). Artech House Books, 46 Gillingham St., London, SW1V 1AH, UK. Adamy is an electrical engineer and experienced speaker. He avoids discussing specific technologies, rather he stresses that good speaking requires practice, respect for the audience, and telling the audience what they came to learn in language they can understand and visual aids they can read. Both Chapters 4 and 5 are dedicated to the use of visual aids. This is a fine book for people with little or no experience in making presentations.

Axtell, R. E., T. Briggs, M. Corcoran, & M. B. Lamb, (1997). *Do's and taboos around the world for women in business*. New York: John Wiley & Sons, Inc. Because much of the business transacted with other cultures involves relationships, this book could as easily be attached to the chapters on relationships as to this one. There is specific advice about meeting protocol, sexual harassment, dining, and gift giving as well as how to conduct business abroad. After a self-test on culture-gender awareness, and six chapters on general concerns, the authors have individual chapters on 14 specific countries; 10 European countries are handled in one chapter. The authors include three chapters on women in the world of work, seven chapters on the international assignment, a chapter of tips to help independent businesswomen who want to work abroad, and a whole part devoted to additional resources. This is a comprehensive, helpful book.

Bolles, Richard N. (2003). *What color is your parachute?* Berkeley, CA: Ten Speed Press. Published annually, this book has sold millions and millions of copies. It is a complete guide to the job hunt, and with each edition it continues to get better. Bolles includes an interview checklist, a complete discussion of salary negotiation, and many resources for seeking additional information. In this practical book, Bolles supports the theme that those who get hired are often those who know the most about how to get hired. Job hunting is more than winning interviews.

Curtis, J. C. (2000). *Strategic interviewing: Skills and tactics for savvy executives.* Westport, CT: Quorum Books. Curtis, manager of her own consulting firm, Executive Expertise, in Athens, Georgia, helps you ask the crucial questions and get at critical answers. Her easily remembered, step-by-step procedure is easy to recall and apply. How do you work within a framework of solid communication skills? How do you not just ask questions, but listen intelligently for crucial answers? Curtis uses practical examples and numerous exercises in this book designed for professionals.

Edenborough, R. (2002). *Effective interviewing: A handbook of skills and techniques,* 2nd ed. London, UK: Kogan. Edenborough takes a comprehensive look at the entire range of interview situations and reveals how the process of interviewing has developed. He offers practical advice on the use of interviewing in contexts such as recruitment, selection, performance management, counseling, and conducting surveys. Edenborough's gives specific advice on selecting the best interviewing methods, developing and applying appropriate techniques, linking interviewing with other professional methods such as psychometrics, questionnaire surveys or assessment centers, and appreciating the effectiveness and application of interviewing skills and techniques. The book is designed for employers, personnel and human resource professionals, and anyone whose job involves interviewing.

Gray, J. (2002). *Mars and Venus in the workplace: A practical guide for improving communication and getting results at work.* New York: HarperCollins. Although I am reluctant to add this book to any reading list because of the author's lack of sources,

footnotes, references, or bibliography, I think it can contribute to successful communication at work simply because his insights may offer a greater understanding that men and women communicate differently no matter the context and a greater respect for each other. This has the potential of increased cooperation, and, perhaps, better techniques for making the best impression. We caution readers that many of the generalizations and conclusions here are the author's own and merit no more than a superficial response. With all of that said, the book is well written, interesting, and full of communications charts and practical advice. Just be cautious in your use of his information. If it inspires increased understanding or tolerance then, perhaps, it has been useful.

(No author). (1999, June 8). "More information on. . .interviews." U.S. Department of the Interior. Retrieved March 24, 2003, from http://www.doi.gov/octc/ivmore.html. This website is an excellent place to begin looking for information. It includes a guide to web browsing information on developing a career strategy; advanced Internet tips; job listings by the federal government, state governments, and the private sector; a personality instrument; and occupational exploration opportunities. It also covers job hunting tools such as networking, job fairs, résumés, cover letters, and interview tips. The site offers articles of interest, a career reading list, a user survey, FAQs, and lists of related Web pages, articles, and books.

Mostafa, J. (2000). *Word processing: Letters & mailing.* (Essential Computers). New York: Dorling Kindersley. This is a 72-page easy-to-follow guide to Microsoft's word-processing program, Word. If you have little or no experience using Word, Mostafa uses a step-by-step format with pictures, to guide readers through their first letter, working with text, changing the layout, appearance, storing letters, printing, letting Word help, and using mail merge. In addition to the step-by-step explanation, there are description and explanation boxes and a glossary at the end of the book. Very useful.

Wellington, S. (2001). *Be your own mentor: Strategies from top women on the secrets of success.* New York: Random House. Catalyst, of which Wellington has been president since 1993, is a nonprofit research and advisory organization that works to advance women in business. It is the leading source of information on women in business. In this book, Wellington—based on her work at Catalyst, whom she claims as a coauthor—covers topics such as wise up, you can if you plan, get-ahead basics, style matters, become known, your number one success strategy, networking, making your life work, find a mentor /be a mentor, conduits to top leadership, what to expect at a firm, and wisdom from the pioneers. Not only are there basic success strategies, but the quotations from top women executives makes this a "must read" for anyone interested in "making it" in corporate life. It is practical, specific, and interesting.

Whiteley, R. C. (2001). *Love the work you're with: Find the job you always wanted without leaving the one you have.* New York: Henry Holt and Company. Whiteley bases his approach on the theory that your career growth, happiness, and company's competitive advantage all depend on how engaged and energized you feel about work. This book gives you tools to assess your current outlook, identify your stumbling blocks, and rekindle the spirit you brought to your job on day one. This is a practical, hands-on approach filled with stories from real workplaces, exercises to encourage enthusiasm and renewed commitment, and lists of specific suggestions for improvement and change. Whiteley is a treat to read because of his enthusiasm and encouragement.

Part Three

Communicating in Groups

Chapter 10

Small Groups: Characteristics

Objectives

After reading this chapter, you should be able to:

- Describe the situations in which group decision making is superior to individual decision making.
- List the characteristics of a small group.
- Distinguish between different types of groups.
- Describe the factors that often determine small-group effectiveness.
- Explain how the physical setting can help a group function better.
- Explain how a group becomes cohesive.
- Explain the difficulties groupthink can create.
- List and explain the steps in group problem solving.
- Identify the strengths and weaknesses of using online discussion groups.

Key Terms and Concepts

Use the Communicating Effectively CD-ROM and Online Learning Center at mhhe.com/hybels7 to further your understanding of the following terms.

Brainstorming 362	Learning group 356	Small groups 347
Bulletin boards 354	Mailing lists 354	Social group 352
Cohesiveness 359	Netiquette 346	Synchronous
Commitment 359	Norms 351	communication 354
Consensus 368	Questions of fact 364	Task-oriented group 352
Groupthink 359	Questions of policy 365	Usenet newsgroups 354
Information-sharing	Questions of value 365	Web conferencing 354
group 355	Rules 351	Web forums 354

When Samantha received her instructions, they read as follows:

1. Introduce yourself to the other members.
2. Keep your messages brief.
3. Stay on the topic being discussed.
4. Emphasize the positive aspects of communication. (Thank others for their messages.)
5. Acknowledge where your ideas came from.
6. Keep your own perspective.
7. Encourage interaction by inviting comments on your work or by asking open questions about an issue.
8. Give and receive feedback. Give people feedback when they respond inappropriately (Sharpe, 1999, pp. 1–2).

As one of the requirements for the small-group segment of her basic course, Samantha had to participate in an online group discussion, and these (the above list) were the guidelines she received—netiquette for online discussions. **Netiquette** (or net etiquette) includes the common practices, customs, conventions, and expectations expected of individuals using the Internet (Chadwick, 2001). Samantha was about to join thousands of others online who were experiencing online learning—"the ability to discuss topics with other students" (Sharpe, 1999, p. 1).

In assigning Samantha to participate in an online group discussion, Samantha's course instructor was aware of the popularity of interest groups. "Global communities of interest have been assembled through use of mailing lists, electronic bulletin boards, chat lines, discussion forums, Internet Usenet or Bitnet Newsgroups, and so on. Traditional communities of geographic proximity are augmented by these communities of interest, where hobbies, medical conditions, professions, athletic and sporting news, automobiles, movie and video heroes, and virtually any other subjects of interest are discussed and debated with worldwide perspective and participation. A posting in an Internet Newsgroup, for example, may be read within a few hours by tens or even hundreds of thousands of individuals from among the 500 to 600 million (or more) Internet subscribers. These communities of interest are formed without regard to geographic proximity or political boundaries. And in the foreseeable future, if costs continue to decline and accessibility continues to expand, the only limits will be the levels of interest themselves. The associations thus formed are without precedent for humanity and promise great potential for cooperative problem solving, skills exchange, and unified action. These dynamic communities of interest may be long term or short term because associations are formed to meet particular needs, and dissolved when they are no longer pertinent" ("Help with". . ., 2001).

To show you the popularity of groups on the Internet, your authors entered the following words into the Google search engine and came up with the number of Web pages indicated: The word *groups* had 54,600,000 hits, the word *discussion* had 37,900,000, and the words *group discussion* had 4,930,000 (March 24, 2003); the words *online group discussions* had 1,670,000 hits and *e-mail group discussion* had 1,900,000 (March 24, 2003). Although the information in this chapter involves face-to-face interactions, much of the material relates directly to online group discussion as well. There are three reasons for beginning this chapter with an example of online discussion rather than face-to-face discussion:

1. It reveals the popularity of discussion as a process.

2. It emphasizes the direction that discussion has taken—away from face-to-face groups and toward Internet opportunities. (This has to do with the time it takes to meet with people, the availability of Internet discussion groups, and the number of people actually taking advantage of online discussion groups.)

3. It reveals the similarities between online discussion and face-to-face discussion.

Although we will be making references to Internet interest groups throughout this chapter—because of their popularity and availability—in preparing for face-to-face group discussion, Internet groups can help you discover a topic, access experts, find current issues, examine opposing issues, discover current trends, and answer questions about your topic.

We will be more specific about using Internet groups primarily for the purpose of finding information, rather than establishing short- or long-term relationships with others, later in this chapter. Such groups can be an important source of information; however, those who have never used Internet groups need to move carefully—using the same care as shown whenever involved in Internet relationships. Also, being involved in too many Internet groups at the same time can be overwhelming. Just being involved in one active group can fill your e-mail box with responses on a daily basis, and forgetting to unsubscribe to a group when going on vacation may inadvertently fill it beyond capacity.

Small groups are gatherings of 3 to 13 members who meet to do a job, solve a problem, or maintain relationships. Small groups are essential in helping society function efficiently, and many of us—especially those of us with Internet access—spend several hours each week communicating in such groups. Not only do we participate in chat rooms, mailing lists, newsgroups, web forums, and other interest groups; we might also take part in a seminar discussion, talk with a group of co-workers about improving job conditions, discuss with family members how to make the household run more efficiently, or discuss a variety of topics and issues with a group of friends. Some will even surf the Net just looking for a place where they can express themselves on any number of ideas. Many of us, too, belong to service or professional groups. Often these groups involve both the completion of tasks and social life. Some are singularly social. Whatever groups we belong to, we want them to function efficiently if they are task-oriented groups, and we want them to be enjoyable and satisfying if they are social. If a group is task-oriented, participation should be pleasurable, but we want to meet, get on with the job, and then spend some time socializing with other group members.

This chapter and the next one discuss how groups work. In this chapter, we note the characteristics of small groups and how such groups go about solving problems (Beebe & Masterson, 2003; Brilhart & Galanes, 2000; Ellis & Fisher, 1994; Wilson & Hanna, 1998). We recognize and acknowledge groups such as marriage-encounter workshops, counseling groups, and growth groups that, in general, have no real collective goal. Also, we recognize groups that exist solely to satisfy the social needs of their participants. Most of these—including the social groups formed in online chat rooms—are informal and seldom have an agenda except enjoyment or friendship. In Chapter 11, Group Leadership, Participation, and Conflict Management, we concentrate on how to effectively lead or participate in a group.

■ WHY DISCUSS?

When a group has a job to do, its main form of communication is discussion. Group members meet to exchange information and ideas in an effort to better understand a particular issue or situation. The executive council of the Student Activities Organization discusses how many major activities it wants to sponsor for the forthcoming academic year; the tenants' committee discusses ways of improving the apartment complex; the social committee discusses security arrangements for an upcoming concert.

Not all people like discussion. Many find it time consuming and boring. What, then, is the value of discussion?

In a democratic society, one of the first assumptions is that no one person will make the decisions for everyone. Discussion is a way for everyone to participate and be heard. It is a forum where ideas are proposed and then modified in response to group feedback.

Group decision making is often superior to individual decision making. Those who study small groups have found that people who work in groups accomplish more than people who work alone (Baird & Weinberg, 1977, p. 126). Other research has found that students learn better in classroom discussion groups. When exam time comes, they will do better and find the task more enjoyable if they join a study group.

Often a group can do a job more efficiently than an individual. The study group is a good example: Rather than outlining every chapter, each member of the group can work on one chapter and share the outline with other members. Or take the case of the executive council of the Student Activities Organization discussing how many major activities to sponsor for the forthcoming year. This is clearly a group project; no one individual can do the job as well. First, the group talks about how many activities per year it has sponsored in the past and how popular the activities were—a member of the group has compiled this information. The group's treasurer offers a report on how much money the group currently has and how much income the activities are likely to generate. The group's social chairperson discusses a list of possible activities. If preparation for this discussion were left to one individual, it would be an overwhelming job.

If you have worked in a group, you probably have discovered that motivation increases when everyone works together (Flynn & LaFaso, 1972, pp. 102–3). If five roommates decide to redecorate their apartment, it is much more fun if everyone pitches in and helps. Also, the five roommates are likely to come up with more ideas about how to do things than would be the case if only one person takes on the project. People are also likely to be more motivated when others are depending on them (Baird & Weinberg, p. 125). For example, if one roommate has to strip the windowsills before the others can paint, he or she is likely to get the job done so that the others can go ahead with what they have to do.

People working in groups have opportunities to ask questions when an idea or issue is not clear. In addition to their learning faster, group members are able to absorb more information (Harnack, Fest, & Jones, 1977, p. 14). Not only does more information become available, but group members can help decide which information is important.

We can see how this works in a practical situation. Let's say that the university is responding positively to student requests for greater campus security. The administration appoints a task force of 10 people to work out the details of how this will be done. The group is made up of community and campus police, administrators, faculty, building and grounds staff, and students. When the group meets, its members agree that they first must locate the dangerous places on campus. Members of the police force will provide statistics and identify locations where problems have occurred as well as supply facts about staff availability and patrol areas. Administrators will provide information about current security costs and projected funding for the next year. Building and grounds staff members will provide campus maps to determine needs for additional lighting as well as additional patrols. Students will conduct a campus poll and query members of the undergraduate student senate to determine the needs, since this is where the request for greater security originated. Because members of the committee will split up the jobs, no one person will be responsible for too much work. When they meet again, the group members will have enough information to begin work on making specific proposals for change.

When you see how effectively a group can solve a problem, it's no surprise that groups are so important. In one study of 200 top-level and midlevel managers in eight different organizations, the researchers found that senior managers spent an average of 23 hours a week in meetings and midlevel managers, 11 hours (Goleman, 1990, pp. 37–41). If one-quarter to one-half of each workweek is devoted to meetings, it's important that we all learn how to work in groups.

■ CHARACTERISTICS OF SMALL GROUPS

All small groups have common characteristics. These groups reflect the culture in which they function; they have norms—expectations that group members have of how other members will behave; and they have rules—formal and structured directions for behavior.

Cultural Values

When Americans think they should solve a problem at work or in the community, their first instinct is to form a group. Once the group begins to function, everyone is more or less equal. If someone wants to talk, he or she is given a chance. If all in the group cannot agree on a solution, the group takes a vote and the majority decides.

This kind of group-forming and group-operating behavior seems so natural that we don't think twice about it: It is part of our culture. We should not assume, however, that other cultures work the same way. When one of our authors asked a Polish friend why the Poles didn't organize child care cooperatives, her friend replied, "In Poland, we never work in groups."

Most societies have a dominant problem-solving mechanism, but it may differ greatly from culture to culture. In many countries men are much more likely than women to make decisions about workplace and community issues. In many of these same countries, only elder members of the group can participate in decision making.

Seventy percent of the world lives in a *collectivist* society—a society whose loyalties are to the family or, more broadly, to the clan, the tribe, or the caste (Goleman, 1990). In such groups, problem solving and decision making are most likely to occur within the family or the clan. If a group is formed that includes members from different clans or families, the way the participants work to solve a problem would depend on their perception of how the solution would affect their own families or clans.

Americans who join a group in another country cannot assume that the group will function in the same way that an American group does. In a campus setting, when American students work with international students, they should also be sensitive to the different ways the work of the group may be perceived. In some cases it might be appropriate to explain at the start how American groups work.

Group Norms

Norms are the expectations group members have of how other members will behave, think, and participate. Norms are informal—they are not written down. Members assume that others understand the norms and will follow them.

A daily staff meeting of the editors of a college newspaper shows how norms operate. All the editors (associate, managing, and city editors, as well as editors of the opinion, campus, and sports sections) look to the editor-in-chief not only to set the agenda for the meeting but to begin it, to recognize participants, and to maintain control throughout the meeting. The editor-in-chief assumes that all editors will attend each meeting, be on time, bring the necessary information that pertains to their areas, and generally act in a polite and responsible manner. In other words, they will follow the norms of behavior for their daily staff meeting. The editor's manner and demeanor set the tone for all meetings.

In familiar settings, we take group norms for granted. But if we join a group where the norms are not so obvious, we might sit back and listen until we figure out what the group norms are. For example, a new person joining an online discussion group should sit back and read to try to get a sense of how the group operates before he or she participates. Different chat rooms, user groups, newsgroups, and web forums each have their own group norms of how people using those interest groups should behave.

Norms are important because they give a group some structure. If members know how to behave, the group will function more efficiently. Also, outsiders can look at the group's norms to see whether they want to join the group. If, for example, you feel comfortable only in informal settings, you will probably not want to join a group that has numerous rituals and ceremonies.

Group norms also govern how participants communicate with each other. This may be especially true in male-female interactions. It is important that group members be treated equally and that all members be given sufficient consideration and concern by all others. Any differences in the way people are treated should be based on their needs or roles in the group and not on gender.

Group Rules

Unlike norms, **rules** are formal and structured directions for behavior. Rules may dictate what jobs group members should do, how meetings should be conducted, how motions should be introduced, and so on. The rules help a meeting to progress and ensure that everyone can be heard but that no one person will monopolize the floor. Sometimes, when order and decorum are especially important, a group will appoint a parliamentarian to see that the rules are properly interpreted and followed.

On the Web

A Sample Acceptable-Use Policy

A short, generic, Web page with no author, and no identification other than a URL, offers the following acceptable-use policy:

You may not use University Computer equipment to

- Acquire, store or display any obscene, racially offensive, or otherwise objectionable material.

- Attempt improper or unauthorized access to any other computer system.

- Willfully prevent or impair the use of the University's computer equipment for legitimate purposes by other users.

- Do anything that might bring the University or its members into disrepute.

- Engage in any illegal activity.

Source: (No author) "Acceptable use policy." Retrieved March 24, 2003, from http://www.scit.wlv.ac.uk/resources/aup.html.

For Internet usage, there are *acceptable-use policy (AUP) statements* that govern behavior online. Indeed, these are lists of group rules. To see a variety of them, enter the words *acceptable use policy* into the Google search engine. When we did (March 24, 2003), there were 2,650,000 Web pages uncovered. Some policy statements cover 10 pages, some less than 1 page as the On the Web box reveals.

Not all groups have rules. Informal groups such as book clubs have norms such as meeting at different homes, providing food, and being prepared to discuss a particular book. A community group such as the Junior League, on the other hand, has rules, bylaws, voting, minutes to approve, and even penalties for not attending regularly. These distinctions between groups are likely to be based on the degree of informality or formality or perhaps on size. Formal and large groups generally have both norms and rules. Small and informal groups usually have norms but few rules.

■ TYPES OF GROUPS

View "Small Group Communication," clip #6, to see a task-oriented group in action.

From your own experience, you can probably distinguish several different kinds of groups. For example, you are probably a member of informal social groups. **Social groups** are groups designed to serve the social needs of their participants. When you were young, you went to school with members of a social group of friends, you met and socialized with friends at work, and you frequently saw friends from your place of worship. All these were social groups; all had norms associated with belonging, but there were few, if any, rules. These are informal groups.

Many groups are **task-oriented**—that is, they serve to get something specific accomplished. Task-oriented groups often have problem-solving or decision-making goals. *Problem solving* involves using some specific procedure—such as the one we discuss later in this chapter—to resolve the difficulty (problem) under consideration. *Decision making*, of course, occurs within the process of problem solving whenever alternatives emerge and choices must be made. When a group is designated as a "decision-making

Many groups are task-oriented; they serve to get something specific accomplished.

group," its task is recommending action—making clear choices among several possibilities.

A task-oriented problem-solving group in the workplace might be designated to solving the problem that smoking presents. That is, what should be done to protect nonsmokers and yet protect the rights of smokers as well?

On the Web

Types of Online Groups

In the text, we mention social, task-oriented (problem-solving and decision-making), information-sharing, and learning groups as different kinds of face-to-face groups. On the Internet, there are different types of groups as well. It should be noted that names for some kinds of online groups vary.

Web conferencing or **web forums** are group discussions that use text messages (and sometimes images) stored on a computer as the communication medium. Participants type messages for others to read instead of speaking them. Unlike the case with face-to-face discussions, messages that are typed into the computer software are recorded. In online group discussions, participants have the opportunity to consider and respond to messages posted by others.

Synchronous communication is group discussion in which all group members are virtually present and communicate at the same time. Most forms of synchronous communication are text-based. Group members type their messages. Voice-based synchronous communication uses speakers and microphones and does not depend on text. Video-based synchronous communication uses speakers, microphones, and video cameras.

Bulletin boards are group discussions originally designed for swapping files and posting notices. Each message is treated independently and is not linked to others of the same topic. Although classified as a form of group discussion by some, bulletin boards are not well adapted to discussion. They require the use of special software for participation. Examples are Spinnaker and WebLine, neither of which is free.

Usenet newsgroups (often referred to just as usenet) are group discussions that handle individual messages sorted by broad subject areas. They use standardized protocols. Because messages can be replicated around the world, usenet newsgroups are not useful for private discussions. Because their functions have been integrated into Web browsers, you subscribe to newsgroups through your Internet or corporate network host provider, and the provider decides what newsgroups it will allow on its system. Therefore, you have access to only the newsgroups that your provider subscribes to.

Mailing lists are group discussions that are completely passive. The discussion arrives through e-mail. The main distinction between a newsgroup and a mailing list is that you go to the newsgroup site to which you subscribe to read the discussions, but the discussions in a mailing list come to you via e-mail. A mailing list is an automated electronic mail program that takes a message sent to it and sends that message to all subscribers' e-mail boxes. Anyone with an e-mail address can belong to a mailing list.

To find an interest group that satisfies your informational needs, you might use one of the following online searchable directories. No single directory covers all the groups available, so you might use more than one of these to ensure a comprehensive search:

1. Liszt Mailing List Directory: www.liszt.com/

2. Deja News: www.deja.com/

3. Tile.Net: www.tile.net/tile/listserv/

4. Publicly Accessible Mailing Lists: www.NeoSoft.com/internet/paml/

5. ONElist: www.onelist.com/

6. Usenet FAQs on WWW: www.cis.ohio-state.edu/hypertext/faq/usenet/top.html

7. Usenet Info Center Launch Pad: sunsite.unc.edu/usenet-i/home.html

Source: (No author) "Types of group communication tools," University of Illinois. Retrieved March 24, 2003, from http://illinois.online.uillinois.edu/stovall/GroupTools/GT/index.html.

A task-oriented decision-making group might be charged with presenting a variety of possible alternatives to management, yet this group does not solve the problem. That is left to management.

Many decision-making groups operate in our society. Juries are one example. Groups can be delegated to decide who is to receive an award, who might be a guest speaker, or what kind of activities the group might like to support. A classroom professor experienced the operation of a decision-making group when students in one class met and recommended to him that the date of an examination be changed from the day after homecoming weekend to any of three possibilities the group presented. He presented the three alternatives to the class, and a vote determined the new date.

There is another important kind of group meeting as well. The **information-sharing group** can be found in corporations, schools, churches, families, and service clubs, in social fraternities and sororities, and among faculty in departments on campus. Whenever people meet to be informed and to inform others, to express themselves and to listen to others, to get or give assistance, to clarify or hear clarification of goals, or to establish or

Another Point of View

The Internet is, perhaps, the world's most available discussion forum, and yet it isn't free from problems:

In 2001, anyone with a modem and Internet access can participate in an electronic forum, and anyone with an anonymous e-mail account can shield his or her true identity. That makes for a lot of 'Timmie Tees' (the nom de Web of Tim Thomson, a 48-year-old real estate broker and father of one from near Phoenix who wreaked havoc in cyberspace by using offensive language and has been suspended or expelled from online communities at least 40 times). On huge services like AOL, and smaller forums like Café Utne and Salon.com's Table Talk, a small but vocal group of folks are having a blast manipulating their online personas and exercising their First Amendment rights. But they are also creating a huge headache for virtual communities. High-traffic websites must hire costly moderators and customer-service representatives to quell disturbances caused by personal attacks, spamming off-topic posting, obscenities and, not infrequently, bashing of the moderators themselves. AOL, for example, enlists more than 10,000 users to help monitor online behavior, and it pays staff members to supervise these volunteers.

Questions

1. How common do you think are personal attacks, spamming off-topic posting, obscenities, and the bashing of moderators at chat room or electronic bulletin-board sites?

2. Do you think chat room and electronic bulletin-board sites are important for establishing communities and creating small-group discussions?

3. How can troublemakers be expelled from Internet small-group discussions?

Source: D. Feldman, "Chat room exiles." *On Monthly* (Time Special Issue), February 15, 2001, pp. 65–67.

maintain working relationships, information sharing becomes the purpose. Such groups are necessary when people plan to do business together over a long period.

In either task-oriented or information-sharing groups, there is a closely interrelated social dimension as well. The degree to which members concern themselves with the task or with information sharing affects the social interaction of the group. Likewise, the degree to which members show concern for relationships within the group has a direct effect on task accomplishment or information sharing. In some faculty meetings, department members converse, tell jokes, and communicate informally before the formal agenda begins. This behavior establishes an effective social climate before the information sharing takes place.

Yet another type of group—not discussed in detail in this chapter—is the **learning group**, in which the purpose is to increase the knowledge or skill of participants. While the most obvious is the study group, reading clubs, the League of Women Voters, and Bible study groups are also learning groups. A group of Scuba divers or skiers and an investment club are examples of skill-development learning groups.

■ SMALL-GROUP EFFECTIVENESS

Why do some groups succeed and others fail? Why do some come up with creative solutions for problems while others fall short? Why do some groups have members who get along and other groups have members who are always fighting?

Research shows that effective small groups have certain characteristics in common: a sense of solidarity, an ability to focus on their task, and a task that is appropriate for their particular group (Goleman, 1990).

Solidarity can come from members' sharing common interests (baseball trivia, exercising), knowing one another at work, or sharing some social time together before and after group meetings.

Focus comes from a leader or member who tries to keep the group directed toward its subject. This is the person who says, "That's an interesting point, but our problem is to. . . ."

Appropriateness exists when a group and its task are well matched. For example, a student group cannot solve the problem of a deficit in the university budget. However, it might be able to solve a problem like screening strangers who enter dormitories or finding a better way to publicize elections for student senators.

In addition to having solidarity, focus, and task appropriateness, a truly effective group must be of a workable size, must meet in appropriate surroundings with suitable seating arrangements, and must inspire its members to feel cohesiveness and commitment.

Workable Size

A group works best when all its members can communicate and interact with one another. For a group to be effective, it should have from 3 to 13 members. Research indicates that an ideal size for a group is five members (Thelen, 1979, p. 142; Stephen & Mishler, 1952). If a group has too many members, it cannot work effectively to solve problems or do the job at hand. It should be broken up into smaller groups—each with its own job to do. The student government, for example, is usually divided into committees: the social committee, the food advisory committee, the constitutional revision committee, and so on. The committees then study the issues and make recommendations to the larger body.

A group may be too large for all its members to participate in group discussions, decisions, and actions. When this occurs, it is time to break the group into still smaller units. With the student social committee, for example, some members could check out the availability of certain musical groups, while other members could conduct a poll to see which musicians the students would like to have on campus.

Groups can also be too small. When there is a lot of information to gather, or when the task requires specialized skill or knowledge from its members, it is important to have enough members to do the job. For example, if a department is completely computerized, it may be faced with many decisions. Some people might be assigned to find the best kind of computer software—or the best available software for updating what the department already has. Then the question may be how to get everyone to use the system or to check their e-mail. Others might be assigned to establish computerized networks with other departments or programs on campus or to develop instructions for getting onto electronic bulletin boards. If there are enough members to investigate each of these areas, no single person will have too much to do.

An Appropriate Meeting Place

The place where a group meets often influences the general atmosphere of the meeting. A group that meets in a classroom or a conference room will probably be more formal than a group that meets in someone's room or apartment.

The meeting place can be chosen on the basis of who the group members are and what they want to accomplish. Members who know each other well might want to meet in someone's home; when members do not know each other well or if the group wants to attract new participants, it would be better for the group to meet in a public place.

Sometimes the meeting place will be determined by what the group wants to accomplish. A parents' group seeking citywide support for a tax increase in order to add new classrooms to the high school might meet in the high school cafeteria. Travel Abroad, a group of interested citizens who enjoy sharing slides and talks about their travels, might gather in the meeting room of the local public library.

Suitable Seating Arrangements

Seating of group members should not be left to chance, with each member choosing a chair. Donald C. Stone, a professor of public service, believes

Circular tables facilitate discussion because group members can see one another's faces.

that a seating plan is important if people are to pay attention at meetings (Lawren, 1989). For small groups, Stone recommends seating people where they can all see one another's faces. A circular table would serve this function, as would classroom desks or small tables placed in a circle. For larger groups, Stone recommends a U-shaped arrangement of tables. In this arrangement people should sit only on the outside of the U. Otherwise, they will have their backs to one another.

Stone also makes recommendations about chairs. The perfect chair, he says, is one that has a little padding on the seat. If the chairs have hard seats, people will not be comfortable in them for very long; if the seats are too soft, group members might be tempted to doze off.

Working Together

Working with others in a group, answer the following questions about groups:

1. Why is it that some groups succeed and others fail?

2. What is it about groups that succeed that makes them succeed?

3. What is it about groups that fail that makes them fail?

Divide your group answers into two columns, one labeled "Strengths" and one labeled "Weaknesses." List as many items as you can. When your lists are complete, arrange the items in each list so that the most important items are listed first and the least influential items are listed last.

Cohesiveness and Commitment

As a positive force, **cohesiveness** is the feeling of attraction that group members have toward one another (Beebe & Masterson, 2003, p. 113). It is the members' ability to stick together, to work together as a group, and to help one another. **Commitment** is the willingness of members to work together to complete the group's task. When members are committed, the group is likely to be cohesive. There are few more powerful and satisfactory feelings than the feelings of belonging to a group and of being loyal to that group.

Although cohesiveness is often a matter of group chemistry, an effective group leader can help cohesiveness develop the first few times the group meets. A good leader will make certain that all members are introduced and, if appropriate, given a chance to say something about themselves. Cohesiveness will also be helped if members have a chance to do a little socializing before and after the meetings. Finally, during the discussions, a good leader will try to draw out the quieter members. The more everyone participates, the better the chance for group unity to develop.

Groupthink

Workable size, appropriate meeting place, suitable seating arrangements, and cohesiveness and commitment are positive aspects of small-group effectiveness. Groupthink is a negative aspect. Social psychologist Irving Janis, having made a careful study of groups, found that cohesive groups can become victims of **groupthink,** a group dysfunction in which the preservation of harmony becomes more important than the critical examination of ideas (Janis, 1972, p. 9). Janis's point is simply that groups can bring out the worst as well as the best in people (p. 3). Because groupthink can limit group effectiveness, group members need to be sensitive to its operation.

There is a potential cultural element involved in groupthink. In a culturally diverse group, it could be that cultural norms may be silencing dissenters (Greenhalgh, 2001). "For example," writes Leonard Greenhalgh in his book, *Managing Strategic Relationships,* "Asian cultures emphasize interpersonal harmony. In such cultures, it's considered impolite to contradict what someone has just said. Saying 'I disagree' risks loss of face for the person you're disagreeing with" (p. 237). The point is that someone who is interculturally insensitive may misinterpret silence in a diverse group for indifference, and the silent person may be ignored. That's why it is so important to draw out the views of all group members in culturally sensitive ways.

Although our society depends on groups to make decisions, and we spend more and more time in groups, not all group decisions are superior. Group decisions can be just or unjust, fair or discriminatory, sensitive or insensitive to the needs of others; they can be responsible or irresponsible, respectful of or in violation of people's rights. In a dormitory, for example, students on one floor decided unanimously to designate a lounge area as a permanent "no-talk study area" where students could go at any time if they needed total quiet for study. When the ruling was put into effect, students

Consider This

In his book *Victims of Groupthink,* Irving Janis describes characteristics of small groups that generally result in ineffectiveness, low-quality decisions, and failure to attain objectives.* Janis identifies eight symptoms that characterize groupthink and should be avoided. Although he does not intend the following to be ethical standards, examine them from that point of view:

1. Avoid the "illusion of invulnerability," which fosters "excessive optimism and encourages taking extreme risks."

2. Avoid rationalizations that hinder members from reassessing their basic assumptions before reaffirming commitment to previous decisions.

3. Avoid "an unquestioned belief in the group's inherent morality," a belief that inclines members to "ignore the ethical and moral consequences of their decisions."

4. Avoid stereotyping adversaries' views as "too evil to warrant genuine attempts to negotiate, or as too weak and stupid" to thwart your efforts against them.

5. Avoid pressure that makes members feel disloyal if they express "strong arguments against any of the group's stereotypes, illusions, or commitments."

6. Avoid individual self-censorship, which minimizes for each person the importance of his or her own doubts or counterarguments.

7. Avoid a "shared illusion of unanimity concerning judgments conforming to the majority view." This illusion results both from "self-censorship of deviations" and from the "false assumption that silence means consent."

8. Avoid the emergence of "self-appointed mindguards." These are members "who protect the group from adverse information that might shatter their complacency about the effectiveness and morality of their decisions."†

Questions

1. Would it seem to you that groups following Janis's guidelines might be more healthy, humane, and reasonable?

2. Do Janis's suggestions appear to you to be clear, appropriate, and applicable as potential ethical guidelines?

3. After reading his guidelines, can you think of any other guidelines that might serve a similar purpose?

Sources: *Irving L. Janis, *Victims of Groupthink* (Boston: Houghton Mifflin, 1982), pp. 174–75.

†Richard L. Johannesen, *Ethics in Human Communication,* 4th ed. (Prospect Heights, IL: Waveland Press, 1996), pp. 169–70.

found they had eliminated the meeting place of a number of important campus groups that could find no other convenient place to meet.

Two students on the dorm floor knew beforehand about the groups that met in the lounge. Because of the high cohesiveness, solidarity, and loyalty of the deciding group, however, these students chose not to speak up. Their decision to remain silent was a direct result of groupthink.

The essential point about groupthink is that it helps us understand why some groups do not exhibit the kind of critical thinking essential to ethical and responsible problem solving and decision making. It should be clear, too, that groupthink can occur in groups of all kinds. Although our example is a dormitory group, such actions can occur in clubs, committees, boards, teams, or work units. Groupthink is sometimes hard to detect, but detection is worth the effort. When you are part of a group, you want that group to be the best. Groupthink can hinder a group's best efforts.

■ DISCUSSION IN GROUPS

Most groups that work efficiently have a process they typically follow for discussing a problem. Different procedures can work equally well; what is important is that the steps help the group focus on the problem. Many groups use a sequence of steps similar to the one shown in Figure 10–1. Let's look at each of these steps in some detail.

Choosing a Topic

If you are in a class, you may be required to pick a topic your group can discuss. How do you choose a topic? How do you find a subject that all group members will find interesting enough to work on?

Your first approach might be to look at your own school. Are there any problems or improvements your group might like to tackle? How's the housing? Does registration run smoothly? Does the bookstore have fair prices? Are computers available to all students 24/7? Any of these questions might lead to an interesting discussion.

Take a look at the community. Are there any problems there? How do students get along with the townspeople? Are students good neighbors? Do the banks cash out-of-town checks without adding a service charge? Do the local merchants realize how important students are to the economy of the town? Are there issues in the city council or county commissioners' office that might affect the school?

If your group is interested in attacking a broader social issue, the supply is almost limitless. World peace, foreign policy in the post–cold war era, abortion, and attacking the federal deficit are all issues that are hotly debated and will continue to be debated in the future. Discussing one of these topics in your group might be a good way for everyone to become informed about an important issue.

Figure 10–1

Solving a Problem

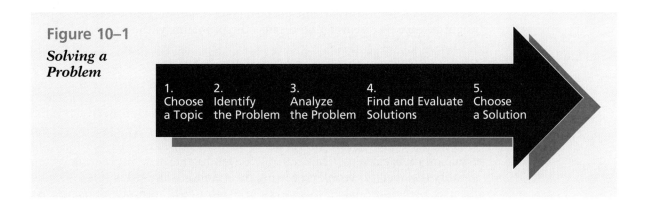

1. Choose a Topic
2. Identify the Problem
3. Analyze the Problem
4. Find and Evaluate Solutions
5. Choose a Solution

Working Together

Brainstorming Guidelines

- Have someone record all ideas.
- Keep your mind open to *all* ideas, both your own and others. Let the ideas flow freely.
- Do not belittle *any* ideas.
- Only once your team has exhausted *all* ideas, crazy or otherwise, you should stop generating and recording and start evaluating which ideas are real possibilities and which ones should be discarded.
- As you pare down your list of ideas, consider how an extreme idea might be interpreted in another way that might be useful.
- Eventually, you want to end up with a manageable number of alternative solutions, something like three to five of them. It might be that you can mix and match parts of ideas into new alternatives.
- Throughout the whole process, make sure that *everyone* is encouraged to participate and that everyone's input is treated with respect. Remember that each team member has something to contribute. Some of the best ideas may come from people who are introverts rather than extroverts. They may be slower to express their ideas because they tend to develop the ideas more fully internally before expressing them. Also, everyone has different experiences to bring to a problem.

Source: J. Fritz, "Brainstorming guidelines," August 2001. Retrieved March 24, 2003, from http://www.os2cs.unb.ca/profs/fritz/cs3503/storm35.htm.

When a group cannot find a topic that all members consider interesting, it should try brainstorming. In **brainstorming** all members of the group suggest ideas—however far out they might seem. The goal of brainstorming is for the group to be as creative as possible. No one should make judgments about the ideas suggested during the brainstorming session. If members fear that their ideas might be condemned, they will be less willing to share some of their wilder thoughts.

Once the group runs out of ideas, it's time to stop brainstorming and take a look at the topics that were generated. Sometimes one idea is so good that everyone says, "That's it." More commonly, however, the group will have to evaluate the ideas. Each topic should be assessed in terms of whether all members are willing to work on it and whether it can be narrowed enough to permit comprehensive research. For example, taking on the problems of the country's landfills (garbage dumps) is too big a job. However, the group might be able to research and discuss the problems with the local landfill.

Identifying the Problem

Once the group has a topic, its members can work toward identifying a specific problem. At this point, much of the work focuses on narrowing the problem so that it can be covered thoroughly. For example, let's say a group of students want to work on reducing crime. They narrow the problem to crime on their campus. They narrow it even further to rape, and they then identify the specific problem: getting the campus administration to accept the need for additional lighting on campus. Notice that through this process

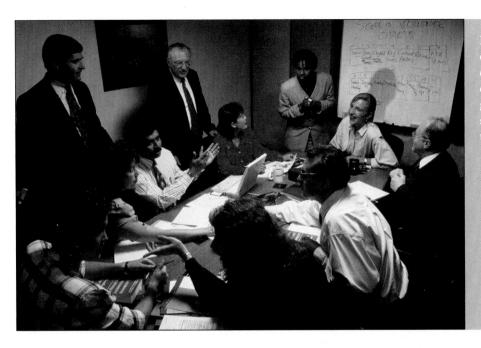

Brainstorming can occur anytime during a group's existence. The goal of brainstorming is simply to generate ideas.

of narrowing and focusing, the group has come up with a topic it will be able to handle and discuss in the time it has.

The most important thing the group can do in this stage is identify a problem that is manageable. One of the biggest mistakes groups make is choosing a problem that is so broad that it cannot be adequately covered.

Analyzing the Problem

Asking the First Questions

Groups can take several approaches to analyzing problems. Sometimes it is useful to know what has caused the problem; other times it's enough to acknowledge that the problem exists. For example, a group that wanted to raise student awareness about donating blood did not need to explore why the American Red Cross needs blood. The problem was that students were not donating blood. Another group became interested in establishing a pregnancy crisis center because several local newspaper articles indicated that pregnant students had nowhere on campus to turn for assistance. This group, too, acknowledged that a problem existed.

Before making a final choice of topics, a group might want to find out how extensive the problem is and how many people are affected by it. For instance, citizens in one community wanted to establish an exchange of guns for toys. However, a neighborhood survey discovered that few people owned guns. In checking with the local police, the citizens discovered that few gun-related deaths occurred in their community. The group discovered that guns affected so few people in its area that it did not pursue its plan.

The group should also ask whether anyone else is trying to solve the problem now or has tried to solve it in the past. For example, a group that wants to solve the problem of poor student preparation for college should check with local school administrators to see if someone has been, is, or will be working on this problem—as well as whether or not administrators consider it a problem. Perhaps the group can add to the work that other people have already done or are in the process of doing.

Once the group has gone through this initial analysis, it should decide whether to proceed or to find a new topic. If it decides to proceed, it's ready to begin defining terms.

Defining Terms

The group should define any terms related to its problem that might be vague or ambiguous. For example, a classroom group decided that the campus mailroom took too long to deliver mail. Since individual members in the group defined "too long" in various ways, the group had to arrive at a precise meaning for the term. After some discussion they agreed that "too long" was anything over 24 hours. A community group that wanted to start a program to teach illiterate persons how to read and write first had to define "illiterate." Did it apply only to people who could not read or write? What about a person who could do some reading and writing but not enough to function in ordinary society? From a practical point of view, was this person also illiterate?

Seeking Out Information

To understand a problem fully, a group will need to seek outside information. The kind of information will vary depending on the problem or task. To get information, individual members may each investigate a different aspect of the problem. First they might decide to interview people who have had experience with the problem. For example, if they were trying to find out why library hours had been cut, one group member could interview the director of the library and others could interview students or faculty to see if they were affected by the reduced hours.

Many subjects require research that extends beyond personal experience. A group that is discussing the problem of harmful household products being dumped in landfills would find it useful to interview an expert, such as a chemistry professor. Groups can also find background information on their subjects in the library and on the Internet. Chapter 13, Finding Speech Material, has many suggestions on both library and Internet research—especially investigations involving the Internet.

A group will work more efficiently if every member prepares for each meeting. Then when the group meets, all members will be ready for discussion and able to move on to the next task.

Wording the Final Question

Once the problem is analyzed, the next step is to phrase it as a question. A well-worded question should summarize the group's problem; it should be simply and clearly worded; and it should focus on a single central idea. It should use neutral terminology and present a specific problem for the group to solve. Depending on the topic, it should take the form of a question of fact, a question of value, or a question of policy.

Questions of fact deal with what is true and what is false. Examples of these questions are the following: How can we protect the drinking water supplies of our largest cities? In what ways can we reduce gun-related deaths in our nation? What are the methods necessary for making our homeland secure? Does sexism affect our lives? What are note-taking skills?

Questions of value are questions of whether something is good or bad, desirable or undesirable: Is recycling a beneficial activity? To what extent is the violence depicted on television and in video games harmful to people in our society? Is fraternity or sorority membership worthwhile?

Questions of policy are questions about actions that might be taken in the future. Such questions are often asked in institutional settings, such as schools, businesses, or organizations, and they usually include the word *should:* Should colleges increase the number of required courses? To what extent should business and industry assume the responsibility for cleaning up the environment? Should all students be required to have real-world work experience as part of their college education? Should businesses be required to hire more minority workers?

Note that many questions of policy also involve fact and value. For example, "Should students be required to take a course in AIDS education?" is a question of policy, but it also has questions of fact and value built in. The questions of fact might include these: Is there enough information on AIDS to justify a course? Can AIDS awareness be taught? Can the institution handle the number of students who would take a required course? Would such a course make a difference? The questions of value might include this one: Is teaching AIDS awareness beneficial and important?

When a group is engaged in fact-finding, it is most likely to use questions of fact. For example, if some students are curious about how much money is spent on college athletics, their fact-finding questions might include these: What percentage of the student activity fee is spent on athletics? What percentage of the total college budget is spent on athletics? What percentage of salaries paid at the college goes to coaches? These and other fact-finding questions will help them to gather information about how much money is budgeted for athletics.

When a group is going to make recommendations, it will use questions of value or questions of policy. A group considering the parking problem on campus might ask these questions: Should first-year students be permitted to bring cars on campus? Should faculty and staff be given the first choice of parking spots? Should everyone be required to pay for parking stickers? Research into these questions will help the group move to the point where it can make recommendations.

Finding and Evaluating Solutions

Most problems do not have a single easy solution. Sometimes there are a number of alternatives, and the way a group looks at these alternatives is an important factor in the group's effectiveness. Not only must a group suggest alternatives that are realistic and acceptable, but it must also look at both the negative and the positive consequences of all the alternatives.

At other times a group may have difficulty finding appropriate solutions. If members cannot come up with good solutions when they work together, they may find it helpful to work separately for a while, with each member coming up with two or three solutions to present at the next meeting. Some

Consider This

Sample Problem-Solving Outline

I. Choose a topic.

  A. Look at your immediate situation.

  B. Examine your community.

  C. Look at broader social issues.

  D. Use brainstorming as a way to creatively generate ideas.

II. Identify the problem.

  A. Narrow the topic so that it can be covered thoroughly.

  B. Identify a problem that the group can manage.

III. Analyze the problem.

  A. Use any of the following approaches:

    1. Does a problem exist?

    2. What has caused the problem?

    3. How extensive is the problem?

    4. How many people are affected by the problem?

    5. Is there anyone else who is trying to solve the problem now or has tried to solve it in the past?

  B. Define vague or ambiguous terms.

  C. Seek out information.

IV. Find and evaluate solutions.

  A. Most problems have a number of solutions.

  B. Discard solutions that are impractical.

  C. List each solution along with its advantages and disadvantages.

V. Choose a solution.

  A. Ideally, groups should work toward consensus—the point at which all group members agree.

  B. If gaining consensus is impossible, group members may have to choose their solutions by putting ideas to a vote, with the majority determining the outcome.

research has shown that when people work alone, they often come up with more innovative ideas than they would in a group (Goleman, 1990).

Sometimes a group can think of several solutions, but some will have to be discarded because they are impractical. In a group that wanted to teach adults to read and write, for example, someone suggested that unemployed elementary schoolteachers should be hired to teach illiterate adults. Although everyone agreed this was a good idea, no one could think of a way to get the money to pay the teachers.

To see if proposed solutions are practical, the group should list each one along with its advantages and disadvantages. Some of the questions a group can ask about proposed solutions include these: Will the solution solve the problem? Is it practical? Is permission necessary to put the solution into effect? Who will implement the solution? How much money will it cost? How much time will it take? If a solution doesn't pass such scrutiny, the group will have to keep working until it finds one that does.

To see if decisions are practical, the group should consider the same types of questions raised regarding solutions. Solutions and decisions are similar because they are both group products or outcomes. Some questions regarding a group's decisions might be the following: What are their relative merits and demerits? What is the best decision the group can support? How will the group's decision be put into effect? To what extent does it satisfy the

Assess Yourself

How Effective Will You Be in Small-Group Discussions?*

Directions: Indicate the degree to which you agree or disagree with each statement by the following scale: 5 = Strongly agree; 4 = Mildly agree; 3 = Agree and disagree equally; 2 = Mildly disagree; 1 = Strongly disagree. Circle your response following each statement.

1. I dislike participating in small-group discussions.	5 4 3 2 1 0
2. I recognize and respond in an appropriate way to differences in values, class, culture, ethnicity, lifestyle, point of view, and personal characteristics.	5 4 3 2 1 0
3. People are quite critical of me.	5 4 3 2 1 0
4. In general, I am comfortable while participating in small-group discussions.	5 4 3 2 1 0
5. I understand the concept of conflict, and I use strategies for handling it.	5 4 3 2 1 0
6. I often feel "left out," as if people don't want me around.	5 4 3 2 1 0
7. I am tense and nervous while participating in group discussions.	5 4 3 2 1 0
8. I possess effective relationship skills including trust, risk taking, empathy, listening, sharing, responsibility, respect for others, and expression of feelings.	5 4 3 2 10
9. People seem to respect my ideas and opinions about things.	5 4 3 2 1 0
10. I like to get involved in small-group discussions.	5 4 3 2 1 0
11. I understand the importance of working effectively with others and the need for courtesy and cooperation to accomplish a task.	5 4 3 2 1 0
12. People seem to like me.	5 4 3 2 1 0
13. Engaging in a group discussion with new people makes me tense and nervous.	5 4 3 2 1 0
14. I am willing to be both an effective and flexible small-group member.	5 4 3 2 1 0
15. Most people seem to understand how I feel about things.	5 4 3 2 1 0
16. I am seldom calm and relaxed while participating in group discussions.	5 4 3 2 1 0

Before Simply Totaling Your Score on This Survey, Go to the CD-ROM or website, and Follow the Directions There.

 Go to the *Communicating Effectively* CD-Rom to see your results and learn how to evaluate your attitudes and feelings.

Sources: For questions 1, 4, 7, 10, and 13, I am indebted to J. C. McCroskey, *An Introduction to Rhetorical Communication,* 4th ed. (Englewood Cliffs, NJ: Prentice Hall, 1982) McCroskey's Personal Report of Communication Apprehension-24 (PRCA-24) scale was published in J. P. Robinson; P. R. Shaver; & L. S. Wrightsman, *Measures of Personality and Social Psychological Attitudes* (San Diego: Academic Press, 1991), pp. 170–73. For questions 2, 5, 8, 11, and 14, I am indebted to "Group Effectiveness: Interpersonal, Negotiation, Teamwork," ICANS (Integrated Curriculum for Achieving Necessary Skills), Washington State Board for Community and Technical Colleges, Washington State Employment Security, Washington Workforce Training and Education Coordinating Board, Adult Basic and Literacy Educators, P.O. Box 42496, 711 Capitol Blvd., Olympia, WA 98504. Retrieved March 24, 2003, from http://www.litera-cynet.org/icans/chapter05/groupeffectiveness.html. For questions 3, 6, 9, 12, and 15 I am indebted to W. F. Fey, "Acceptance by Others and Its Relation to Acceptance of Self and Others: A Revaluation," *Journal of Abnormal and Social Psychology,* **50,** 1955, pp. 274–76. The "Acceptability to Others" scale was published in J. P. Robinson; P. R. Shaver; & L. S. Wrightsman, *Measures of Personality and Social Psychological Attitudes* (San Diego: Academic Press, 1991), pp. 409–11.

group's criteria for an effective decision? How will the effectiveness of the decision, once put into effect, be measured?

Choosing a Solution

Ideally the group should work toward **consensus**—the point at which all group members agree. This must be done, of course, while balancing concerns regarding groupthink, defined previously as a group dysfunction in which the preservation of harmony becomes more important than the critical examination of ideas. If gaining consensus is impossible, group members may have to choose their solutions by putting ideas to a vote, with the majority determining the outcome. Some groups decide on a solution too quickly because they want to get the task done. This is a mistake: A group is only as good as its solution (Cline, 1990).

Chapter Review

A small group is made up of people who get together to solve a problem. Groups can often solve problems better than individuals because they generate more ideas and the work can be divided among the members.

Small groups have norms and rules, and they vary from one culture to another. Small groups are often more characteristic of a democracy than of other forms of government.

For a small group to be effective, it must have a common goal, a workable size (usually from 3 to 13 members), an appropriate meeting place, and suitable seating arrangements. Groups that work effectively are cohesive. However, when group members start to think too much alike, there is the danger of groupthink.

Most groups that meet together to solve problems use a problem-solving sequence to structure their work. A common sequence is that the group chooses a topic, identifies the problem, analyzes the problem, finds and evaluates solutions, and chooses the best solution.

Questions to Review

1. In what situations, or what times, can you justify the use of a group as opposed to an individual for effective decision making or problem solving?

2. What are both the cultural and group conditions that would encourage you to participate in a group?

3. Which of the various characteristics of small groups are likely to lead to group success or failure?

4. From your own experience, what are the group traits that contribute most to group effectiveness?

5. If you want to use any of the online Web

forums or interest groups as possible research or information sources for face-to-face problem-solving groups, what precautions should you heed as you participate in the online group?

6. What step or steps are likely to cause the most difficulty in effectively completing the problem-solving outline?

  Go to the self-quizzes on the *Communicating Effectively* CD-ROM (side 2, track 10) and the Online Learning Center at mhhe.com/hybels7 to test your knowledge of the chapter concepts.

References

Baird, J. E., Jr., & S. B. Weinberg, (1977). *Communication: The essence of group synergy.* Dubuque, IA: Wm. C. Brown.

Beebe, S. A., & J. T. Masterson (2003). *Communicating in small groups: Principles and practices,* 7th ed. Boston: MA: Allyn & Bacon.

Brilhart, J. K., & G. J. Galanes (2000). *Effective group discussion,* 10th ed. Dubuque, IA: Wm. C. Brown.

Chadwick, T. B. (2001, September 21). "How to conduct research on the Internet." Infoquest! Information Services. Retrieved March 24, 2003, from http://www.tbchad.com/resrch.html.

Cline, R. J. W. (1990). "Detecting groupthink: Methods for observing the illusion of unanimity." *Communication Quarterly* 38: 112–26.

Ellis, D. G., & B. A. Fisher (1994). *Small group decision making: Communication and the group process,* 4th ed. New York: McGraw-Hill.

Flynn, E. W., & J. F. LaFaso (1972). *Group discussion as a learning process.* New York: Paulist Press.

Goleman. D. (1990, December 25). "The group and the self: New focus on a cultural rift." *New York Times,* 37, 41.

Greenhalgh, L. (2001). *Managing strategic relationships: The key to business success.* New York: The Free Press (a division of Simon & Schuster, Inc.)

Hare, A. P., E. F. Borgatta, & R. F. Bales eds. (1965). *Small groups: Studies in social interaction.* New York: Knopf.

Harnack, R. V., T. B. Fest, & B. S. Jones (1977). *Group discussion: Theory and technique,* 2nd ed. Englewood Cliffs, NJ: Prentice-Hall.

(No author) (2001, January 1). "Help with Internet e-mail and mailing lists." City of Grand Prarie, Alberta, Canada. Retrieved March 24, 2003, from http://www.city.grande-prare.ab.ca/h_email.htm#Frinding_And-Subscribing_toMls.

Janis, I. L. (1972). *Victims of groupthink.* Boston: Houghton Mifflin.

Lawren, B. (1989, September). "Seating for success." *Psychology Today,* 16–20.

Sharpe, R. (1999, May 27). "Contributing to online discussions." University of Plymouth. Retrieved March 24, 2003, from http://sh.plym.ac.uk/eds/LO/LOnet6.html.

Stephen, F. F., & E. G. Mishler (1952). "The distribution of participation in small groups: An exponential approximation." *American Sociological Review* 17: 598–608.

Thelen, H. A. (1979, March). "Group dynamics in instruction: Principle of least group size." *School Review,* 57, 142.

Wilson, G. L., & M. S. Hanna (1998). *Groups in context: Leadership and participation in small groups,* 5th ed. New York: McGraw-Hill.

Further Reading

Beebe, S. A., & J. T. Masterson (2003). *Communicating in small groups: Principles and practices,* 7th ed. Boston, MA: Allyn & Bacon. Beebe and Masterson emphasize teamwork, technology, and ethical collaboration in this relevant, practical, up-to-date textbook that provides a balanced approach between principles and practice. It is well-written, well-documented, and illustrated, and covers the essentials of small-group processes and problem solving from group formation, relating in groups, and group climate, to problem solving, managing conflict, and leadership.

Brilhart, J. K., G. J. Galanes, & K. Adams (2000). *Effective group discussion: Theory and practice,* 10th ed. Dubuque, IA: Wm. C. Brown. An excellent, comprehensive textbook on small groups and group discussion. The text contains a balance between empirically grounded theories of the dynamics of small-group communication and specific, practical procedures and techniques for improving the functioning of groups, all in the systems approach framework. The authors write about work groups, committees, task forces, self-directed work teams, and other groups whose goal is to find solutions to problems, produce goods, and create policies.

Frey, L. R., ed. (2003). *Group communication in context: Studies of Bona Fide Groups.* 2nd ed. Mahwah, NJ: Lawrence Erlbaum Associates, Inc. Any group, whether family, community, expedition team, social support, organizational, interorganizational or international, must be studied and understood within the numerous contexts in which it is embedded. Here, original research studies conducted on and about communication are presented that cover youth community groups, Internet support groups, climbing expedition teams, families, neighborhoods, and school boards. The researchers use a variety of methodological approaches. A great reference for the serious student of group communication.

Frey, L. R., ed. (2001). *New directions in group communication.* Thousand Oaks, CA: Sage Publications. Frey offers works that scholars have not previously explored. The first part of the book presents new views and extends current positions by focusing on new theoretical and conceptual directions. The second part examines new research methodologies, and the third part looks at antecedent factors affecting group communication. Parts four and five offer insight into group communication processes and practices, and the final part, six, covers group communication contexts including communication patterns in top management teams.

Greenhalgh, L. (2001). *Managing strategic relationships: The key to business success.* New York: The Free Press (a division of Simon & Schuster, Inc.) Although primarily written for managers, Greenhalgh includes two chapters relevant to the small groups and group leadership chapters of this textbook. In Chapter 6, Managerial Negotiation, he discusses the need for managing relationships and, thus, dealing with the conflicts that arise in them. He writes about the objectives and phases of negotiation, and relational ethics in negotiation. In Chapter 7, Group Decision Making, he writes about the complexity of organizational decisions, criteria for evaluating organizational decisions, the process of group decision making, creative concensus, and the leadership function in group decision making, as well as several other topics. This is a superb resource for business managers and for those outside of business as well.

Janis, I. L. (1983). *Groupthink: Psychological studies of policy decisions and fiascoes.* Boston: Houghton Mifflin. Although Janis focuses on foreign relations, his thesis concerns the psychological effects that groups have on individual and group thinking. Numerous case studies are provided. This classic book is an insightful volume full of discussion applications.

_____ (1972). *Victims of groupthink.* Boston, MA: Houghton Mifflin. This is the classic book that introduces the idea of groupthink, the nondeliberate suppression of critical thoughts as a result of internalization of the group's norms. Here, Janis presents the eight symptoms of groupthink–invulnerability, rationale, morality, stereotypes, pressure, self-censorship, unanimity, and mindguards—discusses the consequences, and, finally, the remedies.

Joubert, L. "Intelligence report: Listserves." Retrieved March 24, 2003, fromhttp://nml.ru.ac.za/carr/~leonie/INTELLIGENCE.HTM. Joubert first answers the question, "What are listserves?" and then the article covers searching for lists and subscribing and unsubscribing. It gives a few examples of results or nonresults from lists, compares listserves to newsgroups, offers some of the jargon used, provides conclusions, and then lists, without annotation, some useful sites.

Parks, C. D., & L. J. Sanna (1999). *Group performance and interaction.* Boulder, CO: Westview Press. The authors address recent changes in the field of groups and group decision making from a social psychological perspective. It is an introductory survey of the latest developments in groups research, discussions on computers and in groups, groups in the workplace, and jury decision making. The topics they discuss touch on the disciplines of social, industrial, and organizational psychology, and they are developed around the twin themes of interaction and performance relating to groups engaged in activities.

Renz, M. A., & J. B. Greg (1999). *Effective small group communication in theory and practice.* Boston: Allyn & Bacon. The authors combine discussions of theory with practical applications. Utilizing a clear writing style, they use interesting and engaging narratives to help you understand the relevance and importance of small groups in all walks of life. They give attention to ethical issues, teams, technology, classic and contemporary research, and provide practical tools, as well, for those involved in small-group communication.

Wilson, G. L., & M. S. Hanna (1999). *Groups in context: Leadership and participation in small groups,* 5th ed. New York: McGraw-Hill. The authors provide a comprehensive and up-to-date introduction to group discussion. They effectively combine theory, research, and practical guidelines; however, the unique perspective of this volume is the application of group discussion to a wide variety of career, community, and social contexts. It is a useful, well-written, well-designed textbook.

Chapter 11

Group Leadership, Participation, and Conflict Management

Objectives

After reading this chapter, you should be able to:

- Explain the ways in which a leader can influence followers.
- Explain the elements likely to make a person a leader.
- Tell what is meant by functional leadership.
- Describe the responsibilities of group members within functional leadership.
- Distinguish among the traditional leadership styles of authoritarian, democratic, and laissez-faire.
- Explain what is meant by, what is the point of, and what are the advantages of situational leadership.
- Distinguish between telling, selling, participating, and delegating.
- List the procedures that should be established at the beginning of a group meeting.
- Explain how a leader can help a group to progress.
- Distinguish among task, maintenance, and negative roles and give examples of each.
- Explain how conflict can have some value for a group.
- Explain the ways in which conflict can be managed in a group.

Key Terms and Concepts

Use the Communicating Effectively CD-ROM and Online Learning Center at mhhe.com/hybels7 to further your understanding of the following terms.

Agenda 390	Functional leadership 380	Participating 386
Authoritarian leader 382	Hidden agendas 391	Referent power 377
Coercive power 376	Laissez-faire leader 384	Reward power 376
Conflict 397	Leader 376	Selling 386
Delegating 387	Leadership style 380	Servant leadership 378
Democratic leader 383	Legitimate power 377	Situational leadership 384
Dysfunctional	Maintenance roles 395	Substantive conflict 398
(individual) roles 396	Neutrality 389	Task roles 393
Expert power 377	Objectivity 389	Telling 385

As a freshman in college, Trenton applied himself, focused on his classes, and did well. One goal was personal: Trenton wanted to prove to himself that he was college material. Another goal was that he wanted to prove to his father that he wasn't "good for nothing." Although he knew his father believed in him, he also knew deep down that his father didn't think he would succeed in college. There was a third goal, however, more important than both of these, that Trenton shared with no one. Trenton wanted to be a leader. He had worked at a large number of jobs throughout high school and during summers, and he knew he didn't want to be an hourly wage earner for the rest of his life.

During his freshman year there had been few opportunities for leadership. Yes, he joined committees in his dormitory, but being a freshman prevented him from occupying leadership positions. Also, he went to other informational meetings on campus and joined some other groups; most were inconsequential, but they provided him with useful contacts and a variety of resources he could use in the future.

As Trenton was walking across campus one day, he saw a poster on one of the kiosk bulletin boards. "Sophomore Leadership Series," the headline on the poster exclaimed in large letters. Trenton read on: "This is a leadership development opportunity for sophomores who are interested in learning more about themselves as leaders and as contributing members of teams. The goals of the series are to:

- Provide you with an understanding of teamwork.
- Expose you to leadership concepts.
- Challenge you by choice.
- Demonstrate effectiveness as a team member.

The advertisement drew Trenton's attention further. "The series consists of nine sessions, each building one on the other. Many sessions will consist of a minipresentation, with the rest of the time spent in small groups collaborating and participating in team-building exercises. You'll laugh, you'll compromise, you'll learn about yourself and others!" The meeting time and place (7 PM to 8:30 PM on Thursday evenings in the Student Union) were listed. "Attendance at each session is both essential and expected," the poster stated, and the first meeting was the following Thursday. Trenton wrote down the necessary information in his day book.

Although Trenton did not like meetings, this one turned out to be different. Everyone connected with the Sophomore Leadership Series wore navy-blue shirts with the name and logo printed on the front—from the greeter who gave Trenton a pad of paper and a pen that carried both the name "Sophomore Leadership Series" and the logo, to those who assisted with the name tags, and to all the speakers. Briana began the meeting exactly on time, and she began by dispelling Trenton's major concern: "Nobody likes meetings," Briana said, "most of all me." And with that comment, she turned on a slide about successful meetings that read:

- Prepare ahead of time.
- Have a reason for the meeting.
- Distribute an agenda to participants.
- Give participants at least one day's notification.
- Have participants ask themselves what is expected of them and how they can prepare.
- Limit attendance and designate a leader.
- Keep a clock in the meeting room, and have a specific start and end time.
- Encourage everyone to talk, while keeping with the agenda.
- Foster rigorous discussion, debate, or brainstorming, while respecting each person's opinion.
- Use visual aids.
- Follow up. Meeting leaders should let participants know of any outcomes.
- Evaluate the meeting at the end, and ask for input.

"This is our agenda for all the meetings we will have, and you can hold us to it. We are responsible," Briana said. "We don't want to waste your time, so our goal will be to make the most of the time we have together, and to always give you valuable information and insights that will make our meetings productive and useful. If you use the pad we have provided for you to copy down the information on the slides, you will end up with powerful information on meeting management, leadership effectiveness, team building, and team motivation," Briana said. "That's what this is about. If you want to become either a leader or the best darn group member you can be, then the Sophomore Leadership Series is what you are looking for. We will begin by looking at what leaders are made of."

And that is precisely how this chapter begins as well. We begin our discussion answering the question, what is a leader? We then look at how leaders influence followers, how people become leaders, and approaches to leadership. Approaches include functional, traditional (authoritarian, democratic, and laissez-faire), and situational leadership styles. Our final four sections cover the leading of, participating in, conflict in, and the evaluation of groups.

■ WHAT IS A LEADER?

If we were asked to make a list of all the leaders in our lives, most of us could probably come up with at least a hundred. Some of the people on our list hold recognized leadership positions: the president of the United States, a state senator, the principal of our elementary school. Others do not have formal leadership positions but are leaders because a group acknowledges them as such: the student who organizes a study group to prepare for an examination, the employee who puts together a car pool, the friend who gets people together to purchase tickets for a group to attend a rock concert. The characteristic that all these leaders have in common is that they exert some kind of influence. A **leader,** then, is a person who influences the behavior of one or more people.

Why is one person more influential than another? Why are some people leaders and others followers? Where do leaders get their power to influence others? What kind of power do they have?

■ HOW LEADERS INFLUENCE FOLLOWERS

For an example of leadership in a group, view "Small Group Communication," clip #6 on the CD.

Some leaders influence their followers through sheer force of personality. Others wield influence because they are in a position of power in an organization and the people they lead are their subordinates. Most often, however, leadership is a combination of factors. Researchers have identified five sources of influence for leaders: reward power, coercive power, legitimate power, expert power, and referent power (Arnold & Feldman, 1986, pp. 120–21).

Reward Power

A leader can have influence if he or she can reward followers; this is known as **reward power.** In an organization, rewards can take such forms as promotions or pay raises. If the leader is liked and admired, he or she can reward followers by praising them, giving them approval, recognizing them, or giving them attention. On the campus newspaper staff, for example, the editor rewards her subordinates by giving them good stories to cover and printing their articles on the front page.

Coercive Power

Coercive power is the power to punish. In an organization the leader can punish followers by demoting them or refusing to raise their pay or, more drastically, by firing them. Leaders can also exercise coercive power by criticizing their followers or refusing to pay attention to them. For example, a manager may not assign new projects to employees who have not "paid their dues." Or, an employee who is not willing to work on a weekend might not get new projects.

Legitimate Power

In a formal organization, a leader is influential because he or she is "the boss." The people who report to the leader must comply because of the organizational hierarchy and its rules. This constitutes **legitimate power.** In the military, for example, the lower ranks must always defer to the higher ranks; ability and personality are not factors.

Expert Power

Expert power denotes the influence and power an expert has because he or she knows more than anyone else. For example, Shin and Nikisha have formed a group of international students to study the problem of not having a common meeting place on campus. Although the group has six other members, Shin and Nikisha lead the group because they have done the most research on the problem.

Referent Power

Leaders with **referent power** enjoy influence because of personality. Members look up to them, want their approval, and try to emulate them. For example, a student who writes a humor column for the campus newspaper is greatly admired. Because of this widespread admiration, many students defer to her judgments on a variety of subjects.

Figure 11-1 shows whether these five sources of influence come from organizations or from personality and where they overlap.

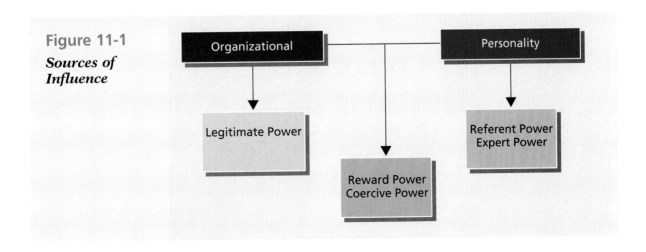

Figure 11-1

Sources of Influence

■ HOW PEOPLE BECOME LEADERS

What makes a person a leader? Why do some people always take on leadership roles, regardless of the situation they are in? Why do people rise to leadership positions in organizations? One reason could be a true motivation to serve others. Although this sounds altruistic and idealistic as well, there are people in this world who have a holistic understanding, who want to build shared visions, encourage effective self-management and interdependence, who want to learn from their mistakes, encourage creativity from everyone, question assumptions, promote shared trust, and embrace humility (McGee-Cooper, & Looper, 2001). These people are known as **servant-leaders,** people who "work for the well-being and growth of all employees and are committed to creating a sense of community and sharing power in decision making" (Abrams, 1999, p. 36). See the Another Point of View box on page 379 about servant-leadership.

Perhaps servant-leaders are few and far between in today's world where pluralism, consumerism, increased mobility, fragmentation, democracy, and increased access to news and information characterizes most westernized societies, and in our own society that demands of its leaders technical know-how, business savvy, and leadership and management capabilities. With the chaotic pace of today's society, the demands for time-saving immediacy, the constant push for more and better, and the emphasis on what we do rather than who we are, any leader today must operate in complex and risky conditions faced with unprecedented challenges.

Robert A. Baron and Paul B. Paulus, who write about organizational theory, believe leaders arise because of their personality traits and the situations in which they find themselves. These two factors work together in what they call the *functional approach to leadership* (Baron & Paulus, 1991, pp. 214–45). We examine functional leadership in some detail in the section that follows labeled, Approaches to Leadership. Here, we look at the elements Baron and Paulus consider predictors or precursors to functional leadership.

Personality Traits

We have all heard the term *born leader*, and we all know individuals who fit this description. Most people like and admire these individuals. They take charge of situations, they are the people others turn to, and they are the ones who come up with the most creative solutions. They can cut through a discussion to identify the essence of the problem, and they show the ways in which the group can make a decision. All these traits are *internal*—they are found in the personality of the leader.

Situational Factors

In many situations people emerge as leaders because they have the competence and the skill to solve the problem at hand. The person who emerges as leader is the one who is best able to meet a specific group's needs. These characteristics are *external* in that they depend on the situation and on the kind of skill or expertise needed to solve the problem. For example, if a

Another Point of View

Servant leadership is based on leadership through serving rather than managing or controlling. According to Larry C. Spears, CEO, The Greenleaf Center for Servant-Leadership, there are 10 characteristics of the servant leader (abridged):

- *Listening.* He or she listens receptively to what is being said and unsaid.
- *Empathy.* The servant-leader strives to understand and empathize with others.
- *Healing.* . . . One of the great strengths of servant-leadership is the potential for healing one's self and one's relationship to others.
- *Awareness.* General awareness, and especially self-awareness, are strengths of the servant-leader.
- *Persuasion.* Another characteristic of servant-leaders is a reliance on persuasion, rather than on one's positional authority, in making decisions within an organization. The servant-leader seeks to convince others, rather than coerce compliance.
- *Conceptualization.* Servant-leaders seek to nurture their abilities to *dream great dreams,* . . . to encompass broader-based conceptual thinking, . . . to provide the visionary concept for an institution.
- *Foresight.* Closely related to conceptualization, the ability to foresee the likely outcome of a situation . . . by understanding the lessons from the past, the realities of the present, and the likely consequence of a decision for the future.
- *Stewardship.* The servant-leader assumes first and foremost a commitment to serving the needs of others by using openness and persuasion rather than control.
- *Commitment to the growth of people.* The servant-leader is deeply committed to the growth of each and every individual within his or her organization.
- *Building community.* The servant-leader seeks to identify some means for building community among those who work within a given institution" (pp. 2–4).

Questions

1. To what extent could servant leadership work for small, problem-solving classroom discussions?

2. Does servant leadership appear to be something easy to implement? Why or why not?

3. Would you ever want to serve under a servant-leader? Why or why not?

L. C. Spears, "On Character and Servant-Leadership: Ten Characteristics of Effective, Caring Leaders." The Robert K. Greenleaf Center for Servant-Leadership, Indianapolis, IN, 2002. Retrieved March 24, 2003, from http://www.greenleaf.org/leadership/read-about-it/articles/On-Character-and-Servant-Leadership-Articles-Book-Reviews.html.

group of students is assigned to make a videotape and only one student knows how to run a video camera, he or she will be the leader—at least until everyone else has learned.

Although a person may become a leader solely on the basis of outstanding personality or skills, most people become leaders when their personalities or skills are appropriate for a particular circumstance or when they can fulfill a need of the group. Hence the name *functional leadership*—suitability of a leader's personality, skills, or knowledge to the needs of a group. Situational leadership is discussed in the section, Approaches to Leadership, which follows.

In this on-site situation, which leadership style is likely to be the best one? On what factors is leadership style likely to depend in this situation?

■ APPROACHES TO LEADERSHIP

There are a number of different approaches to leadership. Here, we discuss functional leadership first, in which responsibility for leadership falls on the shoulders of all group members and moves among them as the group finds it suitable. Then we examine three traditional leadership styles: authoritarian, democratic, and laissez-faire. **Leadership style** is simply the manner in which a leader exerts control over a group. Styles can range from telling participants exactly what to do to—the authoritarian style—to depending on participants to point the way—the laissez-faire style. Finally, we discuss situational leadership, in which leaders adopt different leadership styles depending on the situation. The advantage of situational leadership is that it places responsibility on leaders to determine the appropriate leadership style; it relies on them to assess each situation. No one leadership style is best for all situations; how a leader acts should depend on the job to be done, the group members responsible for the job, and the circumstances in which the group finds itself.

Functional Leadership

We tend to place too much responsibility on the leader of a group and too little on participants. Every member of a group should be a leader in some area. We call this sharing of expertise, when leadership varies with the task of the group and moves from one individual to another as the group finds it suitable, **functional leadership.**

The advantage of functional leadership is that the group's concern is no longer the "property" of any one individual; it belongs to the group as a whole. Group needs vary from moment to moment. How those needs can be fulfilled by group members will also vary. Also, with functional leadership, it is difficult to know for certain who is leading the group at any moment. It doesn't matter. What matters is whether group needs and goals are being satisfied. This means that leadership is active and changing, that the focus of participants is on the group rather than on an individual leader, and that the importance of sharing and member involvement is emphasized.

Functional leadership focuses on the strengths of individual group members. To be ready to be leaders at any moment requires that members be persuasive and adaptive; be able to convince the group they can contribute to the direction of the group; foster agreement, cooperation, or understanding; or influence the group's success in any capacity. Functional leaders must be responsible.

Functional leaders, too, must be aware and sensitive to group needs: What can I do to help the group right now? What skills do I have that will help move the group forward? How can I get us all to work together?

Effective functional leaders are committed to group goals, as opposed to meeting their own needs. They look for opportunities to help the group in any way they can. Functional leaders will try to draw out nontalkers, summarize contributions, help resolve confusion and conflict, and keep groups moving toward their goal. Those leaders are group-centered, active members who contribute to any group. They are well liked because they make everyone feel good and make the group look good.

Let's say the International Student Association meets for the first time in the fall and decides to set an agenda of programs and activities. The club decides that its three priorities are to recruit more members, plan a sightseeing trip to Washington, DC, and present a panel on world peace. The executive committee gets together to discuss which people in the organization will be best to work on each project. Ranjan volunteers to be their recruiter. Everyone likes him, he has numerous contacts, and he is usually good at persuasion. Ranjan, then, becomes leader of this particular activity because of his personality and because he wants to do it. One committee member says that Ming would be good to head the group that will plan the trip to Washington, D.C., because she has been to Washington several times and knows the city well. Ming agrees to lead this group. Luis says he would like to organize the panel on world peace and contact speakers. In previous work with the association, Luis has always done an outstanding job when he handled such activities. He is goal-oriented, and he presents himself in a professional way. He is therefore right for a job that requires both personality and competence. Although leaders do not always emerge in such a clear-cut way in real life, this example shows how the functional approach to leadership works. Often people emerge or can be encouraged to step forth to assume the leadership roles groups need filled.

According to research, a group's ultimate performance on a task depends on three factors: (1) the difficulty of the task, (2) the skills and abilities of group members, and (3) how the group members interact (Salazar, 1996, p. 156).

Some readers may think that one advantage of a group is that the responsibilities outlined in the Consider This box on page 382, Responsibilities of Group Members, can be distributed among group members. What we are saying is that *each* member should fulfill *all* these responsibilities. If this minimum list of responsibilities is assumed by each group member, there will be far more assurance of a successful group discussion.

Consider This

Responsibilities of Group Members

Group members need to:

Be prepared before the meeting. They must have:

- Gathered the necessary information.
- Done the required reading.
- Performed the important thinking.

Think carefully during the discussion process. They must:

- Show concern for the discussion process.

- Be objective.
- Listen carefully.

Be willing to share their ideas and reflections with the group. They must realize that:

- Ideas not openly shared with others serve no useful purpose to the group.
- Ideas are useful only when offered to the group for consideration and discussion.

Support the group's recommendations and say so while the group is deliberating.

When members have critical information because it contributes substantially to the group decision-making process, it should be discussed. Each member needs to take responsibility for making certain that all other members have the opportunity to provide their information. This may require a specific request, such as "Leslie, did you have any information you wanted to present?" Research has shown that when a group member has relatively low status, sometimes his or her critical information is never entered into a discussion and, thus, is never discussed. This can result in a poor group decision (Hollingshead, 1996, p. 213).

Traditional Leadership Styles

Today's complex and changing social and business environments require a special style of leadership. Like yesterday's newspapers, traditional styles are outdated; however, that does not necessitate throwing out the baby with the bathwater. That is, it does not mean these styles are no longer effective in certain instances; it means, rather, that they have been around a long time, they are well-known approaches to leadership, and not only do you need to be familiar with them—despite their datedness—you need them in your leadership toolbox for flexibility, breadth, and potential usefulness. Remember, they have been around so long because they have always been considered worthwhile. Keep them in mind, too, as you read the section that follows on situational leadership. Not only do traditional leadership styles offer an anchor for that section, they provide a useful reference point as well. Here, we will look at authoritarian, democratic, and laissez-faire leaders.

Authoritarian Leaders

The **authoritarian leader** holds the greatest control over a group. He or she takes charge by deciding what should be talked about and who should talk.

This leader approves some ideas and discards others. Most of the discussion in the group is directed to the leader for approval.

Although this style of leadership does not sound very desirable, there are situations where it can work quite well. Often an authoritarian leader gains the leadership position because he or she is the only group member with expertise. Sometimes a group starts out with an authoritarian leader but later operates more democratically. For example, members of a committee are meeting for the first time in the academic year, and only one person has served on the committee before. In the beginning this member may have to be more authoritarian, but group members will start to play greater roles as they gain experience. Sometimes authoritarian leadership results from gender differences, as noted in the following On the Web box.

An authoritarian leader is often the best type of leader when a group must do a job very quickly. For example, a group is meeting to write a grant proposal that is due in two days. One person takes charge of the project and appoints other members to do various tasks. This is the most efficient way to get the job done in the available time.

Authoritarian leaders will be ineffective if group members are equal in experience, knowledge, or status. Such members are likely to resent an authoritarian leader and not cooperate.

Democratic Leaders

A **democratic leader** is one who lets all points of view be heard. Rather than decide things personally, he or she will offer ideas and let the group react to them. Ideally, such a leader keeps the discussion on track but makes a real attempt to let all members be heard. The group is never told what to do, though the leader may suggest a direction to take. Leadership

On the Web

Gender Differences

Jennifer Coates, in her book, *Women, Men and Language* (New York: Longman Inc., 1986), studied men-only and women-only discussion groups and found that when women talk to each other, they reveal a lot about their private lives. They also stick to one topic for a long time, let all speakers finish their sentences, and try to have everyone participate. Men, on the other hand, rarely talked about their personal relationships and feelings but "competed to prove themselves better informed about current affairs, travel, sports, etc." The topics changed often and the men tried to "over time, establish a reasonably stable hierarchy, with some men dominating conversation and others talking very little" (*"Gender Differences..."*)

Questions

1. Is it helpful to understand gender differences when involved in a mixed-sex discussion group?

2. When you notice in a group discussion that a point of view, comment, or suggestion is a result of a gender difference rather than a result of the content being discussed, is it a wise thing to point that out, or is it better to remain silent?

Source: "Gender Differences in Communication," The Ladies Room, Geocities.com. Retrieved March 24, 2003, from http://www.geocities.com/Wellesley/2052/genddiff.html.

in a democratic group is often functional: It may vary with the task and may even move from one individual to another when the group finds this appropriate. All members have a chance to contribute, and information can move among them as well as back and forth to the leader.

Democratic groups work best when members are equal in status and experience and when there is sufficient time to solve the problem. Due to its open nature, a democratic group provides its members more opportunity for originality and creativity than an authoritarian group. Since members share in the decision making, there is also greater motivation. Because members identify with the group, they are more interested in helping the group achieve its goal.

Laissez-Faire Leaders

The **laissez-faire leader** does very little actual leading. He or she might call the group together, but that's about it. Such a leader neither suggests any direction nor imposes any order on the group. In some groups there is a reluctance to name one person as leader. Support groups, such as groups for people with cancer or for people who were abused as children, might feel uncomfortable with an acknowledged leader since the members attend for the purpose of helping one another. As members of the group, they want to be able to respond to a particular member's problem rather than be tied to a schedule or topic. However, these groups could fall into a pattern where the discussion is so unstructured that they don't provide very much help to anyone.

Situational Leadership

In the most simple terms, a **situational leader** can adopt different leadership styles depending on the situation (Zigarmi, Zigarmi, & Blanchard, 1985). In his book *E-Leader*, Robert Hargrove (2001) recommends a "balanced" leadership style, by which he means one that can be shifted in various situations by asking, "Who do I need to be in this matter?" (p. 7). Leaders may need to be directive, empowering, collaborative, facilitative, or whatever, and he makes it clear that there is no one right way to manage. The major difference between functional leadership and situational leadership has to do with how leadership arises in a group: In functional leadership, leadership emerges as the group finds it suitable. In situational leadership, leadership occurs because a leader assesses the situation and determines what is needed.

If you think about it, it is a situational style that you use in your dealings with others. For example, if you find yourself in a teacher-assigned group, in which you have a short amount of time to research a topic and the other group members seem to be uninspired and unmotivated, you will tend to provide the needed direction to get the group going. For many people, this is obvious: They are satisfied only if the task is accomplished, and if they must direct others to get it done, they do.

At the other end of the continuum in situational leadership, assume you are part of a team at work that has been assigned a project. All group participants have a good attitude and have the ability. In this case, each member volunteered to do part of the task, and you—as an active member of the

Another Point of View

Is there a style of leadership appropriate for the age of the Internet and our information-based society? Manz and Sims suggests there is.

What kind of leader is needed for an information-based organization that operates in a rapidly changing world? How can highly independent and physically dispersed telecommuters be effectively led? What kind of leadership is appropriate for leading empowered team members who are supposed to be leading themselves? Is there another model? We believe there is.

We begin with the idea that true leadership comes mainly from within a person, not from outside. At its best, external leadership can provide a spark and support the flame of the powerful self-leadership that dwells within each person. At its worst, it disrupts this internal process, damaging the person and creating conflicts between inner and external influences.

The perspective demands that we come up with a new measure of leadership strength—the ability to maximize the contributions of others by helping them to effectively guide their own destinies, rather than the ability to bend the will of others.

Questions

1. Would the kind of leadership described in the passage above—basically, leading others to lead themselves—be appropriate in classroom discussion groups?

2. To what extent do you believe that leadership comes mainly from within a person, not from outside? In your interpretation of this statement—that leadership comes mainly from within a person, not from outside—does this seem to mean that some people are never destined to be leaders?

3. From your reading of this quotation, what are the strengths and weaknesses of a group leader (external leadership) of a classroom group discussion? As you read the section, Approaches to Leadership, which style do you think best capitalizes on the leader's ability to maximize the contributions of others by helping them to effectively guide their own destinies?

Source: C. C. Manz, and H. P. Sims, Jr., *The New SuperLeadership: Leading Others to Lead Themselves.* (San Francisco, CA: Berrett-Koehler Publishers), p. 4.

team—participate equally along with the others. No direction is needed by you; it is supplied by all members of the group participating equally.

These two situations present the two extremes of situational leadership in which there is, in the first group, low membership maturity—meaning little willingness to participate and little (seemingly) ability to contribute—and, in the second team, high membership maturity. More important, however, the two situations reveal that there is no best way to lead for every situation. The point of situational leadership is that the talented leader employs the most appropriate style based on the context—which is a combination of task, situation, and group. This is most easily demonstrated in a figure. See Figure 11-2.

The first situational leadership style (square 1) is labeled **telling** in which the leader is focused more on the task and less on the group. It is similar to the authoritarian style in which the leader states the problem, takes charge of the task, and tells group members what to do. If you were concerned about your grade, placed in a task-oriented group in which other members did not appear willing or able to complete the task if left alone, you might resort to manipulation or even coercion to get the job done.

Working Together

Come to some conclusions regarding the following questions:

1. Which of the styles of leadership discussed in this section, Approaches to Leadership, do you think is the most effective and why?

2. What specific behaviors do the different styles of leadership discussed in this section require of leaders?

3. Are there leadership behaviors that you consider inappropriate under any circumstance? Why or why not?

4. If you were in a situation in which a leader was using a leadership style you considered inappropriate or ineffective, what could you do, as a member of the group, to try to change the situation?

The second situational leadership style (square 2) is labeled **selling.** In this style, leaders state the problem and decide what to do, but they sell the other group members on the idea to gain majority support. Leaders must explain how the idea will benefit the group and then persuade others to go along. The major differences between telling and selling are:

<table>
<tr><td align="center">*Telling*</td><td align="center">*Selling*</td></tr>
<tr><td>

- One-way communication
- Use of manipulation and coercion for control
- Negative environment
</td><td>

- Two-way communication
- Use of persuasion and explanation for group support
- Positive reinforcement
</td></tr>
</table>

The third situational leadership style (square 3) is **participating.** Using this style, leaders state the problem but immediately consult with group members. With all group members participating, leaders offer support and the group

Figure 11-2

Situational Leadership Styles

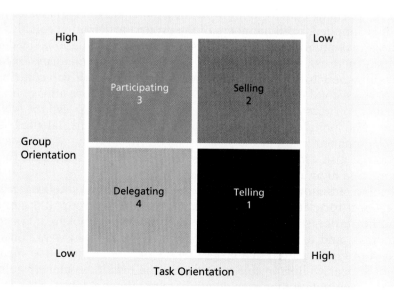

determines the best thing to do only after hearing all members' ideas and reactions. Notice in this style the increased focus by the leader on the group and the corresponding diminished focus on the task. In addition, leaders relinquish much of the structure of how the job will be done; this becomes the members' primary responsibility. There is a close relationship between the participating style and functional leadership because leaders are not focused on either the group or the task. Leaders are part of the group and because the group is responsible for the group and the task, leadership moves from one individual to another as the group or task determines suitability.

The fourth situational leadership style (square 4) is **delegating.** Leaders hang back and let members plan and execute the job. Leaders are not heavily involved with either the group or the job. As noted in the second example that began this section—members are part of a team at work who have been assigned a project—this style of leadership is utilized in more mature, established groups where members can run their own show.

The advantage of situational leadership is that it places responsibility on leaders to determine the appropriate leadership style. And this responsibility is assumed only after looking at all the factors involved. From looking at the lists below, it looks as if there are far too many factors to consider in any given situation; however, most are common sense, and most are factors we would examine unconsciously anyway:

Leadership Factors	*Group Factors*	*Situational Factors*
Knowledge	Combination of	Time
Skills	member personalities	Restraints of organization
Attitude	Values	Environment
Experience	Expectations	Size or duration of job
Background	Willingness to make	Conflict of goals
Values	decisions	Emergencies
Personal goals	Ability to make decisions	Hazards
Group goals	Individual needs	Desirability of the job
Confidence	Group needs	Justice
in members	Interest	Legality
Pressures from	Competition	Removal of alternatives
outside	Confidence	Lack of alternatives
Time	Resources	
Resources	Workload	
Personality	Spirit	
Sensitivity	Communication	
Weight of	Fatigue	
responsibility		

Consider This

In a chapter entitled "Leadership as a Work," Peter F. Drucker, a professor of management at the Graduate Business School of New York University for 20 years and since 1971, Clarke Professor of Social Science at Claremont Graduate School in California, ended the chapter discussing the final requirement.

The final requirement of effective leadership is to earn trust. Otherwise, there won't be any followers—and the only definition of a leader is someone who has followers. To trust a leader, it is not necessary to like him. Nor is it necessary to agree with him. Trust is the conviction that the leader means what he says. It is a belief in something very old-fashioned, called "integrity." A leader's actions and a leader's professed beliefs must be congruent, or at least compatible. Effective leadership—and again this is very old wisdom—is not based on being clever; it is based primarily on being consistent.

Questions

1. For a leader of a discussion group in the classroom, what does consistency mean? How can the group leader be perceived as consistent?

2. What specific things can a leader of a group discussion in the classroom do to gain the trust of group members?

3. Because of the brevity of a group discussion in the classroom—as compared, for example, with a group discussion in a business or organization that could go on for days, weeks, or months—does trust of leaders really matter? Is it something classroom group leaders should be concerned about?

Source: P. F. Drucker, *The Essential Drucker.* (New York: HarperBusiness (an imprint of HarperCollins Publishers, 2001), p. 271.

If the leader is part of the group, many of these factors are readily apparent. Assessing leadership, group, and situational factors may be as easy as in the examples that opened this section. On the other hand, they could be complex when some of the factors above are not readily apparent. In addition, leaders must factor in the possibility of change. Another factor may be trust, as the Consider This above by Peter Drucker explains. Sometimes groups mature or gain awareness or acquire a new vision once they have met or, perhaps, over a number of meetings. These changes cannot be ignored. Whatever the case, the more one understands leadership styles, the factors one must consider, and the options one has available, the easier decision making becomes.

■ LEADING THE GROUP

The role of a group leader is to help the group get the job done, but to do this leaders must have a certain sense of detachment. They need to look at the group from different perspectives than other members do—the perspectives of "Is the group functioning as well as it should?" "Is the group making progress?" "What can I do to make the group work better?" Leaders can help groups work better when they stay neutral and objective, keep the group on track, delegate responsibility, encourage social interaction and perform ethically, as the On the Web box, page 389, suggests.

Neutrality and Objectivity

Since the point of view of group leaders can affect all group procedures, if they suspend judgment and encourage full consideration of all viewpoints, they are likely to appear neutral. **Neutrality** means not taking sides but allowing the weight of members' evidence determine the outcome of group decision making. Most group participants prefer leaders who are not authoritarian. Dogmatic leaders who push their ideas on others come across as arrogant and closed-minded. Members prefer open-mindedness and give high marks to leaders who encourage evaluation, examination, and differing interpretations.

A second point of view of leaders that can affect group procedures is **objectivity,** basing conclusions on facts and evidence rather than on emotion or opinions. Group work will be effective only if conclusions are based on valid evidence. If the goal of groups is to investigate problems systematically and realistically, then leaders' objectivity can make a difference. Discussion will break down when members of groups refuse to accept verified data, disregard reasoning that has been found valid, or reject values tested by human experience.

Neutrality and objectivity are important principles that can guide and direct group activity. The lack of either can have negative results. For example, when leaders are not neutral, they have the potential for imposing their ideas or agenda on group members. When objectivity doesn't exist, group members may not agree on the data concerning the problem, the interpretation of the data, or the values involved in the situation, and they may not be able to reach an agreement on a solution to the problem. Without neutrality and objectivity, groups cannot achieve their greatest potential.

Establishing Procedures

Every formal small-group meeting should be conducted according to a plan that organizes the group's work. This plan, called the group's *procedures,*

On the Web

Ethics of Effective Group Leadership

1. Do not use groups for your own advancement by putting your goals ahead of the group's goals.

2. Don't take credit for the work of others.

3. Do respect others in the group. Groups are effective because of the participation of all, not because of the domination of one person.

4. Work as hard as or harder than the others in the group. Do your fair share.

5. Graciously take whatever responsibility is given to you.

6. Don't force your leadership role onto a group.

Source: R. Gwynne, "Small Group Leadership," Department of Speech Communication, University of Tennessee, Knoxville. Retrieved March 24, 2003, from http://web.utk.edu/~gwynne/Small_Group_Leadership.html.

specifies how the group should operate. Most informal groups, such as book clubs, do not follow a plan.

If the group is meeting for the first time, the person who has convened the group should ask the members to elect a leader. If the members do not know one another, it is a good idea for all participants to introduce themselves before a leader is chosen. If appropriate, the convener might also ask members to tell why they joined the group and what they would like the group to accomplish.

Many groups function more efficiently if someone volunteers or is elected to act as secretary. This person keeps a record of what goes on at every meeting. This record can take the shape of formal minutes that are read at the next meeting or a simple list of topics the group has discussed that members can refer to when necessary. At all meetings, if group members make motions to pass resolutions, each resolution should be recorded exactly as the member worded it, along with the tally of votes for and against it.

After the members have been introduced and someone agrees to take notes, the leader can briefly state what the group's work will be for that meeting. Once the work has been outlined, the discussion is ready to begin.

Many groups structure their time with an **agenda**—a list of all the items that will be discussed during the meeting. In Chapter 10, Small Groups: Characteristics, we discussed the problem-solving sequence. This is an excellent sequence for a group with a single problem to solve. Many groups, however, have a variety of matters to handle during a meeting. These groups are more likely to use an agenda that begins with the reading and approval of the minutes from the last meeting and proceeds to reports of officers, boards, and standing committees; reports of special (ad hoc) committees; special orders; unfinished business; and new business. Figure 11-3 shows a typical agenda.

Throughout the meeting, the leader should give everyone a chance to participate. If the leader includes everyone in the first meeting, it is a good sign that all members' opinions are welcome.

Wood County Area Arts Council
Meeting Agenda
February 1, 2003
A. Approval of January 4, 2003, minutes
B. Treasurer's report
C. Social Chair's report
   1. Valentine's Day update
   2. April social activity plans
D. Special Projects Chair's report
   1. Verdant Gardens Art Project
   2. Council Museum Tour
E. Arts report
F. Committee reports
   1. Program Committee
   2. Fund-raising Committee
G. Correspondence
H. Executive Director's report
I. Unfinished business
   1. Public awareness program
   2. Support for a council brochure
J. New business

Figure 11-3

Agenda

The purpose of the agenda is to keep the meeting on track so that all topics can be covered in the time available. Also, an announced agenda allows group members to anticipate and prepare for the subjects to be discussed.

If possible, group members need to be aware of hidden agendas, because they can interfere with the group's process. **Hidden agendas** are unannounced goals, subjects, or issues that are important to individual members or subgroups but are not on the group's public or stated agenda. For example, in a classroom group one member is more interested in social life than in the topic the group is supposed to be discussing. This person often asks questions about dorm life, football games, or other weekend activities.

In such situations, in order to avoid embarrassing any one member, the group leader might say something like "It might be better if we all tried to stick with the group's assigned topic for now," or "We have a limited amount of time. If we could all keep our comments directed to our topic for today, we might be able to complete our task." Most hidden agendas lose their force when recognized. Often they can be acknowledged and controlled subtly, without causing group members embarrassment or loss of face. It is important not to publicly chastise or condemn group members on whose participation the group must depend.

Helping the Group to Progress

Groups cannot move ahead when members spend too much time dealing with trivia or with a single aspect of a problem. An effective small-group leader will move the group toward the next topic when a sufficient amount of information has been presented, when information is being repeated, or when the discussion becomes too trivial. The leader might say, "I think we are beginning to repeat ourselves. Let's move along to the next issue."

Helping the group move along requires some assertiveness on the part of the leader. Leaders must be willing to interject themselves and enforce the group's agenda. This requires some discretion and diplomacy because group members do not like to be bossed. A leader might say, for example, "Excuse me for interrupting you, Sabrina, but I wonder if we might hear what some of the others are thinking."

Summarizing is one good way to help the group progress. Doing so alerts the group to where it has been, what it has accomplished, where it is now, and where it is going. A final summary and a statement of goals for the next meeting is also a good way to close each group meeting: "Today we had a disagreement over whether we should lease our equipment to outsiders or permit only our own students to use it. At our next meeting, I think we should work to resolve this issue."

Raising Questions

One of the ways a leader can be most helpful is by raising pertinent questions. Sometimes, during discussion, it is easy for a group to lose sight of its original goal. A group of students, for example, might be discussing the issue of date rape and get diverted to the subject of unfriendly law enforcement officials. If the group leader says, "Is this directly related to the problem?" the group will realize that it is not and will get back on the subject.

Sometimes a group will try to discuss a subject but will lack sufficient information. A group discussing faculty and student parking might realize that it doesn't know how many parking places are assigned to each category. The leader may ask someone to find this information. If it is not known, he or she may ask members to count the spaces in the various lots.

Information that the group receives must be evaluated. Some information may be insignificant, irrelevant, or invalid. Appropriate questions for the leader to ask include these: How recent is the information? Who is the source? Might the source be biased? Facts and opinions should be scrutinized carefully for possible errors or misinterpretation.

Focusing on Answers

To accomplish its task, a group needs answers. If the function of the group is to solve a problem, members need to keep their attention on possible solutions. An effective group leader will focus members' attention on the need for answers and will support members who work toward answers.

Focusing on answers involves evaluating alternatives by considering their advantages and disadvantages. A useful leadership role is played by members who ask such questions as these: What consequences are likely to occur? What are the costs going to be? What barriers have to be overcome? How serious are the barriers?

Sometimes solutions call for a plan of action. If your group decides that the only solution to its problem is to demonstrate against the administration, members would be faced with making plans for that demonstration. How are you going to publicize your grievances, get recruits, and carry out the protest? Effective leadership helps a group plan carefully for the action it has decided to take.

Delegating Responsibility

Many people do not want to become leaders because they think that leadership involves too much time and trouble. These people often see a leader as the one who does all the work. This should not be true in any group. A good leader should be able to delegate responsibility to the group's members. If a group is going to do research, for example, the leader could assign some members to go to the library, some to interview experts, and others to coordinate and present the information to the group.

Some leaders do not delegate because they believe they are the only ones who can do the job right. If you are one of these people, you should consider taking a risk and letting some of the other people do some of the work. You might be surprised how well they do it. Also, sharing the work makes participants feel more involved and committed.

Encouraging Social Interaction

Social interaction occurs in a group when people feel recognized and accepted by other members. The more friendliness, mutual trust, and respect exhibited, the more likely the members are to find pleasure in the group and work hard to accomplish its goals. Further, group discussions are more likely to be of high quality when group members participate fully in the process (Mayer, 1998). The use of first names and of such words as *we, us,* and *our* will help group members feel a sense of belonging. The group leader can also strengthen social interaction by encouraging shy members to speak, by complimenting worthwhile contributions, and by praising the overall accomplishments of the group. Group leaders should also plan to leave a little time before and after a meeting so that members can socialize.

■ PARTICIPATING IN GROUP DISCUSSION

To see an example of the importance of task roles, view "Small Group Communication," clip #6 on the CD.

Groups, like individuals, can be defined as mature or immature. Often an immature group is a new one. It is overly dependent on its leader and, in the beginning, is often passive and unorganized. As the group matures, it is able to function independently of its leader, and its members become actively involved and capable of organizing their discussions (Hersey & Blanchard, 1982, pp. 152–55).

Although most groups have a specified leader, the leader does not have total responsibility for giving the discussion a direction or for moving the group along. In most groups, an individual member may temporarily take over the leadership from time to time. For example, a member who temporarily leads a group may have more information or experience in a certain area than the usual leader.

Individual group members continue to play the same roles in groups as they do in any other communication. A person who likes to take charge is likely to want the role of group leader, while a person who is shy will be as hesitant in a group as in any other kind of communication. In addition to the roles we play in life, however, some roles are specific to small-group communication. Kenneth Benne and Paul Sheats (1948), pioneers in the classification of functional roles in groups, have identified the various behaviors associated with leadership in organizations and groups. For people interested in improving their skill in functional leadership, the task and/or maintenance roles Benne and Sheats describe offer a variety of different possibilities (pp. 41–49).

Task Roles

Task roles are roles that help get the job done. Persons who play these roles help the group come up with new ideas, aid in collecting and organizing information, and analyze the information that exists. Task roles are not limited to any one individual; they may be interchanged among the members as the group goes about its job. Following are some of the common task roles.

Initiators-Expediters. Members who act as *initiators-expediters*–by suggesting new ideas, goals, solutions, and approaches—are often the most creative and energetic of the group. When the group gets bogged down, they

Another Point of View

There are gender issues connected with task and maintenance roles, of course. The following might be categorized under the task role "Information Giver:"

Many women don't realize until they've moved a few rungs up the workplace ladder that men sometimes simply ignore what women say. If you haven't experienced this yet, you may be shocked the first time it happens to you. In fact, it can still be a surprise to me (although luckily it doesn't happen very often anymore). The story we hear over and over is that a woman offers an idea in a meeting and no one responds. The meeting proceeds as if she hadn't spoken. Later in the meeting, a man at the table rephrases the woman's idea, people grab at it, and it takes off. The man, of course, gets the kudos. This happens more frequently than you may imagine, which will offer small comfort when it happens to you. In any case, you must find a way to deal with it.

Questions

1. Have you ever been in a group discussion where this has happened? What did you think about it?

2. What are some strategies that can be used for getting yourself heard in a group or meeting?

3. When you are in a group, and when a person makes a comment that gets no response from anyone in the group, yet later in the group discussion the very same point is made by someone else—as if the point were never made before—is there anything that can be done right there and then, that would protect or at least recognize the person who first made the comment, and yet not admonish, chastise, or embarrass the person who has most recently made the very same comment? What might be said or done?

Source: S. Wellington, *Be Your Own Mentor: Strategies from Top Women on the Secrets of Success,* (New York: Random House, 2001), p. 90.

are likely to make such statements as "What if we tried. . . ." or "I wonder if . . . would solve our problem."

Initiators-expediters often can suggest a new direction or can prevent the group from losing sight of its objectives. They are not afraid to jump in and give assistance when the group is in trouble. Often, too, they are the ones who hold the light so that others can see the path.

Information Givers and Seekers. Individual members may both seek information and give it. Since lots of information will lead to better discussion, many members will play the roles of information givers and seekers. *Information givers* are often the best-informed members of the group. They might have had more experience with the subject or even be experts on it.

The more complex the subject, the greater the group's need for *information seekers.* These are people who are willing to go out and research the subject. They might agree to interview experts, go to the library, or initiate an Internet investigation. If the group has very little information on a subject, it might be necessary for several members to play the role of information seeker.

The roles of information giver and seeker are the most important in any group. The information the group gets provides the foundation for the entire discussion. The more group members who play these roles, the better the quality of group discussion.

Critics-Analyzers. *Critics-analyzers* are individuals who look at the good and bad points in the information the group has gathered. These people see the points that need more elaboration, and they discover information that has been left out.

The critic-analyzer is able to look at the total picture and see how everything fits together. People who play this role usually have an excellent sense of organization. Often they can help keep the group on track: "We have mentioned this point twice. Maybe we need to discuss it in more depth." "Maybe we should go back and look at this information again. Something seems to be missing."

Maintenance Roles

People who play **maintenance roles** focus on the emotional tone of the meeting. Since no one wants to spend his or her entire time being logical, gathering information, and doing the job, it is important that some emotional needs be met. People who play maintenance roles meet these needs by encouraging, harmonizing, regulating, and observing.

Encouragers. *Encouragers* praise and commend contributions and group achievements: "You really did a good job of gathering this information. Now we can dig in and work."

The best encouragers are active listeners. They help in rephrasing points to achieve greater clarity. They do not make negative judgments about other members or their opinions. Encouragers make people feel good about themselves and their contributions.

Harmonizers-Compromisers. Members who help to resolve conflict in the group, who settle arguments and disagreements through mediation, are the *harmonizers-compromisers.* People who play this role are skillful at discovering solutions acceptable to everyone. Harmonizers-compromisers are especially effective when they remind group members that group goals are

Knowing this is a work-related, task-oriented, problem-solving group, what are the task and maintenance roles being played at this point in the discussion by each of the group members?

Consider This

Dysfunctional Roles

Occasionally, things in a group do not proceed as planned. There may be many reasons for weak discussions. One may be that a person or persons in the group are playing "individual" or dysfunctional roles. Recognizing these roles will help both leaders and members suppress, control, or compensate for their influence. **Dysfunctional, or individual, roles** include the following:

- The *aggressor* may work in many ways—deflating the status of others; expressing disapproval of the values, acts, or feelings of others; attacking the group or the problem it is working on; joking aggressively; showing envy toward another's contribution by trying to take credit for it; and so on.

- The *blocker* tends to be negativistic and stubbornly resistant, disagreeing and opposing without or beyond "reason" and attempting to maintain or bring back an issue after the group has rejected or bypassed it.

- The *recognition-seeker* works in various ways to call attention to himself or herself, whether through boasting, reporting on personal achievements, acting in unusual ways, struggling to prevent his or her being placed in an "inferior" position, and so on.

- The *self-confessor* uses the audience opportunity which the group setting provides to express personal, non-group-oriented, "feeling," "insight," "ideology," and so on.

- The *playboy* makes a display of his or her lack of involvement in the group's processes. This may take the form of cynicism, nonchalance, horseplay, and other more or less studied forms of "out of field" behavior.

- The *dominator* tries to assert authority or superiority by manipulating the group or certain members of the group. This domination may take the form of flattering others, asserting a superior status or right to attention, giving directions authoritatively, interrupting the contributions of others, and so on.

- The *help-seeker* attempts to call forth a "sympathy" response from other group members or from the whole group, whether through expressions of insecurity, personal confusion, or depreciation of himself or herself beyond "reason."

- The *special-interest pleader* speaks for the "small-business man," the "grassroots" community, the "housewife," "labor," and the like, usually cloaking his or her own prejudices or biases in the stereotype which best fits his or her individual need.

Just one cautionary note regarding a group's move to suppress individuals playing any of these roles: By suppressing such action, a group may also inhibit, restrict, or suppress comments, suggestions, or input from some of the group's best participants. Participants who play a dysfunctional role at one point may play highly constructive, contributing roles at other points.

If members find themselves playing any of these dysfunctional, or individual, roles and they realize such role playing is not in the best interests of the group as a whole, self-discipline is one of the best ways to control the influence. Consider the good of the whole as more important than the good of any individual part of that whole.

Source: Kenneth D. Benne and Paul Sheats, "Functional Roles of Group Members," *Journal of Social Issues* 4(2) (1948): 41–49.

more important than individual needs: "I know you would like the library open on Sunday morning, but we have to find the times that are best for everybody."

Regulators. As their name implies, *regulators* help regulate group discussion by gently reminding members of the agenda or of the point they were discussing when they digressed: "We seem to be wandering a little. Now, we were discussing. . ."

Good regulators also find ways to give everyone a chance to speak: "Vilma, you haven't said anything. Do you have any feelings on this subject?" Sometimes the regulator has to stop someone who has been talking too much: "Roberto, you have made several interesting points. Let's see what some of the others think of them." A regulator who is too authoritarian, however, might find that others resent him or her. In this role, it is important to word statements or questions tactfully.

Observers. Observers aid in the group's cohesiveness. They are sensitive to the needs of each member: "I think we have ignored the point that John just made. Maybe we should take some time to discuss it."

■ CONFLICT IN GROUPS

When individuals meet in a group to solve a problem, there's no guarantee of agreement. **Conflict**—expressed struggle between at least two individuals who perceive incompatible goals or interference from others in achieving their goals—might arise at any stage of discussion: in defining the problem, in deciding how to go about solving it, or in choosing the solution.

Group conflict generally occurs for one of several reasons: procedure, power, or work distribution.

- *Procedure.* The first source of conflict, and perhaps the easiest to eliminate, is differing views on procedure. How often should the group meet? What form should the minutes take? To keep such conflict from occurring, the group members should discuss and resolve issues of procedure at the first meeting. If they do so, the group is not likely to face further conflict in this area.

- *Power.* The second source of conflict is the desire of individual members for power. Research has found that in business and corporate settings a group often becomes a focal point for power struggles (Goleman, 1990, pp. 37, 41). However, power struggles are not so common in classroom groups. If one person wants power, the problem is often solved by making him or her the chair. If this doesn't solve the problem and members continue their power struggle, the group will probably not work very efficiently.

- *Work distribution.* The third source of conflict, and one of the greatest in classroom groups, is that some members often work harder than others. When a lot of work must be done and some people do very little, the harder workers feel anger and hostility—especially if the group is working for a grade. Like power struggles, this kind of conflict is difficult to resolve. Since few students are willing to tell the instructor about such inequality, the harder workers' only hope is to confront the group members who are not working and use peer pressure to persuade them to change. If this approach doesn't succeed, it might console the harder workers to know that most instructors have a good idea of who does the work and who doesn't.

Although these three kinds of conflict can interfere with group work, not all conflict is harmful. The fourth kind of conflict, conflict about substantive issues, can be rewarding. Let's look at substantive conflict more closely.

The Value of Substantive Conflict

Substantive conflict occurs when people have different reactions to an idea. It is likely to occur when any important and controversial idea is being discussed. As in all exchanges of ideas, people's opinions and perceptions are influenced by their culture, upbringing, education, and experience. These perceptions cause them to react differently to ideas and can create conflict in a group. For example, a classroom group is assigned the question of whether a physician should be able to help a suffering patient commit suicide. Even though group members may not have read anything on this subject, when they hear the discussion question, they are still likely to have opinions based on their perceptions. Ricardo, 18 years old and a devout Catholic, is shocked by the possibility. He thinks, "What's there to discuss? Everyone should be against this idea." However, Maria, another group member, who is 40 years old and has returned to school, has another reaction. She thinks, "I wish someone had helped my mother to die. She went through terrible suffering in the last weeks of her life."

Although two group members start out strongly disagreeing, they will not necessarily continue to do so. When the group members begin their research, they read current cases and report their findings to the group. One group member researches the events in the life of Dr. Jack Kevorkian and provides a case-by-case historical base for group analysis. Another member brings in a *Time* magazine article about a devout Catholic family who let their mother commit suicide. Still another student discovers the case of a doctor who told his patient how many barbiturates she would need to take to kill herself. The doctor had been treating this patient for many years and knew that her disease would not respond to treatment.

As the group discovers this information, Maria and Ricardo find that because they have more information, their opinions are beginning to shift. Maria realizes that a physician-aided suicide may take different forms, some less preferable than others. Ricardo is also adjusting his point of view. Maria has told the group about her mother's suffering, and Ricardo, finding himself very moved by her account, begins to question his previous position.

However this group resolves its question, the conflicts of substance between Maria and Ricardo have had a good effect on the group—especially since both have been willing to hear new information and listen to different points of view. By the time the group completes the project, its members will have a better understanding of the ideas and can make a better decision. Also, because group members have worked together to learn and the learning has been rewarding, the group has become more cohesive.

Although conflict in a group may be disruptive, it can work in the group's favor. Substantive conflict can help group members to see other points of view and motivate them to seek additional information.

Managing Group Conflict

There are times when conflict can slow a group down or even bring it to a screeching halt. When conflict arises, the group leader has to step in and try to help group members resolve it. The approach the leader takes should depend on the seriousness of the conflict. Robert Blake and Jane Mouton, who have written about ways to resolve conflict, suggest five ways of managing it (Blake & Mouton, 1978, p. 11). See Table 11-1.

Avoidance

Sometimes groups argue over points that are so minor they are not worth the time they take up. If the leader sees this happening, she or he should suggest that the issue doesn't seem very important and that the group should move to another topic. For example, when one group disagreed about the time its banquet should begin, the leader pointed out that there was little difference between 6:30 PM and 7 PM and that it would be more productive to choose the earlier time and move on. Another method of resolving simple conflicts is flipping a coin.

Accommodation

Accommodation occurs when people on one side of an issue give in to those on the other side. If a leader sees accommodation as a possibility, he or she should attempt to find out how strongly people feel about the sides they have taken. If the issue is not really important to one side, the leader might suggest that that side give in. For example, when a group was planning a children's day, members argued over whether they should spend money for a clown or for pony rides. The members who favored pony rides decided that children would also enjoy a clown, so they were willing to give in.

Competition

Competition can cause considerable harm to a group and must be channeled to promote group goals. It occurs when members on one side care more about winning than about the other members' feelings. When a leader sees competition rising, she or he should try to deflect it before members get entrenched in their positions. Sometimes individual members feel competitive with one another, and they use the group sessions to work out their feelings. If this is happening, the leader might point out to each member privately that the conflict is keeping the group from working together.

Collaboration

In *collaboration*, conflicting parties try to work together to meet each other's needs. Collaborators do not attack one another; instead, they try to understand opposing points of view and work hard to stay away from anything that might harm the group's relationships. For example, a faculty committee was asked to choose a curriculum proposal to send to the state for funding.

Table 11-1 *Conflict Management Approaches, Objectives, Rationales, and Outcomes*

Approach	Objective and Typical Responses	Supporting Rationale	Likely Outcome
Avoiding	Avoid having to deal with conflict. "I'm neutral on that issue. Let me think about it."	Disagreements are inherently bad because they create tension.	Interpersonal problems don't get resolved. They can cause long-term frustration which will be manifested in a variety of ways.
Accommodating	Don't upset the other person. "How can I help you feel good about this? My position isn't important enough to risk bad feelings between us."	Maintaining harmonious relationships should be our top priority.	Other person is likely to take advantage of you.
Competing	Get your way. "I know what's right. Don't question my judgment or authority."	Better to risk causing a few hard feelings than to abandon a position you're committed to.	You will feel vindicated, and the other party will feel defeated and possibly humiliated.
Collaborating	Solve the problem together. "This is my position. What's yours? I'm committed to finding the best possible solution."	Positions of both parties are equally important. Equal emphasis should be placed on quality of outcome and fairness of decision-making process.	The problem will most likely be resolved. Both parties will be committed to solution and satisfied that they have been treated fairly.
Compromising	Reach an agreement quickly. "Let's search for a mutually agreeable solution."	Prolonged conflicts distract people from their work, take time, and engender bitter feelings.	Participants become conditioned to seek expedient rather than effective long-term solutions.

Source: J. Ware & L. Barnes, "Managing interpersonal conflict." In L. A. Mainiero & C. L. Tromley, *Developing Managerial Skills of Organizational Behavior,* (Englewood Cliffs, NJ: Prentice-Hall, 1989), pp. 53–62. Adapted from: (No author). *Inls 180: Communication Processes: Notes on Conflict Management.* Spring 1998. Retrieved March 24, 2003, from http://www.ils.unc.edu/daniel/180/conflict.html.

Since the committee received two proposals—one for a women's studies minor and the other for a leadership minor—the members had to make a choice. Both proposals were well thought out and clearly written, but members of the committee were divided as to which proposal they favored. After many hours of discussion, they decided to choose the women's studies proposal, but they saw many points in the leadership proposal that could make the women's studies proposal even stronger. By combining the two proposals, they had a true collaboration.

Compromise

In *compromise*, each side has to give up something to get what it wants. This involves a kind of bargaining in which each side makes an offer of what it will sacrifice. Compromise will work only when each side believes that what it gets is fair and that it has gained at least a partial victory. For example, a fraternity was planning its annual banquet and dance. One side favored holding it at the Elks hall and making it a formal party, whereas the other side wanted to hold it at a rustic lodge and make it a casual party. The group finally compromised: The party would be held at the Elks, but it would be informal.

■ EVALUATING GROUP PERFORMANCE

Since you are learning how groups work, toward the end of each meeting your group should evaluate its performance. The first and most important question your group should ask is whether it made progress toward finishing its job or solving its problem. Your instructor may have evaluation forms to help you answer this question. Another way of evaluating group work is to have each member take one minute to write down what the group has accomplished during its session and then compare the notes with other members.

If the group has not made progress during its session, it is useful to answer the following questions: Did members stick to the topic? Did everyone come prepared with the material the group needed? Was everyone able to participate and contribute? Did the atmosphere encourage members to try to understand other members' points of view? Was time used efficiently? Was the leader skillful in helping members participate and voice their opinions? If the group answers "no" to any of these questions, it will have an idea of where it needs to make improvements.

The group should also consider whether the process of group work has been rewarding. Do members feel good about what they accomplished? Were they satisfied with the roles they played? Would they like to work with this group again?

Successful work in groups can be rewarding, exhilarating, or, even fun. The key is putting the good of the group ahead of any individual self-interest. Group work gives you a chance to play an active role in your own learning. Therefore, when you have an opportunity to work in a group, make your best effort. Even working in a classroom setting prepares you for the workplace and for participation in the life of your community.

Consider This

Managing Cultural Differences

With the shift in our nation's demographics, the makeup of the workforce has changed as well. Never before has it been so diverse. While such diversity can serve as a strategic advantage for organizations, it is likely to pose challenges for those working in groups, whether small groups, large groups, or team efforts.

The Challenges of Diversity

Diversity poses challenges when group members bring stereotypes and prejudices to groups. It poses even greater challenges when the group-member constituency consists of people with differing educational, economic, and cultural backgrounds.

How does a group leader develop trust, value differences, and devise not just ways to benefit from member diversity, but ways, too, to improve group efficiency, facilitate effective communication, and succeed in group efforts? Although the answers may appear easy, they are difficult to apply in practice.

Attitudes That Encourage Diversity

Much of what can be accomplished in circumstances where diversity exists, depends on attitude. For example, how much more is likely to be accomplished if one appreciates and values diversity? If one appreciates and values the natural communication styles of others? If one appreciates and values the potential contribution and resources of a diverse audience?

Such an attitude is likely to facilitate an open exchange of ideas and active listening to the views of others. Also, it is likely to assist in anticipating communication differences. When differences can be anticipated, it is less likely leaders will be blind-sided in group situations. They will be able, instead, to take responsibility, consider the good of the group or organization as a whole, put the need for effective communication first, believe that the end of group deliberation will be successful for all, and strive, first, to understand others before being understood by others.

Behaviors That Support Diversity

Leaders must reveal behavior that is consistent with both attitude and circumstance. Some important considerations for leaders having to deal with diversity include speaking slowly and clearly; using simple, frequently used words; being very careful with translations; avoiding slang, colloquialisms, and idiomatic expressions; making one point at a time; and adapting in the best manner possible, their tone of voice, style, and behavior to what is culturally acceptable to their listeners.

Success in Dealing with Diversity

Cultural, gender, and racial differences can hamper group efficiency; however, with the proper attitude and careful application of the behaviors (skills) above, group work is likely to improve, communication is likely to become more fluid, and levels of commitment to the group and organization are likely to grow stronger.

Assess Yourself

Do You Have What it Takes to Be a Leader?*

Directions: Indicate the degree to which you agree or disagree with each statement by the following scale:

5= Strongly agree
4 = Mildly agree
3 = Agree and disagree equally
2 = Mildly disagree
1 = Strongly disagree

Circle your response following each statement. When you have finished all seventeen statements, add up your responses, and put your total points in the "Total Points" blank.

Statement	Response
1. I easily and comfortably question others' ideas and opinions.	5 4 3 2 1
2. I strive to find out and meet the needs of other group members.	5 4 3 2 1
3. I feel good when I measure the results of my hard work, rather than counting the time it took.	5 4 3 2 1
4. I feel comfortable thinking of others' needs.	5 4 3 2 1
5. I readily listen to the opinions of others.	5 4 3 2 1
6. I feel comfortable sharing power and control.	5 4 3 2 1
7. I seek out and move on to new opportunities.	5 4 3 2 1
8. I express my feelings easily to others.	5 4 3 2 1
9. I am able to easily share my accomplishments with others.	5 4 3 2 1
10. I am aware of my own strengths and weaknesses.	5 4 3 2 1
11. I feel comfortable with conflict.	5 4 3 2 1
12. I feel comfortable with change and making change.	5 4 3 2 1
13. I make goals.	5 4 3 2 1
14. I am able to motivate others.	5 4 3 2 1
15. I am constantly looking for ways to improve.	5 4 3 2 1
16. I feel comfortable knowing people look at me as a model for what is good.	5 4 3 2 1
17. In general I am a confident person.	5 4 3 2 1

TOTAL POINTS _____

Go to the *Communicating Effectively* CD-ROM to see your results and learn how to evaluate your attitudes and feelings.

Source: Adapted from "Leadership Self-Assessment," ICANS (Integrated Curriculum for Achieving Necessary Skills), Washington State Board for Community and Technical Colleges, Washington State Employment Security, Washington Workforce Training and Education Coordinating Board, Adult Basic and Literacy Educators, P.O. Box 42496, 711 Capitol Blvd., Olympia, WA 98504. Retrieved March 24, 2003, from http://www.literacynet.org/icans/chapter05/leadership.html.

Chapter Review

One characteristic that all leaders have in common is that they exert influence; thus, a leader is a person who influences the behavior of one or more people. They exert influence by rewarding followers, threatening to punish followers, using their position of power, knowing more than anyone else, or because of their personality. One theory of leadership is that people become leaders because of their personalities and the situations in which they find themselves. These two factors work together.

There are five approaches to leadership. Functional leadership occurs when each member of the group takes on leadership responsibilities depending on the group's task. There are three traditional leadership styles: Authoritarian leaders take charge of a group, especially in situations where the group has little information or experience. Democratic leaders give everyone a chance to participate in decision making, especially in situations where members are equal in status, education, and experience and when there is sufficient time to solve the problem. Laissez-faire leaders do little leading. This kind of leadership works best in self-help groups. Situational leaders can adopt different leadership styles depending on the situation. Using the telling style, they focus more on the task and less on the group. In the selling style, leaders state the problem and decide what to do, then sell the other group members on the idea. Using the participating style, they state the problem but immediately consult with group members. In the delegating style, they hang back and let members plan and execute the job.

A group leader has six responsibilities: to establish procedures, keep the group moving, raise questions, focus on answers, delegate responsibilities, and encourage social interaction.

Participants in group discussion play a variety of roles. Members in task roles focus on getting the job done; members in maintenance roles are concerned with the emotional tone of the group.

Substantive conflict in groups can be disruptive, but it can also help group members come to better decisions. One important task of a group leader is to manage conflict. He or she should determine how serious the conflict is and take one of the following approaches: avoidance, accommodation, competition, collaboration, or compromise.

Questions to Review

1. What are the five sources of influences for leaders?

2. How do people become leaders?

3. As a member of a group, what are your obligations to functional leadership in the group? What are the group elements that are likely to affect your commitment to functional leadership?

4. Have there been any examples of functional leadership in groups where you have been a member? Did it work well? Badly? Can you explain why?

5. Compare and contrast functional leadership with the authoritarian, democratic, and laissez-faire leadership approaches. What are the overall strengths and weaknesses of functional leadership when placed side by side with these other leadership approaches?

6. What value do you see in situational leadership?

7. Can you distinguish among telling, selling, participating, and delegating?

8. What are the differences among leadership factors, group factors, and situational factors when it comes to deciding on a leadership approach? Which are likely to have the greatest influence on deciding which situational leadership style to use?

9. With respect to actually leading a group discussion, what aspects would be the most troublesome for you to accomplish? Why?

10. Why is it that most people have difficulty playing a wide variety of task and maintenance roles when they are participating in group discussions?

11. When a member or members of your group are playing dysfunctional roles, as the leader of the group, how would you go about controlling their behavior so that the good of the group as a whole is not seriously threatened or jeopardized?

12. Do you see the value of conflict? What do you normally do when faced with conflict situations? As a leader of a group, what personal strengths or weaknesses would you anticipate in managing group conflict?

13. Overall, do you rate yourself as an effective group leader? Effective group member? Why or why not? What growth areas could you emphasize to increase your effectiveness as a leader? As a member?

Go to the self-quizzes on the *Communicating Effectively* CD-ROM (side 2, track 10) and the Online Learning Center at mhhe.com/hybels7 to test your knowledge of the chapter concepts.

References

Abrams, R. (1999). *Wear clean underwear: Business wisdom from mom.* New York: Villard Books (a division of Random House, Inc.).

Arnold, H. J., & D. C. Feldman (1986). *Organizational behavior.* New York: McGraw-Hill.

Baron, R. A., & P. B. Paulus (1991). *Understanding human relations,* 2nd ed. Boston: Allyn and Bacon.

Benne, K. D., & P. Sheats (1948). "Functional roles of group members." *Journal of Social Issues* 4, 41–49.

Blake, R. R., & J. S. Mouton (1964). *The managerial grid.* Houston: Gulf Publishing.

_____ (1978). *The new managerial grid.* Houston: Gulf Publishing.

Goleman, D. (1990, December 25). "The group and the self: New focus on a cultural rift." *New York Times,* 37, 41.

Hargrove, R. (2001). *E-leader: Reinventing leadership in a connected economy.* Cambridge, MA: Perseus Publishing.

Hersey, P., & K. H. Blanchard (1982). *Management of organizational behavior: Utilizing human resources,* 4th ed. Englewood Cliffs, NJ: Prentice-Hall.

Hollingshead, A. B. (1996). "Information suppression and status persistence in group decision making: The effects of communication media." *Human Communication Research* 23:2, 193–219.

Mayer, M. E. (1998, Summer). "Behaviors leading to more effective decisions in small groups embedded in organizations." *Communication Reports.* 11:2, 131.

McGee-Cooper, A., & G. Looper (2001). "Innovations in management series." Pegasus Communications. Book review by L. C. Spears (2002). *The essentials of servant-leadership: Principles in practice.* The Robert K. Greenleaf Center for Servant-Leadership, Indianapolis, IN. Retrieved March 24, 2003, from http://www.greenleaf.org/ leadership/read-about-it/Servant-Leadership-Articles-Book-Reviews.html.

Salazar, A. J. (1996, December). "Ambiguity and communication effects on small group decision-making performance." *Human Communication Research* 23:2.

Zigarmi, P., D. Zigarmi, & K. H. Blanchard (1985). *Leadership and the one minute manager: Increasing effectiveness through situational leadership.* New York: William Morrow & Co.

Further Reading

Belasco, J. A., & J. L. Stead (1999). *Soaring with the phoenix: Renewing the vision, reviving the spirit, and recreating the success of your company*. New York: Warner Books. The authors base their advice for renewing companies on five overarching principles. Create your own future, utilize your connections, help others learn, help others succeed, and take ownership of your company and your life. Their program includes practical ways to motivate employees, make learning an adventure, create a culture that celebrates performance, and build a customer-focused, people-based organization. An excellent, readable, motivational book by two business professionals.

Borisoff, D., & D. A. Victor (1998). *Conflict management: A communication skills approach*, 2nd ed. Boston: Allyn and Bacon. The authors offer useful advice on how to manage the conflicts that arise on the job and in personal relationships. They provide a five-step model (assessment, acknowledgment, attitude, action, and analysis) for approaching and analyzing interpersonal conflict, and then they apply the model repeatedly to different topics. A book grounded in theory and yet full of readable, practical advice.

Fisher, R., J. Richardson, & A. Sharp (1999). *Getting it done: How to lead when you're in charge*. New York: HarperBusiness. The authors advance the idea of lateral leadership, which consists of five elements: clarifying the purpose of what you're trying to accomplish; understanding how to harness the power of organized thought; learning how to integrate thinking and doing; getting yourself and your team engaged; and learning how to give feedback on what's been accomplished. A practical guide for leading through ambiguity and unclear lines of authority.

Greenhalgh, L. (2001). *Managing strategic relationships: The key to business success*. New York: The Free Press (a division of Simon & Schuster, Inc.). Most effective leaders today must be managers of others. Greenhalgh focuses on what managers need to know—and do—to be effective in their daily lives. He brings together perspectives from clinical psychology, economics, social psychology, anthropology, political science, organizational behavior, business history, sociology, legal studies, industrial psychology, labor studies, feminist studies, organization theory, and marketing. Greenhalgh claims that relational negotiations are crucial to managerial effectiveness, and this is precisely why his book treats negotiation in the transactional context, and why this book is so important for all leaders to read.

Hargrove, R. (2001). *E-leader: Reinventing leadership in a connected economy*. Cambridge, MA: Perseus Publishers. Hargrove contends that the most profound implication of the Internet revolution has to do with leadership. What is both interesting and useful in this book is the number of shifts leaders need to make to succeed in the new e-economy. Each chapter includes a shift from: (1) CEO as steward to CEO as entrepreneur, (2) game-player to game-changer, (3) top-down to lateral leadership, (4) production-builder-in-chief to brand-builder-in-chief, (5) a "me" point of view to a "you" point of view, (6) being a great e-tailer to being a great logistician, and (7) being a manager/technician to being a coach/mentor. With short sections, comfortable vocabulary, and sections that outline the changes necessary, this is a useful and insightful book.

Kelsey, D., P. Plumb, & K. Rudy (1999). *Great meetings!: How to facilitate like a pro*. Portland, ME: Hanson Park Press. This is a user-friendly resource book designed to help meeting leaders, facilitators, and participants. More than just a "how-to-have-a-meeting" book, this is a toolbox for group development. The authors present specific steps for planning and facilitating meetings. Their topics include: what is facilitation, getting to know your group, preparing for a meeting, designing a great meeting, problem-solving process tools, maximizing your group's potential, promoting positive communication, managing conflict, intervening, and using graphics. Straightforward and engaging.

Lulofs, R. S., & D. D. Cahn (2000). *Conflict: From theory to action*. Boston: Allyn and Bacon. This text is based on the assumption that effective behavior in conflict situations requires that participants analyze the situation and choose behavior appropriate to it, without sacrificing their own values and beliefs. This book covers all the essentials in an effective, thorough, and well-researched manner, and it adds to what others have done. Each chapter provides brief narratives and longer case studies—personal descriptions of conflict situations—that help readers apply the theory discussed. A solid volume for serious students.

Manz, C. C., & H. P. Sims, Jr. (2001). *The new super-leadership: Leading others to lead themselves.* San Francisco: Berrett-Koehler Publishers. This is a practical, how-to approach for developing leaders. In Chapter 2 the authors review the strengths and weaknesses of other styles of leadership and clearly differentiate the SuperLeader from previous leaders. This is an easy-to-read motivational book that even approaches the problem of self-leadership and offers strategies for leading the one in the mirror. With numerous examples and a number of effective profiles, they provide a user-friendly approach to effective leadership in today's business world.

(No author, no date). "Module V: Leading a multicultural organization." Retrieved March 24, 2003, from http://p2001.health.org/Cti03/cti03ttl.htm. Although this module is intended for workshop participants, the information provided on leading a multicultural organization (pp. 6–8) is invaluable. Besides the simple observations, there is material on the three important considerations in developing empowering leadership—trust, power, and influence—as well as information on barriers to empowering leadership. There are many good insights here that would be important to anyone who must lead in a multicultural environment.

(No author, no date). "A toolkit for volunteer leaders: Small group dynamics L-4." University of Nebraska–Lincoln. Retrieved March 24, 2003, from http://4h.unl.edu/volun/arlen/small.htm. The article discusses communication, content versus process, decision influence, task versus relationship, roles, membership, feelings, norms, group atmosphere, and group maturity. There is an observation sheet, questions for discussion, guidelines for leading small-group discussions, as well as group techniques.

Zigarmi, P., D. Zigarmi, & K. H. Blanchard (1985). *Leadership and the one-minute manager: Increasing effectiveness through situational leadership.* New York: William Morrow & Company. Although only 112 pages in length, although the information is presented in a storylike manner, and although the date makes it look seriously out-of-date, this is a classic book on situational leadership. Situational leadership and its use in management is defined explicitly with the help of common examples in a business environment. Becoming a situational leader involves (1) starting with goals that are clear to both the leader and followers, (2) working with people to diagnose both their competence and commitment, (3) deciding what leadership style is most appropriate for the individual, and (4) following through with reprimands or praisings. This is a synthesis of major leadership styles, and it is written in a very simple, but clear, style.

Part Four

Communicating in Public

Chapter 12

Getting Started

Objectives

After reading this chapter, you should be able to:

- Choose a topic for a speech.
- Narrow the topic to make it manageable.
- Assess whether the topic is appropriate for the audience, you, and the speech occasion.
- State a general purpose for your speech.
- Distinguish between an informative speech and a persuasive speech.
- State a specific purpose for your speech.
- State a central idea for your speech.
- Make some inferences about your audience's knowledge, attitudes, and interests.

Key Terms and Concepts

Use the Communicating Effectively CD-ROM and Online Learning Center at mhhe.com/hybels7 to further your understanding of the following terms.

Audience analysis 434	General purpose 427	Persuasive speech 428
Central idea 431	Informative speech 427	Specific purpose 429
Demographic analysis 437	Partitioning 425	Web portal 418
	Personal inventory 416	

■ A QUICK GUIDE TO PUBLIC SPEAKING

PREPARATION

Focus on your audience. The focus of all public speaking is the listeners—to gain a response from the audience. If you can get them to think, feel, or act in a certain way, you have achieved a measure of success. To accomplish this, you need to discover as much as you can about them and adapt your speech to their specific needs and interests.

Find a good topic. Select a topic that interests both you and your listeners and one on which you can complete some research.

Choose your purpose and central ideas. Choose your general purpose (to inform, to persuade, etc.), your specific purpose (what you want to achieve with your listeners), and your central ideas (a one-sentence statement of your message) with your specific audience in mind.

Carefully organize your speech. Devise two or three main points you want to explain and develop that will support your central idea.

Find strong support. Use personal experience, examples, facts, expert opinions, and statistics to develop each main point.

Use transitions. Smooth bridges are needed to help listeners know where you have been in the speech, where you are, and where you are going. Anytime you jump to a new point, it is helpful to have a signpost indicate the move: "My second reason is. . . ."

Have an effective introduction. Begin your speech with information that will grasp listener attention and make them want to listen to the rest of your speech. Fascinating stories, intriguing questions, interesting facts and statistics, or engaging quotations are great attention-getters.

Develop a strong conclusion. Summarize the key points of your speech. Because it comes last in the speech, what you say in your conclusion is most likely to be remembered by your listeners.

Use an outline. Put all parts of the speech (introduction, main points, transitions, and conclusion) into an outline. Everything in the outline should explain, illustrate, or prove your central idea.

Prepare a speaking outline. From your complete outline, prepare a key-word outline that you will use when you deliver your speech.

Practice until you feel comfortable. Go over your speech using your key-word outline only. Speak your ideas differently each time you give your speech. Don't memorize it word-for-word.

Delivery

Reveal self-confidence. Strength comes from knowing your material, feeling you have something to share with your listeners, and having a positive attitude about yourself.

Channel your nervousness. Use it as a source of energy. Take a few deep breaths on the way to the lectern, pause before beginning your speech, and strive to be vital, enthusiastic, and involved.

Begin your speech. Walk confidently to the lectern. Arrange your notes, get your first sentence firmly in your mind, look directly at your listeners, and begin your speech. Throughout your speech, maintain eye contact, be expressive, and speak clearly.

Use your notes sparingly. Notes should never be a crutch. Avoid reading them or staring at them absentmindedly. Use them occasionally to pick up your next point.

End your speech with strength. After your conclusion, pause a few moments and, if appropriate, ask if there are any questions. The impressions you give as you move away from the lectern contribute to the overall effectiveness of you and your message.

FROM GRADE SCHOOL THROUGH HIGH SCHOOL JANE AVOIDED *speaking up in class or any public speaking. She wasn't shy; in fact she was outgoing and popular. She was comfortable with friends. Even in front of crowds, as a cheerleader, she was usually at ease, feeling confident of her talent, as long as she didn't have to speak. But answering questions in class was hard. Talking to teachers and older people was not easy for her. And when she had to speak in front of class, she felt very nervous, both before the speech and especially during it. She got tense, her voice quavered, she forgot what she wanted to say, her knees got weak, she thought she would really mess up. . . .*

Jane really wanted to be an actress and majored in Theater and Speech Communication in college. She knew she had to conquer the speech phobia. She tried and tried to confront the fears by talking in certain classes. Her determination to over-come stage fright also motivated her to prepare carefully for small parts in plays. She even tried out for the debate team but didn't make it. Later she had a chance to appear on the campus radio as a news announcer. She was scared, but she did it.

Eventually, as a senior, Jane became one of the anchorpersons on the campus TV news. She was very attractive; other students seemed envious; and she gained confi-dence. A few months after she graduated, she found work as a TV reporter for a small station. It was scary but two years later she was coanchor of the local evening news. As she became more experienced, she noticed an interesting thing happening—she became less and less uptight while performing, but she remained very anxious and dis-organized before going on the air. There was almost a panic reaction, difficulty concen-trating, dry mouth, and an upset stomach as she prepared to read the news. When it was airtime, she settled down. It surprised her to discover that many seasoned profes-sionals experience intense stress prior to performing (Tucker-Ladd, 1996–2000).

There are likely to be many different reactions to this case study. Some students read it who have experienced some of the same anxieties Jane experienced. Some read it and empathize with Jane and, perhaps, even envy her determination and goal pursuit. Some may even wish they could do the same thing Jane did. Some, too, read it and say very clearly and loudly, "Not me. That's not for me. No way. I am not a performer. I don't like performing. I will never be a performer." No matter how you respond to the case study, this chapter will serve as a starting point for getting accustomed to speaking in public.

Whether you are preparing a classroom report, conducting a business meeting of a dormitory, sorority, or fraternity, recruiting other students to become resident advisors, making a plea for additional school equipment, defending your section's work to the board of directors of your company, or just giving a toast at someone's wedding, you are giving a public speech. Such speeches are probably not going to be given in large auditoriums before vast audiences, but they are part of the routine of school, work, and life. People give speeches like this every day. They make presentations (to committees or boards of directors), hold workshops (for community members or professionals), or conduct seminars (for people who want to learn something). Whatever the purpose, all these forms of speaking have a speaker and an audience.

Public speaking involves the same elements as other forms of communication: sender-receivers, a message, a channel, and feedback. The speaker is the main sender-receiver, although audience members also respond as sender-receivers by providing nonverbal feedback or asking questions. The message in public speaking is the most structured of all communication. The speaker works on the message beforehand, planning what he or she will say. The usual channel is the voice and gestures, but some speakers enhance the channel by using graphics such as computer-generated visuals, posters, or slides. Feedback to a speech usually comes from the entire audience rather than from one or a few individuals. Typical feedback would be applause or laughter.

Public speaking has some of the characteristics of transactional communication, although its transactional nature differs from that of interpersonal and small-group communication. When an audience is small and the speaker can see everyone, continuous and simultaneous communication between the speaker and the audience can exist. However, when an audience is very large, it's a stretch to say that all the communication between the speaker and the audience is continuous and simultaneous. Let's say, for example, that several instructors on campus require their classes to go to hear a speech. The auditorium, which holds 500 people, is packed. One group of students sits in the back, in the shadows. This group has no intention of listening to the speaker. Because the auditorium is large, the speaker isn't aware of them and is unable to say something that will engage their attention. In this situation there is probably little communication between the speaker and these members of the audience.

The transactional element of roles is also present in public speaking. When you get up to give a speech to an audience, you may not be aware that if there are a hundred individuals present, they are perceiving not just one you at the lectern, but one hundred separate you's. Steve Allen, who because

Consider This

"On February 29, 2000, 90-year-old Doris 'Granny D' Haddock completed a 14-month walk from Los Angeles to the steps of the Capitol in Washington, D.C.—a feat undertaken in order to draw attention to the need for national campaign finance reform" (Haddock & Burke, 2001, front cover). At many stops during her walk, she gave speeches supporting her cause, and because of her success and the national publicity she received, she was asked to give the opening address at the Reform Party national convention. Here is what she claimed was responsible for her success in giving public speeches:

If I am any good at giving a speech, it is because I took my studies seriously at Emerson in Boston, where I went to college and where they took great pains to teach me proper elocution (the art of correct intonation, and inflection, in public speaking). . . .

Questions

1. Can you predict, as you are reading this book right now, how much public speaking you may become involved in in your life? Because of your career? Because of your community work? Because of your leadership ability?

2. Do you think training in communication—such as you are receiving in this course—should be a requirement for all college graduates? Why or why not?

3. What could be done—or what approach could be taken—that would convince you to take your communication course more seriously? Is your education dependent on the ability of your instructor? Is it dependent on your own desire to learn? Is it dependent on whether or not you think you can apply the material you are learning in the real, practical world that you will face after you leave college?

Source: Haddock, D., and D. Burke. *Granny D: Walking across America in my 90th year.* New York: Villard Books (a registered trademark of Random House, Inc., 2001), p. 120.

of his career as a comedian and an actor was often asked to give speeches. Here, he offered an interesting perspective on the role of the speaker:

I learned very early in my experience as a speaker—as distinguished from an entertainer—that if there were five hundred individuals present, they were perceiving not one Steve Allen at the lectern, but five hundred separate me's.

To give a few illustrations:

A young woman, to whose father I might bear a physical resemblance, might perceive me primarily as a male, to some degree physically attractive.

An elderly conservative Republican gentleman in the front row might perceive me primarily as a notorious Democrat or liberal.

A tailor in the audience might perceive me as someone attired unfashionably.

A fan of my television comedy program might perceive me as too stuffy and serious on this particular occasion.

A poorly educated person might perceive me as someone who uses too many big words.

One of my sons might perceive me as just "Dad."

My wife might perceive me as having put on a bit too much weight recently (Allen, 1986, p. 40).

■ SELECTING A TOPIC

The "Topic Helper" in the CD can help you prepare your speeches.

Many people do not have to select a topic for a speech—the topic develops from the work they are doing, the hobbies they are pursuing, or the interests that engage them. People are often asked to speak on their area of expertise, but the specific topic is left up to them. Dr. Randolph Shine, a prominent local psychiatrist, is asked to give a speech for the Alliance for the Mentally Ill, and he chooses the subject of how families can provide the necessary support for the mentally ill. Sherill Goldman, an active volunteer for local organizations, is asked to speak to the Literary Society, and she decides to talk about the rewards of and need for volunteer work.

Since you are in a speech communication course, you will have to make several speeches during the course of the term, and the choice of topic will probably be left up to you. Choosing the topic is one of the most difficult parts of making a speech, so let's take a look at how to go about it.

The most important consideration in choosing a topic is to find a subject that interests you. If the subject is one that you like, you are going to be more motivated to research it and your presentation will be more lively. How do you find a subject that is interesting and that will also lead to an effective speech? Let's look at some areas you should investigate.

Making a Personal Inventory

The first place to look for a topic is within yourself. You can begin by making a **personal inventory,** which involves appraising your own resources. What are you interested in? Would your interest make a good speech? Sometimes a hobby will lead to a good speech. A hobby can make you an expert about any number of subjects—rap musicians, computer games, or Elvis memorabilia.

Another area you might examine is how you spend your free time. If you listen to music or play an instrument, you might have the basis for a speech. Are you interested in nutrition, or do you like to cook? Maybe you can tell your audience something about food that they would find interesting.

Have you done anything unusual? One student gave a speech on how to teach a cat to do tricks—something most cats are reluctant to do. Have you been to any unusual places, or have you done something unusual, such as foraging for food in the woods?

Sometimes people have unique skills. Do you have the ability to make old cars run? Are you familiar with laser technology and how it works? Are you particularly good at entertaining children? Do you have any innovative ways of studying that you can share with others?

Often books, magazines, newspapers, or the Internet will offer possibilities for speech topics. Hundreds of thousands of articles are published in

Topics of personal interest, such as car maintenance and repair, often make for the best speeches because the speaker will be highly motivated.

magazines and newspapers every year. Most of these articles are about what people are currently interested in, and they can lead to ideas for speech topics. To get some idea of the range of topics covered, take a look at the *Reader's Guide to Periodical Literature.* In it, you will find hundreds of different subjects to choose from. Of course, the Internet offers even more.

What newspapers and magazines do you read? What sections do you turn to first? Are there issues in these sections that might result in good speeches? For example, if you always read the sports section, you know that scores and accounts of games are unlikely to provide material for speeches because scores and accounts alone are just numbers with little or no other substance. Well-written sports pages, however, also include stories on important issues in sports. Typical examples: Are the public pressures on athletes too great? What percentage of college athletes graduate? How should we define *amateur?* Should college athletes be paid?

Newspapers, magazines, and the Internet are also the best sources of information for what is going on in your city or state, the nation, and the world. Even though you might not ordinarily pay attention to this kind of news, take an hour or so someday to leaf through a big-city newspaper or a newsmagazine such as *Time* or *Newsweek.* Accessing CNN, NBC, CBS, or Fox online can provide new ideas, too. What's going on in the community or in the nation that might affect you and the people you know? For example, what is the local zoning board up to? Do you know that this is the board that decides how many people can live in a single dwelling? This is certainly an issue that affects students, who often need to save money by living with four or five others.

What is the state legislature up to? If you are attending a college or university supported by state money, this is an important question, since your state legislature wiil decide how much money your college will get and even how much tuition you will be paying. The federal government also makes many decisions that affect us all (health care and welfare reform, taxes, war, the environment) and many that affect college students in particular (drinking age and student loans). What about the world stage? What effect has the end of the cold war had? How do you view America's position toward Afghanistan? Iraq? China? France?

Whenever you seek a speech topic, remember that you will do best with material you know something about. While you are making a personal inventory, your emphasis should be on discovering interests and skills that you have and would like to share with others. Figure 12-1 diagrams the various sources where speech topics might be sought.

Using the Internet to Discover a Topic

There are numerous strategies you can use to discover topics via the Internet. One is no better than another; they are simply different approaches. Perhaps the easiest is to enter the words *speech topics* into the Google search engine. We received 5,500 hits (March 25, 2003), but we realized many of these were commercial sites advertising a list of topics that a particular speaker was announcing that he or she would be willing to speak on. However, we found three sites—and there are dozens more—where you can get a quick shot of mental adrenalin:

1. J. M. Books (2001). "Here Are Over 850 of the Best Topics We've Seen." Retrieved March 25, 2003, from http://www.schoolelection.com/persuasive/speechtopics2.htm.

2. C. Gesell-Streeter, "Public Speaking: Help with Speech Topics." Gesell Webspinning, Cincinnati State Technical and Community College. Retrieved March 25, 2003, from http://faculty.cinstate.cc.oh.us/gesellsc/publicspeaking/topics.html.

3. (No author), "Speech Topics," District 70, Eastern Division, Area 35, Port Stephens, Toastmasters International. Retrieved March 25, 2003, from http://ww1.tpg.com.au/users/schleter/tie_sptc.htm.

A second approach is to begin with your **Web portal** (Smeraglia, 2000). Your Web portal is the home page your browser displays when you first connect to the Net. "Which portal you start with may be determined by your service provider (e.g., AOL.com, MSN.com, or ATT.net), or by your browser (Netscape.com). These home pages are called portals because they are designed to act as a gateway for your exploration of the Web. . . ." (Smeraglia, 2000, p. 2). The advantage of beginning with your Web portal is that portals typically offer an alphabetical directory of topics designers of the portal thought might interest you. In addition, there are links to news, sports, and entertainment headlines, stock-market quotes, travel agencies, and local weather reports. Note, too, that the home page of any search engine is a second-level Web portal—second level simply because it requires your browser, the first level, to be activated before you can get to the search engine. Search engine home pages, too, include either a list of categories, or links to lists of categories. If you click on any of these categories, a more

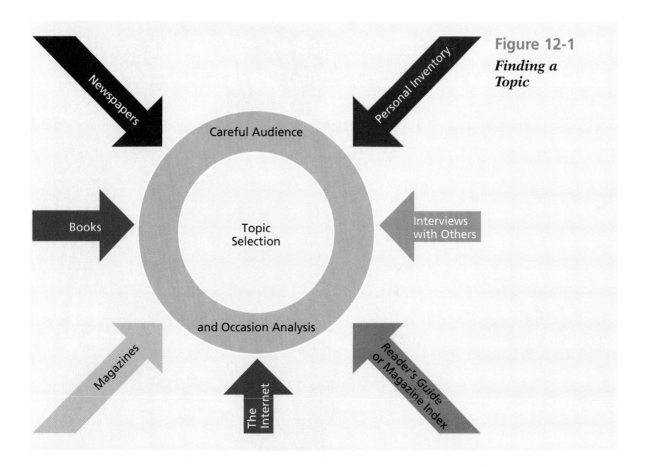

Figure 12-1
Finding a Topic

(Diagram labels: Newspapers, Personal Inventory, Careful Audience, Books, Topic Selection, Interviews with Others, Magazines, and Occasion Analysis, The Internet, Reader's Guide or Magazine Index)

specific list of categories appears until—sometimes sooner and sometimes later, depending on how specific the category is—there is a list of Web pages that contain information.

We chose Google as the search engine. We like the Google home page because it is simple, clean, and without clutter. This time, we entered nothing in the search window. Instead, just under the Google title there are four categories: (1) Web, (2) Images, (3) Groups, and (4) Directory. We clicked on Directory, and we were taken to a new page which revealed how Google organized the web by topic with these categories: arts, business, computers, games, health, world, home, kids and teens, news, recreation, reference, regional, science, shopping, society, and sports.

Inspired by the September 11, 2001, (9/11) terrorist attack, we clicked the category Travel under the Recreation category above. We thought, perhaps, a possible speech topic would be how terrorist threats have affected travel. When we arrived at the next page, still under the Google Web Directory, of course, we were presented with 13 new categories all related to travel: destinations, discounters and consolidators, guides and directories, image galleries, lodging, preparation, publications, specialty travel, tour operators, transportation, travel agents, travel warnings, and travelogues.

We clicked travel warnings, and we were taken to our fourth page and the three additional top-of-the-page headings were society, issues, and terrorism.

The Internet offers many opportunities related to speech topics. On the Internet you can brainstorm for them, find them, narrow them, as well as investigate and research them.

Clicking terrorism, a fifth Web-directory page appeared, and we were faced with 18 new categories: articles and reports, biological and chemical terrorism, counterterrorism, criminal terrorism, cyberterrorism, directories, environmental terrorism, incidents, news and media, nuclear terrorism, preparedness, research centers, rewards, suicide terrorism, terrorist organizations, travel warnings, U.S. domestic terrorism, and war on terrorism.

We clicked travel warnings, as a subcategory of terrorism, and the sixth Web-directory page gave us seven new websites, the first of which was from the U.S. Department of State: Travel Warnings and Consular Information Sheets. At the website, there were information sheets for 157 different countries. We found the information sheets for each country both complete and specific. Under Mexico, we found an information sheet labeled "Spring Break in Cancun" where 100,000 American teenagers and young adults spend their spring break each year. This information sheet (retrieved March 25, 2003, from http://travel.state.gov/cancun.html), is a "must read" for anyone planning to travel to Cancun. Although it did not relate directly to terrorism, it provoked thoughts of a different speech topic—

alerting students to travel concerns in foreign countries—with the possible title being "Paradise or Nightmare?—Spring Break or Spring Broken?"

Originally, we planned to look at some aspect of terrorism as a direct result of the 9/11 attack. But, we were no more tied to that topic than to a topic about spring break in a foreign country. We could have investigated, too, different types of potential terrorist attacks or how the average person can be prepared for terrorism—if, indeed, that is possible. This is precisely what makes using the Internet to discover a speech topic such a unique and interesting adventure.

One caution regarding use of the Internet to find a topic, and this caution is designed to protect your time and energy: Be careful you do not chew away valuable research and preparation time in Internet distractions such as surfing the web. There are many other distractions, too. You need to focus on your task: trying to settle on a topic and then narrowing it. (See the topic heading, Narrowing the Topic, which follows.)

You may think that the procedure we followed is necessarily lengthy or circuitous, however, the entire process can take less than five minutes. What is far more interesting, though, is how many potential subjects you can discover along the way. Sure, we had a specific, original direction, but if you did not, there are literally thousands of possible side trips which can reveal fascinating speech topics. On this short Internet journey alone, we found many other directions that would be fun to pursue.

In his last article for *ComputerScene Online*—in its last scheduled issue—Rene E. Smeraglia (2000) in his column, On the Net, writes about "Getting directions: Reading the road signs on the information superhighway," and gives the following suggestions for getting the most from search engines:

> *"You can help search engines find the right answer by following a few tips. First, ask the simplest query you can. If you want to know about global warming, just use those two words. This makes it less likely that a "confounding" word will change the results. Try to avoid words that show up on almost every page, like "Internet" and "Web." These don't add anything to the search. Don't use capital letters unless you are sure the result you want is also capitalized. And if you don't get the right answer right away, take a few moments to look at the Help or Advanced features of the search engine. Good search tools, such as Google (http://google.com), will let you search for particular file types (like image files), or limit the search results to certain languages or dates" (p. 3).*

All search engines have a home page—check out HotBot, Excite, InfoSeek, Lycos, AltaVista, MSN.com, Savvy Search, or Yahoo for example—and each home page has a set of categories. Many of these categories are the same or similar to those on the home pages of other search engines. Clicking any of them can lead you to enough new categories that you probably would not have time in a single day to pursue all the potential links available. For example WebCrawler, the metasearch engine that uses other search engines—AltaVista, Direct Hit, Looksmart, and About—has a category labeled Relationships, and clicking on that category brings up a menu of 20 topics: advice, weddings, alternative lifestyles, cyber-relationships, marriage, long distance, divorce, friendship, quotations, flirting, web rings, romance, kissing, e-zines, questionnaires, light side, anger management, etiquette, dating, and personal pages. We found all these sites interesting, relevant, and potentially significant for college-aged students—or, the very people who will be your audience for your speeches.

The Internet provides more than simply a starting place for discovering a topic. In Chapter 13, Finding Speech Material, we examine it as a research resource. Also, we discuss how to assess websites and what to look for in evaluating the quality of a website. One point here—common knowledge to active Internet users, of course—is that just because something is on the Internet does not make it correct or of high quality; you must be careful of the information you retrieve from the Internet. Everyone there is a publisher!

Internet Brainstorming

In Chapter 10, Small Groups: Characteristics, we discussed brainstorming in groups. You can brainstorm all by yourself, too, or, as we intend to demonstrate, you can brainstorm using the Internet as well. Brainstorming is a technique of free association. The goal of brainstorming is quantity—to come up with as many ideas as possible (Osborn, 1979). You take a subject—relationships is a good example—and you enter the word *relationships* into a search engine. We'll use Google once again.

Since traditional brainstorming requires mental agility on your part—writing down everything that comes into your mind regarding a topic or category—Internet brainstorming lets the computer do the free association for you. Entering *relationships* into Google produced 11,600,000 Web pages (March 25, 2003). Internet brainstorming involves surfing the website descriptions for words of interest such as:

Dating	Romantic	Cyber-
Building	Harmony in	Help with
Managing	Singles and	Addictive
Problems in	Bad	Sex in
Families	Establishing	Love and

These words—in addition to many other possibilities—were generated on the first two pages of the thousands Google produced. It is obvious from any one of these categories that hundreds of different speeches using different angles, approaches, or slices of the pie could be generated. Each category is too broad, as it stands, for a single speech; each category must be narrowed.

■ NARROWING THE TOPIC

A common mistake made by beginning speakers is trying to cover a topic that is too broad. If you want to talk about a social issue, such as crime, racial equality, or educational reform, you will discover so much relevant and interesting material that you would not even be able to read it all, let alone cover it in a single speech. If you tried to cover the entire topic, your treatment would be so superficial that your speech would not be very meaningful.

Let's say you want to speak on the subject of education. On Google (March 25, 2003) the word *education* brought up 73,900,000 Web pages—an enormous number. So, let's say you want to limit your speech to just elementary education (2,520,000 Web pages), high-school education (4,270,000 Web pages), higher education (4,010,000), college education (3,940,000), or university education (4,250,000)—all very broad topics as well. Special education netted 5,120,000 Web pages, and bilingual education netted 529,000. Learning problems resulted in 3,330,000 hits; learning disabilities, 1,270,000, and dyslexia—a specific learning disability—318,000 Web pages. With any of these topics, you are still faced with the problem of narrowing, the process of finding the specific aspect of a subject that will best meet the time restraints and other demands of the speaking situation.

Let's just take the topic dyslexia—a reading disorder that results in either inability or difficulty learning to read. Well-known dyslexics include William Butler Yeats, Albert Einstein, George Patton, John Irving, Charles Schwab, and Nicolas Negroponte. How many different approaches could be taken to this seemingly, already-narrowed topic? Possibilities—and these are just a few—include:

- The positive aspects of dyslexia.
- Tools to overcome dyslexia.
- How to evaluate and assess dyslexia.
- How to teach people with dyslexia.
- Sources for help for the dyslexic—resources and websites.
- Myths of dyslexia.
- History/discovery of dyslexia.
- Compensated dyslexics (those who perform as well as nondyslexics).
- Researching dyslexia, the use of functional magnetic resonance imaging (fMRI).
- Gender differences in dyslexia.
- Helping the families and communities of the dyslexic.
- Discrimination against dyslexics.

The point isn't that one of these narrowed topics is better than another, nor that many more narrowed topics can be discovered, the point is that even with a seemingly already narrowed topic, there is still more narrowing that can be done. Even with a choice of one of the topics mentioned earlier, more narrowing may be needed to make the topic relate directly to the audience for the speech or to the community where the speech will be given.

Let's examine further the process of narrowing using the word *relationships* that we began looking at in a previous example. After Internet brainstorming and developing such a general list (above)—which might take as long as 5 or 10 minutes at the most—look at the list with a more critical eye. You can now eliminate from the list any topics that don't really interest you or that you know little about. For example, based on your own experience and background in relationships, you might eliminate managing, problems in, families, bad, addictive, and sex in as potential topics.

This is what the process of narrowing a topic is all about. This leaves the following list:

Dating	Romantic	Cyber-
Building	Harmony in	Help with
Singles and	Establishing	Love and

Let's say you have had several cyber-relationships, and you think this topic would relate well to your audience for this speech. Also, you think that some of the other categories might also relate to cyber-relationships; however, you might come up with a whole new set of potential categories, so instead of making a commitment here to talking about cyber-relationships, instead, you go back to the computer to brainstorm further for ideas—but, in this case, narrowing it to cyber-relationships specifically.

By further Internet brainstorming, too, you might come up with subdivisions of the major topic—that is, other subareas of the major topic—that you might enjoy talking about or that might encourage further investigation. Entering Cyber-relationships into Google produced 233,000 Web pages (March 25, 2003). Surfing these pages produced a whole new list of categories:

Advice	Communication	Cybersex
Internet affairs	LDRs (Long-distance relationships)	Virtual romance
Safety		Extramarital relationships
Chat rooms	Advantages of	Deception in
Unrealistic expectations of	Emotional fulfillment	Emotional super-highway

Now, thinking must proceed along some new lines. With only a couple of cyber-relationships in your experience, you may not feel comfortable with giving advice about them, but there is a great deal of information on the Internet regarding advice; you could throw in a couple of pieces of advice during your speech. The same goes for safety, but most people know about Internet safety issues—advice, safety, and deception could occupy one subpoint of the speech labeled precautions.

You could begin your speech talking about your own experiences in chat rooms and what "dating" in a virtual environment involves. It would be at this point you could discuss communication—both advantages and disadvantages—emotional concerns, and even potential unrealistic expectations. You could answer the question, too, "What does relating with someone else via the Internet involve?" That is, what are the advantages and disadvantages?

With it somewhat clear now as to how to begin your speech, somewhat clear that you want to discuss precautions, you could include a third part of your speech on virtual romance. Here, you could talk about Internet affairs, extramarital relationships (if you so choose), and the emotional superhighway. You could even mention cybersex, since there is so much information on the Internet covering this topic—and it would hold the attention of your listeners.

Although it may be premature at this point to think of titles for your speech, titles may pop out at you as you begin to surf websites. For example, this speech could have a title something like "Cyber-relationships: Date, Relate, and Find Your Soulmate." Note that at this point this is a tentative title that can be changed at any time during the speech preparation process. It has a "neat" rhythm or flow to it that might just work. The only advantages of having a title at this very early stage are, first, that it can help guide your research and investigation, and second, it can contribute to the **partitioning** of your speech—how you choose to divide the speech into parts. The major weakness of having a title this early is that it could prove to be restrictive, creating a set of blinders that hinders you from looking beyond the title for other possibilities. Our feeling, in general, is that when you find a good title, write it down, then be flexible as you continue your research, and be open to other possibilities. With the above title, for some reason, there is power in any list of three, and the words date, relate, and soulmate have some of this mysterious power. Three is better than either two or four when it comes to this mysterious power of three.

Sometimes when you use the Internet to brainstorm, you find that your list does not yield anything you want to talk about. In this case, brainstorm again about another subject. It might take two or three brainstorming sessions before you find a topic you really like that is sufficiently narrow to be discussed effectively in a brief speech. Whatever topic you discover, it will probably have to be narrowed to just the aspects you want to cover in your speech.

By starting with a subject you find interesting, you work with it or different aspects of it, and you narrow it in a way that makes it manageable for a speech. And once you have it sufficiently narrowed, then you can begin putting your speech topic through various tests.

■ TESTING THE TOPIC

Appropriate for the Audience?

To determine whether a topic is appropriate for an audience, you have to ask whether you can speak about it on a level the audience can understand. Does the subject require specialized or technical knowledge? Can you talk about it in a language everyone will understand? Can you make the topic interesting for your audience? Does the audience have enough background to understand the subject? Answers to these questions will help you decide whether the topic will be appropriate.

Appropriate for You?

A topic is appropriate for you if it meets this test: Can you get involved in it, and is it interesting enough to motivate you to do the necessary research? A student studying air traffic control would probably have a high interest in air disasters—especially those caused by mistakes on the part of traffic controllers. A student studying restaurant administration would probably find it interesting to research the causes of food poisoning. Someone with a collection of African coins would be motivated to learn even more about the subject.

Another Point of View

Here is some advice found in a college public-speaking textbook published in the mid-1960s:

Generally, women are more interested than men in subjects related to the feminine gender, such as women's clothing, cosmetics, housework, the rearing of children, the local ladies' aid society, home decoration, etc. On the other hand, men show strong masculine interests in rough competitive sports like football. More than women, men tend to enjoy technical and scientific subjects, particularly those related to mechanics, electronics, and engineering. Since more men than women serve as chief breadwinners for their families, they are more apt to be interested in matters pertaining to occupations and professions—but remember the possible exceptions.

Questions

1. Is any of the advice from this 1965 textbook relevant today? Why or why not?

2. What problems will you encounter if you stereotype listeners according to their gender?

3. Are there topics today that are more appropriate for one gender than for the other? What are they?

4. In what ways can speakers make topics relevant to both sexes?

Source: Win Kelley, *The Art of Public Address* (Dubuque, Iowa: Brown, 1965), p. 25.

To give a good speech, you are also going to have to speak with confidence and expertise. Do you know about the subject? Can you learn enough about it to give a speech? There is nothing worse than getting up before an audience and realizing that you don't know what you are talking about!

Appropriate for the Occasion?

The first consideration here is whether you are giving the right kind of speech for the occasion. An after-dinner speech, for example, should have a light touch and not be too long, since it will occur when members of the audience have just eaten and are not feeling their most alert. On the other hand, if you are giving a speech at a seminar, this will be an opportunity to speak on a more complex topic. In a classroom setting, you will probably be given only a limited time to speak, so you have to decide whether you can cover your topic adequately in the time you have.

If you are speaking at a special occasion, you should tie some aspect of the speech into the occasion itself. If the speech is for some kind of ritual occasion such as a graduation, bar mitzvah, or bat mitzvah, certain conventions are expected of the speaker. At a graduation, a speaker typically has some words for graduates about the future. At a bar mitzvah, or bat mitzvah, a Jewish ceremony initiating a young person into religious adulthood, it would be appropriate to praise the young adult and his or her parents.

Another consideration is whether you can fit the speech into the time limits of the occasion. Usually a speaker is given some idea of how long to speak. In a speech class, this is always true. You must consider whether you can cover your topic or whether you need to narrow it down more so that you can cover it adequately within the time allowed.

For many of us, making a final decision about a topic is difficult, especially when we are faced with several good options. When you are deciding on a topic for your speech class, however, it is important that you choose a single topic well ahead of the date when the speech is due. If you don't, you will waste a lot of time doing unfocused and unusable research on several topics. If you have several topics that seem equally appropriate and you just can't make up your mind, put all the topics in a hat and draw one out. Once you have picked a topic, stick with it.

Briefly, let's see how the topic of cyber-relationships holds up with respect to the three questions proposed at the beginning of this section, "Testing the Topic." Is it appropriate for your audience? Because most in your audience will be Internet-savvy and relationship-oriented, there is no doubt your topic will be appropriate for your audience. Is it appropriate for you? Because of your experience in two cyber-relationships, and because you are Internet-addicted, you think that further investigation of the topic will be both interesting and educational. Finally, is it appropriate for the speech occasion? Since yours will be a classroom assignment, it will be fully appropriate.

■ SELECTING A PURPOSE

Whenever you give a speech, you should have a good idea of your purpose or reason for speaking. Having this purpose in mind beforehand is very much like planning a trip: If you know where you're going, you can plan the route ahead of time. In the same way, having a purpose for your speech will help you look for materials, organize and outline your speech, and adapt your speech to the needs and interests of your audience.

There are three stages in working out the purpose for your speech: (1) Selecting the general purpose, (2) Selecting the specific purpose, and (3) Stating the central idea.

The General Purpose

When you are asked to state a **general purpose** for your speech, you should tell whether you intend to inform or to persuade. **Informative speeches** generally concentrate on explaining—telling how something works, what something means, or how to do something. A speaker who gives an informative speech usually tries to give his or her audience information without taking sides. For example, if a speaker is giving an informative speech about using animals for research, he will not state whether he is for or against doing so; he will let members of the audience make up their own minds. When the subject is controversial, the informative speaker will present all sides of the issue. In an informative speech about running for fitness, for example, you could give the advantages (physical fitness and feeling good) and the possible disadvantages (shin splints and other injuries).

Many of the important decisions in speechmaking require that speakers answer questions they ask themselves.

In a **persuasive speech** the speaker takes a particular position and tries to get the audience to accept and support that position. For example, a speaker tries to persuade her audience members that they should oppose welfare reform. Someone else tries to persuade audience members to support making volleyball a varsity sport or to sign a petition against chemical dump sites in the community. In a persuasive speech, the speaker concentrates on looking for the best information available to support his or her point of view.

Often the same subject could lead to either an informative or a persuasive speech—depending on your wording of the topic and your approach. Say your subject is the ethics of abortion. If you choose as your topic "ethical issues of abortion" and cover the ethics on both sides of the issue, the wording of your topic and your approach are appropriate for an informative speech. But if your topic is "abortion: the wrong choice," you clearly have a persuasive speech, because you have made up your mind and are in favor of one particular side of the issue. Here are some other subjects that are phrased first as informative (I) and then as persuasive (P) topics:

I: Latino Interests and Concerns

P: Latinos Must Form Their Own Political Party

I: Environmental Conservation Means Energy Efficiency

P Energy Efficiency Requires People to Change Their Habits

I: Stress Reduction Programs Can Be Successful

P: People Need to Learn How to Control Stress in Their Lives

Sometimes it's difficult to fit a speech firmly into an informative or a persuasive slot. In a persuasive speech, informative material often plays an important role. If you are speaking in favor of political candidates, it is natural to use information about their backgrounds and voting records. In an informative speech, even when you try to present both sides, one side might seem more persuasive than the other to some audience members.

With respect to the topic cyber-relationships, the general purpose is to inform; however, it could be framed as a persuasive speech as well. For example, what if your purpose was to persuade your audience members to avoid cyber-relationships—that the weaknesses far outweigh any advantages? Or, what if your purpose was to persuade them to proceed with extreme caution? You could also persuade them that the Internet offers a superb way to find an appropriate soulmate. But, if you simply want to talk about your experiences, offer some precautions, then discuss virtual romance—with a title like date, relate, and find your soulmate—you are simply aiming to inform.

The Specific Purpose

After you have decided whether the general purpose of your speech is to inform or to persuade, you must then decide on a **specific purpose.** The statement of your specific purpose will help you focus on precisely what you want to accomplish; that is, it will help you define exactly what you are going to inform or to persuade your audience about. In deciding your specific purpose, you should follow four guidelines:

1. *State your purpose clearly and completely.* Examples of a specific-purpose statement are:

   To inform my audience about the value of home schooling.

   To explain to audience members how to halt the spread of germs.

   To persuade audience members to support laws that protect victims of crimes.

   To persuade audience members to become educated consumers.

2. *State your purpose in terms of the effect you want to have on your audience.* What information do you want to give to your audience, or what do you want your listeners to think or do when the speech is over? In

an informative speech the main effect you seek is to have your audience remember the information. For example:

To inform audience members about the ways they can help the handicapped.

To inform audience members about how they can help stop family violence.

In a persuasive speech, however, the effect you might want is to have audience members take direct action:

To persuade my audience to stop driving after drinking alcohol.

To persuade my audience that reduced mental stress will reduce the risk of heart attacks and heart disease.

3. *Limit your purpose statement to one idea.* Keeping your purpose statement limited to one idea will help you narrow your topic and keep it specific. Notice that each of the above examples has only one idea. If a speaker's topic was "to inform my audience about the value of daydreams and how to use them to escape and relax," the speaker would have two topics to cover rather than one, and the speech would lack focus.

4. *Use specific language in your purpose statement.* The more precise your language, the clearer the ideas will be in your mind. For example, "to persuade my audience to fight crime" is too vague a topic. By *crime*, do you mean drugs, kidnapping, murder, or something else? You could rephrase your purpose like this:

To persuade my audience that everyone can help control drunk driving.

To inform my audience that drivers who drink are too impaired to drive.

Once you have determined your statement of purpose, you should subject it to some tests. Does it meet the assignment? You might discover, for example, that your opinions on a subject are so strong that you are unable to talk about it without favoring one side over the other. This means your subject is better for a persuasive speech than for an informative one. If you have been assigned an informative speech, you should keep this subject for a later time.

Another important test is to ask whether you can accomplish your purpose within the time limits of the speech. If your speech purpose is too broad to fit into the allotted time, you will have to either narrow the topic further or find a new topic. One speaker discovered, for example, that her purpose, "to inform my audience about physical fitness," was too broad; too many issues were involved. She rephrased her purpose: "to inform audience members about how low-impact aerobics can improve their health."

In deciding on the specific purpose for the speech on cyber-relationships, it should be easy to do based on the brainstorming and narrowing that has taken place earlier: *To inform my classmates about my experiences with, precautions about, and how the emotional superhighway relates to cyber-relationships.* In this way, the statement is clear and complete; it is phrased in terms of the effect you want to have on your classmates; it is

Working Together

Discuss the ethical implications of the following speech topics. To what extent should speakers pay attention to the values implied in their topic choices? Are the following topics appropriate for speeches?

- How to break into "secure" sites on the Internet.
- How to get out of paying a speeding ticket.
- How to make a bomb.

- How to shoplift without being detected.
- How to destroy others' credit ratings.
- How to get into an athletic event without paying.
- How to lie without being detected.
- How to cheat on college examinations.
- How to get out of paying income taxes.
- How to make a false ID card.

limited to one idea; and, you have used very precise language—except, perhaps, the use of the words *emotional superhighway*, which are an all-inclusive way to discuss virtual romance, emotional commitments, and cybersex.

The Central Idea

Whereas the specific purpose expresses what we want to accomplish when we give the speech, the **central-idea** statement establishes the main thrust of the speech. The central idea is much like the thesis statement students learn about in writing courses. Everything in the speech relates to the central idea. In an informative speech, the central idea contains the information you want the audience to remember; in a persuasive speech, it tells audience members what you want them to do.

The difference between a specific purpose and a central-idea statement is illustrated in the following examples. Notice that the central idea explains the why or the how of the specific purpose:

Specific purpose: To persuade audience members to protect themselves against unsuccessful and unhappy marriages.

Central idea: Unsuccessful and unhappy marriages occur because people do not take the time to become friends first, communicate honestly with each other, resolve conflicts constructively, learn to work around problems, discover an enduring attraction, contribute equally to the relationship, trust each other, and take their commitment seriously.

When the central idea was stated, it was clear that it encompassed too many points to cover in a single speech. So the speaker rephrased it in such a way that the ideas could be grouped:

Central idea: Unhappy marriages may occur because of weak communication.

Specific purpose:	To inform my audience about how to drug-proof children.
Central idea:	People can do three things to help drug-proof children: (1) talk about drugs and their effects, (2) help children deal with peer pressure, and (3) work with parents and the community.
Specific purpose:	To persuade my audience that careful preparation will lead to a better vacation.
Central idea:	Those who want effective vacations should pack light and smart, prepare for emergencies, and be adaptable.

The central idea should be stated in a full sentence, should contain one idea, and should use precise language. Sometimes it is not possible to come up with a central-idea statement until you have finished organizing and outlining the speech. When you start working on your speech, you should have a tentative central idea in mind; when you have finished organizing and outlining the speech, you can refine it.

Julia decided on a topic and a specific purpose right away. She had several books on happy, healthy, 80-year-olds who gave reasons why they had lived such happy, healthy lives. Also, her own grandparents fit this profile. Julia decided to give a speech with the specific purpose "to inform my audience how to live to be 100 by starting right now." Julia knew her central idea would contain information about all the ways that people can stay healthy, but the specific concepts did not emerge until she had a rough outline:

I. *Exuberant, hopeful, and fun-loving folks maintain strong friendships and care about others.*

II. *Robust, vital folks pay attention to their bodily needs for sleep, diet, and exercise.*

III. *A key to always looking and feeling young is loving what you do.*

Once Julia had completed her outline, she knew her central idea would be "to live a happy, healthy life until you are 100, maintain strong friendships, pay attention to your bodily needs, and love what you do."

Regarding the speech on cyber-relationships, the central idea could be phrased simply: To inform my audience about cyber-relationships. Or, it could be expanded slightly to include the three major ideas: To inform my audience about my experiences with, precautions about, and the emotional ramifications regarding cyber-relationships. The latter is better for three reasons: (1) It is more specific, (2) It gives more direction regarding how you will construct the speech, and (3) It shows exactly what you want to share with your listeners. Of course, your research on cyber-relationships has not begun, and although your general purpose (to inform) will not change, because your assignment involves giving an informative speech, your specific purpose and central idea could be tweaked or even changed dramatically depending on what you find during your investigation.

It is important to have a specific purpose and central idea to guide your research and investigation, but just like having a title early in the preparation process, you must not let the specific purpose and central idea bind you unnecessarily. Part of the thrill of using the Internet for research—and your authors consider Internet use both exciting and entertaining—is being flexible and responsive to what you discover. Because millions of Web pages are added to the Internet daily, you never know what you are going to find, and what you find on one day may not be what you find on another. You will enjoy the process of discovery more knowing that you can be open, flexible, and adaptable to what you discover.

■ ANALYZING THE AUDIENCE

Margaret Hernandez is the director of an organization called Citizens for a Better Environment. The organization has decided that its priority for the year is to conduct a campaign to get people to avoid buying products with excessive packaging or with packaging that is difficult to recycle. Since much of the campaign will consist of educating the public, Ms. Hernandez has scheduled several speeches throughout the community. She will speak to all kinds of audiences: on Monday to sixth-graders in a middle school, on Wednesday to senior citizens, on Thursday to a college class, and on Friday to landfill managers in a statewide meeting.

In her speeches Ms. Hernandez always talks about packaging. However, she does not make the same speech to every audience. Instead, she adapts her material to make it appropriate for each particular group. Before she makes the speech to sixth-graders, she finds out from their teacher that they have started a unit on recycling in their social studies class, and so they have some knowledge of the need to recycle. Ms. Hernandez decides to talk about two product packages that sixth-graders are likely to know about: peanut butter and catsup. In this speech she discusses how important it is to recycle plastic and points out that the children can help the recycling effort by urging their parents to make recycling a family activity.

When Ms. Hernandez goes to speak to senior citizens, she assumes that many of them eat frozen dinners that can be heated in the oven or microwave. She brings in one brand of dinner that has three layers of packaging and uses this as a starting point to talk about the problems of packaging. She takes a similar approach with the college students. This time, however, she uses a package of microwave popcorn, a popular item in the dormitory. She asks students to imagine how large the trash pile would be if, in one week's time, half the students in the dorm made microwave popcorn in throwaway containers. Before she leaves, she gives the students a handout on how to make popcorn in containers that can be reused.

When Ms. Hernandez prepares to talk to the landfill managers, she knows that her speech should take a different direction. Since they run the landfills throughout the state, they are well aware of the problems of too much trash and garbage. Ms. Hernandez decides that her focus with this group will be on public education. Because there are only two branches of Citizens for a Better Environment, she tells the managers how to set up similar organizations in their own communities. She also recommends some activities they can engage in to educate the public.

The Role of the Speaker

In all the above examples, Ms. Hernandez was playing the role of the speaker. Whenever you play this role, the audience has certain expectations of you. When an audience comes to hear you, it expects that you will be knowledgeable about your topic and that you will present what you know in an interesting way. Ms. Hernandez is a competent speaker not only because she knows her subject but also because she knows her audiences.

What Ms. Hernandez has done is use audience analysis to adapt her subject matter to the specific characteristics of each group. **Audience analysis** is the process of finding out what the members of the audience already know about the subject, what they might be interested in, what their attitudes and beliefs are, and what kinds of people they are. In your role as speaker you should consider audience analysis one of the most important parts of your preparation.

Audience Knowledge

One important aspect of audience analysis is taking into account how much the audience is likely to know about a subject. In a practical sense, speakers can make only an educated guess about an audience's knowledge. They can assume that if they are talking to a lay audience and pick a topic related to a specialized field of knowledge (electromagnetic radiation, electronic book technology, laser surgery, ergonomics, behavioral psychology), they will have to explain and define a lot of basic terminology before going into the subject in any depth. For example, when Sam spoke to his class about dietary fat, he had to explain such terms as *saturated, polyunsaturated,* and *hydrogenated* before he could talk about anything else.

On some subjects speakers can assume that audiences have a base of general knowledge. For instance, if you are speaking about vitamins, you can assume that most people know vitamins are good for them and even that vitamin C is particularly good for preventing and treating colds. But a general knowledge about other vitamins should not be taken for granted.

Speakers should realize that although people have general information about many subjects, they usually don't know the specifics. Most people know, for example, that the Constitution guarantees us the right to free speech. Yet if you were to ask them what *free speech* means, they would probably be a little fuzzy on a definition or on what is encompassed by the term. Would they know, for example, that the courts regard ringing a bell or burning a flag as a form of free speech?

Here is another example: When speaking to a college audience about her recent trip to mainland China, Ming assumed that most of her listeners would know approximately where China is located and that most of them would know that China is ruled by a Communist government. She figured, however, that most of them would not know much about such important Chinese ideas as communal farming or the Cultural Revolution, and so she took some time to explain them. Once she had given this background information, her speech and slides about what she had seen and done made much more sense.

On the Web

What Do Teens Want?

Here are the demographic conclusions of Mark Hoppus and Tom DeLonge, the two founders and lead performers of Blink 182, the pop-punk trio whose CD, *Enema of the State* sold well over 5 million copies. In addition to building Blink's business side and managing other bands, the two have founded a popular clothing and accessories Web business called Loserkids. com. These are their (abbreviated) rules of thumb for relating to teens—teen demographics, if you will.

Blink-182 Rule #1: Teens don't like what they sense they're supposed to like. Hoppus believes that most businesses that target teens come off as phony, condescending, or disrespectful.

Blink-182 Rule #2: Teens are fickle. Deal with it. Everyone wants something different from what they had before.

Blink-182 Rule #3: Listen. Even though most of us tend to think of teens as being opaque, the truth is, they're pretty open about what they want, notes Hoppus. The problem is often simply that adults don't listen.

Blink-182 Rule #4: Adults really can influence teens. Teens don't despise the idea of growing up. In fact, says DeLonge, they can't wait to grow up and are quick to idolize people who are older than they are and who embody their own aspirations.

Blink-182 Rule #5: Think subculture. Teenagers often seem like professional rebels. But DeLonge observes that even teens who are determined to stand out usually harbor an intense desire to blend in as well.

Blink-182 Rule #6: Lighten up. Teenagers relate to humor, silliness, and irreverence more easily than to any other styles, says Hoppus.

Questions

1. Do you think these "rules" would ensure that you could reliably connect with teenagers?

2. Are there rules left out that you would add? Any rules here you would delete? Why or why not?

Source: D. H. Freedman, "What do teens want?" *Inc magazine*, December 1, 2000. Inc.com Retrieved March 25, 2003, from http://www.inc.com/search/21117.html.

In a college speech class, you can get some idea of how much your audience knows about your subject by asking your friends and classmates what they know. If you have been asked to speak before a group you belong to, you can ask a couple of members what they know about the subject. If they don't know very much, you can assume that your audience won't either and that you will have to start by giving basic information. When you are speaking to community or professional groups, often the program chairperson who is responsible for finding speakers will be able to give you some information about the audience members' level of knowledge and also about what is likely to interest them.

Audience Interest

Some subjects seem to be inherently interesting. Books on the nonfiction best-seller list usually are about diet, exercise, and money. If you look at the topics covered by popular magazines, you will discover that self-help or self-improvement is the category of articles that appears most often. However, most of us do not want to be limited to speaking about physical fitness, diet, and self-help. Instead, we have to find a way to make other subjects appealing to our listeners.

One way to interest your listeners in a topic is to point out that it has importance and relevance to them. Jan, an English major and a tutor in the Writing Center, wants to give a speech on the importance of writing skills. She knows that most students would like to improve their grades, but she also knows that most of them do not want to listen to a lecture on English composition. She decides to call her speech "Five Tips for Better Grades on Papers" and concentrates on giving specific and practical advice.

Another way to attract an audience's interest is to get listeners involved in the subject. Christian wants to persuade his audience that a cheap way to travel and see America is to get involved in American Youth Hostels. He begins his speech with some specific stories about staying in various hostels across the country. He goes on to tell how many students take advantage of hostels, where they are located, and what staying in hostels involves—the commitment to helping out by cooking meals and cleaning up. Even though his audience might not have had an interest in the subject to begin with, his examples are so compelling that he creates interest. Christian concludes his speech by writing on the chalkboard the URL for the American Youth Hostels home page (http://www.hiayh.org/ushostel/usmap.htm), where, he tells the class, you can select a region of the United States by clicking a map, selecting a state, and, finally, clicking a city. The address of the hostel, a picture of it, and both a map and written directions appear as well as a description, price, open and closed dates, office hours, managers, and contact points (phone, fax, or e-mail) for making reservations, if necessary.

Since you will be speaking on a subject that interests you, it might be useful to spend some time thinking about why you find the topic so intriguing. What things about it caught your attention in the first place? If you can re-create your own enthusiasm for a subject, you will have a better chance of exciting your audience's interest too.

Audience Attitudes and Beliefs

When planning your speech, you also need to consider your audience's attitudes and beliefs about your subject. Often you will be speaking before an audience that shares your beliefs, such as when you speak before your club or your church group. The Sierra Club, a conservation group, will appreciate a speech on the environmental position of the federal government. The Marketing Club will be interested in hearing from a local sales representative who has surpassed all previous sales records. Fellow employees will be interested in listening to a speech by an expert on profit sharing. College students will favor a proposal requiring instructors to put copies of their examinations on file at the library. These subjects tie into the attitudes and beliefs of the audience members.

But sometimes your listeners may not have any particular attitudes or beliefs about your subject. They may not have enough information to make up their minds, or they may not care enough to have an opinion. The latter will be especially difficult to deal with. If you want to appeal to an indifferent audience, you will have to try especially hard to make your listeners feel that the speech has relevance and importance to them and use captivating examples and illustrations. Alexis, for example, wanted to speak to his class about the importance of voting in the student government election. He knew that most of his listeners believed that voting was a good idea but that, when election day came, few of them would actually vote. To motivate them, he began his speech by pointing out that student government controls three areas of high interest to students: concerts, athletics, and food service. Then he gave a captivating scenario of how voting or not voting could directly affect choices they make.

Sometimes your own beliefs run contrary to those of your audience, and your speech may be met with hostility. If you think your audience may be opposed to your ideas on a subject, you have to plan your speech carefully. Robin, for example, knew that her classmates would be opposed to the idea of expanding the number of class periods during the day because it meant both earlier and later class periods. Yet, by researching her topic carefully and presenting reasons for the expansion (to make more courses available to students), she was able to show that an expansion was necessary. The members of her audience might not have been happy about the expansion, but they had a better understanding of the reasons for it. In his speech, Kamil set out to persuade members of his speech class that the college should increase the amount of support it gives to student government. He expected his audience to be resistant to the idea because of the number of letters by concerned students printed in the college newspaper. However, he was able to show that interest in student government was increasing, that student government had a positive effect on campus concerns that directly related to students, and that more money could be used in advantageous and responsible ways. Not all his classmates were persuaded, but after the speech was over, several told Kamil they thought his ideas were worth considering.

People's attitudes and beliefs affect how speeches are received. Sometimes, despite our "free" society and despite the protection of free speech, our ideas are not considered acceptable. Just because free speech *should* exist does not mean that it *does* exist.

Since people's attitudes and beliefs will affect how your speech is received, it is absolutely essential that they be considered when your speech is in the planning stage. Important clues to people's attitudes and beliefs can be discovered through attention to audience demographics.

Audience Demographics

Even if you have no specific information about your audience's knowledge, interest level, and attitude toward your subject, certain factual information about the audience members can tell you a great deal. **Demographic analysis** reveals data about the characteristics of a group of people, including such things as age, sex, education, occupation, race/nationality/ethnic origin, geographic location, and group affiliation.

When you work with demographic information, you generalize about the entire audience; your generalizations might not be true of individual members. For example, on the basis of demographic data you have gathered, you might generalize that the ages of your speech class audience are between 18 and 27—even though one member is in his 50s. In the same way, you can make generalizations about the class's educational level or about its racial composition. Then on the basis of such generalizations, you can make some predictions about what might interest the people in this audience and what they might be knowledgeable about.

One caution about generalizing: There is a great deal of change going on in the world today, with concurrent changing demographics. This means that analyzing audiences is even more important than it was in the past, but it means also that we have to be sensitive and responsive to the differences we discover. Analyzing without sensitivity and responsiveness has the same effect as not analyzing at all. What good is it, for example, to discover that audience members are extremely well informed on a topic, very gender-sensitive, or made up of a majority of people of different ethnic groups, if there is no willingness to change one's approach because of this new information? Let's consider each of the demographic characteristics in turn.

Age

As a speaker, you need to have a sense of the age range of your audience because interests differ with age. College-age people are usually interested in school, future jobs, music, and interpersonal relationships. Young parents are often interested in subjects that might affect their children, such as school bus safety and school board policy. Middle-aged people tend to be focused on their jobs, and older adults tend to be interested in issues related to leisure activities and health. However, not all subjects are age-related. Computers, elections, and world and national news, for example, have interest for most age groups because they affect everyone.

Sometimes the same subject can be of interest to various age groups if it is adapted to each group's particular concerns. Take the subject of nutrition. If you were speaking to an elementary school audience, you would probably not go into detail about vitamins and minerals because you would have problems keeping the attention of the children. Instead, you might use puppets (one that eats junk food and another that eats good food) or put your speech into a story with characters the children could identify with. If you talked about nutrition to pregnant women, you could adapt your speech to the needs of a fetus, assuming that every mother-to-be has a high interest in having a healthy baby. When you speak to older adults, you could talk about their particular nutritional needs, such as the importance of calcium to avoid bone deterioration.

It is sometimes difficult to generalize with respect to age. Look, for example, at "college-age" people. The average age of college students is no longer about 20. It is now around 26, and it is likely to go higher with more adults going back to school. Students and others need to be sensitive in their classrooms and in workplaces to age differences and need to avoid stereotyping in their speeches.

Gender

The gender of audience members can also be important. In a speech that's open to the public, you will probably have both men and women in your

Consider This

Christina Hoff Sommers, the W. H. Brady Fellow at the American Enterprise Institute in Washington, D.C., has a Ph.D. in philosophy from Brandeis University and was formerly professor of philosophy at Clark University in Worcester, Massachusetts. Here, she concludes by summarizing her section of the book labeled "Where the Equity Enthusiasts Go Wrong":

The natural gender differences between men and women mean we cannot hope to get statistical male-female parity of competence and aptitude in all fields. The same seems true of preferences: there will always be far more women than men who want to stay home with children; there will always be more women than men who want to be kindergarten teachers rather than helicopter mechanics. Boys will always be less interested than girls in dollhouses. This does not mean that our sex rigidly determines our future. The anthropologist Lionel Tiger has it right when he says, "Biology is not destiny, but it is good statistical probability."

Questions

1. Do you believe that gender differences between men and women are a social construct—that is, they are culturally determined—or do you believe that men and women are innately distinguished by gender? (Sommers suggests that "If all gender differences were culturally determined, you would expect to find some societies where females are the risk takers and males play with dolls. There would be societies in which females, on average, would do better in math and young males would be more verbally adept than females. But where are they?")

2. Can you see, from this excerpt alone, the importance of speakers knowing the gender of their audience members?

Source: C. H. Sommers, *The war against boys: How misguided feminism is harming our young men*, (New York: Simon & Schuster, 2000), pp. 88–89.

audience. If you have either an all-male or an all-female audience, it will probably be because you are talking to a club or organization whose members are all of one sex. The topic of your speech will then be influenced more by the organization itself than by the sex of its members. For example, the American Association of University Women has long been interested in education. If you were speaking to this group, its interest in education would be more important than the fact that the group is all-female.

Speakers must be sensitive and responsive to the gender issue. If you deliver a speech to a mixed audience but do not acknowledge the presence, and appeal to the needs, of both genders, not only will you miss the mark, but your speech may even seem sexist and inappropriate. For example, many volunteer organizations once included mostly homemakers. A speech to one of these organizations now needs to address working women's less flexible, more demanding schedules, which limit women's time for volunteer commitments.

Education

The audience's level of education is important to a speaker because it gives some idea of the group's knowledge and experience. We can assume that the more education people have, the more specialized their knowledge.

Lawyers, doctors, and Ph.D.s all have specialized knowledge; however, they might have little information about subjects other than their own. Your main consideration when you prepare a speech is whether your audience has the same knowledge you have or whether you will have to start with the basics. For example, if you are a biology major, don't assume that your speech class will know what the terms *homeostasis* and *morphology* mean. Although people might have a general idea of what these words mean, they might not know their precise scientific definitions.

Occupation

The occupation of audience members may influence how you approach some topics. Sometimes occupation indicates an area of specialized knowledge: Paramedics and nurses know about the human body; lawyers know about legal rights; social workers know about social problems. A person's occupation can also indicate interest in a subject. Most professional groups would probably be interested in a speech about ethics in their profession. Factory workers might be interested in the workings of a union or how to form one. If you are speaking to an occupational group, try to adapt your speech to that audience's job interests.

Race/Nationality/Ethnic Origin

Politicians speak to whole audiences made up of a single racial or ethnic group. To identify with these groups, they eat knishes with Jews, burritos with Mexicans, and soul food with African-Americans. When they speak to one of these groups, they try to identify with the listeners' goals and aspirations.

If you are speaking to a group with members from diverse backgrounds, you should be particularly careful in your use of language. If your audience includes foreign students, they may have problems understanding slang and colloquial expressions. If you are in a class with people from different ethnic groups, some of your classmates might not understand experiences that are typical of your own group. For example, not everyone has gone to summer camp, and not everyone has eaten *kim chi*.

It used to be that awareness of cultural diversity usually occurred as a result of foreign travel. Today, however, there is a continuous flow of immigration to the United States. Ethnic populations are increasing, and these new racial and ethnic populations tend to hold on to their own customs (Gonzalez, Houston & Chen, 2000). Not only that, the Internet promotes both diversity and, at the same time, ethnic identity. Although there are numerous sites from cultures other than yours, there are also sites where those from other cultures can gather information and seek contact with people like themselves. This creates increasing challenges for speakers.

One thing speakers cannot do is reduce all cultures, or even one culture, to a single type. In their book *Our Voices*, Alberto González, Marsha Houston, and Victoria Chen make it clear that "there is not 'one' style of any particular ethnic group any more than there is 'one' style of Anglo-American communication" (Gonzalez, Houston & Chen, 2000, p. xvi). What this means, more than anything else, is that speakers need to be sensitive and responsive to diverse audiences. The more information and knowledge they have about their listeners, the better they will be able to specifically adapt their speeches to the needs of those audience members.

Geographic Location

Your audience's geographic location may affect the content and approach of your speech. If the federal government is giving money to improve airport runways, find out if some of this money is coming to the local airport. If the nation has been hit with a crime wave (or a heat wave), has this been a problem in your local area? If you have a chance to speak in a town or city other than your own, the audience will be pleased if you know something about its area. Ralph Nader, the consumer advocate, always does some geographical research before he speaks. When he spoke on the environment to upstate New Yorkers, for example, he mentioned specific environmental problems in their own area.

Group Affiliation

Knowing the clubs, organizations, or associations that audience members belong to can be useful because people usually identify with the goals and interests of their own organizations. If you speak to a group, you should be aware of what it stands for and adapt your speech accordingly.

If you speak to the local historical society, its members will expect you to speak on a subject that has some historic angle for their area. The campus journalism society will be interested in a speech dealing with the theory (e.g., freedom of the press) or practice (e.g., using computer-assisted reporting) of journalism. Some groups have particular issues or themes for the year, and they look for speakers who can tie their speeches into these themes.

Consider This

Here is a brief survey you can use to gather information about your audience. Although this survey is designed primarily for classroom use, you can easily adapt it to a broader audience by changing some questions and adding others. Have students circle the correct response or add a response in the blank labeled "Other."

1. I am:
   A. Female
   B. Male

2. My approximate age is:
   A. 18–22
   B. 23–29
   C. 30–39
   D. Over 40

3. My primary ethnic background is:
   A. Anglo
   B. African-American
   C. Hispanic
   D. Native American
   E. Asian
   F. Other _____

4. My marital status is:
   A. Single
   B. Married
   C. Divorced
   D. Other _____

5. I live:
   A. In my parents' home
   B. In my own apartment or house
   C. In a dormitory
   D. In a fraternity or sorority

Consider This (continued)

6. I am involved in: (*Circle all that apply.*)
   A. Athletics
   B. Student government
   C. A fraternity or sorority
   D. Intramural activities
   E. An honor society
   F. Other _____

7. I currently:
   A. Go to school full-time
   B. Go to school full-time and work part-time
   C. Go to school part-time and work part-time
   D. Go to school part-time and work full-time
   E. Other _____

8. To what extent are you liberal or conservative in your religious orientation? (*Circle the number that most closely reflects your attitude.*)
   Liberal 5 4 3 2 1 Conservative

9. To what extent are you liberal or conservative in your political orientation? (*Circle the number that most closely reflects your attitude.*)
   Liberal 5 4 3 2 1 Conservative

10. How involved or committed are you on this issue?

    _____
    (*Write the topic of your speech here.*)
    Highly involved 5 4 3 2 1 Not involved

11. How informed are you on this issue?

    _____
    (*Write the topic of your speech here.*)
    Highly informed 5 4 3 2 1 Poorly informed

12. How interested are you in this issue?

    _____
    (*Write the topic of your speech here.*)
    Highly interested 5 4 3 2 1 Not interested

■ ANALYZING THE OCCASION

When planning your speech, as well as doing audience analysis, you need to consider the occasion at which you will be speaking. Factors to take into account when analyzing the occasion include the length of the speech, the time of day, and the location of the speech.

Length of the Speech

Always stick to the time limit set for the speech. If you are giving a speech in class, you will probably be told the amount of time you can speak. If you are asked to give a speech to a group or organization, you should ask how long you will be expected to speak. When the audience has an expectation of the length of your speech, it will get restless if you go on too long or will be disappointed if you run short. If your speech topic is too complicated to be covered in the allotted time, you should narrow your topic or find another subject to speak on.

More than one speaker hasn't known when to stop. Mortimer J. Adler has written about the time he was giving lectures on philosophy to college students. Student interest in the subject was great, but not great enough to sit through each of Adler's two-hour lectures. When Adler returned the next year to deliver another series of lectures, the students hid alarm clocks in the lecture hall. After an hour, all of the alarms went off. At the second lecture, a student pulled the main switch after an hour and blacked out the lecture hall. Adler got the message; he cut his remaining lectures to a listenable length (Adler, 1983, pp. 71–72).

Time of Day

The time of day should also be a consideration when you are choosing your topic. In a classroom setting, students seem to be less alert in the early morning and late afternoon. If you are in a class that meets at one of these times, you have to pay special attention to the appeal of your presentation. An interesting topic or a topic handled in an interesting manner can get the attention of even a sluggish audience. Probably most public speeches occur at night. Since people are usually somewhat tired, the speaker has to take special care to find material that will hold the audience's attention.

Physical Setting of the Speech

The place where the speech will be given might also be a consideration. If you are not familiar with the room, you might want to take a look at it before you speak. Is the lectern where you want it? Are the chairs arranged the way you want them? Is there a public address system? Do you know how to turn it on? Changes are easier to make before the audience arrives.

A speaker we witnessed gave a speech in a large gymnasium. Arriving moments before the speech was to be delivered, he discovered the public address system had not been set up. Also, the lectern was placed in the middle of the gym instead of closer to the audience as he preferred. The final insult was that the public address system, once working, could be heard by only the center portion of the large audience. People seated at either end of the gym could not hear. The disaster could not be rectified in time to save the speech.

Consider comfort for the audience in a location. Many a politician has given a speech from courtyard steps, where there is no place for the audience to sit. If you are in a location where the audience cannot be comfortable, be prepared to give a short speech and get to the point before you lose your audience.

 Assess Yourself

Do You Have Confidence as a Speaker?

Directions: This instrument is composed of 30 items regarding your feelings of confidence as a speaker. After each statement there is a "True" and a "False."

Try to decide whether "True" or "False" *most* represents your feelings associated with your *most recent* speech, then put a circle around the "True" or "False." Work quickly and don't spend much time on any statement. We want your *first impression* on this survey.

When you are finished, go to the website and compare your responses with those on the website to determine your results.

1. I look forward to an opportunity to speak in public.	True	False
2. My hands tremble when I try to handle objects on the lectern.	True	False

Assess Yourself (continued)

3. I am in constant fear of forgetting my speech.	True	False
4. Audiences seem friendly when I address them.	True	False
5. While preparing a speech I am in a constant state of anxiety.	True	False
6. At the conclusion of a speech I feel that I have had a pleasant experience.	True	False
7. I dislike using my body and voice expressively.	True	False
8. My thoughts become confused and jumbled when I speak before an audience.	True	False
9. I have no fear of facing an audience.	True	False
10. Although I am nervous just before getting up to speak I soon forget my fears and enjoy the experience.	True	False
11. I face the prospect of making a speech with complete confidence.	True	False
12. I feel that I am in complete possession of myself while speaking.	True	False
13. I prefer to have notes on the platform in case I forget my speech.	True	False
14. I like to observe the reactions of my audience to my speech.	True	False
15. Although I talk fluently with friends I am at a loss for words on the platform.	True	False
16. I feel relaxed and comfortable while speaking.	True	False
17. Although I do not enjoy speaking in public I do not particularly dread it.	True	False
18. I always avoid speaking in public if possible.	True	False
19. The faces of my audience are blurred when I look at them.	True	False
20. I feel disgusted with myself after trying to address a group of people.	True	False
21. I enjoy preparing a talk.	True	False
22. My mind is clear when I face an audience.	True	False
23. I am fairly fluent.	True	False
24. I perspire and tremble just before getting up to speak.	True	False
25. My posture feels strained and unnatural.	True	False
26. I am fearful and tense all the while I am speaking before a group of people.	True	False
27. I find the prospect of speaking mildly pleasant.	True	False
28. It is difficult for me to search my mind calmly for the right words to express my thoughts.	True	False
29. I am terrified at the thought of speaking before a group of people.	True	False
30. I have a feeling of alertness in facing an audience.	True	False

 Go to the *Communicating Effectively* CD-ROM to see your results and learn how to evaluate your attitudes and feelings.

Source: G. L. Paul, *Insight vs Desensitization in Psychotherapy* (Stanford, CA: Stanford University Press, 1966.). In J. P. Robinson, P. R. Shaver, & L. S. Wrightsman, *Measures of Personality and Social Psychological Attitudes* (San Diego: Academic Press, 1991), pp. 188–90.

Chapter Review

Whenever you are scheduled to make a speech, it is important to find a topic that interests you. Two techniques will help you discover topics: making a personal inventory, which means taking a careful look at what interests you, and Internet brainstorming, which is a method of generating ideas through free association using the Internet.

Once the topic is narrowed, you should test whether it is appropriate for the audience, whether it is appropriate for you, and whether it is appropriate for the occasion.

Once you have an idea for a topic, you should narrow it so that it can be adequately covered within the time set for your speech. Narrowing the topic means taking some specific aspect of the subject and speaking about it.

Every speech should have a general purpose, a specific purpose, and a central idea. The general purpose relates to whether the speech is informative or persuasive. The specific purpose focuses on what you want to inform or persuade your audience about. The central idea captures the main idea of the speech—the idea you want your audience to retain after the speech.

Audience analysis is the process of finding out what the audience knows about the subject, what it might be interested in, what its attitudes and beliefs are, and what kinds of people are likely to be present. Useful demographic information about an audience includes age, gender, education, occupation, race/nationality/ethnic origin, geographic location, and group affiliation.

In analyzing the speech occasion, the speaker should consider the length of the speech, the time of day, and the physical setting where the speech will take place.

Questions to Review

1. What is the connection between public speaking and transactional communication, and why is it important to regard speaking as a transaction?

2. What makes choosing a topic for a classroom speech so difficult? What are the elements that need to be considered when choosing a topic?

3. How can the Internet be used to assist in searching for a topic?

4. Once a topic is selected, how should you go about testing it? Why is testing the topic an important consideration for speakers?

5. What distinguishes the general purpose, specific purpose, and central idea? Given the topic "Students and Body Piercing,"

create a hypothetical general purpose, specific purpose, and central idea.

6. What are the most effective ways to gain knowledge about your audience?

7. What must be discovered about listeners? Is it clear to you why information about audience members is so important to speakers?

8. Do the suggestions in this chapter sound reasonable to you when you are faced with having to give a speech? Explain.

mhhe•com/hybels

Go to the self-quizzes on the *Communicating Effectively* CD-ROM (side 2, track 10) and the Online Learning Center at mhhe.com/hybels7 to test your knowledge of the chapter concepts.

References

Adler, M. J. (1983). *How to speak, how to listen*. New York: Macmillan.

Allen, S. (1986). *How to make a speech*. New York: McGraw-Hill.

Gonzalez, A., M. Houston, & V. Chen (2000). *Our voices: Essays in culture, ethnicity, and communication (An intercultural anthology)*, (3rd ed.) Los Angeles: Roxbury.

Osborn, A. (1979). *Applied imagination: Principles and procedures of creative thinking*. New York: Scribner's.

Smeraglia, R. E. (2000). "Getting directions: Reading the road signs on the information superhighway." On the Net, *ComputerScene Online*, Continuing Education, I.T. Training, University of New Mexico. Retrieved June 8, 2002, from http://www.computerscene.com/editorial/onthenet.htm.

Tucker-Ladd, C. E. (1996–2000). "Chapter 5: Signs of stress," "Psychological self-help/mental health net." Retrieved March 25, 2003, from www.mhnet.org/psyhelp/chap5/chap5c.htm.

Further Reading

Asher, J. (2001). *Even a geek can speak: Low-tech presentation skills for high-tech people*. Atlanta, GA: Longstreet Press. Asher, president of Chambers and Asher Speechworks, a nationally recognized communications training firm, in this funny, insightful, and enjoyable book, includes sections on defining your goals, eliminating jargon, and enlivening your stage presence. Here you will find dozens of entertaining, real-life examples designed to inspire managers, entrepreneurs, and all types of tech "geeks" to improve themselves.

Brown, M. "Presentations." The Writing Center, Rensselaer Polytechnic Institute, Troy, New York. Retrieved March 25, 2003, from http://www.rpi.edu/dept/llc/writecenter/web/presentation.htm. Brown offers snapshots of the following aspects of developing and delivering presentations: understanding your task and audience, structuring your presentation, framing your presentation, selecting visuals, and practicing for your speech. She includes specific, practical ideas.

Dowis, R. (1999). *The lost art of the great speech: How to write one—How to deliver it*. New York: AMACOM. Dowis claims that speechmaking is not all delivery techniques. In this book, he provides specific guidance on how to write a dynamic speech. Although important, splashy slides, confident body language, and a lot of eye contact are unimportant if the speech is rambling, illogical, or just plain boring. Dowis's advice will help readers give powerful, on-target speeches, designed to capture an audience's attention and drive messages home. Dowis cites great contemporary and historical speeches and includes an appendix that lists resources for speakers and writers.

Eggleston, S. (2001, July 6). "Fear of public speaking: Stress myths and magic." (Trail by Fire). Retrieved March 25, 2003, from http://www.the-eggman.com/ writings/fearspk1.html. In a 3-page website, Eggleston offers a delightful, humorous, anecdotal, personal look at the fear of public speaking.

Esposito, J. E. (2000). *In the spotlight: Overcome your fear of public speaking and performing*. Bridgewater, CT: Strong Books. In this enthusiastic, sensitive, wise, and passionate guide, Esposito helps readers overcome their fears and discover new-found freedom and power in self-expression through the use of elements of CBT, interpersonal psychotherapy, and homework exercises. This book is conversational yet authoritative, and it is concise yet comprehensive.

Hoff, R., & B. Maguire (1992). *'I can see you naked': A new revised edition of the national bestseller on making fearless presentations*. Kansas City, MO: Andrews McMeel Publishing. Although somewhat dated, Hoff's book continues to be the bestselling, popular book on the subject. It is easy-to-read, full of humor, uses a comfortable writing stye, and is easy to understand and apply. He covers first impressions, delivery, and audience analysis (which includes language use and setting analysis). He spends less time with the process of organization. The book is full of terrific, practical tips.

Orman, M. C. (1996–2002). "How to conquer public speaking fear." Retrieved March 25, 2003, from www.stresscure.com/jobstress/speak.html. Orman is a medical doctor, but in this nine-page website, he offers an examination of public-speaking fear from a personal-experience perspective, not a medical one. He begins by discussing 10 key principles to always keep in mind, reveals 11 "hidden" causes of public-speaking stress, and then suggests the best way to practice: "Go out and speak in public."

Smith, P. (Ed.) (2000). *Onward!: 25 years of advice, exhortation, and inspiration from America's best commencement speeches.* New York: Scribner. In this well-edited, interesting, inspirational, and educational anthology, Peter J. Smith includes highlights from such speakers as Art Buchwald, Isaac Asimov, George Plimpton, and Madeleine L'Engle in the 1970s, up through the Dalai Lama, Ruth Bader Ginsburg, Andy Rooney, and Madeleine Albright in the 1990s. There are highlights, too, from Studs Turkel, Shirley Chisholm, Desmond Tutu, Gary Larson, Jodie Foster, Ronald Reagan, Annette Bening, Ann Richards, Alan Greenspan, Mumia Abu-Jamal, and more. There are over 200 excerpts from the best commencement addresses given during the last twenty-five years.

Wagstaffe, J. (2002). *Romancing the room: How to engage your audience, court your crowd, and speak successfully in public.* Three Rivers, MI: Three Rivers Press. James Wagstaffe is a trial attorney who teaches practical speech communications at Stanford University and is a regular columnist for the *Los Angeles Daily Journal* and the *San Francisco Daily Journal.* Based on his personal encounters, and as a public-speaking expert, Wagstaffe has sections on establishing common ground with an audience, using visuals and stories to captivate audiences, avoiding filler words and distracting voice patterns, and winning an audience by substance, not sound bites. The book is full of anecdotes, sage advice, and ingenious tricks of the trade.

Walters, L. (2000). *Secrets of superstar speakers: Wisdom from the greatest motivators of our time.* New York: McGraw-Hill. Walters answers the question, "What makes the cream-of-the-crop motivational speakers stand above the rest?" Based on interviews, she offers detailed profiles of 19 superstars including Mya Angelou, Les Brown, Jack Canfield, Deepak Chopra, Stephen Covey, Sir Winston Leonard Spenser Churchill, Elizabeth Dole, Mark Victor Hansen, Lou Holtz, Vince Lombardi, Sr. and Jr., Earl Nightingale, Norman Vincent Peale, Christopher Reeve, Anita Roddick, Tony Robbins, Brian Tracy, Dottie Walters, and Zig Ziglar. This book, although packed with wisdom and insight, is designed for virgin public speakers or those who want a refreshing booster.

Chapter 13

Finding Speech Material

Objectives

After reading this chapter, you should be able to:

- Complete the necessary steps before doing research on the Internet.
- Use a variety of methods for obtaining information on the Internet.
- Access a number of different online computer databases.
- Recognize the importance of determining website credibility.
- Ask the essential questions necessary to judge the quality of Internet information.
- Make use of efficient procedures for taking notes on Internet information.
- Recognize the various kinds of supporting materials.
- Use the supporting materials that are most appropriate for your topic and your audience.

Key Terms and Concepts

Use the Communicating Effectively CD-ROM and Online Learning Center at mhhe.com/hybels7 to further your understanding of the following terms.

Comparison 471	Hypothetical	Statistics 475
Computer	example 475	Study 479
database 457	Internet 459	Subject directory 461
Contrast 472	Metasearch engine 463	Supporting material 470
Definition 473	Polls 479	Testimony 478
Example 473	Search engine 462	

THE DEADLINE FOR THE SPEECH WAS FAST APPROACHING, and despite all her other class assignments, work schedule, and her new friend Curtis, Prudence Gibson knew she had to move quickly if she was to complete her speech on time. She had been reviewing possible topics for almost a week now, but none of them met the criteria of being appropriate to her, the class, and the occasion. Sitting at her computer terminal, alone in her room, sending e-mail messages to her high school friends back in her hometown, a topic suddenly occurred to her: the Internet. The problem was the topic wasn't new, and Prudence realized most people in her class were likely to be computer-literate. Prudence had been using computers since junior high school—to write her papers, to keep in touch with her friends, to shop, and, occasionally, to play games. "What can I talk about that will offer a new perspective, new information, or new insights to my classmates?" she wondered to herself.

Suddenly a thought occurred to her: OWLs. She had learned about OWLs in high school when her librarian, Mrs. Smith, introduced her to them as an aid to writing a paper for her social studies class. Mrs. Smith told her about *online writing laboratories* (OWLs) because Prudence had asked her so many questions about research techniques, proper language usage, and the citation of sources. Prudence wondered how many of her classmates were already familiar with OWLs. "Probably some of them," she thought to herself, answering her own question. "What can I do with OWLs that would make my speech different?" she wondered some more.

The answer came to her in a flash. "I can talk about how OWLs can contribute to making effective speeches." She would investigate OWLs, and she would show how the advice and suggestions could help those who use these sites to prepare better speeches. At this point, Prudence did not know if what she wanted to do would even work, but since she was already working online at her computer, she decided to begin her exploration at once.

Prudence began by entering *online writing laboratories* into the Google search engine. There were only 74 Web pages reported, but the OWL at the University of Maine suggested using key words *writing lab* or *writing center*. The key words *writing lab* produced 1,390,000 Web pages, and *writing center* produced 1,310,000 pages. The first Web page listed when *writing lab* was entered was for the Online

Writing Lab at Purdue University (http://owl.english.purdue.edu/). Prudence found this to be the most complete OWL she discovered on the Internet. She typed *other online writing labs* into the Purdue search engine and discovered links to 77 other writing labs (March 25, 2003)—more sources for information than she could pursue in any reasonable amount of time.

Prudence spent an hour visiting various websites, making her assessments of the information she discovered, and printing out documents she thought might prove helpful as she prepared her speech. As she began amassing information, she began thinking about how she was going to organize her speech. She wanted to do this rather quickly because it would help her focus her research. Right now, she was simply printing out anything that looked like it might help her, and her pile of information was growing quickly. Even her literature base was growing. That is, some of the websites referred to articles that had been written about OWLs.

Every time she encountered one of these references, she would make certain she had the entire citation so that she could return to the site if she chose to later, and, too, so that she would be able to include it in her references at the end of her written speech. (See the Consider This box below).

When Prudence accessed the OWL of Purdue University she typed *About Online Writing Labs (OWLs)* into the search engine and found 1,222 pages. Clicking the OWL Resource Page, she discovered close to 20 scholarly articles written about OWLs, most of which had a URL attached so that Prudence would be able to access the articles online. (See Figure 13-1.) Regarding

Consider This

Citations

Make certain you have the author, the date of the article or handout if available, or the update of the website if available, the title of the article or handout, the source of the article (e.g., Online Writing Lab (OWL), Purdue University), the date you retrieved it from the Internet, and the entire URL.

You'll need the proper citations when you submit information for an assignment, and you may need them, too, if you plan to return to the website. If the URL is incorrect, you may be able to trace the article or handout by entering the author, title (or both), or the source into the Google search engine.

Figure 13-1

OWL Home Page of Purdue University

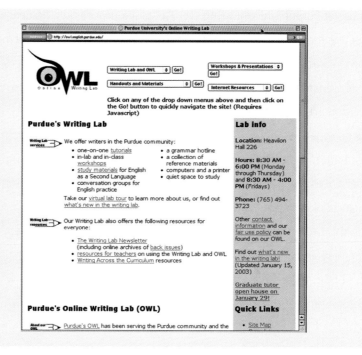

Prudence's assessment of the Purdue University OWL, she soon discovered her evaluation of that site was correct: It was one of the most cross-referenced OWL sites of any she found, and a number of websites mentioned that the Purdue University site had been used as a model when other sites were constructed.

Prudence was getting closer to preparing an outline. Her general purpose was to inform. Her specific purpose was to introduce her listeners to OWLs, to the general benefits of OWLs, and to the aspects of OWLs that would help them prepare their speeches. Her central idea was to show her classmates the value of OWLs in the preparation of their speeches. At this point, then, she began making a list of things she wanted to do in her speech. First, she wanted to offer an introduction to OWLs. Second, she wanted to let her listeners know about the benefits of using OWLs. Third, she wanted to introduce specific aspects of OWLs that would help them prepare their speeches.

With these three ideas in mind, Prudence looked over the stack of printouts that she had accumulated to see if she could divide the stack into these three areas. She could. With the arrangement in front of her, she typed a rough first draft of an outline on her computer. Along with each entry, Prudence typed in the reference from which she obtained the information so that she could easily return to the resource at a later time. This would allow her to put together footnotes or endnotes of sources used for her speech when her outline was complete. Just as important, too, she knew she would be able to cite her sources at appropriate places when she was actually delivering the speech. Her rough first draft of the outline looked like this:

I. *Online writing labs (OWLs) are becoming increasingly common in writing programs of colleges throughout the United States (Arnold, N. (1999, March 14). "OWLS: A New Medium for Teaching Writing; A New Mode of Writing." Retrieved June 5, 2002, from http://www.eln.org/,n_arnold/OWLs.html (July 18, 1999).*
   A. *OWLs are a medium for teaching writing (Arnold).*
   B. *OWLs can be found in many different forms. ([No author]. (n.d.). "A beginner's guide to the OWLs of North America." Retrieved June 5, 2002, from http://www.filebox.vt.edu/users/cbaugh/foyer.htm).*
   C. *OWLs are used primarily by upper–middle-class males (Blythe, S., Spring 1996). "Do OWLs Leave Some Students Out?" Kairos: A Journal for Teachers of Writing in Webbed Environments, 1(1) Retrieved June 5, 2002, from http://www.english.ttu.edu/Kairos/1.1/index.html (July 18, 1999).*

II. *OWLs have important benefits for their users.*
   A. *The first obvious benefit is that an OWL is not limited by geographic distance or time constraints. (Johnson, P. J., (Spring 1996). "Writing Spaces: Technoprovocateurs and OWLs in the Late Age of Print." Kairos: A Journal for Teachers of Writing in Webbed Environments 1(1)]. Retrieved June 5, 2002, from http://english.ttu.edu/Kairos/1.1/index.html).*
   B. *Some OWLs offer online tutoring so users can get e-mail responses to their needs (Arnold, p. 3 of 5).*
   C. *There are MOOs, too—meaning multiuser dungeon, object-oriented—which is a chat software program in which users create a room (dungeon) to talk within. These are real-time virtual environments (Arnold, p. 3 of 5).*
   D. *They offer a solid collection of links for Internet-based academic research, including information on how to evaluate Internet research sites. (Harris, R., 1997). "Evaluating Internet Research Sources." Southern California University. Retrieved June 5, 2002, from http://www.sccu.edu/faculty/R_Harris/evalu8it.htm).*

III. *OWLs can provide important information for speech preparation.*
   A. *Although there are clear differences between preparing a written paper and preparing a speech—like the degree of formality, or the exacting concern in writing for sentence construction, punctuation, and spelling (not that these shouldn't be a concern of ours in our outlines)—there are still a number of important similarities, and it is in these similarities that OWLs can offer assistance. (Personal experience.)*

B. *Let me briefly summarize or, perhaps, annotate a number of the resources I discovered at OWL sites that would help us in preparing speeches:*

1. *Presentation overview. (Brown, M., n.d.). "Presentations." The Writing Center, Rensselaer Polytechnic Institute. Retrieved June 5, 2002, from http://www.rpi.edu/web/writingcenter/presentation.html).*

2. *Using the Web to conduct research. (Jordan-Henley, J., 2001, June 6). "Using the Web to Conduct Research." Roane State Community College. Retrieved June 5, 2002, from http://www2.rscc.cc.tn.us/,jordan_ii/OWL/researchguide.html#Appraisal).*

3. *How to appraise websites. (No author, 2002, May 25). Evaluating websites. Writer's Roosts, Writing Center, The University of Kansas. Retrieved June 5, 2002, from http://www.writing.ku.edu/resources/evaluate.html).*

4. *Coping with writing anxiety. (No author, 2002). "Coping with Writing Anxiety." Purdue University OWL Handouts. Retrieved June 5, 2002, from http://owl.english.purdue.edu/handouts/general/gl_anxiety.html).*

5. *Avoiding sexist language. (No author, 2002). "I Didn't Mean to Say That! Avoiding Sexist Language." Undergraduate Writing Center, The University of Texas at Austin. Retrieved June 5, 2002, from http://uwc.fac.utexas.edu/media/handouts/sexist-lang.pdf).*

6. *Eliminating wordiness. (Leonard, M., April 2002). "Eliminating Wordiness." Undergraduate Writing Center, The University of Texas at Austin. Retrieved June 5, 2002, from http://uwc.fac.utexas.edu/media/handouts/wordiness.pdf).*

7. *Audience analysis. (Zimmerman, D. J., 2002). "Audience analysis." Writing Center, Colorado State University. Retrieved June 5, 2002, from http://writing.colostate.edu/references/processes/audmod/pop10g.cfm.*

8. *Developing an outline. (No author, 2002). "Developing an Outline." Purdue University Writing Lab. Retrieved June 5, 2002, from http://owl.english.purdue.edu/handouts/general/gl-outlin.html.*

Within approximately two or three hours, using the Internet as her sole basis for research, Prudence had put together the rudiments of an informative speech with 10 different current sources—all of which, to her, appeared to be credible and valuable. Also, she had references for at least 10 other offline resources to pursue on her morning trip to the library. Prudence printed out her tentative outline, and with the outline in hand, she began to think about fleshing out the details of the outline and preparing both an introduction and a conclusion.

What pleased Prudence about her speech was that she had discovered much new information that would help her, she was supplying information that was likely to assist members of her audience, and the entire process had occupied so little time. With a couple of days left before the speech was to be delivered, Prudence now had plenty of time to access other databases, fill in the details, and learn her material.

When the time came for Prudence's speech, her audience listened with obvious interest. She was pleased she had hit the appropriate mark. While some of her listeners were already informed, most learned something completely new to them. It was clear that she had done considerable research and knew quite a lot about her topic. After the speech was over, several people asked her questions, and at the end of class someone even asked to examine some of the website printouts she had enlarged and used as her visual aids. By doing her research on a topic with which she already had some familiarity, and pursuing, too, a topic in which she had developed a great deal of interest, Prudence had come across as a *credible*—that is, believable—speaker.

No doubt you would like to have the same reaction from your class that Prudence had. You would like to be thought of as credible and knowledgeable. The key to having this happen lies in the research you do for your speech. The more diligent you are about finding relevant material and adapting it to your audience, the more successful you will be when you give your speech.

■ RESEARCHING YOUR TOPIC: WHERE TO LOOK

Once you have decided on the topic, specific purpose, and central idea of your speech, it is time to begin looking for useful information. The four most common sources you can draw on for relevant material are your own personal experience and observation, interviews, the library, and the Internet. Because there is an enormous amount of information to be obtained from the Internet, it is accessible 24/7, it is a comfortable and easy way to access information, it is cost-effective, and it is the resource of choice for finding information, we will devote most of the space on researching your topic to using the Internet.

Drawing on Personal Experience and Observation

If you have chosen a topic in which you have a strong interest, the first thing you should ask yourself is whether you have had any direct experience with the subject. Your own experience can provide interesting and valuable material. For example, Prudence selected a topic she had become familiar with in high school. When Dan spoke to his speech class on the subject "Preventing Fires in Your Home," he drew heavily on his experiences as a volunteer firefighter. Not only did he describe the tragedy of a family being burned out of their home, but he also gave some facts and figures on the causes of home fires that he had learned during his training period.

When Kelly spoke of the danger of drunk drivers, she too gave facts and figures: how many innocent victims are killed each year by drunks on the road. Then she stunned her classmates by telling them that her own sister had been one of those victims. Because Kelly spoke from personal experience, her example became much more vivid and real than it would have been if she had used only statistics from a book or an article.

Sometimes we do not put enough value on personal experience; we think that if it happened to us, it can't be important. However, relating personal experiences to the subject of a speech can often provide the most interesting material of all.

Interviewing

Interviews can be an excellent source of speech material. Because you can talk directly to decision makers, conducting interviews is one of the best ways to gather material on campus-related topics, such as why three people are put in dorm rooms intended for two or what energy-saving devices are used on campus. Interviews are also a good means of getting up-to-date information from experts. For example, if a war breaks out in the Middle East, you can interview the person on campus who is most knowledgeable in this area. In addition, if the subject is complicated, you can ask questions about points you don't understand.

One advantage of the Internet is that it provides contact with authorities and others around the world on a 24-hour basis. Using interest groups such as mailing lists, news groups, live chat groups, and Web forums, you can ask people questions, share ideas, sound off, and just plain converse with others on almost any topic imaginable. Since the Internet is not limited by geography or time constraints, you can post a question and receive an answer from anywhere in the world in less time than it would take to get the answer from a book, from a face-to-face talk with an authority, or from another resource.

Using the Library

The library can be a rich source of material, and any library—whether large or small—has millions of pieces of information. Fortunately for users, all libraries organize their information in essentially the same way, so when you learn how to use one library, you can use this skill in any library. Today, however, most library resources can be found on the Internet, and, unfortunately, users cannot use the same methods for accessing Internet information as they do when using libraries. But, just as with libraries, once you learn how to access information on the Internet, you can access it in much the same way from any computer around the world. Likewise, the methods of using computer catalogs are similar, although not identical, from library to library on the Internet.

There are two basic things you need to know about using the library. The first has to do with computer databases, and the second has to do with how

On the Web

Online Databases

There are many online databases. Here are three websites that provide links to numerous online databases—indexes, bibliographies, dictionaries, encyclopedias, and full text articles. In their electronic versions, they can be searched more quickly and with more sophistication than in their paper versions.

1. (No author), "General Research Division: Guide to Computer Databases," Humanities and Social Sciences Library, The New York Public Library, December 15, 1999. Retrieved March 25, 2003, from http://www.nypl.org/research/chss/grd/election.html

2. (No author), "Online Databases," University Libraries, Boston College, May 15, 2002. Retrieved March 25, 2003, from http://www.bc.edu/libraries/resources/databases/.

3. (No author), "Online Databases," King County Library System, Puget Sound area, Washington State, April 30, 2002. Retrieved March 25, 2003, from http://www.kcls.org/erout/erout.html.

to use them. Most information that can be found in brick-and-mortar libraries can now be found online; however, it is more accessible and efficient to find it on the Internet.

Computer Databases

This section on library usage is brief because literary, musical, artistic, reference materials, and periodical and newspaper collections are all stored in **computer (or online) databases**—which are a collection of items of information organized for easy access via the computer. Databases vary in their content as well as in their arrangements and protocols. The reason is that there are many database producers and vendors, and each of them has their own corresponding software.

For most classroom speeches, computer databases will supply most of the necessary resources. If in-depth research is necessary, or if the speech assignment requires the use of books and other offline information, it may be necessary to go beyond or outside what the computer has to offer. This is neither good nor bad; however, it is likely to slow down the process of speech preparation.

Using Computer Databases

On the computer, the two common types of databases are *citation databases* and *full-text databases*. ERIC (Education Resources Information Center), SocioFile (for publications in the broad field of sociology), and PsycLIT (for citations to and abstracts from journals and other literature in psychology, as well as citations to dissertations) are citation databases. (All three are discussed in the On the Web box on page 458. *Encyclopedia Britannica*, *Facts on File*, and *World Almanac* are full-text databases.

Most computer databases are not 100 percent full text. Usually, only a percentage of the articles or entries are provided in their entirety. Some databases have arrangements with companies that will supply articles from

On the Web

Internet Databases

- *Yahoo: www.yahoo.com/.* Yahoo is everybody's "favorite" subject guide; it is one of the first places that people register their sites so that it is fairly comprehensive, but its large size can make it unwieldy for precision searching. You can look for documents by moving through the menu categories or do a keyword search at any category level. You can search by Intelligent Default, exact phrase, AND, OR, limiting by date.

- *LookSmart: www.looksmart.com/.* LookSmart has reviewed and organized more than 2 million Web pages into a number of categories (200,000 organized hierarchically) covering everything from gardening and books to motor racing and space exploration in order. You can search by either keyword or drill down through the categories. The keyword search results give you both a list of relevant categories as well as the relevant sites.

- *Gary Price's Direct Search (Search Tools and Directories): gwis2.circ.gwu.edul,gprice/direct. htm.* This is a guide to direct links to numerous interfaces of resources that are not easily searchable from general search tools because they are located in databases or other "hidden" places. Categories include library archives and catalogs, full-text book sources, humanities, science, social sciences, bibliographies, government, business/economics, ready reference, and news sources and serials. Price also maintains a List of Lists, Speech and Transcript Center, Internet Accessible Audio/Visual, and NewsCenter, all linked to from the Direct Search pages.

- *About.com:www.About.com.* Formerly known as the Mining Company, this site contains hundreds of guides on many topics, all put together by experts on each subject. You can search for information by keyword, or drill down through 36 categories to find what you want.

- *Librarians Index to the Internet: http://lii.org/.* This is an extensive index to great sites on the Internet compiled by librarians at the University of California and elsewhere. You can subscribe to a weekly list of new sites added to the index, which serves as a great way to keep up to date on good reference resources.

- *WWW Virtual Library: Data Sources by Subject:vlib.org/Overview.html.* This is another site where each subject is compiled and hosted by an expert in the field. The drawback to this distributed search guide is that the subject guides are erratically and infrequently updated.

- *Argus Clearinghouse for Subject-Oriented Internet Resource Guides (UMich):www.clearing house.net/.* This site also contains Resource Guides to the Internet by subject authored by experts in the field. This is usually the first place I [Terry Brainerd Chadwick] start on a research project in a field that I am unfamiliar with. These guides are great because they usually include an explanation of the subject and/or how to use the Internet, and usually have sections for ftp, telnet, gopher, e-mail, and WWW resources. The site reviews and rates the resource guides.

Source: Terry Brainerd Chadwick, "How to Conduct Research on the Internet," (InfoQuest! Information Services), September 21, 2001, www.tbchad.com/resrch.html (March 21, 2003). This information has been condensed, but quoted directly, from Chadwick's website.

the database for a fee. If a title you are searching for is not available in full text, there are several options:

1. Check local libraries for the source.
2. Utilize the library's document delivery service.
3. Utilize the library's interlibrary loan area.

4. Check to see if the discipline has a CD-ROM that contains the article. (The discipline of speech communication, for example, has one that includes abstracts for every communication-related journal from its inception. The CD-ROM carries the full text for a number of the journals.)

Researching on the Internet

There were more than 3,000 times the number of people online in 2000 than the number who were online in 1993 (State of the Internet 2000). There were more than a half-billion online users in 2001, and some industry estimates predict that the number of Internet users worldwide in 2005 will pass the one-billion mark. "Approximately two million more people become Internet users every month, and over half of the population is now online" (A Nation Online, 2002). More than 700 million users will live outside of North America (State of the Internet 2000). People "worldwide are using the net on a frequent basis for business, research, shopping, personal correspondence, social interactions, entertainment, listening to radio, and communications and information-sharing functions of every description" (State of the Internet 2000).

For children, the Internet has become integrated into their daily routines, which involve school, entertainment, communication, and play. "As children get older, they become far more likely to use the Internet to engage in such activities. As a result, teenagers and young adults in school are now among the highest number of Internet users" (A Nation Online, 2002). For 18–24 year olds, "Internet use is heavily affected by whether or not they attend school or college. Among those in school or college, 85 percent use the Internet, compared to 51.5 percent of those who are not in school" (A Nation Online, 2002).

Not only are computers having an influence on our lives, but they have greatly changed the methods of research as well. This section will focus on the **Internet,** a group of networks connected to each other. In our discussion, we assume that you are already familiar with the Internet. We consider it, with that assumption in mind, our job to offer ways to organize, facilitate, and expedite searches.

The Internet provides users with thousands of online databases—those collections of information that can be read on a computer screen—and libraries of images, sounds, computer programs, books, and animation, as the On the Web box on page 458, and the section on using the library indicates. The amount of free information available over the Internet is staggering. In mid-2000 an Internet company in Washington, D.C., reported there were 2.1 billion unique, publicly available pages on the Internet (Nelson & Coleman, 2000, p. 133). The amount of information available would make you think you could find just about anything you wanted or needed on the Internet, and that is probably true; however, just like trying to find the proverbial needle in the haystack, trying to find a specific bit of data located somewhere in those 2.1 billion pages can prove to be a difficult, if not a merely challenging, task. The best way to learn about the Internet, in case our assumption about familiarity with the Internet is false, is to jump in and start exploring it. Nothing replaces hands-on experience.

On the Web

Online Periodical Databases

As you begin searching for information on the Internet, it is difficult to know exactly which databases will ultimately be most helpful. This is because there are so many and because your choice of topic will dictate which databases you need to access. However, here are three that cover education, sociology, and psychology:

- *ERIC Database* is the world's largest source of education information. This database contains more than 1,000,000 abstracts of documents and journal articles on education research and practice, beginning in 1966. ERIC indexes more than 750 professional journals. Because the database is updated monthly, you can be certain the information you receive is timely and accurate. At the following website, you can begin a search, discover other avenues for searching ERIC, and order ERIC documents and journal articles: ericir.syr.edu/ithome/database.htm.

- *SocioFile Database* indexes publications in the field of sociology. It abstracts articles starting in 1974 from 2,000 journals in 30 different languages and from about 55 countries. The literature found in SocioFile focuses on the behavior and characteristics of groups; some of the subject areas covered include social and organizational groups, social problems, and family and socialization, as well as sociological topics in the fields of anthropology, philosophy, social psychology, economics, demography, political science, community development, and business. It is updated bimonthly. One of the most complete guides to using SocioFile is www.library.pitt.edu/research/guides/socio-web.html.

- *PsycLIT Database* includes documentation of material dating from 1974 to 1983 from approximately 1,400 journals in 29 different languages. PlusNet covers 1984 to the present. New material is added every three months. It provides citations to and abstracts from journals and other literature in psychology and covers topics such as behavior, developmental psychology, educational psychology, social psychology, occupational psychology, health, anthropology, communications, sport psychology, language and linguistics, and treatment and rehabilitation. One of the best guides to using PsycLIT is www.apa.org/psycinfo/yellow.html.

To find other guides and routes to these databases, simply enter the database name into the AltaVista (or any) search engine. In general, we have found that the best guides are produced by libraries, so look for *library* and *edu* in the domain name of the URL.

Looking for Information

There are a number of ways of looking for information on the Internet. The following pages detail six.

1. Join an e-mail discussion, interest group, or Usenet newsgroup.   The following URL is a web-based directory that will help you locate e-mail discussion groups and Usenet news groups: www.liszt.com/.

2. Go directly to the site if you have the address.   Simply type the URL into the "Open" window of your Web browser. Internet Explorer instructs users to "Type the Internet address of a document or folder, and Internet Explorer will open it for you."

3. Browse the Internet. One way to browse is to enter "How to do research on the Internet" into one of the search engines, and then click on some of the Web pages that result. A good place to begin exploring is at the following URL: http://library.albany.edu/infomine.ucr.edu/.

4. Explore a subject directory. INFOMINE, from the University of California, Riverside, is a good example of an academic subject directory. Entering http://infomine.ucr.edu/ into the open window of Internet Explorer will bring up the INFOMINE home page from which you can browse a dozen databases: biological, agricultural and med sciences, business and economics, cultural diversity and ethnic resources, electronic journals, government information, instructional resources (K–12), instructional resources (University), Internet enabling tools, maps & GIS, physical sciences, engineering, CS, math, social sciences and humanities, and visual and performing arts.

5. Conduct a search using a Web subject directory, search engine, or metasearch engine: **Subject directories** include human-selected Internet resources and are arranged and classified in hierarchical topics. How do you know which to use—a subject directory or a search engine? Check out Table 13-1, which follows. In their list of Internet Subject Directories, the University at Albany Libraries (http://library.albany.edu/internet/subject.html), lists 14 academic and professional directories and 15 commercial

Table 13-1
Subject Directories or Search Engines (Searching the Internet, 2002)

Subject Directories	Search Engines
When you have a broad topic or idea to research.	When you have a narrow or obscure topic or idea to research.
When you want to see a list of sites on your topic often recommended and annotated by experts.	When you are looking for a specific site.
When you want to retrieve a list of sites relevant to your topic, rather than numerous individual pages contained within these sites.	When you want to search the full text of millions of pages.
When you want to search for the site title, annotation, and (if available) assigned keywords to retrieve relevant material rather than the full text of a document.	When you want to retrieve a large number of documents on your topic.
When you want to avoid viewing low-content documents that often turn up on search engines.	When you want to search for particular types of documents, file types, source locations, languages, date last modified, etc.
When you want to take advantage of newer retrieval technologies such as concept clustering, ranking by popularity, link ranking, and so on.	

directories and portals. In their Recommended General Subject Directories, the University of California–Berkeley Library http://www.lib.berkeley.edu/ TeachingLib/ Guides/Internet/ SubjDirectories.html), discusses five: the Librarians' Index (www.lii.org), Infomine (Infomine.ucr.edu), Academic Info (www.academicinfo.net), Yahoo! (www.yahoo.com), and About.com (www.about.com/), and at their website they compare these five based on their size, type, and search functions.

Search engines are special tools designed to help you find information on the Internet. They are likely to be your first Web guides when you are searching something by keywords. They are, perhaps, the most direct way to find what you are looking for on the World Wide Web. Each of the following search engines is explained on its home page or at a page that is accessed by clicking an icon that says About, About Us, or at the Google search engine, we first clicked Search Solutions, and on that page there is a left-margin icon All About Google that provides the explanations you are looking for.

- Alta Vista: www.altavista.com/
- Excite: www.excite.com/
- MSN: www.msn.com/
- Google: www.google.com/
- HotBot: www.hotbot.com/
- Infoseek: infoseek.go.com/
- Lycos: www.lycos.com/

- MetaCrawler: www.go2net.com/search.html
- Northern Light: nsearch.com/
- Profusion: www.profusion.com/
- Yahoo: www.yahoo.com/

As a research tool, it is worthwhile to investigate each of these search engines with the purpose of discovering its unique qualities or search capabilities. Another way to do this is to visit one of the following websites that list and annotate some of the major search engines:

- L. Barlow, (2002, May 17). "The spider's apprentice: How to use Web search engines." Monash Information Services. Retrieved March 25, 2003, from http:/ /www.monash.com/spidap3.html.
- (No author). (2002, January 22). "The major search engines." Search Engine Watch.com. Retrieved March 25, 2003, from http:// searchenginewatch.com/links/major.html.
- (No author). "The major search engines." Mimech.com, Web Search Guide. Retrieved March 25, 2003, from http://mimech.com/search-engines/major-engines.asp.

These three sites are not necessarily the best. When we entered the *Major Search Engines* into the Google search engine, 1,320,000 Web pages were produced (March 25, 2003); thus, it would be an easy task to locate other sites that annotate major search engines and provide you the kind of search that best suits your topic or idea. Even an investigation of these types of search-engine-review sites would be informative, educational, and useful before engaging in your research. One key message that is most important to anyone using search engines to investigate topics and ideas is: "Never quit a search after using just one search engine. A site with information you need may not be indexed on one engine, but may be on another" (Woods, 1999, p. 38).

Metasearch engines transmit your search requests to a number of different search engines and their databases of websites at the same time. Metasearch engines do not have their own databases, nor collect web pages, accept URL additions, or classify or review websites. Within a few seconds of your search request to a metasearch engine, you get back a compilation of results containing matching sites from all the search engines queried. This can save you a lot of time, and it can provide you with an overview of the kinds of documents available.

There are many limitations of metasearch engines. For example, most cannot take advantage of all the features of individual search engines. They may not support phrase searches, may not allow query refinement, may not conduct an exhaustive search, nor bring back all the pages from each of the individual search engines. The main advantage of a metasearch engine is the overview it can offer as you begin your investigation.

There are many metasearch engines, and entering *Metasearch Engines* into Google produced 196,000 Web pages (March 25, 2003); thus, discovering those available is an easy task, and getting some brief annotations on each of them is also convenient by accessing articles that list and annotate them. We have listed some of the major ones here along with their URLs, and if asked to recommend several, they would be MetaCrawler, MetaFind, and Dogpile because they have help files, FAQs (frequently asked questions), and search tips all available online.

- Ask Jeeves: www.askjeeves.com/
- Debriefing: www.debriefing.com
- Cyber411: cyber411.com/
- Dogpile: www.dogpile.com/
- Highway 61: www.highway61.com/
- Inference Find: www.infind.com
- Internet Sleuth: www.isleuth.com
- Verio Metasearch: search.verio.net/
- Mamma: www.mamma.com/
- MetaCrawler: www.go2net.com/search.html
- MetaFind: www.metafind.com/
- ProFusion: www.profusion.com/
- SavvySearch: www.savvysearch.com

For a "Guide to Metasearch Engines," as well as brief annotations for each of those mentioned earlier, we recommend Jian Liu's (1999) article listed in the references for this chapter.

6. Ask a research question at a research site. If all the above approaches to looking for information on the Internet have not captured the information you desire, frame your inquiry as a research question such as "Where can I find _____?" or "What is the name of _____?" and go to any one of the top eight research sites on the Internet, according to Sherry Morreale (2001, p. 8), the associate director of the National Communication Association.

Electric Library:
http://www.elibrary.com

Refdesk.com:
http://www.refdesk.com

Bigchalk.com:
http://www.bigchalk.com

Research-It:
http://www.itools.com

The Argus Clearinghouse:
http://www.clearinghouse.net

Learn2.com:
http://www.learn2.com

Infoplease.com:
http://www.infoplease.com

Ehow:
http://www.ehow.com

Enter your research question into the search window at any one of these sites, and the personnel at the site will respond. Usually, you leave an e-mail address, and they send you your answer. In most cases, we have found, responses are both quick and accurate.

Based on a survey by Opinion Research Corporation International for SuperPages.com, reported by Cindy Hall and Quin Tian (2001) in *USA Today* Snapshots, the Internet tools used most to research or find a product are first, search engines (81 percent), second, going directly to the website (71 percent), third, using an unbiased consumer site (47 percent), and four, using an online directory (35 percent). Based on our Internet work, we would agree with these results; using a search engine is easy, convenient, and fast—and you let the search engine do the work for you.

Computer databases put an immense amount of information at your fingertips 24 hours a day, 7 days a week.

Doing Research on the Internet

Prudence Gibson, in the chapter's opening example, was fortunate to discover a topic that was already narrowed, since this made her Internet search more effective and efficient than would normally be the case. Regardless of the nature of your topic, however, there are a number of useful steps for engaging in research on the Internet. Just as in doing any research, it is best to begin by defining and understanding your problem. The more preparation you can do prior to going online, the more successful your online experience is likely to be. Having a general purpose, a specific purpose, and a central idea—as Prudence did—can be a big help. Here are steps for doing research using the Internet adapted from an online website authored by Terry Brainerd Chadwick (2001), entitled "How to Conduct Research on the Internet," one of the most complete and up-to-date guides available online. We have adapted her comments to make them relate directly to speech preparation.

1. *Define your goals.* Be specific about the information you need. Breaking a topic into its component parts will make your information search clear and easier to conduct.

2. *Determine the types of information you need.* Knowing the kinds of information you want will help you choose the resources and tools that will best meet your needs. For example, are you looking for statistics, in-depth books, magazine articles, expert comments, or biographies?

3. *Identify keywords, phrases, and subject categories.* Play with your search terms; use synonyms; try distinctive terms; apply alternative spellings. Search by topic, subtopic, company, product, a person's name, and so on.

4. *Read the instructions, tips, and techniques for using the search tools you have chosen.* If you understand the types of information each tool covers and the kinds of search options you have available, you will expedite your search.

5. *Use more than one source and search tool.* Although there is duplication among sources on sites, queries performed on different search engines usually produce different results.

6. *Practice netiquette.* Be considerate of others in doing your research.

7. *Review your progress.* Look at some of the most promising records, and see if there are other terms that you can use to sharpen or widen your search. Compare what you've learned with what you decided you wanted to learn in step 1. Make adjustments or redirect your focus if necessary.

8. *Practice critical thinking!* Evaluate the information you find. Don't accept what you read as the truth; get confirming sources, ask questions, talk to experts, probe for motivations, and use your intuition. If something just doesn't sound right, check it out further.

Evaluating Information on the Internet

Now that you can access the information you want and need from the Internet, you need to be aware of the precautions regarding use of such

On the Web

When we entered the words *evaluating information on the Internet* into the Google search window, we received 1,210,000 Web pages (March 25, 2003). This is an incredibly important issue because, as noted previously in this book, anyone can be a publisher on the Internet. We have selected three websites that will provide additional insights and information.

1. (No author), "Bibliography on Evaluating Web Information," University Libraries, Virginia Tech, December 31, 2002. Retrieved March 25, 2003, from http://www.lib.vt.edu/research/evaluate/evalbiblio.html#examples. This site lists links to over 70 sites that provide information on evaluating information on the Internet in addition to more than 10 that offer samples of evaluation forms.

2. E. E. Kirk, "Evaluating Information Found on the Internet" The Sheridan Libraries, The Johns Hopkins University, June 5, 2002. Retrieved March 25, 2003, from http://www.library.jhu.edu/elp/useit/evaluate/index.html.

3. N. Lederer, "How to Evaluate a Web Page," Colorado State University Libraries, January 2, 2002. Retrieved March 25, 2003, from http://manta.library.colostate.edu/hoto/evalweb.html.

material. As we have noted previously in this book, the fact that something is on the Internet does not make it credible, valid, or worthwhile. Just as in any library, along with all the good information there is plenty of bad information as well. The old saying "You can't tell a book by its cover" can be updated to "You can't judge the worth of information by the appearance of a website."

The stature of researchers can be measured not in the quantity of information amassed but in the quality of that information. To ensure that you are gathering material of high quality, you must pursue answers to some important questions. These questions can be divided into the six categories discussed here.

1. Reliability. What is the source of the information? Did the information come from an academic, government, or commercial site? Here, it may be helpful to know how to decipher a URL—especially the domain name part of a URL. In the United States, the domain name for Internet providers usually ends with three letters (called the *zone*). These letters indicate the type of organization supplying the information at a site. For example, commercial organizations end with *.com;* educational institutions end with *.edu* (such as "umich.edu"); networking organizations end with *.net;* U.S. government sites end with *.gov;* military sites end with *.mil;* and organizations that don't fall into any of these categories end with *.org.* Outside the United States, domains include a country code.

As of November 16, 2000, ICANN, the Internet Corporation for Assigned Names and Numbers, a nonprofit corporation founded to assume responsibility for the management of top level domain names such as .com, .edu., and .net., assigned seven additional top-level domain names: *.aero,* for airports and airlines, *.biz,* for commercial establishments and businesses, *.coop,* for nonprofit cooperatives, *.info,* for unrestricted use, *.museum,* for museums, *.name,* for individuals, and *.pro.,* for accountants, lawyers, and physicians.

A general rule—very general—is that an educational institution is likely to offer information designed to teach or help learners, whereas a commercial organization is likely to offer information designed to sell or market a product. We would tend to ask about information posted at a commercial site, "What's in it for them?" or "What is their agenda?"; we would be less inclined to ask the same question regarding information posted at an educational site. Remember, this is a general rule only; however, it attempts to get at the issue of reliability.

2. Authority. Who sponsors the site, who manages it, and what are their credentials? The sponsors should clearly have some expertise in the subject area of their site or in the subject area being written about. Sometimes a site will give the author's credentials, such as his or her educational background, past writings, or experience in the area. Sometimes, too, there is a mail-to link for the submission of questions or comments.

If no credentials are offered, write down the name of the author. Enter the name into a search engine such as Google. Often, you will find that the author has a home page that can be quickly accessed, and in many cases the necessary credentials appear on that page. If no credentials are available, you need to reserve judgment about the value of the information you have discovered. There is no need to discredit an unknown source, but you should, at the very least, make your listeners aware of the situation.

3. Currency. How up to date is the site? Has it been updated recently? The most recent date should be clearly listed somewhere on the site—often it is at the bottom of the Webpage, but sometimes it is necessary to go to the home page to get a date. If you are using Google, the most recent date is sometimes included in the Web page listing on the original menu page. But the fact that a website is recent doesn't mean the information contained there is recent—it could be reprinted from somewhere else. You need to discover, if you can, how old the information is and when it was first published.

4. Objectivity. What is the purpose of the organization sponsoring the document or information? Is the purpose purely to collect and publish data? Are there political, ideological, or other agendas? Is the information presented objectively, or does it represent the biases of its author? Is there evidence to support the conclusions? Is the coverage thorough? If you have questions about the data, are you able to call the provider and ask for the identification of the original source of the data? Can you ask about data-collection techniques? (Chadwick, 2001).

5. Validity. Is the information at the site confirmed by information at other sites? One way to make certain that information is sound is to find it repeated at a number of different websites or in other sources. Does the work update other sources or add new information? A goal of researchers is to ensure that their information compels serious attention and acceptance; thus, it must be supported by generally accepted authority (Ormondroyd, Engle, & Cosgrave, 2001).

6. Intuition. Think clearly about the website you have chosen and the information found there. Websites are rarely refereed or reviewed; thus, you must be the judge. Avoid information from sources, for example, that use citations poorly. If sites are unsigned or badly written, this may be a sign, as well, that you should not use the information. Is the source too elementary, too technical, too advanced, or just right for your needs? Remember, even children publish on the Web. Does the information strongly or directly contradict other information you have found? Are there relevant and appropriate links to additional sites? Have you checked them out? Is the article organized well? Are the main points clearly presented? Are there any other weak presentational aspects that would lead you to suspect the information presented? (Jacobson & Cohen, 1996).

Your speech can be vastly improved by using legitimate sources just as it can be severely damaged by using inappropriate sources (Jordan-Henley, 2001). Your credibility is reflected just as much in the sources you choose to use as it is in the information you get from those sources; thus, your judgment in selecting quality sources is important. No one else is responsible for making the appraisals; you must be both accountable and answerable. The matter is in your hands, and the judgments are necessary and important not just to establish your own credibility but to ensure the fair and just treatment of your listeners, to support the responsibilities required for living in a free and open democratic society, and to uphold the set of moral and ethical principles that govern human behavior. This may sound dramatic, but it shows how important these judgments are.

An excellent Web page that thoroughly covers the many aspects of evaluating Internet-based information and provides samples to test your ability to assess quality, is the one created by Don E. Descy at Minnesota State University: D. E. Descy, "Evaluating Internet Based Information." Minnesota State University, Mankato, 1999. Retrieved March 25, 2003, from http://www.lme.mankato.msus.edu/class/629/Cred.html.

Taking Notes on Internet Information

Instead of decreasing the amount of paperwork involved in research and investigation, the Internet has increased it dramatically, and the reason is both clear and simple. Previously, researchers would take notes simply because copying an entire book or article was an expensive, cumbersome, and unnecessary task. We could be selective and make the decisions about what was important and necessary as we discovered the information. The selection process required examination, analysis, judgment, and critical thought—usually at the time of the discovery rather than later. After all, you would never want to write out in longhand and note form any more information than necessary because of the time the process required.

The Internet has changed all that. Now, with printers hooked directly to computers, it is simple to hit the Print key and copy the entire article that is desired with just a click of the mouse, leaving the selection process until later. After all, the article desired contains all the essential reference information (author, date, title, source, and the date the information was retrieved). Not only do we not have to be judicious (unless we are short of either paper or printer ink), but we can produce hundreds of pages in a very short span of time.

The Internet has actually increased the research burden that falls on speakers' shoulders. First, never before has so much information been so readily available and accessible. Speakers have a burden to pursue the research links that look promising. There is no excuse for giving shallow speeches that do not include concrete evidence. The second burden has to do with evaluation. Because everyone knows there is information "published" on the Internet that is suspect, speakers must assume the responsibility—using the criteria outlined in this chapter—of evaluating the information they discover and plan to share with their listeners. They are a crucial ethical and judgmental link between Internet information and audiences; they cannot just present information and expect listeners to make those assessments themselves. Not only does the audience not have enough information to do it, but often, the information comes at them so quickly it is impossible to make the decisions necessary "on the hoof," and too, most listeners expect speakers to have assumed this burden. Speakers have an ethical responsibility to make these assessments.

The third burden has to do with revealing their sources of information. Since most online sources are available to everyone, listeners must be given enough information so they can check out the Internet sites for themselves. Failing to cite the sources within the speech itself—not just in the outline submitted to instructors—does not provide this important access. Remember, that was why Prudence Gibson, in the chapter's opening example, included in her outline the URL for each piece of information she planned to share with her listeners.

Acknowledging these three responsibilities may, indeed, be a cause for creating a huge paper stream for the research for any single speech effort. After all, if you print it now, you can think about it later while, in the meantime, you pursue additional links. Also, you will have the information you need to make those critical evaluative judgments later. Finally, if you print it now, in most cases you have the essential reference, bibliographic, or citation sources you need. (Sometimes, of course, you need to get this essential information from a link on the website you are visiting.)

But, if you press your Print button and discover the Web page you are printing is actually 33 pages long, and all you wanted was a date or a set of statistics that appear about halfway through the document, you probably have printed 31 or 32 more pages than you need. One way to avoid this problem is to activate your browser's Print Preview feature *before* hitting the Print button.

Your Print Preview link is on your File drop-down menu. Using Print Preview, you can find the page that contains the information you are looking for. You may have to zoom in to read the text and the page numbers that appear in the footer, but, you can print just the page (or pages) you need. Just remember if you do this, you need to copy down the reference information and attach it to the page you are printing.

Another way to avoid printing a 33-page document for less than a page of important information, is to highlight just the text you are interested in, and then copy and paste that information to another application such as Word, Word Perfect, or Notepad, using the keyboard shortcuts, Control, C, to copy, and Control, V, to paste it. Then print it from there. The information missing when you use this application may be the author's name, date of the material, title, source, retrieved date, and URL. To avoid this oversight, as soon as we are going to copy and paste information that we need in a research project, we write by hand the essential reference, bibliographic,

Working Together

Where do speakers find good material to use for their speeches? The answer, of course, is anywhere and everywhere. Once we become sensitive to seeing and hearing good examples, illustrations, aphorisms, and anecdotes in everyday life, we become amazed at how much information there is to discover.

When working with others as a group, have one member suggest a topic he or she is considering for an upcoming speech. Then have the group come up with as many ideas as possible for finding information on that topic on the Internet:

- Possible keywords to enter for a search.
- Websites that might supply important information.
- Kinds of reference resources that might have facts.

- Internet chat rooms or interest groups that might be valuable.
- Ways to browse for additional insight into the topic.
- Online media, news, magazine, or newspaper resources that could contribute.
- Sources from which expert or authoritative opinions could be sought.

How successful was the group? Think how quickly ideas will accumulate if members of the group always carry a notepad and jot down incidents when they see or hear them—or useful places on the Internet to get information? Some of the very best ideas for speeches are simple, everyday things to which people can easily relate—not sophisticated, erudite, or scholarly ideas which do not directly relate.

or citation information on a sheet of paper. We then type this information at the top of the page where we plan to paste the material so that when we print out the information desired, the essential source information is directly tied to it.

■ SUPPORTING MATERIAL: WHAT TO LOOK FOR

Once you have learned where to look for information, your next project is to find supporting material for your speech. **Supporting material** is information that backs up your main point and provides the essential content of the speech. To find effective material, you need to return to the specific purpose of your speech. Miguel Grillo had an interest in art that started when he was quite young and growing up in western Nebraska. He found it a treat to go to Denver or Lincoln to see the wonderful collections housed in the museums there. At the University of Nebraska in Lincoln, he majored in studio art and minored in anthropology, and he probably would have pursued archaeology had he not had to go out and make a living. His interest in online art museums began at the same time as his interest in computers. For his speech, he decided on this specific-purpose statement: "To inform the audience about how to enjoy online art museums." Next, he had to find supporting material that would help him achieve his goal of informing the audience about online art museums.

Before Miguel began to look for material, he thought about what might work in his speech and made some notes about what to look for. His notes looked something like this:

How many online art museums are there?	Look for names and Web addresses (URLs).
What kinds of collections exist?	What can you expect to find online?
What issues or policies are important regarding online art museums?	Mention some of the issues and policies.

By thinking out the speech beforehand, Miguel saved himself time because he wouldn't need to examine every website that pertains to museums. He not only had a good idea of what he was looking for, and thus could pass over information that did not serve his purpose, but also was able to narrow his keyword searches. In his searching, too, he found some interesting material he hadn't thought about. Because it fit into his speech, he used it. For example, Miguel found science museums, history museums, and museum indexes; thus, he could talk about the contribution of the Web to other interests besides art. And because the number of online art museums was rapidly expanding, Miguel found several he had never accessed previously and added them to his list of websites. He even found a site that evaluated online art museums; using its evaluations, he could select just the best sites for use in his speech.

Every speech you put together should have supporting material for the main content of your speech. Some of the material you will find through Internet research; other material can come from your personal experience or from interviews.

In the sections that follow, we discuss a few types of supporting material. Every time you prepare a speech, you should decide which types will work best for each particular speech.

Comparison

Comparisons point out the similarities between two or more things. For example, Sidney, who spoke about the use of peer evaluation in one of his classes, used this comparison:

> *Think of peer evaluation as a reflection of real life. Like real life, it includes people who take it seriously and those who do not; opportunities to assist friends and hurt enemies; and even a wide range of possible, and often contradictory, viewpoints—none of them necessarily accurate, but all of them contributing to an understanding of what is being evaluated.*

You can often use comparisons to help your audience imagine something that is outside its experience. For example, Gretchen wanted her audience to understand that the human body, even in its scrubbed and sanitized condition, is not clean—from a microbial standpoint:

> *Our bodies are like a microbial version of Jurassic Park. Microbes thrive, for example, on the desert of the forearm, in the cool woods of the*

scalp, and in the tropical forest of the armpit. Life on humans, however, is most abundant in the tropics. Trillions of bacteria, viruses, protozoa, and fungi thrive in the warm, hairy, humid terrain of the armpits and groin.

Sometimes a comparison can show us a new way of looking at something. Mario Cuomo (1998), in a graduation speech at Iona College, used a comparison he borrowed from the president of his alma mater, Father Flynn. Asking Flynn how he should approach his graduation speech, Flynn replied:

"Commencement speakers," said Father Flynn, "should think of themselves as the body at an old-fashioned Irish wake. They need you in order to have the party, but nobody expects you to say very much" (p. 92).

Contrast

Contrasts point out the differences between two or more things. A contrast might reveal how using the Internet is different from using the library or how online medical advice is different from medical advice from one's private-practice, real-life doctor. Here, Avery Austin uses contrast in his classroom speech to show how blogs—Web-based chronicles with time-stamped postings—are different from anything that previously existed:

You are all familiar with books where authors write, and those interested in what an author has to say, purchase and read his or her book.

Blogs are a form of self-publishing—where I can get 150 to 200 people in a day to gather in one spot and read what I have to say.

You are all familiar with magazines and newspapers where writers can share their ideas and viewpoints with their readers.

Blogs are vehicles for any of us to share ideas with others, and there are no magazine or newspaper editors to scrutinize or judge what is printable—where I can be my own editor and make these judgments myself.

You are all familiar with e-mail and instant messages.

Blogs are ways for publishing my ideas regularly—opinions, timely news, insights and information. It is personal journalism at its finest.

You are all familiar with personal Web pages which must be updated regularly.

Blogs are as easy to update as sending an e-mail, so blog writers—or bloggers—can update weekly, daily, sometimes even several times a day.

You are all familiar with the main draw of the Internet—consuming things.

Blogs are not about consuming things; they make use of the Internet for a new form of communication—you can speak, and there's a potential that you can reach a lot of people. It's really about connecting to people.

Avery ended his speech by writing on the chalkboard some of the websites where the blogger-naive can begin. For example, he wrote Blogger.com, a site, he said, that offers free software to create blogs on your own Web page. He said Blogger was founded by Evan Williams and has more than 250,000 registered users. He wrote Livejournal.com, which, he said, lets users create blogs on its site. Lura.net, is an example of a blog page where Lura Lee has links to her friends. Blogdex.media.met.edu, Avery said, is Cameron Marlow's index of the most popular links from blogs, and Portal.eatonweb.com includes a Blog index that is organized by subject.

Definition

A **definition** is a brief explanation of what a word or phrase means. Use definitions whenever you suspect that some people in your audience might not know what you are talking about. After you define something, it also might be appropriate to give an example. In the speech excerpt below, the student gives a definition followed by an example:

Fatigue is decreased ability of an organism to perform because of prolonged exertion. Have you ever studied and studied for a tough examination only to go into the examination completely tired out and exhausted? Fatigue may seem physical to you, but often it's a sign of mental distress—especially if you are particularly fearful about the exam.

Samuel Hazo, president of the international poetry forum, in an honors day convocation speech, "The Office of Citizen," defined liberal education through etymology, or through the derivation or history of the word, in this way, "Liberal education," he said, "is derived from the Latin word for 'free'—'libra.' But 'libera' is derived from the Latin word for 'book'—'liber.' This implies to me that the Romans saw a connection between books and freedom itself. They recognized that books put people's minds in motion, and that people so moved would be capable of thinking for themselves and arriving at their own conclusions" (Hazo, 2002, p. 479).

Examples

An **example** is a short illustration that clarifies a point. Commonly used in speeches, examples can come from personal experience, from research, or from imagination.

Personal Experience

Often you will choose a topic for a speech because you have some personal involvement in it. Ask yourself whether you can provide any examples from your own experience. Nothing beats "I know what I'm talking about because I've been there," as you can see in this excerpt from a speech against drinking and driving:

Three years ago, I was a senior in high school. One night my best friend, Jeff, called and asked if I wanted to go out to the lake and have a few beers. Since I had planned to see my grandmother, who was in the hospital, I told him I couldn't go but to give me a rain check.

There was no next time. That night Jeff and three of my other friends were killed in an accident. According to the police report, they hit a tree while going 75 miles an hour. All of them had alcohol in their blood.

Consider This

One of the authors of this textbook (Richard), like his coauthor, has been writing about public speaking for over a quarter of a century, and he has been a practicing public speaker for longer than that. He writes here in the first person:

If there is a single piece of advice I would give to all speakers that will help guarantee their success, it would be this: Use examples. I remember the number of times I would be talking to a lecture hall of 300 or more students when I would suddenly realize the room was silent—deathly silent. Inevitably, those were the moments I was telling a personal story, citing an example, or sharing information directly related to them. I think some speakers may forget the value of these moments. Examples are one of the best means for arousing interest and keeping attention. They disarm hostility, paint pictures in listeners' minds, make information memorable, and in the case of classroom lectures, lighten up heavy material.

They have personal rewards, too. Not only do they help speakers connect with their listeners and make them more likable, they leave a positive impression as well.

Questions

1. Can you remember being a member of a large audience when the entire room went silent as it listened to a speaker's story or example? Do you remember the story or example being shared?

2. Do you have any vivid memories of public speakers you have heard? Why are your memories of them so vivid? Did these speakers share interesting stories and examples with their audience?

3. Have you been able to come up with a story or example for the speech you are planning to give in this class? Is the story or example one you know class members will relate to?

Not all personal examples will be so dramatic. Another student uses a commonplace experience to make her point in a speech about how college students are affected by credit cards:

> *Let me show you something. I have twelve different credit cards here. Look at them. Did you know that is two more than the average American consumer? I added up my debt on these twelve cards, and it comes to nearly $5,000. That's $1,100 more debt than the average American household. Then I cried.*

Research

Often if you have not had personal experience with a topic, you can use the examples you find in your research. When you do this, however, be sure to cite your source. A common way of doing this is to say, "In the latest issue of *Newsweek*. . . ." or "According to the January 2003 issue of *Popular Science*. . . ." If the source is from the Internet, you could say, "In an Internet article, entitled. . . .(give short title), Jonathan Keller stated. . ." A student who was giving a speech on why the hair dye industry should be regulated used this example that she found during her research:

> *A current issue of the magazine In Health tells about a woman who was dyeing her hair. As soon as she applied the dye, her vision blurred, her face swelled, and she began to feel dizzy. Suddenly, she couldn't*

No matter the general or specific purpose of the speech, no matter the subject matter or occasion, and no matter the formality or informality of the presentation, examples are one of the best means for arousing interest and keeping attention.

breathe and passed out. Fortunately her son was in the house and called the paramedics. It turned out that she had had an allergic reaction.

Hypothetical Examples

Sometimes speakers use **hypothetical examples**—examples that are made up—to illustrate a point. A speaker should always tell the audience if an example is hypothetical. When one student spoke about the need to avoid suntanning, he involved his audience in his example. The words *imagine yourself* cue the audience that the example is hypothetical:

> *Imagine yourself at the beach in the summer. The sand, the glistening water, and the sun beating down on you. As you sit up from your beach towel, you scan the beach and notice a sign that catches your attention that reads, "Save the Whales!" That sign should also read, "Save Your Skin!" Although the effects of tanning may not show up for ten to twenty years, the health risks and problems that tanning causes can be serious.*

Statistics

Statistics—facts in numerical form—have many uses in a speech. Being factual material, they are a convincing form of evidence. Quite often, a speaker who uses statistics is seen as someone who has done his or her homework.

Sometimes statistics can support your speech in a way no other information can. Ramon Ramirez had read the headlines "College Students of America Wade Deeper into Sea of Booze," "Students Major in Bingeing,"

Another Point of View

Statistics need to be used cautiously, in part, because distorted, biased, or incorrect statistics may not only attract media attention, but they can be circulated quickly on the Internet and become "fact by repetition." Here, Professor David J. Hanson of the Sociology Department, State University of New York, discusses the problem:

Typically, inflated statistics are associated with talk of epidemics, threats to our youth, and similar alarmist language. Often they are promoted by groups with laudable sounding names such as the Center for Science in the Public Interest. But many such groups, which may have underlying social or political agendas, tend to exaggerate the extent and growth of problems in which they have a vested interest and, typically, a proposed solution.

Problems widely seen by the public as being of epidemic proportion justify ever larger budgets, increased staffs, higher salaries, more power, and greater organizational prestige.

Questions

1. Who might have a vested interest in exaggerating statistics? Why?
2. What kinds of cautionary measures can you take in your research, to make certain that you are not using exaggerated—distorted, biased, or incorrect—statistics?

Source: D. J. Hanson, "Underage Drinking," Sociology Department, State University of New York, Potsdam, 2001. Retrieved March 25, 2003, from http://www2.potsdam.edu/alcohol-info/Youth/Youth.html.

(Hanson, 2001) and "Grim Results of Alcohol Abuse on Nation's College Campuses" (Grim results, 2002). On the Internet, he came across an article published by the online version of the *Tampa Tribune,* "Grim Results of Alcohol Abuse on Nation's College Campuses." Among the other statistics Ramon cited about college drinking in his speech, was that drinking by college students ages 18 to 24 during the last year contributed to about 1,400 deaths and 500,000 injuries, 70,000 cases of sexual assault or date rape, more than 600,000 students being assaulted by another student who had been drinking, 400,000 students who had unprotected sex, 2.1 million students who drove a car while under the influence of alcohol, more than 150,000 students who developed an alcohol-related health problem, and between 1.2 and 1.5 percent of students who tried to commit suicide in connection with drinking or drug use. Also, he noted that drinking contributed to about 25 percent of college students having academic problems, including missing class, falling behind, doing poorly on exams or papers, and receiving lower grades overall (p. 1).

With these impressive data, based on a three-year study conducted by the National Institute on Alcohol Abuse and Alcoholism's Task Force on College Drinking (Grim results, 2002), Ramon could emphasize how important it is to establish and enforce campus standards on drinking and, thus, create a healthy environment. He could talk about promoting healthy behavior through both individual and group approaches and, too, the need for universities to share information on drinking prevention programs with demonstrated effectiveness.

Using the Internet, statistics are easy to find. There are numerous statistical sources available and most computer databases supported by your campus library, or libraries that make their information available to the public online, include statistical databases in their lists of reference works. Often, however, you don't have to make a special search for statistics; the sources you use for your speech will have figures you can use. For example, Ramon simply entered *Alcohol Abuse on College Campuses* into the Google search engine and received 25,600 Web pages (June 9, 2002) for his effort.

Rules for Using Statistics

Use the Best Possible Sources.   The headline "World's Food Supply Failing to Keep Pace" will be much more believable if it comes from the *New York Times* than from one of the tabloid newspapers by the checkout stand in your local supermarket. Although tabloids occasionally break an authentic "big" story, their credibility for most listeners is still suspect. Get your statistics from well-respected sources.

Make Sure the Information Is Up to Date.   Figures on military spending in 1993 are useless—unless you want to compare them with figures for the current year. If you do this, you must account for inflation.

Use Statistics That Show Trends.   We can often tell what is happening to an institution or even a country if we have information from one year to another. There is even a Trends Research Institute, based in Rhinebeck, New York, with its own *Trends Journal,* designed to follow major trends in every area of life. It can be accessed online: G. Celente, "Discover the future: See tomorrow's trends today." The Trends Research Institute, 2002. Retrieved March 25, 2003, from http://www.trendsresearch.com/.

Another classroom speech on alcohol focused on college binge drinking, Emily Asher quoted an online publication of the Harvard School of Public Health (Trends. . . . , 2002), to show that when prevention efforts are in place, college binge drinking can be kept at a stable level—even though the rate of college binge drinking remains high. She quoted the article:

> *The 2001 Harvard School of Public Health College Alcohol Study surveyed students at 119 4-year colleges that participated in the 1993, 1997, and 1999 studies. Responses in the four survey years were compared to determine trends in heavy alcohol use, alcohol-related problems, and encounters with college and community prevention efforts. In 2001, approximately two in five (44.4 percent) college students reported binge drinking, a rate almost identical to rates in the previous three surveys. Very little change in overall binge drinking occurred at the individual college level.*

Use Concrete Images.   When your numbers are large and may be hard to comprehend, using concrete images is helpful. William Franklin (1998), president of Franklin International, Ltd., speaking to members of the Graduate School of Business at the Japan Business Association and International Business Society in New York, reduced demographic information he had to the following:

> *If we shrink the world's 5.7 billion population to a village of 100 people—with all existing human ratios remaining the same, here is the resulting profile.*

Of these 100 people, 57 are Asian, 21 European, 14 from North and South America, and eight from Africa.

51 female, 49 male

80 live in substandard housing.

70 cannot read.

Half suffer from malnutrition.

75 have never made a phone call.

Less than one is on the Internet.

Half the entire village's wealth would be in the hands of 6 people.

Only one of the hundred has a college education.

You are in a very elite group of only 1 percent who have a college education (p. 719).

Testimony

When you cite **testimony,** you use another person's statements or actions to give authority to what you are saying. Experts are the best sources of testimony. Suppose you are planning to speak about NCAA violations and you get some information from the athletic director of your school. When you use this information in your speech, tell your audience where it came from. Because the information is from an expert, your speech will have more authority and be more convincing than it would be if you presented only your own opinions.

Testimony can also be used to show that people who are prominent and admired believe and support your ideas. For example, if you want to persuade your audience to take up swimming for fitness, it might be useful to mention some famous athletes who swim to stay fit. If you want people to sign your petition to build a new city park, mention other citizens who are also supporting the park.

Testimony can be made up of direct quotations. You can quote what public figures or celebrities are saying, or you can quote historic figures by using books of quotations found in the reference section of the library. Billy O. Wireman, president of Queens College, quoted Robert Frost in his speech to the Georgetown College Founders' Day Convocation. Wireman said, "In the spirit of honoring those Hall of Fame inductees who have made distinctive contributions to Georgetown, let's reflect on a familiar poem by Robert Frost, which includes the following lines: 'The woods are lovely, dark and deep. But I have promises to keep, and miles to go before I sleep . . . and miles to go before I sleep.'" The Frost quotation gave Wireman the title for his speech, "Promises to Keep" (Wireman, 1999, p. 345).

Try to use quotations that are short and to the point. If they are too lengthy, your speech could end up sounding like everyone but yourself. If you have quotations that are long and wordy, put them into your own words. Whether you quote or paraphrase, always give credit to your source. In her speech "We, The People: Prize and Embrace What Is America," Farah M. Walters, President and CEO of University Hospitals Health System and University Hospitals of Cleveland, speaking to the Women's City Club of Cleveland,

Cleveland, Ohio, used the words of Eleanor Roosevelt—who, Walters said, began her public career at the listeners' sister organization, the Women's City Club of New York—saying to these ladies, "As individuals, we live cooperatively and, to the best of our ability, serve the community in which we live. Our own success, to be real, must contribute to the success of others. When you cease to make a contribution, you die" (Walters, 2000, p. 144).

Polls

Polls are surveys of people's attitudes, beliefs, and behavior. Quite often polls are conducted on controversial subjects. If you want to know how the American public feels about campaign financing, health care reform, or term limits, you will probably be able to find a poll that tells you.

National polls can also provide useful information about what particular segments of the population think or know about an issue. There are numerous polling organizations. Often, however, a single poll may yield far more information than is necessary for a speech. Since that much information would be overwhelming for listeners, you must decide how much or how little to use. Try to select responses that will appeal precisely to your classmates' ages and socioeconomic circumstances.

When your statistics come from a survey, it is important to find out how many and what kinds of people were questioned. For example, if you discovered survey results saying that 30 percent of the American public eats with chopsticks, you might find the statistic fairly startling and be tempted to use it—until you note that the survey included only 100 people and that many of them were Chinese immigrants.

Studies

As the term implies, a **study** is an in-depth investigation of a subject. The subject might be anything—from how white rats run mazes to how newspapers present political news. Studies are reported in popular magazines, newspapers, and academic journals. If you are interested in finding out what research has been done in a particular field, check the indexes of periodicals in that field. Studies are also reported on the Internet. For example, a table at one website (see Table 13-2) shows data from a study conducted by the National Association of Colleges and Employers; it provides comparative information on the top 10 majors (based on the number of offers their graduates have received) and their average starting salaries.

■ ADAPTING SUPPORTING MATERIAL TO YOUR AUDIENCE

Because each kind of supporting material may work better with some audiences than with others, you should keep your audience constantly in mind as you develop your speech.

Consider, for example, a speech about antiques. If you are going to speak to dealers, you should give highly technical information from dealer newspapers such as *Antique Review* or magazines such as *Antique Collecting*. If you will be talking to people who buy antiques, you might discuss potential

Table 13-2
Comparative Salaries According to Major—Based on the Number of Offers Received, April 23, 2002

Major	Average Salary Offers
Accounting	$40,293
Mechanical engineering	48,654
Economics/Finance	40,047
Business administration	35,209
Electrical engineering	50,387
Chemical engineering	51,254
Marketing	35,374
Civil engineering	40,848
Management information	43,732
Systems	50,352

Source: "Salary Survey" is a quarterly report of starting salary offers to new college graduates in 70 disciplines at the bachelor's degree level. The survey compiles data from college and university career services offices nationwide. C. Luckenbaugh and J. Bohovich, "Accounting Majors Getting Most Job Offers," NACE (National Association of Colleges and Employers, April 23, 2002), Press Room, 62 Highland Avenue, Bethlehem, PA 18017–9085. Retrieved June 10, 2002, from http://www.naceweb.org/press/display.asp?year=2002&prid=158.

rip-offs and how to detect a good deal—such as items that are currently "hot" or that have a strong return on the dollar. You might even introduce them to a magazine specifically for buyers, *Magazine Antiques*. If you will be speaking to antique admirers, you might point out the aesthetic aspects of antiques and how one can use antiques as conversation or accent pieces in decorating. In a speech to students, you could talk about the value of antiques, the role they play in our society, or the art of antique collecting.

You also need to consider the attitudes of the audience toward your topic. If your audience is suspicious of you or your message, you will probably do best with facts and figures and with quotations and testimony from people your audience respects. Citing evidence in the form of statistics and facts will give you a better chance of persuading listeners to accept your point of view.

Finally, you should consider what kind of supporting material will hold your audience's attention. If you are speaking to a young and potentially restless audience, examples and narratives will probably hold their attention best.

Since audience members often come from a variety of backgrounds, no one form of supporting material will work uniformly well. If you have an adult audience with different levels of knowledge and different attitudes, you should use a variety of supporting material. In the following extract, the speaker begins with a statistic and then goes on to give an example:

A California study of 3,000 divorced couples found that one year after the divorce, the woman's income had dropped 73 percent while the man's had increased 43 percent.

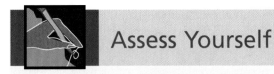

Assess Yourself

Are You Internet Savvy?

Please indicate with a T or an F which of the following statements is either true or false. Place a 0 (zero) next to the number if you do not know the answer.

1. Basically, there is one way of looking for information on the Internet—using Netscape Navigator or Internet Explorer (each one a type of browser)—to access the World Wide Web.

2. If you had a broad topic or idea to research, the best place to start your investigation is with a search engine.

3. One difference between a subject directory and a search engine is how the information in the resource or database gets there.

4. Search engines are likely to be your first Web guides when you are searching for something by keywords.

5. Each search engine has its own unique qualities and search capabilities.

6. Once you have searched for a topic or for a piece of information using a search engine, you can cease your Internet search.

7. A metasearch engine is one designed specifically to research ideas rather than topics.

8. The main advantage of a metasearch engine is the overview it can offer as you begin your investigation.

9. There are specific locations on the Internet where you can frame your research inquiry as a research question and can get the exact answers you are looking for.

10. The best Internet research investigation should begin prior to going online.

11. One suggestion for doing research on the Internet involves playing with your search terms.

12. Netiquette is simply the process of following an exact research protocol when using the Internet.

13. One weakness of the Internet is letting it become a substitute for critical thinking.

14. All information that appears on the Internet is credible, valid, and worthwhile.

15. The stature of an Internet researcher can be measured by the quantity of information he or she accumulates.

16. All information found on the Internet should be evaluated.

17. One way of testing the reliability of information you discover on the Internet is by looking at the domain name (or zone) part of a URL.

18. Reliability, authority, currency, objectivity, and validity are sufficient criteria for evaluating information on the Internet.

19. To question the objectivity of information discovered on the Internet, you would want to know how up to date the site is.

20. Your credibility as a speaker is reflected just as much in the sources you choose to use as it is in the information you get from those sources.

 Go to the *Communicating Effectively* CD-ROM to see your results and learn how to evaluate your attitudes and feelings.

Karen Jackson is one of these women. Last year she was living with her three children in a comfortable middle-class neighborhood. Now she is living in a slum and needs food stamps to feed her children.

Presenting a variety of supporting material is like offering a variety of fruit in a fruit bowl. Some people will like the bananas; others, the apples; and still others, the peaches or grapes. The point is that everyone will be pleased to find something that appeals to him or her.

Chapter Review

When you are putting together material for your speech, you should consider drawing on four areas: your own experiences, interviews with others, computer databases, and resources found on the Internet. Depending on the topic, one of these sources might provide better information than others; however, it is likely that whether you choose to use your own experiences or interviews with others, computer databases and resources found on the Internet will offer substantive and important additional information.

The Internet is a fast, efficient, and cost-effective means of locating a wealth of research information. You can find information on the Internet by joining an e-mail discussion group or Usenet group, going directly to specific sites, browsing the Net, exploring subject directories, using search or metasearch engines, or, by asking a research question at a research site. In addition, computer databases on nearly every subject provide easy access to collections of information.

When doing research on the Internet, you should define your goals, determine the types of information you need, identify key words, phrases, and subject categories, familiarize yourself with using search engines, use more than one source and search engine, practice netiquette, review your progress, and practice critical thinking. Always evaluate the quality of Internet information on the basis of reliability, authority, currency, objectivity, validity, and your own intuition. Be wary of statements, facts, statistics, or opinions that look exaggerated, sensational, or outside the realm of common sense. Most can be quickly validated using other Internet sites.

Note taking from the Internet often involves simply pressing the Print button and capturing a copy of the information you need. In most cases, this provides you with all the necessary citation or reference information—(author, date, title, sponsoring source, retrieval date, and website address (URL)—and then you can make more specific selection choices—with relevance, importance, and significance—later. The Internet has increased the research burden on those who use it: to pursue the research links that look promising, to evaluate the information discovered, and to reveal sources of information to listeners.

Supporting material forms the main content of every speech. Supporting material includes the following: comparisons, which are similarities between two or more things; contrasts, which point out differences; definitions, which give the meaning of words or phrases; examples, which illustrate points; statistics, which are facts in numerical form; testimony, in which the statements or actions of others are used to give authority to a speech; polls, which indicate what a selected group of people think, feel, or know about a subject; and studies, which are in-depth investigations.

When choosing supporting material for a speech, you should consider which kinds will be appropriate for the audience. To make this choice, consider the audience's level of knowledge and attitude toward your topic, and ask yourself which material will best hold the audience's attention.

Questions to Review

1. Can you think of a speech topic for which you can do your primary or essential research on the Internet? Where would you begin your search for information, and why?

2. What are six ways of looking for information on the Internet? Does one of these ways appear to be more efficient or effective than the others? Which one? Why?

3. What steps are important to complete before doing research via the Internet? Why are these steps important?

4. What are the precautions regarding use of the information found on the Internet? Why is it necessary to be cautious using Internet information?

5. What are the specific questions you need to ask to make certain the information you get from the Internet is of high quality? When you discover information that does not meet the standards, what should you do?

6. Why is the process of determining website credibility so important?

7. What are the research burdens placed on researchers who use the Internet to discover information?

8. What are some of the different kinds of computer databases available online? Why is it necessary, in doing research for a speech, to access a variety of different types of databases?

9. What are the differences among comparison, contrast, personal experience, examples, statistics, testimony, polls, and studies? What are the benefits of using a variety of different kinds of supporting material for a speech?

10. Why is it so necessary to adapt your supporting material to your audience?

/hybels

Go to the self-quizzes on the *Communicating Effectively* CD-ROM (side 2, track 10) and the Online Learning Center at mhhe.com/hybels7 to test your knowledge of the chapter concepts.

References

Chadwick, T. B. (2001, September 21). "How to conduct research on the Internet." Infoquest! Information Services. Retrieved June 7, 2002, from www.tbchad.com/resrch.html.

Cuomo, M. (1998). "Graduation speech at Iona College." In A. Albanese and B. Trissler, eds. *Graduation day: The best of America's commencement speeches* New York: Morrow, 72–73.

Franklin, W. E. (1998), (September 15). "Careers in international business: Five ideas or principles." *Vital Speeches of the Day* 64:23.

(No author). (2002, April 13). "Grim results of alcohol abuse on nation's college campuses." *The Tampa Tribune* (Online Edition). Retrieved March 25, 2003, from http://tampatrib.com/News/MGAJP4ALYZC.html.

Hall, C., & Q. Tian (2001, January 16). "Searching on the Internet." USA TODAY Snapshots. *USA Today,* D1.

Hanson, D. J. (2001). "Underage drinking." Sociology Department, State University of New York, Potsdam. Retrieved March 25, 2003, from http://www2.potsdam.edu/alcohol-info/Youth/Youth.html.

Hazo, S. (2002, May 15). "The office of citizen: Thinking things through." *Vital Speeches of the Day.* 68:15, 478–80.

(No author). (2000, November 27). "The importance of libraries." *The Blade* (Toledo, Ohio), 6A.

Jacobson, T., & L. Cohen (1996, April). "Evaluating Internet resources." Libraries, University at Albany. Retrieved March 25, 2003, from http://library.albany.edu/internet/evaluate.html.

Jordan-Henley, J. (2001, June 6). "Using the Web to conduct research." The RSCC Online Writing Lab, Roane State Community College. Retrieved March 25, 2003, from http://www.rscc.cc.tn.us/owl/researchguide.html.

Liu, J. (1999, June). "Guide to metasearch engines." Reference Department, Indiana University Libraries. Retrieved March 25, 2003, from http://www.indiana.edu/~librcsd/search/meta.html.

Morreale, S. (2001, February). "Morreale's mailbag: Administrators & students' resources/news." *Spectra*, 8.

(No author). (2002). "A nation online: How Americans are expanding their use of the Internet." National Telecommunications and Information Administration (NTIA), U.S. Department of Commerce, Washington, DC. Retrieved March 25, 2003, from http://www.ntia.doc.gov/ntiahome/dn/html/toc.htm.

Nelson, S. L., & P. Coleman (2000). *Effective executive's guide to the Internet: The seven core skills required to turn the Internet into a business power tool.* Redmond, WA: Redmond Technology Press.

Ormondroyd, J., M. Engle, & T. Cosgrave (2001, September 18). "How to critically analyze information services." Olin Kroch, Uris Libraries, Research Services Division, Cornell University Library. Retrieved March 25, 2003, from http://www.library.cornell.edu/okuref/research/skill26.htm.

(No author). (2002, April 22). "Searching the Internet: Recommended sites and search techniques." Libraries, University at Albany. Retrieved March 25, 2003, from http://library. albany.edu/internet/search.html

(No author, no date) "State of the Internet 2000." United States Internet Council (USIC) and International Technology and Trade Associates (ITTA). Retrieved March 25, 2003, from http://www.usic.org/.

(No author). (2002). "Trends in college binge drinking during a period of increased prevention efforts: Findings from 4 Harvard School of Public Health College alcohol study surveys: 1993–2001." School of Public Health, Harvard University. Retrieved March 25, 2003, from http://www.hsph.harvard.edu/cas/Documents/trends/.

Walters, F. M. (2000, December 15). "We, the people: Prize and embrace what is America." *Vital Speeches of the Day* 67:5, 143–47.

Wireman, B. O. (1999, March 15). "Promises to keep: Applying old values to a new era." *Vital Speeches of the Day* 65:11.

Woods, M. (1999, October 23). "Search engines do a pretty lame job of finding information." *The Blade* (Toledo, Ohio), Living Section.

Further Reading

Ackermann, E., & K. Hartman (2000). *The information searcher's guide to searching and researching on the Internet and World Wide Web,* (2nd ed.) Wilsonville, OR: Abf Content. In this 438-page book, the authors untangle the links, sites, and search engines on the Net. Their techniques and strategies will aid computer novices in undertaking quick, efficient, and in-depth online research. The authors cover in detail all the top search engines and information portals. There are also sections on the fundamentals of e-mail, electronic interest books, and file transfers. There are many useful exercises for practice as well.

(No author). (2002). "Bartleby. com." Retrieved March 25, 2003, from http://www.bartleby.com/. This is a source for free online literature, verse, and reference books. You can access complete electronic versions of the latest editions of the *Columbia Encyclopedia,* the *American Heritage Dictionary, Roget's II: The New Thesaurus,* the *American Heritage Book of English Usage,* the *Columbia World of Quotations, Simpson's Contemporary Quotations, Bartlett's Familiar Quotations,* as well as the *King James Bible, Oxford Shakespeare, Gray's Anatomy,* Strunk's *Elements of Style,* the *World Factbook,* and *Columbis Gazetteer.*

Berkman, R. I. (2000). *Find it fast: How to uncover expert information on any subject online or in print,* 5th ed. (Harper Resource Book). New York: Harper. This is a popular guide to conducting an information search on any subject. Berkman gives step-by-step instructions on where and how to locate almost any information you need. He includes excellent coverage of library usage and electronic searches, as well as typical research problems. If you are new to doing research, this book will open your eyes to all the possibilities available.

Branscomb, H. E. (2000). *Casting your net: A student's guide to research on the Internet,* 2nd ed. Boston: Allyn & Bacon. Branscomb offers a comprehensive guide to conducting academic research on the Internet. The author assumes familiarity with standard research procedures such as library usage, note-taking skills, and general computer literacy. His focus is specifically on the Internet: search engines, Usenet, the World Wide Web, listservs, and e-mail. He takes readers through the process of finding a topic, shaping and narrowing the focus, drafting and revising papers, and integrating and documenting source material. Practical, useful, relevant information.

Glossbrenner, A., & E. Glossbrenner (2001). *Search engines for the World Wide Web,* 3rd ed. Berkeley, CA: Peachpit Press. This is, by far, the best source for discovering information on the major Internet search engines. It is an easy guide because it takes a visual approach. It works like a reference book because you can look up what you need quickly and efficiently and get on with your work. The authors also take a concise, straightforward approach, and they have a companion website at www.peachpit.com/vqs/search that includes links to search engine resources and updates. Sales of the authors' books number over a million copies, and they have been alerting readers to the power and possibilities of online information since 1982. This is an excellent book full of useful, understandable material.

Hock, R. (2001). *The extreme searcher's guide to Web search engines: A handbook for the serious searcher,* 2nd ed. Medford, NJ: CyberAge Books from Information Today. Hock tells you what you need to know to get valuable and speedy results from Web search engines. He tells you how to assemble high-quality queries, conduct a Boolean search, perform proximity searches on Lycos, and limit a HotBot search to information no more than a week old. He profiles 10 of the most well-known search engines and details their syntaxes, strengths, weaknesses, and special features. The book is thoughtfully written and very readable.

Kirk, E. K. (2001, October 30). "Evaluating information on the Internet and the Web." Milton S. Eisenhower Library, Johns Hopkins University. Retrieved March 25, 2003, from http:users. mwc. edu/~khartman/educan98.html. Elizabeth Kirk is the electronic and distance librarian for the Milton S. Eisenhower Library at Johns Hopkins University, and she brings a wealth of useful information to this comprehensive website. This is one of the most complete sources we discovered on evaluating Internet information. The website is thorough, well written, to the point, and up to date. This is a site for your favorites list.

Nelson, S. L., & P. Coleman (2000). *Effective executive's guide to the Internet: The seven core skills required to turn the Internet into a business power tool.* Redmond, WA: Redmond Technology Press.

This is a very basic introduction to understanding the Internet environment, making Internet connections, browsing the Web, communicating with electronic mail, using search services, understanding other Internet services, and publishing on the Web. The entire focus of the book is on the steps and skills needed to get started, use, and continue to learn about the Internet.

Robbins, C. (1999). *Advanced Internet research one-day course.* New York: Ddc Publishing. In this 224-page book, with 160 pages of lecture material, Robbins covers complex query terms, requiring and prohibiting operators, multiple keyword query terms, search engine discrepancies, searching mailing lists (listserv), searching newsgroups (Usenet), multisearch engine interfaces, specialized databases, commercial (fee-based) search engines, commercial search engine pricing models, case sensitivity, and static, dynamic, and sluggish database types. This book covers the essentials of Internet research.

Sacks, R., & R. Basch, eds. (2001) *Super searchers go to the source: The interviewing and hands-on information strategies of top primary researchers— online, on the phone, and in person.* Medford, NJ: CyberAge Books (Information Today, Inc.). Sacks and Basch interview 12 of the best primary researchers in the business (journalists, reporters, writers, private investigators, educators, a librarian, and more) who reveal their strategies for integrating online and offline resources, identify experts, get past gatekeepers to obtain information, and use primary research tools and techniques to get the most complete results from interviews, public records, printed material, online databases, Internet sites, and direct observation. Here are close to 400 pages of examples, case studies, strategies, and stories. The stories are practical; some are hilarious!

(No author). (2000). "SpeechTips.com." The Online Speech Store. Retrieved March 25, 2003, from http://www.speechtips.com/. At this site you can obtain a free guide to speech writing and public speaking for eulogies, graduations, best-man and father-of-the-bride toasts, and any other public speaking occasions. There is specific, practical information for each of the three steps of speech presentation: planning, writing, and delivery. Also, there is a link to complete speeches, content guides, and toasts at SpeechSuccess.com.

Chapter 14

Organizing and Outlining the Speech

Objectives

After reading this chapter, you should be able to:

- Organize and outline your speech.
- Identify the six patterns of organization for a speech, and choose the best one for your purpose.
- Explain the function of an introduction and be able to write one.
- Explain the function of a conclusion and be able to write one.
- Explain the function of transitions and be able to write them.
- Use both full-sentence and key-word formats to outline a speech.
- Write a reference list for your speech.

Key Terms and Concepts

Use the Communicating Effectively CD-ROM and Online Learning Center at mhhe.com/hybels7 to further your understanding of the following terms.

Body (of speech) 493	Introduction (of speech) 502	Problem-solution order 498
Cause-and-effect order 496	Key-word outlines 513	Reference list 513
Conclusion (of speech) 509	Main points 492	Spatial order 495
Full-sentence outline 513	Minor points 492	Time order 494
	Motivated sequence 500	Topical order 501
	Outline 512	Transitions 511

SOFIA MENA LEARNED HOW TO ORGANIZE HER IDEAS IN A high school English course. Mrs. Donna Blawat, her teacher, told the class that a good outline gets you started right, keeps you underway, and gets you to your destination. Mrs. Blawat emphasized two fundamentals: (1) Keep it simple, and (2) Make sure that whatever organizational pattern you choose is instantly intelligible to your readers.

Sofia decided to put Mrs. Blawat's ideas to work as she began to prepare her first major speech project for the semester. She selected a topic she knew would be important and relevant for her listeners: anxiety. Her roommate, Mai Trieu, always seemed to be anxious. Also, she knew that investigating the topic might help her reduce the anxiety she herself often experienced around exam time. This interest alone was enough to spark her curiosity.

Sofia remembered that her father, who was taking a series of night courses in accounting, had two books on the subject: (1) Marty Sapp's *Test Anxiety* (University Press of America, 1999), and (2) Ed Newman's *No More Test Anxiety* (Learning Skills Publications, 1996). She had looked them over during her last visit home, and she asked her mother to give her information on both of them and to bring them to campus after Sofia had decided on this topic. Also, she had seen recently a *Time* magazine cover on "understanding anxiety" (June 10, 2002), so she knew she could get plenty of information. She asked her mother to bring that copy of *Time* as well.

The first thing Sofia did, however, was to use the Internet to brainstorm about the subject. She was surprised when Google produced 702,000 Web pages for the words *test anxiety* and 254,000 pages for the words *reducing anxiety* (June 10, 2002). What she also discovered was that many college-campus counseling or learning centers provide information for students. It was easy for Sofia to come up with possible angles:

Why do we worry ourselves sick?	*Effects of test anxiety.*
Causes for test anxiety.	*Methods of reducing test anxiety.*
Physical, emotional, behavioral, and cognitive signs of test anxiety.	*Coping strategies.*
	Regulating your arousal level.

From the list she generated, Sofia decided to narrow her topic to methods of reducing test anxiety. She knew, for example, her listeners knew what the causes and effects were, but she thought she could shed some light on methods to reduce it. With this subject narrowing, she entered *Methods of Reducing Test Anxiety* into the Google search engine, and she came up with 98,700 websites (June 11, 2002). There were a number of relevant titles: "Test Anxiety: Friend or Foe?," "Test Anxiety," "General Study Skills," "Understanding Academic Anxiety," "Study Tips, Strategies, and Techniques," and one just called "Anxiety." Most of the sites that interested her were from educational sites; many were written some time ago but had recent update dates; a number of the sites included effective examples Sofia could use to maintain the attention of her listeners; and several were sites cross-referenced with numerous links from other sites—which indicated to Sofia that these articles seemed to be well respected by counseling and learning professionals. Sofia was off to a good start.

She turned on her printer, and she began printing out some of what she discovered. All the pages looked useful and interesting, but it was far more than she would need for her five-minute informative speech. She had so much material that she knew she was going to have to limit her topic even further. After printing out nearly a dozen online articles, Sofia stopped to look more specifically at the information she was getting.

Sofia decided that each main head in the body of her speech would be one phase in dealing with anxiety, and within that phase she would mention a number of methods. Although her single bold point would be that there are specific, simple ways for dealing with anxiety, she also knew that one of the best methods was to start early and maintain both your mental and physical health.

Sofia decided to deal with three phases: (1) long-range planning, (2) short-range planning, and (3) the day of the test. Given her time limit (five minutes), she decided she would have to keep the information under each main point brief, but she would try to deal with some methods she could illustrate with a personal experience or an example—to maintain listener interest.

Looking over the stack of printouts Sofia had in front of her, she separated the information into three piles. As she was dividing up the information, she discovered some that would work for the introduction and conclusion to her speech, and she labeled it at once so she wouldn't forget. Because she was working at her computer, Sofia began typing a rough draft of her outline. She knew it was early, but having an outline allowed her to discard printouts that were not currently relevant, focus specifically and intently on information she wanted to include, and organize her thinking at this early stage.

I. *There is an important long-range approach for dealing with test anxiety.*
   A. *Maintain your physical health through exercise, diet, and rest.*
   B. *Sustain your mental health by focusing on past testing successes and engaging in positive self-talk.*
   C. *Bolster your confidence by believing you will do well, knowing the information backward and forward, taking self-tests, and having another student quiz you. (Health, Exercise, Diet . . ., 1998).*

II. *The short-range approach for dealing with test anxiety is more familiar to us all*
   A. *The best strategy for coping with test anxiety is preparation. "Students who are amply prepared or overprepared for tests almost always perform better than unprepared students" (Preparation . . . , 1998).*
   B. *Overlearn the material to be tested; break large amounts of material into manageable tasks; know the test format; and continue to take practice exams and write practice essays (Jackson, n.d.).*
   C. *View the test realistically: It is not a measure of your self-worth, your ability to be successful, or your future happiness. It is merely a single measure of what you know (II. Reducing . . . , 1999).*
   D. *Establish a study schedule. Do not think about what you should have studied yesterday. Know exactly how much time there is before the exam; know exactly how much information you need to cover; and write down a specific daily schedule to accomplish your goal (II. Reducing . . . , 1999).*

III. *There are important last-minute activities you can engage in to relieve test anxiety on the day of and at the test.*
   A. *Be rested and comfortable. If you take a test when you are hungry or tired, you won't perform well (Test anxiety, 2002).*
   B. *Expect some anxiety. Being concerned will help you do your best on a test (Skills that can help . . . , 1996).*
   C. *Know what to expect. Learn ahead of time the kind of test it will be, where and when it will be held, and what materials to bring. This helps eliminate the element of surprise (Test taking strategies, 2002).*
   D. *Relax as much as you can. If you're too nervous to think or read carefully, try to slow down physically. Take several deep breaths. Then start to work. (Some facts psychologists know . . .; Test taking, 2002).*
   E. *Avoid contact with others—especially worried test takers. Test anxiety is contagious and unproductive (Test anxiety, 2002).*
   F. *Read the instructions carefully; make sure your copy is complete; answer the easiest questions first; read each test question carefully; review the test questions and your answers to them before you turn in your test (Test anxiety, 2001).*

For her conclusion, Sofia summarized her ideas and then alerted listeners to a variety of books and Web pages on the topic. She saved one of her best comments for the end. Sofia's college had a psychological counseling center with specialists who dealt with students experiencing high levels of test anxiety. Not only did she come prepared with this information; she had created a flyer that indicated the location and hours of the counseling center and the names of the available psychologists. Since hers was not a persuasive speech, she did not try to persuade students to seek help; she simply told them where to find more information, material, and assistance.

Sofia filled in the details of her outline, and wrote it out completely for her instructor. She condensed the outline to just key words and put them on several 3" × 5" cards. She began practicing her speech using the cards. Because she had been so thorough in her research, she was so familiar with her material, and she had chosen an important and relevant topic, she could speak on it conversationally and comfortably without having to rely on her note cards.

When the time came to give her speech, her delivery was smooth. Sofia felt strong and in control. The structure of her speech was easy for her to remember and instantly intelligible to her listeners. After the speech, several classmates told her she had done a terrific job. One student asked her a question she had not answered in her speech: "Is use of the college counseling center free of charge?" "Not only is it free," Sofia replied, "but they never release the names of students who go for help."

■ PRINCIPLES OF ORGANIZATION

Relate Points to Your Specific Purpose and Central Idea

The points you make in your speech should relate directly to your specific purpose and central idea. In this outline of a speech entitled "The Challenge to Excel," notice that all the main points do this:

For help in outlining your material, use the computerized "Outline Tutor" on the CD.

Specific purpose:	To inform my classmates about the four things required to excel.
Central idea:	No matter what people's abilities are, there are four things they can do to excel.
Main ideas:	I. Learn self-discipline.
	II. Build a knowledge base.
	III. Develop special skills.
	IV. Bounce back from defeat.

Distinguish between Main and Minor Points

When organizing your speech, distinguish between main points and minor points. If you do this, the speech will flow more naturally and will seem logical to your listeners. The **main points** are all the broad, general ideas and information that support your central idea; the **minor points** are the specific ideas and information that support the main points. Say that the purpose of your speech is to persuade audience members to learn to incorporate computer-generated graphics into their research papers. The central idea of your speech is that they can illustrate their ideas better and more efficiently by using a computer. Your main point would have this broad, general idea: "Computers help you draw faster, revise drawings more easily, and produce a better-looking, better-illustrated paper." Your minor points will explain the main point in more specific terms: (1) Most people do not draw very well; (2) A computer enables you to draw like a professional, even if you don't have drawing skills; and (3) Revising and changing drawings is easy and efficient. All these minor points help explain the ways in which the computer is more effective and efficient for illustrating ideas.

If you have difficulty distinguishing between major and minor points, write each of the points you want to make on a separate index card. Then spread all the cards out in front of you and organize them by main points, with minor points coming under them. If one arrangement doesn't work, try another. This is the advantage of having each point on a separate card.

Phrase All Points in Full Sentences

Writing all your points in full sentences will help you think out your ideas more fully. Once your ideas are set out in this detailed way, you will be able to discover problems in organization that might need more work.

Give All Points a Parallel Structure

Parallel structure means that each of your points will begin with the same grammatical form. For example, on a speech about alcohol, the speaker started each suggestion with the words *what alcohol:*

What alcohol is.

What alcohol feels like.

What alcohol does to your body.

In his commencement address to the California Institute of Technology in Pasadena, California, Tom Brokaw, network news broadcaster, used parallel structure in this manner:

It is not enough to wire the world if you short-circuit the soul.
It is not enough to probe the hostile environment of distant galaxies if we fail to resolve the climate of mindless violence, ethnic and racial hate here in the bosom of Mother Earth.
It is not enough to identify the gene that predetermines the prospect of Alzheimer's disease if we go through the prime of life with a closed mind (Brokaw, 1999).

Working Together

For each of the following sets of sentences, identify the main point with an *M* and the minor or supporting point(s) with an *S*:

1. _____ There are thousands of different kinds of dolls.

2. _____ *Nesting dolls* is the term for dolls that fit inside each other.

3. _____ Baby dolls resemble infants.

1. _____ Don't wear anything that glitters.

2. _____ Don't wear all-black or all-white clothing.

3. _____ If you are appearing on television, be careful what you wear.

1. _____ The amount of agricultural land under cultivation does not support the population.

2. _____ Famine can occur for many reasons.

3. _____ Population exceeds the food sources.

4. _____ Unusual weather, such as drought, occurs.

In each of the next sets there are two main points. Find them and match them with the correct minor points.

1. _____ Certain signs indicate that your pet is too fat.

2. _____ Cut back food by one-third.

3. _____ It tires easily after a little exercise.

4. _____ Put your pet on a diet.

5. _____ Use low-calorie fillers such as rice or cottage cheese.

6. _____ It looks fat (or everyone calls it "Butterball").

1. _____ Some studies indicate that people who drink coffee in large amounts are more prone to heart disease.

2. _____ Caffeine can cause birth defects such as cleft palate and bone abnormalities.

3. _____ Decaffeinated coffee is a good alternative to coffee with caffeine.

4. _____ If you want to break the caffeine habit, cut down by a cup or two a day.

5. _____ People who drink large quantities of coffee may be endangering their health.

6. _____ You can break the coffee–caffeine habit.

Answers: The main points are:
- There are thousands of different kinds of dolls.
- If you are appearing on television, be careful what you wear.
- Famine can occur for many reasons.
- Certain signs indicate that your pet is too fat.
- Put your pet on a diet.
- People who drink large quantities of coffee may be endangering their health.
- You can break the coffee–caffeine habit.

■ PATTERNS OF ORGANIZATION

Once you have researched your speech, decided on a specific purpose, and listed the main points, you are ready to choose an organizational pattern. This organizational pattern will mainly affect the **body**—the main part of the speech. (Introductions and conclusions are discussed later in the chapter.)

The "Speech Preparation Checklist" on your CD can help you prepare your speeches.

The body of the speech is made up of your main points. Most classroom speeches should not have more than four or five main points, and many will

The speech topic, the audience, and the amount of time available are factors to consider when determining your pattern of organization.

have no more than two or three. Your choice of how many main points to use will depend on your topic. If you want to cover a topic in depth, use fewer main points. If you want to give a broad, general view, you might want to use four or five main points.

There are many ways to arrange the main points in your speech. Your choice will depend on what best suits your material. In this section we discuss six possible arrangements: time order, spatial order, cause-and-effect order, problem-solution, motivated sequence, and topical order.

Time Order

Time order, or *chronological order,* is used to show development over time. This pattern works particularly well when you want to use a historical approach. For example, in a speech about what to do if you are the victim of a crime, the speaker arranged her main points in chronological order:

Specific purpose:	To inform my audience about what to do if they are victims of a crime.
Central idea:	If you become a victim of a crime, there are some things you should do.
Main points:	I. Try not to panic.
	II. Attract attention; scream or yell "Fire!"
	III. Protect your own safety; if there is a weapon or you don't know whether there is, don't resist. If there is no weapon, fight back, kick, or run.
	IV. Report all crimes immediately to the police; don't disturb any evidence.

Another Point of View

Throughout this chapter, and you will see it again and again in this textbook, your authors stress the need to let your listeners know where you are going in your speech. Here, is another point of view written by C. M. McKinney (2002) at the Advanced Public Speaking Institute:

I suppose most of my readers know by now that when I'm speaking in public I push the limits most of the time to make sure my audience stays awake. It should be no surprise to you then that I will attack another common old style snoozer technique (and I know I will get letters from educational theory folks, but that is OK) . . . that is, telling the participants what you are going to cover during your presentation. I SAY LET 'EM FIGURE IT OUT AS YOU GO. If they think they know where you are going during a public speaking engagement, then it is easy for them to "zone out" since they "think" they know what you are going to say. The way I do it is to make them won-der, "What in the heck is he going to do next?" which forces them to stay alert to find out (p. 1).

Questions

1. Do you think McKinney has a valid point? Can you be well organized and still leave your listeners wondering what you're going to do next?

2. Are there other ways to keep listeners alert and awake besides keeping your organizational scheme a secret? What techniques could you, as a speaker use, to make certain your listeners stayed alert, and yet reveal your method of organization to them—or, at least let them know where you are going?

Source: C. M. McKinney, "Public Speaking: Make 'Em Wonder," Advanced Public Speaking Institute, Box 2630, Landover Hills, MD 20784, 2002. Retrieved March 25, 2003, from http://www.public-speaking.org/public-speaking-letemwonder-article.htm.

Time order is often used to explain a process. The process could be anything from how to wrap a gift to how to apply for a student loan. One student used time order for describing the process of making beer:

Specific purpose:	To inform my audience of how beer is made.
Central idea:	Making beer involves three stages: mashing, boiling, and fermenting.
Main points:	I. Mashing occurs in three stages, each raising the temperature of the finely mashed malt to a new level.
	II. The wort (what is left after mashing) is boiled in a copper tank or kettle.
	III. Fermenting begins when the yeast is "pitched" into the wort.

Spatial Order

When you use **spatial order,** you refer to a physical or geographical layout to help your audience see how the parts make up the whole. To help your audience visualize your subject, you explain it by going from left to right or from top to bottom, or in any direction that best suits your subject.

For example, a student decided that spatial order is the best way to explain how speakers should "stage" their presentations. She organized her speech around three aspects of a speaker's presentational environment. Her focus was on presentations that included the use of visuals such as slides, overheads, movies, or computer displays.

Specific purpose: To inform audience members about how to be fully effective by staging their presentations.

Central idea: Speakers need to approach their environment from three angles: space, lighting, and mechanics.

Main points:
I. Speakers should control the space as much as possible (location of speaker, screen, and visuals).
II. Speakers must have control over the lighting, since proper lighting is important to relaxed viewing.
III. Speakers must have control over the mechanics of how projection systems work and where controls are located.

Notice how the speaker moved from the largest aspect of presentational concern—space—to the next smaller concern—lighting—to the smallest or most defined concern—location of the mechanics of controlling the equipment. This is a well-thought-out spatial order.

Spatial order works particularly well when the speech focuses on a chart or diagram. When using the visual support, the speaker naturally moves from top to bottom or from left to right. For example, when a student spoke on the topic "What Credit Reports Look Like," she used a spatial order and worked from top to bottom:

Specific purpose: To inform my audience about what credit reports look like.

Central idea: The credit report is, essentially, divided into three parts.

Main points:
I. At the top of the page is background information such as name, address, and employment.
II. The second part of the page lists information about accounts and payment history.
III. The bottom part of the page, under "Credit History," lists who uses and pays for the credit account, whether it is a joint account, and if one person is authorized to use it while another person is liable for payment (as with students and their parents).

Cause-and-Effect Order

A speaker who uses **cause-and-effect order** divides a speech into two major parts: cause (why something is happening) and effect (what impact

Consider This

In their scholarly book, *Blessing for a Long Time: The Sacred Pole of the Omaha Tribe,* the authors discuss the *uki'te,* a term used to designate the form or order in which the tribal organization ceremonially camped, in which each one of the villages, or clans, had its definite place.

In regard to the accompanying figure, the authors explain that the "*hu'thuga* [or dwelling place] was divided into halves or moieties that corresponded to the two 'grand divisions' of the tribe. The Sky people camped in the northern half of the *hu'thuga.* The Earth people camped in the southern half. The entrance of the *hu'thuga* faced east when the tribe had stopped to conduct its ceremonies."

Questions

1. If you were giving an informative speech about the camps of the Omaha tribe, can you see how easy it would be to arrange the speech in a spatial pattern?

2. By using just the information provided in this figure, what other kinds of patterns of arrangement could form the basis for a speech?

Source: Robin Ridington and Dennis Hastings (In' aska), *Blessing for a Long Time: The Sacred Pole of the Omaha Tribe* (Lincoln: University of Nebraska Press, 1997), p. 112.

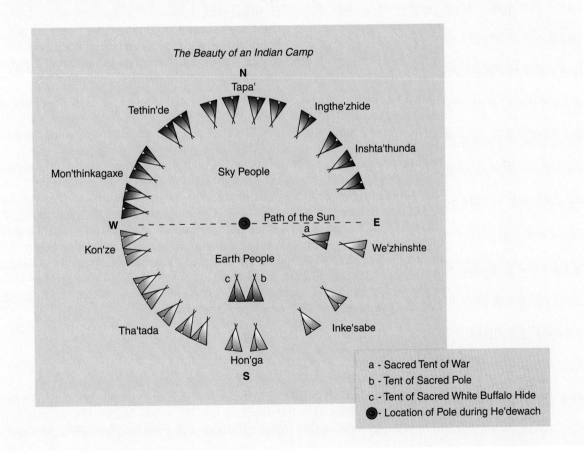

it is having). Notice the cause-and-effect order revealed in items I and II under "main points" in the following outline:

Specific purpose: To inform my audience about the effects that using DNA for paternity testing is having.

Central idea: Everyone needs to be aware that the fast, cheap, and accurate use of DNA technology (247,000 cases of DNA-based paternity testing per year) can have serious human costs. (DNA testing goes mainstream, 2000)

Main points:

I. The development of DNA analysis in the 1980s moved the science forward, and fatherhood can be determined with a better than 99 percent probability. The tests can be completed within days on the basis of mouth swabs or blood samples, and developments in the mid-1990s improved speed and accuracy.

II. The effects are both negative and positive. Negatively, divorces have become more contentious and family ties strained as parents seek to avoid child-support payments by testing children. Also, the time-honored legal concept of parenthood is being reevaluated in courtrooms. Positively, DNA testing has helped resolve inheritance disputes and clear up family mix-ups (Willing, 1999).

You do not always have to start with the cause and end with the effect. In this speech on "DNA and Daddy," the speaker could have begun with the positive and negative effects of DNA testing and ended by showing how all these situations came about. Along with noting the advances in DNA technology, the speaker could point out, as well, that all the interest in and use of this new technology is fueling a $100 million annual business in DNA testing. When you enter *DNA Testing* into the Google search engine, you get 688,000 websites; when you enter *DNA testing and paternity*, you get 38,000 (March 25, 2003), most of which are commercial sites advertising their willingness to do the testing. If you are using a cause-and-effect order, begin with the aspect most likely to capture the audience's attention. Considering the likely interest of college students in a technical subject like DNA testing, the speaker giving the "DNA and Daddy" speech would probably be better off beginning with the examples and ending with the technology.

Problem-Solution Order

Like speakers who use a cause-and-effect arrangement, a speaker who uses a **problem-solution order** also divides a speech into two sections. In this case, one part deals with the problem and the other deals with the solution. For example, look at this outline for a speech entitled "Lose Weight Fast:"

Specific purpose: To inform audience members that by eating high fiber, moving around, and pumping iron, they can lose weight fast.

Central idea: You don't have to starve yourself, become a competitive athlete, or engage in other extraordinary measures in order to drop unwanted weight.

Main points:
I. When I asked how many in here would like to shed 10 pounds fast, you all raised your hands, but unfortunately there are too many highly hyped, too-good-to-be true diets and fads that are unsafe. Some diets are safe and reputable; others are not.

II. You can eat as much as you want of vegetables, fresh fruits, grains, and unrefined starches. Rather than taking special programs in aerobics, dancing, or Tai Bo, you need to make movement, such as increased walking, a regular and habitual part of your daily activities. You need to change fat into muscle by regular (20-minute) strength-training routines.

The speaker let listeners know that some authors of diet books have presented an approach that might be good for some people but may be unsafe for many others. What the speaker stressed, and what is important when anyone undertakes any major change, is that if you want to lose weight fast, you need to concentrate on small, intelligent changes. That is the only way to see a big difference fast—faster than you may think—and, even more important, it is the only way you can expect to keep the weight off.

When Carla Davies, who lost an older brother to suicide, looked up *Suicide* on the Google search engine, she received 3,630,000 websites (March 25, 2003). At one site, she read about suicide among 15–19-year-old adolescents, so she entered that—*suicide among 15–19-year-old adolescents*—into Google, and she had effectively narrowed her search to 4,390 sites. At the site Crisis and suicide: Youth suicide facts (American Association of Suicidology, Youth Suicide Fact Sheet, 2001), Telephone Counseling and Referral Service (retrieved March 25, 2003, from http://www.tcrs211.org/ suicide/statsyouth.htm), she made most of her startling discoveries—for example, that within every 1 hour and 57 minutes, a person under the age of 25 commits suicide—12 every day (Crisis and suicide, 2001). Carla wasted no time, and she tentatively outlined a speech entitled "Suicide Is a Threat That Needs Our Attention" (Suicide is a threat . . . , 1999, p. 3).

Here is another example of a problem-solution order from Carla's speech titled "Suicide Is a Threat That Needs Our Attention" (Suicide is a threat . . . , 1999, p. 3)

Specific purpose: To persuade audience members that they need to learn more about suicide.

Central idea: You need to know about suicide because it is the third leading cause of death among 15- to 19-year-old adolescents, has experienced a 300 percent increase over 30 years, and—overall—claims about 30,000 lives a year (Suicide statistics, 1999; Crisis and suicide, 2001).

Main points:
I. Most people are unaware that suicide is the eighth leading cause of death in our nation and

claims 30,000 lives each year. What are the statistics that reveal the magnitude of the problem?

II. Most people are unaware of the at-risk profile or the risk factors associated with potential suicide victims. Who is at risk, and what is a hypothetical profile of someone who might attempt it?

III. Most people are unaware of the intervention protocol which, if followed, can help reduce suicide risk among students. What are recommendations students can follow that can help in the early stages of the problem?

IV. Most people are unaware of the specific suicide prevention guidelines. What are some do's and don'ts that offer a way for each of us to help solve the problem of suicide?

V. Most people are unaware of the wealth of resources available for help. What are some of the services available on this campus? In the community? On the Internet?

Motivated Sequence

The **motivated sequence,** developed by Professor Alan H. Monroe in the 1930s (McKerrow, Gronbeck, Ehninger, & Monroe, 2003), is also a problem-solving pattern of arrangement. The sequence is designed to persuade listeners to accept a point of view and then motivate them to take action. The full pattern has five steps:

1. Attention:	The speaker calls attention to the topic or situation.
2. Need:	The speaker develops the need for a change and explains related audience needs. This is the problem-development portion of the speech.
3. Satisfaction:	The speaker presents his or her solution and shows how it meets (satisfies) the needs mentioned.
4. Visualization:	The speaker shows what will result when the solution is put into effect.
5. Action:	The speaker indicates what kind of action is necessary to bring about the desired change.

Any persuasive problem-solving speech can be adapted to the motivated sequence. Notice how the speaker uses this pattern in "To Cheat or Not to Cheat: That Is the Question":

Specific purpose:	To persuade my listeners that they should take a strong stand to eliminate academic dishonesty.
Central idea:	Unless you are willing to take a strong stand to eliminate academic dishonesty, cheating is likely to continue and will hurt us all.

Main points:

I. Attention. The decision to cheat or not can be difficult to make—especially when you are under a lot of pressure.

II. Need. Often students face the temptation to be academically dishonest daily, whether it be cheating or helping others to cheat.

III. Satisfaction. Students need to focus on the value of honesty, the importance of integrity in academic matters, and the privilege of a college education.

IV. Visualization. Academic honesty is important to educational growth: Aim for learning, grades that represent solid effort, feelings of self-worth and integrity, and a clear conscience about never having helped others to cheat.

V. Action. Think about academic honesty. If you have ever cheated, don't do it again. If you haven't, don't start. Being honest in your work makes you feel better about yourself.

Topical Order

When your speech does not fit into any of the patterns described so far, you will probably use a topical pattern of organization. You can use a **topical order** whenever your subject can be grouped logically into subtopics. Here are some examples: four ways to save money for college, three systems for selecting a major, inexpensive ways to travel abroad, five foods that help you live longer. Sofia Mena's speech, the chapter's opening example, was arranged topically, too.

In the next sample, a student uses a topical order in a speech entitled "Native Americans." Topical order is one choice for this speech, which treats Native American culture, beliefs, respect for the planet, and contributions. Time order would work if the student were to consider the history of Native Americans. A spatial order would work to compare and contrast various Native American tribes from different geographic locations, to describe where the tribes are now located, or perhaps to show how a living site is laid out spatially. A problem-solution order might work if the student wanted to look at the problems faced by Native Americans and suggest various solutions to these problems. In this example, topical order is used to examine feelings about adoption among Native Americans.

Specific purpose: To inform my audience about the importance of family in Native American culture.

Central idea: To protect their values, continue their traditions, and maintain their families, Native American tribes are trying to keep children from being adopted by outsiders.

Main points:

I. Native American tribes have values that are different from those of mainstream American society.

On the Web

Which organizational pattern might you use for each of the following speech topics, and why?

1. Explaining the process of using the Internet to someone who has never used it before.

2. Using the Internet to discover how to overcome procrastination.

3. Explaining how to find your way around a website *or* how most websites are arranged.

4. Explaining how a chat room on the Internet operates.

5. Clarifying the history and development of the Internet.

6. Explaining how a search engine functions with respect to tracking down and reporting websites.

II. Native Americans believe their traditions will die out if their children are adopted by outsiders.

III. Native Americans want to maintain their families, for values and traditions must be taught to children while they are young.

In a persuasive speech on what can be done to conserve natural resources, a student speaking on the topic "Conservation: What You Can Do" used a topical order to show what can be done:

Specific purpose: To persuade my audience that everyone can contribute to conserving natural resources.

Central idea: Conservation means practicing the four Rs of reduce, reuse, repair, and recycle.

Main points:
   I. Reduce consumption and waste.

   II. Reuse what can be reused.

   III. Repair what can be fixed.

   IV. Recycle what can be recycled.

■ THE SPEECH INTRODUCTION

The **introduction** is the opening statement of your speech. It gives the audience members their first impression of you, it introduces them to the topic, and it motivates them to listen. The introduction is very important: If you don't hook audience members in the beginning, you might never get their attention.

It is possible to outline an introduction. The outline would be especially valuable to beginning speakers who want to make certain everything important is included.

There are no hard-and-fast rules for introductions. If you have a wonderful idea for one, use it. If you need some guidance, try to use some or all of the following techniques in your introduction:

Get attention.

Announce your topic.

Preview your central idea and main points.

Establish your credibility.

We think it is useful to write out the complete text of your introduction, because this gives you added confidence when you begin your speech. However, your instructor might want you to do it differently, so be sure to follow your instructor's directions.

Stating Your Purpose, Central Idea, and Main Points

In most situations, a speaker will use the introduction to tell what he or she is going to talk about. When a speaker does this, the audience can turn its attention to the topic and begin to concentrate. Although you don't have to mention the topic in your very first words, you shouldn't wait too long. By the time you reach the end of your introduction, your audience should know what you intend to accomplish and the central idea of your speech. By including this information in your introduction, you are providing a signpost about the direction you will be taking. For example:

> *The physical abuse of children is a serious problem in this country, and today I want to talk about how bad the problem is and some of the things we can do about it.*

In your introduction, you might also want to preview your main points. Not only does this give members of the audience a sense of your direction, but it also helps them to follow your speech more easily. The student speaking on the physical abuse of children previewed her main points this way:

> *Since this problem covers such a broad area, I would like to limit my talk to three areas: parental abuse of children, social agencies that deal with abuse, and what the ordinary citizen can do when he or she suspects a child is being abused.*

Getting Attention

In addition to telling your audience what you are going to talk about, your introduction should arouse attention and interest. Gaining attention is not just a matter of getting audience members to listen to your first words—they would probably do that anyway. Rather, it is a matter of creating interest in your subject. You want your listeners to think, "This really sounds like an interesting subject" or "I am going to enjoy listening to this speech."

Notice in the following example how Sofia Mena began her speech "Dealing with Test Anxiety." She designed her introduction to get the attention of her listeners:

> *I have heard it over and over again until I am getting sick of it. "It's just not fair. I didn't ask to be here. I don't deserve this kind of treatment." Have you heard students saying things like this? Although my speech today is titled "Dealing With Test Anxiety," it could just as well be called "Taking Responsibility for Your Life." Throughout my speech today, I want you all to keep one thought in the back of your mind:* You are responsible for your own learning. *With that thought in mind, all*

Getting the attention of your audience is a matter of creating interest in your topic.

the information I will be sharing with you today on dealing with test anxiety will make sense. It will make sense because it places the responsibility squarely on your own shoulders. Whether it's long-range approaches, short-range approaches, or day-of-the-exam approaches to dealing with test anxiety, all the methods I will be discussing today are designed to empower you, so that you have control. But they cannot empower you, they cannot put you in charge, unless you accept the responsibility for your own learning. What's more, all my comments today will help you with next week's examination.

Here, Mena has given her central idea—alerting listeners to methods for dealing with test anxiety—and even given a brief synopsis of her speech—long-range, short-range, and day-of-the-exam approaches. But she has done something even more important. She has connected with the audience members—getting their attention by asking them to keep a thought in mind—"You are responsible for your own learning"—and by talking about placing the responsibility squarely on their shoulders and saying she is empowering them with ideas. This is an especially powerful introduction that was carefully planned.

Certain techniques are proven attention getters. Let's look at others and at the functions they serve. Note that sometimes a speaker might use more than one of these techniques.

Use Some Humor

Research shows that speeches with some humor produce a more favorable reaction to the speaker (Gruner, 1985). Often a speaker will use humor in his or her introduction. Notice how Garrison Keillor (1998), no stranger to humor himself as the creator and host of *A Prairie Home Companion*—the radio program centered on the events of the fictional town of Lake Wobegon, Minnesota—began his commencement address to Gettysburg College:

> *I bring you greetings from Lake Wobegon, to all of you in the German branch of the Lutheran Church—we pray for you daily without ceasing. It's a great pleasure for all of us on this platform to be part of your day— the Class of '87. And to be here as witnesses at this grave and solemn moment in your lives.*
>
> *When I graduated from college, I sat about where you are and watched a candidate for summa cum laude honors walk up the stairs to be recognized, and step on the inside hem of his gown. And walk all the way up the inside of it. It was something that we all remembered, who saw it, as an object lesson in how talent and intelligence might fare in this world. And some of us had tears in our eyes as we saw it (p. 181).*

Use an Example

Short examples often work quite well in introductions. They may be personal examples, or they could have happened to someone else. A student used this example to spark interest in her speech:

> *Gilbert is 42 years old. He has three children, ages 17, 10, and 4. Gilbert never read to his two oldest children or helped them with their schoolwork. If they asked for help with reading, Gilbert's reply was, "Ask your mother." Last week everything changed. Gilbert read* The Cat in the Hat *to his four-year-old. It was the first time Gilbert had ever read to one of his children. In fact, it was the first time Gilbert had read anything aloud at all.*
>
> *Gilbert had been illiterate. For the past four months he has been learning to read through a program in the literacy council. I am Gilbert's teacher.*

Refer to the Occasion

If you are asked to speak for a special occasion or if a special occasion falls on the day you are speaking, make a reference to it, as when a speaker said, "I am very honored to have been asked to give a speech for Founders' Day." Although still a week before the exam, Sofia Mena said, in her introduction to her speech on text anxiety: "What's more, all of my comments today will help you with next week's examination."

Because the introduction is so important, it is worthwhile to spend extra time—in addition to preparing the rest of the speech—trying to find something unique or unusual. This is especially true when the speech is a traditional one, like a commencement speech, and it is fairly well known that the attention of audience members is likely to be seriously divided between the speaker and so many other potential diversions—other audience members, celebrations, weather concerns, time constraints, the need for sleep, plans for later, and certainly, boredom. Here is how Robert L. Dilenschneider (2001), president and CEO, The Dilenschneider Group, chose to face the challenge in his commencement address at Muskingum College, New Concord, Ohio:

> *Thank you very much. Muskingum is a great place. I am privileged to be here. And I am thrilled that you asked me to speak today. Thank you. When I took suggestions on what to say here today, two pieces of advice stuck with me.*
>
> *First, my two sons, 15-year-old Geoffrey, and 11-year-old Peter, said, "Keep it short, crisp, and to the point." They reminded me of Robert DeNiro's talk at New York University several years ago when the actor stood up and told several thousand students, faculty, and parents, "Break a leg."*
>
> *And then DeNiro sat down.*
>
> *The second thought came from a friend in Ireland who said, "The students have been lectured to for four years. Don't give them another lecture. They want to get on with the day and their lives" (p. 605).*

Show the Importance of the Subject

Showing audience members that the subject is important to their own lives is a good way of getting and keeping attention. In the example below, not only does the student let her listeners know how important the subject is to them, but she also keeps their attention by building suspense:

> *If I asked you right now, how many of you have done what I am going to talk about today, every one of you would raise your hand. This is a topic that affects everyone. Sometimes it nags at us day in and day out. Often it creates a negative spiral of fear of failure, self-doubt, feelings of inadequacy, anxiety over the expectations that others have of us, and even feelings of being overwhelmed—that tasks seem unmanageable and that we are overextended—trying to manage too much. All of this takes a serious toll on us physically, mentally, and emotionally. We even have some wonderful mental self-seductions for tolerating the discomfort: "I'll do it tomorrow," "What's the harm of a half-hour of TV now? I've still got time," or "I deserve some time for myself." What is this thing that makes us feel we have lost control over our day-to-day routine? It is procrastination.*

Use Startling Information

Using information that startles or surprises your audience is a good device for gaining attention. The only caution is that you do not overdo the use of startling information because it has the potential of losing its effect. In this speech to the International Committee, University Club of Washington D.C., "Terrorism: Addressing Its Root Causes," Tariq Karim (2002), ambassador of Bangladesh, puts the 9/11 terrorist attack in brutal, startling relief:

9/11—A defining moment, setting a global agenda. The dastardly terrorist attacks on September 11, on the twin towers of the WTC and on the Pentagon, were not just an assault on America and Americas. They were heinous attacks on the entire world as well, because innocent citizens from many countries other than the United States were among the casualties. . . indeed, they were an attack on humanity. As a result of those attacks we all stand diminished, not only because of the colossal loss of innocent human lives, but also because they denigrate the core spirit and essential values of a great religion, Islam, in whose name these criminal acts were perpetrated.

The 9/11 attacks brought sharply home the realization that terrorism was not just something that happened elsewhere, in distant lands among alien peoples, but that it has assumed global dimensions, with its perpetrators harboring a global agenda"(p. 425).

Use Personal Examples

Don't be afraid to refer to your own life when you can tie examples from it into your subject. Personal examples make a speech stronger because they are a way of showing that you know what you're talking about. In the next example, the speaker used an example from his own experience to begin a speech about dropping out of school:

Seven years ago I was a teenage dropout. I went away to college because my parents wanted me to. I moved into a dorm, made lots of friends, and began to have a wonderful time—a time that was so wonderful that I only occasionally went to class or studied for an exam. The college, realizing that first-year students take time to adjust, put me on probation for the first year. In the second year, however, I had to settle down.

I tried to study, but I didn't have any idea of what I was studying for. I didn't have a major, and I had no idea of what I wanted to do with my life. Finally I asked myself, "What am I doing here?" I could come up with no answer. So after finishing the first semester of my sophomore year, I dropped out. It was the second-best decision I ever made. The first-best was to come back to school—at the grand old age of 27.

Sometimes examples from your life help tell your audience why you are qualified to speak on your subject. If the audience thinks you have some experience or expertise, you will have more credibility as a speaker:

Today I am here to persuade you never to take up smoking. You might think it is a case of the pot calling the kettle black. In the past you may have seen me smoke at every possible opportunity. All I can say is that if I had one wish, I would like to be a nonsmoker. Why do I want to give it up? Let me tell you what you might not know. Every morning I cough for half an hour when I get out of bed. I have thrown away countless clothes because I have burned tiny holes in them with cigarette sparks. The windows of my house and car are covered with a greasy yellow film from smoke. Worst of all, my favorite cat won't sit in my lap because she hates smoke.

Why haven't I given it up? Because it is a powerful addiction that is very hard to break. But today, here, with all of you as my witnesses, I want you to know that I have just passed my first week without any cigarettes.

Use a Quotation

Sometimes you can find a quotation that will get your speech off to a good start. A well-chosen quotation can also give credibility to your speech. When Patty LaPlomb began her speech "Drinking to Get Drunk," she began this way:

"Students used to drink to have fun, and now they drink to get drunk," says Richard Yoast, the director of drug abuse programs for the American Medical Association. I admit, I enjoy a drink or two—but until I came to this campus, I had never seen the kind of drinking I have witnessed now. Friends of my roommate, for example, miss classes regularly. They've been involved in traffic accidents, and they have damaged property. If you ask me, they are heavy drinkers, but if you ask them, they are moderate drinkers. Henry Wechsler, the psychologist who oversaw a Harvard research study on binge drinkers I'll refer to later, said, "If someone does not think they have a [drinking] problem, they are unlikely to listen to messages directed at people who have that problem" (Marcus, 2000, p. 53).

Manuel Castro collected quotations, so when he faced the prospect of having to give a persuasive speech, he knew it would be an opportunity to put some of them to use. As a member of the campus Student Activities Office staff, Manuel decided to persuade listeners to take advantage of some of the extracurricular activities available on campus. Since he had handouts he could distribute on many of them, the visual-support requirement would be easily satisfied. Here is the introduction he constructed for his speech:

The first student I met on this campus was Stewart Little, my summer orientation leader. He said to our orientation group, "If I could live by only two words, these would be them: Carpe Diem"—or Seize the Day! I know these words aren't new, but because I liked Stewart, his words have stuck with me. Then, you all will remember President Woodward's remarks at our opening convocation: "Life may not be the party you want, but while you're here, you might as well dance!" I loved it. When he was talking about what our college has to offer us, he said, "Most students realize the good things only when they are about to run out." Today I want to tell you about some of the 200 student organizations available to you on this campus and not only how we can seize the day but how we can enjoy the dance, too—before the good things run out and our time here is gone.

My talk today, "Never Rest till Better Be Best" was inspired by my work at the Student Activities Office. But, perhaps even more important than that is the inspiration I received from my grandfather whose name I share. He loved quotations. He said, "Good, Better, Best. Never rest till good be better, and better be best." I have not only taken his words to heart, but I want you to take his words to heart as well. The opportunity is here; the time is now; we need to act.

Additional Tips for Introductions

When writing an introduction to a speech, remember the following points as well:

1. Although you might want to build curiosity about your speech topic, don't draw out the suspense for too long. The audience will get annoyed if it has to wait to find out what you're going to talk about.

2. Keep your introduction short. The body of your speech contains the main content, and you shouldn't wait too long to get there.

3. In planning your speech, be sure to adapt the topic to the occasion and to the audience. Before you start to speak, ask yourself whether there is anything in the situation that you did not anticipate and need to adapt to. For example, did someone introduce you in a particularly flattering way? Do you want to acknowledge this? Did your audience brave bad weather to come and hear you talk? Do you want to thank them?

■ THE SPEECH CONCLUSION

A good **conclusion** should tie a speech together and give the audience the feeling that the speech is complete. It should not introduce any new ideas.

If you have not had very much experience in public speaking, it is especially important that you plan your conclusion carefully. No feeling is worse than knowing that you have said all you have to say but do not know how to stop. If you plan your conclusion, this won't happen to you.

In preparing a conclusion, it may be helpful to follow a model. Like following a model for the introduction, doing so for the conclusion can help ensure that all essential parts are included. This is, perhaps, more important for beginning speakers than for those with more experience. As we said when discussing a model for introduction preparation, speakers who follow models without deviation may find themselves giving lackluster, mechanical speeches.

A conclusion should:

- Signal the end of your speech. (You could say, "The last thing I would like to say. . . ." or "Finally, . . ." Please note that the phrase "In conclusion I would just like to say that. . . ." is overused. Try to find an original signal.)
- Summarize your main points.
- Make a memorable final statement.

This model is designed to show beginning students what they are supposed to work toward as they prepare their conclusions. Try not to let the model stifle your creativity or imagination.

As with introductions, certain kinds of conclusions are used time and time again. When you are working on your conclusion, consider one of the approaches discussed below. Note that even though the conclusions are of different types, speakers should try to give them an inspirational quality. They should make the audience members feel that the speech was terrific and that they would like to hear the speaker again.

Summarize Your Main Ideas

If you want your audience to remember your main points, it helps to go back and summarize them in the conclusion of your speech. The student whose topic was "Five Tips for Improving Term Papers" concluded her speech this way:

> Let me briefly summarize what you should do whenever you write a term paper. Use interviews as well as the Internet, show enthusiasm about the subject, paraphrase quotations, don't pad your paper, have your paper printed on a quality printer, and proofread your paper before you hand it in. If you follow these hints, you are certain to do better in the next paper you write.

Include a Quotation

If you can find a quotation that fits your subject, the conclusion is a good place to use it. A quotation gives added authority to everything you have said, and it can often help sum up your main ideas. In his speech to persuade the audience not to make political choices on the basis of television commercials, the student used a closing quotation to reinforce his point:

> An executive in the television industry once wrote, "Television programming is designed to be understood by and to appeal to the average 12-year-old." Since none of us are 12-year-old viewers, I would suggest that we fight back. There is only one way to do that. Turn off the television set.

Inspire Your Audience to Action

When you give a speech, especially a persuasive one, your goal is often to inspire the audience to some course of action. If this is the goal of your speech, you can use your conclusion to tell audience members precisely what they should do. Notice how Carole McKenna closed the farewell speech she gave to participants in one of her five-day self-improvement seminars:

> You have all had the chance to try out a variety of exercises and activities. Some of you have admitted that you have been "pushed," "stretched," and "challenged" by the ideas, concepts, and opinions. Some of you found them disturbing and troubling. But, where better to encounter these things than a protected environment—a learning environment that stresses exposure and discovery?
>
> The certificate we will give you singles you out as someone who has been part of a unique opportunity. You found skills to practice, knowledge to digest, and feelings to understand. Also, you found each other. Most importantly, I trust, you found yourself. I hope you will now put to use all that you have discovered. You now recognize the truth in the statement "The greatest distance you have yet to cover still lies within you." Use this seminar as the beginning of competition, knowing that the most rewarding competition is with yourself, to improve yourself. Take charge of your life. Good luck to all of you.

Additional Tips for Conclusions

When writing a conclusion for a speech, keep these additional points in mind:

1. Work on your conclusion until you feel you can deliver it without notes. If you feel confident about your conclusion, you will feel more confident about your speech.

2. If you tell your audience you are going to conclude, do so! Don't set up the expectation that you are finished and then go on talking for several more minutes.

3. Don't let the words "Thank you" or "Are there any questions?" take the place of a conclusion.

4. Give your conclusion and leave the speaking area if appropriate. If you don't do this, you will ruin the impact of your conclusion and perhaps even your entire speech. (Leaving the speaking area may not be appropriate if there is a question period following the speech.)

■ SPEECH TRANSITIONS

The final element to work into your speech is **transitions**—comments that lead from one point to another to tell your audience where you have been and where you are going. Transitions are a means of smoothing the flow from one point to another. For example, if you are going to show how alcohol and tobacco combine to become more powerful than either acting alone, you might say:

We all know, then, that cigarette smoking is hazardous to our health and we all know that alcohol abuse can kill, but do you know what can happen when the two are combined? Let me show you how these two substances act synergistically—each one making the other more powerful and dangerous than either would be alone.

Now you are set to speak about their combined effect.

Tips for Transitions

In writing transitions, you should pay attention to these points:

1. Use a transition to introduce main heads and to indicate their order: "First. . . . Second. . . . Third. . . ."; "The first matter we shall discuss. . . ."; "In the first place. . . ."; "The first step. . . ."; "Let us first consider. . . ."; and the like.

2. Write out your transitions and include them in your speech outline. A transition that is written out and rehearsed is more likely to be used.

3. If in doubt about whether to use a transition, use it. Since a speech is a onetime event, listeners cannot go back. Do everything you can to make the job of listening easier and more accurate.

■ PREPARING AN OUTLINE

An **outline** is a way of organizing material so you can see all the parts and how they relate to the whole. Outlining your speech will help you organize your thoughts and discover where your presentation might cause problems in structure.

The Outline Format

Your speech will be organized into an introduction, a body, and a conclusion (with transitions connecting them). Since the introduction and the conclusion deal with so few points, they are usually not outlined, although some people prefer to outline them. As previously noted, outlining can help you see whether all essential parts are included. This is especially important for beginning speakers. We use Roman numerals to designate the main points of the body of the speech, as demonstrated in the examples of speech organization.

Main and Supporting Points

The outline sets forth the major portion of the speech—the body—and shows the content's organization into main and supporting (minor) points. Remember that the broad, general statements are the main points; the minor points contain the more specific information that elaborates on and supports the main points.

Standard Symbols and Indentation

All outlines use the same system of symbols. The main points are numbered with Roman numerals (I, II, III) and capital letters (A, B, C). Minor, more specific points are numbered with Arabic numerals (1, 2, 3) and lowercase letters (a, b, c). The most important material is always closest to the left-hand margin; as material gets less important, it moves to the right. Note, then, that the outline format moves information from the general to the more specific through the use of numbers, letters, and indentation:

I. *University*
   A. *College of Arts and Sciences*
      1. *English*
      2. *History*
      3. *Mathematics*
      4. *Psychology*
      5. *Science*
   B. *College of Business Administration*
      1. *Accounting*
      2. *Economics*
      3. *Finance*
      4. *General Business*
   C. *College of Education*
      1. *Early Childhood Education*
      2. *Elementary Education*
      3. *Secondary Education*
      4. *Special Education*

Another thing you should note about the outline format is that there should always be at least two points of the same level. That is, you can't have just an A and no B; you can't have just a 1 and no 2. The only exception to this is that in a one-point speech, you would have only one main point.

Full-Sentence and Key-Word Outlines

There are two major types of outlines: full-sentence and key-word. A **full-sentence outline** is a complete map of what the speech will look like. All the ideas are stated in full sentences. In a full-sentence outline it is easy to spot problem areas and weaknesses in the structure, support, and flow of ideas. This type of outline is useful as you plan and develop your speech.

Key-word outlines give only the important words and phrases; their main function is to remind the speaker of his or her ideas when delivering the speech. Sometimes speakers will add statistics or quotations to key-word outlines when such information is too long or too complicated to memorize. Some speakers prepare a full-sentence outline on the left and a key-word outline on the right, as in the following example. The key-word outline enables the speaker to avoid having to look at his or her notes all the time.

Produce should be carefully washed before you eat it.	Wash produce
Breads without preservatives should be refrigerated.	Refrigerate bread
Meat should not be eaten raw.	No raw meat

The main points (whether presented in full sentences or by key words) are sometimes put onto cards—one to a card. We discuss the reasons for this in Chapter 15, "Delivering the Speech."

■ THE REFERENCE LIST

At the end of your outline you should have a **reference list** of all the material you have used—and only that which you have used—in preparing your speech. This reference list should include everything you have used in your speech (books, newspapers, magazines, and Internet resources) as well as all the people you have interviewed. At the end of this chapter, after the sample outline, you will find a speech reference list.

The Internet offers a resource that is readily available, easily accessible, and makes it difficult for people to claim they did not know how to cite their sources. In Figure 14-1 we have provided two websites that provide information on the APA reference style, and one of the MLA style; however, do not feel compelled to use our recommendations. Entering *APA reference style* in the Google search engine produced 104,000 websites (March 25,2003), and entering *MLA reference style* produced 82,000.

There are a couple of things that need to be said regarding reference lists. First, adopt a style and be consistent. For example, every book you cite should be recorded using exactly the same style. Every magazine should be recorded using the same style for magazines, and every Internet citation should be consistent as well. Because there are so many different kinds of Internet resources besides websites, if you need reference-list style guidelines for other resources such as e-mail, newsgroups, Internet books (sometimes referred to as e-books), and online magazines (often referred to as e-zines), use the sources mentioned in Figure 14-1 or, as an alternative, enter "citing Internet resources" in your search engine. Google produced 264,000 websites (March 25, 2003). Instructors may have a preferred style they want you to follow, so check, first, to see what the assignment calls for.

The second thing that needs to be said regarding reference lists is to keep careful notes along the way. If you look at the style requirements *before* you begin gathering information, you will have all the data necessary when you begin to put together your reference list. Trying to piece together—if not locate—information at the last minute is both frustrating and time consuming.

Your authors have found that the APA style is much easier to use than the MLA style for a number of reasons. First, there are no footnotes, since you document in parentheses within the text of the document, as you go. That is also where your specific page numbers are entered as well, if you are quoting. Second, as soon as you perform a parenthetical citation in the text of your document, you can enter the same source directly into your reference list, and at the same time you can put the inclusive page numbers if you are citing an article. Computers make this especially easy because you can keep a running reference list ahead of where you are working at the current time, and whenever you use a citation in the text, you can jump ahead and enter the work, alphabetically by the author's last name—and if there is no author, by the first letter or letters of the title— directly into your reference list. When you finish writing your information, you have a complete reference list. Finally, the APA style is much more adaptable to computer work, especially when manuscript pages, or portions of content, are being cut and pasted somewhere else. Using the MLA style, all footnotes forward of any cut and pasted material must change. Although automatic within most word-processing programs, with the APA style no adjustments are necessary.

There are two other reasons why we prefer APA style over MLA style. Third, there is only one style to learn. There is no "footnote style" and then a slightly different "bibliography style," and there aren't two separate lists of essentially the same information. Fourth, because the dates of the sources you use come directly after the author's name—what we would call "up front" in your reference-list citation—it is easy to look over your reference list to make sure that the dates of the information are the most recent available. With all the references in one spot, and with all the dates clearly visible, you can tell if your speech is up to date or out of date. One thing you want in speeches, of course, is recent information. That is why website update dates are so important. Information gets old fast. Up-to-date information will increase your credibility.

There are two major weaknesses to using the APA style over the MLA style that should be mentioned as well. In your reference list, you do not use an author's first or middle name; you only use the last name with first and middle initials. If you want to use first names in your work, make sure you use those in the document (speech) itself. The second major weakness is that footnotes give you a chance to add additional information. You simply write a note, or a helpful additional piece of advice within the footnote. You can do this because the footnote takes you back to an exact spot in your manuscript. Of course, you can do this using the APA style, too; however, you must create a special footnotes section for this information—a section in addition to the reference list.

Rather than viewing the requirement of submitting a reference list as a chore—or, as some students would label it, "busywork"—think of it as a useful, productive exercise. How? Look at your reference list to make sure you have secured information for your speech from a wide range of sources. This not only helps validate the data you are using but lets listeners know, too, that your viewpoints are more credible.

When you have assembled your entire reference list, look at the sources you have accumulated. Do they look like credible sources when you examine the expertise of the authors or the credibility of the websites? How reliable and accurate is the Internet anyway? In 2002, the UCLA Center for Communication Policy surveyed 2,000 national households. Of Internet users, more than 50 percent said most of the information on the Internet is reliable and accurate. Only 7.2% said only a small portion of it is reliable and accurate (Users find . . . , 2003, p. 1A). Using credible sources, of course, adds to your own credibility. Just as important—and maybe more—using poor material, or websites with no credibility can destroy your credibility in an instant. A listener's question that asks who a person is whom you have cited in your speech as a source for a piece of information is a legitimate question—and one that needs to be answered. In Chapter 13, "Finding Speech Material," we not only list a variety of ways to test the quality of Internet information, but we supply additional websites where you can go to get similar kinds of information. There is so much information and so many warnings and cautions about using Internet material that by *not* heeding the guidelines, warnings, and cautions you will enter upon very suspect territory and risk your credibility.

APA Reference Style

Baker, D. S., and L. Henrichsen (n.d.). "APA reference style: Tightening up your citations." Brigham Young University. Retrieved March 25, 2003, from http://humanities.byu.edu/linguistics/Henrichsen/APA/APA01.html.

(No author). (2003). "Using American psychological association (APA) format (updated to 5th edition)." Online Writing Lab, Purdue University. Retrieved March 25, 2003, from http://owl.english.purdue.edu/handouts/research/r_apa.html.

MLA Footnote and Bibliographic Style

(No author). (2003). "Using modern language association (MLA) format." Online Writing Lab, Purdue University. Retrieved March 25, 2003, from http://owl.english.purdue.edu/handouts/research/r_mla.html.

Figure 14-1

Internet Websites for APA Reference-Style Guidelines and MLA Footnote and Bibliographic Guidelines

Sample Outline

To help you do your outline, here is a sample speech entitled "Fearless Public Speaking" by Deirdre Chong-Reed, done in outline form. The topical outline works well for this particular speech because all the main points aid speakers in limiting their fear of speaking in public.

General purpose: To persuade.

Specific purpose: To persuade my listeners that through education, experience, and expression, you can limit your fear of speaking in public.

Central idea: I want my audience to know how to deal with the fear of public speaking so that they, too, can turn their fear into fearlessness.

Fearless Public Speaking

Introduction

Undoubtedly you all already know that the fear of public speaking ranks number one in the minds of a majority of people (Wallechinsky & Wallace, 1993). Far above the fear of death and disease comes the fear of standing, just like this, in front of an audience. The fear is so great it prompted Jerry Seinfeld, in his comedy routine, to remark, "Studies show that fear of public speaking ranks higher than the fear of dying. I guess this means that most people at a funeral would rather be in the coffin than delivering the eulogy" (Ragsdale, 2000). Well, you can't count me among those who fear it. True, you could have, but not now. Not now—because I know too much. In the past two weeks or so I have had one of the best educations I could ask for—an education in how to deal with the fear of speaking in public. And now I am fearless, and I want to help you become fearless, too.

There are some excellent ways to deal with the fear of speaking in public. I'm going to label them education, experience, and expression. When I was very young, I wanted to be a movie star, but I was terrified of the spotlight. My first public humiliation came in the third grade, when, as a top-heavy apple tree in the play "Johnny Appleseed," I fell off the stage. I hid for weeks. Kids can be so cruel. One of them said to me, "You sure made it easier for ole' Johnny to pick your apples." How could I ever be a whole human being again? I might as well have died.

Deirdre first acknowledges what her audience already knows; then she adds the quotation from Jerry Seinfeld—just in case some members of her audience had not yet heard his joke.

Deirdre's personal experience serves as a tie between her topic and herself and establishes her credibility on the topic by stating how long she has spent researching it.

After giving her central idea—helping listeners become fearless—and the three divisions of her speech—education, experience, and expression—she relates a personal experience to provide humor, get attention, and connect her with her listeners.

Well, I had other humiliating experiences connected with public speaking, and if you want to know the truth, it is really amazing—at least to me—that I can stand here before you today and say, "I have really gotten this fear under control!" But how it has happened is what I want to talk about today.

Transition: Almost all of us have experienced the sweaty palms, the stomach wretching, the queasy feeling, and the quivering voice. And most of us, too, do not like making ourselves so vulnerable to others. Getting up here like this is not only intimidating, but it opens us up to criticism—and who would ever choose that? (Ragsdale, 2000). But whether we like it or not, we're going to have to do it, so we might as well learn how to limit the fear. I will be talking about education, experience, and expression.

Body

I. With *education* you can limit your fear of public speaking. This is a broad area and can cover a variety of topics. I will cover three: knowledge of yourself, knowledge of the problem, and knowledge of your topic.

 A. Knowing yourself is important to limiting your fear of public speaking.
  1. Are you focusing on yourself? Often, it is your own fear of failure, exposure, or judgment that causes a fear of speaking in public. Remember: Fear is normal, and you are not alone.
  2. Focus on your audience. According to Morton C. Orman (2002), a medical doctor who writes on "Conquering Public Speaking Fear," this will not only remove the spotlight from you, but it places the emphasis on the very essence of public speaking—giving listeners something of value.

 B. Knowing about the problem of the fears connected to public speaking is helpful to limiting your fear because there is so much helpful information. I want to recommend two terrific websites for you to examine.
  1. The first is the medical doctor I referred to earlier: M. C. Orman "How to Conquer

---

She ends her introduction with a direct confession and a lead-in to her speech.

Her first transition acknowledges the physical traits of public-speaking anxiety and the reasons why it occurs and then reminds listeners of her three main points.

With the first main head, she uses parallel structure and partitions her three subheads as well—knowledge of yourself, the problem, and your topic.

Her two sub-subpoints (1 and 2) relate to each other. The first suggests that you should not focus on yourself, and the second offers the solution: Focus on your audience.

Notice that in subpoints A, B, and C Deirdre also uses parallel structure in the statement of the idea, but the second thing she does is relate that knowledge to her goal: limiting listeners' fears of public speaking.

The two sub-subpoints for subpoint B (1 and 2) give listeners specific Web sources for further

Public Speaking Fear," 2002, http://www. stresscure.com/jobstress/speak.html. The reason for recommending this site is Orman's nine principles—the first of which is "Speaking in public is *not* inherently stressful." He has eight more just as good.

2. The second site is: D. Ullius (1997). "Crossing a Bridge of Shyness: Public Speaking for Communicators. Editorial Eye, EEI Press, Georgetown University." http://www.eeicom.com/eye/shyness. html. In addition to advice, Ullius offers numerous sources for novice speakers.

Transition: Two of the benefits of examining different websites on "The Fear of Public Speaking" are, first, the fear affects people in different ways, and so how you read the information may be completely different from how someone else reads it. But, second, there is so much advice. The advice best for you is likely to be a combination or synthesis of what you read, and, once again, everyone is different.

We've talked about knowing yourself, and we've talked about knowing about the problem of fearing public speaking. Here, I want to talk about knowing your topic.

C. Knowing your topic is important to limiting your fear of public speaking.
1. Most of the sources you will read mention proper and thorough preparation as the key to limiting the fear (Laskowski, n.d.). Laskowski, a professional speaker, suggests that proper presentation and rehearsal reduce the fear of speaking in public by 75 percent.
2. You will know your topic better if you select one with which you are already familiar—or one that you know will help you in some way. I selected this one for a reason unknown to any of you right now: As president of my sorority, I have to give an address to our regional conference in about a month or so. I want to do my best.

Transition: Know yourself; know the problem; and know your topic—all aspects of becoming educated about the fear of speaking in public. But there is another element needed, too, and that is experience.

information. Deirdre wrote these on the chalkboard and covered them with poster board until using them in her speech. In addition to these specific references, Deirdre also gives her Web references throughout the speech—wherever a citation occurs in the outline.

Deirdre's second transition is from subpoint B to subpoint C because she feels listeners would have forgotten where she was after uncovering her two references on the chalkboard. Here, she is simply trying to reorient the audience before continuing.

Notice that the end of the transition gives both subpoints A and B and then gives C, too, which Deirdre repeats—to drive the point home.

In these two sub-subpoints, Deirdre first cites an authority (Laskowski) and a statistic he provides. In the second sub-subpoint, she offers another personal experience to support her point—not that you should select a topic with which you are already familiar, but that you should select one that may help you in some way.

Her third transition in the speech repeats subpoints A, B, and C, relates them to main head I—education—and moves listeners immediately to the second main head—experience.

II. With *experience* you can limit your fear of public speaking. You have heard the old axiom, "Practice makes perfect" (Ragsdale, n.d.). True, you don't need perfection, but practice certainly helps to reduce the fear.

A. Think about what you want to achieve and what you can reasonably achieve in the allotted time (Price, 1998). Cover only what you have time for.

1. As you practice, keep your listeners in mind: organize carefully so that audience members have both a structure and a framework. Illustrate so that listeners can visualize your information (Nordgren, 1996). Keep audience-focused.

2. Practice in front of a mirror or in front of someone else. If you use notes, watch yourself to see how much you are relying on them. "Most people find the more they practice, the more at ease they feel when they give their presentation" (Brown, n.d.). Visualize yourself speaking.

B. Seek opportunities to speak. Whether it's in other classes, in clubs and organizations, in your community, or on the job, the more often you are in front of people delivering messages, the easier it will become (Ullius, 1997). With increasing competence comes greater confidence (Orman, 2002).

Transition: I have talked about the importance of both education and experience in limiting your fear of public speaking. Now, I want to talk about the importance of expression.

III. With *expression* you can limit your fear of public speaking. The first part of expression may be less familiar to you than the last part.

A. The first part of expression has to do with mental preparation—the pep talk you give yourself. Give yourself the four C's for speech success. Tell yourself over and over: "I am capable; I am confident; I am in control; and I want to communicate" (Gater, 1996).

B. The second part of expression has to do with physical preparation.

1. Can you practice your speech in the same location where it will be given?

She begins main head II using the same parallel structure as in main head I.

In sub-subpoints 1 and 2, Deirdre talks about the importance of practice, and she gives specific audience-centered ideas for practicing speeches. Also, Deirdre cites Molly Brown, the author of the quotation in sub-subpoint 2.

Subpoint B offers listeners further practical suggestions for limiting the fear of public speaking. Also, at the end of subpoint B, Deirdre uses a phrase she developed during her research: "With increasing competence comes greater confidence."

Notice how simple and straightforward her transition from main head II to III is. Once again, the topic—expression—was repeated to drive the point home.

Deirdre does not give away her subpoints in her statement of main head III; however, notice, once again, the parallel structure in the statement of subpoints A, B, and C: The first part . . . , the second part . . . , and the third part. . . .

Also, notice how Deirdre uses a convenient method for subdividing the three parts of main head III: mental, physical, and emotional preparation.

2. Can you check to make sure all elements in the physical environment in which you will speak are set up and in order? (McGavern, 2002, p. 9).

C. The third part of expression has to do with emotional preparation—the commitment to your ideas.

1. "A speech that conveys genuine emotions resonates with listeners" (Ullius, 1997, p. 3).

2. "Be yourself. Your audience will forgive your nervousness, but they will be turned off by false modesty or bravado" (Public Speaking, 1999).

3. Maintain eye contact; use natural hand gestures; keep body movement quiet and natural; maintain appropriate voice volume; and maintain a constant rate of speech (Brown, n.d.) . . . And if you make a mistake, keep going. Don't stumble. Pretend it was intended (Ragsdale, n.d.).

4. Turn nervousness into positive energy by harnessing it and transforming it into vitality and enthusiasm (Laskowski, p. 3).

Her point about emotional preparation is especially important because all these ideas relate to speakers' being themselves, being natural, and maintaining a comfortable and relaxed connection with listeners. Not only is a commitment to the ideas essential, but the commitment often has these effects.

Transition: There are three parts of expression: mental, physical, and emotional preparation. The final aspect, emotional preparation, has to do with conveying emotions, being yourself, connecting with your listeners, and turning your nervousness into positive energy.

In the transition from the body of the speech to the conclusion, she first reviews subpoints A, B, and C—mental, physical, and emotional preparation of main head III—and then her most recent point—emotional preparation: conveying emotions, being yourself, connecting with listeners, and turning nervousness into positive energy.

Conclusion

What is interesting here is that you will discover that some nervousness is good! Nerves can empower you. They can help you think of details you might otherwise forget (Eggleston, 1997). They can get you excited about sharing ideas with your listeners. And they can add energy and dynamism to those ideas. You don't want to eliminate your fear of public speaking, you just want to get it under control—to limit it. What's scary is that the fear of public speaking could even cause you to prepare more! And, as you think about these ideas, remember the old saying, "The person who fails to prepare is preparing for failure." So, prepare, prepare, prepare. In that way, you can turn fear into fearlessness.

As she begins her conclusion, she first tells listeners some of the benefits of nervousness. She chooses to use another well-known quotation here, "The person who fails to prepare is preparing for failure," but she uses it to emphasize the importance of preparing. Then she ends by referring once again to the title of her speech "Fearless Public Speaking."

Speech Reference List

Brown, M. (n.d.). "Presentations." The Writing Center, Sage Laboratory, Rensselaer Polytechnic Institute, Troy, NY. Retrieved June 15, 2002, from http://www.rpi.edu/web/writingcenter/text/present.htm

Eggleston, S. (1997, August 12). "Fear of public speaking: Stories, myths and magic." Trial by Fire. Retrieved June 15, 2002, from http://www.access.digex.net/,nuance//fearspkl.html.

Gater, J. (1996, October 7). "Notes on public speaking." Retrieved June 15, 2002, from http://www.cyberus.ca/csbruce/shyness/pubspeak.html.

Laskowski, L. (n.d.) "Overcoming speaking anxiety in meetings & presentations." LJL Seminars, Newington, CT. Retrieved June 15, 2002, from http://www.ljlseminars.com/anxiety.htm

Nordgren, L. (1996, September 23). "Designing presentation visuals." Media Services, Robert A. L. Mortvedt Library, Pacific Lutheran University. Retrieved June 15, 2002, from http://www.plu.edu/libr/media/designing_visuals.html (Jan. 31, 2000).

Orman, M. C. (2002). "How to conquer public speaking fear." Retrieved June 15, 2002, from http://www.stresscure.com/jobstress/speak.html.

Price, R. M. (1998, April 29). "Technical presentations: Hints & suggestions." University of Mississippi. Retrieved June 15, 2002, from http://home.olemiss.edu/cmprice/lectures/badpres.html.

[No author]. (n.d.). "Public speaking." Canadian Association of Student Activity Advisors. Retrieved June 15, 2002, from http://www.sentex.net/casaa/resources/sourcebook/acquiring-leadership-skills/public-speaking.htm.

Ragsdale, L. (n.d.). "Solutions." Retrieved June 15, 2002, from www.geocities.com/BourbonStreet/6411/solutions.html.

—— (n.d.). "What is the one thing you fear most?" Retrieved June 15, 2002, from http://www.geocities.com/BourbonStreet/6411/target1.html (Jan. 31, 2000).

—— (n.d.). "Why do we fear public speaking?" Retrieved June 15, 2002, from http://www.geocities.com/BourbonStreet/6411/fears.html (Jan. 31, 2000).

Ullius, D. (1997). "Crossing a bridge of shyness: Public speaking for communicators." *Editorial Eye*, Georgetown University. Retrieved June 15, 2002, from http://www.eeicom.com/eye/shyness.html.

Wallechinsky, D., & A. Wallace (1993). *The book of lists*. New York: Bantam.

Assess Yourself

How Much Do You Know About Organizing a Speech?

1. What is the primary reason for organizing a speech? A well-organized speech:
   A. promotes clear communication.
   B. is an easier way to prepare any speech.
   C. provides more of a challenge for listeners.
   D. allows for the preparation of an outline of the speech.

2. What is one of the advantages of organizing your speech? Organizing it will give you:
   A. believability.
   B. a point of view.
   C. total comprehension.
   D. an emotional advantage.

3. Once you have written your general and specific purposes, what are the next three levels on which you can organize your speech?
   A. Main head and first two subpoints.
   B. Introduction, main heads, and conclusion.
   C. Evidence, attention factors, and transitions.
   D. Central idea, main points, and supporting material.

4. Which of the following pieces of advice relates to refining your main points?
   A. Restrict each one to no more than two ideas.
   B. Always limit your number of main heads to three.
   C. Make sure all your main points develop your central idea.
   D. Determine your main points by the quantity and quality of your supporting material.

5. If you arranged your main points in a time sequence—for example, dealing with periods of time in history—you would be using which of the following organizational patterns?
   A. Causal.
   B. Topical.
   C. Spatial.
   D. Chronological.

6. Which of the following is the cardinal rule for using supporting material? They must:
   A. hold attention.
   B. enliven your speech.
   C. be easy to remember.
   D. support, explain, illustrate, or reinforce your central idea.

7. Why is it important to make your organization obvious to your listeners?
   A. This isn't important; you should not make it obvious.
   B. Because organization—whatever the topic—convinces.
   C. Because a listening audience can't stop the speech and go back over it.
   D. If you have spent the time on it, the audience should notice your efforts.

8. Why is it important to time your speech in practice?
   A. Speaking is different than reading.
   B. To help you memorize your words.
   C. So you know where to place your emphasis.
   D. To help you better phrase the main heads of your speech.

9. What is the key to effectiveness in presenting your well-organized ideas to your listeners?
   A. Be conversational.
   B. Elevate your language and approach.
   C. Speak slightly below your audience's level of understanding.
   D. Try to talk to your audience as if you are talking entirely to yourself.

10. In the conclusion of your speech—with respect to the organizational pattern you have selected—you should do what?
    A. Repeat your main heads.
    B. Offer listeners new evidence for your position.
    C. Tell them if it was topical, spatial, causal, or chronological.
    D. Be totally spontaneous, natural, relaxed, and comfortable as you think of any additional ideas that may help them understand your speech better.

 Go to the *Communicating Effectively* CD-ROM to see your results and learn how to evaluate your attitudes and feeling.

Chapter Review

The principles of organization include selecting information that relates to the specific purpose and central idea; distinguishing among the introduction, body, and conclusion of the speech; distinguishing between main and minor points; and phrasing all points in full sentences with parallel structure.

Six patterns of organization work well for organizing speeches: time order, using a chronological sequence; spatial order, moving from left to right, top to bottom, or in any direction that will make the subject clear; cause-and-effect order, showing why something is happening and what impact it is having; problem-solution order, explaining a problem and giving a solution; motivated sequence, following the steps of attention, need, satisfaction, visualization, and action; and topical order, arranging the speech into subtopics.

The purpose of the introduction is to set the tone for the speech, introduce the topic, and get the audience's attention. Some attention-getting devices are using humor, giving personal examples, referring to the occasion, showing the importance of the subject, telling startling information, asking questions, and using quotations.

The speech conclusion should signal the audience that the speech is over and should tie all the ideas together. In their conclusions, speakers often summarize main ideas, use quotations, and inspire the audience to take further action.

Speech transitions help an audience follow where a speaker is going. They introduce main heads and may be written into the speech outline.

An outline is a way of organizing material to highlight all the parts and how they relate to the whole. In most cases, the body of the speech is what is outlined—the introduction and conclusion are handled separately.

The outline shows the organization as main and minor points through the use of standards symbols and indentation. Many speakers like to construct two outlines: a full-sentence outline for organizing the speech and a key-word outline to summarize the main ideas and to function as notes during delivery of the speech.

Your outline should be followed by a bibliography—a list of all the material from other sources that you have used in your speech. All the items should be presented in a standard bibliographical form.

Questions to Review

1. Can you tell the difference between an organized speech, presentation, lecture, or report and one that is not organized? What difference does this make in your attentiveness to the speaker? In your understanding of the information? In your overall evaluation of the effort?

2. Is organizing ideas difficult for you? Why or why not?

3. Which pattern of organization was most appealing to you? Why? Which seems to be the most difficult? Why?

4. How important are introductions in speeches? What purposes do they serve?

5. Is it true that if you grab the attention of listeners in the introduction to your speech, you will have their attention throughout the speech? Why or why not?

6. How are transitions used in a speech?

7. Have you ever been moved by a speech? What was it about the speech that moved you?

8. Do you think most speakers follow the examples set in the sample speech regarding outlining and organizing their ideas? Why or why not? What are the barriers or hindrances that restrain people from organizing their speech efforts as well as they could?

9. Faced with an upcoming speech that you have to prepare, do you ever feel overwhelmed with ideas and suggestions? What do you do in situations like that? Do you just go on and prepare in your own way? Or do you actually take and use as many new ideas and suggestions as you can, given the time you have to prepare your speech?

Go to the self-quizzes on the *Communicating Effectively* CD-ROM (side 2, track 10) and the Online Learning Center at mhhe.com/hybels7 to test your knowledge of the chapter concepts.

References

Brokaw, T. (1999, July 15). "Information and communication: A life well-lived. *Vital Speeches of the Day* 65:19.

(No author). (2001) "Crisis and suicide: Youth suicide facts. American Association of Suicidology," Youth Suicide Fact Sheet, 2001, Telephone Counseling and Referral Service. Retrieved March 25, 2003, from http://www.ters211.org/suicide/statsyouth.htm.

Dilenschneider, R. L. (2001, July 15). "Heroes or losers: The choice is yours." *Vital Speeches of the Day* 67:19, 605–8.

(No author). (2000, March 8). "DNA testing goes mainstream." CBSNews.com. CBS Worldwide. Retrieved March 25, 2003, from http://www.cbsnews.com/Stories/Inc./1999/09/19/tech/main 62842.shtml.

Gruner, C. B. (1985, April). "Advice to the beginning speaker on using humor—What the research tells us." *Communication Education*, 34, 142.

(No author). (1998). "Health, exercise, diet, rest, self-image, motivation, and attitudes." Learning Strategies Database, Center for Advancement of Learning, Muskingum College, Muskingum, MI. Retrieved March 25, 2003, from http://muskingum.edu/~cal/database/Physiopsyc.html.

Jackson, K. (n.d.). "Study tips." Psychiacomp. Retrieved March 25, 2003, from http://www.psychiacomp.com/studytips.php.

Karim, T. (2001, May 1). "Terrorism: Addressing its root causes. *Vital Speeches of the Day* 68:14, pp. 425–429.

Keillor, G. (1998). Commencement address—Gettysburg College. In A. Albanese and B. Triller, eds. *Graduation day: The best of America's commencement speeches*. New York: Morrow.

Marcus, D. L. (2000, March 27). "Drinking to get drunk: Campuses still can't purge bingeing behavior." *U.S. News & World Report*, 53.

McKerrow, R. E.; B. E. Gronbeck; D. Ehninger; & A. H. Monroe (2003). *Principles and types of speech communication*, 15th ed. Boston, MA: Allyn & Bacon.

(No author). (1998). "Preparation." Learning Strategies Database, Center for Advancement of Learning, Muskingum College, Muskingum, MI. Retrieved March 25, 2003, from http://muskingum.edu/~cal/database/Preparation.html.

(No author). (n.d.). "II. Reducing test anxiety." NCLEX EDGE-EXAMCO. Retrieved March 25, 2003, from http://www.examco.com/nursing/nclex_book/ii_a.htm.

(No author). (1996). "Skills that can help you get the best grade possible." Test-Taking Skills, Austin Community College. Retrieved March 10, 2000, from http://Irs.austin.cc.tx.us/research/guides/testtake/test.htm.

(No author, no date). "Some facts psychologists know about . . . Test and performance anxieties." Retrieved March 25, 2003, from http://www.psc.uc.edu/sh/SH Test Anxiety.htm.

(No author). (1999, July 29). "Suicide is threat to nation." *The Blade* (Toledo, Ohio), p. 3.

(No author). (1999, June 1). "Suicide statistics." Crisis Intervention Resources Manual, Office of Psychological Services, Bartow County School System, Cartersville, Georgia. Retrieved March 25, 2003, from http://www.bartow.k12.ga.us/psych/crisis/suestats.htm.

(No author). (2002, January 17). "Test anxiety." Counseling Center, University of Illinois at Urbana. Retrieved March 25, 2003, from http://waukesha.uwc.edu/sc/skills/ttanxiety.htm.

(No author). (2001, August 31). "Test anxiety: Overcoming test anxiety." Counseling Center, University of Florida. Retrieved March 25, 2003, from http://www.counsel.ufl.edu/selfHelp/test Anxiety.asp

(No author). (2002) "Test-taking strategies." Academic Services, Southwestern University. Retrieved March 25, 2003, from http://www.southwestern.edu/academic/acser-skills-terstr.html.

(No author). (2003, February 26). "Users find Internet to be reliable, accurate." USA TODAY Snapshots. *USA Today*, p. 1A.

Willing, R. (1999, July 29). "Explosion of technology is straining family ties." *USA Today*, 1A–2A.

Further Reading

Deal, C. (2001, September 15). "Preparing & delivering oral presentations: Organizing and outlining your topic." Hampden-Sydney College Speaking Center Online. Retrieved March 25, 2003, from http://people.hsc.edu/faculty-staff/cdeal/students/orgaout.htm. Claire Deal covers organizational patterns for informative speeches, organizational patterns from persuasive speeches, introductions, conclusions, and transitions. There are not just tips here, but she includes examples as well. A useful starting point.

(No author, no date). "Essay organization." The Citadel Writing Center, The Citadel. Retrieved March 25, 2003, from http://www.citadel.edu/citadel/othersev/wctr/essayorg.htm. This site is designed for writers of papers, but it covers the essentials of getting started, general organization, organizing main points, tips for introductions, and tips for conclusions—the same kinds of things speakers need to be concerned about when preparing a speech for presentation.

McCoy, S., & S. Cogdill (1999, October 5). "Developing an introduction: The top-down model." Literacy Education Online (LEO), The Write Place, St. Cloud State University, St. Cloud, Minnesota. Retrieved March 25, 2003, from http://leo.stcloudstate.edu/acadwrite/intro.html. Here, the authors answer the questions: What is an introduction, what is the function of an introduction, how can I write an introduction, what goes in an introduction, and do all introductions have four sentences? They do the same for conclusions at http://leo.stcloudstate.edu/acadwrite/conclude.html.

McGavern, N. (2002, March 4). "Public speaking pointers: Speaking up." Undergraduate Research Opportunities Program (UROP). Massachusetts Institute of Technology (MIT). Retrieved March 25, 2003, from http://web.mit.edu/urop/speaking.html. This information was taken from *Speaking Up*, MIT Freshman Advisor Seminar 055, and in the ten pages McGavern covers preparation for speaking, writing for speaking, mapping the content of your speech, writing elements and speaking elements, the audience and you, using visuals, and a final section "On the Day of Your Speech—Avoid Panic!" This is a great list of practical suggestions in each of the categories above.

McManus, J. A., & J. MacManus (1998). *Arco's how to write and deliver an effective speech*, 3d ed. (Arco's How to Series) New York: Macmillan. This is a 116-page, practical guide to every aspect of public speaking from researching to writing and delivering polished, professional-sounding speeches.

Morgenstern, J. (1998). *Organizing from the inside out*. New York: Henry Holt and Company (an Owl Book). Morgenstern's basic steps, covered in sections 1 and 2, apply to all projects that require organization: analyze, strategize, and attack. In sections 3 and 4, she shows how to apply these steps. Morgenstern addresses the psychological issues and practical challenges that face you when challenged by chaos. Although she applies her principles to home and mobile offices, bathrooms, closets, kitchens, kid's rooms, garages, schedules, and technology, they remain the same when applied to speech preparation.

(No author, no date). "Outline your points." Virtual Presentation Assistant, Communication Studies Department, University of Kansas. Retrieved March 25, 2003, from http://www.ku.edu/cwis/units/ coms2/vpa/vpa6.htm. Although only one-and-a-half pages long, this handout covers organizational patterns and then provides tips on introductions and conclusions. The University of Kansas's Virtual Presentation Assistant offers tips, suggestions, and links to all aspects of speech preparation and presentation.

Petress, K. C. (n.d.). "The value of outlining your ideas." University of Maine. Retrieved March 25, 2003, from http://www.umpi.maine.edu/~petress/essay/5.pdf. This is an outlining case study Petress prepared for a communication conference paper he was going to present. It shows, with specific examples, how he outlined his ideas in stages, expanding, refining, and sequencing his ideas in parallel layers of complexity as his work stages developed. A practical and helpful explanation of how the development of a complete outline should work.

Stephens, C. (2000). "Building plain language from the ground up—organization: Clarity without clutter." Plain Language Partners, Plain Language Center. Retrieved March 25, 2003, from http://plainlanguage/com/BPL2.html. Stephens offers practical, straightforward suggestions on the plain language process, organization clarity, writing for real people, layout and design, and writing that works. Although her ideas are designed for writers, they apply as well as speakers who desire clarity and a strong connection to audience members.

St. John, R. (1999, October 17). "The public speaker's page: Outlining the speech." Maui Community College. Retrieved March 25, 2003, from http://manicc.hawaii.edu/staff/stjohn/publicspeakers/outliing.html. Ron St. John has links to his infor-mation on organizing the informative speech outline, and using connectives in the informative speech. He provides a sample outline, a check sheet to help you prepare, organize, and outline your speech, and a blank template for outlining your informative speech. There is much more here if you click on the marginal topics listed on St. John's home page.

(No author). (2001, October 8). "Writing speeches." The Writing Center, University of North Carolina at Chapel Hill. Retrieved March 25, 2003, from http://www.unc.edu/depts/wcweb/handouts/speeches.htm. In this excellent and comprehensive online guide to writing speeches, the authors offer more than simply lists and tips. Their focus is on "the *process* of writing a speech—from deciding on a topic to actually delivering the speech. Consequently," they explain, "we've divided this handout into the following sections: prewriting, drafting, practicing, revising/editing, and delivery" (p. 1). The information is well-written, well-edited and well-presented.

Chapter 15

Delivering the Speech

Objectives

After reading this chapter, you should be able to:

- Pay attention to your audience.
- Achieve a conversational quality in your speech.
- Distinguish among the four types of delivery.
- Use body movement, eye contact, facial expressions, and gestures to enhance your speech.
- Identify the elements that affect how you sound, and adjust them to improve your delivery.
- Use visual aids to increase your audience's attention and understanding.
- Employ several techniques to control your nervousness.
- Outline the steps to follow in practicing your speech.

Key Terms and Concepts

  Use the Communicating Effectively CD-ROM and Online Learning Center at mhhe.com/hybels7 to further your understanding of the following terms.

Articulation 545	Flip chart 549	Model 547
Attentiveness 533	Graphs 550	Monotone 545
Computer-generated graphics 551	Immediacy 534	Multimedia 553
	Impromptu speaking 536	Organizational chart 548
Conversational quality 535	Inflection 545	Pace 544
Diagram 548	Manuscript speaking 537	Poster 548
Directness 535	Memory (speaking from) 538	Pronunciation 545
Enunciation 545		Tables 549
Extemporaneous speaking 538		Visual support 546

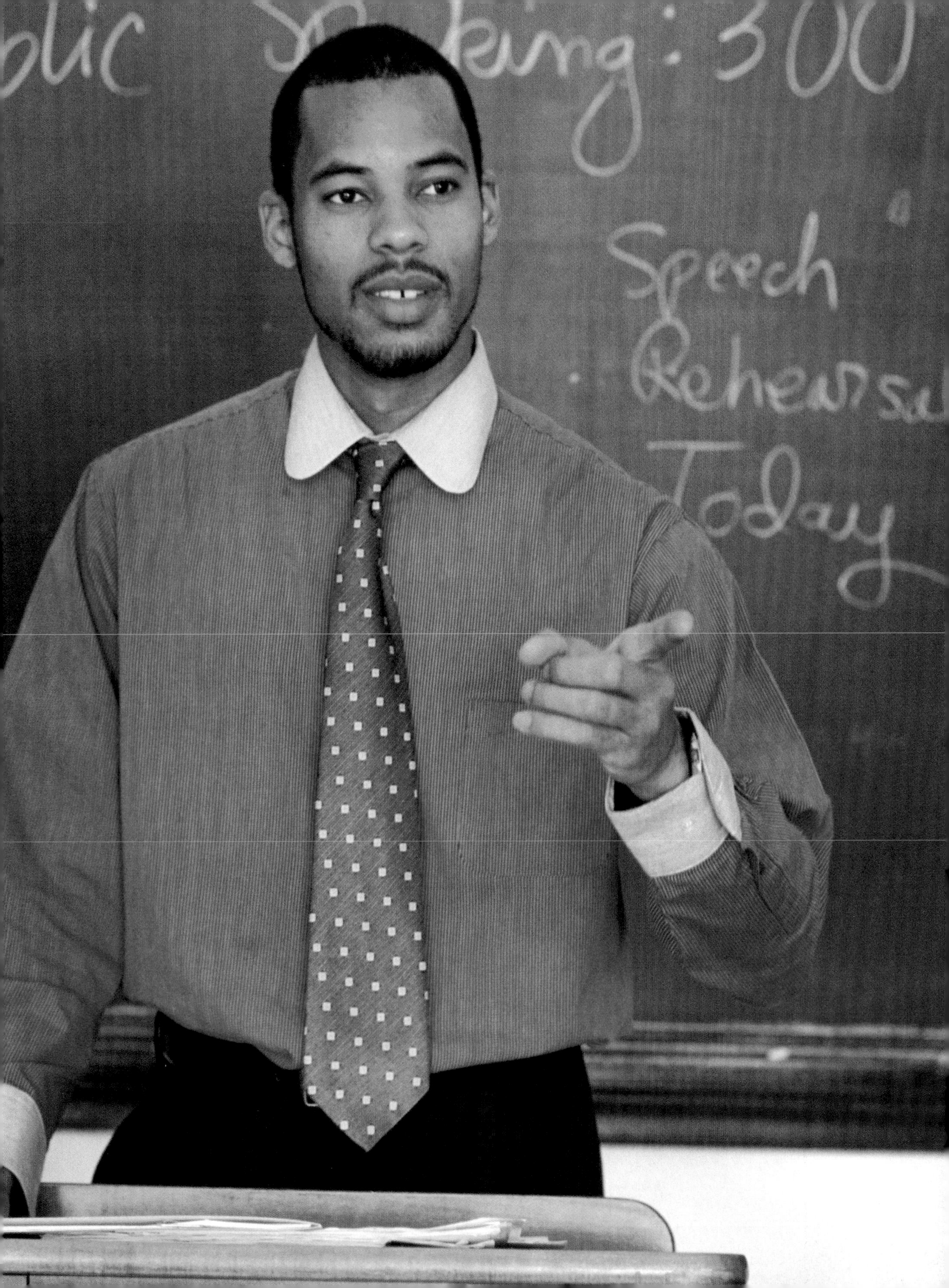
Speech
Today

ALBERTA ROCHON HAD BEEN OUT OF COLLEGE FOR TWO years. She had majored in social work and was employed by the Department of Social Services. Most of her work involved finding foster homes for problem children and helping the children adjust to their new families. Alberta loved her work, and when the Social Work Club at her alma mater asked her to speak, she was excited by the opportunity. She decided to speak on the subject "Foster Care for Problem Kids," and she hoped to inspire some of the future social work graduates to choose the area of foster care for their own careers.

In preparing her speech, Alberta gathered facts and figures about foster care in the state. Because of her work at the Department of Social Services, much information was available to her. Also, using several search engines, she came up with 1,430,000 sites for the words *foster care,* 727,000 for *foster-care programs,* 170,000 for *foster care* in her state, and 85,700 for *foster-care programs* in her state. She even received 380,000 hits for the *Department of Social Services* in her state. Alberta had more than enough helpful information for her speech.

Alberta prepared two charts. One listed characteristics that make up a good foster home. The other was a graph that showed the percentage of children who stay out of trouble once they have been in a foster home. The state Web pages Alberta consulted were filled with factual and statistical information. Also, because of her own work, she had numerous examples and anecdotes about how foster care really works. She organized all this material into a full-sentence outline, choosing items she thought would be particularly interesting to her listeners.

Alberta had not done any public speaking since her speech class in college, but she remembered that practicing her speech beforehand had been very helpful. Once it was organized, and she was comfortable with the transitions she wrote into the outline, she gave the speech in her living room—pretending it was filled with an audience. On the first run-through, she discovered it was 20 minutes long, whereas she had been asked to speak for only 15 minutes. She worked to cut it back and also added another two transitions to make it run more smoothly. When she had finished her editing and revising, she tried giving the speech again, this time in front of a mirror. She found that her speech was the right length and the transitions worked well, but she wasn't using enough gestures. She made notes on the margins of her note cards to move around a little more and use more gestures. This she would practice in her next run-through. Feeling satisfied with her progress, she went to bed. The next morning she woke up remembering three light-bulb jokes she could use in her introduction.

"How many social workers does it take to change a light bulb?"

"The light bulb doesn't need changing, it's the system that needs to change," or

"We don't change light bulbs—we empower them to change themselves," or, finally,

". . . I'll do it, but I have 172 other lightbulbs to change first."

She made a few notes, and then went off to work. During her lunch hour, she shut her office door, ran through the speech again, timed it, and then went back and polished some of her material. As she was speaking, she made an effort to add gestures and move around. This time the speech went so smoothly that she felt confident and went back to her work.

That evening, on her way to give the speech, she was feeling a little nervous, but she told herself that she was in good shape: The speech was well prepared, she knew she could deliver it well, and she was so confident she would welcome—even encourage—questions afterward.

When she arrived in the room where she was to give the speech, she was still feeling a little apprehensive, so she took the remaining time to look over her note cards again.

When she stood up to speak, she started with the humorous anecdote, thus winning the complete attention of the audience. This immediately put her at ease. Alberta felt that she was off to a strong start and that this was going to be a good speech. As she spoke, she remembered to look around the room, particularly toward the back row and corners. She also looked at individual audience members. When she was two-thirds through the speech, she noticed some restlessness, so she added an anecdote. Immediately she had the audience's attention again.

Consider This

In her speech entitled *Taking the Stage™*, Judith Humphrey, President of The Humphrey Group, an executive speech-training firm, explains the essential elements of The Humphrey Group's *Taking the Stage™* program and how important it is to have an 'on stage' mindset.

- The first step is understanding what it means to 'take the stage.' Shakespeare wrote that 'all the world's a stage.'

- A stage can be a podium, the front of a conference room, a telephone, an elevator, or the entrance to a CEOs office. Every time you communicate, you're on stage. When you walk into a room, say "this moment is important."

- Don't just wait for the opportunities to happen—Create them! One of my clients did just that. 'When she was at her customer's office, she asked to see the CEO. Soon she found herself standing at the door of the CEOs office, with two or three minutes to influence him.' That was a performance!

- *Taking the Stage™* begins with an attitude. It starts with the understanding that every single situation is an opportunity to influence, inspire, and motivate people" (p. 436).

Questions

1. Have you ever seized an opportunity—as if it were a stage—and used a situation as an opportunity to demonstrate your best communication skills? What was the situation, and how did it work out?

2. Can you see how important it is to be prepared? Can you see how important it is to be an effective communicator?

3. What would you say are the skills or techniques necessary to detect or determine important situations? Situations where it would be best if you could demonstrate your best communication skills?

4. Have you ever been in a situation that was important, but you didn't know how important it was until later? Did you ever think back to the situation after it had happened, and in your mind, give the speech you wish you had given? What was the situation? If you had known that it was important at the time it occurred, could you have seized the moment? What would you have done?

5. Is it realistic to say "Don't just wait for the opportunities to happen—create them!"? Do you think most people can and would take this advice?

Source: J. Humphrey, "Taking the Stage: How Women Can Achieve a Leadership Presence." *Vital Speeches of the Day,* May 1, 2001, 67:14. *Taking the Stage™* is a trademark of the Humphrey Group Inc. For more information see *www.thehumphreygroup.com.*

When the speech was over, the chairperson asked if there were any questions. With barely a pause, numerous hands went up. Alberta answered dozens of questions—all of them dealing with different aspects of her work. The questions went on for so long that the chairperson had to call a halt—campus security had come to lock up the room. As the audience left the room, the chairperson told Alberta that hers was the best speech the Social Work Club had heard all year. She added, "We'll be sure to invite you back next year." As Alberta drove home, she felt very good about herself. She thought, "I would like to do this again. It was a lot of work, but it really paid off."

■ CHARACTERISTICS OF GOOD DELIVERY

A good speech can bring even more satisfaction to the speaker than it does to the audience. There is nothing quite like the experience of communicating your ideas, having them understood, and having an entire audience respond to you in a positive way. Yet speaking to an audience does not come naturally; it is a skill you have to learn. By now you have begun to master the skill of finding material and putting your speech together; it is time to shift focus to delivering your speech.

Attentiveness

You might wonder how a speaker could be inattentive to his or her own speech. Yet it's quite possible to be present and functioning as a body while not being there in spirit. When Shakela's friend complimented her on the speech she had given in speech class, Shakela replied, "You know, it's almost like I wasn't there at all. I don't remember looking at anyone, and I barely remember what I said."

Not being attentive to your own speech is really a matter of internal noise: You are so overcome with the mechanics and anxiety of giving a speech that you forget that doing so is basically a human encounter between a speaker and listeners.

Attentiveness means focusing on the moment. It means saying to yourself that you have come to tell your listeners something important and that you are going to do your very best to communicate with them. It is also a matter of being aware of and responding to your listeners' needs. To ensure that you will be attentive to your audience, you can do several things:

1. *Pick a topic that is important to you.* If you are speaking on something of great interest and importance to you, it is likely that you will communicate your interest and enthusiasm to your audience. Also, if you can get involved in your subject, you are likely to feel less anxiety about giving your speech.

2. *Do all the work necessary to prepare the best speech possible.* If you work on your speech—organize and practice it—you will be much more confident about it and will feel less anxious when the time comes to give it. Then you will be able to concentrate on delivering your speech.

3. *Individualize your audience members.* Try to think of your audience as individual human beings rather than as a mass of people. As you give the speech, think: "I am going to talk to Kristen, who sits in the second row. Gabriel always looks like he is going to sleep. I am going to give a speech that will wake him up."

4. *Focus on the audience rather than on yourself.* As you speak, look for audience feedback and try to respond to it. The more you focus on the audience members and their needs, the less likely you are to feel anxiety.

Alberta followed these four guidelines when she gave her speech. She selected a topic, "Foster Care for Problem Kids," that was important to her; she did the work necessary to prepare the best speech she could; she looked at individual audience members as she delivered her speech; and she focused on listeners rather than on herself. At one point, noting some restlessness in her audience, she even added an unplanned anecdote to her speech.

Immediacy

Closely aligned with attentiveness is immediacy. **Immediacy** occurs when the communicator is completely focused on the communication situation. When it happens, speakers are thinking about the best way to make their words have an impact and how the audience is responding to what they say.

If you look back on past communication situations, you will probably remember times when you were not focused. For beginning speakers it is easy to lose immediacy. As you begin your speech, you think, "Do they see how nervous I am?" "Maybe I should have dressed up more," or "What if I lose my place?" In such cases, speakers are focused on themselves, not on their audience.

With immediacy, the best questions to ask are along the lines of "Am I being understood?" "Does this point need to be clearer?" "Can that person in the back row hear me?" or "How can I let them know that I really believe what I am talking about?"

Although the judgment will be somewhat difficult to make because so many of the elements are missing here, assess the difference between the following two excerpts from student speeches. Which one appears more immediate, and why?

> *The way humans express themselves sexually is learned at a very young age, and throughout our lives we use very similar, if not the same, reoccurring patterns to express ourselves sexually. However, sexual expression is learned behavior, and it may not mean the same for everyone. To improve people's understanding of each other, it will help us to know how we develop sexual knowledge, feelings, and behaviors.*

This is the second excerpt, and it deals with a similar topic:

> *If you and I are like the average population, sexual activity among all of us here has occurred much earlier than ever before. There has been more pressure placed on us to have sex. You know that you and I can blame our peers, and we can blame the media as well. It doesn't really matter who or what is to blame, the fact is that along with this sexual activity, you and I must accept responsibility for our sexual behavior.*

Both excerpts are about the same length, and they both are about a topic that relates to listeners. But notice the differences. The first speaker uses the pronouns *we* and *our* and the word *people*. These choices are removed from listeners and noninvolving. The excerpt is abstract and lacks immediacy. The second speaker began and ended with *you and I* and even included it in the middle of this quotation; this closes the gap between speaker and audience. Notice, too, the second speaker's use of *here*, which reinforces the speaker's sense of the present. From just a casual reading of both excerpts, the second is more immediate, lively, and liklely to hold audience attention.

Directness

Closely aligned with both attentiveness and immediacy is directness. **Directness** means being natural and straightforward. Your writing teachers have probably told you that you shouldn't choose big words if a small word says the same thing—that your goal is to communicate with readers, not to dazzle them with your vocabulary and knowledge of complicated grammatical structure. The same is true for a speech, only more so. Your audience is going to hear this speech only one time, so you have to be as specific and direct as possible.

The second goal in trying to achieve directness is to be straightforward. Being straightforward means selecting an effective specific purpose and a strong central idea. Then make all of your points and examples relate to them.

Sometimes you come up with a wonderful idea or example, but you find that you can't relate it directly to the main point. One of the hardest things to do in speaking (or in writing) is to get rid of material that is fascinating or wonderful but doesn't work. However, it has to be dropped if it interferes with your directness. (Put it in a file folder, and use it for something else another day.)

Listening to indirect speakers causes listeners to question, "What's the point?" "Where is the speaker going?" "What does this speaker want?" "Why is the speaker being so confusing?" Since we have already devoted a chapter to purposes and central ideas (Chapter 12, Getting Started), we will omit any further discussion of those topics here. Our point is simply that being straightforward is an important aspect of directness, and in most cases it requires some planning.

Conversational Quality

When speakers are attentive, immediate, and direct, in most cases they will sound conversational. When you have a **conversational quality,** you talk to your audience in much the same way that you talk when you are having a conversation with another person. The value of sounding conversational in speaking is that you give the impression that you are talking *with* the audience rather than *at* it. In the next excerpt, notice how the speaker uses conversational language and the word *you* to involve his audience:

> *Have you ever felt embarrassed—I mean really embarrassed—where you never wanted to show your face in public again? Has your face ever turned red when lots of people were watching you? I would guess that you've had this experience once or twice in your life—I know I have. But—don't you ever wonder what happens to our bodies when we're embarrassed?*

How do you achieve a conversational tone in speaking? The most useful way, right from the planning stage, is to imagine giving your speech to one person or to a small group of people. Have a mental picture of this person or persons, and try to talk directly with him, her, or them, in a normal, conversational manner. This will help you achieve the right tone.

There is an important caution, however: A conversational tone doesn't mean being casual. A speech occasion is more formal than most conversations. Even though you're aiming for a conversational tone, you shouldn't allow long pauses or use such conversational fillers as "OK" or "you know." You should also avoid some of the slang and "in" jokes or expressions you would use in casual conversation. Here are a few additional hints on how to achieve a conversational quality:

- When you give your speech, imagine you are giving it to someone you know.

- Use contractions such as *don't, can't, isn't,* and *weren't*. They are more conversational than their two-word counterparts.

- Use words everyone will understand.

- Use an outline rather than writing out your speech word for word.

TYPES OF DELIVERY

Think about a particularly good speech you have heard. Do you remember how it was delivered? From notes? From a manuscript? From memory? Was the speaker making a few brief, off-the-cuff remarks?

There are essentially four methods of delivery: making impromptu remarks, speaking from a manuscript, memorizing the speech, and speaking extemporaneously from notes.

Impromptu Speaking

Impromptu speaking is the giving of a speech on the spur of the moment. Usually there is little or no time for preparation. Sometimes your instructor might ask you to give an impromptu speech in class. Other times you might be asked to give a toast or offer a prayer at a gathering, or you may make a few remarks at a meeting.

If you are asked to give an impromptu speech, the most important thing is not to panic. Your main goal is to think of a topic and organize it quickly in your head before you start to speak.

In finding a topic, look around you and consider the occasion. Is there anything you can refer to? Decorations? A friend? A photo that recalls a time together? Formal occasions usually honor someone or something, and the person or thing being honored can provide a focus for your speech: "I am delighted to be at this yearly meeting of documentary filmmakers. Documentary filmmaking is one of the noblest professions." Other times you might want to refer to the place or the people: "I am happy to be here in Akron again. The last time I was here. . . ." or "I am very touched by the warm reception you have all given me."

In impromptu speaking it's essential to keep your remarks brief. No one expects you to speak for more than a minute or two. The audience knows that you are in a tight spot, and it doesn't expect a long and well-polished speech.

If you are asked to give an impromptu speech, the most important thing is not to panic.

Speaking from a Manuscript

Speaking from a manuscript involves writing out the entire speech and reading it to the audience. When you read a speech, you can get a clear idea of how long it is, so manuscript speaking is a good method when exact timing is necessary. Because a manuscript also offers preplanned wording, political leaders often favor this method when they speak on sensitive issues and want control over what they say. When Louisa, for example, decided to run for president of the student government, she prepared a five-minute speech in manuscript form for her appearance on the campus television station with the other candidates. Louisa knew that having a manuscript would help her stay within her time limit and would also help her say exactly what she wanted to say. However, she knew that she had to be very familiar with the manuscript so that she could break away from it to look directly at the camera.

There are other reasons why some speakers feel it necessary to give a manuscript speech. For example, Lutie Eugenia Sterns, as reported by Brenda Knight, had a bad stammer, but she cared so much about the public library system, that she traveled the state of Wisconsin by train, buggy, and sleigh preaching about public libraries. Sterns wrote out her speeches to avoid the letters she had trouble with, but she was so effective that before she retired to campaign for women's suffrage she had established 101 free libraries and 1,480 traveling libraries. All this in the late nineteenth century (Knight, 2000, p. 31).

Speakers find that it is difficult to sound spontaneous when using a manuscript; if listeners think they are being read to, they are more likely to lose interest. Experienced speakers who use manuscripts are often so skilled at delivery that the audience is not aware the speech is being read. Beginning speakers, however, have difficulty making a manuscript speech sound spontaneous and natural.

Feedback is another problem in speaking from a manuscript. If the audience becomes bored and inattentive, it is difficult to respond and modify the speech; the speaker is bound to the manuscript. A manuscript also confines a speaker to the lectern—because that's where the manuscript is.

Working Together

Working with classmates in a group, have each member of the group practice giving the speech "Looking Through Our Window" (the sample speech at the end of this chapter) using the following technique. Critique each other.

One of the most difficult techniques for a beginning speaker to master is moving one's eyes between the note cards (or manuscript) and the audience. Try to develop the technique this way: You can use any piece of written material for practice. Place it on a lectern or on a box on top of a table like a makeshift lectern. Now, you are going to deliver the material orally to an imagined audience. Look down at the written material and *"snapshot," "eye-photograph," or "snatch" a phrase or group of words—a chunk of words that will be easy to utter in one breath. Bring your head up; pick out a lamp or a chair, pretending it is a single listener, and while looking the listener in the eye, deliver the "snatched" phrase as if in conversation. Pause, look down again, snapshot the next phrase or group of words, bring your head up again, and converse naturally and comfortably with your "listener" again. This is a terrific way to practice a conversational style of delivery.*

Source: James C. Humes, *The Sir Winston Method: The Five Secrets of Speaking the Language of Leadership* (New York: Morrow, 1991), p. 160.

Speaking from Memory

Speaking from memory involves writing out the entire speech and then committing it to memory word for word. It has the same advantages for speakers as the manuscript method: Exact wording can be planned, phrases and sentences can be crafted, and potential problems in language can be eliminated. Also, a memorized speech can be adapted to a set, inflexible time limit. Francisco, who was running against Louisa in the student election, decided to memorize his speech. He felt this was a good idea because he wanted exact wording, but he also wanted the freedom to move around. Feedback was not a problem to Francisco because he was speaking to a television audience via the campus's closed-circuit television station. In other situations, however, responding to feedback can be a problem because it is difficult for the speaker to get away from what he or she has memorized. A speaker who gets off track or is distracted may forget parts of the speech or lose his or her place.

A memorized speech can create considerable pressure. Not only does the speaker have to spend the time memorizing the speech, but he or she is also likely to worry about forgetting it. In addition, making a memorized speech sound natural and spontaneous requires considerable acting talent.

Extemporaneous Speaking

In the **extemporaneous speaking** method, a speaker delivers a speech from notes. The speaker might commit the main ideas of the speech to memory—possibly also the introduction and conclusion—but will rely on notes to remember most of the speech.

Extemporaneous speaking has several advantages. It permits flexibility so that a speaker can adjust to the feedback of listeners. For example, if a speaker sees that several audience members do not understand something, he or she can stop and explain. If the audience looks bored, the speaker can try moving around or using a visual aid earlier than planned. Extemporaneous speaking is the one method of delivery that comes closest to good conversation because a speaker can be natural and responsive to the audience.

One disadvantage of the extemporaneous method is that the speaker may stumble over or grope for words. However, much of this problem can be overcome by rehearsing the speech beforehand. Sometimes speakers want to use exact words or phrases. Although in extemporaneous speaking the speech as a whole is not memorized, there is nothing wrong with memorizing a particularly important sentence or having it written down and reading it from a note card.

For the beginning speaker, speaking extemporaneously is the best method of delivery. In addition to eliminating heavy burdens for the speaker (writing out or memorizing the speech), it enables a natural and spontaneous style of speaking. It also makes the listeners a central element in the speech, for the speaker is more free to respond to them.

■ HOW YOU LOOK

Appearance

As you rise from your chair and walk to the lectern to give your speech, the audience's first impression of you will come from how you look. Audience members will notice how you are dressed, if you walk to the lectern with confidence, and whether you look interested in giving this speech.

On days when you are going to make a speech, it is a good idea to look your best. Not only does looking good give the audience a positive impression of you, but it also gives you a psychological boost.

Try to stay away from clothing that might distract from your speech. For example, avoid T-shirts with writing on them. The message itself may be distracting, and audience members will divert their attention by trying to read or guess what your T-shirt says if some of it is hidden by the lectern. Also, avoid accessories you might be tempted to play with. Scarves or jewelry worn around the neck can be troublesome in this regard.

When you are giving a speech in public, wear what the audience would expect you to wear. If it's a formal occasion, wear dress-up clothing; if it's informal, wear what you think everyone else will wear. If you don't know what others will be wearing, ask the person who has invited you to speak.

Body Language

Movement usually causes a response. Blinking turn signals on a car attract more attention than taillights; most of us prefer motion pictures to still photos; the most interesting commercials show the products working. By the same token, a speaker who uses some movement is likely to attract more attention than a speaker who stands absolutely still. Of course, this does not mean that all movement is good. To be effective, your movement should be carefully coordinated with your speech. For example, if you want to stress your most important point, you might indicate this nonverbally by moving closer to your audience. If you want to create intimacy between you and your audience as you are telling a personal story, you could sit on the edge of the desk for a brief period.

Avoid movement that might be distracting. Probably you have seen a speaker (or teacher) who paces back and forth in front of the room. This movement is not motivated by anything other than habit or nervousness: as a result, it's ineffective.

Speakers cannot move around very much if they depend too heavily on their notes. If you must constantly return to the lectern to consult your notes, you will not be able to move very far. The better you know your speech, the more you will be able to experiment with movement.

When you are planning how to deliver your speech, you should consider whether to include deliberate body movements. If you leave these movements to chance, you might not move at all or might move in a way that distracts your listeners. For example, when Navita planned her speech about battered women, she decided to stay behind the lectern when she talked about policy but to move in front of the lectern when she talked about individual women. So that she wouldn't forget, she wrote reminders about moving on her note cards.

Eye Contact

In North American culture, it is considered extremely important to look into the eyes of the person you are talking to. If you don't, you are at risk of being considered dishonest or of being seen as having something to hide. However, this is not true from culture to culture. There are sharp differences between cultures, although many people are not aware of them. Eye behavior varies according to the environment in which it is learned. People respond to social norms.

In some cultures, for example, there are rules governing whom you should and should not look at. One report says that in Kenya, men and their mothers-in-law must turn their backs to each other—they have no eye contact at all (Knapp & Hall, 1996).

Our point here is simply to underscore the existence of cultural differences. Often, Americans think everyone behaves the same as they do. In situations where cultural diversity exists, difficulties in social interaction and communication may arise if we are not sensitive or responsive to these differences. Eye contact, of course, is just one aspect of cultural diversity. Careful audience analysis may uncover differences in other areas of nonverbal communication, language, rules of social situations, social relationships, and even motivation (Argyle, 1991, p. 43).

Public speakers talk to a broad range of audience members. Speakers in our culture are expected to scan the audience and look directly into the eyes of individual audience members (Argyle, 1991). Not only is this expected, but it is a standard of excellence by which effectiveness often is gauged. Be careful about judging speakers from other cultures by standards that they have not learned and to which they do not personally subscribe.

Facial Expression

Because speakers are their own most important visual support—the visual support listeners are obliged to look at—they have the same responsibility to offer audiences an expressive, not deadpan, face, as they have to offer an expressive, not monotonous, voice. Correspondingly, listeners have every reason to expect an expressive face and an expressive voice.

Facial expressions are not terribly difficult to change. By using a mirror—as Alberta did in the chapter's opening example—or by using videotape, you have a chance to see your own face and to know what you are expressing. This is an area of movement that all speakers need to examine. Certainly, speakers can depend on others to give them a negative reaction, but it may be a reaction that never comes or that comes later than necessary. After all, think about it, how willing are you to tell others they look like a deadpan zombie? Using mirrors or video, speakers can discover this and make the needed changes.

On the Web

"What makes some sales professionals standouts and others merely competent?" asks Marjorie Brody (2002). As we have noted previously in this book, anytime you communicate with others, *you* are involved. *You* are selling yourself and your ideas. Here, Brody, indicates how important that really is.

Sales professionals know that the most effective presentations have to start and finish with the audience's needs as the focus. In a world filled with parity products and services, sales professionals who best present themselves to their clientele come out on top. In a sales situation, it is essential that your client or prospect [audience] be receptive to the communications signals you will be sending, simplified here as the three V's—the Visual, the Vocal, and the Verbal. While all three are important, in some situations what you say may not be as important as how you say it; for still others, the way you look and the facial expressions you use will influence the impression your *presentation leaves. Your ultimate credibility as a sales professional will be determined by how well you master the three V's" (p. 1).*

Questions

1. If you weighed the influence of the three V's versus the influence of the content or substance of a speech, which do you think would carry the most influence with most listeners and why?

2. If you were having to make a decision about how much rehearsal and preparation time you spent on the three V's versus how much rehearsal and preparation time you spent on developing the content of your speech, on which would you spend the most amount of time and why?

Source: M. Brody (2002). "You Can't Sell Anything if You Can't Sell Yourself." Brody Communications, Ltd. Retrieved March 25, 2003, from http://www.marjoriebody.com/show.Article.asp?id = 13.

If someone says to you after a speech, "You looked bored to death while you were giving the speech," obviously facial expression is an area you need to work on. But why wait for the reaction? Since facial expressions often mirror attitude, perhaps you need to change your attitude. Rather than thinking of giving the speech as an assignment, a chore, or more busywork, think of it as a legitimate opportunity to share some important information with people who really care. If you think such a change in attitude doesn't matter, you may be surprised by a negative listener reaction.

Gestures

When we speak, most of our gestures are made up of hand and arm movements. We usually use gestures to express or emphasize ideas or emotions. Most of us are too stiff when we speak and could benefit by using more gestures. The best way to add more gestures to your speech is to practice in front of a mirror. Always aim for gestures that look spontaneous and that feel natural to you.

Posture

Posture is a matter of how a person walks and stands. It can give the audience all sorts of messages. If you drag your feet or slouch, you could be communicating that you are lazy, sick, tired, or depressed—none of which you would want to communicate when giving a speech.

Also remember that the way you sit in your seat, rise and walk to the lectern, and return to your seat after the speech, can leave as much of an impression as the posture you use during your speech.

When giving a speech, we usually don't have a good idea of our eye contact, facial expressions, or general body movement. Because we don't have a very good sense of how we look to others, a speech class is a great opportunity to get some feedback. Try to listen to critical remarks from your instructor and classmates without feeling defensive. If you can learn from your mistakes, you will improve every time you give a speech.

■ HOW YOU SOUND

When members of a speech class have a chance to see themselves on videotape, most of them react more negatively to how they sound than to how they look. Few people really like their own voices.

Our voices reveal things about us that might be far more important than the words we speak (Hahner, Sokoloff, & Salisch, 1993). How loud, how fast, how clear and distinct the message—all are part of the information we send about ourselves.

The voice is also a powerful instrument of communication. Because it is so flexible, you can vary it to get the effect you want. You can speak in a loud voice and then drop to a mere whisper. You can go through basic information quickly and then slow down to make a new and important point.

You can even use your voice to bring about a change of character. Notice how your favorite actress or comedian uses many different voices.

We have some idea of how we look to other people because we can see ourselves in a mirror. Most of us, too, because of voice mail and answering machines, have some idea of how we sound. But that doesn't mean we like all that we hear. When members of a speech communication class were asked to identify the things they most disliked about their voices, the most common complaints were poor articulation, speaking too fast, not sounding confident, and not having enough expression.

Volume

Many students who thought they did not sound confident enough attributed this fault to not speaking loudly enough. As one student wrote, "I sound as soft as a mouse." Her comment reflects the perception in our society that a weak and hard-to-hear voice implies the speaker has little confidence. You don't want people to think that about you. In a public-speaking situation, you have to speak loudly enough for people in the back row to hear you. Because your voice-producing mechanism is so close to your ears, you probably think you are speaking louder than you really are. This means that you probably need to speak in a louder voice than you feel comfortable with.

Always check out the back row to see if people can hear you there. Generally you can tell if they are straining to hear you, and often they will give you some nonverbal sign (e.g., leaning forward or cupping a hand behind an ear) that you need to speak louder. If the place in which you are speaking is unusually large, you could even ask if people in the back can hear. If people have to strain to hear you, they probably will not make the effort unless you have something extraordinary to say.

Using a Microphone

If you are speaking in a large auditorium or in a room with poor acoustics, there might be a stationary microphone at the lectern. You may also have access to a *lavaliere microphone,* which is a small microphone that can be attached around your neck or onto your clothing. Many microphones, too, have a body pack or transmitter. The microphone is attached to your collar or lapel. It has a cord attached to the body pack or transmitter, and the transmitter is often attached to a belt. When turned on, the transmitter sends a signal to a distant amplifier that then sends the signal to the room speakers. This type of microphone is especially useful because you are neither confined to a stationary microphone nor hooked to a leash. Many of the people in reality-TV shows wear these microphones..

The rules for using microphones are simple: Make sure they are turned on, and don't blow into them to see if they work. This could ruin them. If the microphone is a stationary one, make certain it is adjusted to your height, and stand 8 to 12 inches away from it while you speak. It should be adjusted so that you do not have to lean down or over to speak into it. If you have attached a small microphone to your clothing, you will want to test it first to

Another Point of View

One point assumed throughout this textbook is that readers can always improve their communication skills. Even if you're already articulate and poised, there is always room for improvement. Sheila Wellington (2001), writes this about improving communication skills for Hispanic and Asian-American women, in her book, *Be Your Own Mentor:*

Hispanic women . . . find others discounting what they say or that even their accents are mocked. Communications issues for women of color are compounded if they speak with an accent, they say. Asian-American women voice concern at being passed over for managerial positions because they're soft-spoken and are stereotyped as shy and self-effacing. They report that working on their communications skills helps a lot.

- For example: Learn how to pace your speaking. Women sometimes speak too fast. Breathe deeply, which slows you down and allows for more deliberate speech.

- Lower the pitch of your voice. A lower voice commands more attention and respect.
- Do not allow yourself to be interrupted. If someone is interrupting, say, "Just give me a minute to finish and then I do want to hear your pont of view." Remember, say this calmly and firmly, without rancor."

Questions

1. Do you think work on communication skills is a realistic and practical suggestion for women of color?
2. Who else might benefit from the suggestions Wellington provides for improving communication skills?
3. Can you make any other suggestions that might help women of color to overcome the stereotypes and to become more assertive?

Source: S. Wellington, *Be Your Own Mentor: Strategies from Top Women on the Secrets of Success* (New York: Random House, 2001), p. 92.

see if everyone can hear you. Also, in one auditorium, whenever the speaker moved in front of one of the side speakers, there was a loud reverberation. This is another reason for checking out the facilities and equipment before giving a speech. In another situation, the speaker had a handheld microphone but no lectern on which to place notes. Fortunately, the speaker knew the speech so well that she could dispense with the notes altogether.

Pace

Like volume, pace is easy to vary. **Pace** refers to how fast or how slowly a person speaks. If you speak too fast, you may be difficult to understand. If you speak too slowly, you risk losing the attention of your audience. If audience attention seems to be drifting away, try picking up your pace. Usually speakers don't know that they have been going too fast until someone tells them so after the speech is over. If you are told this, guard against the mistake in the future: In your next speech, write reminders on your note cards to slow down.

Ideally a speaker varies his or her pace. Speaking fast and then slowing down helps keep the attention of the audience. Also, don't forget the benefits of pausing. Making a pause before or after a dramatic moment is a highly effective technique. The next time you are watching a comedian on television, notice how he or she uses pauses.

Pitch and Inflection

As we noted in Chapter 6, Nonverbal Communication, pitch is the range of tones used in speaking. **Inflection** is a related concept. It refers to the change in pitch used to emphasize certain words and phrases. A person who never varies his or her speaking voice is said to speak in a **monotone.**

Sometimes a person's voice might not seem very interesting because of lack of inflection. If you listen to professional newscasters or sportscasters, you will discover that they use a lot of inflection. By emphasizing certain words and phrases, they help direct listeners' attention to what is important. Emphasis can also bring about subtle changes in meaning. An English professor wrote the words, "Woman without her man is nothing" on the chalkboard and directed her students to punctuate it correctly. The men wrote: "Woman, without her man, is nothing." The women wrote: "Woman! Without her, man is nothing."

Try reading the following sentence, emphasizing a different word each time you read it; you should be able to read it in at least eight different ways:

You mean I have to be there at seven tomorrow?

The best way to get inflection in your voice is to stress certain words deliberately—even to the point of exaggeration. Try taping something in your normal voice and then in your "exaggerated" voice. You might be surprised to find that the exaggerated voice is more interesting.

Enunciation

Enunciation is made up of articulation and pronunciation. **Articulation** is the ability to pronounce the letters in a word correctly; **pronunciation** is the ability to pronounce the whole word. Not only does good enunciation enable people to understand us, but it is also the mark of an educated person. Most of our articulation problems go back to the people from whom we learned our language. If our parents, teachers, or peers pronounced words incorrectly, we probably will too.

Three common causes of articulation problems are sound substitution, omission of sounds, and slurring. Sound substitution is very common. Many people say "dere," "dem," and "dose" for *there, them,* and *those.* In this case a *d* is substituted for the more difficult *th* sound. The substitution of a *d* for a *t* in the middle of a word is widespread in American English. If you need any proof, try pronouncing these words as you usually do: *water, butter, thirty, bottle.* Unless you have very good articulation, you probably said "wader," "budder," "thirdy," and "boddle."

Some people believe they have a speech defect that prevents them from producing certain sounds. This can be easily checked. For example, if you always say "dere" for *there,* make a special effort to make the *th* sound. If you are able to make it, you have a bad habit, not a speech defect.

People also commonly omit sounds. For example, some people say "libary" for *library,* and some frequently omit sounds that occur at the ends of words, saying "goin" for *going* and "doin" for *doing.*

Slurring is caused by running words together, as in such phrases as "Yawanna go?" and "I'll meecha there." Slurring, as with other articulation problems, is usually a matter of bad speech habits, and it can be overcome with some effort and practice.

Once you are aware of a particular articulation habit, you can try to change it. Changing a habit is not easy, since the habit has probably been a part of your behavior for many years. Sometimes it helps to drill, using lists of words that give you trouble. It also helps to have a friend remind you when you mispronounce a word. After you become accustomed to looking for the problem, you will catch yourself more often. If you have several articulation problems, do not try to solve them all at once. Work on one sound at a time; when you can handle that sound, attempt another one.

Pronunciation is a matter of saying words correctly. Probably you have a bigger reading vocabulary than speaking vocabulary and don't know how to pronounce many of the words you read. If you are in doubt about how to pronounce a word, look it up in the dictionary. The Internet offers pronunciating dictionaries where you can hear the proper pronunciation.

■ USING VISUAL SUPPORT

Visual support includes devices such as charts, graphs, slides, and computer-generated images that help illustrate the key points in a speech. Visual support serves four functions: It helps hold the attention of listeners, it provides information in the visual channel, it helps audience members remember what speakers have said, and it helps speakers in several ways. Visual support often helps speakers by:

1. Providing them with another means for supporting or illustrating content.
2. Adding a different, often interesting, attention-grasping element to the speech.
3. Giving them a chance to move around or demonstrate.
4. Offering them assistance in remembering their information.

A study has shown that visual support also helps listeners remember the information. According to the study, if audience members are given only verbal information, after three days they remember a mere 10 percent of what they were told. If they are shown material without verbal communication, they remember 35 percent of what they see. However, if both verbal and visual information is provided, listeners remember 65 percent after three days. But just because you have visual support does not mean that audience members will automatically give you their attention. Poorly designed or inappropriate visual materials will not keep listeners' attention. They could even have a negative effect by distracting from the information you are giving and weakening your credibility.

Types of Visual Support

Your visual material should help make your topic lively and interesting to the audience. There are numerous types of visual support to choose from. In making your choice, ask yourself which kind of visual material would best illustrate your topic and appeal to your listeners.

The Chalkboard

Since a chalkboard exists in every classroom, it is the most accessible visual support. It works particularly well for writing key words or phrases, drawing very simple diagrams, and giving URLs (web addresses) for speech material.

When you use the chalkboard, it's important that you write quickly to avoid having your back to the audience any longer than necessary. Once you have the word or diagram on the board, turn around, stand next to it, and as you explain, point to it with your hand. Make sure that your writing is large and dark enough for the entire audience to read.

The Actual Object

Sometimes it is useful to use the thing you are talking about as visual support. Audience members like to see what you are talking about, especially if the object is not familiar to them. One student brought a violin and a viola to class to demonstrate the differences in the sounds and the looks of the two instruments. Another, explaining how to make minor adjustments on one's car, brought a carburetor. Still another borrowed a skeleton from the biology department to illustrate a speech on osteoporosis, a bone disease.

Models

A **model** is a replica of an actual object that is used when the object itself is too large to be displayed (e.g., a building), too small to be seen (e.g., a cell), or inaccessible to the eye (e.g., the human heart). A model can be very effective visual support because it shows exactly how something looks. It is better than a picture because it is three-dimensional. A student who was discussing airplanes used in warfare brought in models of planes he had constructed.

A diagram can be valuable in explaining complex ideas.

Figure 15-1

One Cavern's Size

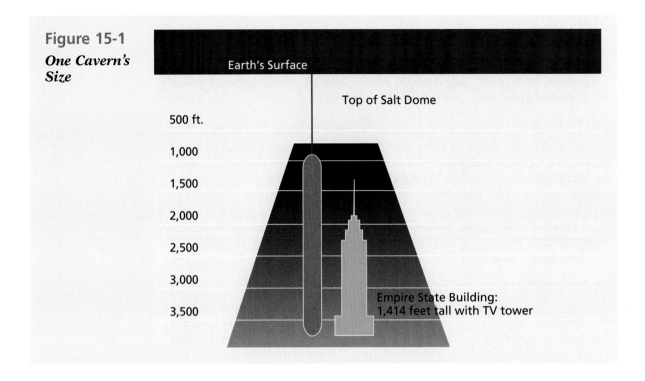

Posters, Diagrams, and Charts

A **poster** consists of lettering or pictures, or both. The purpose of a poster is to enhance the speaker's subject. For example, when speaking about the style of electric cars, a student used a poster showing pictures of one make to show how the batteries had been incorporated into the overall design of the car. A poster may also be used to emphasize the key words or thoughts in a speech. A student who spoke on how to save money on clothes used a poster to list the following points:

- Decide on a basic color.
- Buy basics at one store.
- Buy accessories at sales.

Not only did the poster provide the audience with a way to remember the points, but it also gave, in visual form, the general outline of the speech.

A **diagram** may range from a simple organizational chart to a complex rendering of a three-dimensional object. Diagrams are particularly valuable in showing how something works. For example, in a speech about storing toxic wastes, a student used the diagram in Figure 15-1 to show how waste can be stored in a salt cavern. Including a drawing of the Empire State Building was particularly useful because it gave the viewer an idea of the depth of the mine.

An **organizational chart** shows the relationships among the elements of an organization, such as the departments of a company, the branches of federal or state government, or the committees of the student government. Note how a speaker used the organizational chart in Figure 15-2 to show how the academic side of a university is organized and how a student wishing to

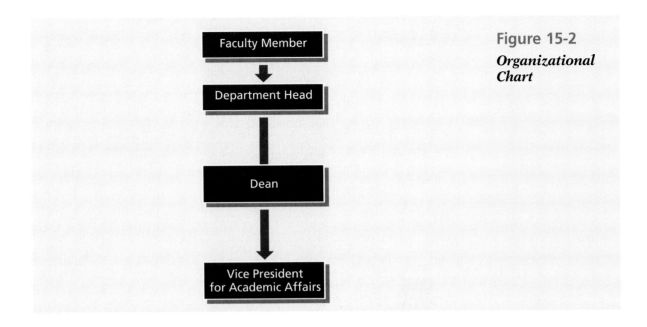

Figure 15-2

Organizational Chart

express dissatisfaction should approach people in a specific order, beginning with a faculty member.

A **flip chart** is a series of pictures, words, diagrams, and so forth. It's called a "flip chart" because it is made up of several pages that you flip through. A flip chart is best used when you have a complicated subject that needs several illustrations or when you want to emphasize several points in your speech.

Tables and Graphs

Tables and graphs are easy to prepare and can be used to condense a lot of information into a useful, understandable form. Perhaps most important, anyone can make this visual support because no special skills are required. With the use of a computer, creating tables, putting information into the tables, changing the tables, and creating titles for the tables can be accomplished through the click of a mouse.

Tables are columns of figures arranged in an order that enables the viewer to easily pick out the information needed. For example, when Tina Amin spoke to her class on the topic "Living Alone," she used a simple table to illustrate problems associated with creating a budget. She said, "My monthly budget is divided into these things" and pointed to the table (see Table 15-1). "This represents costs of $1,360 a month," said Tina. "I work 30 hours a week at the library for $8 an hour, for which I receive $960 a month. I am fortunate to receive an allowance from my parents of $100 a week, or $400 a month—while I am in school—which brings my monthly income to $1,360. So, if I can stick to my very strict budget, I am able to just break even each month. Often, I can cut corners on food, clothing, school supplies, and entertainment—especially if I can find a date who doesn't believe in going 'dutch,' " she said with a sly smile, "and then I can sometimes realize a monthly savings," Tina said.

"When I was asked to move into a larger, more spacious apartment," Tina said, "I simply created a third column for projected expenses. I quickly discovered that on the income I have now, I could not afford to move."

Table 15-1
Tina's Budget:
Expenses

Rent	$ 300
Car payment	250
Food	300
Utilities	100
Clothing	100
Books/school supplies	100
Entertainment	100
Savings	60
Miscellaneous	50
Total	$1,360

Figure 15-3

List of Things
that People Fear

Source: "Snakes
Scarier than Public
Speaking" (USA
TODAY Snapshots),
USA Today, March
26, 2001, p. 1. From
a Gallup Poll of 1,
016 adults February
19–21, 2001; margin
of error +/− 3 per-
centage points.

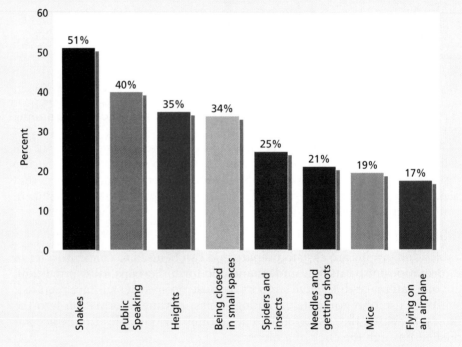

Graphs are used to present statistical material in a visual form that helps viewers see similarities, differences, relationships, or trends. There are three commonly used types of graphs: bar, pie, and line. If you want to see a variety of the graphs available, look in any issue of *USA Today.* The bar graph in Figure 15-3—as the source notes—is from one of these graphs.

A line graph is particularly useful for showing trends over a period of time or for making comparisons. For example, Figure 15-4 shows how many people were online as of February 2002; however, the source notes that "The art of estimating how many are online throughout the world is an inexact one at best. Surveys abound, using all sorts of measurement parameters" (How many online?, 2001, p. 1). So, how did ComputerScope Ltd. get its results? "From observing many of the published surveys over the last two years, here is an 'educated guess' as to how many are online worldwide . . ." (p. 1).

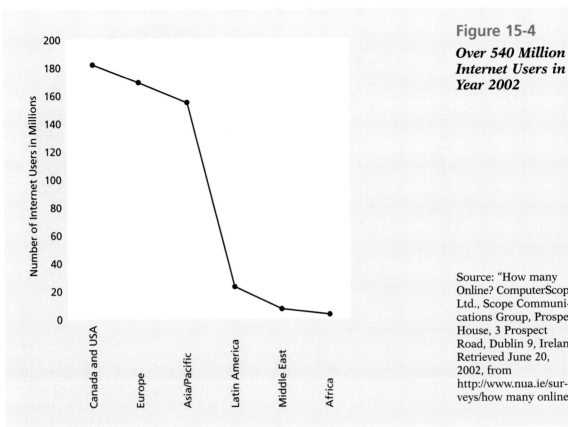

Figure 15-4

Over 540 Million Internet Users in Year 2002

Source: "How many Online? ComputerScope, Ltd., Scope Communications Group, Prospect House, 3 Prospect Road, Dublin 9, Ireland. Retrieved June 20, 2002, from http://www.nua.ie/surveys/how many online/.

In a speech entitled "Let's All Read," Martin used the pie graph in Figure 15-5 to illustrate the fact that nearly half the nation's population doesn't even buy books, much less read them.

Computer Graphics

The computer offers numerous options to speakers. The phrase **computer-generated graphics** refers to any images created or manipulated via computer—art, drawings, representations of objects, pictures, and the like. If you want to create a graph or some other piece of visual support, a computer with a graphics program can generate it. Computers are best for processing numerical data and then converting that data into bar, line, or pie graphs. Having a computer-generated graph enlarged is a relatively simple, inexpensive process; photocopiers can enlarge images, sometimes to 200 percent of the original size. The end product is worth the time, effort, and money. You can emphasize portions of your material by highlighting or coloring in areas. Even darkening the lines of a line graph or adding press-on letters for headings on a large copy can enhance visual presentation and effect.

The average computer user may not yet have the capacity to produce visuals like those seen on television—which often cost thousands of dollars to produce—but well-thought-out visuals, projected on a screen or on a computer, can give your presentation a professional and sophisticated look. And the computer software available today can make even the simplest attempt at slide production extremely professional looking.

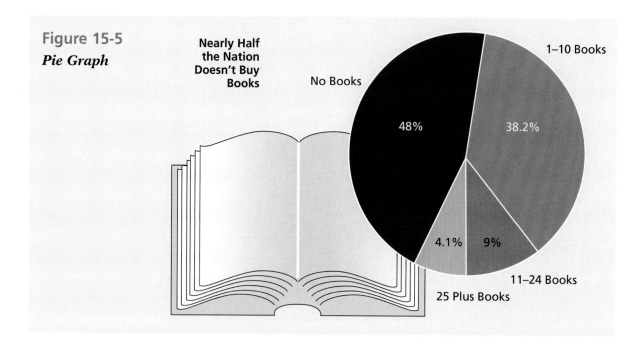

Figure 15-5
Pie Graph

Nearly Half the Nation Doesn't Buy Books

No Books — 48%

1–10 Books — 38.2%

11–24 Books — 9%

25 Plus Books — 4.1%

Before you go to the computer to prepare a presentation, make certain that you already have in mind your general and specific purposes as well as your central idea. Then, around those, organize your main heads—or key points—and examples, facts, statistics, and personal experiences to support your main heads. If you have three points you want to make and the points are relatively equal, you will use a topical outline approach. If you are explaining a process and want to show it developmentally—how one part of the process follows another—you will use the time-order or chronological approach.

Our point here is not to be redundant but, rather, to emphasize that you must be fully prepared before using a computer to create slides. The computer isn't magic. It will assist you best in illustrating and explaining your ideas if you are fully prepared before putting it to use. Remember the old maxim: "Garbage in; garbage out."

Perhaps the most important advice regarding your slides is to make them readable. Follow the "6 × 6 rule." Use no more than six words horizontally, and use no more than six items on a page—less than that, if possible. This will result in a slide that conveys its meaning readily, and it will help ensure that the slide can be seen by the people farthest away. Here, we'll apply the 6 × 6 rule in a bulleted list:

- Keep text larger than 18 points.
- 44 points = titles; 32 = text; 28 = subtext.
- Use no more than three fonts.
- Use dark background and bright text.
- Overheads need light background, dark text.
- Insert tables and graphs when appropriate.

One essential element in any slide presentation is visual variety. How do you obtain variety? You can use diagrams, flowcharts, and graphs to illustrate your ideas. Most software packages offer opportunities to obtain variety. There are clip-art packages that allow you to insert professional-quality graphics into your slides. There are numerous Internet sources where clip art can be downloaded free. With a scanner, you can add cartoons, magazine and newspaper headlines, and photographs. To keep the focus of listener attention on you, not the slides, occasionally intersperse a slide without words or pictures to give audience members a chance to move their necks, refocus their attention, and concentrate on your textual message.

There are numerous software tools available for creating slide shows. One website in particular is valuable, because it is regularly updated and because it includes links to examples of presentations, sites that provide instruction on how to create presentations, sites that offer both the advantages and disadvantages of PowerPoint, sites that discuss other software available for creating presentations, as well as sites for software for creating demonstrations, and, in addition, sites where you can get free or inexpensive presentation software:

> *G. Daniel, and K. Cox, "Tools for Web-Based Presentations," Web Tools Newsletter, March 11, 2002. Web Tools for Learning. Division of Computer Studies. City University of Hong Kong. Retrieved March 25, 2003, from http://webtools.cityu.edu.hk/news/newslett/presentation.htm.*

You can get additional visual variety by enhancing your presentation through the use of **multimedia**—various media (sound, graphics, and animation, as well as text) used to deliver information. You can liven up your message with pictures and music, but you need to be cautious, especially if you are a beginner. Just as a child overplays with a new toy, people tend to overuse software packages. You need enough multimedia to enhance and strengthen your message; too much can overpower and weaken your message—and, perhaps, your credibility. Knowing how much is too much requires some experience, judgment, and plain old common sense. Aim for just enough graphics, sound, and animation to support, elaborate, and focus the point of your message without risk of obscuring or overwhelming your point.

Multimedia products are often interactive—users can choose from a variety of information options. For example, Larry used computer graphics to illustrate parts of the human body for his speech on proper exercise techniques, and he gave his presentation a more professional look by converting computer-generated images into transparencies showing muscles during exercise. He projected these images during his speech. Computer-generated images can show machines, buildings, almost anything.

As we write this, techniques combining CDs with television and computers and computer-generated graphics with video cameras are bringing sophisticated capabilities to the nonprofessional as well as the professional speaker. Many of these resources are already being used in high-quality workplace speeches and sales presentations. Check to see if you have access to such technology.

Although we give more advice about using visual support in the section that follows, there is a major caution that needs to be made regarding the use of such materials: Our caution here builds on that provided by Daniel Goleman (1998) in the Consider This box on page 554. Remember, computer-generated graphics and multimedia are props that should support and enhance your main ideas, not take their place. It is you—the main actor, speaker, and focus of the speech—who must engage your listeners

Consider This

It is important for speakers to connect emotionally with their audiences. Daniel Goleman, in his book, *Working with Emotional Intelligence*, explains how dependence on too much visual support can interfere or subvert this emotional connection:

Those who rely too heavily on the persuasive effects of aids such as elaborate overhead projections or elegant statistical analyses of data also can miss the boat. An audience must be emotionally engaged, but mediocre presenters rarely go beyond the same dry litany of facts, however flashily displayed, and never take into account the emotional temperature of the audience. Without an accurate reading of how a listener is taking in an idea, that idea is in danger of falling on deaf, indifferent, or even hostile ears.

Questions

1. Why do some speakers rely too heavily on visual support?

2. What does Goleman mean when he uses the phrase "the emotional temperature of the audience"? Of what is that emotional temperature composed? How can it be detected? How should speakers respond to it?

3. If the speaker's goal is to persuade listeners, how does he or she know how much visual support is too much?

Source: Daniel Goleman, *Working with Emotional Intelligence* (New York: Bantam Books, 1998), p. 173.

emotionally. Visuals, thus, must be chosen to fit your purpose, your physical setting, and—most importantly—your audience's needs. If they are not, as Goleman says, above, your ideas are in danger "of falling on deaf, indifferent, or even hostile ears" (p. 173).

Projected Material

Videos, slides, and other projected material are useful types of visual support. When you are using projected material, remember that it should enhance, not replace, your speech.

If you decide to use a video, you have two choices: You can use one made by other people, or you can make your own. If you are making a long speech, a preprogrammed video can be a very good visual reinforcement of what you are saying. A student who gave a speech on how applicants are propagandized by college admission tapes followed her speech with the college's own admissions video. The students were amazed at the difference between their perception of the college and the tape's portrayal of it.

If you have access to your own video camera, you can make your own tape and customize it to match your subject and your audience. One student made a videotape illustrating four basic karate moves for his speech. Because video is so easy to work with, he was able to stop the tape, talk about each move, and then go on to the next one. Another student, speaking about parking on campus, made a short video of students trying to find a place in a full parking lot. Her video was an effective way of persuading her audience of the need for additional student parking areas.

You may have slides you could use in a speech, or you may have access to a set of slides that have been commercially produced. Since you are giving a speech rather than a slide show, however, you should limit the number of slides you use. One student who had traveled to China decided to limit her slides to those of the Great Wall. She figured this single site would be of greatest interest to her audience.

Overhead projectors are a very easy way of showing visual material. With an overhead, a page from a book can be projected and enlarged on a movie screen—which is much less complicated than copying from the book onto a chart. You can also draw your information on an ordinary-size piece of paper and then transfer it to a transparency for projection. Whenever you use an overhead projector, you must first make a transparency.

Handouts

When material is complex or when there is a lot of it, audience members may need a handout. For example, a student who spoke about the calories in fast foods gave audience members a handout showing the caloric values of specific foods. Other times a handout is useful to reinforce the points you are making in your speech. A student who spoke about 10 ways to recycle made a handout of her main points and distributed it at the end of her speech.

If you use handouts, choose the best time to pass them out. If you distribute your handouts too early, the audience will read them and ignore you. Also, most people dislike having a handout read to them. If your handout repeats the points you are making, give it out when your speech is over.

You as Visual Support

There are two aspects to "you as visual support." The first has to do with the contribution you make as a speaker. Whether you like it or not, you are on display. When you speak, your verbal and nonverbal demeanor contributes more to if and how your listeners receive your message than anything else you might do. Your look, actions, and sound must add strength and vitality to your message. You need to eliminate anything in your personal presentation that might distract from the positive contribution you can make as your own visual support. As an aside here, if you are asked by an instructor to use specific visual support, you are being asked to use something in addition to yourself!

The second aspect of "you as visual support" has to do with participating in what you are demonstrating. If you want to show your listeners how to do something, you become your best visual support. For example, if you're telling audience members how to improve their golf swing, bring your clubs and demonstrate. If you want to reveal clothing fads, dress the part. One speaker demonstrated several self-defense moves in a speech she entitled, "You Are Your Own Best Defense."

Rules for Using Visual Support

You want visual support that will really work for you. The wrong type could detract from your speech and make it much less effective. When you are considering visual support, keep the following rules in mind:

- *Use visual support to supplement, not replace, the speech.* The visual suport should not become the whole show. It should be a useful addition to reinforce the speech.

- *Use visual support for points that need more explanation.* Look over your speech and decide which details could be better explained visually. Is there a particular statistic you want to stress? Will something be more easily understood if your audience can see it? Will it help your speech to show your main points visually?

- *Show the visual support only when you are ready for it.* Put the visual in an inconspicuous place; then, when you are ready to use it, take it out. When you are finished with it, put it away. You don't want it to compete with you for attention.

- *Make sure everyone can read your visual.* When making a chart, use a dark marker with a thick tip so that you can draw bold lines that will show up. If you have any doubts, check your visual support beforehand. Set it up in the front of the room and stand in the farthest corner to see if you can read it. If you can't read it easily, fix it so you can.

- *Before your speech, check the room to see if your visual support can be easily displayed.* If you are using projection equipment, find the electric outlets and see if the room has blackout shades or curtains. If you are hanging a chart, decide how to hang it. Are you going to need tape or thumbtacks?

- *Practice with your visual support before the speech.* If you are using some sort of chart, stand next to it and point to it with your right or left hand rather than standing in front of it with your back to the audience. Practice using any kind of equipment until you can operate it quickly and easily. If you are using something complicated, such as projection equipment, consider having a classmate run it for you. If you do this, practice with him or her. When practicing with your visual support, check to see how much time it takes. If it is going to take too much time, decide how you will cut back.

- *Talk to the audience, not to the visual.* You may need to look at your visual occasionally, but remember to maintain eye contact with the audience.

- *Maintain control of the speech situation.* Since visuals can take audience attention away from you, keep them simple.

■ CONTROLLING NERVOUSNESS

In studies of what makes people anxious, public speaking always ranks right up there at the top. Winston Churchill, who became one of the most famous statesmen and orators of the twentieth century, fainted dead away the first time he gave a speech. Billy Graham, the most famous and successful evangelist of the twentieth century, was invited to preach his first sermon in a small Baptist church in the community of Bostwick, in northeast Florida. Graham assembled detailed notes from a sermon book—enough to preach *four* 45-minute sermons. "But shaken almost to desperation by the ordeal of actually preaching to a group of ordinary people, he rattled through the notes of all four sermons in less than eight minutes," writes David Aikman, in his book *Great Souls* (1998). "Nobody has ever failed more ignominiously in a first sermon," Graham has said since then.

Twenty-one percent of Americans—more than 40 million people—fear performing in front of audiences. Nervousness affects professional musicians, lecturers, actors, business executives, and people in other lines of work (Woods, 1996). Notice in Figure 15-3 (page 550) that according to a Gallup Poll of 1,016 adults, next to snakes (feared by 51 percent of American adults), 40 percent of Americans fear public speaking (Snakes scarier . . . , 2001). That figure (40 percent) agrees with a Roper Starch Worldwide study (1998) supported by the National Communication Association, conducted four years earlier that found that "almost 40 percent of Americans do not feel comfortable giving a presentation or a speech." The Roper Starch study concluded, too, that with respect to college graduates, "Almost half (48 percent) . . . are very comfortable speaking up at a meeting and 38 percent are very comfortable giving a presentation or speech, as opposed to 22 percent and 10 percent of those who did not finish high school" ("How Americans communicate," 1998). The results say something about the value of a college education!

The reaction to the fear of public speaking is perfectly natural, although it can be unpleasant. Brad Schmidt and Jeffrey Winters (2002) explain the physiological reaction—the actual chemical involvement—in their article entitled "Fear Not":

> *Fear begins in the amygdala, a cluster of cells deep in the most primitive part of the brain that weighs information for emotional content and possible threat. If a threat is sensed, the amygdala sends out immediate signals. Simple reflexes are set off: a jump or a shout. And the adrenal glands in the kidneys begin pumping adrenaline and noradrenaline, two chemicals that act as messengers to trigger reactions all over the body. A rush of adrenaline and noradrenaline causes the heart to race, breathing to quicken, pupils to widen and saliva to dry up. In the extreme, it is common to experience hyperventilation, dizziness, trembling and even nausea (p. 48).*

Speaker anxiety has been well documented. While most people have a normal heart rate of 70 beats a minute, as a person anticipates giving a speech, the rate may increase from 95 to 140. Once he or she begins speaking, it can jump from 110 to 190. As the person proceeds with the speech, however, the heart rate begins to drop (Motley, 1988, p. 47).

No matter how nervous a speaker might be, there is some comfort in the fact that, as studies have shown, most audience members do not realize that a speaker is nervous. Even observers who are trained to look for anxiety cues usually do not see them in a speaker (Motley, 1988). This means that if your palms sweat, your knees shake, or your mouth is dry, you are probably the only one who knows it.

A great deal of research has been done on the subject of anxiety. Researchers have found that about 10 percent of college students have an intense fear of public speaking and will even go so far as to drop a public-speaking course they need in order to graduate. The other 90 percent have fears they can overcome; they are nervous, but their nervousness doesn't impair their ability to make a speech (Page, 1985). Although people who are phobic often need professional help to conquer their speaking phobia, people who have normal anxiety can usually find at least one strategy that helps them deal with their nervousness by themselves.

In a question and answer column Dr. Robert Epstein (2002) was asked a question by a reader, M, New York,: "I suffer severely from stage fright. What can I do? I tried medication, but it just makes me drowsy." Epstein's reply has direct relevance to and application for college students:

> *For onstage situations, I'd avoid medication. You'll probably want all your marbles if you're acting or speaking. In an acting workshop I took in high school, I learned some simple breathing techniques that relax the body and improve the focus before a performance. Since then I've found—and regularly practice—dozens of powerful techniques of this sort. You can learn a variety of stress-management techniques from a qualified counselor . . . or from books such as my Big Book of Stress-Relief Games (McGraw-Hill, 2000).*

Your authors entered *stress-management techniques* into the Google search engine and received 149,000 websites (March 25, 2003). Here are three we found helpful if managing stress is a problem you are facing:

1. (No author), "How to Fight and Conquer Stress," Rose Men's Health Resource, Rose Medical Center, Denver, CO, 80220, 1993. Retrieved March 25, 2003, from http://www.coolware.com/health/joel/stress.html. This site tells you what stress is, what causes it, why it can be harmful, its positive side, quick tips for managing it, things you can do to relax, how to take control of stress through relaxation, plus six additional techniques.

2. (No author), "Stress Management," Counseling Center, University of Illinois, at Urbana-Champaign, 1996. Retrieved March 25, 2003, from http://www.couns.uiuc.edu/Brochurse/stress.htm. This site tells you what stress is, how you can eliminate it, how you can manage it better through the use of six areas of influence plus numerous subpoints under each area.

3. (No author), "Stress Management Techniques." Self Help Counseling Center, Texas Woman's University, July 21, 1999. Retrieved March 25, 2003, from http://www.twu.edu/o-sl/counseling/SH009.html. This is a straightforward listing of 15 strategies for managing stress and a 15-item attached action plan that is both instructive and helpful.

There is a list of additional helpful links at (No author), "Stress Management Websites." Retrieved March 25, 2003, from http://www.siu.edu/departments/bushea/stress.html.

Unfortunately, there is no single, surefire formula that reduces every person's anxiety before a speech. However, some strategies work for many people and are thus worth trying to see if they will work for you:

- *Dress in comfortable clothes.* Wear clothes you feel at ease in—but clothes that show you have made some kind of special effort for the speech. Psychologically, it is important to feel confident and in control.

- *Practice positive self-talk.* Whenever a negative idea appears ("I'll never get through this speech"), replace it with a positive one ("I'm feeling

Working Together

The ultimate goal here is to get people to talk about their thoughts and feelings and to explore creative problem solving. Group members will have a chance to do two things: (1) to express their feelings about having to give a speech in front of their classmates, and (2) through brainstorming, to explore various methods of dealing with such situations.

Here is the scene group members must respond to: "I'm so stressed out. I have been avoiding this class. I hate to give public speeches. Standing up in front of others and having to speak really scares the heck out of me."

Now, go around the group, and have everyone express his or her feelings about this scene.

After everyone has expressed his or her feelings, have everyone brainstorm first about ways

they personally handle such situations of stress, and second, all the possible methods they could use that might also work to help deal with such stress.

Some people who were successful in overcoming the stress associated with having to give a public speech have said they were able to pretend they were an actor playing the role of a confident, poised, successful speaker, with the actual words of the speech being the lines they had to know to play the role of the speaker. In this way, they could not only imagine themselves in front of the crowd feeling confident and poised, but they could carry that feeling with them when they walked to the front of the class to deliver the speech. By playing the role, they displaced their own feelings of anxiety.

nervous, but that won't stop me from doing a good job"). Don't give yourself any negative messages. Don't say, "I know I'm going to blow it" or "I'm so nervous I'll lose my voice." Saying such things, whether out loud or to yourself, feeds your fears and makes them worse than they already are.

- *Be well prepared.* Do not wait until the last moment to put your speech together. And don't just go over the speech in your mind. Stand up. Say the speech aloud, using notes only as many times as you need to remember your main points.

- *Concentrate on your message.* When you believe you have something important to share with your listeners, it is easier to get excited about what you plan to tell them. Along with concentrating on your message, focus on your audience. Think about really communicating with your listeners about your important message. The point is to take your focus from yourself and aim it at the message and toward your listeners.

- *Picture yourself doing well.* Use positive mental imagery. If you can imagine yourself walking to the front of the room, speaking to a responsive audience, hearing your words flow without hesitation, and receiving a positive response from listeners, you have a visual image of success. Replay this visual image of success often.

- *If your anxiety is high, ask your instructor if you can speak first or second.* Being among the first to speak means you have less time to worry. Sometimes anxiety increases if you have to sit and wait to speak.

- *Take several deep breaths on the way to the front of the room.* An increased respiratory rate because of nervousness can cause you to feel short of breath. It can also inhibit good vocal production. Taking several deep breaths can break this cycle and have a calming effect.

- *Remember that your audience is made up of people just like you.* They want you to do well; they are supportive. Nervous, uncomfortable speakers make listeners ill at ease and embarrassed; that is why planning and thorough preparation are so important.

- *If possible, move around.* Moving releases nervous energy and restores a feeling of calm. Don't pace, and don't make extraneous, nonpurposeful movements, but try to gesture and move when you use transitions and personal examples.

- *Pick out friendly faces, and make eye contact with these people.* An encouraging, supportive expression on a listener's face can do wonders to promote confidence and reassure speakers that they are on the right track.

- *Give yourself a reward after your speech, and congratulate yourself for having succeeded.* Even though your speech may not have been perfect, remind yourself that you were able to do it. Remember, you're human, and humans aren't perfect.

■ PRACTICING YOUR SPEECH

Practice will help you give a better speech. You may be hesitant to practice—probably because you feel silly talking to an empty room. Yet if you go into a store to buy a new piece of clothing, you probably spend a lot of time in the dressing room looking at it from several angles. By practicing a speech, you are doing the same thing: You are trying it on to see if it fits; if it doesn't, you will have time to make the necessary alterations.

How can you practice delivery so that you will feel comfortable with the content and language of your speech and yet not get so locked in that your words sound memorized or mechanical? Below is a plan that seems to work well for most speakers.

Preparing Your Speech

Before you give your speech in a practice session, you should do the following:

1. Prepare the content thoroughly. Your speech will be no better than the effort you've put into it. Do you have a clear statement of purpose? Do the materials you have collected support this statement of purpose? Have you done enough research to provide support for each of your main points?

2. Organize your content into a full-sentence outline. Have you made the proper distinction between main idea and supporting points? Does your outline flow clearly and logically? Are you quite clear about what you are going to say in your introduction and conclusion? Is your conclusion worded in such a way that you can end the speech and sit down without feeling awkward?

3. From your full-sentence outline, prepare a key-word or short-phrase outline that you can use while you rehearse and also while you give your speech. Put your key-word outline on a series of 3" x 5" cards using one side only. Can you follow the speech from this outline? Have you written out phrases or quotations that you want to quote precisely? Can you read the cards easily?

Trying Out Your Speech

During the tryout sessions, emphasis should be on the content of the speech and whether it is working the way you imagined it would in your head. (There is often a big difference between the way we imagine something will sound and the way it really sounds.) In these sessions you want to actually say the words—stop to clear up imprecise language, maybe add a transition, try out the conclusion. It will take you a while to get through the speech because you will be making corrections as you go along—especially the very first time.

Daniel Schacter (2001), in his book *The Seven Sins of Memory*, states that "Everyday experience and laboratory studies reveal that emotionally charged incidents are better remembered than nonemotional events" (p. 163). This means that if you have selected a subject that you care about or one you can become emotional about or, to put it a bit differently, a subject to which you can become emotionally attached, you are far more likely to remember your ideas. As you are trying out your speech, give the content and the way you have structured and phrased your ideas your special attention. As Schacter says, "when we fail to attend to or elaborately encode incoming information [the speech you are trying to learn] we stand little chance of remembering it later" (p. 163). This will help you make the most of your rehearsal times.

One other technique to use when trying out your speech is visualization—the deliberate attempt to see your successful performance in your mind's eye (Manz & Sims, 2001). Charles Manz and Henry Sims, Jr., state that "Visualization may be particularly useful the next time you make a speech or deliver a briefing. Try to engage in a mental rehearsal by visualizing yourself delivering the speech in a very effective manner" (2001, p. 112). According to Annie Murphy Paul, however, in an article entitled "Self-Help: Shattering the Myths," (2001), visualization by itself is not sufficient. Paul, citing Shelley Taylor, a psychologist at UCLA, says that in addition to visualization, you need to figure out what steps are necessary to accomplish your goal and mentally rehearsing those steps—even "running through the steps you've laid out once a day" (p. 64). The "Virtual Presentation Assistant" at www.ukans.edu/cwis/units/coms2/vpa/vpa.htm contains step-by-step instructions for preparing and presenting a speech.

Consider This

Many speakers think their work is done after they say the final words of their conclusion. However, some of the most valuable work begins *after* the speech is over. This is the time to ask whether you reached your goal and to discover what effect you had on your listeners. Here are some questions that you need to ask yourself after you give a speech:

1. Did I follow the plan for my speech? Did I stick to my outline and cover the material I wanted to cover? Did I keep my central idea in mind?

2. Was my speech completed in the time allotted? If it was too long, did I go too slowly or did I have too much material? If it was too short, did I talk too fast or did I have too little material?

3. Did I pay attention to my audience? Do I have a sense of how audience members responded to my speech? If they started losing interest, did I do anything to try to reengage them?

4. Did I make eye contact with the audience? Was I conscious of using appropriate gestures to make certain points?

5. Did I have a well-defined conclusion? Did I communicate to my audience that the speech was finished?

6. The next time I speak, what things should I change?

Your answers to these questions should help you improve every time you get up to speak. Remember, the goal of your speech communication class is to make you an effective communicator. Reaching this goal involves having the information that will help you improve, but it also involves your putting this information to work for you.

You should practice delivering the speech until you feel comfortable with it. As you practice, try to use wording that sounds natural to you. Every time you speak, your wording should be a little bit different—otherwise, your speech will sound mechanical. Also, as you practice, you should become less and less dependent on your notes. Try to consult them as little as possible.

If you think you will need a lot of practice to feel comfortable with your speech, it is better not to rehearse it all at one time. Put the speech away for a few hours or even overnight. The next time you approach it, you may be surprised to find fresh ideas or ways of solving problems that hadn't occurred to you before.

Practicing Actual Delivery

The next stage is to actually deliver the speech. As you practice your delivery, try to imagine an audience.

1. Stand against one wall and look over your "audience." Remember to establish eye contact with people in all parts of the room.

2. Check your starting time. In this practice session you want to find out how long your speech is.

3. Deliver the speech all the way through without stopping. As you speak, remember to look at your "audience."

4. When the speech is over, check your ending time.

5. Analyze your performance: Did any parts of the speech give you difficulty? Did the speech seem clearly organized? Check your outline. In giving the speech, did you leave anything out? Was your outline clear and easy to follow? How about time? Do you need to add or delete any material to make the speech the proper length?

6. Make the necessary changes, and practice the speech again.

Sample Speech

In this speech, "Looking through Our Window: The Value of Indian Culture," by Marge Anderson (1999), chief executive of the Mille Lacs Band of Ojibwe, notice the power behind the words. This speech was delivered to the First Friday Club of the Twin Cities, sponsored by St. Thomas Alumni, St. Paul, Minnesota. As you read it, imagine yourself delivering it. Try to imagine how Ms. Anderson might have delivered it. Can you give it with feeling and strength—as if *your* culture depended on it? Anderson's is a two-point speech supported with numerous examples.

General purpose: To inform.

Specific purpose: To increase the understanding of my listeners about the Indian culture.

Central idea: To demonstrate how Indians see the world and their place in it and how Indian businesses allow Indians to give back to others.

Aaniin. Thank you for inviting me here today. When I was asked to speak to you, I was told you are interested in hearing about the improvements we are making on the Mille Lacs Reservation, and about our investment of casino dollars back into our community through schools, health care facilities, and other services. And I do want to talk to you about these things, because they are tremendously important, and I am very proud of them.

But before I do, I want to take a few minutes to talk to you about something else, something I'm not asked about very often. I want to talk to you about what it means to be Indian. About how my people experience the world. About the fundamental way in which our culture differs from yours. And about why you should care about all this.

The differences between Indians and non-Indians have created a lot of controversy lately. Casinos, treaty rights, tribal sovereignty—these issues have stirred such anger and bitterness.

I believe the accusations against us are made out of ignorance. The vast majority of non-Indians do not understand how my people view the world, what we value, what motivates us.

They do not know these things for one simple reason: They've never heard us talk about them. For many years, the only stories that non-Indians heard about my people came from other non-Indians. As a result, the picture you got of us was fanciful, or distorted, or so shadowy it hardly existed at all.

It's time for *Indian* voices to tell *Indian* stories.

Now, I'm sure at least a few of you are wondering, "Why do I need to hear these stories? Why should I care about what Indian people think, and feel, and believe?"

I think the most eloquent answer I can give you comes from the namesake of this university, St. Thomas Aquinas. St. Thomas wrote that dialogue is the struggle to learn from each other. This struggle, he said, is like Jacob wrestling the angel—it leaves one wounded and blessed at the same time. Indian people know this struggle very well. The wounds we've suffered in our dialogue with non-Indians are well documented; I don't need to give you a laundry list of complaints.

We also know some of the blessings of this struggle. As *American* Indians, we live in two worlds—ours, and yours. In the 500 years since you first came to our lands, we have struggled to learn how to take the best of what your culture has to offer in arts, science, technology and more, and then weave them into the fabric of our traditional ways.

But for non-Indians, the struggle is new. Now that our people have begun to achieve success, now that we are in business and in the headlines, you are starting to wrestle with understanding us.

Your wounds from this struggle are fresh, and the pain might make it hard for you to see beyond them. But if you try, you'll begin to see the blessings as well—the blessings of what a deepened knowledge of Indian culture can bring to you. I'd like to share a few of those blessings with you today. Earlier I mentioned that there is a fundamental difference between the way Indians and non-Indians experience the world. This difference goes all the way back to the Bible, and Genesis.

In Genesis, the first book of the Old Testament, God creates man in his own image. Then God says, "Be fruitful, multiply, fill the earth and conquer it. Be masters of the fish of the sea, the birds of the heaven, and all living animals on the earth."

Masters. Conquer. Nothing, *nothing* could be further from the way Indian people view the world and our place in it. Here are the words of the great nineteenth century Chief Seattle:

> *You are part of the earth, and the earth is a part of you. You did not weave the web of life, you are merely a strand in it. Whatever you do to the web, you do to yourself.*

In our tradition, there is no mastery. There is no conquering. Instead, there is kinship among all creation—humans, animals, birds, plants, even rocks. We are all part of the sacred hoop of the world, and we must all live in harmony with each other if that hoop is to remain unbroken.

When you begin to see the world this way—through Indian eyes—you will begin to understand our view of land, and treaties, very differently. You will begin to understand that when we speak of Father Sun and Mother Earth, these are not new-age catchwords—they are very real terms of respect for very real beings.

And when you understand this, then you will understand that our fight for treaty rights is not just about hunting deer or catching fish. It is about teaching our children to honor Mother Earth and Father Sun. It is about teaching them to respectfully receive the gifts these loving parents offer us in return for the care we give them.

And it is about teaching this generation and the generations yet to come about their place in the web of life. Our culture and the fish, our values and the deer, the lessons we learn and the rice we harvest—everything is tied together. You can no more separate one from the other than you can divide a person's spirit from his body.

When you understand how we view the world and our place in it, it's easier to appreciate why our casinos are so important to us. The reason we defend our businesses so fiercely isn't because we want to have something that others don't. The reason is because these businesses allow us to *give back* to others—to our People, our communities, and the Creator.

I'd like to take a minute and mention just a few of the ways we've already given back:

- We've opened new schools, new health care facilities, and new community centers where our children get a better education, where our elders get better medical care, and where our families can gather to socialize and keep our traditions alive.

- We've built new ceremonial buildings, and new powwow and celebration grounds.

- We've renovated an elderly center, and plan to build three culturally sensitive assisted living facilities for our elders.

- We've created programs to teach and preserve our language and cultural traditions.

- We've created a Small Business Development Program to help Band members start their own businesses.

- We've created more than twenty-eight hundred jobs for Band members, people from other tribes, and non-Indians.

- We've spurred the development of more than one thousand jobs in other local businesses.

- We've generated more than fifty million dollars in federal taxes, and more than fifteen million dollars in state taxes through wages paid to employees.

- And we've given back more than two million dollars in charitable donations.

The list goes on and on. But rather than flood you with more numbers, I'll tell you a story that sums up how my people view business through the lens of our traditional values.

Last year, the Woodlands National Bank, which is owned and operated by the Mille Lacs Band, was approached by the city of Onamia and asked to forgive a mortgage on a building in the downtown area. The building had been abandoned and was an eyesore on Main Street. The city planned to renovate and sell the building, and return it to the tax rolls.

Although the Band would lose money by forgiving the mortgage, our business leaders could see the wisdom in improving the community. The opportunity to help our neighbors was an opportunity to strengthen the web of life. So we forgave the mortgage.

Now, I know this is not a decision everyone would agree with. Some people feel that in business, you have to look out for number one. But my people feel that in business—and in life—you have to look out for *every* one.

And this, I believe, is one of the blessings that Indian culture has to offer you and other non-Indians. We have a different perspective on so many things, from caring for the environment, to healing the body, mind and soul.

But if our culture disappears, if the Indian ways are swallowed up by the dominant American culture, no one will be able to learn from them. Not Indian children. Not your children. No one. All that knowledge, all that wisdom, will be lost forever.

The struggle of dialogue will be over. Yes, there will be no more wounds. But there will also be no more blessings.

There is still so much we have to learn from each other, and we have already wasted so much time. Our world grows smaller every day. And every day, more of our unsettling, surprising, wonderful differences vanish. And when that happens, part of each of us vanishes, too.

I'd like to end with one of my favorite stories. It's a funny little story about Indians and non-Indians, but its message is serious: You can see something differently if you are willing to learn from those around you.

This is the story: Years ago, white settlers came to this area and built the first European-style homes. When Indian People walked by these homes and saw see-through things in the walls, they looked through them to see what the strangers inside were doing. The settlers were shocked, but it makes sense when you think about it: Windows are made to be looked through from both sides.

Since then, my people have spent many years looking at the world through your window. I hope today I've given you a reason to look at it through ours.

Mii gwetch.

Source: M. Anderson, (1999, August 1). "Looking through Our Window: The Value of Indian Culture." *Vital Speeches of the Day,* 65:20, 633–34. Used with permission of Marge Anderson and *Vital Speeches of the Day.*

Assess Yourself

Delivery Self-Evaluation Form

How effective is your delivery? Give a qualitative evaluation for each of the following seven factors by placing a numerical score next to each of the factors that best represents your delivery. Select an event, a situation, a context, and a time when you recently gave a speech or presentation, and give yourself a self-analysis by using the following delivery criteria: 7 = Outstanding; 6 = Excellent; 5 = Very good; 4 = Average/good; 3 = Fair; 2 = Poor; 1 = Minimal ability; 0 = No ability demonstrated.

1. *Did you reveal commitment?* That is, did you act like you were in charge? Did you know what you were doing? Did you offer your listeners a strong "presence"? Did you begin your speech well? _____

2. *Did you select an audience-centered topic?* That is, were your listeners interested in your topic? Were they attentive to you? Was the topic significant? Was it relevant to your audience? _____

3. *Did you have a clear focus?* Was the focus of the speech clarified for your listeners? Did you stick to the focus? Was all speech material related to the focus? Did the focus relate to your listeners? _____

4. *Did you select strong supporting material?* Did your supporting material hold your listeners' attention? Did your supporting material relate directly to the focus of your speech? Did your supporting material appear significant, relevant, and recent (new)? _____

5. *Did you organize your speech well?* Was the organization of your speech clarified for your listeners? Were the transitions between your points clear? Did you follow the same organizational pattern throughout the entire speech? _____

6. *Did you use effective language?* Was your speech easily understood by your listeners? Were any necessary terms defined for your listeners? Was the language appropriate for your audience throughout your speech? _____

7. *Were your ideas presented effectively?* Were you poised and relaxed? Did you use strong facial expressions? Did you use strong gestures? Did you use your notes well? _____

Total Points: _____

 Go to the *Communicating Effectively* CD-ROM to see your results and learn how to evaluate your attitudes and feelings.

Chapter Review

Good delivery in a speech involves attentiveness—focusing and paying attention to giving the speech. It also involves achieving a conversational quality in your speech.

The four ways of delivering a speech are speaking impromptu, with very little preparation; speaking from a manuscript; speaking from memory; and speaking extemporaneously, from notes. For the beginner, extemporaneous speaking is the best type of delivery because it permits the speaker to depend on notes and still sound spontaneous.

All speakers should be aware of how they look and what they can do to look better. Speakers should concentrate on what they wear and on their body movement, eye contact, gestures, and posture so that they appear at their very best.

How the speaker sounds is also an important consideration in public speaking. Speakers should pay special attention to volume, pace, pitch and inflection, and enunciation. If they find they have a problem with one of these areas, they should work to improve it.

All speakers should consider using visual support for their speeches. Visuals help hold attention and clarify information. Common types of visual support include the actual object, models, chalkboards, posters, diagrams, charts, tables, graphs, computer-generated graphics, videos, and handouts. When using visual support, make sure that it can be easily seen and that it enhances the speech rather than overpowers it.

Practically everyone is nervous about giving a speech. Most people, however, can overcome their nervousness. Some ways of handling speech anxiety are to acknowledge that the anxiety exists, practice positive self-talk, anticipate difficult situations that could arise, practice the speech beforehand, focus on the audience while speaking, and reward yourself once it's over.

The final step in getting ready to deliver a speech is to practice it. Your practice should include rehearsing delivery of the speech, imagining an actual audience, checking the speech for clarity and organization, and checking its length.

Questions to Review

1. How can the speaker's attentiveness, immediacy, and directness contribute to a conversational tone?

2. Why is conversational tone important? At what point does it become too casual?

3. Of the different types of delivery (impromptu, manuscript, memory, and extemporaneous), with which are you most comfortable? Why? Which do you find the most difficult? Why?

4. If you were motivated to improve your speaking ability, which of the different types of delivery would you concentrate on, and why?

5. Weigh the value of how you look when it comes to giving speeches. How important is it? How about the importance of how you sound?

6. What visual support is best for your speech? Why? Would it simplify, clarify, and enhance the speech? In what ways?

7. What have you found to be the best methods for controlling nervousness when giving (or getting ready to give) a speech?

8. What method do you use for practicing speeches? Is it significantly different from the method suggested by the authors?

9. Can you sense the emotion Marge Anderson's listeners must have felt when they heard her speech, "Looking through Our Window"? Would you feel comfortable giving a speech similar to this one but defending your traditions, culture, or religion? Could you give such a speech with feeling? Why or why not?

mhhe.com/hybels

Go to the self-quizzes on the *Communicating Effectively* CD-ROM (side 2, track 10) and the Online Learning Center at mhhe.com/hybels7 to test your knowledge of the chapter concepts.

References

Aikman, D. (1998). *Great Souls: Six Who Changed the Century*. Nashville, TN: Word Publishing.

Argyle, M. (1991). Intercultural communication. In L. A. Samovar and R. E. Porter, eds. *Intercultural communication: A Reader*, 6th ed. Belmont, CA: Wadsworth.

Epstein, R. (2002, January/February). "Q&A: Ask Dr. E." *Psychology Today*, 78.

Goleman, D. (1998). *Working with emotional intelligence*. New York: Bantam Books.

Hahner, J. C., M. A. Sokoloff, & S. Salisch (1993). *Speaking clearly: Improving voice and diction*, 4th ed. New York: Random House.

(No author). (1998, Summer). "How Americans communicate." Roper Starch Worldwide, National Communication Association. Retrieved March 25, 2003, from www.natcom.org/research/Roper/how_americans_communicate.htm.

(No author). (2001). "How many online?" Computer-Scope Ltd., Scope Communications Group, Prospect House, 3 Prospect Road, Dublin 9, Ireland. Retrieved March 25, 2003, from http://www.nua.ie/surveys/how many online/.

Knapp, M. L., and J. A. Hall (1996). *Nonverbal communication in human interaction* 4th ed. Fort Worth, TX: Holt, Rinehart and Winston.

Knight, B. (2000). *Women who love books too much: Bibliophiles, bluestockings and prolific pens*. Berkeley, CA: Conari Press.

Manz, C. C., & H. P. Sims Jr. (2001). *The new superleadership: Leading others to lead themselves*. San Francisco, CA: Berrett-Koehler Publishers.

Motley, M. T. (1988, January). "Taking the terror out of talk." *Psychology Today*, 47.

Page, W. T. (*1985, Spring*). "Helping the nervous presenter: Research and prescriptions." *Journal of Business Communication* 22:2, 10.

Paul, A. M. (2001, March/April). "Self-help: Shattering the myths." *Psychology Today*, 62–68.

Schacter, D. L. (2001). *The seven sins of memory: How the mind forgets and remembers*. Boston: Houghton Mifflin Company.

Schmidt, B., and J. Winters (2002, January/February). "Fear not." *Psychology Today*, 46–54.

(No author). (2001, March 26). "Snakes scarier than public speaking." (USA TODAY Snapshots). *USA Today*, 1.

Woods, M. (1996, September 30). "A cure for stage fright." *The Blade* (Toledo, Ohio), 29.

Further Reading

Blair, G. M. (n.d.). "Presentation skills for emergent managers." VLSI Design, Department of Electrical Engineering, The University of Edinburgh. Retrieved March 25, 2003, from http://www.ee.ed.ac.uk/~gerard/Management/art1.html. Useful, basic information here on speech preparation, but more emphasis on delivery including a discussion of the eyes, the voice, expression, appearance, and stance. The section "The Technique of Speech" covers making an impression, repeat, repeat, repeat, draw a sign, draw a picture, jokes, plain speech, short and sweet, the narrative, rehearsal, and relaxation.

(No author). (2002). "*Delivery*." Presenters University, InFocus Corporation. Retrieved March 25, 2003, from http://www.presentersuniversity.com/courses/cs_delivery.cfm. Offers 28 articles on topics related to delivery skills such as presentation disasters, body language, hecklers, how women sabotage their effectiveness, dress, using technology, stage fright, vocal effectiveness, and much, much more. Advice comes from professionals in the field. There are also eleven items/articles on delivery applications.

(No author, no date). *"Designing effective oral presentations."* The Rice On Line Writing Lab (*Rice Owl*). Retrieved March 25, 2003, from http://www.rut.rice.edu/~riceowl/oralpres.html#top. Covers all aspects of speech preparation and presentation including information on conversational style and visual aids. In part 2, there is a full section on "Choose an Effective Delivery Style" and using "Techniques to Enhance Audience Comprehension," "Using Visual Aids," and "Practice, Practice, Practice." Useful, practical advice for beginners.

Feierman, A. (n.d.). "The art of communicating effectively." Presenting Solutions, San Clemente, CA 92673. Retrieved March 25, 2003, from http://www.presentingsolutions.com/effectivepresentations.asp. Feierman assembles the basic rules of good presentations: KISS (Keep it simple stupid), rehearsing, don't memorize, use your notes sparingly, dress for success, pace yourself, and presentation tools. This is a website full of practical advice that will serve as a refresher for most users.

Finkelstein, E. (2001). "How to develop charisma." PowerPointers. Retrieved March 25, 2003, from http://www.powerpointers.com/showarticle.asp?artcleid=375. Finkelstein breaks down charisma into its 12 individual qualities including self-confidence, enjoyment, liveliness and energy, knowledge, stage presence, avoidance of vocalized pauses, commitment to subject, expansiveness, strong rapport, positiveness, organization, and honesty.

Gottesman, D., and B. Mauro (2001). *Taking center stage: Masterful public speaking using acting skills you never knew you had.* New York: Berkley Publishing Group. The authors are directors of Center Stage Communications, a consulting firm specializing in applying acting techniques to the business world. They offer serious advice on such issues as defining and clarifying objectives as well as suggestions for overcoming stage fright. They claim that real actors find the truth in the situation and bring many different aspects of themselves to

each role and then live their role as honestly as they can within the fictional parameters of the play. Contains numerous exercises.

Humes, J. C. (2002). *Speak like Churchill, stand like Lincoln: 21 practical secrets of history's greatest speakers.* Rocklin, CA: Prima Publishing. Humes attempts to unlock the secrets of history's greatest speakers. As an author, historian, world-renowned speaker, and the speechwriter for five American presidents, he reveals some of the tricks famous speakers have used to speak, persuade, and win listeners to their side.

Jacobi, J., and W. G. Parrett (2000). *How to say it: With your voice.* Englewood Cliffs, NJ: Prentice Hall Press. The authors use a practical, systematic approach to improving your voice. Through self-tests, skill-building exercises, and sample speeches, they help readers pinpoint and overcome common problems such as sloppy pronunciation, a rapid-fire pace, childlike lilt, nasal whine, monotonous tone, and off-putting accents. Their information on building vocal strength and variety for holding listener interest is especially valuable. This is a useful, practical, applied book full of suggestions.

Laskowski, L., ed. (2001). *10 days to more confident public speaking.* New York: Warner Books. This is basically a book on delivery. There is information on overcoming nervousness, discovering your own natural style, establishing immediate rapport with your audience, practicing new conversational techniques, blending humor and anecdotes into your talks, and using special techniques to memorize your speech. There is a section, too, on writing a speech that builds to an unforgettable conclusion. If you want to be shown how to be your own laid back, comfortable, unique self in front of an audience, this book will help.

Tham, M. (2002, April 22). "Presentation skills." Chemical and Process Engineering, University of Newcastle Upon Tyne, United Kingdom. Retrieved March 25, 2003, from http://lorien.ncl.ac.uk/ming/dept/tips/present/present.htm. Tham offers great links to websites covering the topics "Homegrown Advice and Tips," "General Advice, Tips, and Guidelines," "Public Speaking," and "Overcoming Fear and Shyness." The links are interesting and worthwhile.

Chapter 16

The Informative Speech

Objectives

After reading this chapter, you should be able to:
- Get the attention of listeners.
- Increase listener understanding.
- Aid listener retention.
- Use specific strategies for defining ideas in informative speeches.
- Use specific strategies for describing ideas in informative speeches.
- Use specific strategies for explaining ideas in informative speeches.

Key Terms and Concepts

 Use the Communicating Effectively CD-ROM and Online Learning Center at mhhe.com/hybels7 to further your understanding of the following terms.

Anecdote 588	Describe 580	Informative speech 573
Color 581	Etymology 577	Rhetorical questions 592
Comparison 579	Example 578	Shape 581
Composition 582	Explaining 584	Size 581
Contrast 579	Fit 582	Weight 581
Definition 576	Function 580	

LENA AJOUZ BEGAN HER INTEREST IN GRAPHIC ART IN A class in high school as a result of an excellent teacher who recognized and nurtured her talent. She capitalized on her interest when her mother, a real-estate agent, upgraded her own computer and gave Lena her old one equipped with a Pentium 4 processor, 2.40 gigahertz-M, 256 DDR SDRAM memory, 80GB 7200RPM Hard Drive, with a 64MB NVIDIA GeForce2 MX400, AGP graphics accelerator video card. Long ago, Lena had established her own Web page, and she upgraded her site and regularly changed information, dates, and links to other sites. Because link addresses tend to change, she checked them often for linkrot—when a link expires and no longer connects one to the appropriate Web page. Once Lena was comfortable setting up her own website, she set them up for her friends. When it came time for her informative speech, she talked about the process of creating Web pages. Because of how integral the World Wide Web has become in everyone's life, she called her speech, "You Can't Spit Without Hitting a URL."

Before Bruce McNee decided to go back to school, he was involved in two marriages that ended in divorce. The second marriage was shorter than the first. Now that he felt far enough away from the experiences, he could look at and talk about them objectively. Although he was aware that the statistic that half of American marriages are doomed to failure is, as one pollster (Louis Harris) labeled it, "one of the most specious pieces of statistical nonsense ever perpetuated in modern times" (Petersen, 1999), Bruce knew that the topic would interest the class because everybody wants a successful marriage. His speech, "Until Death Do Us Part," was based on his own experience, of course, but Bruce also talked to two divorce lawyers, consulted a number of online statistical sources for current information and statistics, and read newspaper reporter Stephanie Staal's book *The Love They Lost: Living with the Legacy of Our Parents' Divorce* (Dell, 2000). Staal's parents divorced when she was 13, and in this book she shares the stories of 120 "Generation Ex" adults whose parents divorced. Another book Bruce heard about through an Internet online divorce-support chat group: Edward Baiamonte and Ted Baiamonte's *The 91% Factor: Why Women Initiate 91% of Divorce, End Most Relationships, and What Can Be Done About It,* 3rd ed. (American Political Press, 1999), which discussed 30 couples with severe relationship problems. He felt he had concrete information to share with his classmates.

Lena and Bruce have something in common: They are gathering information. Like the majority of people in the United States, much of what they do is concerned with producing, processing, and distributing information. As a matter of fact, there is more information thrown at us each day than we can ever hope to absorb. You might wonder why you should even want to contribute to the overload?

The single, clear answer is this: The purpose of an informative speech is to provide listeners with information that will help them make decisions as individuals and as citizens. The need for high-quality information demands skill in our ability to produce and deliver it. Although some of this information is delivered in written form, much of it is oral: The teacher before the class, the radio or television reporter broadcasting to an audience, the professional sharing ideas with colleagues, the employer explaining policies to employees, the politician clarifying issues or defining approaches to problems—all of them need oral skills to convey information.

The **informative speech**—one that defines, clarifies, instructs, and explains—is a common phenomenon in our society. If we are going to prosper in the information society, the ability to give an informative speech is a necessary skill. The need to increase understanding is a universal one.

You are likely to encounter informative speeches in a variety of contexts. You're probably familiar with the *lecture,* which is simply an informative talk given before a class audience. One is unlikely to escape college or university without experiencing a number of lectures, since the lecture remains the most common form of class presentation. The next is a *lecture/demonstration,* an informative talk that shows listeners how to do something or how something works. Teachers show how to prepare an assignment; sales representatives show how their products work; supervisors show employees how to do their jobs. The last is an *explanation* of ideas or policies. Meredith Kim's speech, "Time Management Strategies," which appears at the end of this chapter, is an example of a speech of explanation. Most of the examples in this chapter, too, come from speeches of explanation.

■ GOALS OF AN INFORMATIVE SPEAKER

With so much information available, it's surprising that listeners don't buckle under from information overload. When listeners are so swamped with information, we face a serious problem as speakers. We have to ask ourselves, "How can I, as an informative speaker, make my information stand out?"

Getting Attention

The first goal of a speaker is to get the attention of audience members. In most public-speaking situations there are many distractions: People come in late; the air-conditioner fan turns on and off; a fly buzzes around the room; the microphone gives off feedback.

Once you have attention, there is no assurance that you will keep it. Attention spans are short. You have probably noticed that as you listen to a speech or lecture, your attention wanders—even when you are interested in the message. Since this pattern of wandering attention is characteristic of most listeners, as a speaker you have to work to get attention back again.

The best way to get and keep attention is to create in your audience a strong desire to listen to your material. Ask yourself whether your material is relevant. Does it apply to the people in your audience? If it doesn't, how can it be adapted to them?

If the audience perceives the information as new, it is more likely to pay attention. "New" doesn't necessarily mean a subject no one has ever heard about—it might be a matter of a new perspective or a new angle. Certain topics are going to provoke a "ho-hum" reaction from the audience. You don't want your audience to think "Not another speech about jogging" (or dieting and nutrition, or getting organized). When Richard Lamm (1998), from the Center for Public Policy and Contemporary Issues at the University of Denver, was asked to deliver an address to the 1998 World Future Society, he chose a title that might—just from hearing it—put many listeners to sleep: "Unexamined Assumptions: Destiny, Political Institutions, Democracy, and Population." So he planned an introduction that ran counter to both his title and his topic, one that he knew would get the attention of his audience. He began:

> A priest was riding in a subway when a man staggered toward him, smelling like a brewery, with lipstick on his collar. He sat in the seat right next to the priest and started reading the newspaper. After a few minutes, the man turned to the priest and asked "Excuse me, Father, what causes arthritis?"
>
> The priest, tired of smelling the liquor and saddened by the lifestyle, said roughly "Loose living, drink, dissipation, contempt for your fellow man and being with cheap and wicked women!"
>
> "That's amazing," said the drunk and returned to his newspaper. A while later, the priest, feeling a bit guilty, turned to the man and asked nicely, "How long have you had arthritis?"
>
> "Oh," said the man, "I don't have arthritis, I was just reading that the Pope did."
>
> The parable, of course, is a lesson on assumptions. (p. 712)

The goal of an informative speech is to give listeners new or in-depth information on a subject.

Although audience members knew the name of the guest speaker, knew his credentials, and knew the title of his speech, on the basis of all that information most of them would never have expected his speech to begin with a joke that involved a drunk, a priest, and the pope.

Increasing Understanding

Since the goal of an informative speech is to give the audience new or in-depth information on a subject, it is particularly important that a speaker put together a speech that audience members will understand. Several things will help understanding: language choice, organization, and illustrations and examples.

Language Choice

In our highly technological world, many of us speak a specialized language that is understood only by people in the same field. Because we are so accustomed to this language, we often don't realize that other people don't know what we are talking about. If you are giving a speech that uses technical or specialized vocabulary, you must take the time to define your terms, or consider whether you can avoid technical terms altogether.

Organization

Organization not only helps you put your speech together but also helps listeners understand what you are talking about. A good organizational pattern will show how ideas relate to one another and will help listeners move from one idea to another. You probably know that as a listener your attention will wander if the speaker is rambling or you have trouble finding the main points of the speech.

Illustrations and Examples

Probably the greatest key to understanding is an ample supply of illustrations and examples. If you are going to explain a principle that might be unfamiliar to your audience, use an example to show what it is or how it works. For example, a student who was explaining three basic body types held up pictures to illustrate each type. When he held up a picture of a thin, lightly muscled person, the meaning of the term *ectomorph* was immediately clear.

Helping Retention

An important goal of informative speaking is to have your listeners remember what you said once the speech is over. Listeners are more likely to remember speeches in which they feel some kind of emotional involvement. This involvement might range from sympathy when they hear about an adult who can't read, to high personal interest in a speech about how to get a better job. For the speaker, then, the goal is to involve listeners by speaking about subjects that they can identify with or that have an impact on their lives.

When you want people to remember certain points, it is useful to give these points special emphasis. Sometimes this can be done with verbal cues: "This is my most important point" or "If you remember only one thing I said today, remember this." Sometimes you can use a cue after a point: "Now let me show you how important what I just said can be to you." A point can be emphasized, too, by repeating it, by changing your rate of speech, or by pausing just before you say it (Ehrensberger, 1945).

■ STRATEGIES FOR INFORMATIVE SPEECHES

View clip #7, an excerpt from an informative student speech, "Indian Weddings, Preeti Vilku."

There are different types of strategies for presenting material in informative speeches. Each type requires a special skill. Sometimes all of these types can be found in a single speech; usually at least two will be used.

Defining

A **definition**—an explanation of the meaning of a word or phrase—can often make a critical difference in whether your audience understands your speech. Sometimes a dictionary definition is sufficient; other times you must expand on it by using your own words or those of others. When Marci Kaplan developed her speech, "Get the knowledge, use the power, change your world," she wanted to explain to her class the power of paradox—a statement, doctrine, or expression that is seemingly absurd or contradictory to common notions, according to the dictionary. Rather than use the dictionary definition, she did it this way:

When I came to college, I was just like many of you. I had developed an idea from both my high-school experiences, and from my parents, exactly what I wanted to do here: I wanted to be a business major, go on and get an MBA, graduate, and make big bucks! I had a narrow vision. But as I

Choices of strategies for presenting material in informative speeches depend on the unique combination of speaker, topic, audience, and situation.

took required courses, as I listened to my friends struggling with decisions about what to major in, and as I began to learn about things I had never dreamed about before college, I discovered something unusual, something that was for me unique, something that I want to share with you. It is this: To embrace the power of paradox—wholeheartedly and unreservedly! It is to be single-minded about nothing and open to everything.

The power of paradox is the power of and. *From my limited experience here at college talking to other students—and from listening to both my brothers and my parents talk about their college experiences—students and former students often see either/or when they should be searching for an* and. *Too often, the choices are posed as this college or that one, this major or that one, this set of requirements or that set of requirements. But, do you know what? A truly resilient student shouldn't be all of one thing; he or she shouldn't even be most of one thing. A truly resilient student must be all of many things. All efficiency and all innovation. All optimization and all experimentation. All discipline and all passion. All evolution and all revolution. All involved and all motivated.*

Definition can also go beyond explaining words or phrases. Four useful ways to define concepts in a speech are by etymology, example, comparison, and function.

Etymology

Etymology, the study of the origin and development of words, can be used as a basis for definition. For example, when discussing romantic love and the intense feelings that occur, one speaker pointed out that the word *ecstasy,* which is a common label for emotions during the time of romantic love, is derived from a Greek word meaning "deranged"—a state beyond all reason and self-control (Knapp & Vangelisti, 1996). She went on to show that

On the Web

There are numerous websites where information on different types of supporting material for speeches are explained. Three of those we like the best are:

1. L. Corder, "Stop Bellyaching! It's Only a Presentation: 367 Time-Tested Suggestions for Adding Impact and Excitement to Your Presentation." 2001, Lloyd Corder, Ph.D. Retrieved March 26, 2003, from http:// www.420worldwide.net/book2/ private/ Contents.htm.

Corder lists twelve ways to gain audience attention, four types of supporting material, four rules to follow when using examples, three rules to follow when using analogies, seven questions to ask when using statistics, five rules to follow when using testimony, and much, much more.

2. R. St. John, "The Public Speakers' Page: Supporting the Speech, The Public Speakers' Resources, Kaleo Kumu, 1998. Retrieved March 26, 2003, from http://mauicc/hawaii/edu/staff/stjohn/publicspeakers/support.html.

St. John begins with a definition, then offers general guidelines for supporting materials and then specific guidelines for supporting materials.

3. (No author), "Supporting Your Points," The Virtual Presentation Assistant, Communication Studies Department, University of Kansas, (n.d.). Retrieved March 26, 2003, from http://www.ku.edu/cwis/units/coms2/vpa/vpa5.htm.

This website offers guidelines and links to help users create a credible and well-supported speech. This site also provides links to speeches that contain good examples of support.

the word *deranged* accurately describes the state of mind that exists early in romantic relationships. The *Oxford English Dictionary* is the best source for word *etymologies*.

Dr. Phillip Tompkins, emeritus professor of communication and comparative literature at the University of Colorado, Boulder, delivered his speech, "Thoughts on Time: Give of Yourself Now," to the 50th reunion of the Class of 1951, and in his speech referred to the atomic clock in Boulder at the National Institute of Standards there. Following Tompkins' comment about seeing a play in which an actor portrayed a scientist responsible for the care and feeding of this clock, whose big line in the play is "Time is God's way of making sure everything doesn't happen at once," Tompkins uses etymology to define *time*:

> Yes, that ticking notion of time isn't completely adequate. The Ancient Greeks called it the Chronos, the eternal or ongoing time, and from it we get the word chronological. They contrasted Chronos with Kairos, the opportunity or propitious moment. In this morning's Wichita Eagle the Religion editor, Tom Schaeffer, had a column about Kairos. He quotes a theologian at the University of Chicago, William Schweikert, as saying our plight since 9/11/01 is that we are living amid a kind of rupture in human time (p. 183).

Example

An **example** is something that is used to illustrate a point. When using an example, a speaker often either points to an actual thing or points out something verbally. In this excerpt, Dennis Koslowski (2001), CEO of Tyco International, points out to his listeners that the first thing they will do after graduating will not be the last or only thing they ever do:

> I talk to a lot of young people—including my own daughters—who are in law and business school. On top of the natural anxiety about going out in the world, finding a job, making their way, I'm hearing something that I think is new. It's the fear that one wrong step will send you veering off "the career path"—whatever that is—on a one-way trip to nowhere. Please—don't fall for it. The first thing you do after you graduate will be just that, the first thing. After that will come the second thing. And then the third. Take me for an example. My first job out of college was as an airplane pilot. Since then, including over the past 25 years at Tyco, I have worked for three corporations and held 12 different jobs at Tyco. And today I'm the Chairman and CEO (p. 595).

Comparison and Contrast

Comparisons point out the similarities between two or more things. When Dwight Cushenberry, who grew up in a rural farming community, gave his class speech, "Auctions, 24/7," he not only had numerous experiences with farm auctions and found them exciting, but in his speech, he could compare those with the excitement and thrill of using eBay:

> Most people wouldn't think an old farm boy like me would know very much about computers, but what you don't know is that my father and older brother run a huge farm operation, and they have been using computers for more than a dozen years to manage the entire operation. I was introduced to computers when I was very young, and I've not just used them for playing games, but for getting information, doing some farm-related research on the current price of products, and for writing papers, too.
>
> But eBay—talk about auctions!—eBay has brought the excitement of participating in an auction, to millions. It revved up the old auction spirit in me as well. Just like an old farm auction, you're likely to find just about anything on eBay; just like a farm auction, too, when you use eBay you are part of a community of members. And just like an old farm auction, you are likely to get carried away with the excitement and overpay for something. For me, eBay has been a godsend because it captures all the excitement of an old farm auction, but the real thrill is that you can enjoy the excitement 24/7.

Contrasts point out the differences between two or more things. In her class speech, "Girls Get a Grip," Lenore Ashley used contrast when she talked about the way males and females express their anger:

> Now, you all know how guys express their anger because first, it's obvious, and second, it's consistent. When that bubbling cauldron of hormone-laden emotion explodes, guys will express their anger physically. They'll shove someone's face into a toilet, or they'll push them up against a car. The reason you don't always see females express their anger

Working Together

For each of the following ideas, decide which kinds of definitions would work in a speech—etymology, function, example, or comparison—and have each member of the group offer an example of each one.

an incomparable experience	great instructor
awesome dreams	recession
ethical actions	unbeatable bargain
free speech	war
independence	well done

is because it's more subtle. That doesn't mean it's less effective, and if you're ever on the receiving end of a female's anger, you already know how effective it can be. Females express their anger in nonphysical, indirect, covert forms. And they have many weapons. I not only know the weapons, but I have used each of them at some time: backbiting, exclusion, rumors, name-calling, and manipulation. I know it's ugly; I now know better, but I have learned from the very best, and all I can do now is regret my actions.

Function

With certain topics it's useful to define by **function**—showing how a thing performs or how it can be used. Speakers may stress an object's usefulness, advantages, benefits, convenience, or service. Eugene Finerman (1996), a satirist and professional speechwriter, began his speech on humor, "Humor and Speeches: A Stand-Up History," by defining the function of humor:

A plumber, a jockey and a rabbi walk into a pet store. . . What a cheap trick to get your attention, but that is the charm—and the power—of humor. Humor can engage, entice, coax and persuade. It can ridicule, vilify, agitate and incite. Humor can warm an audience or inflame it. The effective speaker and the astute speechwriter know the value of and place for humor. It is a natural means of communication, and it has served the public speaker for as long as there have been speeches (p. 313).

Describing

To **describe** is to provide a mental image of something experienced, such as a scene, a person, or a sensation. Many times your audience will be able to visualize what you are talking about if you create a picture for them. Here, Anali Abora, a typical undergraduate student, offered a description with which most of his listeners could identify:

I have a confession to make: I stayed up most of the night last night putting the finishing touches on this speech. For me, that isn't that unusual. In general, I get to bed well after midnight or one a.m., and I am up by five or six A.M. I stay up too late, and I wake up unrefreshed. There is no doubt my sleeplessness interferes with not just the amount but with the quality of the work I get done. I know that making decisions and solving problems is more difficult, too, when I'm sleepy. I drive while drowsy, and during this past year I have fallen asleep while driving at least twice. Most of you can probably both identify and empathize with my sleep deprivation. After all, what choice do we have?

Size or Quantity

Size is the measurement or extent of a thing when compared with some standard. Notice how Kellie, a student, described a spider's web in her speech:

I didn't notice it at first because of the dark, but when I saw it against the outside house light, I stood in awe of its magnitude, intricate structure, and beauty. Not only did it stretch from the ground to the lower limbs of one tree, close to six feet off the ground, but several dew-covered fibers—only one-millionth of an inch in diameter each— secured the hundreds of other radiating and evenly spaced fibers between trees as well. This spider's strong and elastic web silk—its stretched strength second only to that of fused quartz—was a geometric orb the size of the front door of our house with the spider sitting motionless in the central hub.

Shape

Shape is the outward form, configuration, or contour of a thing. In a speech on insect control in gardening, one student used the following description of a cabbage worm:

It looks like a brilliant yellow-green caterpillar that begins at a length of an inch or so with about the circumference of your little finger. It has antennae coming from its head with numerous short pudgy feet. As it chomps away at garden cabbage throughout the summer, it extends its length from two to three inches, and it grows in circumference to about the size of the large part of your thumb.

Weight

Weight is the heaviness of a mass, object, or thing. Since people have a hard time visualizing large numbers, speakers need to relate them to something from the listeners' own experience. One speaker was trying to impress her listeners with how much a million was. She said that a class in Des Moines, Iowa, collected 1 million bottle caps. How much did they weigh? According to the speaker, these caps weighed 21½ tons: "They were put into 200 bags and the bags were so heavy it required a moving van to take them away."

Color

Color is a visual attribute of bodies or substances distinct from their spatial characteristics. It is an obvious component of description and serves quickly to call up mental pictures. Here, Aaron Roberts uses the importance of color in website design in his speech "Color My Web:"

> *What do you first think about when you see the color red? How about blue? And yellow? Which of these colors best represents you—who you are? How many of you have websites? Do you realize that your website is the window through which the world can catch its first glimpse of you? Because the Web is for the world, you must take the time and effort to choose colors that best present you to the world. Look at this picture [shows picture to class]—what does this picture convey to you? Now, look at this one? Is there a difference? What is the difference? Do you see the difference color can make?*

Composition

Composition, a description of the makeup of a thing, can be a useful part of description. Notice here how Jeremiah Stamler, in a speech called "Internet Snake Oil," discussed what the composition of a good website is—especially important if you happen to be surfing the Internet for medical sites for information about treatment and rehabilitation:

> *When my roommate came down with mononucleosis, we went right to the Web, but what we discovered was that any fool—or charlatan—with a telephone, modem, and computer can create decent-looking web-sites. Do you know what the composition of a good website is? Well, no site is perfect, but the best ones share five important qualities. First, they are upfront about who they are and what their mission is. Second, the advertising on reputable websites is always clearly separated from the editorial content. Third, both the original source of the information and the date it was posted or reviewed are marked. Fourth, online experts are identified by name, credentials, and institution. And, fifth, confidentiality is treated as more than a technicality. Be aware, too, that some of the most reliable sites are sponsored by federal health agencies. This is just helpful information to know. These five ingredients are what make up a good website.*

Fit

Fit occurs when you describe something by the way parts belong together or by the relationship among parts. A mental picture emerges when listeners can fit all the parts into a proper relationship.

Say you are speaking about the campus newspaper and you want to explain how all the parts fit together. You talk about the responsibilities of the editor and then of the jobs of the features, news, and sports editors and what their relationship is to the editor. Next you talk about the roles of the business manager and advertising department and the relationship these people have to the editor. If you discuss how all these people fit into the overall structure, your audience will have a good idea of how the newspaper works.

Cat O'Shaughnessy, in her speech on "Academic Fraud," talked about the perfect fit between the erosion of conscience at every level of education, and the availability and use of new technology that has opened new avenues to cheat. It is students' boldness in using these new avenues that created O'Shaughnessy's desire to speak on this issue:

Just since I have been in college—and my history is brief—I have heard of students on this campus tampering electronically with grade records, transmitting quiz answers via both pager and cell phone, and the lifting of term papers from hundreds of available websites. We're all familiar with the student who got caught using the video camera hidden in his tie. He broadcast questions to an outside ringer who then called the answers into a silent pager. It's not that I don't understand the pressures to excel we get from both hard-driving peers and parents, and it's not that I don't understand the overload of work we suffer from. But it's this perfect fit between what technology now offers and the pressures we are under that makes cheating not only easy to justify, but hard to resist.

On the Web

A cliché is a phrase, metaphor, or expression that has been worn out by overuse. Often, as we convey information to others, we fall into using clichés because we are familiar with them, because we don't try to think of other alternatives, or simply because it is the best way we can think of to convey an idea. At the Weber State University online writing center, they begin their handout, "Clichés," saying "Clichés are the old coins of language: phrases that once made a striking impression but have since been rubbed smooth by repeated handling" (p. 1).

The Weber State University handout on "Clichés" notes that "The worst offense you can be guilty of is to use cliches in your writing. One cliche," the handout continues, "can make your artistic efforts all seem without value" (p. 2). The same can occur in speeches, of course, so you need to be aware of them. One site said "he/she should avoid them 'like the plague,' for they bespeak a mind that took the easy way out" (*Cliches*, 2000).

Fortunately, the Internet offers numerous websites (Google, 175,000, 3/26/03) where you can not only learn about clichés, but where you can check out the most common clichés as well. Here are some:

1. S. M. Friedman, (2000, December 11). "Cliche Finder." Retrieved March 26, 2003, from http://www.westegg.com/cliche/.

2. (No author). (2003). "Cliches," About, Inc. Retrieved March 26, 2003, from http://quotations.about.com/cs/cliches/.

3. (No author). (2002, June 25). "ClicheSite.com." DigitalCLICK, Inc. Retrieved March 26, 2003, from http://www.clichesite.com/index.asp.

4. J. M. Samuelson. (2002, June 18). "Cliches." Professor of English, Kingwood College. Retrieved March 26, 2003, from http://kcweb/nhm ccd.edu/employee/jsamuels/cliches.htm.

(No author). (n.d.). "Cliches." Weber State University Writing Center, Retrieved March 26, 2003, from http://wsuonline.weber.edu/wrh/cliches.htm.

Explaining

Almost everything that we know how to do was explained to us at one time or another. We were not born knowing how to do such things as cook or play volleyball—someone told us how to do them. Many of the questions we ask are requests for explanations. What does this concept mean? How does this work? How do I get there? **Explaining,** then, is the process of making something clear.

The most common form of explaining occurs when you teach someone to do something. Usually this is a matter of breaking the process down into steps. For example, in a speech on how to make a toasted cheese sandwich with an iron, the speaker used the following steps:

1. Gather what you need: bread, cheese, margarine, aluminum foil, and an iron.
2. Heat the iron to medium-high.
3. Make a sandwich from the cheese and bread. Butter both sides of the bread on the outside.
4. Wrap the sandwich in aluminum foil.
5. Place the iron on each side for about 20 seconds. (Check to see if you need more time.)

Using Numbers

Few people can visualize large quantities, such as millions or billions. Therefore, it's useful if these figures are put into some kind of relationship. *Spider-Man* (the movie) cost about $120 million to make and $50 million to market, and made more than $115 million in its first weekend—by far the most any film ever made in a weekend (and a nonholiday one at that). It was expected to have earned $225 million by its second weekend, making Sony pictures a cool $55 million by its second week of wide release (Stein, 2002). Grossing more than $800 million worldwide, and with *Spider-Man II* in 2004, it is one of the most successful movie franchises in history. Credited for its success was a simple marketing campaign—billboards featuring a masked red-and-blue character and the release date. The real genius was knowing what people cared about: the Date.

To capture the kind of numbers the first *Spider-Man* achieved, you have to be just as careful in planning as you would for a speech. You have to appeal to all segments of your potential audience, and the movie, being half action and half romance, did just that. It split its time between these two themes, and by doing that evenly nailed what Hollywood calls all four demographic quadrants: male, female, under 25, and 25 and over. The opening Saturday night broke down like this: 54 percent male, 46 percent female, 52 percent 25 and over, 48 percent under 25. If you know who your target audience is, it makes it easier to plan a product that appeals exactly to that demographic (Stein, 2002, p. 3).

One student speaker who wanted to impress her listeners about the 800 million pounds of peanut butter eaten each year in the United States said, "That is enough to coat all the floors and walls of the entire Grand Canyon."

The *CBS Evening News* reported that the planet Pluto is so dim that "it is like seeing a candle from 100 miles." Tim, a major in astronomy, wanted to show his audience the power of interstellar lenses. He said, "Interstellar lenses were employed to resolve a pulsar to less than one-millionth of an arc second." He knew his listeners had no idea of the meaning of "one-millionth of an arc second," so he said, "That is the equivalent of looking west from New York and spotting an amoeba in Los Angeles."

When you work with numbers, here are some simple rules to follow:

- If numbers are unusual or surprising, explain why. Usually the best way to do this is to quote an expert.
- Round off large numbers.
- If you have a lot of numbers, try to convert them to percentages.
- Look for opportunities to replace numbers with words. For example, it's easier to understand "Over half the people said. . . ." or "A majority believed. . . ." than "Over 370 people said. . . ."
- Try to relate numbers to something familiar. For example, say, "The number of people killed in the earthquake was equal to the entire student body of this college."
- If possible, try to compare numbers. For example, "Forty-five percent of the seniors but only 3 percent of the first-year students believed . . . ."

Look for trends, especially from one year to another: "In 1990, the average home had the TV on six hours and 53 minutes a day. Just 10 years later, by the year 2000, the TV was on for seven hours and 35 minutes—an increase of close to 45 minutes in ten years—or a nine percent increase" (Trends. . . ., 2002)

Use graphs and other visual aids to make numbers more concrete.

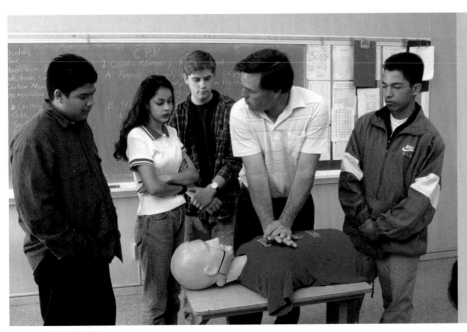

Whether you are using numbers, connecting the known with the unknown, or repeating and reinforcing ideas, when you are explaining, your main goal is making something clear.

Connecting the Known with the Unknown

When listeners are unfamiliar with a subject, a speaker can help them understand it by connecting the new idea to something they already know. For example, when a British student wanted to explain the game of cricket to her American classmates, she started by listing the ways that cricket was similar to baseball. Another student, explaining how people always seem to be looking for new ways to communicate (the known), described the Teledesic proposal (the unknown). This is the proposal by Teledesic Corporation, owned by Craig McCaw and William Gates, to develop a global communications network made up of 840 satellites that would transport information ranging from ordinary telephone calls to high-resolution computerized medical images and two-way videoconferences to and from any spot on the planet.

Repeating and Reinforcing Ideas

Repetition in a speech is important because it helps listeners remember key points. However, if it is overdone, speakers run the risk of boring listeners. Let's look at a format that will enable you to spread out the repetition and reinforcement in a speech.

In your introduction, tell your listeners *what you plan to tell them* in the body of your speech. In the introduction to her speech, "Becoming a Smart Buyer," Heather listed her main points: "Today I want to talk about the four steps to becoming a smart buyer. These steps are find out price, get a receipt, examine service and repair, and read contracts carefully."

In the body of your speech, tell your listeners *your full message* (explain your points). In Bishetta's speech, she explained each of her steps:

> *The first step in dealing with difficult bosses is to understand them. To find out what makes them tick will allow you to speak their language.*
>
> *The second step is to reveal loyalty. Most bosses will give you the freedom to solve problems in your own way as long as they are convinced of your loyalty.*
>
> *The third step in dealing with difficult bosses is to establish strong communication channels. With good rapport, problems can be discussed openly and directly, facts and discoveries can be given, and information that might prove valuable can be shared.*

In your conclusion, tell your listeners *what you told them* in the body of the speech. This is the place to summarize your main ideas. Bishetta concluded her speech by saying:

> *Now you can see how you can go about dealing with difficult bosses. You need to understand them, show loyalty, and establish strong communication channels.*

■ AROUSING INTEREST IN YOUR TOPIC

So many things compete for each listener's attention that even though you might get attention at first, it is not always possible to keep it. Speakers

Consider This

In their book, *Last Night a DJ Saved My Life*, Bill Brewster and Frank Broughton (2000), discuss "The Art of Djing." They claim that when you are dancing to a single record, you appreciate the work of a producer and some musicians. But when you dance to a set of records that have been joined together, you're enjoying the talents of a DJ. As you read this excerpt, think about how similar the work of a talented DJ is to an effective public speaker who has joined together disparate pieces of information.

Imagine a grand tapestry made by stitching together pieces of the finest handmade cloth. Seen up close its beauty comes from the skill of the weavers and embroiderers who made the different fabrics, but seen from a distance it has a beauty of a different scale, a more imposing grandeur that comes from the overall pattern or design. Like the maker of such a tapestry, the DJ is an artist of a different order. The DJ is a musical editor, a metamusician, he makes music out of other music.

Questions

1. Isn't the job of an effective public speaker to stitch all the various speech components together so that when presented as a whole, its imposing grandeur comes from the overall pattern or design?

2. What are the similarities and differences between the effective public speaker and the DJ as an artist?

3. Do quality ingredients necessarily guarantee a quality final product? Why or why not?

Source: B. Brewster and F. Broughton, *Last Night a DJ Saved My Life: The History of the Disc Jockey*. (New York: Grove Press (Grove Atlantic, Inc.), 2000), p. 13.

often give special attention to their introduction so that it reaches out and grasps audience attention. The need, however, is to sustain it throughout the speech. You probably have had the experience of paying attention to a speaker when he or she gets up to speak and then half listening to him or her once the body of the speech began as you wondered what was for lunch, mentally prepared a grocery list, or thought about your schedule for the rest of the day. What you can do, as a speaker, to compete with all these distractions is the subject of this section. Besides arousing curiosity, presenting anecdotes, building anticipation, and building suspense, there are numerous other techniques, too, for holding attention throughout the speech. One of the keys is to think specifically about holding listener attention at every point during speech preparation.

Arouse Curiosity

One way to make sure that you will be listened to is to create a desire to learn about your subject by stimulating your listeners' curiosity. For example, one speaker began her speech with "Have you ever wondered why you get so tired?" Another began his speech with "Do you know how to stop procrastinating?" Another stated "Before this speech is over, I plan to share with you a message that has the potential of changing your life forever."

In her speech "Cons, Scams, and Frauds," Vanessa Monroe began her speech with the question:

> *Who says there are no good jobs out there? Have you checked your e-mail in-box today? I get at least a half dozen job offers every day: Work from home! Start right away! Change your life! One began like this, "One man I know earns between $6,520 to $10,260 every single month, and you can too." Everybody knows that most junk e-mail—spam—is phony. But did you know that much of it is sent to you by con artists? These are real-life bad guys who are after your money. The Internet Fraud Complaint Center (IFCC) estimated that as of 2001, there were over 56,000 victims who suffered cumulative losses in excess of $117 million ("New report shows..." [2002]). What is it that makes these advertisements successful? What I discovered is that some of the very same techniques these advertisers use to be successful are exactly the same techniques which—if we put them to use—would make us successful public speakers! Yes, I'm talking about the advertising techniques of the cons, scams, and frauds; they are not that unusual, and they are incredibly successful!*

Present Anecdotes

An **anecdote** is a short, interesting story based on your own or someone else's experience. Although some speakers use them in their introductions, anecdotes are particularly useful in the body of your speech because they can get back audience attention if it is wandering.

Nicole Gant, a mother who home-schooled both a daughter and a son before returning to school herself, used this anecdote in her speech to her class:

> *The Internet changed everything for home-schooling parents. For me, it was a Godsend. I wanted the best possible curriculum at the least possible cost, and I found the Internet just brimming with sophisticated course material. The Internet not only kept me, but both my children as well, connected to the rest of the world—to libraries, research institutes, and other students and families with similar interests. My kids dissected virtual frogs, worked through a set of college-level genetics problems offered by M.I.T., checked in on a vocabulary-building site that sprinkled their dialogue with SAT–worthy words, and researched the life of Georg Philipp Telemann, who composed the baroque trio that my son, a flutist, plays with friends in an afternoon group. When I look at the moldering set of World Books that formed the intellectual basis for my early education, I just laugh out loud.*

Build Anticipation

One way to build anticipation is to preview your points in the introduction. Gwendolyn Haas, for example, said that she was going to talk about what makes Olympic champions. Then she said in a speech entitled "Olympic Inspiration":

> *The qualities I want to talk about not only make Olympic champions; they are invaluable, too, in school, in the home, or on the job. First,*

champions anticipate. They have a dream of themselves as a champion. They aim high, because often they don't just meet their goals but surpass them. They plan for trouble by anticipating possible setbacks and preparing for them. Second, champions motivate. They are driven not just to be the best but to do their best as well. They never quit because they know the satisfaction of completing a difficult task against the odds. Third, champions activate. They make their own luck because they know luck strikes those best prepared to capitalize on it. They bounce back, and their failures inspire them to try harder.

The audience is now more likely to listen for each of her points: (1) Anticipate, (2) Motivate, (3) Activate. Notice the way Gwendolyn kept them parallel. Framed in the same way, they were easier for listeners to remember.

Build Suspense

Building suspense is one of the best ways of keeping attention. Esteban Estrada decided to speak on drunk driving, and he began his speech with a personal experience:

There was no way I could anticipate what would happen. My girlfriend, Angelica, and I were coming home from dinner out and a movie. We were on State Street, one of the main streets of my hometown, when suddenly we were sideswiped by a car. Not knowing what was going on, and thinking it was inadvertent, we continued driving. Suddenly, the car sideswiped us again. Knowing we were about seven blocks from the police station, we drove there fast. But the car that had been following us disappeared. We waited almost twenty minutes, and thinking it safe, we decided to continue toward Angelica's house. Suddenly, out of nowhere, it was behind us again. We made it to Angelica's and ran inside. The car squealed past, but forgetting the curve leading into the court where Angelica lived, the outlaw car missed the turn, ran one wheel in the gutter and another up a driveway, and broke the front axle. The police were called; all three teenage boys had been drinking.

Esteban then went on to talk about the penalties in the state for driving while drunk, such as fines, a police record, possible license suspension, prison, and more.

Other Techniques for Getting Attention

Most of these ideas have been discussed elsewhere; they are gathered here to highlight the way they can help get attention in informative speeches. When thinking about the *content* of your speech, think specifically of the needs, wants, and desires of your listeners. Also, in content, tie old ideas to new ones. One student talking about food additives (an old idea), for example, tied it to chemicals found naturally in foods that cut the risk of cancer and heart attack (a new idea). Another student did the same, but the new idea had to do with brain foods—natural foods that stimulate thinking.

Two other ways to think about content are relating the new to the old and using conflict. Eduardo Gaigher related the new to the old when talking about how the Internet revolution (the new) has changed the local library (the old) and how Internet access (the new) relates to support of the First Amendment (the old) especially when it comes to cyberporn (the new) and censorship (the old). He was also able to work conflict into his speech as he traced some of the issues raised in community debates between free-speech advocates and antiporn taxpayers.

Monica Castillo, a former telemarketer, used conflict—good versus bad—when she talked about the use of telemarketing to sell products (good) and contrasted that to the use of telemarketing to rip off the public (bad). Contrasting right versus wrong, benefits versus detriments, or strengths versus weaknesses uses conflict to hold attention.

Speakers can use their *evidence* to hold attention when they select their information with listeners in mind. Meredith Kim's speech on time management at the end of this chapter demonstrates this well. Notice, for example, that her introduction begins with evidence from a Web page that she credits immediately after her opening lines—and yet the evidence was selected with her listeners in mind. In Kim's introduction alone, there is a quotation, statistics, and personal experience. Within her first main head, she includes opinion and personal experiences, and she gives another statistic in the transition to the second main head. Speakers need to select their evidence with variety in mind. Use opinions, statistics, facts, and personal experience—all in one speech, as Kim did. Mixing up the information keeps audience interest high. If listeners can predict what will come next, the speech becomes too routine and boring.

In using evidence, speakers also need to be concrete rather than abstract. It would be easy, for example, to talk about increases in automobile accidents, gun-related deaths, or minority enrollments in colleges (abstract) without citing any exact statistics to prove these increases (concrete). Because the abstract is general and lacks detail, it does not hold attention.

Choosing examples that are immediate is another way to use evidence to hold attention. *Immediacy* means closeness or nearness in time or space. Shelly gave a speech on the importance of psychological counseling, and she scheduled an interview with an on-campus psychologist before her speech to make her example more immediate. In this way she could talk not only about how to go about making such appointments and where and when the services were provided but also about what topics are of most concern to students on her campus. Thus, the subject of psychological counseling became immediate.

Finally, when speakers choose evidence, the novel example may hold attention better than the common one. Nadia, talking about the benefits of algae and Irish moss, stopped during her speech and asked her listeners how many ate them every day of their lives. No one raised a hand, so she questioned them: "How many of you eat ice cream? How many of you like chocolate milk? How about ketchup? Do you eat cheese? How many of you did not raise your hand? Then, do you brush your teeth every day? The thickening agent in all of these," said Nadia, "is carrageenan—or algae or Irish moss. Look on the side of a carton of chocolate milk, and you will see it listed there." Her novel questions helped create audience interest.

Organization also helps keep the attention of listeners. Speakers who follow a precise order or emphasize the form or structure of their information are more likely to keep their audience with them. Organization is so important that we spent a whole chapter discussing it. When speakers use transitions and internal summaries, and relate their material to their central idea, it helps listeners follow the speech. When listeners can't follow a speech, their minds will tend to wander. Making only a few points and using some repetition also help sustain interest throughout a speech.

Content, evidence, and organization are important, but so is *style* or language, as you learned in Chapter 5, Verbal Communication. We would suggest rereading that chapter before you give your speech.

Finally, speakers can get attention through their *delivery*. This does not mean delivery at the expense of quality content. Taking an active role in getting your audience involved helps. If you speak clearly and move around, your speech will be more dynamic. Speakers must realize that they play an important role in creating interest, activity, and motivation. When you are the fifth speaker in an 8 A.M. class on a Monday, people aren't going to listen to you just because you are there.

Don't forget that it isn't a single element that holds listener attention; it is the combination of elements working together. That is why this section on content, evidence, organization, style, and delivery is so important. Getting attention and arousing interest should be an all-consuming, ongoing, always present task of effective speakers—not something tacked on as an afterthought.

■ GETTING LISTENERS INVOLVED

At all points in the development of a speech or presentation, speakers need to think about the audience, audience responses, and audience involvement. Before we discuss three ways to get the audience involved—external to the speech itself—we need to remind speakers of the methods for getting audience involvement that are within the speech:

1. Choose a topic that is inherently interesting—one that is both significant and relevant and has attention-holding value in and of itself.

2. Select examples, personal experiences, and stories that are interesting and relevant to listeners.

3. Use an organization scheme that is simple, clear, and easy for listeners to follow.

4. Incorporate transitions that guide listeners to what has been said, what is going to be said, and the purpose or central idea of the speech.

5. Make certain that all judgments and decisions regarding speech material are made with listeners in mind.

The three methods that we label "external to the speech itself" really are not truly external, because they are so closely tied to the internal content. But the difference between the following three areas and those just mentioned is that the next areas involve the overt physical or mental participation of audience members. They are getting the audience to participate, asking rhetorical questions, and soliciting questions from the audience.

Get the Audience to Participate

In a speech on aerobic exercises, the speaker had listeners try several of them. In a speech on self-defense, the speaker had the class practice a few simple moves. In a speech on note taking, the speaker had listeners take notes and, as they did so, taught them some shortcuts and simplified procedures.

As every magician knows, choosing someone from the audience to participate in an act is a good technique for keeping attention. Speakers can do this too. In a speech on first aid, the speaker called for a volunteer from the audience so that she could point to pressure points. For a speech entitled "Appearance Sells," one student asked three classmates to come to class dressed in a certain way: one was to dress in casual attire; another, in dressy clothes; and the third, in business wear.

Ask Rhetorical Questions

Some speakers use **rhetorical questions**—questions audience members answer mentally rather than out loud. Meredith Carey used rhetorical questions in her speech, "Recover, Refocus, Regenerate":

> *I was there when they lowered my grandmother into the ground; I was very close to my grandmother, and it hurt deeply knowing she was gone forever. I knew that the fights between my parents were leading to separation, but their divorce was devastating for me because I loved them both so much, and even the idea of divorce really shocked me. And going away to college—leaving my friends, the town and home where I grew up, and my boyfriend all the way through high school—almost ripped me apart. Have changes like these shaken you to the core? Have there been other changes in your lives that have freaked you out? What do you do with all your feelings of rage? Hurt? Sorrow? What do you do when you feel like you are drowning in a sea of anger? Or in an ocean of despair? Are you a person who likes regularity in your life? Predictability? Can you cope with all these changes? Are you prepared for even more changes in your lives?*

Solicit Questions from the Audience

Another device is to solicit questions from the audience after the speech. A question-and-answer session encourages listeners to get involved. You might even tell your listeners at the beginning that you will take questions when you finish, which may encourage them to pay attention in preparation for asking questions.

Here are some useful guidelines if you plan to solicit questions from your audience: First, make sure you listen to the full question before answering it. Sometimes speakers will cut off a questioner or will focus on irrelevant details instead of the main thrust of the question. Second, if a question is confusing, ask the questioner to rephrase it. If you are still confused, rephrase it yourself before answering it. For example, say, "Let me make sure I have heard you right; what you are asking is. . . . Am I right?" Finally, in responding to questions, try to keep your answers brief and to the point. This is no time for another speech. As a final check, it's also a good idea to ask, "Does that answer your question?"

Sample Speech

In this speech by Meredith Kim, notice several things. First, notice how well organized her speech is, and how she has incorporated transitions to help her listeners. Second, notice how she has incorporated her sources into her speech both to help her listeners find sources on the topic and to add to her own credibility. Third, notice how she has used her own personal experiences to hold listener attention.

General purpose: To inform.

Specific purpose: To inform my class about the purpose of time management strategies, the advantages of time management strategies, and specific time management strategies.

Central idea: Inability to manage their time is one of the major concerns of most college students. I intend to explain a specific, practical approach to time management.

Time Management Strategies

Introduction

Suppose that you had a bank that credited your account each day with more than $80,000. The money is yours, but you cannot carry over any balance or keep any cash through the next day. You must draw out and use every cent each day or lose it! What would you do with such a resource?" This is how the Web page "Time Management," from the University Counseling Services at Kansas State University, begins. (Time management. . ., 1996)

What would you do with $80,000 a day?

The Kansas State University Web page continues, "Everybody has such an account; it is called time. There are 24 hours, 1,440 minutes, or 86,400 seconds in each day. There are no extensions or overdrafts, and anyone who fails to make use of the time deposit loses it. It is up to you to determine how to make use of this precious commodity. Planning and acting to get the best out of your resource, which is available only once, is called time management" (Time management. . ., 1996).

I wish I were a better manager of my time. I've never been very good at it, and that is why I pursued this topic, "Time Management Strategies." I'm always feeling anxious, frustrated, and guilty, and the only way I discovered to attack my problem was to learn more about it—the purpose of time management strategies, the advantages of

Kim begins her speech with a quotation from an Internet source, which she cites immediately after her first four sentences. It is especially good for a college audience, who would find this opening comment attention grasping.

Kim continues using this same source because the statistics regarding time are useful, and the analogy between money and time seems to work effectively.

She ends her introduction with a confession, "I wish I were a better manager of my time," and then promptly outlines her forthcoming speech: (1) purpose, (2) advantages, and (3) some specific strategies. Her comments about using the Web help establish her credibility.

time management strategies, and some specific time management strategies. Thinking this is a problem common to everyone, I went straight to the Web, and I found the best information available there was from colleges and universities that want to help their students succeed.

Transition: Let me first explain the purpose of time management strategies.

Her transition from introduction to body eases listeners into her first point.

Body

I. Time management strategies fulfill a number of functions.

Notice how her main head sets up her subpoints.

A. One purpose is to plan activities and schedule time for completing them, according to the "Time Management" Web page from the Center for Advancement of Learning at Muskingum College in New Concord, Ohio (Time management. . . ., 1998). All the Web pages I consulted mentioned planning and scheduling.

Kim cites her source for each of her functions.

1. My life seemed to be controlled by external events. I would look for clear-cut signals to motivate me such as deadlines and expectations others had for me. This is a myth clarified in the "Time Management" Web page by the SUNY Potsdam Counseling Center (Time management, 2000).

For sub-subpoints 1 and 2, Kim uses her personal experiences.

2. I had to realize that I—and I alone—was responsible for initiating control. I had to evaluate what had to be done within a given time frame and what could be postponed (Time management, 2000).

For sub-subpoint 2, Kim confesses once again. This time it is that she has not been responsible.

B. A second purpose is to help people become more punctual, according to the Center for Advancement of Learning at Muskingum College (Time management, 1998).

Notice how Kim uses parallel structure to frame her subpoints: one purpose, a second purpose, and a third purpose.

1. One of the signs of time wasting, according to the "Time Management" Web page of the Department of Computer Science, School of Engineering, University of Virginia at Charlottesville, is missed appointments and the need to reschedule them (Robins, n.d.).

Even for her sub-subpoints Kim uses parallel structure: one of the signs, and a second sign.

2. A second sign of time wasting is appearing late and/or unprepared for meetings—like classes, according to this same Web page (Robins, n.d.).

Continue to examine how Kim is able to cite her sources within her speech—a strong point of her speech.

C. A third purpose of time management strategies is to aid us in remembering obligations, meetings, appointments, and special events, according to the Center for Advancement of Learning (Time management, 1998).

Transition: The "Time Management" website for the Department of Computer Science at the University of Virginia states that people waste about two hours per day. (Robins, n.d., p. 2) By planning activities, becoming punctual, and remembering things, we can cut out much of that wasted time.

But, if you think about it, the main reason for managing time is to provide structure to our life. I know I don't have enough structure, and I know I want it. So, what are the advantages of time management strategies?

II. Time management strategies have a number of advantages.

A. One advantage, according to the Center for Advancement of Learning at Muskingum College, is that the strategies don't take much time to implement (Robins, n.d., p. 2).

1. I purchased a semester planner, which took me about an hour to complete. (*Shows semester planner.*)

2. The weekly grids (*shows grids*) take about 15 minutes to fill out.

3. It now takes me about 10 minutes a week to keep schedules up to date—maybe a little longer because I'm still new at it.

B. A second advantage of time management strategies is a reduction of stress, according to the Center for Advancement of Learning at Muskingum. (Robins, n.d., p. 2)

1. There are fewer stressful situations resulting from procrastination.

2. There are fewer stressful situations resulting from overextending—or trying to do too many activities.

C. The third advantage of time management strategies is that they serve as a useful memory aid. (Robins, n.d., p. 2)

1. With this semester planner, which I am now depending on, I am reminded of my obligations. I used to try to remember

For her transition, Kim adds an additional piece of evidence—a statistic about wasting time that ties into one of the subpoints she has already developed. Then she summarizes her first three subpoints.

In her transition, too, she adds an additional personal insight—the need for more structure.
The end of Kim's transition forecasts her next main head.

Kim uses the same structure to phrase her main heads.

Her subpoints are once again phrased in the same way: one advantage, a second advantage, and a third advantage. This helps her remember them, and it helps her listeners follow her ideas.
The sub-subpoints (1, 2, and 3) under subpoint A give detailed personal experience with a semester planner—which she also uses as visual support. Her explanations are specific and detailed.

Regarding reduction of stress, Kim's sub-subpoints are actually personal experience, but they are not phrased in that way.

Kim could use additional personal experience with her semester planner under her third subpoint—the third advantage of time management strategies.

them all—even though I was not very good at it.

2. I know the days when assignments are due, but I also know the specifications for each assignment. I know the times for all my meetings. I write down routine activities as well as birthdays, anniversaries, and other special dates.

Transition: They don't take much time; they reduce stress; and they aid memory. Overall, time management strategies have given me a sense of balance. They're not going to make me a perfect student, but they offer great peace of mind—and a valuable tool that I did not previously have.

Now, I want to be concrete and practical, and I am going to ask all of you to think along with me. I want to give you "A Personal Time Survey" I found on the "Time Management Tips" Web page of George Mason University (Knight, 1998, pp. 1–2). This is the survey that convinced me that "Time Management Strategies" would be a useful topic for a speech for this class.

III. Time management strategies are useful only when *you know* that you need them. I have constructed a handout that captures the entire "Personal Time Survey," from George Mason University, and I want to go over it with you item by item. (*Hands out survey forms.*)

A. This survey shows the amount of time you spend on various activities. Just estimate the amount of time you spend on each item and, when asked on the form, multiply it by seven—so it equals time spent on the activity in one week.

1. _____ × 7 = _____ Number of hours of sleep each night
2. _____ × 7 = _____ Number of grooming hours per day
3. _____ × 7 = _____ Number of hours for meals/snacks per day including preparation time
4. _____ × 5 = _____ Total travel time weekdays
5. _____ Total travel time weekends
6. _____ Number of hours per week for regularly scheduled functions (clubs, church, get-togethers, etc.)

The first thing Kim does in her transition is summarize. Then she relates the effect of time management strategies to her own behavior.

Kim uses her transition to introduce a new tactic—a survey she found on the Internet that she says convinced her to give this speech. She thinks this survey will be new information for her listeners.

Because the information of the survey is complicated and lengthy, Kim puts it on a handout that she distributes.

The first subpoint under main head III introduces the first survey, and each of the sub-subpoints is one aspect of the survey.

One reason we decided to include this survey is because people who were *not* in Kim's audience can take the survey and use the information just as Kim's listeners could. It still has the same meaning. Although Kim guides her listeners through each step of the survey, with the handout in front of them, they can also proceed at their own pace.

7. _____ × 7 = _____ Number of hours per day for chores, errands, extra grooming, etc.
8. _____ Number of hours of work per week
9. _____ Number of hours in class per week
10. _____ Number of average hours per week socializing, dates, etc. Be honest!
11. _____ Now add up the totals
12. Subtract the above number from 168: − _____ = _____

Transition: The remaining hours are the hours you have allowed yourself to study. Now, you need to know your study needs as well.

B. This survey will determine how many hours you need to study each week to get A's. Use this rule of thumb: 2 hours per hour for an easy class; 3 hours per hour for an average class; 4 hours per hour for a difficult class.
1. _____ × 2 = _____ Per week for an easy class credit hours
2. _____ × 3 = _____ Per week for an average class credit hours
3. _____ × 4 = _____ Per week for a difficult class credit hours
Total Weekly Study Hours _____

C. Compare this number to your time left from the previous survey. Remember as you make the comparison that it's not only the quantity of study time but also it's quality.

Transition: If you are at all similar to those people in my dorm to whom I have already administered these surveys—if you're being honest—then you have very little time in your life for what you are here for—studying. There are numerous suggestions for how to better manage your time. I am not trying to persuade you to use any one or even all of them. After all, this is an informative speech. My purpose here is to indicate some of the techniques available.

IV. There are numerous time management strategies.

A. My first time management strategy is using a semester planner. All you really need, according to the Web page "Using Time

Notice how brief Kim's transition between the two parts of the survey is: It concludes the survey just discussed, and immediately alerts listeners to what is to come. Transitions do not need to be lengthy and elaborate.

The second part of the survey is on the handout as well. Although the information is clear, she keeps a close eye on her listeners to make sure they are progressing at the pace she is setting and to see that all understand.

The final subpoint draws the two survey results together.

Her transition from main head III to main head IV is valuable for several reasons: (1) It gives her listeners a reference base with which to compare their survey responses; (2) She provides a clear lead-in to her final main head; and (3) She lets her listeners (and her instructor) know she is treading on the fine line between informative and persuasive speaking.

Kim is able to tie her semester planner into her last main point. This allows her not only to show the planner once again but also to make some general suggestions about how to use it.

Management Techniques," by the School of Allied Health Professions at the University of Wisconsin—Milwaukee, is a large monthly calendar that has good-size blocks of space for each date. (Using time management. . ., 1997) (*Shows one.*)

1. Block out any fixed time commitments like exams, according to "Time Management and Making a Master Schedule," by the Counseling and Psychological Services Center at the University of North Carolina at Chapel Hill (Time management and making. . ., 2002).

2. Block out time for the basics of daily living such as eating, sleeping, personal maintenance, and travel (Time management and making. . ., 2002).

3. Plan and block out study time for each final test or paper. Use one-hour blocks, and know your high-energy times (Time management and making. . ., 2002).

4. Balance your activities by scheduling distressing times that allow you to unwind (Time management and making. . ., 2002)

5. Keep your schedule flexible (Time management and making. . ., 2002). A time schedule that is not personalized and honest is not a time schedule at all.

B. Make "To do lists," according to "Ten Tips for Better Time Management" from the Learning Center, School of Liberal Arts, at Purdue University (Ten tips for better. . ., 1996).

1. Prioritize the items (Ten tips for better. . ., 1996).

2. Keep the list short—five to six items, both academic and personal (Ten tips for better. . ., 1996).

3. Set small specific goals—like reading only five pages in a psychology chapter ("Ten tips for better. . ., 1996).

C. Find your productive time, says the "Stress Manager" page of the Faculty and Staff Assistance Program at the University of Michigan (Successful time management, n.d.).

Kim knows that some of the ideas for blocking out time in a semester planner are new to her listeners—like blocking out time for the basics of daily living, planning destressing times, and keeping the schedule flexible.

In making all her choices, Kim tries to keep her listeners in mind. She knows that time management itself is not a new topic, so she tries to offer ideas that might be new or different.

Rather than simply present an idea and move on, which Kim could have done, she tries to provide a little bit of explanation or description as her sub-subpoints.

Because each of Kim's ideas under subpoint C and subpoint D were found on different websites, Kim took careful notes, and her outline/speech notes reflect where she obtained each individual piece of information. This is important for her outline and for her instructor, and it is important, too, because Kim wants to incorporate as many relevant sources into her speech as possible. Not only does this reflect the wide search she engaged in to obtain her information; it reflects, too, how much information is available on the Web.

The additional benefit is that Kim's credibility with her audience is high. Not only do her listeners respect her, but they listen more closely to her ideas.

1. Determine the time of day when you are most productive (Successful time management, n.d.).
2. Schedule your hardest assignments for that time (Successful time management, n.d.).

D. Control your study environment, says the study skills, self-help website at the Cook Counseling Center, Division of Student Affairs, Virginia Polytechnic Institute and State University. (Control. . ., n.d.)

1. Use a regular study area, says the website entitled "25 Ways to Get the Most Out of Now," from the Academic Services of the University of San Francisco, California (Ellis, n.d.).
2. Keep your study area neat, says the University of Michigan website (Successful time management, n.d.).
3. Study where you'll be alert, it also says at the "25 Ways" website (*Ellis,* n.d.).
4. Avoid interruptions, says the website labeled "Managing Your Time" from the University of Bradford in the United Kingdom (Managing your time, 1999).
5. Don't exhaust your attention span. You protect your attention span by varying your activities, the website from the University of Bradford also says (Managing your time, 1999).
6. Avoid postponing important tasks, it also says at the University of Bradford website (Managing your time, 1999).

Transition: My strategies include using a semester planner, making "To do lists," finding your productive time, and controlling your study environment. There are so many more—like doing the most important things first, not wasting time with insignificant details, learning to say no to friends who try to get you to do something else, and relaxing. Often, we take more time worrying about something that needs to get done than the actual time it takes to do it.

Her transition from her final main head, IV, into her conclusion summarizes the information under her final main head alone, not her entire speech. Also, she uses it to mention four more items. Kim had more information than she could fit into her speech, but she is concerned that her listeners might not have heard some of the ideas she has left out, so she covers them quickly as a list.

In her conclusion, Kim first summarizes the ideas in her speech. Then she tells her listeners how to obtain more information.

Conclusion

We've learned the purpose of time management strategies, we've learned the advantages of time management strategies, and we've learned several important time management strategies. If you want more information on this important topic, enter "time management" into any search-engine location window.

A lot of time management has to do with attitude: How badly do you really want to change? A lot of time management has to do with your habits: Are you willing to change your current habits? And, a lot of time management, too, has to do with responsibility: Are you willing to take responsibility for your life? Once scheduling becomes a habit for me, I'll adjust my attitude to it. Remember, it is easier to find something to do with extra time than to find extra time to do something. Understanding time management strategies is the first step in putting them to use.

Speech Reference List

(No author, no date). "Control of the environment." Cook Counseling Center, Division of Student Affairs, Virginia Polytechnic Institute and State University. Retrieved June 25, 2002, from http://www.ucc.vt.edu/stdysk/control.html.

Ellis, D. (n.d.). "25 ways to get the most out of now." The Chemistry Department, Chemistry and Environmental Science, Lake Superior State University. Retrieved June 25, 2002, from http://dalton.1ssu.edu/unsem/timetips.htm. From: D. Ellis, (1994). *Becoming a master student*, 7th ed. New York: Houghton Mifflin, 74–79.

Knight, D. (1998, March 25). "Time management tips." Counseling Center, George Mason University. Retrieved June 25, 2002, from http://www.gmu.edu/departments/csdc/time.html.

(No author). (1999, September 1). "Managing your time." Student Development Web Pages, University of Bradford, United Kingdom. Retrieved June 25, 2002, from http://www.brad.ac.uk/admin/studev/time.html.

Robins, G. (n.d.). "Time management." Department of Computer Science, School of Engineering, University of Virginia, Charlottesville. Retrieved June 25, 2002, from http://www.cs.virginia.edu/helpnet/Time'time.html.

Kim has trodden softly on the line between informative and persuasive speeches. This would have made a strong persuasive speech if Kim had asked her audience to change their attitudes and habits and take responsibility for their lives, but she hasn't done that. She has alerted listeners to what is necessary and remained at the "understanding" level.

(No author, no date). "Successful time management." Stress Tips, Faculty and Staff Assistance Program (FASAP), University of Michigan. Retrieved June 25, 2002, from http://www.umich.edu/~fasap/stresstips/1.html.

(No author). (1996, April 10). "Ten tips for better time management." Learning Center, School of Liberal Arts, Purdue University. Retrieved June 25, 2002, from http://www.sla.purdue.edu/studentserv/learningcenter/handouts/tentpstm.htm.

(No author). (1996, January 16). "Time management: Academic success through time management." University Counseling Services, Kansas State University. Retrieved June 25, 2002, from http://www.ksu.edu/ucs/timemng.html.

(No author). (1998). "Time management." Center for Advancement of Learning, Learning Strategies Database, Muskingum College, New Concord, Ohio. Retrieved June 25, 2002, from http://www.muskingum.edu/~cal/database/time.html.

(No author). (2000, June 21). "Time management." Counseling Center, State University of New York (SUNY), Potsdam. Retrieved June 25, 2002, from http://www.potsdam.edu/COUN/brochures/time.html.

(No author). (2002, March 18). "Time management and making a master schedule." Counseling and Psychological Services, University of North Carolina, Chapel Hill. Retrieved June 25, 2002, from http://www.unc.edu/depts/unc_caps/TimeMgnt.html.

(No author). (2001, September 26). "Using time management techniques." The College of Health Sciences, University of Wisconsin-Milwaukee, Milwaukee, WI 53201. Retrieved June 25, 2002, from http://www.uwm.edu/SAHP/studentinfo/usingmgmt.html.

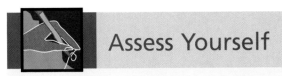
Assess Yourself

Have You Followed a Complete Program for Speech Preparation?

The assumption underlying this evaluation form is that you have selected an outstanding subject, developed a specific purpose and central idea for your speech, created main points that support your central idea, done sufficient research and investigation to discover supporting material that supports your main points, organized your speech effectively, and prepared an outline for your speech—all prior to using this form.

Answer "Y" for yes, "N" for no.

_____ 1. Have you prepared an outline for your speech at least three days before you plan to give the speech?

_____ 2. Have you converted the key parts of the outline to note cards?

_____ 3. Have you read through your outline several times to become familiar with the structure and flow of your ideas?

_____ 4. As you began to rehearse the delivery of your speech, did you check the time?

_____ 5. Using your notes, did you begin speaking and not stop until you completed your speech?

_____ 6. Did you check the time once again to see how long your speech took?

_____ 7. Once you completed your first complete run-through of the speech, did you go back and look at your outline to analyze your effort?

     _____ A. Were any key ideas omitted?

     _____ B. Were some ideas discussed too long or too briefly?

     _____ C. Did all your ideas receive proper and appropriate clarification and support?

     _____ D. Did both your introduction and conclusion flow smoothly?

     _____ E. Were you able to feel the presence of your future audience?

_____ 8. Did you make certain your notes were an effective tool for you?

     _____ A. Did you put too many notes on a single card?

     _____ B. Did you record just key ideas or key words?

     _____ C. Are your notes written large enough for you to see them from a distance?

     _____ D. Did you record brief quotations or important statistics on your notes?

     _____ E. Did you write on one side of the cards only?

     _____ F. Did you clearly number each of your cards so that their order is easy to determine?

_____ 9. Did you continue rehearsing the speech using your notes as you will in the final speech?

_____ 10. Are you saying the speech differently each time you rehearse it, letting your ideas trigger your words?

_____ 11. Have your rehearsed using all the props or visual support that you will be using in your speech?

_____ 12. Have you visited the exact location where you will be giving your speech? Are you certain all the props and visual support will work as you intend them to in the location?

_____ 13. Did you review your notes quickly, one last time, before going before your audience to give the speech—checking, of course, to see that all your notes are in order?

_____ 14. Do you feel relaxed, confident, and in control of your information?

Go to the *Communicating Effectively* CD-ROM to see your results and learn how to evaluate your attitudes and feelings.

Chapter Review

Our society needs high-quality information, and one way of producing and delivering it is through the informative speech—a speech that defines, clarifies, instructs, or explains.

When giving a speech, one of the speaker's goals should be to attract and maintain attention by presenting information that is relevant and interesting to the audience. The speaker should work to increase understanding through careful language choices, coherent organization, and the use of illustrations and examples. Finally, the speaker should use emphasis and repetition to help the audience retain the information.

There are numerous strategies for presenting information. Definitions, which explain the meaning of a word or phrase, can be done using etymology, the study of the origin and development of words, example, something used to illustrate a point, comparison, which points out the similarities between two or more things, contrast, which points out the differences, or function, which shows how a thing performs or how it can be used. Descriptions, which provide a mental image of something experienced, can be accomplished using size, shape, weight, color,

composition, or fit. Explanations, the process of making something clear, can occur by using numbers, connecting the known with the unknown, and repeating and reinforcing ideas.

Regardless of the type of informative speech, arousing interest in your topic is essential. We discussed arousing curiosity, presenting anecdotes, building anticipation, building suspense, and a variety of other techniques. More often than not, just as speakers should use more than one strategy to clarify or explain an idea, they need to use more than a single strategy for arousing interest in their topic.

A speaker can get his or her audience involved in the speech by thinking about listeners at all stages in the development of the speech. There are methods for doing this that do not ask for listeners' overt physical or mental involvement, such as selecting an interesting topic and examples, choosing a simple and clear organizational pattern, and using transitions. Three methods that do involve overt physical and mental involvement are inviting volunteers to participate in the speech, asking rhetorical questions, and soliciting questions from the audience.

Questions to Review

1. How many informative speeches have you heard in the past week? In what contexts have most of them been delivered? Were most of them effective? What made them effective or ineffective?

2. What are the biggest challenges that having to give an informative speech presents to you?

3. What questions can you ask yourself about your information and research to determine if the material is relevant?

4. What kinds of strategies are used in informative speeches?

5. Of the different strategies for informative speeches, which ones do you feel most comfortable using and why?

6. What are the best methods for arousing *your* interest in a speaker's topic? What is likely to grab *your* attention?

7. Do you think Meredith Kim's speech, "Time Management Strategies," was effective? Why or why not? Do you think she used too many sources? Why do you think she chose to use so many?

8. What suggestions would you offer to a beginning speaker on how to prepare and present an informative speech? Of the suggestions provided in this chapter, which ones do you consider most important?

mhhe.com/hybels

Go to the self-quizzes on the *Communicating Effectively* CD-ROM (side 2, track 10) and the Online Learning Center at mhhe.com/hybels7 to test your knowledge of the chapter concepts.

References

Ehrensberger, R. (1945). "An experimental study of the relative effects of certain forms of emphasis in public speaking." *Speech Monographs* 12, 94–111.

Finerman, E. (1996, March 1). "Humor and speeches: A standup history." *Vital Speeches of the Day* 62:9, 313–15.

Foster, J. (1993, May 23). "Graduation speech to Yale University." In A. Albanese, and B. Trissler, eds. (1998). *Graduation Day: The best of America's commencement speeches.* New York: Morrow.

Lamm, R. (1998, September 15). "Unexamined assumptions: Destiny, political institutions, democracy, and population." *Vital Speeches of the Day* 64:23.

Knapp, M. L., & A. L. Vangelisti, (1996). *Interpersonal communication and human relationships,* 3rd ed. Boston: Allyn and Bacon.

Koslowski, D. (2001, July 15). "Think carefully: Do the right thing, not the easy thing." *Vital Speeches of the Day* 67:19, 594–96.

(No author). (2002, April 9). "New report shows what Internet scams cost Americans most." FBI National Press Office, U.S. Department of State, International Information Programs. Retrieved March 26, 2003, from http://usinfo.state.gov/topical/global/ecom/02040901.htm

Petersen, J. A. (1999, August 12). "Better families." Quoted on the Christianity Net home page, "Preaching Resources." Copyright 1996 by *Christianity Today, Inc./LEADERSHIP Journal*—Summer 1996. Vol. 17:3, p. 69. Retrieved March 26, 2003, from http://patriot.net/~crouch/adr/50percent.html.

Stein, J. (2002, May 20). "Summer movies." *Time* Magazine. Retrieved May 13, 2002, from http://www.time.com/time/covers/1101020520/story.html.

Tompkins, P. K. (2002, January 1). "Thoughts on time: Give of yourself now." *Vital Speeches of the Day* 68:6, 183–85.

(No author). (2002). "Trends in television." Nielsen Media Research, Television Bureau of Advertising, Inc. Retrieved March 26, 2003, from http://www.tvb.org/tvfacts/trends/tv/timespent.html.

Further Reading

Bly, R. W. (2000). *Getting started in speaking, training, or seminar consulting.* New York: John Wiley & Sons. Bly provides a step-by-step procedure on acquiring what you need to know to become a polished and highly paid speaker. It is a how-to book on creating a presentation, establishing yourself as an authority, selling yourself, winning speaking engagements, setting fees, writing contracts, handling financial and legal aspects, promoting yourself on the Internet, working with bureaus, agents, reps, and office assistants, and boosting your speaking income with information products.

Glickstein, L. (1999). *Be heard now! Tap into your inner speaker and communicate with ease.* New York: Bantam Books. Glickstein approaches public speaking as a creative, interactive process that relies on the speaker's natural presence and willingness to be "in the moment." He believes the key to successful public speaking lies in an emphasis on self-realization and authenticity. His is a compassionate, realistic approach.

Kirby, T. (2001). "117 ideas for better business presentation." The Executive Speaker Company. Retrieved March 4, 2003, from http://www.executive-speaker.com/kirb117.htm. The ideas here are grouped by category. Categories include controlling nervousness, keeping attention, opening remarks, question and answer sessions, visual aids, introductions, humor, manuscript speaking, using notes, microphones, dress, rehearsal and practice, speaking to young learners, technical talks, on-camera techniques, style, enthusiasm, and further tips.

Nelson, P. (2002, May). "Public speaking resources." Toastmasters International, Edmonton and Area. Retrieved March 26, 2003, from http://www.ecn.ab.ca/toast/resource.html. Links here are to books and videos for speakers as well as websites for speakers, trainers, and learners like online public-speaking courses and tutorials, resources to enrich your performance, other communication programs and sites, training, and learning organizations.

Orman, M. C. (2002). "How to conquer public speaking fear." Retrieved March 26, 2003, from http://www.stresscure.com/jobstress/speak.html. The purpose of this report is to help readers overcome their fear of public speaking. Orman discusses 10 key principles to keep in mind: Public speaking is not inherently stressful; you don't have to be brilliant to succeed; all you need is two or three main points; you need a purpose that is right for the task; the best way to succeed is not to consider yourself a public speaker; humility and humor can go a long way; when you speak in public, nothing "bad" can ever happen; you don't have to control the behavior of your audience; in general, the more you prepare, the worse you will do; and your audience truly wants you to succeed. Well written, with practical advice.

(No author). (1999, August 9). "Public speaking." Canadian Association of Student Activity Advisors (CASAA). Retrieved March 26, 2003, from http://www.sentex.net/~casaa/resources/sourcebook/acquiring-leadership-skills/public-speaking.html. "Effective public speaking skills can be learned by following a few simple points," begins the material at this website. Sections include "Better Speech Tips," and "Speech Recipe," which have one headline, one expandable thesis or plan, three points to support your thesis or plan, and one conclusion. Although insufficient with respect to long-term results and long-range effectiveness, this site is a great place to get started.

(No author). (1998, July 20). "Public speaking bibliography." COM 225 Public Speaking Page, Maricopa College. Retrieved March 26, 2003, from http://www.mc.maricopa.edu/~cfay/bib225.html. This page offers links to general Web references, newspapers, biographical sources, statistics almanacs, dictionaries and thesauruses, subject indexes, atlases and gazetteers, encyclopedias, quotations and stories, government sources, and public-speaking resources. There is a link to a list of controversial topics, too.

(No author). (1999). "Public speaking resources." Commcentral, The McGraw-Hill Companies. Retrieved March 26, 2003, from http://www.mhhe.com/socscience/speech/commcentral/mgpubspeakresour.htm/. There are links here to 28 websites including advice to speakers, *Bartlett's Familiar Quotations,* Congress, ethos, logos, pathos, figures of speech, national press club's archives of speeches, preparation steps, preparing presentations, public speaker's page, public-speaking links, public-speaking workbook, quotations and stories, resources for public speaking, statistics, women in rhetoric, and a lot more.

Swain, M. R. (2001, September 6). "Public speaking resources & links." Salina Library, Kansas State University. Retrieved March 26, 2003, from http://www.sal.ksu.edu/library/publicspeak.htm. A list of six links to websites and online resources including the Virtual Presentation Assistant, Advanced Public Speaking Institute, the PBS show "Standard Deviant" episode on public speaking, Allyn & Bacon's Public Speaking Website, the History Channel's Speech Archives, and the Kansas State University Lecture Series.

Templeton, M., & S. S. Fitzgerald, (1999). *Schaum's quick guide to great presentations.* New York: McGraw-Hill. Templeton and Fitzgerald have written a basic public-speaking book in a tradebook style that covers all the essentials. Chapter 5, Presenting Data, is especially useful for the number of illustrations included. Filled with do's and don'ts, suggestions, exercises, hints, tips, and lists, the book offers much practical information.

Walch, S. (1998). "Main menu: Online public speaking workbook." Department of Speech Communication, Pennsylvania State University. Retrieved March 26, 2003, from http://www.personalpsu.edu/users/s/b/sbw3/workbook/workbook/workbook_menu.htm. This website is the link page to information on the communication process, selecting an appropriate topic, a purpose for communicating, researching your topic, audience analysis, formulating a residual message, developing your main points, structuring your speech, connectives, conclusions, introductions, visual aids, and practice and delivery. Solid, useful advice—a great resource.

Chapter 17

The Persuasive Speech

Objectives

After reading this chapter, you should be able to:

- Explain how persuasion relates to the communication model.
- Define *persuasion* and describe its purpose.
- Distinguish among values, beliefs, and attitudes, and explain the purpose of each.
- Explain what makes persuasion difficult.
- Describe each of the strategies persuaders can use.
- Describe specific techniques for building your credibility.
- Briefly outline the seven ethical standards persuaders should follow.

Key Terms and Concepts

Use the Communicating Effectively CD-ROM and Online Learning Center at mhhe.com/hybels7 to further your understanding of the following terms.

Analogy 625	Deductive reasoning 621	Influence 610
Attitudes 614	Dynamism 638	Logical appeal 621
Beliefs 613	Emotional appeal 625	Motivation 611
Causal reasoning 625	Ethics 639	Persuasion 608
Comparative-advantage order 635	Expertise 637	Target audience 620
	Hierarchy of needs 626	Trustworthiness 639
Credibility 637	Inductive reasoning 622	Values 612

CHRIS WORKS FOR THE GREEK LIFE OFFICE. BASICALLY, HIS job involves presenting speeches about the importance of Greek-letter organizations. Although it sounds as though Chris gives informative speeches, the speeches have a twofold persuasive purpose: to refute stereotypes and to get students to attend rush information night. Chris stresses that people who belong to Greek-letter organizations are more likely to remain in college to receive a bachelor's degree. Also, he says, fraternity or sorority membership has a substantial positive effect on persistence in studies, satisfaction with instruction and social life, and overall satisfaction with college. After Chris finishes talking and answers questions, he circulates a sign-up sheet to get commitments for rush information night. Chris's speeches have proved to be a successful recruitment device for the Greek Life office, and the office has already recruited other speakers because of Chris's success.

Allyson Migani was an honor-roll student and defensive sweeper for her college field hockey team. Because of her outstanding ability, she was nominated for the chance to participate in the U.S. Scholar-Athlete Games. She accepted the invitation and became one of over 1,600 prep scholar-athletes from all 50 states, as well as hundreds more from around the world, to take part in the event. Allyson met people from places such as England, Ireland, and Australia. At the games, she heard speeches on ethics and sportsmanship, global responsibility, and community service. But the speech that affected her most was on an international exchange program set up specially for outstanding athletes. Not only did she apply and receive acceptance for an exchange position in South Africa for the coming year, but the cost of her trip was picked up by one of the sponsors of the Scholar-Athlete Games. Allyson visited the cultural-diversity center on her campus and was given information on a wide variety of cultural-awareness programs available to students on her campus. When the time came for her persuasive speech, Allyson persuaded her classmates to become more involved and active in available cultural-awareness programs. All this was triggered by her participation in the Scholar-Athlete Games.

Both Chris and Allyson are engaged in **persuasion**—the process of trying to get others to change their attitudes or behavior. Most likely, you are involved in some sort of persuasion every day of your life. You try to persuade someone to join you for lunch or to join your study group. Others are involved in trying to persuade you: Radio commercials exhort you to buy, telephone salespeople offer bargains on a variety of goods and services, professors try to persuade you to turn in your papers on time, and candidates for student government try to persuade you to vote for them.

Since persuasion runs through every aspect of our society, you need to study how it works. Understanding persuasion will help you evaluate the persuasive techniques of others. Studying persuasion also will help you develop your own persuasive messages in the most effective way possible.

■ PERSUASION AND THE COMMUNICATION MODEL

Often when we think of persuasion, we think of a communicator having an influence on a listener or on many listeners, such as a salesperson on a purchaser or a politician on a group of potential voters. This view emphasizes the source of the communication as the main influence in the persuasion process. However, sometimes when we think of persuasion, we think of people buying products ("Okay, I'll buy the larger TV with the clearer picture"), changing their attitudes ("Maybe Paula is the better candidate"), or

Consider This

Why is persuasion so important? Daniel Goleman, in his book, *Working with Emotional Intelligence*, explains:

No matter how intellectually brilliant we may be, that brilliance will fail to shine if we are not persuasive. That is particularly true in fields where entry has high hurdles for cognitive abilities, like engineering and science, medicine and law, and executive ranks in general. As the director of research at one of Wall Street's largest brokerage firms put it to me, "To get into our business you need to be highly adept at numbers. But to make things happen, that's just not enough—you have to be able to persuade" (p. 173).

Questions

1. What traits does a person who is a skilled persuader possess? Are they strengths you find in yourself now, or are they traits you need to develop if you want to be a skilled persuader?

2. In the quotation, the director of research was talking about the need to be highly adept at numbers but added, "to make things happen, that's just not enough—you have to be able to persuade." Can you think of any business, profession, or occupation where this is *not* the case? No matter where you end up after your formal education, won't persuasive ability be necessary to "make things happen?"

Source: D. Goleman, *Working with Emotional Intelligence.* (New York: Bantam Books, 1998).

altering their beliefs ("All right, maybe student demonstrations can make a difference"). This view emphasizes the receivers of persuasive messages as the main part of the persuasion process.

When we emphasize the message in a persuasive situation, we might say, "That is a powerful statement" or "What a great speech!" And yet the focus of persuasion should not be on the sender, the receiver, or the message. All share in the persuasive process, even though one may play a more important role than the other two. You might not have purchased the product if the salesperson hadn't been terrific. The salesperson might not have sold the product if the receiver hadn't been ready, willing, and able to purchase it. Or the persuasive message might just have been the right message at the right time.

The point of this discussion is that what happens in the sender as he or she delivers the message and adjusts to feedback is often just as important as what happens in the receiver. To be an effective persuader means that you need to be concerned about all three elements, not concentrate on one to the exclusion of the others. Only when all three combine with one another successfully does effective persuasion occur.

■ WHAT IS PERSUASION, AND WHAT IS ITS PURPOSE?

Listing all the persuasive messages that have affected you over the past 12 hours is really a difficult task. Advertisers have tried to get you to buy their products; you may have turned down a telemarketer offering a new credit card or a person selling magazine subscriptions; a friend may have asked for a loan of $5; your family may have tried to get you to come home for the weekend; a newspaper editorial may have convinced you to attend this weekend's athletic contest to show your school spirit; your dormitory friends may have persuaded you to go downtown with them; an instructor may have told you to keep up with your reading; a Girl Scout may have asked you to buy cookies.

It is impossible to escape persuasive speaking, and persuasion has consequences. Change can occur when persuasion takes place. *Persuasion* is the process that occurs when a communicator (sender) influences the values, beliefs, attitudes, or behaviors of another person (receiver).

The key to understanding persuasion is influence. **Influence** refers to the power of a person or thing to affect others—to produce effects without the presence of physical force. For example, lending a friend $5 could cause a change in your character: It might make you realize that lending money is not so painful and thus make you more understanding or charitable in the future. The newspaper editorial on this weekend's athletic contest could have changed your thoughts about school spirit and your role in it. Your dormitory friends could have changed your mood for the day and given you something to look forward to tonight. An instructor could have changed your habits by getting you to read regularly rather than cramming at exam time. Influence implies a degree of control over the thinking, emotions, and actions of others. *Social influence* is what occurs when a person's values, beliefs, attitudes, or behaviors are changed because of the behavior or presence of another person.

To fully understand persuasion, you need to understand influence and motivation. Persuasion involves influence, but you are unlikely to do something just because someone else affects you in some way. That is where motivation comes in. **Motivation** is the stimulation or inducement that causes you to act. For example, let's say you decide to go downtown with your dormitory friends to avoid being annoyed and irritated by their pestering if you don't go. Maybe, too, you agree because that way you have someone to go out with. Let's say you decide to keep up with your reading because doing so will help you do better in a course. From these hypothetical instances alone, it becomes clear that we are motivated to do what we do.

Persuasion, influence, and motivation are closely linked. As persuaders, if we can relate our goals to things that persuade, influence, or motivate our listeners because they lead to desirable outcomes, we are far more likely to be successful. But if it were truly this simple, people would be pulled and pushed so often that a numbing effect might eventually block out persuasive efforts. Brent, for example, was called so often by telemarketers, who often acted as if they knew him, that he decided to respond with "Is this a sales call?" and (if the answer was "yes"), "We don't accept solicitation by phone, and please take this number off your calling list." Elvin contacted his post office to request that he receive no junk mail.

It should be clear that any persuasive effort involves ethics. Sometimes ethical choices are clear from common knowledge and good judgment alone. Sometimes ethical choices are not clear. When involved in making decisions that may be questionable, you should consult other people if possible. If students in your class are planning something new, thinking about taking an unusual risk, or attempting to push the frontiers of acceptability, they are well advised to clear their decision or choice with their instructor first.

There is no doubt that persuasion plays a significant role in people's lives, and it does have consequences. Before we discuss specific strategies that persuaders can use to influence and motivate others, we need to look at values, beliefs, and attitudes because these are precisely what persuaders are trying to influence.

■ VALUES, BELIEFS, AND ATTITUDES

When a persuasive message taps into our values, beliefs, and attitudes, not only are we more responsive to the message, but we are more likely to like or accept the sender. When persuasive messages do not tap into our values, beliefs, and attitudes, we are less responsive to them. For example, we tend to respond positively to people who share our values. If you believe in the importance of recycling, you are more likely to be receptive to a speaker who advocates recycling. Thus, persuaders who have investigated audience values, beliefs, and attitudes are more likely to be effective if—and this is the big "if"—they can adapt to them and use them effectively in their presentations.

Marcus, as he was thinking about subjects for a persuasive speech, considered talking to his class on the topics of welfare, Medicare, and the

If a persuasive speaker can tap into our values, beliefs, and attitudes, we are more likely to respond to his or her message.

graduated income tax. As he used the information he gained from his own classroom audience analysis, he came up with an entirely different set of subjects; topics more closely tied to students' values, beliefs, and attitudes included suicide, racism, and political indifference.

Values

Values are our beliefs about how we should behave or about some final goal that may or may not be worth attaining (Rokeach, 1968, p. 124). This definition divides values into two types: (1) *instrumental values,* which guide people's day-to-day behavior, and (2) *terminal* values (final goals that are or are not worth attaining).

Instrumental and terminal values are fairly easy to distinguish. Values that guide day-to-day behavior are similar to those that are learned in scouting organizations—loyalty, honesty, friendliness, courage, kindness, cleanliness, thrift, and responsibility. Terminal values may vary, but some are shared by all human beings: freedom, the value of world peace, family security. Other enduring values include inner harmony, happiness, safety, personal security, achievement, progress ("Every year things are getting better and better"), enlightenment (the value of the scientific method and rationality), and patriotism.

When Raymond V. Gilmartin (1999), chairman, president, and CEO of Merck & Company, gave his speech "Innovation, Ethics and Core Values" to the Harvard Magazine/Conference Board in New York City, he first outlined what Merck meant by *leadership,* having defined a wide range of behaviors that support and demonstrate leadership—such as setting clear objectives, recognizing the performance of employees, and responding to the needs of its customers. Then he said:

> *Heading our list of traits is the requirement that the leadership at Merck should demonstrate a high degree of integrity and ethics and should encourage fairness, teamwork and treating others with dignity and respect. Even though we believe those traits have been an unstated part of Merck's culture for many years, they are now, for the first time, part of a comprehensive management system that is applied to recruitment, development, performance evaluation and management selection (p. 210).*

Gilmartin added that Merck is incorporating a formal ethics component into its corporatewide training and development programs. That is the way, Gilmartin claims, that Merck is working to make core values and ethics an integral part of how it does business. Notice how Gilmartin has emphasized enduring values such as integrity, fairness, dignity, and respect. If asked, we're certain Gilmartin would say, "We want these to be the values that guide our leaders' day-to-day behavior."

There are two points to think about when considering terminal values. First, they are not likely to be changed because of one brief, persuasive speech; they change only over time. Second, the degree to which you can tie your approach or appeal into widely accepted terminal values may help determine whether you achieve your goals. If you can show that your approach is consistent with, supports, or reinforces the values your audience members hold, they are more likely to accept the new approach as a natural outgrowth of the values they already support. For example, Marcus chose racism as his topic because he could relate it to so many terminal values his classmates support: freedom, equality, friendship, inner harmony, and happiness.

Beliefs

Often, it is values that determine beliefs. They may also anchor beliefs. For example, if one of our values is patriotism, this value might result in a variety of beliefs. We might believe in a capitalistic economy, a democratic form of government, a public education system, and the Judeo-Christian religious tradition.

Beliefs are statements of knowledge, opinion, and faith. A statement of knowledge is "I believe [know] that if I let go of this book, it will drop to the floor." A statement of opinion is "I believe [have an opinion] that vitamin supplements help keep us healthy." A statement of faith is "I believe [have faith] that there is a God."

Where do we get our beliefs? Beliefs can come to us from a variety of sources. Besides our own observations, we depend on the observations of our parents, teachers, religious leaders, and friends—especially as we grow up. As adults, we depend more on the observations of professionals, scientists, and journalists. The point here is that we seldom develop beliefs in isolation from other people. Our interactions have much to do with what we observe, how we observe it, and the conclusions we draw from our observations.

If you compare values with beliefs, you realize that beliefs are, in general, easier to change than values. Values are central; they are more securely anchored. The fact that beliefs are easier to change does not necessarily mean they can and will be changed. While statements of knowledge can be changed with more knowledge (examples, statistics, or testimony) and statements of opinion can be changed in the same way, statements of faith are less likely to be changed—at least by a brief persuasive speech.

Often in ritualistic or commemorative speeches—those designed to honor an occasion or someone in particular—beliefs are pronounced, as in Christopher "Gus" Loria's (2002) speech, "In Defense of Liberty," given at the anniversary of the American flag raising on Iwo Jima to Iwo Jima veterans. Loria is a major in the United States Marine Corps and a NASA astronaut.

> *Because of your sacrifices made on that island.*
>
> *Years later . . . back home . . . America was a place where once again . . . children skipped to school without fear . . . fathers played Saturday morning football with their kids in the back yard . . . and families hurriedly dressed for Sunday morning church services.*
>
> *Because of your sacrifices.*
>
> *America was a place where, once again, Midwestern farmers could plow the land in peace, and East-coast factory workers could share lunch boxes under the bright noon sun . . . a place where ranchers still drove cattle across western plains . . . and California sunsets, of brilliant red and gold, graced the end of a free nation's day.*
>
> *Because of your sacrifices.*
>
> *America was a place where, once again, college kids studied to be doctors and writers, teachers and engineers . . . a place where knowledge merged with compassion to develop new medicines and seek new cures . . . where talent and creativity inspired great books, great art, great music . . . a love of beauty and goodness.*
>
> *America was a place where, once again, its people were known for their courageous commitment to liberty, their adventurous drive towards achievement, and . . . towards those of the world less fortunate . . . their great spirit of generosity.*
>
> *Once again we remembered the America which was forged from a frontier territory . . . a vast landscape upon which the dreams of many nations, and the ideals of many peoples, could, in the spirit of freedom, suddenly find possibility . . . a nation so great as to be unparalleled in human history.*
>
> *America was a place where, once again, dreams were limited only by the scope of imagination.*
>
> *And, prompted by our country's own flag, America was a place which began extending the spirit of freedom to a pursuit of the stars (p. 379).*

Attitudes

Attitudes are groups of beliefs that cause us to respond in some way to a particular object or situation. Let's say you have a group of beliefs regarding

Consider This

Why do persuaders giving a single speech before an audience face inherent difficulties? Read this excerpt from Daniel Yankelovich, one of the world's most famous public-opinion experts, taken from his book, *The Magic of Dialogue*, then answer the questions that follow:

The public, I have learned over the years, forms its judgments mainly through interactions with other people, through dialogue and discussion. People weigh what they hear from others against their own convictions. They compare notes with one another, they assess the views of others in terms of what makes sense to them, and, above all, they consult their feelings and their values. The public doesn't distinguish sharply between facts and values, as journalists and social scientists do. Indeed, dialogue draws heavily on feelings and values. Of course, information is important. But information stripped of feelings is not the royal road to public judgment; dialogue, rich in feelings and values, is (p. 25).

Questions

1. If people form their judgments mainly through interactions with other people through dialogue and discussions, what role does persuasion through public speaking even play? Is it likely to have any influence at all? If so, what? If not, why not?

2. If people don't distinguish sharply between facts and values, then why should public speakers offer listeners facts and values? Wouldn't it be as effective, if not more effective, for speakers just to offer audiences their personal feelings?

3. What does Yankelovich's viewpoint suggest to you as a potential persuader? That is, if information, accompanied by feelings, is the royal road to public judgment, then what might you do, as a persuader—in a persuasive speech—to satisfy what Yankelovich is suggesting?

Source: D. Yankelovich, *The Magic of Dialogue: Transforming Conflict into Cooperation* (New York: Simon & Schuster, 1999).

honesty that are connected to educational experiences—test taking, paper writing, and doing your own work. This might result in the negative beliefs "I don't believe in cheating" and "I don't believe in presenting someone else's work as my own." According to our definition of *attitude*, this group of beliefs would cause you to respond in some way: to speak out in favor of honesty, to discourage friends or classmates from being dishonest, or, depending on the strength of the beliefs or attitude, to report cheating or plagiarism that you observe.

In the excerpt we presented from Loria's speech, "In Defense of Liberty," it is clear that Christopher "Gus" Loria shares people's common beliefs about families, freedom, knowledge, liberty, adventure, achievement, generosity, hope, imagination, discovery, and more. What Loria has done in his speech is create a set of actions that surround the beliefs he is sharing. If attitudes are groups of beliefs that cause us to respond in some way, then, look again at the way Loria grouped his ideas. If you have a group of beliefs that revolve around the importance of family, then you would expect this group of beliefs to cause you to respond in some way. Loria talks about children skipping to school, fathers playing Saturday morning football with their kids, and families dressing for Sunday morning church services—the very actions you would expect people to exhibit if they had a group of beliefs regarding the importance of family.

In the next section on the group of beliefs centered around freedom—although all of his ideas are centered around freedom—Loria talks about Midwestern farmers plowing their land in peace, East-coast factory workers sharing lunch boxes, ranchers driving cattle across western plains, and California sunsets gracing the end of a free nation's day.

In developing your own speech around a group of beliefs notice what is especially interesting in Loria's speech. You could begin with a group of beliefs and develop the actions, or you could begin with a group of related actions, and develop the beliefs from them.

■ WHY PERSUASION IS DIFFICULT

The purpose of this section is threefold: First, it is designed to help you have realistic expectations. Persuaders, especially beginning persuaders, often become too optimistic about what they can accomplish in persuasive speeches. Second, it is designed to motivate you. If you know before you begin putting together your persuasive speech how difficult the process of change can be, you will be more likely to put in the time and effort needed to make the process work. Third, this section is designed to show you some specific difficulties persuaders may face so that you can try to prepare in advance to overcome these hurdles.

One obvious difficulty is the sheer amount of persuasion that occurs. To say that we are besieged by persuasive messages is an understatement. Your persuasive message is likely to be received as just another persuasive message unless you take special care to make it stand out from others.

A second difficulty is that persuasion tends to work slowly, over time. For example, how often have you gone out and bought a product after hearing or seeing just one advertisement for it? How often are you prompted to do anything as a result of just one message? We rarely take action after seeing just one advertisement. Usually we have to see the same advertisement over and over, or, perhaps, different versions of the advertisement that focus on various aspects of the product, until all our questions have been answered and our objections overcome. Persuasive speakers, however, ordinarily do not have the luxury of repeated efforts.

A third difficulty is that the value, belief, or attitude you are trying to change may be deeply entrenched. Many values, beliefs, and attitudes are interconnected. Some are based on family and religious traditions, others on deep personal commitments made early in life or personal experiences we have had. Many early experiences are etched in our memory. Henrik grew up eating fast food; he's not going to change to a nutritional eating plan because of one speech. Letty's family was prejudiced against Catholics; a single persuasive message about ecumenism probably will have little effect. Shocking circumstances, fearful activities, or events that evoke strong emotional reactions often make such imprints. It's unusual for a single speech to shake or change our strongest feelings.

A fourth difficulty is that some people you hope to persuade may have structured their lives around some basic "truth," and thus their habits and

To make a persuasive message stand out it must be made special or unique.

beliefs are entrenched. For example, some people still believe that they can catch a cold by going outside in the cold without wearing a coat. This belief runs counter to everything we know about viruses and how colds are communicated. But changing someone's belief in this "truth" would be difficult, perhaps impossible.

A fifth difficulty is laziness. People, in general, are not easily aroused to action or activity. Getting people to do something—sometimes anything—can be difficult, let alone getting them to change an established way of doing things or an established way of thinking. Most people are inclined to follow familiar, traditional, well-traveled routes. The routine is easier, well known, more comfortable, and perhaps more rewarding—at least, it's predictable to do things the way they've always been done.

A sixth difficulty is that people want freedom of action. A threat to that freedom, like a persuasive appeal that seems coercive—"Do things my way"—causes people to react, maybe even to reject the appeal. People might respond in an opposite way: "I'll show you!" "I don't want to be told how to do it!" The desire for freedom of action is so strong that some people respond negatively to a persuasive appeal even when the point of view expressed is similar to their own.

Many other factors can affect the receptiveness of your audience. Time of day may affect how awake or responsive people feel. Your audience's educational level could affect how much your listeners understand, how complex your argument can get, or how technical your language can be. Socioeconomic level might affect the kinds of subjects to which your audience responds. For example, you might speak to an audience of young people about how to get a job or how to impress an employer or talk to a group of retirees about investments and exotic travel opportunities.

Gender can be a difficulty as well. Some men have trouble dealing with women who show an interest in power; these men lose energy and initiative

(Monedas, 1992, pp. 197–208). Sometimes when speakers are trying to persuade others, they are perceived as dominating or controlling. How do males respond to female persuaders? Diana Ivy and Phil Backlund (1994), who write on the topic of gender, raise the question, "Wouldn't it be great if women could act assertively (even aggressively) without the risk of being perceived as a threat, without being called masculine, or worse?" (p. 61). Ivy and Backlund raise another interesting question: "Wouldn't it be great . . . for a guy to be able to communicate in a nurturing, caring fashion to women and men alike without risking rejection or embarrassment for being unmasculine?" (p. 61). How might women respond to a male speaker who gets emotional? Or to a man who does not conform to traditional male stereotypes of dominance, power, and control? The answers are not clear.

Speakers can turn such difficulties into strengths by carefully analyzing their audiences and using this information in their research and other preparation—in selecting their organizational schemes, choosing their language, and presenting their messages. Our discussion of the difficulties of persuasion points out what we mentioned earlier: Persuasion involves all three elements—sender, message, and receiver—working together.

Effective persuasion requires rigorous audience analysis, careful limiting of the persuasive focus or intent, much time in thorough preparation, great care in selecting the proper argument and evidence, detailed attention to the way the message is constructed, and much practice in effective delivery. Information about the audience can affect the choices you make in each area, although it may not be easy to apply all your information about your audience to each area. But nothing worthwhile in life comes easily; effective persuasion is no exception.

Patrick McLaurin, in an online PowerPoint presentation sponsored by the Wharton Communication Program at Pennsylvania State University (1999), identified some of the challenges to achieving your persuasive goal. Here are some of the audience responses persuasive speakers must overcome:

View clip #8, an excerpt from a persuasive student speech, "Living Wills, Susan Hrabar."

We're doing OK as it is.

We don't have the staff.

We tried that before.

It's not our problem.

It will take too long.

I don't have the authority.

We didn't budget for it.

■ STRATEGIES OF PERSUASION

Now you have a good idea of how persuasion relates to our model of communication; you understand what persuasion is and what its purpose is; you have an idea of how values, beliefs, and attitudes are involved in the process; and you have some indication of how difficult persuasion is likely to be. You now have a foundation for examining strategies. In persuasion, just as in any other form of communication, there are no guarantees. No strategy is foolproof. The best approach is to use all the available strategies to meet the demands of the audience. Obviously, different audiences will require different approaches, so the more strategies you can use, the better.

Determine Your Purpose

Determining your purpose at the outset will provide a focal point for the entire effort. Subtracting a purpose from a persuasive effort is like pulling out the main rod of an umbrella. Without the rod, the whole umbrella collapses. Your purpose should be a highly specific and attainable persuasive goal.

When you begin planning a persuasive speech, one of the first questions you should ask yourself is what you want your audience to think or do. As we have noted in previous chapters, this is called your *specific purpose*. Here are some specific-purpose statements for persuasive speeches:

To Get Audience Members to Believe a Certain Way

- To persuade audience members that state lotteries exploit poor people.
- To persuade audience members that their college theater program is worthwhile.
- To persuade audience members that sex education at the elementary school level needs to be expanded.

To Get Audience Members to Act

- To persuade audience members to attend church.
- To persuade audience members to eat more fresh fruit and vegetables.
- To persuade audience members to write to their congressional representatives in support of stronger gun-control legislation.

If you keep your specific purpose in mind, it will be easier to generate main points for support. As you find support for your purpose, remember that you will want your audience members to respond in one or more of the five following ways:

1. *To change or reinforce beliefs.* A speaker wants to persuade the audience to change a belief or way of thinking or to reinforce a belief and take action. For example, a speaker who wants to convince listeners that state lotteries exploit the poor will provide evidence that poor people are the most likely to spend money on lotteries and that lotteries serve no constructive purpose.

2. *To take action.* For example, a speaker who wants the audience to attend church, eat more fresh fruits and vegetables, or write to congressional representatives will try to motivate listeners to do certain things.

3. *To continue doing what they are already doing.* Some audience members might already be doing what you are asking them to do. For example, if several members of the class are taking theater classes, they might find a speech on supporting the college theater program interesting because it reinforces what they already believe.

4. *To avoid doing something.* The speaker might want audience members to stop buying or wearing fur, to stop watching a particular television program, or to get their legislators to prohibit personal firearms or abolish capital punishment.

5. *To continue not doing something.* This goal is slightly different from the second goal. It works best if audience members are considering taking action that you are against. For example, if they're thinking about playing the lottery (because the payoff has become so large) or skipping church services, you might be able to persuade them not to do so. Your speech might persuade listeners who don't eat red meat not to give in to peer pressure if they're out with a crowd of friends at a fast-food place.

Any audience is likely to include listeners who represent every possible point of view on your subject. When you're planning your speech, you should consider all of them.

Analyze Your Audience

Whether you use your own observations, surveys, interviews, or research, you need to get good information about your audience—as we discussed in depth in Chapter 12, Getting Started. We mention this again here to remind you to appeal to your audience's values, beliefs, and attitudes whenever possible.

The second reason to analyze your audience is to predict its response to your persuasive effort. Many audiences reveal wide diversity. For example, even when speaking about day care to a group of working mothers—women who share a common desire to find good day care for their children—you will find big differences in age, socioeconomic background, and even marital status. Because of the problems of appealing to a diverse, or heterogeneous, audience, it might be helpful to select a target audience.

Your **target audience** is a subgroup of the whole audience that you must persuade in order to reach your goal. You aim your speech mostly at the individuals in this subgroup, knowing that some members of your audience are opposed to your message, some agree with it, some are uncommitted or undecided, and some find it irrelevant.

Politicians always go after a target audience. A legislator may speak at a school and target the people who will vote for a specific issue. A candidate may speak in a factory and target those people who will support a local zoning ordinance that would create more factories and, thus, further employment. Politicians have to do this because their success often depends on how many different constituencies they can appeal to. When uncommitted or undecided individuals are targeted, it is because they are the ones most likely to be influenced by persuasion.

Appeal to Your Audience Using Logic

As we discussed in Chapter 1, The Communication Process, the field of communication traces its roots to the ancient Greeks, who called persuasion "rhetoric." The most important theorist, Aristotle, thought that effective persuasion consisted of three parts: a source's credibility (*ethos*), emotional appeals (*pathos*), and logical appeals (*logos*). We consider these in reverse order, beginning with logical appeals.

A **logical appeal** is one that addresses listeners' reasoning ability. Evidence in the form of statistics or any other supporting material will help persuade the audience. Chapter 13, Finding Speech Material, explains in detail the kinds of supporting material you can use in a logical appeal.

A logical appeal may be argued in several ways: through deductive reasoning, inductive reasoning, causal reasoning, or reasoning by analogy. Causal reasoning and reasoning by analogy are both forms of inductive reasoning, but because of their importance, we will discuss them briefly in separate sections.

Deductive Reasoning

Deductive reasoning moves from the general to the specific. Here is a deductive argument used by one student:

Acid rain is a problem throughout the entire northeastern United States.

Pennsylvania is a northeastern state.

Pennsylvania has a problem with acid rain.

Care is needed, however, with this pattern of reasoning. Have you ever heard someone say, "It's dangerous to generalize"? A faulty premise really is faulty deductive thinking, as in this example:

All college students procrastinate.

Mary is a college student.

Therefore, Mary procrastinates.

Deductive reasoning can form the structure for an entire speech, for just a single part, or for several parts. In his commencement address, "The New Entrepreneurship," to the Olin School of Business, Boston College, Wellesley, Massachusetts, Peter Bell (2001), CEO of Storage Network, Inc., used deductive reasoning for each of the three qualities that entrepreneurs share:

Take the first quality—resilience. You won't find successful entrepreneurs blaming others for their own failure—because they actually use failure as a lesson.

I've suffered a number of complete failures—and they hurt. Like when I was unable to raise enough capital to launch a venture—which eventually caused the company to close its doors. Or when I was unable to turn around a company.

I really hate to fail. I know that there are some people in the world who actually derive pleasure when others fail. But I've learned from my failures. My failures made me work ten times harder. And they've given me valuable experience.

The second quality of successful entrepreneurs is initiative. They don't hide. They're out front. Consider this analogy from baseball. If you look at the fielding percentages of some shortstops, you could be misled by the number of errors they make. That's because some of the greatest short-stops in history put themselves on the line. They go after groundballs and pop-ups that their less driven counterparts don't even attempt. The great shortstops aren't afraid of being visible—even if it means they fail. And entrepreneurs can't afford to be afraid either.

The third quality of successful entrepreneurs is an enormous capacity for perseverance and determination.

I think Ellen Hancock, the CEO of Exodus Communications, is a great example. After 29 years at IBM, where Ellen became the most senior female executive in the company, reporting to the CEO—she left. She joined Apple and Apple fired her. Then she went to National Semiconductor and they fired her, too. But instead of hanging it up, she went to Exodus—a small company with fewer than 20 employees at the time. And she built Exodus into the largest web-hosting company in the world.

I believe Ellen's success story is a terrific illustration of how successful entrepreneurs never quit.

Inductive Reasoning

Another logical technique is **inductive reasoning**—reasoning from the specific to the general. Usually when we use inductive reasoning, we move from a number of facts to a conclusion. Here is how a student used inductive reasoning to persuade her audience that the college should require everyone to take a foreign language:

In some parts of the United States, you need to understand Spanish to get by.

Americans are traveling more and more to countries where a language other than English is spoken.

The mark of an educated person is that he or she can speak, write, and read at least one other language.

Conclusion: Everyone should learn another language.

In her speech to her class, "I Lived to Tell About It," Adrienne Bower used inductive reasoning to arrive at the action step of her speech. She believed that her listeners might reject her conclusions if they heard them first, so she built her case slowly with statistics, facts, opinions, and a personal example. Here is some of the information she provided her audience:

1. *According to the Core Institute at Southern Illinois University, cited in an article in* USA Today, *by Michael P. Haines (2001), the director of the National Social Norms Resource Center at Northern Illinois University, the average number of alcoholic drinks consumed weekly by freshmen in 2000 was 8.5 for males, 3.7 for females. For sophomores, it was 9.1 for males, and 3.8 for females (Haines, p. 15A). Yet, at one institution, the Core Institute reported that 58 percent of students surveyed had consumed five or more drinks at one sitting in the previous two weeks (Lane, 2001). The average, according to the Core Institute, across campuses is 46.5 percent who had consumed five or more drinks at one sitting in the previous two weeks (Lane, 2001, p. A6).*

2. *"Half the students age 10 to 24 questioned in a 1999 study by the Centers for Disease Control said they had consumed alcohol in the preceding month" reported Jeffrey Kluger (2001) in an article "How to Manage Teen Drinking (The Smart Way)" in* Time *magazine. The Core Institute, which surveys 30,000 to 60,000 college students annually, reports that heaviest drinkers are males in fraternities or on athletic teams followed closely by female students in sororities (Lane, 2001).*

3. *"College students are young and irresponsible, and drinking is part of their culture," says Rob Waldron (2000) in an article "Students Are Dying; Colleges Can Do More," for* Newsweek. *Another article in* Time, *"Women on a Binge," by Jodie Morse (2002) includes the line "More college women regularly get drunk," as part of her headline. Morse (2002) also includes the statistic, "Since 1993, women's colleges have seen a 125 percent increase in frequent binge drinking" (p. 56).*

4. *Last year, I was drinking hard lemonade and bottled mixed drinks with friends in the parking lot of Burger King. I didn't know how much my friend Stephanie had to drink, and I thought she was being careful, but she crashed the car on the way back to our sorority. The tree hit the driver's side of the car, and Stephanie died in the hospital of her injuries. You probably read about it last year. Three of my sorority sisters and I lived to tell about it, but it was a harrowing experience I never want to relive.*

   Now, my point is not to try to eliminate drinking from college campuses. "Prohibition didn't work for the nation in the 1920s, and it's a failure on college campuses today," says Michael P. Haines (2001). It isn't going to happen. My point, too, isn't to develop terror campaigns designed to scare students about the hazards of drinking too much. This is another approach that hasn't worked well (Haines, 2001).

   My solution has five parts, and it is based on one common assumption: College-age kids are going to drink: (1) Lower the national drinking age to 18 so that drinking takes place in the open where it can be supervised by police, security guards, and health-care workers (Kluger, 2001, p. 43). (2) Get out the information that heavy drinkers are not in the majority, that most students who drink "do so responsibly, according to a study funded by the U.S. Department of Education" (Haines, 2001). "When students are armed with the truth about the moderate and responsible drinking habits of the majority of their peers," says Haines, "they tend to consume less themselves" (p. 15A). (3) Widely promote a designated-driver program whereby all local bars give free soft drinks to the nondrinker in any group (Lane, 2001, p. 6A). (4) Establish a university policy whereby all college students are sent a birthday card to arrive the day before they become eligible to drink, which wishes them a happy birthday but reminds them to drink responsibly. (5) Drink responsibly. Take full responsibility for yourselves, knowing that moderate drinking habits are " a powerful way to help create a healthier, safer campus culture" (Haines, 2001).

Sometimes it will work best to give the facts and then draw the conclusion (induction); in other cases you might want to start with the conclusion and then support it with facts (deduction).

On the Web

Logical Fallacies in Argument

Fallacy is an improper conclusion drawn from the premise. (A *premise* includes the reasons given in support of a conclusion.)

- *Naturalistic fallacy* occurs when something is identified as being good or desirable because it appears to be a natural characteristic. ("Everyone wants to be wealthy so systems should be designed on the basis of economic incentives.")

- *Fallacy of sweeping generalization* occurs when a general rule is applied to a specific case to which the rule is not applicable because of special features of the case. ("Everyone has a right to his or her own property; therefore, even though Jones has been declared insane, he should keep his machine gun.")

- *Fallacy of hasty generalization* occurs when an isolated or exceptional case is used as the basis for a general conclusion that is unwarranted. ("I had a bad relationship with the first person I ever dated. I'm sure all relationships are bad.")

- *Fallacy of bifurcation* occurs when one presumes that a distinction is exclusive and exhaustive, but other alternatives exist. ("America—love it or leave it." "Companies can either make a profit or be socially responsible.")

- *Fallacy of begging the question* occurs when an argument, instead of offering proof for its conclusion, simply reasserts the conclusion in another form. ("God exists because the Bible says so. I know the Bible is true because it is the work of God.")

- *Fallacy of question-begging epithets* occurs when slanted language is used to reaffirm what we wish to prove but have not proved yet. ("No right-thinking American could support this measure, a cunning plot hatched in backrooms by corrupt politicians.")

- *Fallacy of false analogy* occurs when a comparison between an obscure or difficult set of facts and one that is already known and understood, and to which it bears a significant resemblance, is erroneous and distorts the facts of the case

being argued. ("Why should we sentimentalize over a few hundred Native Americans who were ruined when our great civilization was being built? It may be that they suffered injustices, but, after all, you can't make an omelet without breaking a few eggs.")

- *Fallacy of false cause* occurs when events are causally connected but in fact no such causal connection has been established. ("Most of the company's managers before the bailout were Caucasians. Therefore, the government should demand that more minorities be in upper management before it provides any guaranteed loan.")

- *Fallacy of ad hominem* occurs when an argument diverts attention away from the question being argued by focusing instead on those arguing it. ("The candidate used drugs; thus we shouldn't trust his views on drug control.")

- *Fallacy of appeal to authority* occurs whenever an idea is justified by citing some source of expertise as a reason for holding that idea. ("Of course there shouldn't be government intervention; after all, Adam Smith and Milton Friedman are opposed to government intervention.")

- *Fallacy of mob appeal* occurs when an appeal is made to emotions, particularly to powerful feelings that can sway people in large crowds. ("I [a candidate for public office] almost died of cancer; therefore, you can trust me to be a good president.")

- *Fallacy of appeal to ignorance* occurs when an argument is based on an opponent's inability to disprove a conclusion as proof of the conclusion's correctness. ("I know that God doesn't exist because nobody has yet been able to prove God's existence.")

Sources: C. P. Dunn, "Logical Fallacies in Argument," Department of Management, San Diego State University. Retrieved March 26, 2003, from http://www-rohan.sdsu.edu/faculty/dunnweb/ logicafall.html. Adapted from S. M. Engel, *With Good Reason: An Introduction to Informal Fallacies* (New York: St. Martin's Press, 1976), pp. 66–130.

Causal Reasoning

Another way to reason is causally. **Causal reasoning** is a logical appeal that pertains to, constitutes, involves, or expresses a cause and therefore uses the word *because,* which is either implicitly or explicitly stated. For example, "I failed the class because I didn't complete the assignments," or "The basketball team is losing because it has an incompetent coach." The latter example points out some of the problems of causal reasoning. That the coach is incompetent may be a matter of opinion. The team might be losing because it doesn't have good players or because the other teams have taller players or because there is no way of recruiting good players. The causal pattern can be used for presenting evidence as well as for organizing an entire speech. The cause-and-effect pattern is one of the ways to organize a speech that is discussed in Chapter 14, "Organizing and Outlining the Speech."

Reasoning by Analogy

Finally, you can reason by **analogy.** In this case you compare two similar cases and conclude that if something is true for one, it must also be true for the other. Casey used analogy to try to get his listeners to understand the value of new electronic gadgets. He said, "Think of these as tools to make your life easier. These are just like the tools you've been using all along. The only difference is that these electronic tools are faster and more adaptable to your specific needs."

Often speeches of policy use analogy. Advocates of a policy look to see if the policy has succeeded elsewhere. For example, Katrina Paschalis was trying to get her listeners to understand that a better lifestyle will help prevent cancer. Her goal was to get her listeners to take an active part in their own preventive health care:

> You all know the threat that cancer holds on your life. It is a pervasive threat, but it needn't be scary. It is something you can handle. Think of living a healthy lifestyle as similar to owning a new automobile. Just as you want to keep the inside clean, you want to avoid smoking to keep your own insides clean. Just as you want to make sure all the fuel and other liquids you put into your car are exactly what the manufacturer's warranty requires, you, too, want to make certain you only take in drinks and foods known to be good for you. And just as you want to drive your car with care, you, too, want to use proper physical activity. If you take care of the insides, what you put into it, and how you drive it, you can keep your car in new condition. If you avoid smoking, a poor diet, and physical inactivity, you can prevent half of all the cancers in the USA and, thus, live your life as if in new condition.

Appeal to Your Audience Using Emotion

An **emotional appeal** focuses on listeners' needs, wants, desires, and wishes. Recent research shows that the people who are most successful at persuasion are those who can understand others' motives and desires—even when these motives and desires are not stated. To do this, researchers found, the persuader must be able to understand someone else's feelings without letting his or her own feelings get in the way (Goleman, 1986, pp. C1, C15).

In a public-speaking situation it is impossible to appeal to each individual's motives and desires, so it helps to know that there are some basic needs that we all have.

Appealing to Needs

Psychologist Abraham Maslow (1970) proposed a model that arranges people's needs from relatively low-level physical needs to higher-level psychological ones. This model, referred to as a **hierarchy of needs,** is shown in Figure 17-1. Let's look at the needs in the hierarchy and see how they can help you decide what emotional appeals to put in your persuasive speech.

As you can see at the bottom of the figure, the first needs all human beings have are *physiological needs.* Starving people do not care about freedom; their need for food is so great that it outweighs all other needs. Therefore, physiological needs must be taken care of before other needs can be met. Since we usually assume that basic needs are taken care of, they are generally not a basis for a persuasive speech, although politicians, clergy, and educators may try to persuade citizens to address the unmet basic needs of the poor.

Safety needs are next in the hierarchy. The whole area of safety needs can be useful in persuasion, since all of us have these needs in varying degrees. In the excerpt below, notice how the speaker appeals to the student audience's need for safety:

> *In the last three months there have been six assaults on this campus. Where have they occurred? All in parking lots with no lights. When? At night, after evening classes. Does this mean that you can't take any more evening classes without fearing for your life? Should you leave your car at home so you can avoid the campus parking lots?*

Figure 17-1

Maslow's Hierarchy of Needs

Self-Actualization Needs
(Genuine fulfillment, realization of potential)

Self-Esteem Needs
(Recognition, respect from others, self-respect)

Belongingness and Love Needs
(Friendship, giving and receiving love, affection)

Safety Needs
(Stability, order, freedom from violence, freedom from disease, security, structure, order, law)

Physiological Needs
(Food, water, sleep, and physical comfort)

How many different emotions or needs are being tapped to get results like these?

Belongingness and love needs, the next level, also have a potent appeal. If you doubt this, turn on your television set and note how many commercials make a direct pitch to the need to be loved.

Here is how one student used the need to belong to urge new students to join the Campus Fellowship—a student social group on campus:

> *The first year is the hardest year of college. You are in a new environment and are faced with a bewildering array of choices. I felt this way when I was a freshman. Then I met someone from "The Campus Fellowship" who invited me to one of its meetings. The minute I walked in the door several people met me and made me feel welcome. Today some of these people are my best friends.*

Self-esteem needs stem from our need to feel good about ourselves. We see a lot of persuasion based on these needs in self-help books. Typical themes are that you'll feel good about yourself if you change your fashion style, learn how to climb mountains, practice meditation, and so on. One student appealed to self-esteem needs when she gave a speech called "Try Something New:"

> *I have a friend who, at the age of 35, decided to learn how to play the flute. She had never played an instrument before, but she loved music and thought it would be interesting to give it a try. Now that she has been studying for two years, she told me, "I will never be a great player but this has been a wonderful experience. I enjoy my recordings even more because I know what the musicians are doing. I understand so much more about music. It's wonderful to try something new." I am here today to urge you to try something new yourself. To see what you can discover about yourself.*

On the Web

When we entered "Maslow's Hierarchy of Needs" into the Google search engine, we received 7,740 websites. Without the quotation marks, there were 12,200 hits (3-26-03). Several that we discovered that give great, brief explanations of Maslow's theory include the following:

C. G. Boeree (1998). "Personality Theories: Abraham Maslow, 1908–1970." Psychology Department, Shippensburg University. Retrieved March 26, 2003, from http://www.ship.edu/~cgboeree/maslow.html. Boeree includes a brief biography, an explanation of his theory, and his discussion includes some criticism.

R. Gwynne (1997). "Maslow's Hierarchy of Needs." Department of Speech Communication, University of Tennessee College of Communications, 1997. Retrieved March 26, 2003, from http://web.utk.edu/~gwynne/maslow.HTM.

W. G. Huitt (2002, May). "Maslow's Hierarchy of Needs." Educational Psychology Interactive, Department of Psychology and Counseling, Valdosta State University, Valdosta, GA 31698-0001. Retrieved March 26, 2003, from http://chiron.valdosta.edu/whuitt/col/regsys/maslow.html. In addition to a brief explanation of Maslow's theory, Huitt lists 15 additional references.

At the top of his hierarchy, Maslow puts *self-actualization needs*—the need to realize one's potential and the need to attain fulfillment. These needs involve our desire to do our best with what we have. An admissions director for a community college made this statement in a speech to a group of older women in an attempt to persuade them to go to college:

> *I'm sure that many of you look back at your high school days and think "I was a pretty good writer; I wonder if I still could write," or "I really liked my business courses; I would like to try my hand at bookkeeping again." I believe one of the saddest things that can happen to us is not to be able to try out things that we are good at, things that we have always wanted to do. Our new college program for returning adults will give you a chance to do just that—try out the things you are good at.*

You have the best chance of choosing the right emotional appeal if you have done a thorough job of researching your audience. For instance, safety needs tend to be important to families, especially those with young children. On the other hand, younger audiences, such as college students, generally focus more on belonging, love, and self-esteem needs. If you focused on safety needs to encourage a college audience to buy savings bonds, the students probably wouldn't find your speech very interesting. Self-actualization needs probably appeal most to older audiences. Adults who are approaching midlife are the most likely to ask themselves whether they have made the right choices for their lives and whether they should make some changes. Age, of course, is only one factor to consider in assessing needs. The more information you have about your audience, the better your chance of selecting the right emotional appeals.

Appealing to Other Emotions

Appeals can also be made to other emotions that all of us feel. In each of the examples that follow, the speaker is appealing to a common emotion.

In his commencement address, "Realize Your Dreams," Barry L. Ray (2001), field staffing manager for Frito-Lay, Inc., worked near the top of Maslow's hierarchy, on self-esteem needs—but rather than recognition, respect from others, or the typical self-respect, Ray sought to get listeners to believe that there was actually something deep within them, a reserve energy, that would serve them in times of need:

> *PERSEVERANCE: Now after you have found your passion, after you have committed yourself to pay the price of preparation, you must yet stand before the alter of perseverance . . . for life is a marathon. There are steep hills and sharp curves. There will be road blocks and curve balls so you needn't ever believe that your dreams will roll in on wheels of inevitability.*
>
> *As you go forward from this place today, some of you will have as your chief stock in trade, your extraordinary brilliance, an uncommon intellect. For others of you, your chief calling card will be irrepressible charm and the unmerited grace of magnificent looks. There are others of you who will go on to build impressive networks of contacts, but I would submit to you today that the world belongs to those who are the masters of perseverance.*
>
> *You name the field; you name the endeavor; history is the story of the fact that you're going to have to have something deep within, a reservoir that you can call on, for there comes a time when intellect alone is not enough. There comes a time when charm and good looks are not enough. There comes a time when an impressive network is not enough, but instead you must have something deep within which tells you to keep on keeping on, something that tells you that it's always darkest before the dawn, something that reminds you that you're made of the right stuff (p. 672).*

In another speech, the speaker worked to get her audience to feel angry about the shortsightedness of eliminating welfare payments to women who are in college. She stated:

> *During the time I was in college I received approximately $15,000 in welfare and food stamps from the government. Since I have been out of college and working I have paid approximately $60,000 in federal and state taxes. This means that to this date the government has received $45,000 by investing in me and my future. Wouldn't you like an investment that pays back three times the amount you put into it? Also, don't forget I have twenty more years of earning so the government is going to make a lot more money from me.*

Sometimes you can appeal to a collective emotion. One student urged student listeners to attend an honors convocation by appealing to their pride:

> *The most unsung heroes and heroines of this campus are those who have academic achievements. Do you know that fifteen students from this school have scholarships to medical school next year? That for the past six semesters students from this campus have gone on highly competitive federal internships? That we are ranked as number four in the nation for our writing program?*

Working Together

The following is the conclusion to a speech entitled "Reading as if for Life." Read the speech, and as you read it, think about the various emotions to which the speaker, Charles M. Reed (2001), is appealing. As a group, list all the possible emotions, then once a list is created, organize the list with the most important emotion you think Reed is appealing to listed first, the second most important one listed second, and so on.

> Please allow me to summarize the main thrust of what I've said today: In a rapidly changing world the practices of reading, writing, arguing, analyzing arguments, speaking, listening, and seeing as if for life are the most durable, the most "down-home," useful practices you can take away from four years at Brenau.

Your professional knowledge will need to be constantly transformed to keep pace with the rate of technological change, but the basic practices mentioned just above—these liberal arts, for that's precisely what I've been talking about—will endure, will serve you well every day of your life. So, far from amounting to cultural frills or genteel refinement, the liberal arts in your general education requirement can actually help to preserve and enhance the parts of your life you'll most cherish (p. 86).

Source: C. M. Reed, "Reading as if for Life: Preparing Young Women for the Real World," *Vital Speeches of the Day* 68:3, November 15, 2001, pp. 84–87.

When you are going to give a persuasive speech, think about the emotions you can appeal to. Emotions are powerful tools in persuasion. If you can find a good way to use them, they will add strength and power to your speech.

Choose Your Language Carefully

How audience members respond to your message is likely to depend on your ability to motivate them. Remember, people are not inclined to think or act the way you want them to unless they are motivated. In Chapter 5, Verbal Communication, we discussed the importance of language; here we simply want to underscore the importance of language for appealing to listeners' emotions.

Try to keep language in mind as you select supporting material. You want to find emotion-arousing material for both your introduction and your conclusion. You want to stimulate the emotions of your listeners with special words. And you want to create emotional pictures that will make people feel what you are talking about.

Now look at a very carefully worded conclusion. Don't be put off by the sophistication of the language or the structure of the sentences. Consider this example as a challenge for you. Realize, first, that it was constructed by Gene Fendt (2002), a professor of philosophy at the University of Nebraska. Realize, second, that it was delivered at the Explorations Lecture Series, sponsored by the Office of the Vice Chancellor for Academic Affairs.

Realize, third, that the title of the speech is "Two Figures of the Imagination: Their Consequences for the Arts." Realize, finally, that Fendt began his speech with a short parable by Plato from Plato's *Republic*, 596c, in which Plato discusses the imagination in Republic 10. This, then, is the conclusion to his speech:

> *So what? What should we do? Let us, then, practice crying with the best of them. Our object is not to be variety, but truth; not difference, but accuracy to the occasion. To educate students in some other thing than this is to arrange their marriage to failure and their slavery to opinion. And we know who those are who are best at crying the occasion, we have known for hundreds, and in some cases thousands of years. That is to say, in order to train our demi-urgic imagination we must practice what the masters in our favored medium have practiced: geometry, calculus and differential equations, for example; or control of the hand in drawing a line; government of the tongue in speaking one. We must become familiar with the tools the old masters used, both to see what those tools, that tongue, those media enabled and to see where they failed and how. Only if we do this first will the demi urge of our own imagination be able, on the occasion, to cry accurately, articulately, or with any hope of that universal choric agreement that every great artist aims at, and some, on occasion, achieve. In that achievement Beauty and Truth are one, Justice and Peace kiss (p. 448).*

In a completely contrasting example, look at the way Martin Luther King Jr. (2001) used language in the last speech he gave, "I've Been to the Mountaintop," just before he was assassinated the next day. The speech was delivered at Bishop Charles Mason Temple, Memphis, Tennessee, April 3, 1968. In the speech, he recalled an unsuccessful assassination attempt in which a demented woman stabbed him. X-rays revealed that the tip of the blade was on the edge of his aorta, the main artery, which, if punctured, one would drown in his or her own blood. The *New York Times*, in their report of the incident the next morning, said that if he had merely sneezed, he would have died. Here, King tells why he is happy he didn't sneeze. The expressions in brackets are audience responses:

> *If I had sneezed* [Yes], *I wouldn't have been around here in 1961, when we decided to take a ride for freedom and ended segregation in interstate travel* [All right].
>
> *If I had sneezed* [Yes], *I wouldn't have been around here in 1962, when Negroes in Albany, Georgia, decided to straighten their backs up. And whenever men and women straighten their backs up, they are going somewhere, because a man can't ride your back unless it is bent.*
>
> *If I had sneezed* [Applause], *if I had sneezed, I wouldn't have been here in 1963* [All right], *when the black people of Birmingham, Alabama, roused the conscience of this nation and brought into being the Civil Rights Bill.*
>
> *If I had sneezed, I wouldn't have had a chance later this year, in August, to try to tell America about a dream that I had had.* [Yes],
>
> *If I had sneezed* [Applause], *I wouldn't have been down in Selma, Alabama, to see the great movement there.*

If I had sneezed, I wouldn't have been in Memphis to see a community rally around those brothers and sisters who are suffering. [Yes] I'm so happy that I didn't sneeze (pp. 221–22).

Selecting language that evokes pictures in listeners' minds also will help motivate listeners. Look at the images created by the language in Lance R. Odden's speech, "Talk to Your Children about the Tough Stuff:"

Remember that the innocent freshman pledge who died at MIT last year had been told to drink a beer and a bottle of bourbon. Remember the three students who died in the Virginia college system with no one learning from the previous experience. Remember the deaths of the students at LSU. Remember the rape, which was alcohol induced, at a local high school party. Note that just last Tuesday, in Denver, an 18-year-old girl died after having consumed over a liter of tequila (1999, p. 301).

Odden ended his speech with a story to show how alcohol use on campus affects everyone, not just those who do the drinking. Again, examine the way he used language to create images in listeners' minds:

Let me illustrate this with one story. Ten days ago, one mid and five upper-mid boys went on a legal weekend to one of your homes. The host family is a wonderful one. Most of the boys would seem to be bright and naive. After a nice dinner, good conversation and some pool, the boys went to visit a friend at a nearby girls' school. They were to be back by midnight. Before going to the school, in the woods in back of their host family's house, they drank a half gallon of vodka in cups cut with orange juice. A couple of the boys only had a drink or two, the others had more—a lot more, as it turned out—and by the time they got to the girls' school, two of the boys had passed out, and a third was in trouble. Fortunately, one boy stayed to assist his friends, but two went off to find girls, and one more, intoxicated, went off on his own. Fortunately, a neighbor saw the boys in trouble and summoned help, leading to three students being taken to the hospital. The alcohol level of the two boys who passed out was .031. Their brains were comatose. Had they not been discovered, they would have died. These are wonderful boys; they had not been partyers. They followed the lead of the cool guys. Neither their parents nor any Taft faculty member would have predicted this (p. 304).

■ STRUCTURE YOUR MATERIAL EFFECTIVELY

How you decide to structure your material may depend on the material itself; it may depend on your own interests or intentions; or it may depend on the situation or assignment. The most important consideration, however, is your listeners' attitude, or how you expect your audience to react. Let's review the organizational schemes most commonly used in persuasive speeches: cause-and-effect order, problem-solution order, and motivated sequence. (We cover these and other organizational formats in Chapter 14, Organizing and Outlining the Speech.) Here we will discuss several topics related to persuasive speaking: questions of fact, value, and policy; one-sided versus two-sided arguments; and order of presentation.

Questions of Fact, Value, and Policy

Chapter 10, Small Groups: Characteristics, discussed using questions of fact, value, and policy in group discussions. Now let's see how these questions can be used for persuasive speeches.

Questions of Fact

A *question of fact* deals with what is true or false. One student used a question of fact when he spoke on the topic "Do Extraterrestrial Beings Exist in Our Universe?" The purpose of his speech was to persuade the audience that the chances appear highly probable.

Questions of Value

A *question of value* is concerned with some aspect of a moral issue: whether something is good or bad, right or wrong, beneficial or detrimental, and so on. Note how a student used a question of value to discuss the topic of plagiarism:

Specific purpose:	To persuade my audience that plagiarism of any kind is unacceptable.
Central idea:	Plagiarism may have short-term gains, but it does long-term harm.
Main points:	I. People's professional careers have been ruined when it was revealed that they had cheated in college.
	II. People who plagiarize deny themselves the opportunity to learn new skills.
	III. Plagiarism is theft; rather than take someone's possessions, you steal his or her ideas and work.

Questions of Policy

A *question of policy* deals with specific courses of action and usually contains such words as *should, ought,* or *must.* Here are the main points for a speech based on a question of policy:

Specific purpose:	To persuade my audience that all students should be granted a one-term work-experience opportunity as part of their college education.
Central idea:	A work experience will give students a realistic understanding of the workplace before they graduate.
Main points:	I. Work experiences are an effective way to give students real-world college.
	II. Work experiences provide students with useful contacts outside college.
	III. Work experiences offer students a better base for understanding their education.
	IV. Work experiences develop skills that may not be developed in college.

The sample persuasive speech by Juanita E. Hill, "Unlock Your Full Potential," presented at the end of this chapter (pages 642–649), is arranged in a topical manner as is the example above. Also, it is clearly organized around a question of policy: Students should unlock their full potential by expanding upon their current talents and abilities, exploring new frontiers and possibilities, and experimenting with new thoughts and behaviors. One of the strengths of Hill's speech is the way she has tied each of the main heads of her speech (expand, explore, and experiment) with transitions. Her speech is an example of a tightly structured, well-supported presentation.

One-Sided versus Two-Sided Arguments

Should persuaders present one side or both sides of an issue? When you know your listeners basically support your ideas, one side may be sufficient. For example, a student knew that she didn't have to persuade her audience of the pros and cons of speed dating. Instead, she came up with some unique ideas for how her listeners could find dates.

There are occasions, however, when speakers should present both sides of the picture. Often the presentation of both sides will boost credibility: The speaker is likely to be perceived as fairer and more rational. When an issue of public importance is controversial, it's a good idea to present both sides, since most people will probably have heard something about each side. When a student spoke on gun control, he presented both sides because he knew there were strong feelings for and against. Another speaker chose to present both sides of the sex-education issue. She thought sex education should be taught at home, but she wanted to let her audience know that others preferred it to be handled in the schools.

There has been extensive research comparing the one-sided speech with the two-sided speech. The results seem to indicate that (1) A two-sided speech is more effective when the listeners have at least a high school education; (2) The two-sided speech is especially effective if the evidence clearly supports the thesis; and (3) The two-sided presentation is more effective when listeners oppose the speaker's position, but the one-sided approach is more effective when listeners already support the thesis (Thompson, 1978; Hovland, Lumsdaine, & Sheffield, 1949).

Ethical considerations should sometimes be taken into account when deciding whether to present two sides. For example, if presenting only one side will suppress key information, then presenting two sides is essential, but you may need to refute the side you don't agree with.

Order of Presentation

Certain ways of organizing speeches seem to be especially effective for a persuasive speech. As we discussed in detail in Chapter 14, Organizing and Outlining the Speech, the *problem-solution order* works well for persuasion. It lets the speaker build tension by describing the problem and getting listeners involved in it; then the speaker can relieve the tension by providing a solution.

Another organizational pattern that works well for persuasion is the **comparative-advantage order.** When using this pattern, a speaker presents several proposed solutions to a problem and then persuades the audience to choose a particular solution by emphasizing its advantages. For example:

If you follow the newspapers, magazines, and books, you know there are many ideas about how to live a better life. One is to follow a better diet. Another is to get more sleep. A third is to exercise more. A fourth is to develop better time-management skills. But I have a solution that draws strengths from each of these, and that is self-discipline. I favor this last solution because. . . .

The *motivated sequence* was discussed in some detail in Chapter 14, Organizing and Outlining the Speech, but because of its popularity and usefulness for persuasion, we will review it here. The five steps of the Monroe motivated sequence, which is based on the problem-solution form, suggest five specific main points for developing a speech. Any problem-solving speech can be adapted to this form.

1. The *attention* step's purpose is to gain the attention of the audience. You do this by following the suggestions in the section, The Speech Introduction, in Chapter 14.
2. The *need* step points out a problem that affects audience members. In this step you create a sense of urgency about the problem.
3. The *satisfaction* step gives relief to the audience by providing a solution to the problem.
4. The *visualization* step lets the audience see how much better things would be if this solution is put into effect.
5. The *action* step urges the audience to go out and take some action that will help solve the problem.

Since the motivated sequence follows the human thought process, it is extremely easy to use. In fact, you might be using it without even realizing it. Here's how Maria tries to persuade her roommate, Carlotta, to move from the dorm to an off-campus apartment:

Attention: Do you realize how small this room is? We don't have anyplace to store our clothes—let alone our books, CDs, and DVDs.

Need: We really need a space where we can spread out a little and invite our friends in without sitting nose to nose.

Satisfaction: See all the ads for off-campus housing? We can get an apartment in town for a little bit less than we are paying for the dorm.

Visualization: Just imagine—if we had our own apartment, we could each have a separate room. We could have all our friends over at one time.

Another Point of View

In their book *You've Only Got Three Seconds*, Camille Lavington and Stephanie Losee (1997), in a section entitled Preparing a Speech, explain how you can lead listeners through a decision-making process that ends with their endorsement of your plan. The structure of the interaction between audience and speaker should proceed through seven steps: listen, assess, bridge, adapt, acknowledge, empower, and endorse. As you read Lavington and Losee's description of pitching a fund-raising strategy to a philanthropic organization, compare and contrast their series of steps with those of the motivated sequence:

Now we're looking at this process from the point of view of a member of the audience rather than that of the speaker. A board member first listens *to the new strategy. He then* assesses *whether the plan will preserve the dignity of the cause while attracting enough dollars to finance the next year's activities. The board member thinks about previous fund-raising drives and wonders whether the new campaign will be a* bridge *from the previous one; will the continuity of the charity's image be broken by departing from what worked in the past? He then recognizes how to* adapt *one aspect of the fund drive to make it fly (you've got him here!). As he discusses his ideas with the presenter, he* acknowledges *the merits of the strategy. Satisfied that the changes he's requested will be made, he* empowers *the presenter by outlining the* resources he'll devote to the effort. After the presentation has ended, he puts his political power behind the new fund-raising drive to demonstrate his endorsement.

Questions

1. Does the motivated sequence view the process of persuasion from the point of view of the speaker or the point of view of the audience? What support do you have for this position? Which point of view makes more sense for persuaders? Why?

2. Could a speaker use the motivated sequence and still attain or cover all the steps in the sequence above?

3. Is the system described above simple and easy to understand, or is it too complex? Justify your answer.

4. Let's say you have a new study method that, if followed, will guarantee students A's in their courses. We'll call it "The Complete Study System." Using this topic, trace the steps (as presented above) that your listeners would follow to achieve endorsement of your ideas. Can Lavington and Losee's steps be adapted to listeners in a classroom situation?

Source: C. Lavington, and S. Losee, *You've Only Got Three Seconds: How to Make the Right Impression in Your Business and Social Life*. (New York: Doubleday, 1997).

Action:	Here's the list of apartments that are for rent. Let's start making some appointments to go and see them.

Now see how one student speaker developed a persuasive speech using the motivated sequence:

Specific purpose:	To persuade my audience that the campus newspaper should be funded directly by the activity fee rather than by student government.

Central idea: When student government funds the newspaper, it often tries to control the news.

Main points:

I. Attention: This week the student government says it will stop funding the newspaper unless the newspaper stops criticizing it.

II. Need: This has been a problem for a long time. Whenever the government doesn't like what the paper says, it closes the paper down.

III. Satisfaction: The only way to solve this problem is to fund the paper directly with money from the student activity fee. If the student government doesn't control the funding, it can't control the newspaper.

IV. Visualization: The newspaper will be able to play its proper role as watchdog of government, and all of you will no longer find that the paper has not come out because the government has closed it down again.

V. Action: I have a petition addressed to the president of this university. I hope all of you will sign it.

■ BUILD YOUR CREDIBILITY

The likelihood of our being persuaded depends greatly on the person doing the persuading. You can probably think of people in your own life who are particularly persuasive. Why are some people more persuasive than others? Research on persuasion says we are more likely to be effective as persuaders if listeners consider us to be credible. **Credibility,** or believability, consists of four qualities: expertise, dynamism, trustworthiness, and ethics. Let's look at each of them.

Expertise

Someone who has **expertise** possesses special ability, skill, or knowledge. That is, he or she is an expert. A speaker who is perceived as an expert on his or her subject gains much credibility. For example, let's say that on the news one night you see a woman talking about the effects of long-term exercise on health. The anchorperson introduces her by saying that she is a medical doctor from Johns Hopkins Medical School who has been studying the effects of exercise. Since the results of her study are interesting, you listen closely. The next day you hear a student give a persuasive speech about the value of exercise. Some of his comments, however, contradict some of what you heard on the evening news. Which speaker do you believe? In this case there isn't much doubt. You believe the physician because she is an expert.

Expertise Based on Personal Experience

When you are a speaker trying to persuade an audience, it will help your credibility if you can show some expertise about your subject. Expertise does not depend only on book learning or specialized training; you can be an expert because of your personal experience. Nancy, for example, speaks of her own experience with alcoholism:

> *One night I went to a party. I remember the early part of the evening but that's about all. The next thing I remember was waking up in my own bed. I didn't remember the end of the party or how I got home. When I woke up that morning and realized I didn't remember anything, I knew I was in serious trouble.*

You don't always have to relate such a dramatic experience as Nancy's. One student who had done volunteer work with the Red Cross persuaded classmates to serve as volunteers. Another student persuaded several classmates to petition the dean of students for better food in the cafeteria. She knew that the food was poor, as did many members of her audience. Thus she used both her experience and the experience of audience members to make her point.

Expertise Based on Commitment

Another way to show expertise is by establishing your commitment to your topic. Listeners are more inclined to believe speakers who have taken actions that support their positions. If you can show that you have contributed to a charity, you are more likely to persuade others to contribute. If you are trying to persuade people to become scout leaders and can point out that you have been a scout or have worked with scouts for many years, people are more likely to take you seriously.

Expertise through Research

Expertise can also be developed through research. By interviewing and by reading articles and books, you can quote acknowledged experts, thereby making your speech more credible. When you are using information derived from experts, make that clear in your speech with such references as:

According to Dr. John Smith, a noted authority in this area . . .

From an article in last week's *U.S. News & World Report* . . .

From Daniel Goleman's best-selling book, *Working with Emotional Intelligence* . . .

Dynamism

Speakers with **dynamism,** another aspect of credibility, show a great deal of enthusiasm and energy for their subjects. For example, when a student tried to get his classmates to become more politically active, he spoke of his own work in a local politician's primary campaign as one of the most exciting times of his life. He described his experience so vividly that the audience was able to feel his excitement.

It's easy to be dynamic about a subject you're enthusiastic about. When Hanna spoke about the Australian exchange program, she started this way:

When your classmates are fighting snow and ice, you will be on the sunny beaches of Australia. When it's winter here, it's summer there. You'll have a chance to talk with people who speak your language. You'll have a chance to see how a different political system works, and you'll have a chance to visit spaces that are more wide open than you've ever dreamed of. A semester in Australia will change your life.

Much of the dynamism in a speech will be created nonverbally. A speaker who stands up straight, projects his or her voice to the back of the room, and doesn't hesitate will be seen by the audience as more dynamic than one who doesn't do these things. Watch for the most dynamic speakers in your class, and make some mental notes on how they convey their energy and enthusiasm nonverbally.

Trustworthiness

A speaker with **trustworthiness** is perceived as reliable and dependable. Sometimes we have no way of knowing whether a speaker is trustworthy unless he or she does something unreliable, such as showing up an hour late for a speech. In a speech communication class, however, after a month or so, most students can identify classmates who are reliable and dependable. These are people who come on time for class, give their speeches on time, pull their weight in a group, and give evidence that they have spent time preparing for a speech. Because of their previous behavior in class, they are perceived as trustworthy and therefore worth listening to.

Ethics

Ethics are a matter of conforming to acceptable and fair standards of conduct. Ethics are particularly important to persuasion because you are trying to change people—often in a significant way. If your audience doesn't perceive you as ethical, your speech will fail. Here are some ethical principles that are particularly useful in persuasive speaking:

1. Treat your audience with respect. Assume that audience members are intelligent and mature and will respond to a well-reasoned and well-organized appeal.

2. Take care not to distort or exaggerate your facts. Find the best facts you can, and let them stand on their own.

3. Avoid lying or name calling. Even if you think that the opposing side is stupid or vicious, it's unacceptable to say so.

4. Avoid suppressing key information. If you discover important information that doesn't support your view, include it but find a way of refuting it.

5. If you have something to gain personally from your persuasive speech, tell your audience what it is.

Working Together

Apply the ethical principles you have just read about to each of the following situations:

1. Is it ethical to give a speech advocating a position with which you disagree?

2. Is it ethical to present a speech just to fulfill an assignment—a speech that you feel no commitment to or responsibility for?

3. Why are student speakers under obligation to provide listeners with ideas that are logically developed and well supported?

4. Why are student speakers responsible for being fully knowledgeable about their topics?

5. Should student speakers concern themselves with the consequences of their speaking? Why or why not?

6. Show respect for your opponent or the opposing side. Do not dismiss ideas from the opposition; show how your ideas are better.

7. Take time to develop and organize the best possible speech you can. Make it worth the audience's time to listen to you.

■ THE INFLUENCE OF THE INTERNET ON PERSUASIVE COMMUNICATION

Along with the Internet has come an information glut. According to Kelly Mooney and Laura Bergheim, in the book *The Ten Demandments* (McGraw-Hill, 2002), we are captives of our multiple choices, ensnared in our wide-open lines of communication, and victims of the messages that clog our e-mail boxes. In this generation of instant information and news, there are new demands on persuaders because listeners have new expectations and needs. The items in the following list of things persuaders must do to adapt to listeners in the age of the Internet may not be new; they simply require a new emphasis or focus. To be successful, persuaders must:

1. *Create immediate respect and integrity.* Without respect and integrity on the Internet, listeners will mouse click to another source just as easily as they can divert their attention from what is taking place in front of them.

2. *Form an emotional bond with listeners.* With no emotional bond, there is no need for listeners to stay tuned. If you are fired up about what you believe in, your listeners will become fired up as well.

3. *Use listeners' time wisely.* With so many resources available to listeners, consider yourself just one more—nothing more and nothing less—unless you prove otherwise. An efficient use of time adds value to whatever product is discussed.

4. *Filter the noise for them by organizing the chaos.* So much information available becomes little more than noise—clutter—to many people.

5. *Put what is most important front and center.* Because it is fast, the Internet has helped nurture short attention spans. When they are drowning in a glut, they need a life preserver in their face.

6. *Offer the necessary facts, figures, and additional information.* What they need and want is available to them if they want to pursue it; persuaders need to efficiently and effectively offer what they need and want with the necessary support.

7. *Bring in others' ideas and opinions; avoid dominating your speech as the single, sole source of information and opinion.* The Internet offers links; when you link your ideas to those of others, you provide a strong foundation for belief and action. A site with links simply says, "Click here for more information."

8. *Make certain listeners have ways to get further information; give them the citations necessary.* Because they are unlikely to make up their mind on the spot (because they don't have to do so), they need specific instructions on where additional information can be found. The easier it is to get, the more likely it will be sought.

9. *Present material in understandable, bite-size units that are easily digestible.* From kids' television shows to *USA Today* and the Internet, not only have short attention spans been nurtured, but listeners want information that is prepackaged and ready to put into the oven, onto the table, or into their minds.

10. *Give listeners personal attention.* Remember ". . . the Internet . . . has altered the landscape of consumer relationships by giving people experiences, services, and product options tailored to their tastes and needs as never before" (Mooney & Bergheim, p. 167).

11. *Talk to listeners in a language they can understand.* There can be no ambiguity or misunderstanding, because the connection between persuader and listener is but a mouse-click option. Translate jargon; avoid difficult words; keep it simple.

12. *Exceed their expectations by offering them an enthusiastic, relevant responsiveness to their needs.* Persuaders' information must somehow rise above the noise and clutter to make a difference. Enthusiasm can be an effective persuader.

13. *Deliver a quality product.* Whether it is the speech as a whole, the ideas, suggestions, solutions, or the supporting material, listeners expect quality—quality draws them in. The Internet offers so many options, listeners are accustomed to making quick quality decisions. Whether these quality decisions are right or wrong is irrelevant; decisions will be made.

14. *Simplify their decision by making solutions and approaches fair, easy, and understandable.* If accepting the belief or pursuing the action requested is the least bit difficult, it is unlikely to take place.

15. *Help listeners see your solutions or approaches in action—in situations with which they can easily identify.* The Internet is both a verbal and visual medium.

16. *Give listeners freedom.* Avoid high pressure, pushy persuasion. Technology has given customers a greater sense of control. Acknowledge their need to move at their own pace and, thus, release them from their over-scheduled, over-committed, stress-filled lives.

Mooney claims that in today's Internet-dominated world ". . . what really counts in the long run is the sense of being known as an individual, understood as a unique human being, and treated with the respect that each and everyone of us deserves" (Mooney & Bergheim, p. 174).

Sample Speech

The following speech was given by Juanita E. Hill in her summer required public-speaking class. Ms. Hill is a friend of the authors, and her speech is used here with her permission.

General Purpose:	To persuade.
Specific Purpose:	To inspire my class to unlock their full potential by expanding upon their current talents and abilities, exploring new frontiers and possibilities, and experimenting with new thoughts and behaviors.
Central Idea:	The three keys to unlocking your full potential are expanding your talent and ability, exploring new frontiers and possibilities, and experimenting with new thoughts and behaviors.

Unlock Your Full Potential

Introduction

I confess that I am neither a normal nor an average college student. I am returning to college after raising a family, but I want you to know that it wasn't my own desire for a college education that motivated my return—although my desire had to be strong. More than anything else, it was my father who inspired my return. He told me when I was very young that "My life is exactly what I choose it to be." He said, "No matter what the circumstances, I am in charge of how I feel and how I act." Although he was an electrician and without a college education himself, he knew its value, he never let me forget it, and he instilled the desire in me.

Hill begins her speech by reaching out for audience attention with a personal example. What makes the introduction even more effective is her inclusion of two of the specific quotations from her father that inspired her—and might inspire her listeners as well.

About accepting responsibility for yourself and your behavior, Jerry O'Connor of Oregon State

In her second paragraph, she immediately turns to a quotation to reveal the importance of accepting

University said it best, "If what you say and do is prompted by others, or if nothing is ever your fault because others allegedly 'pushed' you, you really cannot claim to be an adult, just a poor follower" (O'Connor, 2002, p. 4). There is an outstanding website called "Tools for Personal Growth: Accepting Personal Responsibility" by Doctors James J. Messina and Constance M. Messina who have listed 18 ways for accepting personal responsibility, and I have written their website URL on the chalkboard: http://www.coping.org/growth/accept.htm.

Because I have been away from college for about 10 years, I have had a chance to think about its value, to reflect on its possibilities, and to consider its potential. So, in this speech I want to be personal, but I also want to inspire and persuade, because I believe that each of you has far more potential locked within you than you recognize, acknowledge, or act upon. It's there, but it lies unknown, untapped, and often unrealized. Today, I have the keys to unlocking your full potential, and I have organized my speech around the words expand, explore, and experiment.

I. **Expand** your talents and abilities.

To expand is to increase your range, scope, volume, and size. The fact that you are here—in college—means that you have special talents and abilities. Expanding means doing better than merely resting on your laurels, and better, too, than doing the best you can with what you have: It means expanding, enlarging upon and growing those talents and abilities. But how do you do that?

A. At the website for Student Affairs and Services of Memorial University, the University of Newfoundland, Canada, they state that the students who are most successful in college have uncovered the secret of how to make the most out of their university experience: "the more they involve themselves in the life of the university, the greater their sense of personal satisfaction" (Student experiences, n.d.). At the Career Services and Arts and Sciences Advising Services at the University of Tennessee, they state that "With planning, you can combine course work, internships, campus activities, part-time

responsibility. Even better, she gives listeners a website that she writes on the chalkboard about accepting responsibility.

Notice in paragraph three of the introduction how Hill depends on "triplets"—groups of three words—to help convey her ideas: think about its value, reflect on its possibilities, and consider its potential. She uses the words recognize, acknowledge, and act upon. She uses unknown, untapped, and unrealized. And, finally, the main ideas of her speech form a triplet: expand, explore, and experiment. Hill is obviously concerned about the language she uses.

In each case, when Hill introduces a main head, she also briefly defines the term she is introducing. Doing this each of the three times she introduces a new main head not only reveals the use of parallelism—setting her ideas in parallel or similar form—but it alerts listeners, too, to the new main head.

Beginning with the first main head, subpoint A, Hill depends on evidence from the Internet to support her ideas. What is as important as the evidence itself, is her citation of the source she is using within her speech. This increases the value of the information, increases her credibility, and gives audience members a chance to evaluate her sources—and, thus, her information.

employment, volunteer work, and a variety of other activities that will enhance your future career opportunities" (Undecided . . . , n.d.).

B. Follow the first rule of the college game, according to the Wayne State University website: "Go to class" (O'Connor, 2002). On this campus, it seems to me, the common thinking is to skip class. More than lack of relevancy or lack of interest, it seems like the way to fit in. But I can tell you from my own experience, a pattern of good attendance and participation, just like it says at the Wayne State website, develops "the essential habits of collegiate success" (O'Connor, 2002, p. 1).

In main head one, subpoint B, Hill combines her personal experience with support from a Wayne State University website.

C. Another "rule" from the Wayne State website is "Accept constructive criticism" (O'Connor, 2002). You will never again be faced with the number of growth possibilities as you will in college: "Constructive criticism is not meant to be personal, and it will help you reach your potential" (O'Connor, 2002, p. 2). Don't worry about the source; don't worry about its nature; and don't worry about its intent; if you don't get constructive criticism, seek it out.

In main head one, subpoint C, Hill again combines her personal experience with support from the same Wayne State University website.

Transition: Involve yourself, go to class, and accept constructive criticism are three of the ways you have for expanding your talents and abilities. Now I'll look at three ways you have to explore new frontiers and possibilities.

In her transition from main point one to main point two, Hill briefly summarized her three subpoints and forecast her next main head. It is a good idea to do this because listeners have a difficult time following the organization of the speech. More important, however, may be how this helps them keep track of the ideas during the speech.

II. **Explore** new frontiers and possibilities.

Notice how Hill keeps the phrasing of her main heads parallel with each other.

To explore is to search through or travel over new lands for the purpose of discovery. Exploring involves seizing the college experience with both hands and milking it for all it's worth (Miller, 1999).

A. Perhaps the most value you can get from a college education—and something you will never again have offered to you in such quality and quantity—is group activities. Our college talks about opportunities for meeting new people in freshman orientation: recreational, sports, music, and drama activities. There are special activities for engineering

In main head two, subpoint A, Hill remembers her college orientation, but she obviously used a website, as well, to help supplement the ideas she remembered. Her goal was to cover all her bases.

students, business students, and education students, too. There are cultural and religious associations as well as volunteer service organizations. Almost every department has a club or organization as well for those who share similar passions and perspectives. And, last but not least, there are fraternities, sororities, a student government association, a student newspaper, and both a student radio and television station as well (Participating . . . , n.d.).

B. The "Top 10 Tips for Academic Success" website at Rutgers University, Newark, New Jersey, suggests "including courses of interest in your next registration that may not be in your presently desired major" (Top 10 Tips . . . , n.d.). We become so limited by required courses in majors and minors, we often forget about exploring new possibilities.

In main head two, subpoint B, she used the website at Rutgers University to give herself and her ideas credibility.

C. "The single most important skill for life success is communication," says the Wayne State University website. (O'Connor, 2002, p. 2). And there are two distinct ways to use those communication skills to explore new frontiers and possibilities:

1. Communicate with your professors. These are people "who will evaluate your work, supply references, and guide your intellectual development" (O'Connor, 2002, p. 2).

2. Communicate in class. When you don't know or understand, ask questions. "There are no dumb questions concerning subject matter" according to Jerry O'Connor, of Oregon State University (O'Connor, 2002, p. 3).

In main head two, subpoint C, Hill notes the importance of communication to life success, but she gives listeners distinct ways to use their communication skills: communicating with their professors, and communicating in class.

Transition: So, to summarize this section on exploration: participate in a variety of group activities, include courses of interest—not just required courses—in your next registration, and develop your communication skills, and use those skills in communicating with your professors and in class. We've looked at ways for expanding your interests and abilities, and we've looked at ways to explore new frontiers and possibilities. Now, let's look at three ways to experiment with new thoughts and behaviors.

In the transition between main head two and main head three Hill first summarizes the three subpoints of main head two, then reviews both main head one and two before forecasting main head three.

III. **Experiment** with new thoughts and behaviors.

To experiment is to test in order to confirm or disprove something that may be in doubt.

A. You will never in your life have the opportunities for testing yourself as you do in college. For example, I have never been a political person, and yet I ran for a student-government office and won, and now I am also the student representative to the Board of Trustees. It began as an experiment because I doubted both my ability and my interest in government, but I have found it fascinating, to say the least.

In main head three, subpoint A, Hill again uses personal experience. But notice that after she uses it, she ties the idea back to main head three: "It began as an experiment. . . ."

B. You can experiment, too, by volunteering. Near this college or on campus here, are day care centers, nursery schools, state hospitals for persons with mental retardation, Head Start programs, YWCA child-care programs, public-interest groups, host-family programs for international students, homeless shelters, nursing homes, and retirement communities (Social life . . . , n.d.).

In main head three, subpoint B, Hill again emphasizes the subject of main head three: to experiment. What is interesting is how much research and background information Hill has about the volunteer opportunities available on or near her campus. She proves again she has done her homework.

C. Another area for experimentation involves your major. Some students "change their minds several times before honing in on a major that fits" (Carter et al., 1998, p. 2). Experimenting now may mean happiness for a lifetime. What you may not realize is, "Many employers are more interested in your ability to think than in your specific knowledge, and therefore may not pay as much attention to your major as they do to your critical-thinking skills" (Carter et al., 1998, p. 2). To experiment, start again, thinking about a major by:

1. Taking a variety of classes.
2. Not ruling out subject areas not classified as "safe."
3. Getting to know your self, interests, and abilities.
4. Working with advisors.
5. Seeking opinions from instructors, friends, family members, and other students.
6. Developing your critical-thinking skills.

(Carter et al., 1998, pp. 1–2)

In main head three, subpoint C, Hill not only encourages students to experiment by thinking again about their major, but she gives them six specific ways to do it.

Transition: You can experiment with new thoughts and behaviors by trying things that you've never tried before—testing the waters, so to speak. Remember, you are not the same person you were when you were growing up; thus, just as tastes change, your needs and interests change, too. To discover these changes, you need to break out from habits, routines, and past expectations. Engage in volunteer activities, explore new and different majors, and, above all, develop your critical-thinking skills: "Critical thinking is the most crucial ingredient in any recipe for school and career success" (Carter et al., 1998, p. 1).

In the transition from main head three to the conclusion, Hill tells her audience why experimenting is so important: tastes, needs, and interests change, and to discover these changes, she gives them outlets: break out from habits, routines, and past expectations. Then she summarizes main head three.

Conclusion

In her online article, "Taking Responsibility for Your Self," Marie T. Russell, publisher of *InnerSelf Magazine* and *The Natural Yellow Pages* (1987–2002), begins her article asking the questions "Are you enthusiastic about life? Do you wake up excited to face another day? Are you interested in your work and are you involved in it with intensity, energy, and zeal? Are you doing what you would choose to do were you to make a completely fresh start? Are you committing your time to activities you enjoy?" (Russell, 2002). I am convinced her questions are relevant to each one of us. If we find ways to unlock our full potential, the answers to all these questions can be a resounding and enthusiastic YES.

Hill was obviously concerned with audience attention as she began her conclusion, because she cited an authority and immediately used the authority's questions to question her own listeners—to reestablish their interest and to again grab their attention.

In my introduction I wrote on the chalkboard that URL of the outstanding website of Messina and Messina that provides 18 ways for accepting personal responsibility. Here, I want to suggest a book by Brian Tracy (2002) called *Focal Point.* Tracy says that "Among the most important personal choices you can make is to accept complete responsibility for everything you are and everything you will ever be" (p. 12). Tracy says—and this is an important key—"The acceptance of personal responsibility is what separates the superior persons from the average person" (p. 12).

In the second paragraph of her conclusion, Hill refers back to her introduction and underscores the URL referred to there, but adds an additional book by Brian Tracy called *Focal Point.* Also, she reinforces the importance of personal responsibility.

I began my speech by telling you how my father inspired me—or, should I say, put the desire within me. There is more. He had a favorite saying that he had me write on one of my drawing pads when I was five years old, but he reinforced it over

In the third paragraph of a fairly lengthy conclusion, Hill refers back to her introduction by again giving a quotation from her father—a very effective saying, as it turns out, that we are certain Hill believes her listeners will find endearing.

and over throughout my life, and I committed it to memory. It goes like this:

Whatever you are, be that.

Whatever you say, be true.

Straightforwardly act,

Be honest in fact,

But, be nobody else but you.

By assuming full responsibility for your life—all your actions and feelings—you will live a fulfilling life. As Dr. Frank Pittman says, in his book *Grow Up!,* "Without responsibility there can be no happiness" (Smalley, 2002). Tracy (2002) says "Personal responsibility is the preeminent trait of leadership and the wellspring of high performance in every person in every situation" (p. 12). But, there is another benefit of assuming full responsibility for your life that you may not realize as you sit here today, and it is both related to happiness and to leadership, and that is that by assuming full responsibility for your life, you have the possibility of unlocking your full potential.

In the final paragraph of her speech, Hill quotes first from Dr. Frank Pittman on the importance of responsibility and its relation to happiness. Then, she immediately backs up that quotation with one from Brian Tracy who connects responsibility to leadership. Hill summarizes her speech and ties assuming full responsibility not just to happiness and leadership, but, to the possibility of unlocking listeners' full potential—a very effective final sentence.

Speech References

Carter, C.; J. Bishop; & S. L. Kravits (1998). "Major exercise: Self-awareness—How can you start thinking about choosing a major?" From their book *Keys to Success,* 2nd ed. Prentice-Hall, Inc., Upper Saddle River, NJ, pp. 62–64. Retrieved July 4, 2002, from http://www.neiu.edu/~empower/essayassess/major.htm.

Messina, J. J., and C. M. Messina (2002). "Tools for personal growth: Accepting personal responsibility." Coping.org Tools for Coping with Life's Stressors, 6319 Chauncy Street, Tampa, FL 33647. Retrieved July 4, 2002, from http://www.coping.org/growth/accept.htm.

Miller, W. (1999, October 6). "Expand your horizons and join an organization." *The Daily Cougar* Opinion Online 65:32. University of Houston, Houston, TX. Retrieved July 4, 2002, from http://www.stp.uh.edu/vol65/32/opinion/oped-index.html.

O'Connor, J. (2002, March 19). "Rules of the college game." University Advising Center, Wayne State University. Retrieved July 4, 2002, from http://sdcl.wayne.edu/uac/hndbk/rules.html.

Hill cites twelve references for her speech. Five of those from the Internet had no date on them—typical of some Internet sources. One source was from 1998, another from 1999—both fairly recent—and five were from 2002, as recent as Hill could discover—considering that she gave her speech in the summer of 2002.

Using the Internet for retrieving information, recent material is readily available on almost any topic. It is important, as you seek information to support your ideas that the most recent material of the highest quality be used.

Of the 12 sources Hill used, fully half of them came from education-sponsored websites. This does not mean that the websites are automatically credible, however, it adds to their credibility, and it suggests, too, that there is likely to be no commercial interests involved. As speakers select websites to support their information, the origin of their material must be of utmost consideration.

(No author, no date). "Participating in campus life." California Technical College. Retrieved July 4, 2002, from http://www.isp.caltech.edu/NAFSA/Ch8Campus Life.html.

Russell, M. T. (2002). "Taking responsibility for yourself." InnerSelf Publications, Altamonte Springs, Florida & Delta, British Columbia. Retrieved July 4, 2002, from http://www.innerself.com/Reflections/takingresponsibilityforyours.htm.

Smalley, M. (2002). "Why taking responsibility for yourself is so important." Crosswalk.com, Inc. Family Living Channel. Retrieved July 4, 2002, from http://family.crosswalk.com/partner/ Article Display Page/0,,PTID74451|CHID194886|CIID5.

(No author, no date). "Social life at the university." The Assembly of Turkish Student Associations, Washington, DC. Retrieved July 4, 2002, from http://www.atsadc.org/nafsa/social.html.

(No author, no date). "Student experiences." Student Affairs and Services, The Smallwood Centre, Memorial University, the University of Newfoundland, Canada. Retrieved July 4, 2002, from http://www.mun.ca/student/StudentExperience.html.

(No author, no date). "Top 10 tips for academic success." Rutgers University, Newark. Retrieved July 4, 2002, from http://www.newark.rutgers.edu/dsanwk/10tips.htm.

Tracy, B. (2002). *Focal point: A proven system to simplify your life, double your productivity, and achieve all your goals.* New York: AMACOM (American Management Association).

(No author, no date). "Undecided students." The University of Tennessee. Retrieved July 4, 2002, from http://www.artsci.utk.edu/advising/deg prog/undecid.html.

Assess Yourself

Are You a Credible Speaker?

Please give a qualitative evaluation for each of the following factors by circling the numerical score which in your judgment best represents your personal position on each factor based on the last or most recent speech you have given: 7 = Outstanding; 6 = Excellent; 5 = Very good; 4 = Average/good; 3 = Fair; 2 = Poor; 1 = Minimal reaction; 0 = No ability or position on this factor. Total your numerical score, place it in the "Total Points" blank in the space below, then go to the website to determine your credibility.

1. Are you generally perceived to be a person of goodwill? 7 6 5 4 3 2 1 0
   A. Do you treat others courteously?
   B. Do you generally display acceptance, approval, and appreciation?
   C. Do you generally consider yourself equal to others?

2. Did you do things prior to your previous speech to develop your credibility? 7 6 5 4 3 2 1 0
   A. Were you aware of your image in all contacts with your audience members prior to your speech?
   B. Did you make your listeners aware of your qualifications?
   C. Did you set a favorable tone prior to your speech?

3. In your past speech, did you build your credibility through quality   7 6 5 4 3 2 1 0
   communication?
   A. Did you strive for believability in your message?
   B. Were your feelings, meanings, intentions, and consequences clear?
   C. Did you maintain respect for the thoughts and feelings of
      your listeners?

4. In your past speech did you intentionally raise your perceived   7 6 5 4 3 2 1 0
   competence by doing the things the listeners perceived as competent?
   A. Did you quote people who are acknowledged experts on your topic?
   B. Did you list facts and issues pertinent to your topic?
   C. Did you use any of the special vocabulary of the experts?

5. Did you pay special attention to the organization of your speech?   7 6 5 4 3 2 1 0
   A. Did you have—and reveal—one clear, powerful central thesis?
   B. Did you reveal the structure of your speech to your listeners?
   C. Did the pattern of organization you followed remain
      consistent throughout your speech?

6. Did you mention your personal involvement in, your prior commitment   7 6 5 4 3 2 1 0
   or your active current commitment to the topic of your speech?
   A. Did you specifically let your listeners know your personal experiences
      with your topic?
   B. Did you specifically let your listeners know the personal actions you
      have taken in the past which are clearly compatible with your basic
      orientation?
   C. Did you tell your audience what you are doing or will do as a
      consequence of your orientation to your topic?

7. Did you reveal a solid knowledge base on your topic?   7 6 5 4 3 2 1 0
   A. Did you appear qualified, informed, and authoritative?
   B. Did you have fresh, clear, relevant, and specific supporting material?
   C. Did you specifically refer to your research effort during your speech?

8. Did you do things during your speech to build your trustworthiness?   7 6 5 4 3 2 1 0
   A. Did you self-disclose—within the limits of interpersonal safety,
      of course?
   B. Did you compliment your audience?
   C. Did you appear honest, kind, friendly, pleasant, earnest, and sincere?

9. Did you do things deliberately in your speech to appear forceful, bold,   7 6 5 4 3 2 1 0
   and dynamic?
   A. Were you poised, relaxed, and fluent?
   B. Did you reflect a clear emotional commitment to your ideas?—
      complete ego involvement?
   C. Were your nonverbal cues (face, voice, gestures, and body movement)
      completely supportive of your ideas?

10. Was the evidence you used in your speech significant, relevant, and   7 6 5 4 3 2 1 0
    interesting to your listeners?
    A. Did you objectively evaluate your evidence in terms of its usefulness?
    B. Did you tell your listeners who the authorities of your evidence
       were, and why those authorities should be respected?

                                                          Total Points: _____

 Go to the *Communicating Effectively* CD-ROM to see your results and learn how to evaluate your attitudes and feelings.

Chapter Review

Persuasion is the process that occurs when a communicator influences the values, beliefs, attitudes, or behaviors of another person. The focus of persuasion should be on the sender, the receiver, and the message, because all three share in the persuasive process. It is only when all three combine with each other successfully that effective persuasion occurs.

The key to understanding persuasion is influence, the power of a person or thing to affect others—to produce effects without the presence of physical force. Persuasion involves motivation as well. Motivation is the stimulation or inducement that causes a person to act. We are motivated to do what we do in order to reduce tension, meet needs, or achieve goals or because we want personal growth, mastery of the environment, and self-understanding. These are useful motivators for persuaders to keep in mind.

We are more likely to respond to persuasive messages that tap into our values, beliefs, and attitudes. Values are types of beliefs, centrally located within one's total belief system, about how one ought or ought not to behave or about some end state of existence that is or is not worth attaining. Instrumental values guide people's day-to-day behavior, while terminal values are central to our culture. Beliefs are simple propositions, conscious or uncon-

scious, expressed in what people say or do. People often begin statements of belief with the phrase "I believe that . . ." Attitudes are relatively enduring sets of beliefs about an object or situation that predispose people to respond in some preferential manner. Persuaders who are sensitive and responsive to the values, beliefs, and attitudes of listeners are more likely to be successful.

Effective persuasion, even though it happens on a daily basis, is difficult. Speakers who understand why it is difficult to change values, beliefs, and attitudes can put the process into perspective and work to create a receptive mental attitude. Difficulties include the sheer amount of persuasion that occurs; how slowly persuasion tends to work; how deeply entrenched values, beliefs, and attitudes may be; the truisms that may guide listeners; laziness; and the desire for freedom of action. These difficulties should increase persuaders' willingness to invest time, effort, and care in their preparation for speeches.

There are specific strategies persuaders can use to be effective. In preparing a speech, you must determine your purpose, analyze your audience, appeal to your audience using logic, appeal to your audience using emotion, structure your material effectively, select your language carefully, build your credibility, and be ethical.

Questions to Review

1. Think of a recent persuasive message that you have heard. How did the speaker influence and motivate you?

2. What are the differences among values, beliefs, and attitudes?

3. For you, which values, beliefs, or attitudes are the ones most likely to be stable? Most likely to change?

4. For you, which of the difficulties of persuasion listed in the chapter would likely make you most resistant to someone else's persuasion? How might you as a speaker overcome (or approach) this particular difficulty?

5. Besides those discussed in this chapter, are there other factors that make persuasion difficult?

6. As a persuader, which strategies do you feel most comfortable using when persuading others?

7. As an audience member, which strategies would work best in speeches trying to persuade you? Or which ones would likely hold your attention better than others?

8. When you compare logic, emotion, and credibility (*logos, pathos,* and *ethos*), on which do persuaders most often depend?

9. How do questions of fact, value, and policy differ?

10. On a controversial topic, which would work best: a one-sided or a two-sided argument? Why?

11. If you were speaking on the value of a college education, what techniques for building your credibility would you use if you were talking to a high school audience?

12. Have you ever heard persuaders who were not ethical? What did they do?

13. For you to be ethical in persuasion, what principles should you follow?

14. In what ways has the Internet influenced persuasive communication?

15. Would you likely be persuaded by Juanita E. Hill's speech? Why or why not?

Go to the self-quizzes on the *Communicating Effectively* CD-ROM (side 2, track 10) and the Online Learning Center at mhhe.com/hybels7 to test your knowledge of the chapter concepts.

References

Bell, P. (2001, July 1). "The new entrepreneurship: From exuberance to reality." *Vital Speeches of the Day* 67:18, 572–75.

Fendt, G. (2002, May 1). "Two figures of the imagination: Their consequences for the arts." *Vital Speeches of the Day* 68:14, 444–48.

Goleman, D. (1986, February 18). "Influencing others: Skills are identified." *New York Times.*

Haines, M. P. (2001, July 23). "Facts change student drinking." *USA Today,* 15A.

Hovland, C. I., A. Lumsdaine, & F. Sheffield, (1949). "Experiments on mass communication." Vol. 3 of *Studies in Social Psychology in World War II.* Princeton, NJ: Princeton University Press, 213–14.

Ivy, D. K., & P. Backlund. (1994). *Exploring gender speak: Personal effectiveness in gender communication.* NY: McGraw-Hill.

King, M. L., Jr. (2001). "I've been to the mountaintop." In C. Carson and K. Shepard, eds. *A call to conscience: The landmark speeches of Dr. Martin Luther King, Jr.* New York: IPM (Intellectual Properties Management, Inc. in association with Warner Books, a Time Warner Company), 207–23.

Kluger, J. (2001, June 18). "How to manage teen drinking (the smart way)." *Time,* 42–44.

Lane, T. (2001, December 3). "Colleges develop better awareness of drinking risks." *Blade* (Toledo, Ohio), 1.

Loria, C. J. (2002, April 1). "In defense of liberty: Then and now." *Vital Speeches of the Day* 68:12, 377–80.

Maslow, A. H. (1970). *Motivation and personality,* 2nd ed. New York: Harper & Row.

McLaurin, P. (1999, August 18). "Identify the persuasive challenges to achieving your goal."

Wharton Communication Program, Pennsylvania State University. Retrieved March 26, 2003, from http://rider.wharton.upenn.edu/~commprog/lecture1/sldoiz.htm.

Monedas, M. (1992) "Men communicating with women: Self-esteem and power." In L. A. M. Perry, L. H. Turner, & H. M. Sterk, eds. *Constructing and reconstructing gender: The links among communication, language, and gender.* Albany, NY: State University of New York Press, 197–208.

Mooney, K., with L. Bergheim. (2002). *The ten demandments: Rules to live by in the age of the demanding customer.* New York: McGraw-Hill.

Morse, J. (2002, April 1). "Women on a binge." *Time Magazine,* 56–61.

Odden, L. R. (1999, March 1). "Talk to your children about the tough stuff: We are all in this together." *Vital Speeches of the Day* 65:10, 301–4.

Ray, B. L. (2001, August 15). "Realize your dreams: Find your passion for life." *Vital Speeches of the Day* 67:21, 671–72.

Rokeach, M. (1968). *Beliefs, attitudes, and values: A theory of organization and change.* San Francisco: Jossey-Bass.

Strauss, G. (2002, June 27). "America's corporate meltdown." *USA Today,* A1.

Thompson, W. N. (1978). *Responsible and effective communication.* Boston: Houghton Mifflin.

Waldron, R. (2000, October 30). "Students are dying; colleges can do more." *Newsweek,* 16.

Further Reading

Carson, C., & K. Shepard, eds. (2001). *A call to conscience: The landmark speeches of Dr. Martin Luther King, Jr.* New York: IPM (Intellectual Properties Management, Inc. in Association with Warner Books, a Time Warner Company). This is a collection of King's most influential and best-known speeches. In addition to such speeches as his "Address to the First Montgomery Improvement Association Mass Meeting," "Address at the Freedom Rally in Cobo Hall," "I Have a Dream," "Acceptance Address for the Nobel Peace Prize," and "I've Been to the Mountaintop," there are 12 important introductions by some of the world's most renowned leaders and theologians such as Andrew Young; His Holiness, the Dalai Lama; Senator Edward M. Kennedy; and Mrs. Rosa Parks. King's speeches provide examples of effective use of language, emotion, and structure. This book is a unique and unforgettable record of the words that rallied millions of people.

Cialdini, R. B. (2000). *Influence: Science and practice,* 4th ed. Boston: Allyn & Bacon. This is a book about the psychology of compliance answering the question, what is it that causes people to say "Yes" to a request. Although written in a narrative style, Cialdini includes scholarly research along with the techniques and strategies he learned as a salesperson, fundraiser, and advertiser. He organizes his compliance techniques into six categories based on the psychological principles that direct human behavior: reciprocation, consistency, social proof, liking, authority, and scarcity. Easy to read with numerous anecdotes.

Johannesen, R. L. (2001). *Ethics in human communication,* 5th ed. Prospect Heights, IL: Waveland Press. Johannesen begins with a consideration of ethical responsibilitiy in human communication. In separate chapters he discusses political perspectives, human nature perspectives, dialogical perspectives, situational perspectives, religious, utilitarian, and legalistic perspectives, some basic issues, interpersonal communication, communication in organizations, formal codes of ethics, feminist contributions, and intercultural and multicultural communication. His chapter on "Some Basic Issues" is especially practical and insightful. This is a thoughtful, clear, and comprehensive introduction to ethics.

Kahane, H., & N. Cavender, (2001). *Logic and contemporary rhetoric* (with InfoTrac): *The use of reason in everyday life.* Belmont, CA: Wadsworth Publishing Company. The goal of Kahane and Cavender is to promote clear thinking. The strength of this book is in the guidelines the authors offer for using and developing logical argument. More than most other available sources, this book helps readers both identify and eliminate fallacies of reasoning. An outstanding resource.

Larson, C. U. (2001). *Persuasion: Reception and responsibility* (with InfoTrac), 9th ed. Belmont, CA: Wadsworth Publishing Company. Larson begins with theoretical premises including a look at persuasion in today's world, ethics, approaches to research, making, using, and misusing symbols, and tools for analyzing language. In part two, identifying persuasive first premises, he examines the tools of motivation, content and cultural premises as well as nonverbal messages. In the final part, applications, he discusses persuasive campaigns or movements, becoming a persuader, modern media, propaganda, and advertising. This is a comprehensive, well-written textbook.

Mills, H. A. (2000). *Artful persuasion: How to command attention, change minds, and influence people.* New York: AMACOM. This is a pragmatic guide to the fundamentals underpinning persuasion. Mills includes numerous case studies, public relations strategies, and personal examples as he explains how master persuaders create powerful, memorable messages and how successful persuaders exploit the psychological triggers that cause people to subconsciously move from "No" to "Yes." This is basic, fundamental information designed for beginning persuaders.

(No author, no date). "Module 6: Persuasive speaking." Saskatchewan Education, Regina, Saskatchewan. Retrieved March 26, 2003, from http://www.sasked.gov.sk.ca/docs/comm20/mod6.html. Although intended for teachers to implement at the eleventh-grade level, this website contains great summary information on the principles of persuasion, using persuasive strategies, listening critically to persuasive speaking, planning and presenting persuasive talks, and both a "Sample Teacher Assessment Checklist for Persuasive Talk" and a "Sample Peer or Teacher Assessment for Persuasive Talk" form. The forms are useful for identifying the important factors in persuasive speaking.

O'Keefe, D. J. (2002). *Persuasion: Theory and research.* Beverly Hills, CA: Sage Publications. In this 304-page scholarly book, O'Keefe includes ten chapters: (1) persuasion, attitudes, and actions, (2) functional approaches to attitude, (3) belief-based models of attitude, (4) cognitive dissonance theory, (5) theories of behavioral intention, (6) elaboration likelihood model, (7) the study of persuasive effects, (8) source factors, (9) message factors, and (10) receiver and context factors. He offers an excellent examination of attitudes, approaches to attitudes, as well as models and theories of attitude and attitude change.

Perloff, R. M. (2003). *The dynamics of persuasion: Communication and attitudes in the 21st century,* 2nd ed. Mahwah, NJ: Lawrence Erlbaum Associates, Inc. Perloff offers a comprehensive introduction to persuasive communication and attitude change. Part I covers definitions and major concepts as well as the applications of persuasion to everyday life. Part II explores the major theories, related research, and critical analysis. Part III examines advertising and communication campaigns. The book is designed for the serious student of persuasion.

(No author, no date). "Persuasive speech links." Chapman University. Retrieved March 26, 2003, from http://www.chapman.edu/comm/faculty/thobbs/com202/Speechlinks.html. The value of this website is that it offers 76 links to other websites that are related to persuasive speaking.

Slagell, A. R. (2002). "Lecture notes: Speech Communication 212; Fundamentals of Public Speaking, Spring 2002." Department of Speech Communication, Iowa State University. Retrieved March 26, 2003, from http://www.public.iastate.edu/~astagell/spcm212/Lecture.html. Dr. Amy R. Slagell has created a website for students in these two courses. Click on the links to the Persuasive Unit, "Introduction to Persuasive Speaking," "Methods of Persuasion: Supporting Material and Logos," and "Methods of Persuasion: Putting It All Together a Review and Examples of Logos, Ethos, and Pathos in Speech Making." Her lecture notes offer excellent overviews and summaries of the entire persuasive process.

Williams, R. H. (2001). *Magical worlds of the wizard of ads: Tools and techniques for profitable persuasion.* Tenafly, NJ: Bard Press. In this 240-page book, there are 101 brief chapters designed to appeal to those in business, marketing, advertising, sales, and persuasion. Williams offers a creative reference source for writers looking for tips for improvement, for clergy looking for inspiring sermon stories, teachers seeking interesting and unique perspectives on historical and cultural figures and events, and those who want to stimulate their thinking. This is a book for those who enjoy ideas and creative thinking.

Appendix

Mass Communication and Media Literacy

Appendix Objectives

After reading this appendix, you should be able to:

- Define *media literacy*.
- Explain how the media relate to the communication model.
- Identify the reasons for studying media literacy.
- Distinguish how the media shape attitudes and influence behavior.
- Tell how assessment relates to the media.
- Employ the tools for assessing or evaluating information on television, in the newspapers, and on the Internet.
- Explain how ethics relates to the media and identify who is responsible for maintaining ethical standards in the media.

Key Terms and Concepts

 Use the Communicating Effectively CD-ROM and Online Learning Center at mhhe.com/hybels7 to further your understanding of the following terms.

Asynchronous communication 663	Media literacy 660	Virtual reality 674
Gatekeepers 667	Synchronous communication 663	

Media literacy is the ability to access, analyze, evaluate, and communicate information in all its forms.

After Anna Kahlo's freshman year in college, when she knew she was going to be in an apartment from her sophomore through senior years, she immediately put a cable modem into it. That cable modem was 30 times as fast as her previous dial-up and twice as fast as her previous DSL, and virtually as fast as the T-1 line used at the architectural office where she served as a part-time receptionist and file clerk. Downloads that used to take her hours, now take minutes, and her cable modem is on all the time. It constantly brings Anna faxes, voice mail, e-mail, and, in addition, it alerts her to incoming phone calls. Anna does her shopping on her cable modem, listens to Internet Radio—her favorite station is Klassic Radio from Hamburg, Germany. She listens on http://windowsmedia.com/radiotuner/default.asp. "It's a great station," says Anna, "Always 'up' music. Lots of music. No commercials. And mercifully little talking."

Not only did Anna listen to music, she downloaded music files, watched her stocks, did research on her stocks, listened in when executives reported their results, heard analysts asking probing (and occasionally rude) questions, listened to the answers, read magazines and newspapers, talked to her family and her boyfriend, and maintained her daily agenda, all on the Internet via her cable modem. This morning when Anna checked her daily agenda, there were so many items she decided to download it to her PDA (personal digital assistant) so she could carry it with her and access it during the day.

Anna's PDA was integrated and synchronized with her computer, and from it she had instant access to hundreds of contacts. Anna's hand-held PDA recognizes her handwritten notes, appointments, and contact information, and it can be uploaded to her computer for further work. Anna's PDA replaced all her low-tech predecessors like her card indexes and appointment calendars. It has huge data capacity, graphics, handwriting recognition, phone and fax capability, even wireless Internet access. Anna uses her PDA to take class notes, which she uploads to her computer at her apartment or via a phone connection and then she coordinates those notes with her memory, the audio recordings she makes on her pocket-sized recorder, and any online notes or outlines available from her instructors and professors at the class website. The PDA allows Anna to supplement her audio recordings with details from any slides or projected material that she captures in her PDA notes.

Her agenda downloaded instantaneously, and Anna logged onto her Theatre 202 website where her professor maintains contact with each class member through a class chat room. Not only that, in addition to the syllabus, he has additional readings that can be downloaded, special events and opportunities listed for class attention, pages of links to related websites, checklists and evaluation forms to be used when viewing campus theatrical performances, a list of FAQs (frequently asked questions) along with his answers about lectures, class activities, assignments, and anything else that arises, test-preparation suggestions and recommendations, and a special list of criteria to be used to evaluate the script he posted a week ago for the next class-period's discussion. Just as he had said in class, he had posted dialogue from a popular movie script. After her agenda downloaded, Anna printed a copy of the evaluation criteria and the script so she could work on it during her spare time during the day. Her printer stopped just in time for her to walk across campus to class.

In Anna's first class, a lecture class in mass communication, the lecturer presented all his information using PowerPoint; thus, it was easy for her to take notes. The lecture was highly organized, and the lecturer presented personal experiences as well as examples from the mass media—some of the information on an overhead projector with which she was familiar—to expand on the slide presentation and keep listener interest. At one point he added a video clip from a popular television advertisement. It was a multimedia performance.

After class, she and her friend Yoshiko went to a nearby computer lab to review a new CD-ROM she had purchased for her computer-studies class. It was a new software program that would be used in class the next day. Since Yoshiko had already taken the class, she was able to give Anna some useful tips on how to use the new software and what applications would be relevant. She also shared her class notes from the term before, so Anna knew what to expect in tomorrow's class. This helped Anna gain perspective and revealed the significance of the exercise.

Anna and Yoshiko had lunch together. They sat near a television that was playing the most popular soap. Following lunch, they went to the rec center for an hour of exercise before their afternoon classes. Their exercise involved following a videotaped aerobics workout. They had a choice of which version to use, depending on how long and how hard they wanted to exercise. They chose the 45-minute moderate version since they did not want to wear themselves out. Following the exercise, they went their separate ways, planning to meet early the next morning.

When Anna was alone, she quickly found a computer terminal where she checked, first, for messages. Following that, she immediately spent time preparing for her afternoon theatre-appreciation class by reading the evaluation criteria first, then the dialogue the professor supplied, and then making notes on the computer—her responses to each of the evaluation criteria: (1) Major characters and roles? (2) Main theme or essential message? (3) Techniques used to hold audience attention? (4) Lifestyles, values, or points of view represented? (5) Possible differences in understanding this piece by different people? (6) Anything omitted from this dialogue? (7) How does it compare with other scripts we have evaluated? (8) Major themes previously discussed also portrayed here? (9) Anything that is unrealistic here? and (10) What does the script reflect about society in general? Using the computer and the criteria, Anna was able to construct a four-page response paper in just less than an hour of uninterrupted work. She finished her paper just in time for her afternoon classes.

Anna had both her political science and theatre-appreciation classes in the afternoon. In the first, the class viewed a video of a recent campus visit by a major politician preceded by a short PowerPoint presentation about the politician's background and viewpoints. In the second, her theatre course, her instructor conducted an oral evaluation of the movie script using a computer projection system he displayed on a screen in front of the class. He then presented a taped critique of this portion of the movie by a New York film critic.

Following the movie, Anna returned to her apartment, checked and responded to her e-mail messages, and took time to respond to the longer inquiries she had read in the morning regarding her political science

On the Web

At a website "What Caused the Internet's Growth?" (2000), the author cites the availability of the personal computer in the early 1980s as the first significant contribution to the growth of the Internet. Then, in the late 1980s, it was an increase in communications capabilities as well as an increase in personal computer capabilities. In the early 1990s it was graphical interfaces (Windows 3.1; Mac OS7 and OS/2; and the browser), and finally, affordable high-speed communications for everyone.

The second part of this website (2000) shows the years it took to reach 50 million users worldwide of various media. For example, it took the telephone 74 years to reach 50 million users; radio took 38 years; the personal computer took only 16 years; television took 13 years; and, the World Wide Web took only 4 years. John Zeglis (2000), senior vice president of AT&T, says "in only six and one-half years, 100 million people logged on to the Internet."

Sources: (No author), "What Caused the Internet's Growth?" Seminars@grizbiz.com, April 19, 2000. Retrieved March 26, 2003, from http://www.grizbiz.com/edintro/eyhh12.htm; and J. Zeglis, "LEGOs Anyone?" A speech delivered to SUPERCOMM 2000, Atlanta, Georgia, June 6, 2000. Retrieved January 27, 2001, from http://www. att.com/speeches/item/0.1363.3007.00.html.

research. She then began reading the printouts for her political science research paper and began an outline, working on her computer. If her outline was complete enough, she knew she could simply fill in details and transitions and then add an introduction and conclusion to complete the paper. Since she was getting tired, she stopped her course work and looked through a copy of *USA Today*, which she had purchased on campus, and she clicked on the television once again to catch a late news show and a weather report.

This is a typical day for Anna, and the day is dominated by various media. As a media-literate person, she reads, analyzes, evaluates, and produces communication in a variety of formats—all in one day. She enjoys what she does in a deliberately conscious way. Not only is she comfortable with the various media, but they are so naturally integrated into her life that she barely notices them and, thus, is in control of her daily experiences.

■ WHAT IS MEDIA LITERACY?

To be literate, according to the dictionary, is to be able to read and write. The notion of literacy in society has traditionally been related to the information forms of the culture. For example, in the era of the printing press, *literacy* mostly meant the ability to read, write, and print. Soon after computers were introduced, *media literacy* meant the *technical* ability to operate a computer (Freed, 2002, p. 1). Today, however, most Americans get much of their information from multiple media. They seek information from a combination of television, radio, newspapers, the Internet, and word of mouth (Wiggins, 2001). Dan Bricklin (2002), a software designer and cocreator of VisiCalc, the first electronic spreadsheet, says "The Internet has succeeded in becoming a tool that many regular people turn to in lieu of alternatives for communicating and for finding information." Computers, distance education, CD-ROM, and other related formats utilize a combination of images and text. Because of this, a wider definition of what it means to be literate is necessary. **Media literacy** is the ability to access, analyze, evaluate, and communicate information in all its forms— both print and nonprint (*Resource Guide*, 1999, pp. 6–7; A Few Words . . . , 1999; Hobbs, 1998). Thus, it provides important communication skills for today and tomorrow. To be literate within this definition means that you must learn to receive, comprehend, analyze, and evaluate media messages as well as use technology to create messages. Assumed within this definition, but perhaps not obvious, is a basic understanding about the nature and power of interactivity itself (Freed, 2002, p. 2).

This definition of *media literacy* embraces the broader dictionary definition of *literacy*, meaning "having or showing extensive knowledge, experience, or culture," for how can you possibly exhibit the skills under the new definition of media literacy without these traits? It is, indeed, the trait of showing extensive knowledge, experience, or culture that moves people from merely recognizing and comprehending information to the higher-order critical thinking skills implicit in questioning, analyzing, and evaluating that information (Considine, 1995). Perhaps there is even an additional aspect, too. Critical thinking does not necessarily imply using the

Media literacy involves more than merely recognizing and comprehending information, it involves, too, the use of critical thinking skills in questioning, analyzing, and evaluating that information.

EF/JD042626 Copenhagen Denmark: Danish college student doing his homework on laptop computer. June 23, 2002 ©Francis Dean / The Image Works

critical-thinking skills in your communication with others. To paraphrase Marshall McLuhan, media guru of the 1960s, in his book *The Medium is the Massage,* the medium massages the message as the message massages the medium—meaning we shape the mass media as the mass media shape us (Freed, 2002; McLuhan, 1967). This truly recognizes the power of interactivity. More than that, it acknowledges our personal and collective power.

But why focus, you might wonder, primarily on the Internet and not the other media? A special report in *Newsweek* magazine on "e-life" (September 20, 1999) explains it this way:

> *Was there a single moment when we turned the corner? When we moved from a culture centered on network television, phones with wires, information on paper and stock prices based on profit into a digital society of buddy lists, streaming video, Matt Drudge and 34-year-old billionaires in tennis shoes? (Special report, 1999).*

No is the answer to the question posed; there was no single moment. But the evolution was rapid. The appetite was obviously present, but it required the right food to satisfy the hunger. The Internet proved to be the perfect nourishment. When the technology was presented, it was as if the table

Another Point of View

There is some disagreement about what media literacy actually means:

Some people think of media literacy purely in terms of a defensive mechanism to help our children navigate their way through the minefield of insidious, pejorative, and God-knows-what-else kinds of advertising that they're hit with every time they turn on the TV. Give our kids the tools to understand how the media are trying to manipulate them, and they will be able to fend off the commercial propaganda, so the thinking goes.

Questions

1. How is this perception of media literacy limited? Negative?

2. What would you view as the most important part of media literacy? Why?

3. In what ways will media literacy help people get along in the world a whole lot better?

Source: D. Bicket (2002, January 3). "So What Is This All About Anyway?" K.I.S.S. of the Panopticon: Core Concepts, School of Communications, University of Washington. Retrieved March 26, 2003, from http://www.com.washington.edu/cmu/panop/home6.htm.

were already set, the participants to the banquet were seated, and their forks were raised as if poised to dig in. As of September 2002, the estimate was that worldwide there were 605.6 million people on the Internet. In the United States and Canada, the estimate was 182.67 million (How many online?, 2003). Another website said 561 million people were online as of March 2002 (Global Internet statistics, 2002). Of course, statistics like these are not only in continual flux, but they are, in general, only estimates. The point is, however, that it is clear that people's forks were raised as if poised to dig in to a full-course spread; the Internet afforded them a feast. The growth of the Internet led futurist Paul Saffo of the Institute for the Future, a think tank in Menlo Park, California, to state, "We'll remember 1999 as the year the Internet ceased to be a technology and became a medium of wide acceptance" (Iwata, 1999).

What is remarkable is that almost everything we've ever done that has to do with communication and information has been digitized from schools and businesses to operating rooms, labs, banks, and the halls of government. This isn't just a change of tools. "The Internet is built on both a philosophy and an infrastructure of openness and free communication; its users hold the potential to change not just how we get things done, but our thinking patterns and behavior" (Special report, 1999). It isn't as if the participants to the banquet knew what the nourishment would be; indeed, they were indulging in sustenance of a very different nature than previously available, even though it satisfied needs already present.

It is because people are working, shopping, playing, researching, and communicating on the Internet that media literacy demands our attention. Although we label this phenomenon "media literacy," and although we give it a new definition to encompass all the effects it has, realize that this digital, Net-based, computer-connected gestalt is the way many people live their lives today, just as Anna does in the opening example. It is a normal, comfortable, accepted, and expected way of daily living. In his article "Deep

Literacy," Ken Freed says "The smart people with an interactive sensibility will be the best prepared to survive and thrive in the stormy years ahead" (Freed, 2002, p. 5).

Our focus here may be more on the Internet than on other media, but we want to make it clear that we are not lumping "the media" together as a single entity. When we use the word *media*, we are referring to many forms of communication including newspapers, magazines, and billboards, radio, television, videocassettes, video games, and computer games. Almost everything we know about people, places, and events that we cannot visit firsthand comes from the media. We rely on them for entertainment and pleasure. Perhaps even more important, it is the media that tell us about who we are, what we believe, and what we want to be.

■ HOW DO THE MEDIA RELATE TO THE COMMUNICATION MODEL?

Our discussion will focus on the Internet because it is the newest of the media, even though it bears a lot of similarity to the media that have come before. At the Centre for Learning and Teaching website entitled "Computer Mediated Communication (CMC)" (Riddy, 2002), there is a one-to-one comparison of face-to-face groups versus electronic groups that we have reproduced on page 664 as Figure A-1.

Under the second item in the chart—the comparison between synchronous and asynchronous communication—perhaps a word of explanation is in order. **Synchronous communication** occurs when people *are* directly connected, as in a telephone conversation, a face-to-face encounter, or a real-time, online group format such as those offered by any of the instant-message providers. **Asynchronous communication** is communication in which the people are not directly connected with each other at the same time. Most of the exchanges between people on the Internet consist of asynchronous communication.

If you examine the comparisons in Figure A-1 you will note that Internet usage relates to the communication model in the same ways that both interpersonal *and* group communication do. Most of the differences in the channels of communication are obvious, but the differences in the social cues to communication—especially the social leveling and the differences in turn taking—are important. The Internet could easily be labeled "the great leveler." It is precisely because of this that source validation for information gained from the Internet becomes so important. This comment refers to an earlier one in this book about anyone can be a publisher on the Internet. Another aspect of leveling, too, is that often in face-to-face communication the assertive, highly confident individual may have an edge with respect to credibility or gaining an audience for his or her ideas—even, perhaps, at having greater opportunities (turns) for talking. On the Internet, assertiveness traits are often not detected; so, shy, nonassertive individuals have an equal opportunity for self-expression.

The fact that the Internet is two-way also is important. The other media such as radio, television, and newspapers are one-way, with restricted

Face-to-face group	Electronic group
Channels of communication	
Uses a variety of channels: words, intonation, posture, etc. to convey meaning and emotion	A single channel: textual. This is why some see electronic groups as cold and impersonal. Emotion can be conveyed by symbols or smileys: :) happy : (sad/frown
Synchronous: all are physically gathered in a given place at a given time.	Asynchronous: time and place for communication is at the discretion of individuals.
Essentially verbal, but with a great deal of nonverbal cues like intonation, posture, facial expressions and hand movements.	The mode of communication is a mixture between verbal and written text. This is now known as interactive writing. E-mail texts can be spontaneous and can tolerate misspellings and grammatical errors as with spoken texts. E-mail can also support thought-out prose as in written texts.
Social cues to communication	
Members of a face-to-face group are aware of social cues to status in their environment and with their group leader.	Electronic groups experience a social leveling, as many of the cues to social status are removed.
You need to wait your turn in a face-to-face group and you may even miss the opportunity to say something.	There is no need to wait your turn in electronic groups; you contribute when you feel like it with either a spontaneous or a thought-out response.

Figure A-1

Communication in Face-to-Face and Electronic Groups

access to the sender or transmitter. Restricted access simply means that not everyone has a radio station, television station, or newspaper to communicate his or her ideas. But, when things are put on a Web page, or expressed in a chat room, you are potentially communicating with a group of senders—anyone—who are on the Net, and *they* can communicate with you—even though their communication with you may take a different form (see Figure A-1) than it would if face-to-face. Ken Freed, in his article "Deep Literacy," says "Knowing our actions affect the whole world tends to influence our interactions" (Freed, 2002, p. 2).

The characteristics of mass communication differ from those of the Internet in some ways, although the most important way is that message flow is typically one-way in mass communication. Another important distinction is the possibility of gatekeepers in mass communication. This will

In mass communication:

Machines are involved in translating messages from one channel to another.

The message is usually restricted to one or two channels only.

The messages are public.

Message termination is easy.

Messages involve multiple decoding before they are received.

Audiences are large.

Audiences are heterogeneous.

Audiences are spread over a wide geographic area.

Source and receiver are not in the same physical presence.

Audience members are anonymous to one another.

Source and receiver are, for the most part, anonymous to each other.

Receivers are self-defined because they choose what film to see, paper to read, or program to watch.

Message flow is typically one way.

The messages that are sent are not unique for each receiver; they are usually the same.

Noise is likely to be semantic, environmental, or mechanical.

Figure A-2

Mass Communication Characteristics

be discussed in a forthcoming section of this chapter. We have listed the characteristics of mass communications in Figure A-2.

"The communication cycle [underlining his] explains the relationship at the heart of the creative process that generates our life experiences," says Freed. "Studying the communication cycle reveals how senders and receivers interact, how the give and take cycle alters senders and receivers alike" (p. 4). For example, how is one affected by having to type a message to another person (computer format) if one is a poor typist? How is one affected by communication that is devoid of the nonverbal cues of emotion (content)? How is one affected by the miscommunication that results from misleading or faulty encoding and decoding? How is one affected by differences in geographical distance which may alter some of the ways or kinds of communication that take place? There is no doubt that we affect others with every Internet transaction. We not only create a private as well as a public reality by our choices, but "our interactions spin the web of culture" (Freed, 2002, p. 4) as well.

All of the components of the communication model remain intact, even though there are obvious differences in the channels of communication and in the social cues to communication, as depicted in Figure A-1. Although these differences could be viewed as a restriction when face-to-face and electronic communication are compared, we think the restrictions are easily offset by the increased audience one can have, the lack of geographic boundaries, the social leveling, and the possibility of providing thought-out responses. Thought-out responses, if taken seriously, have the potential of increasing both the precision and accuracy of communication—and maybe even the wisdom, too.

One author believes that the lapse in time that occurs in asynchronous communication may be our most valuable asset (McCluskey, 1999). Alan McCluskey, in an online article, "Building Shared Intelligence for Networked Decision Making," says that the lapse in time "makes possible the careful thinking that is required for decision making in an increasingly complex environment" (1999). Another author, Robert L. Dilenschneider, takes issue with any increase in wisdom or thought. In a speech "The Coming Age of Content and Critical Thinking," Dilenschneider says ". . .To an alarming extent, these communications breakthroughs (the Internet, the World Wide Web, e-mail, voice mail, cell phones, pagers, personal computers, Palm pilots, coaxial and fiber optic cables, communication satellites) have weakened our ability to communicate substance and ideas." He says that "being bombarded as we are with message without content and critical thinking wastes our valuable time, saps our energy, and ultimately, deludes us into thinking that content and critical thinking are irrelevant" (Dilenschneider, 2001, p. 208).

Returning to differences between face-to-face and electronic communications for a moment, in one study that compared the Internet and face-to-face communication, Lisa Flaherty, Kevin Pearce, and Rebecca Rubin found that use of the Internet as a communication channel is not perceived by users as a functional alternative to face-to-face communication. "The face-to-face channel," they found, "has more social presence than the Internet; the possibility of immediate feedback with face-to-face interaction conveys greater personal closeness" (Rubin, 1998, p. 264).

■ WHY STUDY MEDIA LITERACY?

The Internet has transformed how Americans live, think, talk, and love. It has transformed how they go to school, make money, see the doctor, and elect presidents. It is the largest and most diverse information resource in the world today; as a content provider, it has no equal. These two facts alone would be sufficient justification for studying media literacy, but there is more.

The Media Provide Instant News

When a news event takes place, interested parties immediately post messages on the Internet for others to read. Whereas in traditional journalism decisions flowed from the top down, with editors deciding what to cover and where to send reporters to collect facts, with the Internet news starts at the bottom and is generated by people close to or with an interest in the news topic. Because of the Internet, anybody with a computer can become a reporter, editor, or publisher. For example, when a storm hits a particular area, various news groups and residents in the area will post information about storm damage on the Internet. A weather report could suggest that part of the country is totally snowed in, whereas a check of the Web page of a ski resort in the same area could reveal that the area suffered little effect from the storm, roads to the resort have been cleared, and visitors to the resort will not be inconvenienced.

If you think of organizations, owners, editors, news directors, and reporters as **gatekeepers,** those in control of what information becomes available over the media, then you would think the Internet eliminates the gatekeeper; however, this is not entirely true. Even search engines play a role in gatekeeping. There is a website (Wiggins, 2001) that offers evidence of the role that Google played in what happened after the September 11, 2001, attack. "The important point to note here," says Richard Wiggins, senior information technologist at Michigan State University, "is that someone at Google was playing the role of editor, selecting major, authoritative sources, and updating the context to match users' needs as they changed over time. This is an entirely new role for Google" (Wiggins, 2001). It cannot be said that "On the Internet, there are no evaluators of information" simply because everyone who puts information onto the Internet is an evaluator. In addition, any person or organization that plays a role in mass media places information on the Internet, and all have some kind of bias (Goldberg, 2001).

And, there is yet another aspect of gatekeeping going on on the Internet and often not in full view of Internet users. Because cyberspace travelers must pay gateway companies for securing access to the passageways of the electronic domain, gatekeeping companies have become more powerful—as the example of Google, above, demonstrates. According to Jeremy Rifkin, author of *The Age of Access*, "The world's leading entertainment, software, and telecommunications companies, aware of the commercial potential of being the gatekeepers, have positioned themselves at the entry point to the new world of electronic commerce and are buying up the more successful access providers and search engine companies." "They realize," says Rifkin, "that whoever controls the gates to cyberspace exercises vast potential control over people's day-to-day lives in the twenty-first century . . ." (Rifkin, 2000, pp. 178–79).

In general, on the Internet you do not necessarily have the protection of gatekeepers. Some of the information is accurate; some of it must be used at your own risk. The keys to keep in mind are these: The fact that something is on the Net doesn't mean it has any credibility. The other key is: No gatekeepers means no censorship. This, of course, can be both an advantage and a disadvantage. One textbook writer on mass communication (Dominick, 1999) said you should think of the Internet in much the same way as you would a big city. It may be a nice place to take your family, but just as in any city, there are places all of you can go, and there are places where you would not want to take your children (p. 341).

The Media Shape Culture

There is a rapidly growing global economy. Even America's standard of living—as in no time previously in our history—depends upon growing markets in the Pacific Rim and the Third World. Americans cannot afford to approach people in these areas ignorantly or arrogantly. Television and other mass media bring us closer to the rest of the world, but sometimes the frame and filter through which we see this world and its people dwells on gloom, doom, famine, flood, and disaster. Too often, we feel, this picture of

The Internet is the largest and most diverse information resource in the world today.

human misery and suffering minimalizes and marginalizes the richness, diversity, achievements, and cultures of the world's people. The Internet and World Wide Web (WWW) provide a new window through which we can view other cultures. They can help people seek new information, explore it, analyze it, discuss it, and even ask questions about it. In addition, they can help them explore the way the media construct their window on the world. Is it fair? Is it accurate? Access to information—whether it is the raw data being transmitted by firsthand observers, broadcast news, or news analysts—is so readily available that people can evaluate perceptions, prejudices, and stereotypes like never before. What is the impact of mass media—no matter what delivery vehicle is involved—on public opinion? On your opinion? On your communication?

Ken Freed, responding to the coming global digital networks, offers a poignant view of the possibilities:

> The world Internet is transforming how we think and feel about ourselves and each other. Interactive broadband media—in all of its many devices for data, voice and video—soon will surpass the impact of one-way TV and movies as the fountainheads of popular culture. Consider the use of smart cellphones among teens in Europe for a glimpse of the future. How we do business in daily life is being forever changed. We need to understand interactive media simply to function and flourish in our interactive world. Anyone who's not media literate may perish (2002, p. 2).

On the Web

1. Access each of the following websites of the major television networks:

   ABC-TV: www.abc.com
   CBS-TV: www.cbs.com
   NBC-TV: www.nbc.com
   Fox TV: www.foxworld.com
   CNN: www.cnn.com

   Information on programming and scheduling is available at www.tvnet.com.

2. Choose a news story that is current and that you are pretty certain will be covered by all the networks. Read what one network says about the story or subject.

3. Now check out the other networks and their coverage of the same story or subject.

4. Answer the questions below.

Questions

1. Is the coverage identical? Why or why not?

2. What are the differences? How do you account for the differences?

3. Can you see how a person's opinion or point of view can be slanted by the way a story or subject is covered?

4. In what ways can readers or viewers make certain the news they receive—the news on which they base their own opinions and points of view—is objective, unbiased, and accurate?

The Media Shape Attitudes

The influence of the media can be obvious as we adopt the language or aphorisms of a star we follow or buy a product advertised in or on the media. But the influence of the media can be subtle as well, perhaps even pernicious (highly destructive or injurious), when it unconsciously shapes our thoughts and visions. Why pernicious? Because the media must follow conventions that are often out of sync with real life. For example, imagine how pernicious it would be for people already possessing a low self-concept to compare themselves with the physical models of actors and actresses on television and realize that they don't measure up? Besides cosmetics, air brushing, and blurred shots, some facts are directly manipulated. When *TV Guide* put Oprah Winfrey on a cover, they gave her Ann Margret's body. CBS aired a concert where a computer was used to make Whitney Houston look less painfully thin (Johnson, 2002).

There are other examples, too, of how the media shape attitudes, and some of it occurs because of direct manipulation. Money and ratings, of course, are usually behind it. For example, there was widespread reporting that "road rage" was on the increase, but there was no hard evidence that it had increased. It was based, instead, on media mentions of aggressive driving—a simple case of the pot getting hot so the kettle can too (Johnson, 2002). John Stossel gave one example of manipulation: "Watch my program on killer bacteria! Lawn chemicals! Danger in the grass!" he reported to Johnson, instead of saying "It's not likely to kill you" (Johnson, 2002, p. 3D).

Another Point of View

In his article, "Progress has given us more bad than good," Joseph Sainton, a retired electronics engineer from Sylvania, Ohio, claims that "Progress, when you look back over the last 50 years, has probably done more to us that it has for us." He claims, further, that:

. . . The most damaging progress of all has been wrought by electronic technology which is clearly dedicated to the enfeebling of the human intellect. Idiotic video games that corrupt young minds, the hypnotic attraction to the Internet, to computers, to digital this and that, to RAMs and ROMs and dot coms, all meant to make zombies of weak minds.

Mind-numbing television has us continually consumed and intellectually impoverished. The electronic picture tube has become the light of our lives, entertaining us, nurturing our fantasies, raising our children, and filling every empty moment of our soon-to-be empty lives (p. 11).

Questions

1. If you were to compose an argument to refute this viewpoint expressed by Sainton, what would your ideas be?

2. Did this excerpt make you wonder at what proof Sainton has that electronic technology enfeebles the human intellect?

J. Sainton, "Progress Has Given Us More Bad than Good. *The Blade,* (Toledo, Ohio, March 4, 2000.)

Think about the other ways the media shape your attitudes. You can learn from the media that your nation is strong and decent, that the political process you participate in is reliable, that the technological achievements during your lifetime are often remarkable. The media can teach you what it means to be a man or a woman, what families are supposed to be like, or what it means to grow old. It is because you receive these messages over and over that you may unconsciously come to accept them as truth without really thinking about them. The images you receive, comprehend, and, perhaps, unconsciously filter shape your attitudes—sometimes superficially, as when you respond to a product or circumstance you saw on a televised news magazine like *60 Minutes, 20/20,* or *Dateline.* But the effect can be more profound than that as you subconsciously adopt some of the values you see depicted over and over on soap operas, dramas, talk shows, and movies. Think, for example, about the attitudes you have toward members of the opposite sex, relationships, dating, marriage, and sex. The effect can be especially profound when you don't even realize it is happening. The media have that kind of power and influence.

The Media Influence Behavior

There is no doubt that the media have had a major influence on our lives. Just a few of the influences according to Michael C. Kearl (2002) include changes in the way housewives use their leisure time. As an escape mechanism, it changes the way people relieve societal stress. It changes, too, the way people educate and entertain themselves, the way children receive cultural enrichment, the way people view the abnormalities of everyday life, and the way people seek emotional release and relaxation. The media tend to communicate life in emotional rather than intellectual or rational terms; thus, they require little critical thinking and deliver satisfying, enjoyable experiences, in a way that stimulates your feelings not your mind and provokes the imagination over real-life experiences. According to the research findings reported by Kearl (2002), the behavioral effects of the media are similar for all classes of people in all residential locations, and no matter how much media is absorbed. It tends to have a greater effect on adult behavior than children's, a greater effect on blue collar workers' overt behavior than that of white collar workers, and has a greater effect on the behavior of suburbanites, or non-city dwellers, than on city dwellers, reinforces materialism, allows the elderly to relate to current affairs, and shatters families. Professor Kearl also suggests that although the connection between viewing violence and viewer aggression is often mixed in the research results, there is historically increasing support for the connection.

The point of this long list isn't the specifics as much as the combined influence of the media. There are so many effects on our lives, you would expect even more and, certainly, more will be discovered. Also, as the media—especially the Internet—become more and more intrically intertwined in our lives, there have to be trade-offs with the routines, habits, and behaviors that we currently take for granted. Recognize, too, that the effects are likely to apply to different people in different ways. For some, we are

Another Point of View

Does the media influence behavior? Here is a report, "Internet Intrudes on College Students" from *USA Today* (2001), citing the results of a study printed in the *Journal of Communication*:

Most college students say that the Internet doesn't interfere with studies, but about 10 percent to 15 percent say they don't feel in complete control of their computer use and that it has hurt their schoolwork. A study of 572 college students finds that those who stay up late chatting or playing games on the Internet are more likely to miss class and report lower grades. Students who say they are Internet-dependent are seven times more likely to use real-time communication tools—like chat rooms, instant messaging and gaming rooms; students who report the Internet interfered with school were nine times more likely to use those tools. The study, in the June (2001) issue of the Journal of Communication, *finds the problem affects freshmen the most, with many*

saying they use the Internet to combat isolation and loneliness of college life by staying up late and using instant messaging to keep in touch with high school chums and family.

Questions

1. To what extent does the Internet intrude on your college studies? Does it hurt your schoolwork in any way? Do you feel the interference with your college studies is worth the sacrifice considering the value of what you get from using the Internet?

2. If the Internet does not intrude on your college studies, what are the things you do to prevent its intrusion? Are these things, too, which any college student could do?

Source: (No author). "Internet Intrudes on College Students" (A Better Life: Health, Education & Science), *USA Today*, May 23, 2001, p. 100.

certain, the media are used as a supplement and counterpoint to, and, perhaps, a checkpoint of reality. For others, the media become reality. Many people live in the imaginary world of the screen, the interface, and networks, and for them, their world has become an "aesthetic hallucination of reality" (Rifkin, 2000, p. 197).

Whether it be your language, interpersonal communication, relationships, sexual behavior, or something else, the Internet influences behavior. And, as it creeps deeper and deeper into your everyday life—as it surely will—you need to keep in mind this fact: Media influence behavior. It may mean nothing to you; however, it could have deep implications of which you are not fully aware.

The Media Connect Us with the Global Community

There is no doubt that the Internet links people from around the world cheaply. It offers a connection to the global community, and because of that connection individuals are likely to identify with the world and feel more concerned with what happens to it. As a facilitator of intercultural communication that is widely available, easily accessible, and deeply penetrating—with respect to how deeply into cultures it is likely to delve and how many people will have access—there has never been such a tool (McCluskey, 1999).

There may be another aspect of the "global community" that may escape a first look. The communications gap between the developed nations and the developing nations may well divide the world into the informationally rich and the informationally poor. Columnist David Kline (see Golding, 1996) in the high-tech magazine *Hot Wired* writes that "the future may become a wonderland of opportunity only for the minority among us who are affluent, mobile, and highly educated. And it may at the same time become a digital dark age for the majority of citizens—the poor, the non-college educated, and the so-called unnecessary" (p. 70). So, it may well be that the media will not connect us with the entire global pie, but only with one particular slice of it.

Connecting with just one slice of the global pie has its own dangers, however, writes Thomas L. Friedman, *New York Times* News Service, in an article "Global Village Idiocy, Courtesy of the Internet." Writing from Jakarta, Indonesia, Friedman says "Internet users are only 5 percent of the population—but these 5 percent spread rumors to everyone else. They say, 'He got it from the Internet.' They think it's the Bible." Friedman adds,

> *If there's one thing I learned from this trip to Israel, Jordan, Dubai, and Indonesia, it's this: Thanks to the Internet and satellite TV, the world is being wired together technologically, but not socially, politically, or culturally. We are now seeing and hearing one another faster and better, but with no corresponding improvement in our ability to learn from, or understand, one another. So integration, at this stage, is producing more anger than anything else (Friedman, 2002, p. 7A).*

The point is simply that because the Internet has an aura of "technology" surrounding it, the uneducated believe information from it even more. For example, the lie that 4,000 Jews were warned not to go into the World Trade Center on September 11, 2001, was spread all over the Internet. It is now thoroughly believed in the Muslim world (Friedman, 2002).

The Media Promote Responsible Citizenship

"It certainly directly addresses responsible citizenship in a democratic society, since it (media literacy) argues that a responsible citizen is an informed member of the community," says the statement at the website entitled "Media Literacy and North Carolina Curriculum Connections" (Considine, 2002, p. 1). This is the case many states make in their request for additional funding for, and attention to the needs of schools for, computers. The North Carolina statement is typical, and it adds:

> *The citizen must be able to do more than simply access information. An informed citizen must be able to detect bias and to understand the commercial pressures that shape not only what news is presented, but how it is presented. Hopefully such a citizen might also access alternative sources of information (Considine, 2002, p. 1).*

In a White House publication, a critical statement underscored the relationship between media literacy and responsible citizenship: media literacy "may offer young people positive preparatory skills for responsible citizenship. For example, media literacy can empower youth to be positive contributors to society, to challenge cynicism and to serve as agents of social change" (*Helping Youth . . .* , 2001, p. 8).

There is more to responsible citizenship, however, than having access to information. Look how many qualified voters have access to information, and look how many actually vote! Clearly, too, responsible citizenship involves more than voting. "It involves informed decision making. Media literacy promotes the critical thinking skills necessary to understand the complex issues facing modern society," says David Considine (1995, p. 9).

The Media Create Productive Workers

In an information economy, the term *productive workers* will increasingly mean workers with the technological skills required to utilize computer-related technology to access, store, produce, and disseminate information. Without these skills, many citizens will be left behind—how far behind will depend on how fast the information economy develops and the supply-and-demand nature of the marketplace. Although more and more media-literate individuals are being nurtured, the need for them is growing exponentially—thus, the current gap between supply and demand.

■ HOW DOES ASSESSMENT RELATE TO THE MEDIA?

Appearing in the PBS broadcast "Media Literacy: The New Basic," former CBS news anchor Walter Cronkite said that schools should teach healthy skepticism (Considine, 2002). There is not likely to be a single teacher who wouldn't believe in the truth of Cronkite's comment. The only question might be, How can the media, or more specifically, the Internet, promote healthy skepticism?

Accessing websites is meaningless, even dangerous, without the ability to filter, interpret, and accept or discard information and the media messages located at the sites. Just as the ability to effectively deliver a speech is a worthless commodity if speakers have nothing to say or if their purpose is unethical, possessing the technical skills to create a website or PowerPoint presentation is not enough. Not only do speakers need substantive content to convey, but, in addition, they need to understand graphic design, screen display, and other elements that will determine how well the program is processed.

As noted in Chapter 9, Communicating at Work, in the "Presentations" section, and again in Chapter 15, Delivering the Speech, in the "Using a Computer" section, it is easy for the special effects of a presentation or speech to overwhelm, and even drown, the content. This point cannot be overstated! As Plato eloquently articulated it, consider how "true speech is banished, the authentic gold driven out by the tinny dross of what is pleasing and immediately popular" (Elshtain, 1995, pp. 99–100). This can be just as true when assessing websites as when preparing to make a presentation; one easily can be overcome by what is pleasing and popular, while what is rich, authentic, and to be treasured is ignored or neglected. Remember, too, that that was one of the findings Professor Kearl uncovered, which we reported in the section, "The Media Influence Behavior." We noted, there, that "The media tend to communicate life in emotional rather than intellectual or rational terms; thus, it requires little critical thinking and delivers satisfying, enjoyable experiences in a way that stimulates your feelings not your mind and provokes the imagination over real-life experiences." If that is true, in general, then the media cannot be counted on to increase or polish one's critical-thinking skills.

Another aspect of assessment has to do with what is occurring as a result of virtual reality and imagineering. **Virtual reality,** like imagineering, is a computer-generated alternate reality. The proverbs "You can't judge a book by its cover" and "A picture is worth a thousand words" are even truer today than previously. Why? Because today's technologies represent fusions of sight and sound that make it difficult to discern illusion from reality and fact from fiction. Special effects merge the past with the present, color with black and white, and the dead with the living. These technologies are not just employed in the entertainment industry; they are also evident in broadcast news. For example, reporters in a TV studio can be magically transported via computer onto the White House lawn or to any country or location desired. That location can lend power, authority, and credibility to the reporter and story. This is essential information that is necessary when you are looking for factual information that can be relied on. Here is how David Considine, coordinator of Media Studies in the graduate program in media literacy at Appalachian State University, views these new technologies:

> While such techniques (as those noted above) may render the program more visually pleasing, they represent the emergence of infotainment and the decline of objective, neutral, and reliable news. Given these trends, responsible citizens need to possess the ability to question the accuracy and authenticity of information in all its forms, not just print (Considine, 1995).

What needs to be understood is that media are constructions—constructions that have commercial purposes. The phrase "The camera never lies"

Working Together

1. Working with others as a group, assign one or two members of the group to one of the following Web pages:

   - J. Alexander, & M. Tate (2001, July 25). "Evaluating Web Resources," Wolfgram Memorial Library, Widener University. Retrieved March 26, 2003, from http://www2. widener.edu/Wolfgram-Memorial-Library/webevaluation/webeval. htm.

   - S. Beck (2002, June 5). "Evaluation Criteria: The Good, the Bad & the Ugly or, Why It's a Good Idea to Evaluate Web Sources," Humanities & Social Sciences Services Department, New Mexico State University Library, New Mexico State University. Retrieved March 26, 2003, from http://lib.nmsu.edu/instruction/evalcrit.html.

   - E. Grassian (2000, September 6). "Thinking Critically about World Wide Web Resources," UCLA College Library, Regents of the University of California. Retrieved March 26, 2003, from http://www.library.ucla. edu/libraries/college/help/critical/.

   - J. R. Henderson (2002, May 28). "ICYou See: T is for Thinking—A Guide to Critical Thinking about What You See on the Web," Ithaca College Library, Ithaca College. Retrieved March 26, 2003, from http://www.ithaca.edu/library/Training/hott.html.

2. Each group member should answer each of the following questions about the website:

   - How good is this website for evaluating information?

   - If this were *all* the information you had for evaluating information, would it be sufficient? Why or why not?

   - If you were to add additional information to this website to increase its effectiveness, what would you add?

3. Following a complete discussion of each of the websites, conduct a full group discussion to determine which of the four websites the group thinks is the best one for gaining information about evaluating information. (If a member of the group can suggest another website that can be evaluated or is, perhaps, better than those listed above, let him or her make the suggestion.)

is no longer true—if it ever was. Because of competition, because of the need to entertain as well as inform, because of time constraints, and because of the many other forces that operate (e.g., the dynamics of the marketplace), all media are carefully assembled, edited, selected, and designed constructions. Although they show us a world, it is a selected and often unrepresentative view, even though it seems to be true (Considine, 1995). Even when the reporting appears firsthand on the Internet, this does not mean that it hasn't been carefully assembled, edited, selected, and designed.

It should be clear that any "real understanding of media content cannot be divorced from the economic context and financial imperative that drives the media industry" (Considine, 1995). In a large class, one of the authors of this book was discussing newspapers and threw off the comment that "newspapers are primarily advertising." A student raised his hand and challenged the comment. The response to the challenge was simple: "A good way to check this out is to purchase a daily newspaper and see for yourself." The student reported back, "I never realized how much advertising a daily newspaper contains." While we may lament the commercialization of the Internet, tabloidism, or infotainment, the media industry would claim that it is giving the public what it wants. In the case of newspapers, it is the advertising that keeps them affordable; the advertising virtually subsidizes the cost of the paper. Does it in any way drive or influence the content within?

■ HOW SHOULD ONE ASSESS THE MEDIA?

The area of assessment is essential to media literacy. In this section we will look at assessment from three perspectives: (1) evaluating information in general, (2) assessing information delivered via mass media such as television and newspapers, and (3) assessing information found on the Internet.

Evaluating Information

The first perspective involves examining information in general. There are standard criteria for doing so, regardless of the format in which the information appears (Evaluating information . . . , 1999). Below are some of the standard criteria for evaluating information. These include relevancy, recency, reliability, and availability.

Relevancy
- How relevant or useful is the information I am looking at for the topic I am studying?

Recency
- How current is the information?
- Is it up to date enough for my needs?

Reliability
- What is the source of the information?
- Do other sources support this information?
- Is this a reputable source or author?
- What are the author's credentials?
- Is this person an authority in this field?

(*Note:* To determine the author's credibility, look for background information on the person. It might be included elsewhere in the information source or might be in biographical sources that can be accessed via the Internet. Sometimes this information can be accessed through a website in the person's name.)

Availability
- Is this information available online or at another location that is readily accessible?
- What other resources are available on this topic?
- Have you sought out ways to find other sources?

Assessing Information on Television and in the Newspapers

The criteria above are designed for assessing information in its generic form, that is, no matter what the delivery system. A second important area is the assessment of information delivered via mass media such as television and newspapers. The important question is, How can you become a more critical consumer of mass media? There are two factors that intervene in the assessment process that automatically affect any evaluation that occurs. The first involves the gatekeepers we referred to previously in this chapter, and the second factor is economics. The following are some of the questions you need to ask:

- *How is the information you discovered affected by the decisions of professional communicators?* Whether you are watching television or reading a newspaper, someone decided not only what topic you see or read but also how that topic is presented.

- *Is the information you discovered a product of sensationalism?* Strive to gather your information from a variety of sources—television in addition to newspapers and, perhaps, weekly newsmagazines as well. There are differences, even between networks and between different newspapers, in how stories are covered.

- *How is the information you discovered affected by economic or financial considerations?* It may be difficult to detect the influence of the profit motive on information delivered via the media; it can influence which stories are carried or not carried or what is said or done to attract viewers (of broadcasts) or buyers (of newspapers).

- *How is the information you discovered affected by bias?* Some publications have biases that affect their presentation of information. One of the best ways to detect bias is, once again, to get your information from a number of sources.

- *How can you influence the information you discover?* To say you need to be wary of what you hear, see, or read is truly an understatement. All media are subject to human error and bias. As a consumer of mass media, you influence the information you discover by thinking for yourself. Remember, it was Walter Cronkite who advocated the need for healthy skepticism. Skepticism means that knowledge in a particular area is uncertain. It means suspended judgment, systematic doubt, or a disposition to incredulity.

Assessing Information on the Internet

There are criteria, too, for evaluating information on the Internet. Because this aspect of media literacy is so important, using a search engine to discover the criteria will produce an abundance of available Web pages. For "Assessing information on the Internet" Google supplied 809,000 Web pages; for "Evaluating information on the Internet" Google provided 1,200,000 (March 26, 2003). Assessment and evaluation of Internet information is important, too, because new Web pages are placed on the WWW at incredible speeds; the quantity is remarkable, and the quality should always be suspect. Don E. Descy, a faculty member in the Library Media Education Department at Minnesota State University, Mankato, Minnesota, in one of his early articles in his online column "All Aboard the Internet" explains the problem—which is as true today as when it was first written:

> *The Internet is not like a library, a newspaper, an encyclopedia, or even a bookstore. In all of these someone reviews, reads, and/or filters the news, information, and books that we find. This is not the case on the Internet. Almost anyone can place almost any information on the Internet. No one filters it. No one checks it for accuracy. No one can be really sure of who is producing the information or why they are placing it on the Internet. Evaluating what one reads on the Internet is a critical task. Because of the fluid nature of the Internet, it is a difficult task (Descy, 1996).*

The WWW offers a wealth of information, but not all of it is equally accurate or reliable. In most cases, you need to use the same critical evaluative skills in looking for information on the Internet as you would use in evaluating a book, an article, a movie, or a television show. Specific criteria to consider are discussed below (Kirk, 2002).

Authorship?

This is the major criterion used in evaluating information. Who is presenting it? If your goal is to find information with some type of critical value, you must determine the basis of the authority with which the author speaks. The author could come from your own field of study and have a well-known, well-regarded name that you recognize. No problem. However, when you come across an author you are unfamiliar with, how do you find out about his or her credibility? Here are the questions you need to answer:

- Is the author mentioned in a positive way by another author or person you trust?
- Did you link to the author's Web/Internet document from another document you trust?
- Does the document you are reading give you the author's position, institutional affiliation, and address?
- Does the document you are reading give you a link to another document that enables you to judge the author's credentials?
- Is there an address, telephone number, or e-mail address for the author so that you can request further information on his or her work and professional background?

Publishing Body?

In traditional publishing, the author's manuscript undergoes screening to verify that it meets the standards or aims of the publisher. Often, this process includes peer review. Documents published on the Internet do not undergo such a process. Therefore, you need to ask questions to assess the role and authority of the publisher, which on the Internet means the *server,* or computer, where the document is located:

- Does the name of any organization appear on the document you are reading? (Are there headers, footers, or distinctive watermarks showing that the document is part of an official academic or scholarly website? Can the webmaster be contacted from this document?)

- Can you link to a page where the name of the organization appears? Is it on the same server? In the same directory? (Look at the URL and see if it relates.)
- Is this organization recognized in the field in which you are studying?
- Is the organization suitable for addressing the topic at hand?
- What is the relationship of the author and the publisher/server? Was the document prepared as part of the author's professional duties (i.e., within his or her area of expertise)? Is the relationship a casual one? A fee-based one? (A casual or fee-based arrangement tells you nothing about the author's credentials within an institution.)
- Can you verify the identity of the server where the document resides? (Internet programs such as *dnslookup* and *whois* may be of some help.)

Is the Web page a product of an individual's personal Internet account, rather than being part of an official website? If so, approach the page and the information contained there with great caution.

Point of View or Bias?

Information is rarely neutral. Every writer wants to prove his or her point and will use data and information to do so. Because the structure of the Internet allows for easy self-publication, the variety of points of view and biases will be the widest possible. The following questions can help you determine point of view or bias:

- What is the URL of the document? Is the document located on the Web server of an organization that has a clear stake in the issue at hand?
- Is the document located on the Web server of an organization that has a political or philosophical agenda?

Referral to and/or Knowledge of the Literature?

What is the context in which the author places his or her work? The context reveals what the author knows about his or her discipline and its practices. This allows you to evaluate the author's scholarship or knowledge of trends in the area under discussion. The following are suggested questions:

- Does the document include a bibliography?
- Does the author allude to or display knowledge of related sources, with proper attribution?
- Does the author display knowledge of theories, schools of thought, or techniques usually considered appropriate in the treatment of his or her subject?
- If the author is using a new theory or technique as a basis for research, does he or she discuss the value and/or limitations of this new approach?
- If the author's treatment of the subject is controversial, does he or she know and acknowledge this?

Accuracy or Verifiability of Details?

The ability to verify details is especially important if you are reading the work of an unfamiliar author, presented by an unfamiliar organization, or if the information is presented in a nontraditional way. The following are some questions to ask:

- For a research document, is there an explanation of the research method that was used to gather and interpret the information?
- Is the methodology outlined in the document appropriate to the topic? Does it allow the study to be duplicated for purposes of verification?
- Does the document rely on other sources that are listed in a bibliography? Or does it include links to the other sources themselves?
- Does the document name individuals and/or sources that provided nonpublished data used in the preparation of the study?
- Can the background information that was used be verified for accuracy?

Currency?

Currency refers to the timeliness of the information. In printed documents, the date of publication is the first indicator of currency. For some types of information, currency is not an issue: Authorship or place in the historical record is more important (e.g., T. S. Eliot's essays on tradition in literature). For many other types of data, however, currency is extremely important, as is the regularity with which the data are updated. The following are the questions to ask:

- Does the document include the date or dates on which the information was gathered?
- Does the document refer to clearly dated information?
- Does the document include information on the regularity of updates, if the data require this?
- Does the document include a publication date or a "last updated" date?
- Does the document include a date of copyright?
- If no date is given, can you view the directory in which the document resides and read the date of latest modification?

Using an Internet Search Engine?

If you use a search engine such as Google, AltaVista, InfoSeek, Lycos, Yahoo, or any of the services that rate WWW pages, here are some questions to ask:

- How does the search engine decide the order in which it returns the information requested?
- How does the search engine look for information? How often is the information updated?
- How does the search engine evaluate Web pages?

Not every attempt to find good, solid, useful information on the Internet will be successful. Finding reliable information is a process that requires

On the Web

This is an opportunity to put into practice the criteria outlined in the text for assessing websites. Begin by visiting each of the following websites:

- R. B. Farnsworth (2001, October 4). "Mankato, Minnesota: Home Page." Retrieved March 26, 2003, from http://www.lme.mankato.msus.edu/mankato/mankato.html.

- (No author) (2002, January 25). "McWhortle Enterprises, Inc.," McWhortle Enterprises, Inc., Washington DC, 20091. Retrieved March 26, 2003, from http://www.mcwhortle.com/about.htm.

- (No author) (1996). "The Greatest Thing since Cut Cheese©"), Real Aroma, Agency.com Ltd. Retrieved March 26, 2003, from http://www.realaroma.com.

- (No author) (1998). "Moon beam enterprise and the lunar travel agency," DreamWeaver Studios. Retrieved March 26, 2003, from http://www.dreamweaverstudios.com/moonbeam/moon.htm.

Now apply the Internet evaluation criteria to these websites in terms of these questions:

1. Who is the author of the site?
   a. Is there an author of the site? If there is no author, is there a sponsor? If a sponsor, answer the following questions about the sponsor—assuming they are responsible for the content of the site.
   b. Does the site provide a way to contact the author or sponsor?
   c. Does the author or sponsor seem reliable? Why or why not?
   d. How does the author or sponsor establish his or her credibility?

2. Is the author or sponsor the publishing or producing body?

3. What point of view is being conveyed at this website?

4. What is the accuracy or verifiability of the details of this website?

5. Is the information current? When was the information on the website last updated?

6. Is the site entertaining, engaging, thought-provoking? Why or why not?

strategy and flexibility. Assessing material is primarily a matter of common sense. The critical-thinking skills needed to master everyday life are the critical-thinking skills needed in media literacy as well. Soon media literacy will be such an automatic, accepted, and integrated part of everyday living that survival itself will depend on critical-thinking skills. Without these skills, how will people be able to retrieve the kind of information they need to survive?

■ HOW DO ETHICS RELATE TO THE MEDIA?

There is a great deal of appreciation for standards in the media because without them the system doesn't work. The questions are "Whose standards?" and "How should they be imposed?" Any discussion of standards,

Consider This

Where does the responsibility for ethics lie? According to media journalist Ken Freed:

The more we feel linked to one another, if only through a PC or TV screen, the more we'll tend to accept responsibility for the public effects of our private media choices. As more of us appreciate our penetrating interactivity, and try to act accordingly, the benefits will be boundless. For starters, unwelcome censorship like the Decency Act would become moot as vile impulses are inhibited by an interactive sensibility guiding us from within. As we feel how deeply we are interconnected, we tend to become more inclined to exercise our free will with self-restraint, to accept the accountability that allows any democracy to flourish. The more we see how we're all in one boat together, the more we'll tend to balance our individual and collective weight to keep the boat afloat. As this worldview spreads throughout society over the next few generations, I can clearly envision humanity eventually living in open communities, where personal democracy prevails, where responsible self-rule makes global sense.

Questions

1. Do you think this view is realistic or idealistic?
2. What are the possible factors that are likely to undermine or otherwise sabotage this approach to ethical behavior?
3. To what extent do you think the Internet or WWW is likely to increase people's feelings of linkage with one another?

Source: K. Freed, "Deep Literacy: A Proposal to Produce Public Understanding of Our Interactivity," Media & Education, *Media Visions Journal,* May 11, 2002. Retrieved March 26, 2003, from http://media-visions.com/ed-deepliteracy.html.

of course, recognizes media's potential influences. Here, David Considine responds:

One of the most traditional approaches to media literacy has been based on the widespread belief that the media "makes" people do things, i.e., that there is a relationship between what we see and hear and what we think and do. When the U.S. government banned cigarette advertising on television, it demonstrated this belief. Today, there is much concern about explicit sexuality, graphic violence, and obscene language in film and television. New technologies merely add to the problem so we now find the U.S. Congress discussing "cyberporn." Some people want to protect impressionable children and adolescents by banning or legislating offensive sights and sounds. Others point to the First Amendment and express concern about censorship (Considine, 1995).

The answer, of course, is media literacy! Surprise. Considine suggests that critical consumption leads to critical production. The answer is education. "Educating students, parents and citizens to recognize the persuasive techniques advertisers use to promote alcohol, tobacco and other potentially harmful products, offers another form of defense (in addition to the V-chip, which blocks out offensive material) (Considine, 1996).

There is no easy answer when it comes to ethics. Ethics are involved at both ends of communication—senders and receivers. That is, consumers of the media should be able to expect an ethical presentation. Unfortunately, with respect to the Internet and many of the sites that appear on the WWW, that is not true today, nor will it be true tomorrow. Let's be realistic: The current situation is *caveat lector*—"Let the reader beware." The best guideline available is simply to be wary of how much credence you attribute to what you see, hear, and read. All media are subject to human error and biases. Consumers must be armed with the kinds of assessment criteria outlined in the section above so that they can, on their own, assess the legitimacy, accuracy, and validity of the messages they receive. Just because citizens are informed doesn't mean they can make such decisions. That is why any answer to the question of how to deal with the ethics of the media requires a multipronged approach consisting of education, clear public standards, and personal responsibility. All are important, and no single element is more or less important than the other elements.

Assess Yourself

Are You Media Literate?

Answer "Y" for Yes, "N" for No, and "O" for I don't know.

_____ 1. Do you understand how mass media work? (Mass media include newspapers, magazines, billboards, radio, television, videocassettes, video games, computer games, the Internet and World Wide Web.)

_____ 2. Do you know how the mass media produce meanings?

_____ 3. Do you know how the mass media are organized?

_____ 4. Are you aware of and responsive to the changing nature of the media in our society?

_____ 5. Do you know the basic conventions of various media? (Conventions are the rules, principles, forms, and techniques of conduct.)

_____ 6. Are you in control of your media experiences?

_____ 7. Can you read, analyze, evaluate, create, produce, and communicate in a variety of media?

_____ 8. Do you have the critical-thinking skills necessary for questioning, interpreting, analyzing, and evaluating both the informational and emotional content derived from the media?

_____ 9. Can you use and are you willing to employ the criteria necessary to evaluate the information gained from the media?

_____ 10. Do you understand the impact of the mass media on the news you receive, the entertainment you enjoy, the vision of yourself you develop, the shopping choices you make, and the critical stance you construct as a means for approaching your physical, social, economic, and political world?

 Go to the *Communicating Effectively* CD-ROM to see your results and learn how to evaluate your attitudes and feelings.

Chapter Review

Media literacy is the ability to access, analyze, evaluate, and communicate information in all its forms—both print and nonprint. To recognize the importance of media literacy is to acknowledge our personal and collective power.

This chapter focuses primarily on the Internet rather than on movies, television, telephones, or the print media because of the newness of the Internet, as well as its worldwide acceptance and use and its numerous applications. Almost everything we have ever done that has to do with communication and information has been digitized and made available on the Internet.

The Internet blurs the traditional boundaries between interpersonal and mass communication. It allows us to do things we couldn't do before—publish, distribute video and audio material, telephone, and use messaging systems. What's more, communication via the Internet relates to the communication model in Chapter 1, The Communication Process, in the same ways that both interpersonal *and* group communications do. Also, communicators interact with the medium's format and content.

The study of media literacy is important because the media (and we are especially referring to the Internet) provide instant news, shape culture, shape attitudes, influence behavior, connect us with the global community, promote responsible citizenship, and create productive workers.

Perhaps the most important part of the media-literacy definition regarding the Internet is assessment. This is because everyone has access to the Internet and seldom are there gatekeepers. Assessment involves filtering, interpreting, accepting, and/or discarding information found on the Internet. Part of the problem in assessment is the use of virtual reality, the fact that the media are already constructions, and the economic context and financial imperative that drive the media industry. These are factors that must be considered.

One assesses the media using certain criteria. Beyond the relevancy, recency, reliability, and availability of information, one assesses information on television and in the newspapers by asking questions regarding the intervention of gatekeepers, the influence of sensationalism, as well as economic or financial considerations and bias, and, finally, noting the importance of suspended judgment, systematic doubt, and a disposition to incredulity. The specific criteria for evaluating a website include questions about authorship, publishing body, point of view or bias, referral to and/or knowledge of the literature, accuracy or verifiability of details, and currency, as well as questions associated with the Internet search engine itself.

An important question today is, How do ethics relate to the media? Dealing with the ethical issue requires a three-pronged approach: (1) education, (2) the establishment of clear public standards, and (3) personal responsibility of both senders and receivers. It would be a relief to know that those offering information for public consumption via the media had high moral values and impeccable ethical standards. However, this is not true today and is unlikely to be true tomorrow—a reality that is one facet of a free society. Thus, it is important to be armed with the tools that will enlighten in an environment of *caveat lector*—"Let the reader beware."

Questions to Review

1. What is media literacy? Why is its definition important?

2. Why does this chapter focus primarily on the Internet and not on the other media?

3. Why does media literacy demand our attention?

4. How does communication via the Internet relate to the communication model?

5. What is meant by the comment that senders and receivers interact "with any medium's format and content"? Do you have any personal experiences with this interaction? How does it alter all participants?

6. Why study media literacy?

7. What role do gatekeepers play, and of what significance are they to the communication that occurs on the Internet?

8. In what specific ways has media shaped your attitudes or influenced your behavior? Can you cite specific examples?

9. Distinguish between asynchronous communication and synchronous communication. Which do you prefer, and why?

10. Do you have any personal experiences of how the media connect us to a global community, of how media promotes responsible citizenship, or of how it creates productive workers?

11. How does assessment relate to the media? Why is this, perhaps, the most important aspect of the definition of media literacy?

12. What standard criteria are used to evaluate information received from any source?

13. What are the criteria for evaluating a website? What questions should be asked?

14. How do ethics relate to the media?

15. Who is responsible for the ethical standards related to the information presented on or acquired from the Internet?

mhhe.com/hybels

Go to the self-quizzes on the *Comunicating Effectively* CD-ROM (side 2, track 10) and the Online Learning Center at mhhe.com/hybels7 to test your knowledge of the chapter concepts.

References

Bricklin, D. (2002). "The Internet is now a dominant tool for regular people." Dan Bricklin's Web Site. Retrieved March 26, 2003, from http://www.bricklin.com/internetregulartool.htm

Considine, D. (1995, Fall). "An introduction to media literacy: The what, why and how to's." Appalachian State University, *Telemedium:* The Journal of Media Literacy, 41:2. Retrieved March 26, 2003, from http://www.ci.appstate.edu/programs/edmedia/medialit/article.html.

Considine, D. (2002, January 29). "Media literacy and North Carolina curriculum connections." Appalachian State University. Retrieved March 26, 2003, from http://www.ci.appstate.edu/programs/edmedia/medialit/medialit_nccuric.html.

Descy, D. E. (1996, October). "All aboard the Internet: Citing electronic resources." Tech Trends (Online) 41:5, 3p. Retrieved March 26, 2003, from http://www.lme.mankato.msus.edu/ded/tt/19eval.html.

Dilenschneider, R. L. (2001, January 15). "The coming age of content and critical thinking: Age of information technology." *Vital Speeches of the Day* 67:7, 209.

Dominick, J. R. (1999). *The dynamics of mass communication.* New York: McGraw-Hill.

Elshtain, J. B. (1995). *Democracy on trial.* New York: Basic Books.

(No author). (1999, May 30). "A few words about 'media literacy.'" Retrieved March 10, 2003, from http://www.cmpl.ucr.edu/exhibitions/education/vidkids/medialit.html.

(No author). (1999, August 2). "Evaluating information sources." Academic Library, St. Mary's University. Retrieved March 26, 2003, from http://library.stmarytx.edu/acadlib/subject/misc/evalinfo.htm

Flaherty, L. M., K. J. Pearce, & R. B. Rubin, (1998, Summer). "Internet and face-to-face communication: Not functional alternatives." *Communication Quarterly* 46:3, 250–68.

Freed, K. (2002, May 11). "Deep literacy: A proposal to produce public understanding of our interactivity." Media & Education, Media Visions Journal. Retrieved March 26, 2003, from http://www. media-visions.com/ed-deeplit.html.

Friedman, T. L. (2002, May 14). "Global village idiocy, courtesy of the Internet." (New York Times News Service). *The Blade* (Toledo, Ohio)., 7A.

(No author). (2002, March 31). "Global Internet statistics (by language)." Global Reach. Retrieved March 26, 2003, from http://global-reach.biz/ globstats/ index.php3.

Goldberg, B. (2001). *Bias: A CBS insider exposes how the media distort the news.* Washington, DC: Regnery Publishing, Inc. (An Eagle Publishing Company).

Golding, P. (1996, July/August). "World wide wedge: Division and contradiction in the global information infrastructure." *Monthly Review* 48:3.

Helping Youth navigate the media age: A new approach to drug prevention. (2001). Office of National Drug Control Policy, Washington, D.C.: ONDCP.

Hobbs, R. (1998). "Media literacy in Massachusetts." In A. Hart, ed. *Teaching the media: International perspectives.* Mahwah, NJ: Lawrence Erlbaum, 127–44.

(No author). (2003). "How many online?" ComputerScope Ltd., Scope Communications Group. Retrieved March 26, 2003, from http://www. nua.ie/suveys/how_many_online/.

Iwata, E. (1999, December 14). "The Net at 30: From the Edge to the mainstream in just a blink." (Cover story). *USA Today,* 1A–2A.

Johnson, P. (2002, July 11). "Media distortion draws Stossel's indignation" (The Media Mix). *USA Today,* 3D.

Kearl, M. C. (2002). "Communication studies." Exercising the Sociological Imagination, Department of Sociology & Anthropology, Trinity University. Retrieved March 26, 2003, from http://www.trinity.edu/mkearl/commun.html.

Kirk, E. E. (2002, June 5). "Evaluating information found on the Internet." The Sheridan Libraries, The John Hopkins University. Retrieved March 26, 2003, from http://www.library.jhu.edu/elp/ useit/evaluate/.

McCluskey, A. (1999, November 2). "Building shared intelligence for networked decision making." Connected. Retrieved March 26, 2003, from http://www.connected.org.html.

McLuhan, M., & Q. Fiore. (1967) *The medium is the massage.* NY: Bantam Books.

(No author). (1999). *Resource guide: Media literacy.* Ontario, Canada: Ministry of Education.

Riddy, P. (2002, May 3). "Computer mediated communication (CMC)." Centre for Learning and Teaching. Retrieved March 26, 2003, from http://www.clt.soton.ac.uk/LTDI/CMC/cme intro.htm.

Rifkin, J. (2000). *The age of access: The new culture of hypercapitalism where all of life is a paid-for experience.* New York: Jeremy P. Tarcher/Putnam (Penguin Putnam Inc.).

(No author). (1999, September 20). "Special report: The dawn of e-life." *Newsweek,* p. 40.

Wiggins, R. W. (2001, October). "The effects of September 11 on the leading search engine." First Monday 7:10. Retrieved March 26, 2003, from http://firstmonday.org/issues/issue6_10/wiggins/ index.html.

Further Reading

Baran, S. J. (2002). *Introduction to mass communication, media literacy, and culture* 2nd ed. New York: McGraw-Hill. In this 535-page textbook, Baran includes four parts: Laying the groundwork; Media, media industries, and media audiences; Supporting industries; and Mass-mediated culture in the information age. This is a well-written, well-organized, well-presented book with numerous pictures, figures, forums, special

sections labeled "Media Echoes," "Cultural Forum" and "Using Media to Make a Difference" to make it not only interesting but fun to read.

Brinson, J. D., & M. F. Radcliffe (2000). *Internet law and business handbook.* Palo Alto, CA: Quality Books, Inc. This 554-page book would be a useful reference for those developing material for the Internet, creating or distributing online products, using material from the Internet, or buying products over the Internet. Although designed for nonlawyers and lawyers alike, it becomes quite technical where appropriate—as when explaining the laws applicable to the use of the Internet. There are numerous examples to help readers understand how laws apply to business, personal, and educational use of the Internet. Those areas most interesting to readers would be the lawful use of material found on the Internet, Web development, using music on the Internet, e-mail and linking issues, and distance learning and educational legal issues—although the range of topics is far greater than these and includes basic legal principles, licensing, e-commerce laws, and legal issues of service providers and content owners.

Dodd, A. Z. (2000). *The essential guide to telecommunications,* 2nd ed. Upper Saddle River, NJ: Prentice Hall PTR. Dodd, formerly a marketing manager at Bell Atlantic and telecommunications manager at a Fortune 500 company and now a faculty member who teaches telecommunications for the nontechnical classes at Northeastern University, has put together a clear, comprehensive, and low-jargon map to the telecommunications territory. She covers basic concepts, telephone systems and cabling, network service providers, local competition, the public network, specialized network services, modems and access devices, the Internet, convergence, and wireless services. Her information is accurate, up to date, and easy to understand.

Ferrington, G. (2002, Spring/Summer). "Media literacy review." Media Literacy Online Project, College of Education, University of Oregon, Eugene. Retrieved March 26, 2003, from http://interact.uoregon.edu/MediaLit/mlr/home/index.html This is a wonderful website for its inclusiveness. Here you will find articles, special features, and hundreds of links to media literacy organizations, media-education, online journals, resource and curriculum guides, lesson plans, curriculum standards, research, and courses as well.

Freed, K. (2002, May 11). *"Deep literacy: A proposal to produce public understanding of our interactivity."* Media & Education, Media Visions Journal. Retrieved March 26, 2003, from http://media-visions.com/ed-deepliteracy.html. Freed offers a thorough, thought-provoking, practical article about developing deep literacy—developing a deep appreciation for the nature and power of our global interactivity. His strategies for deep media literacy include developing a shared media vision, talking about our media choices, and talking about interactivity itself. Benefits include the public relations advantages of helping the world to value interactive media as a force for civility in our "global village" (p. 8)—"ensuring that open markets and free democracies prevail in the centuries ahead" (p. 9).

McGuire, M., L. Stilborne, M. McAdams, & L. Hyatt, (2000). *The Internet handbook for writers, researchers, and journalists—2000/2001 Edition.* New York: Guilford Publications, Inc. This is a guide to what the Internet has to offer writers, researchers, journalists, and students. Whether you are a novice or experienced Internet user, there is a wealth of practical, informative graphics, tips, tricks, and techniques that will prove helpful no matter the subject you are searching for. Clearly, the authors understand the nuts and bolts of successful research and writing. The book is updated through their website at http://www.guilford.com/writernet.

Newton, H. with R. Horak, (2001). *Newton's telecom dictionary: The official dictionary of telecommunications, networking and the Internet,* 17th ed. New York: CMP Books. No other aspect of our lives or, indeed, history, has experienced as much explosive growth as telecommunications. You almost need a map to understand the territory. This book is the map to technical concepts. Newton and Horak use nontechnical business language and focus on what terms mean, what the technology does, what benefits the technology confers, and which pitfalls to watch for, in this 787-page paperback. One of the most valuable portions is the introduction, "Where the Telecom, Networking, Fiber, Internet, Web Explosion is Taking Us," by the author, where he explains both the current status and future of telecommunications. This is an incredibly important and satisfying reference work.

Potter, J. (2001). *Media literacy,* 2nd ed. Beverly Hills, CA: Sage Publications. Potter helps readers establish knowledge structures from which they can consciously filter out negative media effects, while acknowledging the positive instructional and entertainment value of the media. Integrating theory with practice, he includes exercises and examples to support the key ideas of media studies and invites the reader to think like a psychologist, an economist, an advertiser, a journalist, a media critic, a producer, and a policymaker. This book will make you think as you gain a better understanding of the media.

Rifkin, J. (2000). *The age of access: The new culture of hypercapitalism where all of life is a paid-for experience.* New York: Jeremy P. Tarcher/Putnam (Member of Penguin Putnam Inc.). Although much of this book is speculation and prophecy about our future and the future of society, Rifkin will really make you think. His premise, to state it briefly, is that every activity you engage in outside your immediate family is going to be a "paid-for" experience—a commodity. We are headed rapidly to a time when nearly every kind of service will be available through vast commercial networks operating in cyberspace. These changes will have an enormous effect on both communication and culture, and Rifkin produces the evidence to support his theories. Startling and compelling reading.

Silverblatt, A. (2001). *Media literacy: Keys to interpreting media messges,* 2nd ed. New York: Praeger Publishing. Silverblatt answers the question, what are the essential components for critically examining mass media. He offers tips on content analysis and other means of interpreting media efforts. He discusses the influence of the Internet upon various media, provides new concepts and insights into media literacy, and offers an easy-to-understand theoretical framework for the critical analysis of media text. The second part of the book invites readers to apply his framework to a variety of media formats. Well written and full of interesting facts about the world of the mass media.

Glossary

A

abstract symbol A symbol which represents an idea. (ch 1) (10)

accommodation An approach that works toward getting the dominant group to reinvent, or at least change, the rules so that they incorporate the life experiences of the nondominant group. Something that occurs in groups when people on one side of an issue give in to the other side. (ch 3, 11) (83, 399)

accommodation strategies When people are not part of a dominant culture, those processes people use to get the dominant group to reinvent or change the rules through the use of nonassertive, assertive, or aggressive accommodation. (ch 3) (83)

action listening style That kind of listening in which the listener wants precise, error-free presentations and is likely to be impatient with disorganization. (ch 4) (102)

active listener A listener who makes a mental outline of important points and thinks up questions or challenges to those points. (ch 4) (113)

adaptors Nonverbal ways of adjusting to a communication situation. (ch 6) (182)

ad hominem A fallacy that occurs when an argument diverts attention away from the question being argued by focusing instead on those arguing it. (ch 17) (624)

affection A feeling of warm, emotional attachment we have for people we appreciate and care for. (ch 7) (219)

agenda A list of all the items that will be discussed during a meeting. (ch 11) (390)

aggression A physical or verbal show of force. (ch 8) (273)

aggressive talk Talk that attacks a person's self-concept with the intent of inflicting psychological pain. (ch 8) (272)

analogy In reasoning, comparing two similar cases and concluding that if something is true for one, it must also be true for the other. (ch 17) (625)

anecdote A short, interesting story based on an experience. (ch 16) (588)

appeal to authority A fallacy that occurs whenever an idea is justified by citing some source of expertise as a reason for holding that idea. (ch 17) (624)

appeal to ignorance A fallacy that occurs when an argument is based on an opponent's inability to disprove a conclusion as proof of the conclusion's correctness. (ch 17) (624)

appraisal interview A type of information interview in which a supervisor makes a valuation by estimating and judging the quality or worth of an employee's performance and then interviews the employee in connection with the appraisal. (ch 9) (303)

articulation The ability to pronounce the letters in a word correctly. (ch 15) (545)

assertiveness Taking the responsibility of expressing needs, thoughts, and feelings in a direct, clear manner. (ch 8) (286)

assessment The evaluation of what took place during communication. (ch 4) (112)

assimilation When nondominants use assimilation, they drop cultural differences and distinctive characteristics that would identify them with the nondominant group. (ch 3) (81)

assimilation strategies When people are not part of a dominant culture, those processes people use to get the dominant group to reinvent or change the rules through the use of nonassertive, assertive, or aggressive assimilation. (ch 3) (81)

assumption A taking for granted or supposition that something is a fact. (ch 3) (86)

asynchronous communication Communication in which people are not directly connected with each other at the same time. (ch 10, Appendix) (354, 663)

attentiveness Focusing on the moment. (ch 15) (533)

attitudes Deeply felt beliefs that govern how one behaves. Also, a group of beliefs that cause us to respond in some way to a particular object or situation. (ch 7, 17) (217, 614)

attractiveness Having the power or quality of drawing, pleasing, or winning. (ch 6) (184)

audience analysis Finding out what one's audience members know about a subject, what they might be interested in, and what their attitudes and beliefs are. (ch 12) (434)

authoritarian leader One who holds great control over a group. (ch 11) (382)

avoidance A refusal to deal with conflict or painful issues. (ch 8,11) (278, 399)

B

balance One of eight ways couples have for dealing with or responding to dialectical tension that involves a useful approach because it is a compromise that promotes dialogue about both opposing dialectical extremes. (ch 7) (245)

begging the question A fallacy that occurs when an argument, instead of offering proof for its conclusion, simply reasserts the conclusion in another form. (ch 17) (624)

beliefs One's own convictions; what one thinks is right and wrong, true and false. Also, they are classified as statements of knowledge, opinion, and faith. (ch 7, 17) (217, 613)

bid A question, gesture, look, touch, or other single expression that says "I want to feel connected to you." (ch 7) (223)

bifurcation A fallacy that occurs when one presumes that a distinction is exclusive and exhaustive, but other alternatives exist. (ch 17) (624)

body (of speech) The main part of the speech. (ch 14) (493)

body adornment Any addition to the physical body designed to beautify or decorate. (ch 6) (188)

body movement (kinesics) Describes a phenomenon responsible for much of our nonverbal communication. (ch 6) (181)

brainstorming A technique of free association; in groups, when all members spontaneously contribute ideas in a group without judgments being made. The goal of brainstorming is for the group to be as creative as possible. (ch10) (362)

bulletin boards An online group discussion originally designed for swapping files and posting notices. (ch 10) (354)

C

causal reasoning A logical appeal that pertains to, constitutes, involves, or expresses a cause and therefore uses the word *because*, which is either implicitly or explicitly stated. (ch 17) (625)

cause-and-effect order Organization of a speech around why something is happening (*cause*) and what impact it is having (*effect*). (ch 14) (496)

central idea The main idea or thesis of a speech. It establishes the main thrust of the speech. (ch 4, 12) (114, 431)

channel The route traveled by a message; the means it uses to reach the sender-receivers. (ch 1) (11)

chronemics The study of time. (ch 6) (195)

clarity That property of style by means of which a thought is so presented that it is immediately understood, depending on the precision and simplicity of the language. (ch 5) (156)

closed-format Interviews that are highly structured. (ch 9) (307)

closed questions Interview questions that are worded in ways that restrict their answers (e.g., questions that can be answered with a yes or a no). (ch 9) (308)

coculture Because the word *subculture* has the connotation of a culture beneath, lower, or under, we have chosen, instead, to use the word *coculture* to represent nonwhites, women, people with disabilities, homosexuals, and those in the lower social classes who have specific patterns of behavior that set them off from other groups within a culture. (ch 1, 3) (22, 65)

coercive power In an organization, the ability of a leader to punish followers (e.g., by criticizing them, refusing to pay attention to them, using power to demote them, refusing to raise their pay, or firing them). (ch 11) (376)

cognitive dissonance A psychological theory, applied to communication, which states that people seek information that will support their beliefs and ignore information that does not. (ch 4) (104)

cohesiveness The feeling of attraction that group members have toward one another. It is the group's ability to stick together, to work together as a group, and to help one another as group members. (ch 10) (359)

collaboration When people in conflict try to work together to meet the other person's needs as well as their own. (ch 11) (399)

color A visual attribute of bodies or substances distinct from their spatial characteristics. (ch 16) (581)

commitment A strong desire by both parties for the relationship to continue. In groups, it is the willingness of members to work together to complete the group's task. (ch 8, 10) (271, 359)

communication Any process in which people share information, ideas, and feelings. (ch 1) (7)

comparative advantage order A method of arranging a speech that enables the speaker to compare the advantages of one solution over another. (ch 17) (635)

comparison Pointing out the similarities between two or more things. (ch 13, 16) (471, 579)

compatibility Similar attitudes, personality, and a liking for the same activities. (ch 7) (217)

competition Something that occurs in groups when one side cares more about winning than it does about other members' feelings. (ch 11) (399)

complaint Expression of dissatisfaction with the behavior, attitude, belief, or characteristic of a partner or of someone else. (ch 8) (277)

composition The makeup of a thing. (ch 16) (582)

compromise When each side in a conflict has to give up something in order to get what it wants. (ch 11) (399)

computer database A collection of items of information organized for easy access via a computer. (ch 13) (457)

computer-generated graphics Refers to any images created or manipulated via computer—art, drawings, representations of objects, pictures, and the like. (ch 15) (551)

conclusion (of speech) In a speech, the closing remarks that tie a speech together and give listeners the feeling that the speech is complete. (ch 14) (509)

concrete symbol A symbol that represents an object. (ch 1) (10)

conflict Expressed struggle between at least two individuals who perceive incompatible goals or interference from others in achieving their goals. (ch 11) (397)

conflict resolution Negotiation to find a solution to the conflict. (ch 8) (287)

connotative meaning The feelings or associations that each individual has about a particular word. (ch 5) (141)

consensus The point at which all members of a group agree. (ch 10) (368)

content listening style That kind of listening in which the listener prefers complex and challenging information. (ch 4) (102)

context High context occurs when most of the meaning of the message is either implied by the physical setting or is presumed to be part of the individual's beliefs, values, and norms. It is considered low context when most of the information is in the code or message. (ch 3) (77)

contrast Pointing out the differences between two or more things. (ch 13, 16) (472, 579)

control People who attempt to exert control believe that they are always right and that no other opinion (or even fact) is worth listening to. They argue for their point of view, insist their position be accepted, and raise their voices to get people to accept what they believe. (ch 6) (171) Also, control is being able to make choices. (ch 7) (220) Also, people who believe they are always right and that no other opinion (or even fact) is worth listening to. (ch 8) (279)

control messages Messages designed to get children to behave in ways that are acceptable to the mother. (ch 7) (247)

controlling listener These types of listeners don't want to listen at all, and they always look for a way to talk about themselves and their experiences. (ch 4) (105)

convergence An aspect of rate (the speed at which one speaks) demonstrated by how one person will accommodate or adapt to another's rate. (ch 6) (180)

conversational quality When speakers talk to audiences in much the same way they talk when they are having a conversation with another person. (ch 15) (535)

costs and rewards Problems and pleasures of a relationship. (ch 8) (283)

costumes That type of clothing that is a form of highly individualized dress. (ch 6) (188)

cover letter Letters that provide a "cover" to a résumé. (ch 9) (323)

credibility The believability of a speaker based on the speaker's expertise, dynamism, trustworthiness, and ethics. (ch 4, 17) (118, 637)

critical listening Evaluating and questioning what has been heard. (ch 4) (117)

criticism A negative evaluation of a person for something he or she has done or the way he or she is. (ch 8) (276)

critics-analyzers Group members who look at the good and bad points in the information the group has gathered. These members see the points that need more elaboration, and they discover information that has been left out. (ch 11) (395)

cultural identity The degree to which you identify with your culture. (ch 3) (65)

culture The ever-changing, values, traditions, social and political relationships, and worldview created and shared by a group of people bound together by a combination of factors (which can include a common history, geographic location, language, social class, and/or religion). (ch 1, 3) (22, 66)

D

database A collection of information that can be read on a computer screen. (ch 13) (457)

deductive reasoning Reasoning from the general to the specific. (ch 17) (621)

defensive communication When one partner tries to defend himself or herself against the remarks or behavior of the other. (ch 8) (278)

definition A brief explanation of what a word or phrase means. (ch 13, 16) (473, 576)

delegating That style of situational leadership in which leaders hang back and let members plan and execute the job. (ch 11) (387)

deletions The blotting out, erasing, or canceling of information that makes people's perceptions less than perfect because their physical senses are limited. (ch 2) (50)

democratic leader One who lets all points of view be heard and lets group members participate in the decision-making process. (ch 11) (383)

demographic analysis Reveals data about the characteristics of a group of people, including such things as age, sex, education, occupation, race/nationality/ethnic origin, geographic location, and group affiliation. (ch 12) (437)

denial One of eight ways couples have for dealing with or responding to dialectical tension that involves responding to one element of a dialectic while ignoring the other. (ch 7) (245)

denotative meaning The dictionary definition of a particular word. (ch 5) (141)

describe To describe is to provide a mental image of something experienced, such as a scene, a person, or a sensation. (ch 16) (580)

diagram May range from a simple organizational chart to a complex rendering of a three-dimensional object. It is particularly valuable in showing how something works. (ch 15) (548)

dialect The habitual language of a community. (ch 5) (153)

directness Being natural and straightforward. (ch 15) (535)

disciplinary interview A type of information interview that concerns a sensitive area, where the employee is notified, and the interview involves hearing the employee's side of the story and, depending on the outcome, instituting disciplinary action. (ch 9) (303)

discrimination The overt actions one takes to exclude, avoid, or distance oneself from other groups. (ch 3) (80)

disorientation One of eight ways couples have for dealing with or responding to dialectical tension that involves a nonfunctional response that involves couples who have become overwhelmed by the contradictions dialectics present. (ch 7) (245)

displays of feelings Face and body movements that show how intensely we are feeling. (ch 6) (182)

distortions The twisting or bending of information out of shape that makes people's perceptions less than perfect because they only observe a small part of their external environment. (ch 2) (51)

dominant culture Includes white people from a European background. (ch 3) (81)

doublespeak A term that refers to euphemisms created by an institution, such as government, to cover up the truth. (ch 5) (147)

dynamism For speakers, a great deal of enthusiasm and energy for their subject. (ch 17) (638)

dysfunctional (individual) roles Any role played by a group member that can be characterized as aggressor, blocker, recognition-seeker, self-confessor, playboy or playgirl, dominator, help-seeker, or special-interest pleader. (ch 11) (396)

E

elective characteristics The nonverbal, physical characteristics over which you have control such as clothing, makeup, tattoos, and body piercing. (ch 6) (185)

electronic résumé A résumé specifically designed to apply for jobs online that produce interviews. (ch 9) (322)

emblems Body movements that have a direct translation into words. (ch 6) (181)

emotional appeal An appeal that focuses on listeners' needs, wants, desires, and wishes. (ch 17) (625)

emotional intelligence The ability to understand and get along with others. (ch 7) (212)

empathic listening Listening for feelings, in contrast to listening for main points or listening to criticize ideas. (ch 4) (121)

empathy The ability to recognize and identify with someone's feelings. (ch 7, 8) (214, 280)

employment interview An interview used by an employer to determine whether someone is suitable for a job. (ch 9) (316)

encouragers Those group members who praise and commend contributions and group achievements. (ch 11) (395)

enunciation How one pronounces and articulates words. (ch 15) (545)

ethical communication Communication that is honest, fair, and considerate of others' rights. (ch 1) (23)

ethics A matter of conforming to acceptable and fair standards of conduct. (ch 17) (641)

ethnocentrism The belief that one's own cultural group's behaviors, norms, ways of thinking and ways of being are superior to all other cultural groups. (ch 3) (79)

etymology The study of the origin and development of words. (ch 16) (577)

euphemisms Inoffensive words or phrases which are substituted for words that might be perceived as unpleasant. (ch 5) (146)

evaluative statements Statements involving a judgment. (ch 8) (279)

example A short illustration that clarifies a point. (ch 13, 16) (473, 578)

exit interview A type of information interview that occurs at the termination of an employee's employment, and is designed to resolve any outstanding concerns of employers and employees. (ch 9) (303)

expert power The influence and power that an expert has because he or she knows more than anyone else. (ch 11) (377)

expertise Having the experience or knowledge of an expert. (ch 17) (637)

explaining The process of making something clear. (ch 16) (584)

extemporaneous speaking Speaking from notes. (ch 15) (538)

external noise Interference with the message that comes from the environment and keeps the message from being heard or understood. (ch 1) (12)

eye messages As an aspect of nonverbal communication, they include all information conveyed by the eyes alone. (ch 6) (183)

F

fact Something that can be verified in a number of ways, which might include experiments, direct observation, or books by authorities. (ch 4) (119)

factual information Interviews that focus on facts such as who, what, where, and when. (ch 9) (306)

fallacy An improper conclusion drawn from the premise. (ch 17) (624)

false analogy A fallacy that occurs when a comparison between an obscure or difficult set of facts and one that is already known and understood, and to which it bears a significant resemblance, is erroneous and distorts the facts of the case being argued. (ch 17) (624)

false cause A fallacy that occurs when events are causally connected but in fact no such causal connection has been established. (ch 17) (624)

family Two or more individuals who are joined together at a particular point in time through the biological or sociological means of genetics, marriage, or adoption. (ch 7) (239)

feedback The response of the receiver-senders to each other. (ch 1) (11)

femininity versus masculinity That way of contrasting a group of cultures to another group of cultures that involves the division of roles between women and men. (ch 3) (76)

feng shui The ancient Chinese art of improving every aspect of your life by enhancing your environment according to the principles of harmony and energy flow. (ch 6) (173)

file A complete, named, collection of information. (ch 9) (323)

file format Coded in ASCII (pronounced ASK-ee), in plain text, rich text and hypertext, a file format exists so that information can be stored and retrieved electronically. (ch 9) (323)

fit It occurs when you describe something by the way parts belong together or by the relationship among parts. (ch 16) (582)

flip chart A series of pictures, words, diagrams, and so forth. It is made up of several pages that speakers "flip" through. (ch 15) (549)

follow-up questions Interview questions that are based on the answers given by interviewees and useful when interviewers want interviewees to go into a subject in greater depth. (ch 9) (308)

FOXP2 gene The gene directly linked to developing the fine motor skills needed for the development of language and speech. (ch 5) (136)

full-sentence outline A complete map of what a speech will look like. (ch 14) (513)

function How things perform or how they can be used. (ch 16) (580)

functional leadership When leadership varies with the task of the group and moves from one individual to another as the group finds it suitable. (ch 11) (380)

G

gatekeepers Those in control of what information becomes available over the media (e.g., organizations, owners, editors, news directors, and reporters). (Appendix) (667)

general purpose The intention of the speaker to inform or persuade. (ch 12) (427)

generalizations The process of drawing principles or conclusions from particular evidence or facts that makes people's perceptions less than perfect because once people have observed something a few times, they conclude that what has proven true in the past will prove true in the future as well. (ch 2) (51)

graphs Statistical material presented in a visual form that helps viewers see similarities, differences, relationships, or trends. (ch 15) (550)

groupthink A group dysfunction in which the preservation of harmony becomes more important than the critical examination of ideas. (ch 10) (359)

H

harmonizers-compromisers Group members who help to resolve conflict in the group, settle arguments and disagreements through mediation, and attempt to discover solutions acceptable to everyone. (ch 11) (395)

hasty generalization A fallacy that occurs when an isolated or exceptional case is used as the basis for a general conclusion that is unwarranted. (ch 17) (624)

hidden agendas Unannounced goals, subjects, or issues of individual group members or subgroups that differ from the group's public or stated agenda. (ch 11) (391)

hierarchy of needs The relative order of the physical and psychological needs of all human beings. (ch 17) (626)

high context versus low context That way of contrasting a group of cultures to another group of cultures that involves the degree to which most of the information is carried in the context (high) or most of the information is in the code or message (low). (ch 3) (77)

hypothetical example An example that is made up to illustrate a point. (ch 13) (475)

I

illustrators Gestures or other nonverbal signals which accent, emphasize, or reinforce words. (ch 6) (181)

immediacy It occurs when the communicator is completely focused on the communication situation. (ch 15) (534)

impromptu speaking Speaking on the spur of the moment with little time to prepare. (ch 15) (536)

inclusion Involvement with others. (ch 7) (219)

indirect aggression (Also called *passive aggression.*) People who use this form of communication often feel powerless and respond by doing something to thwart the person in power. (ch 8) (273)

individualism versus collectivism That way of contrasting a group of cultures to another group of cultures that involves the degree of integration and orientation of individuals within groups. (ch 3) (76)

inductive reasoning Reasoning from the specific to the general. (ch 17) (622)

inflection A change in pitch used to emphasize certain words and phrases. (ch 15) (545)

influence The power of a person or things to affect others—to produce effects without the presence of physical force. (ch 17) (610)

information givers and seekers Members of groups who either give information or seek it. (ch 11) (394)

information interview An interview in which the goal is to gather facts and opinions from someone with expertise and experience in a specific field. (ch 9) (303)

information-sharing group A type of group which meets to be informed or to inform others, to express themselves and to listen to others, to get or give assistance, to clarify or hear clarification of goals, or to establish or maintain working relationships. (ch 10) (355)

informative speech A speech that concentrates on explaining, defining, clarifying, and instructing. (ch 12, 16) (427, 573)

initiators-expediters Members of groups who suggest new ideas, goals, solutions, and approaches. (ch 11) (393)

instrumental values Those values that guide people's day-to-day behavior (how one should or should not behave). (ch 17) (612)

integration One of eight ways couples have for dealing with or responding to dialectical tension that involves a way that partners simultaneously respond to opposing forces without dilution or delusion. (ch 7) (245)

intercultural communication When a message is created by a member of one culture, and this message needs to be processed by a member of another culture. (ch 1, 3) (22, 68)

internal noise Interference with the message that occurs in the minds of the sender-receivers when their thoughts or feelings are focused on something other than the communication at hand. (ch 1) (12)

Internet A group of computer networks connected to each other. (ch 13) (459)

Internet-ready résumé A résumé specifically designed to apply for jobs online that produce interviews. (ch 9) (322)

interpersonal communication One person interacting with another on a one-to-one basis, often in an informal, unstructured setting. (ch 1, 7) (20, 24)

interview A series of questions and answers, usually exchanged between two people, which has the purpose of getting and understanding information about a particular subject or topic. (ch 9) (301)

intimacy Intimacy is defined by some or all of the following characteristics: spontaneity, self-disclosure, motivation, interdependence, and tension and balance. (ch 7) (241)

intimate distance That distance zone, a range of less than 18 inches apart, that places people in direct contact with each other. (ch 6) (190)

intrapersonal communication Communication that occurs within you; it involves thoughts, feelings, and the way you look at yourself. (ch 1) (18)

introduction (of speech) In a speech, the opening remarks that aim to get attention and build interest in the subject. (ch 14) (502)

J

Johari window A model of the process of disclosure in interpersonal relationships, developed by Joseph Luft and Harry Ingham. (ch 7) (232)

K

key-word outline An outline containing only the important words or phrases of a speech that helps to remind speakers of the ideas they are presenting. (ch 14) (513)

L

laissez-faire leader One who does very little actual leading. This leader suggests no direction for and imposes no order on a group. (ch 11) (384)

language environment The environment in which language takes place, e.g., in a classroom. (ch 5) (145)

leader A person who influences the behavior of one or more people. (ch 11) (376)

leadership style The amount of control a leader exerts over a group. (ch 11) (380)

leading question A question designed to point the interviewee in a particular direction. (ch 9) (309)

learning group The purpose is to increase the knowledge or skill of participants. (ch 10) (356)

legitimate power (Also called *organizational power*) Leaders in formal organizations who derive their influence because they are "the boss" or because of the organizational hierarchy and its rules. (ch 11) (377)

leisure clothing That type of clothing that is up to the individual and that is worn when work is over. (ch 6) (188)

letter of application A letter that accompanies a résumé and other requested materials, such as transcripts and letters of recommendation, when it is known that an employer has an opening which interests a prospect. (ch 9) (326)

letter of inquiry A letter that accompanies a résumé and is designed to determine if an employer has an opening for which you may qualify. (ch 9) (323)

listening Hearing and responding to given information, both intellectually and emotionally. (ch 4) (102)

logical appeal An appeal that addresses listeners' reasoning ability. (ch 17) (621)

long-term orientation That way of contrasting a group of cultures to another group of cultures that involves the trade-off between long-term and short-term gratification of needs. (ch 3) (78)

M

mailing lists Online group discussions that are completely passive. The discussion arrives through e-mail. (ch 10) (354)

main heads The points that reinforce the central idea. (ch 4) (114)

main points All the broad, general ideas and information that support your central idea. (ch 14) (492)

maintenance roles Group members who play these roles focus on the emotional tone of the meeting. (ch 11) (395)

manuscript speaking Writing out an entire speech and reading it to the audience from the prepared script. (ch 15) (537)

map versus territory The map is the personal mental approximation and the territory is the actual land or external reality that people experience. Map versus territory simply contrasts the subjective internal experience with the objective external reality. (ch 2) (54)

mass communication Communication that involves highly structured messages and large audiences, often numbering in the millions. Messages of mass communication are created by many people. (ch 1) (21)

media literacy The ability to access, analyze, evaluate, and communicate information in all its forms—both print and nonprint. (Appendix) (660)

memory (speaking from) This type of delivery involves writing out the entire speech and then committing it to memory word for word. (ch 15) (538)

message The ideas and feelings that a sender-receiver wants to share. (ch 1) (9)

metamessage The meaning, apart from the words, in a message. (ch 5) (161)

metasearch engine A special tool designed to help you find information on the Internet that transmits your search request to a number of different search engines and their databases of websites at the same time. (ch 13) (463)

minor points The specific ideas and information that support the main points. (ch 14) (492)

mixed message A message in which the verbal and nonverbal contradict each other. (ch 6) (177)

mob appeal A fallacy that occurs when an appeal is made to emotions, particularly to powerful feelings that can sway people in large crowds. (ch 17) (624)

model A replica of an actual object that is used when the object itself is too large to be displayed (e.g., a building), too small to be seen (e.g., a cell), or inaccessible to the eye (e.g., the human heart). (ch 15) (547)

monotone Little variety of pitch in a speech. (ch 15) (545)

motivated sequence Organization of a speech that involves five steps: attention, need, satisfaction, visualization, and action and works because it follows the normal process of human reasoning. (ch 14) (500)

motivation The stimulation or inducement that causes people to act. (ch 17) (611)

multimedia Refers to various media (e.g., text, graphics, animation, and audio) used to deliver information. (ch 15) (553)

N

national communities Cocultural groupings within a country. (ch 3) (70)

natural delivery The collection of speech and actions that best represents your true self—that is, free from artificiality, affectation, and constraint. (ch 9) (333)

naturalistic fallacy Occurs when something is identified as being good or desirable because it appears to be a natural characteristic. (ch 17) (624)

netiquette (or net etiquette) It includes the common practices, customs, conventions, and expectations expected of individuals using the Internet. (ch 10) (396)

neutral questions Interview questions that do not show how the interviewer feels about the subject. (ch 9) (309)

neutrality Not taking sides (in a group discussion). (ch 11) (389)

noise Interference that keeps a message from being understood or accurately interpreted. (ch 1) (12)

nondominant culture Includes people of color, women, gays, lesbians, and bisexuals, and those whose socioeconomic background is lower than middle class. (ch 3) (81)

nonelective characteristics The nonverbal physical characteristics over which you have no control and cannot change such as height, body proportion, coloring, bone structure, and physical handicaps. (ch 6) (185)

nonverbal communication Information we communicate without using words. (ch 6) (170)

nonverbal symbol Anything communicated without words, e.g., facial expressions or hand gestures. (ch 1) (10)

norms Expectations that group members have of how other members will behave, think, and participate. (ch 10) (351)

O

objective world The actual territory or external reality people experience. (ch 2) (54)

objectivity Basing conclusions on facts and evidence rather than on emotion or opinions. (ch 11) (389)

observers Group members who aid in the group's cohesiveness by being sensitive to the needs of each member. (ch 11) (397)

occupational dress That type of clothing that employees are expected to wear, but not as precise as a uniform. (ch 6) (188)

online résumé A résumé specifically designed to apply for jobs online that produce interviews. (ch 9) (322)

open-ended questions Interview questions that permit the person being interviewed to expand on his or her answers. (ch 9) (308)

open-format Interviews that are relatively unstructured. (ch 9) (307)

opinion A personal belief with which some people may disagree. Some opinions are more reliable than others. (ch 4) (119)

organizational chart A chart that shows the relationships among the elements of an organization, such as the departments of a company, the branches of federal or state government, or the committees of student government. (ch 15) (548)

organizational power (also called *legitimate power*) The ability of a leader to be influential because of his or her place in the organizational hierarchy (e.g., as a boss or supervisor). (ch 11) (377)

outline A way of organizing material so all the parts and how they relate to the whole can be seen. (ch 14) (512)

owned message (also known as an I-message) An acknowledgment of subjectivity by a message-sender through the use of first-person singular terms (I, me, my, mine). (ch 7) (228)

P

pace How quickly or slowly a person speaks. (ch 15) (544)

paralanguage The way we say something. (ch 5, 6) (154, 179)

paraphrasing Restating the other person's thoughts or feelings in your own words. (ch 4) (123)

participating That style of situational leadership in which leaders state the problem but immediately consult with group members. (ch 11) (386)

partitioning How you choose to divide your speech into parts. (ch 12) (425)

passive listener A listener who records but does not evaluate what is heard. (ch 4) (113)

passive listening style That kind of listening in which listeners believe that it involves no work. (ch 4) (105)

patriotism Devotion to one's country. (ch 3) (79)

people listening style That kind of listening in which the listener is concerned with the other person's feelings. (ch 4) (102)

perception How people look at themselves and the world around them. (ch 2) (46)

perceptual filters The limitations that result from the narrowed lens through which people view the world. (ch 2) (51)

personal distance That distance zone, a range from 18 inches to 4 feet, that people maintain from others when they are engaged in casual and personal conversations. (ch 6) (191)

personal inventory Appraising your own resources. (ch 12) (416)

persuasion The process of trying to get others to change their attitudes or behavior; also, the process that occurs when a communicator (*sender*) influences the values, beliefs, attitudes, or behaviors of another person (*receiver*). (ch 17) (608)

persuasive speech A speech in which the speaker takes a particular position and tries to get the audience to accept and support that position. (ch 12) (428)

PETAL In using presentation graphics, 1) develop pertinent materials, 2) choose an engaging format, 3) present your materials in a timely manner, 4) satisfy yourself that they are appropriate to the audience, and 5) ensure that everything is legible. (ch 9) (335)

pitch Highness or lowness of the voice. (ch 6) (180)

policy information Interviews that focus on how things are or should be done. (ch 9) (306)

polls Surveys taken of people's attitudes, feelings, or knowledge. (ch 13) (479)

poster Consists of lettering or pictures, or both. (ch 15) (548)

power distance That way of contrasting a group of cultures to another group of cultures that involves social inequality. (ch 3) (74)

powerful talk Talk that comes directly to the point, that does not use hesitation or qualifications. (ch 5) (157)

precursor Something that precedes or comes before something else. (ch 9) (314)

prediction From past experience with a person, a listener tries to predict what he or she will say next. (ch 4) (109)

prejudice A negative attitude toward a cultural group based on little or no experience. (ch 3) (80)

premise A premise includes the reasons given in support of a conclusion. (ch 17) (624)

presentation A descriptive or persuasive account that is created to communicate ideas in a compelling and graphic manner (e.g., explain concepts, communicate complex data, make recommendations, or persuade and motivate others). (ch 9) (332)

primary questions Interview questions that often come first in the interview or that come first with each new topic the interviewer introduces. (ch 9) (308)

proactive In this style of responding to undesirable behavior, the mother anticipates that the undesirable behavior is coming and tries to divert the child. (ch 7) (247)

problem-solution order Organization of a speech into two sections: one dealing with the problem and the other dealing with the solution. (ch 14) (498)

pronunciation The ability to pronounce a word correctly. (ch 15) (545)

propriety The character or quality of being proper, especially in accordance with recognized usage, custom, or principles. (ch 4) (127)

proxemics The study of how people use space. (ch 6) (189)

proximity Close contact that occurs between people who share an experience such as work, play, or school. (ch 7) (218)

psychological risk Taking a chance on something new, e.g., on a new person or place. (ch 2) (41)

psychological safety Approval and support obtained from familiar people, ideas, and situations. (ch 2) (41)

psychological sets Those types of perceptual filters that are expectations or predispositions to respond by knowing what is about to confront people and preparing for it. (ch 2) (46)

public communication The sender-receiver (*speaker*) sends a message (the *speech*) to an audience. (ch 1) (21)

public distance That distance zone, a distance of more than 12 feet, typically used for public speaking. (ch 6) (192)

Q

quality (of voice) Comprised of all voice characteristics: tempo, resonance, rhythm, pitch, and articulation. (ch 6) (180)

question-begging epithets A fallacy that occurs when slanted language is used to reaffirm what we wish to prove but have not proved yet. (ch 17) (624)

questions of fact Questions that deal with what is true and what is false. (ch 10) (364)

questions of policy Questions that are about actions that might be taken in the future. (ch 10) (365)

questions of value Questions of whether something is good or bad, desirable or undesirable. (ch 10) (365)

R

rapport-talk Type of language women use in conversation, designed to lead to intimacy with others, to match experiences, and to establish relationships. (ch 5) (151)

rate (of speech) Speed at which one speaks. (ch 6) (180)

RDAT In using slides in a presentation, read the visual, describe its meaning or significance, amplify it with an explanation or illustration, and, finally, transition to the next slide. (ch 9) (336)

reactive In this style of responding to undesirable behavior, the mother punishes the child when the behavior appears. (ch 7) (247)

reaffirmation One of eight ways couples have for dealing with or responding to dialectical tension that involves an active recognition by both partners that dialectical tensions will never go away. (ch 7) (245)

recalibration One of eight ways couples have for dealing with or responding to dialectical tension that involves couples in reframing situations so the tugs and pulls on partners do not seem to be in opposite directions. (ch 7) (245)

reference list A list of all the material you have used—and only that which you have used—in preparing your speech. (ch 14) (513)

referent power When leaders enjoy influence because of their personality. (ch 11) (377)

reflected appraisals Messages we get about ourselves from others. (ch 2) (36)

regrettable talk Saying something embarrassing, hurtful, or private to another person. (ch 8) (274)

regulators 1) Nonverbal signals which control the back-and-forth flow of speaking and listening, such as head nods, hand, gestures, and other body movements. (ch 6) (181) 2) Group members who play this role help regulate group discussion by gently reminding members of the agenda or of the point they were discussing when they digressed. (ch 11) (397)

relational dialectics The dynamic interplay between unified oppositions, based on the premise that relationships are organized around the dynamic interplay of opposing tendencies as they are enacted in interaction. (ch 7) (243)

report-talk Type of language men use in conversation, designed to maintain status, to demonstrate knowledge and skills, and to keep center-stage position. (ch 5) (151)

response to a bid A positive or negative answer to somebody's request for emotional connection. (ch 7) (223)

résumé A summary of a person's professional life written for potential employers. (ch 9) (318)

reward power A leader can have an influence if he or she can reward the followers (e.g., through promotions, pay raises, or praise). (ch 11) (376)

rhetorical question A question that audience members answer mentally rather than aloud. (ch 16) (592)

ritual language Communication that takes place when we are in an environment in which a conventionalized response is expected of us. (ch 5) (145)

roles Parts we play, or ways we behave with others. (ch 1) (15)

rules Formal and structured directions for behavior. (ch 10) (351)

S

scannable résumé Résumés that follow specific guidelines so they can be scanned into a computer to create a searchable database. (ch 9) (322)

scripts Lines and directions given to people by parents, teachers, coaches, religious leaders, friends, and the media that tell them what to say, what they expect, how to look, how to behave, and how to say the lines. (ch 2) (35)

search engine Special tools designed to help you find information on the Internet. They are likely to be your first Web guides when you are searching something by keywords. (ch 13) (462)

segmentation One of eight ways couples have for dealing with or responding to dialectical tension that involves a strategy of compartmentalizing different aspects of a relationship. (ch 7) (245)

selective attention The ability to focus perception. (ch 4) (110)

self-concept How a person thinks about and values himself or herself. (ch 2) (34)

self-disclosure Process by which one person tells another something he or she would not tell just anyone. (ch 7) (230)

self-esteem See *self-concept*.

self-fulfilling prophecies Events or actions that occur because a person and those around her or him expected them. (ch 2) (37)

self-perception The way in which one sees oneself. (ch 2) (39)

selling That style of situational leadership in which leaders state the problem and decide what to do, but they sell the other group members on the idea to gain majority support. (ch 11) (386)

semantic noise Interference with the message that is caused by people's emotional reactions to words. (ch 1) (12)

semiopen format Interviews that occur based on a core set of standardized questions that are asked in a standard manner and carefully recorded. (ch 9) (307)

sender-receiver In communication situations, people who simultaneously send and receive messages. (ch 1) (9)

separation When nondominants do not want to form a common bond with the dominant culture, so they separate into a group that includes only members like themselves. (ch 3) (84)

separation strategies When people are not part of a dominant culture, those processes people use to get the dominant group to reinvent or change the rules through the use of nonassertive, assertive, or aggressive separation. (ch 3) (84)

servant leadership People who work for the well-being and growth of all employees and are committed to creating a sense of community and sharing power in decision making. (ch 11) (378)

setting Where the communication occurs. (ch 1) (12)

shape The outward form, configuration, or contour of a thing. (ch 16) (581)

situational leadership People who can adopt different leadership styles depending on the situation. (ch 11) (384)

size The measurement or extent of a thing when compared with some standard. (ch 16) (581)

small-group communication Gatherings of 3 to 13 members who meet to do a job or solve a problem. (ch 1) (21)

small groups Gatherings of 3 to 13 members who meet to do a job, solve a problem, or maintain relationships. (ch 10) (347)

small talk Social conversation about unimportant topics that allows a person to maintain contact with a lot of people without making a deep commitment. (ch 7) (222)

social comparisons When people compare themselves with others to see how they measure up. (ch 2) (37)

social distance That distance zone, a range from 4 to 12 feet, that people are most likely to maintain when they do not know people very well. (ch 6) (191)

social group Groups designed to serve the social needs of their participants. (ch 10) (352)

space and distance Those distances people maintain between themselves and others that convey degrees of intimacy and status. (ch 6) (192)

spatial order Organization of a speech by something's location in space (e.g., left to right, top to bottom). (ch 14) (495)

specific purpose A statement for a speech that tells precisely what the speaker wants to accomplish. (ch 12) (429)

spiraling inversion One of eight ways couples have for dealing with or responding to dialectical tension that involves separating the dialectical forces and responding to one pull now, the other pull later. (ch 7) (245)

statistics Facts in numerical form. (ch 13) (475)

stereotypes Oversimplified or distorted views of another race, ethnic group, or culture. (ch 3) (74)

stress interview A type of information interview which is sometimes part of the job search and is designed to see how an interviewee acts under pressure. It is designed to give interviewers a realistic sense of their response to difficult situations. (ch 9) (303)

study An in-depth investigation of a subject. (ch 5) (149)

style The result of the way we select and arrange words and sentences. (ch 5) (149)

subculture People who are part of a larger culture but also belong to a smaller group that has some different values, attitudes, or beliefs. (ch 1) (22) See coculture. (ch 1, 3) (22, 65)

subject directory They include human-selected Internet resources and are arranged and classified in hierarchical topics. (ch 13) (461)

subjective view The personal, internal, mental map of the actual territory or external reality that people experience. (ch 2) (54)

substantive conflict Conflict that arises when people have different reactions to an idea.

Substantive conflict is likely to occur when any important and controversial idea is being discussed. (ch 11) (398)

support messages Those messages designed to make a child feel comfortable and secure in the family relationship. (ch 7) (247)

supporting material Information that backs up your main points and provides the main content of the speech. (ch 13) (470)

supporting points That material that backs up the main heads. (ch 4) (114)

sweeping generalization A fallacy that occurs when a general rule is applied to a specific case to which the rule is not applicable because of special features of the case. (ch 17) (624)

symbol Something that stands for something else. (ch 1) (9)

synchronous communication Online group discussion in which group members communicate at the same time. All participants are virtually present at the same time (e.g., in a telephone conversation, a face-to-face encounter, or a real-time, online group format). (ch 10, Appendix) (354, 663)

systems theory of family This theory describes a family as a dynamic whole composed of constantly shifting interrelationships but still bounded and rule-governed. (ch 7) (239)

T

tables Columns of figures arranged in an order that enables the viewer to easily pick out the needed information. (ch 15) (549)

target audience A subgroup of the whole audience that you must persuade to reach your goal. (ch 17) (620)

task-oriented group A type of group that serves to get something specific accomplished, often problem-solving or decision-making goals. (ch 10) (352)

task roles Roles that help get the job done. Persons who play these roles help groups come up with new ideas, aid in collecting and organizing information, and assist in analyzing the information that exists. (ch 11) (393)

telling That style of situational leadership in which the leader is focused more on the task and less on the group. (ch 11) (385)

terminal values Some final goal that is worth or not worth attaining. (ch 17) (612)

territory Space we consider as belonging to us, either temporarily or permanently. (ch 6) (189)

testimony Another person's statements or actions used to give authority to what the speaker is saying. (ch 13) (478)

time order Organization of a speech by chronology or historical occurrence. (ch 14) (494)

time-style listening That kind of listening in which the listener prefers brief and hurried interaction with others and often lets the communicator know how much time he or she has to make the point. (ch 4) (102)

topical order Organization of a speech used when the subject can be grouped logically into subtopics. (ch 14) (501)

touch To be in contact or come into contact with another person. (ch 6) (193)

transactional communication Communication that involves three principles: 1) people sending messages continuously and simultaneously, 2) communication events that have a past, present, and future, and 3) participants playing certain roles. (ch 1) (14)

transitions Comments that lead from one point to another to tell listeners where speakers have been, where they are now, and where they are going. (ch 14) (511)

transpection The process of empathizing across cultures. (ch 3) (88)

trustworthiness In the giving of a speech, the speaker is perceived as reliable and dependable. (ch 17) (639)

U

uncertainty avoidance That way of contrasting a group of cultures to another group of cultures that involves tolerance for the unknown. (ch 3) (76)

uniforms The most specialized form of clothing and that type that identifies wearers with particular organizations. (ch 6) (187)

usenet newsgroups (or Usenet) Online group discussions that handle individual messages sorted by broad subject areas that can be subscribed to

through Internet or corporate network host providers. (ch 10) (354)

V

values A type of belief about how we should behave or about some final goal that may or may not be worth attaining. (ch 17) (612)

verbal symbol A word that stands for a particular thing or idea. (ch 1) (10)

virtual reality Like imagineering, it is a computer-generated alternate reality. (Appendix) (674)

visual support Visual material that helps illustrate key points in a speech or presentation. Visual support includes devices such as charts, graphs, slides, and computer-generated graphics. (ch 15) (546)

vividness That property of style by which a thought is so presented that it evokes lifelike imagery or suggestion. (ch 5) (159)

vocal fillers Words we use to fill out our sentences or to cover up when we are searching for words. (ch 6) (181)

volume (of vocal sound) How loudly we speak. (ch 6) (180)

W–Z

web conferencing or web forums Online group discussions that use text messages (and sometimes images) stored on a computer as the communication medium. Messages are typed into the computer for others to read. (ch 10) (354)

web forums (also known as *web conferencing*) Group discussions that use text messages (and sometimes images) stored on a computer as the communication medium. (ch 10) (354)

web portal The home page your browser displays when you first connect to the Net. (ch 12) (418)

weight The heaviness of a mass, object, or thing. (ch 16) (581)

worldview An all-encompassing set of moral, ethical, and philosophical principles and beliefs which governs the way people live their lives an interact with others. (ch 3) (67)

Text and Line Art Credits

Chapter 7

Figs. 7-2, 7-3 From Luft, Joseph, *Group Processes: An Introduction to Group Dynamics*, Mayfield Publishing Company, 1984. Reprinted with permission from The McGraw-Hill Companies.

P. 235 From *Self-Disclosure on Computer Forms: Meta-analysis and Implications* by S. Weisband & S. Kiesler. Copyright © 1999 by ACM Publications. Reprinted with permission.

P. 236 From J. J. Messina & C. M. Messina, "Tools for Personal Growth: Building Trust. Coping.org. Tools for Coping with Life's Stressors. Reprinted by permission of Constance Messina.

Chapter 8

P. 263 From "A Man, A Woman and a Cat: Stages in a Relationship," from an idea in an article by Colin McEnroe, columnist for the Hartford Courant. Reprinted with permission.

P. 284 From Kantrowitz, B. & Wingert, P., "The Science of a Good Marriage," *Newsweek*, April 19, 1999. Copyright © 1999 Newsweek Inc. All rights reserved. Reprinted by permission.

P. 288 From www.tabcom.org/TheVine/1999/10-99/05.htm. Reprinted with permission of TABCOM.

P. 289 Reprinted from "Organizations & Values"by M. Rosenberg, in *Measures of Personality and Social Psychological Attitudes* by Robinson, J. P., Shaver, P. R. & Wrightsman, L. S. , pages 404-406, Copyright © 1991 with permission of Elsevier Science.

Chapter 9

P. 337 From J. Lorence and J. Mortimer, "Job Involvement Through the Life Course," *American Sociological Review*, 50, 1985, pp. 618-738. Reprinted with permission.

Chapter 10

P. 352 From *www.scit.wlv.ac.uk/resources/aup.html*. Reprinted by permission of University of Wolverhampton.

P. 354 From *http://www.uillinois.edu/stovall/ GroupTools/GT/index.html*. Copyright by University of Illinois. Reprinted by permission of Iris K. Stovall.

P. 355 From D. Feldman, "Chat Room Exiles," *On Monthly* (Special *Time* issue, 2/5/01, p. 65). Copyright ©2001 Time, Inc. Reprinted by permission.

P. 362 From www.os2cs.unb.ca/profs/fritz/cs3503/storm35.htm (August 2001) "Brainstorming Guidelines" by J. M. Fritz. Reprinted by permission of Jane Fritz.

P. 367 From *Measures of Personality and Social Psychological Attitudes* by Robinson, J. P., Shaver, P. R. & Wrightsman, L. S., 1991, pages 404-406. Copyright © 1991 with permission of Elsevier Science.

Chapter 11

P. 379 L. C. Spears, "On Character and Servant-Leadership: Ten Characteristics of Effective, Caring Leaders. The Robert K. Greenleaf Center for Servant-Leadership, Indianapolis, In 2002. Copyright © 2002 Larry C. Spears, The Greenleaf Center <www.greenleaf.org>. Reprinted by permission of Larry C. Spears.

P. 383 From Gender Differences in Communication. The Ladies Room, www.geocities.com/ Wellesley/2052/wendiff.html. Reproduced with permission of Yahoo! Inc. YAHOO! and the YAHOO! logo are trademarks of yahoo! Inc.

P. 389 From "Small Group Leadership" by Robert Gwynne, Department of Communication, University of Tennessee, Knoxville, TN, http://web.utk.edu/~gwynne/Small_Group_Leadership.html. Reprinted by permission of Robert Gwynne Ph.D.

T. 11.1 Adapted from INLS 180: Communication Process: Notes on Conflict Management, Spring 1998. Retrieved from http: www.ils.unc.edu/daniel/180/conflict.html.

P. 403 Adapted from ICANS (Integrated Curriculum for Achieving Necessary Skills) from *www.literacynet.org/ icans/chapter05/leadership.html*. Reprinted with permission of the ABLE Network, Office of Adult Literacy.

Chapter 12

P. 412 C. E. Tucker-Ladd, 1996-2000, "Chapter 5: Signs of Stress, Psychological Self-Help/Mental Health Net." Retrieved from www.mhnet.org/psyhelp/chap5c.htm. Reprinted by permission of Clayton Tucker-Ladd.

P. 421 From "Getting Directions: Reading the Road Signs on the Information Super Highway," by Rene Smeraglia, *On the Net*, 6/8/02 from www.computerscene.com/editorial/onthenet.htm. Reprinted with permission.

P. 435 D. H. Freedman, "What Do Teens Want?" *Inc magazine*,Dec. 1, 2000. Retrieved 6/2/02 from http: www.inc.com/search/21117.html. Reprinted with permission.

P. 441 From Gordon L. Paul, *Insight vs Desensitization in Psychotherapy*, Stanford University Press, 1966. Copyright © 1966 by The Board of Trustees of the Leland Stanford Jr. University, renewed 1994. With the permission of Stanford University press, www.sup.org.

Chapter 13

Fig. 13-1 From OWL (Online Writing Lab) home page, Purdue University. Copyright Purdue Research Foundation. Reprinted with permission. All rights reserved.

P. 458 From "How to Conduct Research on the Internet" by Terry Brainerd Chadwick. (InfoQuest! Information Services) June 24, 1999. http://www.tbchad.com/resrch. html. Reprinted by permission of the author.

Photo Credits

Chapter 8

257	Barry Yee/Taxi/Getty Images
261	Michael Newman/PhotoEdit
271	Michael Newman/PhotoEdit
276	David Young-Wolff/PhotoEdit

Chapter 9

299	China Tourism Press/The Image Bank/ Getty Images
304	Bob Daemmrich/The Image Works
311	Loren Santow/ Getty Images
317	Michael Newman/PhotoEdit
333	Dennis MacDonald/PhotoEdit

Chapter 10

345	John Henley/ Corbis
353	Kaluzny-Thatcher/Stone/Getty Images
358	Bob Mahoney/ The Image Works
363	Loren Santow/ Getty Images

Chapter 11

373	Charles Gupton/Getty Images
380	Harry Sieplinga/HMS Images/Getty Images
395	Bill Aron/PhotoEdit

Chapter 12

411	Jose Luis Pelaez,Inc./ Corbis
417	Will Hart/PhotoEdit
420	Peter Cade/Stone/Getty Images
428	Esbin-Anderson/The Image Works

Chapter 13

449	Will & Deni McIntyre/Photo Researchers Inc.
464	Jon Riley/Getty Images
475	Jose Luis Pelaez,Inc./ Corbis

Chapter 14

487	Michael Newman/PhotoEdit
494	A.Ramey/PhotoEdit
504	Chuck Savage/ Corbis

Chapter 15

529	Cleve Bryant/ PhotoEdit
537	B.Stitzer/PhotoEdit
547	Newspapers/The Image Works

Chapter 16

571	Andy Sacks/Stone/Getty Images
575	Michael Newman/PhotoEdit
577	James Schnepf/Liaison/Getty Images
585	Michael Newman/PhotoEdit

Chapter 17

607	Bob Daemmrich/The Image Works
612	David Young-Wolff/PhotoEdit
617	A.Ramey/PhotoEdit
627	G.D.T./Stone/ Getty Images

Appendix

657	Lucidio Studio Inc./Corbis
661	Francis Dean/The Image Works

Index

space and distance, 189–192
and transpection, 88
uncertainty avoidance, 76–77
workforce diversity, 402
Cultural do's and don'ts, 89
Cultural identity, 64–65
and behavior, 74
and intercultural communication, 68–697
Cultural norms, 359
Cultural studies, 5
Cultural values of small groups, 350–351
Culture, 22–23; *see also* Intercultural
communication
and clothing, 186–187
coculture, 64–65
and cultural identity, 64–65
dominant *vs.* nondominant, 81–86
masculine/feminine, 76
and metamessages, 161
nature of, 65–68
perceptual filters, 52
and self-perception, 67–68
shaped by media, 667–668
significance of, 67
and words, 143
and worldview, 67
Cuomo, Mario, 472, 483
Curiosity, arousing, 587–588
Currency, 467
of Internet information, 680
Curtis, D. B., 6, 29, 30, 316
Curtis, J. C., 341
Cushenberry, Dwight, 579
Customs, 52

D

Dalrymple, T., 59
Daly, John A., 252, 274, 294
Dance of Connection (Lerner), 229, 275
Dane, J., 254
Date.com, 261
Dateline, 670
David, Michele W., 268, 293
Davies, D., 35
Davis, L., 295
Davis, M. W., 295
Days of Our Lives, 211
Deal, C., 525
Decision making
and groupthink, 359–361
group *vs.* individual, 349
in small groups, 352–355
DeClaire, J., 223, 224–228, 252, 294
Deductive reasoning, 621–622

Defensive behavior, 280
Defensive communication, 278–282
avoiding, 281–282
certainty *vs.* provisionalism, 280
control *vs.* problem solving, 279
definition, 278
evaluation *vs.* description, 279
neutrality *vs.* empathy, 279–280
strategy *vs.* spontaneity, 279
superiority *vs.* equality, 280
Definitions, 473
comparisons, 579
contrasts, 579–580
etymology, 577–578
examples, 578–579
functional, 580
DeFord, D. H., 294
DeFrancisco, V. L., 178, 203
Delegating responsibility, 392
Delegating style of leadership, 387
Deletions, 50–51
Delivery
after-speech questions, 562
attention-getting, 590–591
attentiveness, 533–534
body language, 539–540
case, 530–532
controlling nervousness, 556–560
conversational quality, 535–356
directness, 535
extemporaneous, 538–539
eye contact, 540–541
facial expressions, 541–542
gestures, 542
immediacy, 534
impromptu, 536
natural, 333–334
personal appearance, 539
posture, 542
practice and preparation, 560–562
practicing actual delivery, 561–562
self-evaluation, 566
speaking from manuscript, 537
speaking from memory, 538
tryout, 561–562
visual supports, 547–556
voice quality, 652–546
DeLonge, Tom, 435
Democratic leaders, 383–384
Demographic analysis
age, 438
of audiences, 437–441
definition, 437
education, 439–440
gender, 438–439